Handbook of Clinical Hypnosis

Handbook of Clinical Hypnosis

Edited by Judith W. Rhue, Steven Jay Lynn, and Irving Kirsch

American Psychological Association • Washington, DC

First printing September 1993
Second printing June 1994
Third printing April 1997

Published by the
American Psychological Association
750 First Street, NE
Washington, DC 20002

Copies may be ordered from
APA Order Department
P.O. Box 92984
Washington, DC 20090-2984

In the U.K. and Europe, copies may be ordered from the American Psychological Association, 3 Henrietta Street, Covent Garden, London WC2E 8LV, England.

Typeset in Goudy by PRO-IMAGE Corporation, York, PA

Printer: Braun-Brumfield, Inc., Ann Arbor, MI
Cover printer: Phoenix Color Corporation, Hagerstown, MD
Cover designer: Berg Design, Albany, NY
Technical/production editor: Olin J. Nettles

Library of Congress Cataloging-in-Publication Data

Handbook of clinical hypnosis / edited by Judith W. Rhue, Steven J.
   Lynn, and Irving Kirsch.
        p.   cm.
     Includes bibliographical references and index.
     ISBN 1-55798-440-9 (acid-free paper)
     1. Hypnotism—Therapeutic use.   I. Rhue, Judith W.   II. Lynn,
Steven J.   III. Kirsch, Irving.
     [DNLM: 1. Hypnosis. 2. Psychotherapy—methods.   WM 415 H2355
1993]
RC495.H356   1993
616.89′162—dc20
DNLM/DLC
for Library of Congress   93-9788
                                                                                      CIP

British Library Cataloguing-in-Publication Data
A CIP record is available from the British Library.

Printed in the United States of America

To my greatest blessings, my children, Martha Kate, Alexandra, Grant, and Steven.
Judith W. Rhue

To my precious daughter, Jessica.
Steven Jay Lynn

To my beloved son, David.
Irving Kirsch

CONTENTS

List of Contributors xi

Foreword xix

Preface xxi

Acknowledgments xxv

I. Foundations and General Considerations 1

    Chapter 1. Introduction to Clinical Hypnosis 3
                 Irving Kirsch
                 Steven Jay Lynn
                 Judith W. Rhue

    Chapter 2. Individual Differences in Response to Hypnosis 23
                 Brad L. Bates

    Chapter 3. Operator Variables in Hypnotherapy 55
                 Billie S. Strauss

    Chapter 4. Expectations and Hypnotherapy 73
                 William C. Coe

    Chapter 5. Prevention and Therapeutic Management of
             "Negative Effects" in Hypnotherapy 95
                 David C. Frauman
                 Steven Jay Lynn
                 John P. Brentar

II. Models of Hypnotherapy 121

    Chapter 6. Psychoanalytic and Psychodynamic Models of
             Hypnoanalysis 123
                 Marlene R. Eisen

Chapter 7. Cognitive–Behavioral Hypnotherapy 151
    Irving Kirsch

Chapter 8. Rational–Emotive Therapy and Hypnosis 173
    Albert Ellis

Chapter 9. An Ericksonian Model of Hypnotherapy 187
    William J. Matthews
    Stephen Lankton
    Carol Lankton

Chapter 10. Cognitive–Developmental Hypnotherapy 215
    E. Thomas Dowd

III. Hypnotic Techniques 233

Chapter 11. Enhancing Hypnotizability and Treatment
    Responsiveness 235
    Jeffrey D. Gfeller

Chapter 12. Clinical Self-Hypnosis: Transformation and
    Subjectivity 251
    Shirley Sanders

Chapter 13. Active–Alert Hypnosis in Psychotherapy 271
    Éva I. Bányai
    Annamária Zseni
    Ferenc Túry

Chapter 14. Hypnosis and Metaphor 291
    Peter Brown

IV. Treating Psychological Disorders 309

Chapter 15. Phobias and Intense Fears: Facilitating Their
    Treatment With Hypnosis 311
    Helen J. Crawford
    Arreed F. Barabasz

Chapter 16. Hypnosis and Depression 339
    Michael D. Yapko

Chapter 17. Hypnotherapy With Children 357
    Daniel P. Kohen
    Karen Olness

Chapter 18. Hypnosis in the Treatment of Anorexia Nervosa .. 383
    Michael R. Nash
    Elgan L. Baker

Chapter 19. ~~Hypnosis in the Treatment of Multiple Personality Disorder .... 395~~
~~Richard Horevitz~~

Chapter 20. The Borderline Patient and the Psychotic Patient 425
Joan Murray-Jobsis

V. Coping With Stress and Trauma 453

Chapter 21. Hypnosis and Storytelling in the Treatment of Child Sexual Abuse: Strategies and Procedures ... 455
Judith W. Rhue
Steven Jay Lynn

Chapter 22. Hypnotherapy With Rape Victims 479
William H. Smith

Chapter 23. Hypnosis in the Treatment of Posttraumatic Stress Disorders 493
David Spiegel

VI. Behavioral Medicine and Sports Psychology 509

Chapter 24. Hypnosis in Pain Management 511
John F. Chaves

Chapter 25. Hypnosis in the Treatment of Obesity 533
Eugene E. Levitt

Chapter 26. Hypnosis and Smoking Cessation: A Cognitive–Behavioral Treatment 555
Steven Jay Lynn
Victor Neufeld
Judith W. Rhue
Abigail Matorin

Chapter 27. Assessment and Treatment of Somatization Disorders: The High Risk Model of Threat Perception 587
Ian Wickramasekera

Chapter 28. Psychological Treatment of Warts 623
Susan C. DuBreuil
Nicholas P. Spanos

Chapter 29. Hypnosis and Sport Psychology 649
William P. Morgan

VII. Issues and Extensions 671

Chapter 30. Training Issues in Hypnosis 673
Peter B. Bloom

Chapter 19 has been deleted from this edition.

Chapter 31. Cross-Cultural Perspectives on Hypnotic-Like
Procedures Used by Native Healing
Practitioners 691
Stanley Krippner

Chapter 32. Forensic Hypnosis: The Application of Ethical
Guidelines 719
Peter W. Sheehan
Kevin M. McConkey

Author Index 739

Subject Index 757

About the Editors 767

CONTRIBUTORS

Elgan Baker, PhD, currently serves as Director of Psychology at the Midwest Medical Center, director of the Indiana Center for Psychoanalysis, and Associate Clinical Professor in the Department of Psychiatry at the Indiana University School of Medicine. He has served as president of the American Board of Psychological Hypnosis and of the Division of Psychological Hypnosis of the American Psychological Association, of which he also is a fellow.

Éva I. Bányai, PhD, is the head of the Department of Experimental Psychology, Eötvös Loránd University, Budapest, Hungary. In 1973, she spent a fellowship year with E. R. Hilgard at Stanford University, where she developed active–alert hypnosis. Dr. Bányai is a past president of the Hypnosis Section of the Hungarian Psychiatric Society and is a member of several governing bodies of the Hungarian psychologists' community.

Arreed F. Barabasz, EdD, PhD, ABPP, is director of the Attentional Processes Laboratory at Washington State University and a professor of counseling psychology. He is a diplomate of the American Board of Professional Psychology (Clinical) and a fellow of the American Psychological Association, the American Psychological Society, the American Association of Applied and Preventive Psychology, and the Society for Clinical and Experimental Hypnosis. He is president of the International Restricted Environmental Stimulation Investigators Society.

Brad L. Bates, PhD, is Associate Psychologist, Behavioral Medicine and Neuropsychology Associates, Tacoma, Washington. Dr. Bates is an advisory editor for the *International Journal of Clinical and Experimental Hypnosis*, author of numerous scientific and clinical papers regarding hypnosis, and recipient of an award for the best research paper on hypnosis, bestowed by the Society for Clinical and Experimental Hypnosis.

Peter B. Bloom, MD, Clinical Professor of Psychiatry, University of Pennsylvania School of Medicine, is a fellow of the Society of Clinical and Experimental Hypnosis and has served as the secretary–treasurer (1980–1992) of the International Society of Hypnosis. In 1994, he will serve as president of the Society. In 1990, he received the Bernard B. Raginsky Award of the Society for Clinical and Experimental Hypnosis for distinguished leadership and achievement.

John P. Brentar, PhD, is assistant mental health director at the Children's Health Council in Palo Alto, California. He received a research excellence award from the American Psychological Association's Division of Psychological Hypnosis. He has written articles and book chapters on negative effects in hypnotherapy, hypnotic rapport, and prescription privileges for psychologists.

Peter Brown, MD, F.R.C.P., is an associate professor in the Department of Psychiatry, the University of Toronto, and head of the Consultation/Liaison Service at Mount Sinai Hospital, Toronto. He is author of *The Hypnotic Brain: Hypnotherapy and Social Communication.*

John F. Chaves, PhD, is professor and head of the Behavioral Sciences Section, School of Dental Medicine, Southern Illinois University at Edwardsville. He is coeditor, with N. P. Spanos, of *Hypnosis: The Cognitive–Behavioral Perspective* and has published extensively in the areas of hypnosis and pain management. He is a fellow of the Society for Clinical and Experimental Hypnosis and the American Psychological Association, and he is past president of the American Psychological Association's Division of Psychological Hypnosis.

William C. Coe, PhD, is a professor of psychology at California State University, Fresno, where he was "Outstanding Professor of the Year," 1988. He has served as president and secretary of the American Psychological Association's Division of Psychological Hypnosis. He has authored four books, including *Hypnosis: A Social Psychological Analysis* (with T. R. Sarbin). His awards include "Outstanding Contributions to Psychotherapy" from the California School of Professional Psychology, Fresno, and "Best Theoretical Paper in Hypnosis" from the Society for Clinical and Experimental Hypnosis.

Helen J. Crawford, PhD, is a psychologist in the Applied Experimental Program, Department of Psychology, Virginia Polytechnic Institute and

State University, Blacksburg, Virginia. She has been president of the Society for Clinical and Experimental Hypnosis and president and secretary of the American Psychological Association's Division of Psychological Hypnosis. She has received awards for research excellence and distinguished leadership and achievement from the Society for Clinical and Experimental Hypnosis.

E. Thomas Dowd, PhD, is professor and director of School and Counseling Psychology at Kent State University. He received his PhD from the University of Minnesota and previously taught at Florida State University and the University of Nebraska. He is editor of the *Journal of Cognitive Psychotherapy: An International Quarterly,* and his scholarly interests are in cognitive therapy, paradoxical interventions and psychological reactance, and hypnotherapy.

Susan C. DuBreuil, MA, is a PhD student in psychology at Carleton University in Canada. She has published research in the areas of hypnosis, the psychology of women, and psychology and the law.

Marlene R. Eisen, PhD, is a therapist in private practice who also teaches hypnotherapy courses for the Illinois School of Professional Psychology and advanced hypnosis courses for the Society for Clinical and Experimental Hypnosis. She presently serves as treasurer of the American Psychological Association's Division of Psychological Hypnosis, and she has published papers on incest, abuse, and hypnotherapy.

Albert Ellis, PhD, is president of the Institute for Rational–Emotive Therapy in New York City, is the founder of rational–emotive therapy, and is the grandfather of cognitive–behavior therapy. He has been president of the Division of Consulting Psychology of the American Psychological Association and president of the Society for the Scientific Study of Sex. He has won many awards, including Distinguished Professional Contributions to Knowledge from the American Psychological Association and the Professional Development Award of the American Counseling Association. He has published more than 600 articles and over 50 books.

David C. Frauman, PhD, is currently in private practice in Indianapolis. He was formerly the director of psychology at St. Vincent Hospital (Indianapolis) and an adjunct faculty member at Indiana University Medical School. He has published many articles on group psychotherapy, hypnotic rapport, role-playing procedures and hypnotherapy, and hypnotic involuntariness.

Jeffrey D. Gfeller, PhD, is an assistant professor of psychology at St. Louis University. He has published hypnosis articles on the topics of individual differences in cognition and hypnotizability modification.

Richard Horevitz, PhD, is the Associate Director of Associated Mental Health Services and director of its Anxiety and Depression Treatment Program. He is on the faculties of psychology and psychiatry at the University of Illinois, Chicago, and is a research associate at the Dissociative Disorders Program, Rush-Presbyterian-St. Lukes Medical Center. He is the immediate past president of the American Psychological Association's Division of Psychological Hypnosis.

Irving Kirsch, PhD, is a professor of psychology at the University of Connecticut. He is the North American editor of the journal *Contemporary Hypnosis,* and a member of the editorial board of the *International Journal of Clinical and Experimental Hypnosis.* In 1993, he served as president of the American Psychological Association's Division of Psychological Hypnosis. He has published more than 75 journal articles and book chapters on hypnosis, behavior therapy, anxiety disorders, depression, and expectancy effects and has presented papers on these topics internationally.

Daniel P. Kohen, MD, is Director of Behavioral Pediatrics for the University of Minnesota Department of Pediatrics and University of Minnesota Hospitals and Clinics, and is Assistant Professor, Departments of Pediatrics and Family Practice and Community Health, University of Minnesota. Dr. Kohen is past president of the Minnesota Society of Clinical Hypnosis and is currently secretary–treasurer of the American Board of Medical Hypnosis. Dr. Kohen has received awards for scientific writing and for excellence in teaching (1992) from the American Society of Clinical Hypnosis.

Stanley Krippner, PhD, is Professor of Psychology, Saybrook Institute, and Distinguished Professor of Psychology, California Institute of Integral Studies, both in San Francisco. He is a fellow of the American Psychological Society, the American Psychological Association, the American Society for Clinical Hypnosis, and the Society for the Scientific Study of Sex. He is coauthor of many books, including *Spiritual Dimensions of Healing, Personal Mythology, Dreamworking,* and *Dream Telepathy.*

Carol Lankton, MA, trained with Milton Erickson and maintains a private practice in Gulf Breeze, Florida. She is an associate editor of the *Erickson Monographs* and an adjunct faculty member in the Department of Psychology at the University of West Florida.

Stephen Lankton, MSW, studied intensively with Milton Erickson, has a private practice in Gulf Breeze, Florida, and is editor-in-chief of the *Erickson Monographs*. He is an adjunct faculty member in the Department of Psychology at the University of West Florida.

Eugene E. Levitt, PhD, is Professor Emeritus of Clinical Psychology at the Indiana University School of Medicine and has served as past secretary–treasurer of the American Board of Psychological Hypnosis and as past president of the American Psychological Association's Division of Psychological Hypnosis. He has been awarded the Morton Prince Award by the Society for Experimental and Clinical Hypnosis and American Board of Psychological Hypnosis, the Bernard E. Gorton Award by the American Society of Clinical Hypnosis, and the Karl Heiser Award by the American Psychological Association.

Steven Jay Lynn, PhD, is a professor of psychology at Ohio University and has a private practice. He is a former president of the American Psychological Association's Division of Psychological Hypnosis. He has received two awards from the Society for Clinical and Experimental Hypnosis for research excellence and for the best hypnosis book published during 1991 (*Theories of Hypnosis: Current Models and Perspectives*).

Abigail Matorin, BA, is a student in the clinical psychology graduate training program at Ohio University.

William J. Matthews, PhD, is an associate professor in counseling psychology at the University of Massachusetts in Amherst. He is an editorial assistant for the *Erickson Monographs*.

Kevin M. McConkey, PhD, is Professor of Psychology and head of the School of Psychology at the University of New South Wales, Sydney, Australia. He is currently president-elect of the Australian Psychological Society and vice-president of the Federation of Australian Scientific and Technological Societies. He has contributed widely to the scientific literature on hypnosis and related phenomena.

William P. Morgan, PhD, is Professor of Kinesiology and director of the Sport Psychology Laboratory at the University of Wisconsin—Madison. He is the current president of the American Psychological Association's Division of Psychological Hypnosis and was the first president of the APA's Division of Exercise and Sport Psychology. He edited the first book of readings in sport psychology, *Contemporary Readings in Sport Psychology*, as well as *Ergogenic Aids and Muscular Performance* and *Exercise and Mental Health*.

Joan Murray-Jobsis, PhD, is a clinician in private practice in Chapel Hill, North Carolina, and is also a clinical associate professor at the University of North Carolina at Chapel Hill. Dr. Murray-Jobsis is a past president and fellow of the American Society of Clinical Hypnosis. She is a diplomate of both the American Board of Professional Psychology and the American Board of Psychological Hypnosis, and she has published extensively in the area of hypnotherapy with borderline and psychotic patients.

Michael R. Nash, PhD, is an associate professor at the University of Tennessee and is actively engaged in clinical training, research, and teaching. A past president of the American Psychological Association's Division of Psychological Hypnosis, he is a fellow of both the Society for Clinical and Experimental Hypnosis and the American Psychological Association. Dr. Nash is coeditor, with Erika Fromm, of *Contemporary Hypnosis Research*.

Victor Neufeld, PhD, is a psychologist at Penrose Hospital, Colorado Springs. He works with neurologically impaired, elderly, and chronic pain patients. Dr. Neufeld has published many articles and chapters on direct versus indirect suggestions, smoking cessation, and imagination and fantasy.

Karen Olness, MD, is the director of General Academic Pediatrics at Rainbow Babies & Childrens Hospital in Cleveland, Ohio. She is a professor of pediatrics, family medicine, and international health. Dr. Olness is president of the Society for Behavioral Pediatrics and president of the Society for Clinical and Experimental Hypnosis. She is past president of the Northwestern Pediatric Society, the Minnesota International Health Volunteers, the American Society of Clinical Hypnosis, and the American Board of Medical Hypnosis.

Judith W. Rhue, PhD, is a professor of family medicine at the Ohio University College of Osteopathic Medicine, and has a private practice. She is a fellow of the American Psychological Association's Division of Psychological Hypnosis and has received awards for research excellence from both organizations and an award for the best hypnosis book published during 1991 (*Theories of Hypnosis: Current Models and Perspectives*), bestowed by the Society for Clinical and Experimental Hypnosis. Dr. Rhue serves on the editorial boards of the *International Journal of Clinical and Experimental Hypnosis* and *Contemporary Hypnosis*.

Shirley Sanders, PhD, is a clinical professor of psychology at the University of North Carolina School of Medicine in the Department of Psychiatry and maintains a private practice in Chapel Hill. She holds the Diplomate in Clinical Psychology (ABPP) and Clinical Hypnosis (ABPH), and has published in professional journals in the areas of hypnotic dreams, hypnosis and creativity, and hypnotherapy. She teaches clinical hypnosis to other professionals both nationally and internationally.

Peter W. Sheehan, PhD, is Professor of Psychology and Pro-Vice-Chancellor of Research and Postgraduate Studies at the University of Queensland, Brisbane, Australia. He is currently president of the Academy of the Social Sciences in Australia, and chair of the Research Grants Committee of the Australian Research Council. He has contributed extensively to the literature on hypnosis and mental imagery, both in book and article form.

William H. Smith, PhD, is director of clinical psychology and of postdoctoral training at the Menninger Clinic in Topeka, Kansas. A diplomate of both the American Board of Professional Psychology and the American Board of Professional Hypnosis, he has served on the teaching faculty of the Society for Clinical and Experimental Hypnosis and the American Society of Clinical Hypnosis.

Nicholas P. Spanos, PhD, is Professor of Psychology and director of the Laboratory for Experimental Hypnosis at Carleton University, Ottawa. He is a fellow of the American Psychological Association, is on the editorial boards of *Contemporary Hypnosis* and *Imagination, Cognition and Personality*, and has published research in a number of areas including hypnosis, pain control, memory distortion, psychopathology, psychology and the law, and the history of psychology and psychopathology.

David Spiegel, MD, is Professor of Psychiatry and Behavioral Sciences at Stanford University School of Medicine and director of the Psychosocial Treatment Laboratory. He is a fellow of the American Psychiatric Association, the American College of Psychiatrists, the Society for Clinical and Experimental Hypnosis, and the American Society of Clinical Hypnosis. He is the author of many papers, chapters, and books, including *Trance and Treatment*.

Billie S. Strauss, PhD, is Director of Training in Psychology and Director of Outpatient Services in the Department of Psychiatry at Michael Reese Hospital and Medical Center, and Associate Professor of Psychology in the Department of Psychiatry at the University of Illinois at Chicago. Dr. Strauss is a diplomate of the American Board of Psychological Hypnosis in Clinical Hypnosis and of the American Board of Professional Psychology in Clinical Psychology, and a recipient of the Morton Prince Award from the Society for Clinical and Experimental Hypnosis and American Board of Psychological Hypnosis. She is secretary of the American Board of Psychological Hypnosis, Director of Training for the Society for Clinical and Experimental Hypnosis, and Advisory Editor to the *International Journal of Clinical and Experimental Hypnosis*.

Ferenc Túry, MD, is a physician in the Department of Psychiatry No. 1, Borsod County Hospital, Miskolc, Hungary.

Ian Wickramasekera, PhD, ABPP, ABPH, is Professor of Psychiatry and Behavioral Sciences at Eastern Virginia School in Norfolk, Virginia. He is Director of the Behavioral Medicine Clinic and Psychophysiological Stress Disorders Research Laboratory, and he received the Morton Price Award from the American Board of Psychological Hypnosis and an award for pioneering research in applied psychophysiology from the Association of Applied Psychophysiology and Biofeedback.

Michael D. Yapko, PhD, is a clinical psychologist in private practice in San Diego, California. He is a national and international trainer in the methods of hypnosis and brief psychotherapy, and is a fellow of the American Society of Clinical Hypnosis and author of many popular works, including *Trancework*, *When Living Hurts*, *Free Yourself From Depression*, and *Hypnosis and the Treatment of Depressions*.

Annamária Zseni, MD, is a physician in the Department of Psychiatry, St. Imre Hospital, Budapest, Hungary.

FOREWORD

The upsurge of interest in the scientific study of hypnosis and of its usefulness in clinical practice that began in the 20th century and accelerated during the second half of the century justifies a handbook of this kind to give a "state-of-the-art" report as we approach the next century.

The editors who undertook this large task have been well prepared for it by their own active involvements in clinical practice, research, and participation in the hypnosis societies devoted to enhancing the scientific knowledge of hypnosis and its applications in clinical practice.

In addition to themselves, they have called upon 37 eminent professionals, each an acknowledged expert in their particular area of specialization, to participate as authors of the 32 chapters that provide comprehensive coverage of clinical hypnosis. The majority of the authors are clinical psychologists with PhDs, along with a few medically trained psychiatrists and at least one social worker. The high ratio of psychologists to other professionals reflects the disproportionate numbers of reputable clinical hypnotherapists who are psychologists by training.

This collection of experts has much to offer the practicing clinician. For the clinician who may be considering adding hypnosis to his or her therapeutic skills, the *Handbook,* with its many examples of inductions, hypnotic methods and procedures, and case studies, provides an excellent introduction to clinical hypnosis. For therapists who are already acquainted with clinical hypnosis, the *Handbook* is an authoritative source of information on specific applications of hypnosis and the treatment of a wide variety of psychological disorders and conditions.

The contributors represent a wide range of points of view. The prevailing split is recognized between those who accept the more conventional view that there is something unique about the condition described as being hypnotized—whether or not is is called a trance—and those who argue that there is little or no distinctiveness to the hypnotic condition because hypnotic phenomena can be understood according to ordinary cognitive and social psychological concepts.

Although this division holds within clinical hypnotherapy, there are many additional aspects on which hypnotherapists differ. These include the role of psychodynamics, the relative significance of persisting individual differences, the personality of the therapist, and how the outcomes of therapy are assessed. The editors rightly feel that the lack of outcome studies on a larger scale is to be regretted.

The range and diversity of viewpoints is something to be celebrated, because it continues to raise the questions appropriate to any therapeutic intervention: How do we know? How good is the evidence? The curious reader can find in this handbook a great deal of information that brings the answers to these questions closer. The *Handbook*'s rich clinical material, integrative summaries of current research, and suggestions for future research are likely to stimulate important contributions to the science and practice of hypnosis well into the next century.

ERNEST R. HILGARD
Emeritus Professor of Psychology
Stanford University
Stanford, California

PREFACE

Hypnosis is a word that conjures many associations. There is a certain magic in the ability of mere words to produce profound changes in a person's mood, thoughts, and behaviors. There is a compelling quality to subjects' reports of involuntary experiences that often accompany hypnotic behaviors. And there is an almost eerie feeling of surprise and amazement when hypnotized subjects demonstrate classical hypnotic phenomena such as positive and negative hallucinations, alterations in pain sensitivity, and amnesia upon command.

No wonder, then, that hypnosis has long been wed to terms like *mystery, mysticism,* and the *supernatural.* Yet, at the same time that the media and stage hypnotists have exploited and advanced these misconceptions of hypnosis, scientists have placed hypnosis on a firm empirical footing, and clinicians have devised ever more creative ways of serving their clientele with hypnotic stratagems and techniques.

No student of contemporary psychology can ignore the surge of interest in hypnosis over the last decade or so. Hypnosis has always captured the attention of some of the most creative thinkers in the field of psychology (Sigmund Freud, William James, Clark Hull, Ernest Hilgard, T. X. Barber, and Theodore Sarbin, among others). It comes as no surprise, therefore, that the scientific community has increasingly recognized that hypnosis is a fruitful and legitimate area of scientific inquiry.[1] That hypnosis has moved into the orbit of mainstream psychology is evidenced by the sharp increase in the number of hypnosis articles published in recent years that span a wide range of disciplines[2] and by the increasing frequency with which

---

[1]Lynn, S. J., & Rhue, J. W. (1991). *Hypnosis theories: Current models and perspectives.* New York: Guilford Press.

[2]Graham, K. R. (1991). Hypnosis: A case study in science. *Hypnosis, 17,* 78–84.

Nash, M. R., Minton, A., & Baldridge, J. (1988). Twenty years of scientific hypnosis in dentistry, medicine, and psychology: A brief communication. *International Journal of Clinical and Experimental Hypnosis, 36,* 198–205.

hypnosis articles appear in leading journals geared to a general audience of psychologists.

This legitimization and "normalization" of hypnosis accounts, in some measure, for clinicians' fascination with integrating hypnotic techniques into their clinical practice. The last decade has witnessed a number of developments, including a boom in the number of professionals who have joined organizations that advance clinical hypnosis, the widespread use of hypnotic techniques to treat psychological and medical disorders, the swell in the ranks of people who attend hypnosis training workshops, and the increase in hypnosis and hypnotherapy courses offered in graduate training programs.[3]

This unprecedented interest in the scientific and clinical foundations of hypnosis is what prompted us to bring eminent scholars and clinicians together to create the *Handbook of Clinical Hypnosis*. There are already many fine books on hypnotherapy available, but they were written from a particular vantage point or are limited to particular applications. We believe the time has come for an authoritative, comprehensive textbook of clinical hypnosis that represents the gamut of theoretical orientations and clinical applications. We also believe the time has come for a book that places theory and research beside the best examples of clinical practice. In this way, we hope to immerse the reader in the nitty-gritty work of hypnotherapy and highlight the evidential basis of the techniques presented. Our goal is to advance a scientifically rigorous yet compassionate approach to hypnotherapy.

In developing the *Handbook*, we thought 'of those individuals from whom *we* would like to learn. With this proviso in mind, we succeeded in assembling authors who are eminent clinical theoreticians, practitioners, and researchers. With this panel of experts, the *Handbook* provides authoritative, virtually encyclopedic, coverage of many topics in clinical hypnosis.

The majority of contributions are organized in a uniform way so as to facilitate comparisons across theories and treatment modalities and to maximize the accessibility of each approach for the reader. Each chapter introduces a particular theory or technique, then discusses clinical applications and case material, and concludes with an appraisal of relevant research and final comments by the authors.

The *Handbook* is divided into sections that cover general clinical considerations, hypnosis theoretical models, hypnotic techniques, specific clinical applications, and contemporary issues. The first section includes chapters relevant to understanding the foundations of clinical hypnosis. Represented here are chapters on basic hypnotic induction techniques, individual differences in responsiveness to hypnosis, operator variables, the

---

[3]Lynn & Rhue, 1991.

role of expectations in hypnosis, and the prevention and management of negative effects in hypnotherapy. The second section presents the major modes and models of hypnotherapy, which include psychodynamic, cognitive–behavioral, rational–emotive, Ericksonian, and cognitive–developmental approaches. The third section is devoted to a variety of hypnotic techniques and approaches that can be used to enhance and generalize treatment gains. The fourth, fifth, and sixth sections of the book describe, respectively, specific interventions that are used in treating a wide variety of psychological disorders ranging from anxiety disorders to multiple personality, the use of hypnosis in the treatment of stress and trauma-related problems and disorders, and the application of hypnotic techniques to behavioral medicine and sports psychology. In a concluding section, issues germane to forensic hypnosis, training, and understanding hypnotic-like techniques from a cross-cultural perspective are discussed.

This book is intended for anyone who wishes to learn about clinical hypnosis. It will introduce the novice hypnotherapist to the basics of hypnotherapy and the many potential uses of hypnosis. It is thus ideally suited for use as a textbook for graduate and postgraduate courses and workshops. For the trained hypnotherapist, and even the seasoned clinician, the *Handbook* can be used as a reference volume that contains many suggestions for applying techniques and strategies relevant to the day-to-day work of the practitioner. Finally, hypnosis researchers and theoreticians will find much of value in this book. We hope that the state-of-the-art summaries of current research, along with the many suggestions for additional research contained in the *Handbook*, will spur creative investigations at the interface of science and practice that will enrich the field for years to come.

JUDITH W. RHUE
STEVEN JAY LYNN
IRVING KIRSCH

ACKNOWLEDGMENTS

This book has benefitted in innumerable ways from the intelligence, wisdom, and support of many people. Without our students prodding us to put together a collection of practical and useful chapters on the topic of clinical hypnosis, it would never have come to fruition. A number of these students, Joseph Green, Steven Kvaal, Abigail Matorin, David Sandberg, and Harry Sivec, contributed in more direct ways by providing us with helpful commentary on a number of the chapters. Ted Baroody, the development editor, APA Books, and Drs. James R. Council and Melvin Gravitz provided us with thoughtful suggestions and incisive commentary on the entire book. Dr. George Allen made useful suggestions on various sections of the book. The APA editorial staff also deserves a word of thanks for their meticulous editorial assistance. We extend our gratitude to our spouses, Jennifer Lynn and Christine Winter, and to our children, Martha Kate, Alexandra, Grant, and Steven Rhue, Jessica Barbara Lynn, and David Kirsch for their love and understanding. We close with a special note of thanks to the late Mrs. Reye Williams for her love and support during the editing of this book.

I

FOUNDATIONS AND GENERAL CONSIDERATIONS

1

INTRODUCTION TO CLINICAL HYPNOSIS

IRVING KIRSCH, STEVEN JAY LYNN, and JUDITH W. RHUE

Hypnotherapy is often treated as if it were a particular approach to psychotherapy, on a par with psychoanalysis, client-centered therapy, behavior therapy, and other therapeutic modalities (see, e.g., Smith, Glass, & Miller, 1980). In the 19th century, hypnotherapy actually was a distinct mode of treatment. Auguste Liébeault (1823–1904), for example, offered his patients a choice between traditional medical treatment, for which a standard fee would be charged, or hypnotherapy, which he would administer without charge (Gravitz, 1991). In those days, hypnotherapy consisted of administering a hypnotic induction and suggesting the alleviation of the symptom for which the patient sought relief.

A careful reading of the chapters in this book will make it evident that this is no longer the case. Although direct suggestion of symptom relief is still used for some purposes (e.g., the treatment of warts; see chapter 28 in this book), it is the exception rather than the rule. More frequently, the use of hypnosis in contemporary hypnotherapy is embedded within some broader therapeutic approach. Thus, one can speak of psychodynamic hypnotherapy, cognitive–behavioral hypnotherapy, or Ericksonian hypno-therapy, as evidenced by the chapters in part 2 of this book.

Just as most psychotherapists identify their orientation as "eclectic," hypnotherapy often involves a blending of ideas and techniques from different theoretical perspectives. Dowd (see chapter 10, this volume, for example), offers an interesting combination of cognitive and Ericksonian concepts, and many of the chapters devoted to the treatment of specific presenting problems include elements of psychodynamic and cognitive–behavioral theory. Thus, most clinical applications of hypnosis can be referred to as "eclectic hypnotherapy." As it is practiced today, *hypnotherapy* can be defined as the addition of hypnosis to accepted psychological or medical treatment. As such, it should be practiced only by professionals who have the appropriate training and credentials to provide the treatment that is being augmented by hypnosis.

DEFINING HYPNOSIS

Our definition of hypnotherapy assumes that one knows what is meant by the term *hypnosis*. What is hypnosis though? For more than a century, hypnosis was defined as a special state that is different from normal waking consciousness (American Psychological Association Division of Psycholog-ical Hypnosis, 1985; James, 1890). However, the question of whether hypnosis is an altered state of consciousness has become the subject of intense controversy (Sheehan & Perry, 1976) and, more recently, even the nature of the controversy has become controversial (Kihlstrom, 1992; Kirsch, 1992). Clearly, defining hypnosis as an altered state begs the ques-tion. A theoretically neutral definition is needed, a definition that is not inconsistent with any prominent theories.

Fortunately, there is general agreement about the kinds of phenomena that are observed in what has been termed the *domain of hypnosis* (Hilgard, 1973). Hypnosis is a situation or set of procedures in which a person designated as the hypnotist suggests that another person designated as the patient, client, or subject experience various changes in sensation, percep-tion, cognition, or control over motor behavior (cf. Kihlstrom, 1985). It is useful to think of these suggestions as being divided into two phases—induction and application—although in practice they may not be entirely distinct. Some responsive subjects report that hypnotic inductions produce an altered state that is much different from the normal waking conscious-ness, but most describe it as a normal state of focused attention (McConkey, 1986). Most people are more responsive to suggestion after an induction than they were before (Hilgard, 1965).

HISTORICAL BACKGROUND OF HYPNOSIS AND HYPNOTHERAPY

Although healing procedures dating back to antiquity have been viewed as precursors of hypnosis, their relevance to the history of hypnosis has not gone unchallenged (Spanos & Chaves, 1991). In any case, there is general agreement that the modern history of hypnosis began with the work of a flamboyant Viennese physician named Franz Anton Mesmer (1734–1815). Mesmer believed that an invisible magnetic fluid permeated the universe, that certain diseases were produced by an imbalance of this fluid within the human body, and that these conditions could be cured by restoring the body's magnetic balance. At first, he did this through the use of magnets, but he later decided that the healer's body, itself permeated with animal magnetism, could redirect the patient's magnetic fluid without the use of magnets. This was accomplished by a variety of means, including touching and making "passes" over the patient's body.

Unlike hypnotized subjects today, Mesmer's patients responded with violent convulsions, termed a "crisis." This seems to have been due to modeling because the first patient magnetized by Mesmer had been suffering from a convulsive disorder. In turn, her responses to the magnets seemed to have been patterned on the behavior of allegedly possessed individuals who were being treated by a well-known priest whose exorcisms were the talk of Vienna at the time.

The trancelike behavior that is associated with hypnosis today was discovered by one of Mesmer's disciples, the Marquis de Puységur (1751–1825). In 1784, Victor Race, a peasant who had come to the Marquis for treatment and who might not have known that a convulsive crisis was the proper response to being magnetized, responded with what appeared to be a deep sleep. It differed from normal sleep, however, in that Victor was able to speak and respond to the speech of others while in this apparent somnambulist state. Artificial somnambulism soon attracted the attention of other mesmerists. As it did, their patients responded with fewer and fewer convulsions and with more and more manifestations of a trance.

In 1785, mesmerism was investigated by a distinguished royal commission in Paris, chaired by the American ambassador to France, Benjamin Franklin. Through a series of surprisingly well-designed, placebo-controlled experiments, the commission discredited the notion of animal magnetism, concluding that the observed effects were caused instead by imagination. Carles D'Eslon, who had represented mesmerism before the commission, astutely responded as follows:

> If Mesmer had no secret than that he had been able to make the
> imagination exert an influence upon health, would he still not be a

wonder doctor? If treatment by the use of imagination is the best treatment, why do we not make use of it?" (quoted in Gravitz, 1991, p. 27)

This comment was prescient, insofar as many of the treatments described in this book capitalize on imagination and fantasy-based techniques to enhance treatment gains.

After the Royal Commission issued its reports, mesmerism fell into decline, attaining the status of a cult. And so it might have remained had it not been resurrected by James Braid (1795–1860), a 19th-century British physician. After witnessing a demonstration and experimenting with some of his own patients, Braid concluded that the mesmerists had discovered an important medical procedure. At the same time, he rejected Mesmer's theory of animal magnetism. He described the somnambulist state as a "nervous sleep" and hypothesized that it was produced by fatigue of the eye muscles, brought about by staring fixedly at a point somewhere above the normal line of vision. In discarding the outmoded theory of animal magnetism, Braid gave the phenomena a new name, *hypnotism*, which was derived from *hypno*, the Greek word for *sleep*.

The most famous 19th-century advocate of hypnosis was Jean-Martin Charcot (1835–1893), one of the most eminent neurologists of the era, director of the Neurological Clinic at the Salpêtrière Hospital in Paris, and teacher of Pierre Janet, Alfred Binet, and Sigmund Freud. Charcot's notion that hypnosis was a neuropathological state that could be produced only in hysterics was buttressed by his producing and removing conversion symptoms through posthypnotic suggestion. Charcot's idea that certain thoughts could be dissociated from conscious awareness led to Freud's adoption of the notion of the unconscious and to Janet's theory of dissociation.

At the same time, Charcot developed the completely erroneous theory that only hysterics were capable of experiencing hypnosis and that it occurred in three stages: lethargy, catalepsy, and somnambulism. These views were successfully challenged by Auguste Liébeault (1823–1904) and Hippolyte Bernheim (1837–1919), from the small town of Nancy, France, who viewed hypnotic phenomena as normal products of suggestion. Despite Charcot's prominence, it was the conception of the Nancy school that became one of the dominant 20th-century views of hypnosis. Charcot had fallen prey to the most common pitfall of hypnosis theory and research. He had observed phenomena that had been directly or indirectly suggested to his patients and mistakenly concluded that what he had seen was part of the essence of hypnosis.

Nevertheless, through Charcot, hypnosis profoundly affected the development of psychotherapy. The precursor to free association, hypnosis was the first "basic tool" of what was to become psychoanalysis. After the abandonment of hypnosis by Freud, its clinical use virtually vanished for decades. The 1930s witnessed two milestones in the history of hypnosis. Hull (1933) launched the first large-scale research program devoted to the topic of hypnosis. During that same decade, one of Hull's students, Milton H. Erickson, began to develop many creative therapeutic techniques that advanced the use and acceptability of hypnosis in clinical practice and are widely practiced today.

Various strands of early hypnosis theorizing have survived and even flourished in contemporary accounts of hypnosis. Hilgard's (1991) neodissociation theory, which was based in part on Janet's theorizing, holds that multiple cognitive systems or cognitive structures exist in a hierarchical arrangement under some measure of control by an executive ego responsible for the planning and monitoring functions of the personality. During hypnosis, these systems may become independent of or dissociated from each other and can be directly activated by the hypnotist's suggestions. This perspective has become one of the most influential contemporary theories of hypnosis. The neodissociation theory has been adopted implicitly, if not explicitly, by many clinicians whose work is represented in this book.

Neodissociation theory vies for support and empirical attention with models proposed by sociocognitive theorists (e.g., T. X. Barber, Chaves, Coe, Kirsch, Lynn, Spanos, Sarbin) who, like Liebault and Bernheim of the Nancy school, argue that hypnotic phenomena are social behaviors that are direct by-products of suggestion. Contributors to this book (e.g., Chaves, Coe, Gfeller, Kirsch, Lynn, Spanos) have demonstrated that techniques derived from a sociocognitive perspective can be used in creative ways in many clinical situations. Of course, much of the modern history of hypnosis is presented in the chapters that follow, which outline major contemporary hypnosis models.

INDICATIONS AND CONTRAINDICATIONS FOR THE USE OF HYPNOSIS IN THERAPY

The chapters of this book demonstrate the wide range of clinical problems to which hypnosis can be applied. These include anxiety disorders, depression, borderline conditions, posttraumatic stress disorder, multiple personality, psychosomatic disorders, pain management, eating disorders, smoking, obesity, and wart removal. Indeed, hypnosis can be used in treating virtually any condition for which a psychological intervention is indicated.

There are many reasons for adding hypnotic procedures to treatment plans. For some clients, the hypnotic context may increase rapport or accentuate positive transference and countertransference (see chapter 3 in this book). For clients with positive attitudes toward hypnosis, the hypnotic context may enhance their confidence in the effectiveness of therapy and thereby produce a placebo effect without the deception that is generally associated with placebos (see chapters 4 and 7 in this book). Hypnotic suggestions can also produce changes in perception among hypnotizable clients. An example of the use of this phenomenon is administering suggestions to decrease the intensity of withdrawal symptoms and increase the aversiveness of tobacco smoke as aspects of smoking cessation treatments (see chapter 26 in this book). It also has been hypothesized that hypnosis heightens the vividness of imagery, thereby enhancing the effectiveness of desensitization treatments (see chapter 15 in this book).

Yet, hypnosis is not a panacea. It is simply not effective with all clients, and it should be used only after careful deliberation on the therapist's part. The use of hypnosis, or any other therapeutic intervention for that matter, should be preceded by an evaluation of the client. At a minimum, this assessment should include information pertinent to the client's mental status, life history, and current psychological problems and dynamics. Important areas of inquiry include the client's treatment motivation, needs, character structure, life situation, beliefs about hypnosis, and perceived strengths and weaknesses. Delving into the archive of life experiences can be a source of useful suggestions that tap into the client's resources, and acquiring knowledge of hypnosis-specific attitudes and expectations can prove invaluable in preparing the client for hypnosis, as described in the next section.

It is essential that the decision to use hypnosis is justified by what is learned in the initial assessment, by the therapist's general theoretical orientation, and by the specific goals and objectives of psychotherapy. Before hypnosis is undertaken, it is imperative that therapists establish a strong therapeutic alliance, know what they wish to accomplish, and have a clear idea about how hypnotic communications can facilitate treatment. Additionally, careful planning and preparation of therapeutic communications and suggestions is essential before hypnosis is induced. Ultimately, the pros and cons of hypnosis must be carefully weighed against those of nonhypnotic treatment.

Therapists would do well to examine their motives for using hypnosis (or any other psychotherapy technique) and to monitor their actions and reactions, as well as those of the client. Given these considerations, in our own clinical practice we do not make the decision to use hypnosis on a casual or cursory basis. Before we induce hypnosis, we routinely ask ourselves a number of questions, the first and foremost of which is, Why use hypnosis at this particular juncture in therapy? What is to be gained? Can hypnosis accelerate treatment? Can it promote generalization of treatment effects? What are the client's motives for requesting hypnotherapy? Is the client's request a test of whether we truly care and will yield to the client's wishes or whims? By contrast, what are our motives? Do we wish to use hypnosis because we feel guilty that we are not doing more for the client? Are we bored or angry with the client and hungering for "fireworks" in therapy that only hypnosis can provide?

Affirmative answers to these latter questions would lead us to reevaluate the use of hypnosis or postpone hypnotherapy until these issues were adequately addressed or resolved. For example, clients sometimes request hypnotherapy thinking that hypnosis will do the work for them. Unrealistic expectations of this sort set up both the therapist and client for failure. The client may feel like a failure when yet one more intervention fails to make a difference, and the therapist can be discredited or diminished when a highly touted intervention meets with little success. The client's experience may lead to the despondent conclusion, "I tried hypnosis and even that didn't work!"

We would be equally suspicious of using hypnosis to bypass the cautions that normally would be considered before abreactive or uncovering work were undertaken. Clients can have intense abreactive reactions during hypnosis, as they can in nonhypnotic contexts. It has been our observation that the hypnotic context may give some clients license to express thoughts and feelings that they ordinarily would not express in psychotherapy. This can be one of the advantages of using hypnosis. However, if therapists are not trained or prepared to work with clients who experience abreactions, then techniques that promote regressive experiences, whether hypnotic or not, ought to be avoided.

It would also be wise for therapists to postpone hypnotherapy or not use hypnosis with borderline or dissociative clients who are not yet stabilized in treatment. Regressive or altered bodily experiences that often accompany hypnosis could well disrupt these clients' psychological equilibrium. As in nonhypnotic treatment, the following questions need to be considered: Is the client's condition sufficiently stabilized to justify treatment that focuses on abreaction or uncovering? Are there conscious or subconscious motivations to resist responsibility for current actions and to affix blame on events or people from the past? Does the client wish to arrive at a facile understanding of his or her problems by way of viewing his or her present through the lens of a past rife with abuse?

Besides these general concerns, there are questions that relate directly to the establishment of a hypnotic context for doing uncovering work: Does the client view hypnosis as a magical cure, as a royal road to the unconscious, or as a window to the past? Does the client's request for hypnosis to recall past events represent an attempt to control the therapy hour in order to avoid dealing with issues that trouble him or her in the present? Many issues pertinent to the indications and counterindications of hypnosis and the management of client reactions are discussed in chapter 5, which is concerned with the prevention and management of negative effects in hypnotherapy.

If the clinician decides to proceed with hypnosis, some clients will nevertheless be ambivalent, resistant, or unable to experience hypnotic effects at all. It is, of course, impossible to know precisely how a client will respond to a hypnotic intervention prior to inducing hypnosis itself. Yet, even when hypnosis is not entirely successful, much can be learned about the client. For example, it is possible to better understand clients' resistance or ambivalence to treatment; their creative abilities and comfort with relaxation, imagination, and fantasy; their feelings about the therapist and the therapeutic alliance; and the needs, wishes, and fears that are projected onto the therapist and the hypnotic relationship. Whether and how this knowledge can be exploited depends in part on the therapist's acumen and the degree to which insight derived from clients' reactions to hypnosis are relevant to the therapist's particular brand of psychotherapy.

Because hypnosis is not a form of psychotherapy in and of itself, the best guarantee of competent practice is adequate training in the psychotherapy used. In the next section we outline some of the "nuts and bolts" of administering hypnotic inductions. This is meant only to be an introduction to the use of hypnotic techniques. The limited information we provide here is not a substitute for supervised training in the use of hypnotic inductions and the administration of therapeutic suggestions.

BASIC HYPNOTIC PROCEDURES

Clinical applications of hypnosis are the subject matter of this book and are amply described in subsequent chapters. In this chapter, we deal with the topics of hypnotic inductions, deepening techniques, and terminating hypnosis sessions. Appropriately enough, relatively little of this book is devoted to these topics. Inducing hypnosis is notoriously easy to learn. This ease has led to a proliferation of self-described hypnotherapists who have learned how to induce hypnosis but have not been adequately trained in psychotherapy. In fact, we were somewhat hesitant about providing detailed instructions here. However, this book is intended for professionals and graduate students and not for a lay audience. Therapists who wish to add hypnosis to their clinical repertoire need to learn the standard procedures of hypnotic induction, and a handbook of this sort would be incomplete without this information. In any case, hypnotic inductions have also been printed in other professional books. Nevertheless, we caution readers against sharing this information with nonprofessionals. Hypnotherapy should be used only by people with appropriate training and credentials.

Introducing Hypnosis

Before beginning hypnosis, it is important to clear up misconceptions about it that are likely to have been picked up from the media. Many people believe that hypnosis is something that is done to them rather than some-thing that they do. They think that hypnotized people lose control of themselves and can be made to do or say whatever the hypnotist wants. They think that they will feel drastically altered, as if they had taken a powerful drug, and they may fear that they will not be able to come out of this altered state. Some believe that subjects who have been hypnotized are unable to remember what occurred. Less common misconceptions in-clude the idea that only weak-willed people are capable of being hypnotized or that hypnosis might weaken one's willpower.

The media is not entirely to blame for these misconceptions. Many of them were believed by mesmerists and early hypnotists. However, clinical experience informed by the results of controlled research in hypnosis has led to a more accurate understanding of the phenomenon. It is now known that (a) hypnosis is not related to sleep, (b) it is something done by the subject rather than by the therapist, (c) subjects retain the ability to control their behavior (Lynn, Rhue, & Weekes, 1990), (d) subjects are aware of their surroundings and can monitor events outside of the framework of suggestions (Lynn, Weekes, & Milano, 1989), and (e) spontaneous amnesia is relatively rare (Simon & Salzberg, 1985) and its unwanted occurrence can be prevented by informing clients that they will be able to remember everything that they are comfortable remembering about the session. This information should always be provided to clients before attempting to induce hypnosis.

A Standard Hypnotic Induction

An astoundingly wide variety of procedures have been used as induc-tions. Some of these methods are rarely, if ever, used now. These include stroking patients, having them ingest "magnetized" substances, waving one's hands over them, and touching them with magnets or in particular ritualized ways. Among the procedures still in use are asking subjects to close their eyes and telling them to sleep, instructing them to relax, having them fix their gaze on an object or their attention on an idea, suggesting various images or automatic movements, asking them to attend to their ongoing experience, commenting on changes in their moment-to-moment behavior, confusing them with indecipherable verbal communications, telling them stories, and so on. These procedures are often used in combination. Most inductions include instructions for deep relaxation, and this has been thought to be an essential component of hypnosis (see Edmonston, 1991). However, inductions stressing physical tension and alertness have been developed, and they seem about as effective as relaxation inductions in enhancing suggestibility (Banyai & Hilgard, 1976; Gibbons, 1974, 1976; Kirsch, Mobayed, Council, & Kenny, 1992).

The following is an example of a standard relaxation-based induction.

It assumes that this is the patient's first experience of hypnosis, that the nature of hypnosis has been explained, that fears and misconceptions have been discussed, that the patient is seated in a comfortable chair or couch, and that permission to induce hypnosis has been granted.

Please make yourself comfortable. Close your eyes and let yourself relax. Take a few slow deep breaths and notice that as you exhale, you can feel yourself becoming more relaxed. You can continue to relax, as I speak to you . . . and each time you exhale, you can feel yourself becoming more and more relaxed . . . more and more relaxed. Soon you will experience hypnosis, and you are probably wondering what that experience will be like. I want to assure you that no matter how deeply hypnotized you become, you will remain in complete control. You will stay in control, even when very deeply involved in the experience of hypnosis. I will make suggestions, but it will be up to you to decide whether you want to experience those suggestions. If you don't like a suggestion that I make, you can choose to ignore it and to not have that experience. But if you want to experience a suggestion, you may find it easier to experience than you ever thought possible. So the choice is always yours, and it's safe to enter hypnosis now, as you allow yourself to relax.

As I speak, you can feel yourself becoming more and more relaxed. But no matter how relaxed you become, you will hear my voice, and you will be able to respond to my suggestions. If you become at all uncomfortable, you can readjust your body and make yourself comfortable again, and that won't get in the way of your experience of hypnosis. If you need to speak to me, you will be able to do so easily, without disrupting your hypnotic experience.

Right now, you might want to relax even more, and as you relax, you may feel a slight tingly feeling in your fingers . . . or in your toes . . . and if you do, it can comfort you because you will know that it is a feeling of relaxation that some people have as they begin to experience hypnosis. Let your body relax. Just begin to feel a spreading sense of calm . . . and peace . . . letting go of all your cares and concerns, let them drift away, like clouds in the wind . . . dissipating . . . breaking up . . . just relaxing . . . more and more . . . feeling more and more at peace . . . more calm . . . more comfortable and secure . . . nothing to bother . . . nothing to disturb . . . more and more deeply relaxed, as you enter hypnosis . . . becoming so deeply involved in hypnosis that you can have all of the experiences you want to have . . . deep enough to experience whatever you want to experience . . . but only the experiences you want . . . just your own experiences.

And you can focus your attention on your toes . . . your right toe . . . and your left toe. Let your right toe relax . . . relax completely . . . and your left toe . . . letting your toes relax . . . more and more . . . more and more relaxed. And let the relaxation spread from your toes into your feet, and let your feet relax. Let them become more and more relaxed . . . as you can feel so calm and at ease. And now pay attention to your ankles and to your calves. I wonder if you can begin to let go . . . let go and relax as you feel perhaps a comfortable sense of warmth in your ankles or your calves . . . or perhaps it is a cool and easy feeling . . . in your right leg or in your left leg. Just let your legs relax . . . more and more relaxed . . . more and more completely relaxed.

And the relaxation can spread into your thighs . . . your thighs can relax more and more . . . just letting go. And you can let your pelvis relax . . . relaxing more and more. Relax your stomach. Let your stomach become completely relaxed. Just let it go loose and limp . . . loose and limp. Notice how it feels. Can you let it feel completely relaxed? . . . can you notice this now or a bit later? And let the relaxation spread upward into your chest. Let all the nerves and muscles in your chest relax completely . . . relaxed . . . loose and limp . . . feel the peace spreading as you feel so at ease . . . so secure . . . your body and mind so relaxed and at peace. And now your back can relax, and your shoulders. Let yourself feel the relaxation in your back and your shoulders . . . more and more relaxed . . . loose and limp . . . completely relaxed.

Let the relaxation spread through your arms, down into your hands and your fingers. Focus on the feelings in your arms and hands. Do your fingers feel more heavy than light or more light than heavy? Focus on your right upper arm . . . right lower arm . . . your right hand . . . and fingers . . . relaxing completely . . . more and more relaxed . . . completely relaxed. And now your left arm . . . relaxing completely, so relaxed . . . completely relaxed. I wonder if you can go even deeper now. Deeper and deeper . . . just as you wish . . . just as comfortable and as deep as you would like to go.

Would it feel even better to relax the muscles of your neck? . . . Just let go and relax . . . loose and limp . . . completely relaxed. And relax your jaw muscles. Just let them go limp. All the nerves and muscles in your jaw relaxing completely. And relax all the rest of the muscles in your face . . . your mouth . . . nose . . . eyes . . . eyebrows . . . eyelids . . . forehead . . . all the muscles going loose and limp . . . loose and limp . . . completely relaxed . . . at peace . . . calm and relaxed . . . completely at ease.

You might like to imagine being somewhere peaceful and relaxing. I like to imagine lying on a quiet beach on a warm sunny day, with a beautiful blue sky and just a few billowy clouds floating by. . . . I can imagine feeling a soft, gentle breeze . . . smelling the salt sea air . . . but you can imagine being anywhere you like. It might be someplace you've been . . . or someplace you'd like to be. Or just a place in your imagination . . . It doesn't matter . . . all that matters is your comfort . . . your peace. Wherever it is, it is so peaceful and calm . . . someplace where you can just be you . . . where you can feel completely at ease and content. And you can imagine yourself actually being there . . .

seeing, in your mind's eye, the things that you would see if you were actually there now . . . feeling the things you would feel . . . hearing the sounds you would hear . . . smelling the smells.

And while you are in your perfect place, I am going to count from one to ten. And with each count you can drift more and more deeply into hypnosis . . . more and more able to experience whatever you want to experience. One . . . drift . . . drift deeper . . . two . . . more and more centered, and balanced . . . three . . . four . . . deeper and deeper . . . five . . . halfway there . . . six . . . seven . . . even deeper than before . . . so deep that you can experience whatever you wish to experience . . . eight . . . nine . . . ten . . . very deep now . . . very deep . . . completely at one with yourself . . . completely engrossed.

This is a basic but completely adequate induction that can be used with individuals or groups. It can be memorized or read verbatim by therapists who are practicing hypnosis in a workshop or class, but except in research settings, becoming familiar with it and paraphrasing it extemporaneously is advised. Behavior therapists will recognize it as a simple relaxation exercise with the addition of the word *hypnosis*. Research indicates that simple memorized inductions of this sort are as effective as the more complicated individualized inductions given to clients by highly skilled hypnotherapists (Van der Does, Van Dyck, Spinhoven, & Kloosman, 1989). Hypnotic talent is a characteristic of subjects, not of hypnotists.

Other Induction Techniques

Eye Closure

The eye-closure induction is a simple variation of the relaxation induction. Instead of having clients close their eyes, they are asked to stare at a target. The target can be provided by the therapist, or clients can be asked to pick a spot on the wall or ceiling, preferably somewhat above the normal field of vision so that some eye strain is provoked. The client is told, "As you begin to enter hypnosis, you will feel your eyes beoming tired and heavy, so heavy that they will feel like closing all by themselves." Additional suggestions for eye heaviness and closure are inserted into typical relaxation instructions, such as the one presented earlier. The vigilant therapist can monitor the client for signs such as blinking, eyelids beginning to droop, or watery eyes. These are then noted verbally, as though they provide evidence that the client is successfully entering hypnosis: "Your eyes are beginning to droop . . . getting heavier and heavier . . . more and more tired . . . they are closing all by themselves as you become more and more deeply hypnotized."

Arm Levitation

The client is told that one arm is becoming lighter and lighter and that soon it may become so light that it will float up into the air. These suggestions can be combined with relaxation instructions and with the eye-closure procedure just described. An image can be described to facilitate arm lightness, such as having a helium balloon tied to one's hand. When movements of the fingers, hand, or arm are observed, the therapist comments on them in a manner similar to that used to facilitate eye closure:

> You can feel the lightness in your finger as it begins to move . . . becoming lighter and lighter. Your whole hand is becoming lighter . . . lighter and lighter . . . beginning to lift . . . lifting . . . more and more . . . lighter and lighter . . . lifting higher and higher.

Although arm levitation provides clients with dramatic evidence of the effects of hypnosis, thereby facilitating positive treatment expectancies (Goldstein, 1981), it may be failed by a substantial number of subjects or require a long time for some to achieve. This problem can be avoided by suggesting that one arm will become light and the other heavy (Kirsch, 1990):

> You may notice that one of your arms is just a bit lighter than the other, and your other arm is heavier. As we talk, your light arm may become even lighter or your heavy arm may become even heavier. And I wonder just how light your lighter arm will feel, and how heavy the other arm will feel. Will your light arm become so light that it lifts up into the air all by itself or will your heavy arm become so heavy that it stays rooted to the arm of your chair? And I wonder which arm feels lighter. Is it your right arm or your left arm? And where do you feel the lightness most? In your wrist or in your fingers? In all of your fingers or especially in one of them?

Overt signs of upward movement in one hand or arm provides a signal to focus on arm levitation. Otherwise, these are abandoned and suggestions for arm heaviness and immobility are stressed. This method has the dual advantage of preventing failure and providing some indication of the client's level of responsiveness.

Deepening Techniques

There are times when the therapist would like a client to feel more "deeply" hypnotized. This may occur, for example, when the client appears to be having some difficulty in achieving a desired therapeutic effect. In these instances, a brief deepening procedure can act as a catalyst, enabling the client to experience phenomena that could not be accomplished earlier.

Deepening techniques and the components of hypnotic inductions are interchangeable, and the only difference between them is the time at which they are used. For example, the counting procedure contained in the standard induction presented earlier is an excellent deepening procedure. It can also be combined with a variety of images, limited only by the creativity of the therapist. For example, one can have the client imagine walking down a flight of stairs or watching waves at the beach and becoming more deeply hypnotized or "twice as deeply hypnotized" with each step or wave. Alternately, simple instructions for becoming more deeply hypnotized will generally suffice:

> And now I would like you to become even more deeply hypnotized . . . more deeply than before. With each breath you take, you can become more and more deeply hypnotized . . . so deep that you will be able to do whatever you need to do in hypnosis today . . . deeper and deeper . . . deep enough to experience anything you wish to experience.

Posthypnotic Suggestions

The nature of posthypnotic suggestions that can be administered is limited only by the imagination of the hypnotherapist. It is often helpful to administer posthypnotic suggestions for relaxation, ego enhancement, and mastery that are linked with a physical movement or gesture such as touching the thumb and forefinger together. When a particular feeling state or sense of mastery regarding a situation is achieved during hypnosis, clients can be instructed to touch their thumb and forefinger together, for example, and to do so in an actual life situation in which they would like to replicate the feelings or sense of mastery. This technique is illustrated in chapter 25 with respect to smoking cessation, but the technique of cue-controlled relaxation, or "anchoring," as it is sometimes referred to, has a wide range of application.

Preparing for Subsequent Sessions

Before ending the initial hypnosis session, it may be useful to prepare the client for subsequent sessions, so that the time required for inducing hypnosis can be reduced. This can be accomplished in two ways: First, clients can be told that hypnosis becomes easier to experience with practice, so that each time they experience hypnosis, they will find it easier and easier to become hypnotized and they will enter hypnosis more and more quickly. Second, a posthypnotic suggestion (i.e., a suggestion to have particular experiences or engage in specific behaviors after hypnosis is terminated) can be given to establish a cue or signal for quickly becoming involved with the experience of hypnosis. For example,

> From now on, it is going to be very easy for you to become hypnotized when you want to. We are going to establish a cue that will allow you

to become hypnotized instantly. We can use any word or phrase you like. I wonder if there is a particular word or phrase that can symbolize this experience for you . . . or whether you prefer that I suggest the phrase. [The client or therapist selects a phrase.] Okay! From now on, the words *hypnosis now* will be a signal to enter hypnosis. But it will only work when I say those words and when you want to become hypnotized. When you want to enter hypnosis and I say the words *hypnosis now,* you will immediately become deeply engrossed in the hypnotic experience. But it won't happen if someone else says those words. If you hear those words in normal conversation, they will have no effect at all. And it won't work if you do not wish to experience hypnosis. But if I say "hypnosis now" and if you are ready to be hypnotized, you will be able to enter hypnosis immediately.

In subsequent sessions, once the client is comfortable and indicates readiness to begin hypnosis, the therapist says "hypnosis now," either alone or embedded in a phrase such as "You can enter hypnosis now," stressing the cue words so that the signal intent is not missed. This can be followed by deepening suggestions as needed by the client.

Terminating Hypnosis

Ending a hypnosis session is even easier than inducing it. One can terminate hypnosis by simply telling the client to "wake up now" or "you can come out of hypnosis as soon as you are ready." More often, a brief counting procedure, spoken in an increasingly energetic tone, is used:

I am going to count backward from five, and with each count you are going to become more and more alert and energized. At the count of one, you can open your eyes. At zero, you will be fully alert and wide awake, feeling better than you did before we began. Five . . . four . . . three . . . feel the energy flowing into you . . . two . . . one . . . open you eyes . . . zero . . . wide awake.

Before ending the hypnosis session, it may be helpful to provide suggestions for general well-being, such as those contained in the counting procedure presented above. Termination can be preceded by pleasant imagery, such as that used in the sample induction. This is especially useful if emotionally stressful work has been done during the session, but it can also be included at other times to promote feelings of well-being and enhance the enjoyment of the hypnotic experience.

At the conclusion of the hypnosis session, it is important to ask clients how they are feeling. As noted in chapter 5 of this book, negative aftereffects are not common, but they are sometimes reported. Although there is no evidence that these are caused by the use of hypnosis (see chapter 5), they require clinical attention whatever their cause.

Novice hypnotists sometimes worry about not being able to bring a client "out" of hypnosis. This is a holdover from conceptions of hypnosis that are no longer held by professionals but that continue to influence the public through inaccurate portrayals in the media. The state of consciousness produced by typical hypnotic inductions is similar to meditative or relaxed states. Asking "What if my client doesn't come out of hypnosis" is like asking "What if my client doesn't stop relaxing?"

It can happen that a particular subject seems to be "stuck" in hypnosis, but this is extremely rare, especially in clinical settings in which a good therapeutic relationship has been established. On the rare occasions in which it does occur, it may indicate that the client is enjoying the experience and does not want it to end. In nonclinical settings, it may be a provocation aimed at seeing what the hypnotist will do. The motive for remaining in hypnosis can be ascertained by simply asking the client, and the answer is likely to provide the therapist with the cues needed to resolve the problem. If all else fails, clients can be told that they will "come out" of hypnosis when they are ready but that they will be charged for the time they remain in the therapist's office.

A Word of Caution

The chapters of this book illustrate a wide variety of hypnotic techniques. These techniques include, but are not limited to, suggested hypnotic dreams, analgesia, metaphors, and communications couched in indirect language. One technique that is widely used by therapists of diverse persuasions is age regression. Events that are remembered during hypnosis may seem particularly compelling to both the therapist and client when they are associated with intense affect reminiscent of childhood displays of emotion. However, memory studies (e.g., Loftus, 1979) have challenged the idea that all events are stored with perfect accuracy in memory. A traumatic history, for example, consists not only of past childhood events but also of the person's interpretations, embellishments, and distortions of those events from the perspective of present events, accomplishments, behaviors, and relationships that constitute life in the present (see chapter 19 in this book). In short, memory is not immutable or preserved like a fly in amber, nor is the mind like a vast storehouse of indelible impressions, facts, and information. Indeed, the memory literature (Laurence & Perry, 1983; Sheehan, 1988) indicates that ordinary memory is fallible and that certain subjects place an inordinate degree of confidence in their remembrances, even to the point of being convinced that events that did not take place actually did occur.

Practitioners of hypnosis need to be cognizant of the fact that hypnosis does not foster a literal reexperiencing of childhood events. Hypnosis is not a key to unlocking the vault of memory. In his exhaustive review of more than 100 years of hypnosis research on temporal regression, Nash

(1987) failed to find any special correspondence between the behavior and experience of hypnotized adults and that of actual children. He concluded that although the products of hypnotic age regression are often clinically useful, the client's response cannot be accepted at face value.

The point here is that hypnosis in no way obviates the hazards of memory distortion associated with ordinary psychotherapy. In fact, hypnosis may exacerbate memory problems. One of the core demands associated with the hypnotic context is to fantasize and imagine along with suggested events and to relinquish a critical, analytical stance in favor of the direct experience of subjective events that arise in response to hypnotic communications. The combination of increased fantasy and decreased objectivity, along with the commonly held belief that hypnosis enhances recall, may promote the confusion of fantasy and historical reality. A 1985 report by the Council on Scientific Affairs of the American Medical Association and subsequent research underscores the fact that hypnosis can increase confidence of recalled events with little or no change in the level of accuracy.

Although hypnotizability augurs well for successful responses to suggestions used to enhance or uncover memories, such as age regression, it is precisely this ability that is associated with increased pseudomemory (i.e., false memories suggested during hypnosis or psychotherapy) rates. Studies from Laurence's (Laurence & Perry, 1983), Sheehan's (Sheehan, Statham, & Jamieson, 1991a, 1991b; Sheehan, Statham, Jamieson, & Ferguson, 1991), McConkey's (McConkey, 1992; McConkey, Labelle, Bibb, & Bryant, 1990), and Spanos's (Spanos, Gwynn, Comer, Baltruweit, & deGroh, 1989) laboratories have shown that high- and medium-hypnotizable subjects are at particular risk for suggestion-related memory distortions and that these hypnotizability effects are not necessarily limited to hypnotic situations.

Our brief discussion suggests that the mere fact that memories are uncovered during hypnosis does not lend them the stamp of historical validity. Indeed, therapists need to exercise vigilance to avoid inadvertently administering suggestions that produce or legitimate pseudomemories. It is essential that therapists evaluate the credibility of purportedly repressed memories uncovered during therapy in light of the client's hypnotizability and the nature of the procedures used to uncover the remembrances.

A Call for Outcome Research

Although relatively little outcome research has been done on the effectiveness of hypnotherapy, the results of existing studies are encouraging. In a meta-analysis of psychotherapy outcome studies, Smith et al. (1980) reported that psychodynamic hypnotherapy produced substantially greater effects than all nonhypnotic therapies. Levitt (see chapter 25, this volume) presents data indicating that hypnotic treatments may enhance the long-term effectiveness of treatments of obesity, which may provide a key to solving a recalcitrant problem in this area. Kirsch (see chapter 7, this volume) reports the results of a meta-analysis suggesting that hypnosis can substantially enhance the effects of cognitive–behavioral therapies, and despite Chaves's (see chapter 24, this volume) caution about the mechanisms involved, the effects of hypnotic procedures on pain have been well documented (Hilgard & Hilgard, 1975).

Nevertheless, the data are sparse, and the studies from which they have been drawn were often poorly designed. In the long run, hypnotherapeutic procedures will stand or fall on the basis of outcome data validating (or failing to validate) their efficacy. It is our hope that a substantial increase in outcome studies will be among the major changes between the publication of this book and its next edition.

REFERENCES

American Psychological Association, Division of Psychological Hypnosis. (1985). *A general definition of hypnosis and a statement concerning its application and efficacy* [Report]. Washington, DC: Author.

Banyai, E., & Hilgard, E. R. (1976). A comparison of active-alert hypnotic induction with traditional relaxation induction. *Journal of Abnormal Psychology, 85*, 218–224.

Council on Scientific Affairs, American Medical Association. (1985). Scientific status of refreshing recollection by the use of hypnosis. *Journal of the American Medical Association, 253*, 1918–1923.

Edmonston, W. (1991). Anesis. In S. J. Lynn & J. W. Rhue (Eds.), *Theories of hypnosis: Current models and perspectives* (pp. 197–237). New York: Guilford Press.

Gibbons, D. E. (1974). Hyperempiria: A new "altered state of consciousness" induced by suggestion. *Perceptual and Motor Skills, 39*, 47–53.

Gibbons, D. E. (1976). Hypnotic versus hyperempiric induction procedures: An experimental comparison. *Perceptual and Motor Skills, 42*, 834.

Goldstein, Y. (1981). The effect of demonstrating to a subject that she is in a hypnotic trance as a variable in hypnotic interventions with obese women. *International Journal of Clinical and Experimental Hypnosis, 29*, 13–23.

Gravitz, M. A. (1991). Early theories of hypnosis: A clinical perspective. In S. J. Lynn & J. W. Rhue (Eds.), *Theories of hypnosis: Current models and perspectives* (pp. 19–42). New York: Guilford Press.

Hilgard, E. R. (1965). *Hypnotic susceptibility*. New York: Harcourt, Brace & World.

Hilgard, E. R. (1973). The domain of hypnosis: With some comments on alternate paradigms. *American Psychologist, 28*, 972–982.

Hilgard, E. R. (1991). A neodissociation interpretation of hypnosis. In S. J. Lynn & J. W. Rhue (Eds.), *Theories of hypnosis: Current models and perspectives* (pp. 83–104). New York: Guilford Press.

Hilgard, E. R., & Hilgard, J. R. (1975). *Hypnosis in the relief of pain*. Los Altos, CA: Kaufmann.

Hull, C. L. (1933). *Hypnosis and suggestibility: An experimental approach*. New York: Appleton-Century-Crofts.

James, W. (1890). *Principles of psychology* (Vols. 1–2). New York: Holt, Rinehart & Winston.

Kihlstrom, J. F. (1985). Hypnosis. *Annual Review of Psychology, 36,* 385–418.

Kihlstrom, J. F. (1992). Hypnosis: A sesqi-centennial essay. *International Journal of Clinical and Experimental Hypnosis, 40,* 301–314.

Kirsch, I. (1990). *Changing expectations: A key to effective psychotherapy*. Pacific Grove, CA: Brooks/Cole.

Kirsch, I. (1992). The state of the altered state debate. *Contemporary Hypnosis, 9,* 1–6.

Kirsch, I., Mobayed, C. P., Council, J. R., & Kenny, D. A. (1992). Expert judgments of hypnosis from subjective state reports. *Journal of Abnormal Psychology, 101,* 657–662.

Laurence, J.-R., & Perry, C. (1983). Hypnotically created memory among highly hypnotizable subjects. *Science, 222,* 523–524.

Loftus, E. F. (1979). *Eyewitness testimony*. Cambridge, MA: Harvard University Press.

Lynn, S. J., Rhue, J. W., & Weekes, J. R. (1990). Hypnotic involuntariness: A social-cognitive analysis. *Psychological Review, 97,* 169–184.

Lynn, S. J., Weekes, J. R., & Milano, M. J. (1989). Reality versus suggestion: Pseudomemory in hypnotizable and simulating subjects. *Journal of Abnormal Psychology, 98,* 137–144.

McConkey, K. M. (1986). Opinions about hypnosis and self-hypnosis before and after hypnotic testing. *International Journal of Clinical and Experimental Hypnosis, 34,* 311–319.

McConkey, K. M. (1992). The effects of hypnotic procedures on remembering: The experimental findings and their implications for forensic hypnosis. In E. Fromm & M. Nash (Eds.), *Contemporary hypnosis research* (pp. 405–426). New York: Guilford Press.

McConkey, K. M., Labelle, L., Bibb, B. C., & Bryant, R. A. (1990). Hypnosis and suggested pseudomemory: The relevance of test context. *Australian Journal of Psychology, 42,* 197–205.

Nash, M. R. (1987). What, if anything, is regressed about hypnotic age regression? A review of the empirical literature. *Psychological Bulletin, 102,* 42–52.

Sheehan, P. W. (1988). Memory distortion in hypnosis. *International Journal of Clinical and Experimental Hypnosis, 36,* 296–311.

Sheehan, P. W., & Perry, C. W. (1976). *Methodologies of hypnosis*. Hillsdale, NJ: Erlbaum.

Sheehan, P. W., Statham, D., & Jamieson, G. A. (1991a). Pseudomemory effects over time in the hypnotic setting. *Journal of Abnormal Psychology, 100,* 39–44.

Sheehan, P. W., Statham, D., & Jamieson, G. A. (1991b). Pseudomemory effects and their relationship to level of susceptibility to hypnosis and state instructions. *Journal of Personality and Social Psychology, 60,* 130–137.

Sheehan, P. W., Statham, D., Jamieson, G. A., & Ferguson, S. R. (1991). Ambiguity in suggestion and the occurrence of pseudomemory in the hypnotic setting. *Australian Journal of Clinical and Experimental Hypnosis, 19,* 1–18.

Simon, M. J., & Salzberg, H. C. (1985). The effect of manipulated expectancies on posthypnotic amnesia. *International Journal of Clinical and Experimental Hypnosis, 33,* 40–51.

Smith, M. L., Glass, G. V., & Miller, T. I. (1980). *The benefits of psychotherapy.* Baltimore, MD: Johns Hopkins University Press.

Spanos, N. P., & Chaves, J. F. (1991). History and historiography of hypnosis. In S. J. Lynn & J. W. Rhue (Eds.), *Theories of hypnosis: Current models and perspectives* (pp. 43–78). New York: Guilford Press.

Spanos, N. P., Gwynn, M. I., Comer, S. L., Baltruweit, W. J., & deGroh, M. (1989). Are hypnotically induced pseudomemories resistant to cross-examination? *Law and Human Behavior, 13,* 271–289.

Van der Does, A. J. W., Van Dyck, R., Spinhoven, P., & Kloosman, A. (1989). The effectiveness of standardized versus individualized hypnotic suggestions: A brief communication. *International Journal of Clinical and Experimental Hypnosis, 37,* 1–5.

2

INDIVIDUAL DIFFERENCES IN RESPONSE TO HYPNOSIS

BRAD L. BATES

Patients differ in their responses to treatment. Dentists, nurses, physicians, social workers, and psychologists alike learn early in their training that no one remedy works for everyone. In fact, the same client may respond differently at different times: A tonic that initially cures may later fail. If this maxim is recognized in medicine, it should be an oath of office for psychotherapists whose very livelihood depends on the existence of individual differences. Each patient is a new psychodynamic puzzle, every behavior is a function of a unique learning history, and we all suffer the slings and arrows of existential misfortune in our own fashion. To meet the challenge of such diversity, the therapist must tailor treatment to the individual needs of each client.

Psychotherapy is an appropriate point to begin a discussion of individual differences in response to hypnosis because the clinical use of hypnosis

The substantive evaluation on which this chapter is based was supported in part by National Institute of Mental Health Grant MH44193 and by a grant from the Institute for Experimental Psychiatry Research Foundation.

I am grateful to David F. Dinges, Martin T. Orne, Emily C. Orne, and Sydney E. Pulver for their helpful criticisms of earlier drafts of this chapter.

is best understood within the more general rubric of psychological treatment. That is, hypnosis should not be considered a distinct school of therapy but a technique that can be used within the larger context of treatment in order to facilitate the therapeutic process (e.g., Gill & Brenman, 1961; Moll, 1889/1958; Weitzenhoffer, 1957). An important implication of this is that professionals should not elect to use hypnosis with a patient whom they would not treat otherwise. A clinician who does so is "acting out the fantasy that hypnosis makes it possible to treat conditions that are beyond the practitioner's expertise" (Orne & Dinges, 1989, p. 1513). As an adjuvant, however, hypnosis can be used by practitioners of diverse theoretical orientations, from psychoanalytic to behavioral; may be combined with most existing treatment modalities, from individual to group to family; and can be used to treat a broad range of conditions. Yet, like any element of therapy, hypnosis is not indicated for every condition and should be used only with the understanding that not all patients will respond to it favorably at all times. Wolberg (1948), in his classic text, *Medical Hypnosis*, made explicit this fundamental observation:

> There is nothing miraculous about the trance state. It has many values; but it does have limitations in terms of the individual's existing motivations and his capacities for change. Therapeutic failures occur with hypnosis as with any other form of therapy. (Vol. 1, p. 418)

How are we to understand the fact that clients respond idiosyncratically to hypnotic treatment? Is it possible to be more precise about the particular individual differences that influence the outcome of therapy? And what are the implications for the way in which we use hypnosis with our patients?

GENERAL FACTORS THAT INFLUENCE TREATMENT OUTCOME WITH HYPNOSIS

Given that hypnosis is not a treatment per se but an ancillary technique, it follows that many of the variables that determine how a given patient will respond to hypnotic treatment are common to psychotherapy in general. Hence, patients' attitudes toward therapy are an important consideration; when hypnosis is added to the treatment regimen, it also becomes necessary to inquire about patients' apprehensions about hypnosis and to correct misconceptions that may interfere with the experience of hypnosis. Motivation for change continues to play a significant role, and issues of primary and secondary gain must be handled judiciously. Because hypnosis can add to patients' belief in magical powers of the therapist, it is critical that both parties remain clear that responsibility for change lies with the client and not the practitioner.

As in nonhypnotic therapy, the therapeutic alliance seeks to provide a context that legitimizes treatment and within which patients feel secure enough to allow meaningful therapy to occur. As Orne and Dinges (1989) noted, "the preconditions of the relationship between therapist and patient for the induction of hypnosis are very similar to the preconditions that make for successful psychotherapy" (p. 1506). The same therapist characteristics that facilitate rapport when hypnosis is not involved—qualities such as flexibility, objectivity, accurate empathy, positive regard for patients, and effective communication skills—are relevant when hypnosis is used.

Involving, as it typically does, a quiet setting, a therapist speaking in a soft voice, and a patient who is relaxed and actively involved in fantasy, hypnosis is frequently experienced as an extremely intimate interaction. Although the incorporation of hypnosis may intensify the transference feelings patients develop toward the therapist (Gill & Brenman, 1961), the transference itself remains similar in nature and should be addressed much as it is when hypnosis is not involved. This point is illustrated by the following case material:

> A patient whose mother had suddenly died one night when he was 4 years old and asleep had great difficulty going into anything but the lightest stages of trance. Every once in a while he exhibited in his light trances a curious, minute, pulling-up movement of his head and shoulders—as if he wanted to alert himself or prevent himself from going down into a deeper trance. At the end of most of his hypnotic sessions, he would become very solicitous about me, asking me how I felt, wondering whether I was tired, remarking that he must be a strain on me. As he was my last patient of the day, we often left the building together, and he would always insist on carrying my briefcase or my books to the car. At first I thought this was gallantry, but then I realized that the behavior, both in and out of a trance, was an expression of the same transference reaction: The patient pictured me as weak, was afraid I might die and leave him . . . as his mother had done. Further hypnoanalytic work revealed his unconscious fantasy that his mother had died because she had to work too hard to support him. The father had deserted the mother a few months after the patient was born.
>
> When he next made this curious head and shoulder movement in trance, I quietly said to him, "You don't need to be afraid of making demands on me. I am strong. I am not going to die." The patient heaved a great sigh, relaxed, and immediately went into much deeper trance. (Brown & Fromm, 1986, p. 211)

As with therapy in general, the manner in which the therapist handles transference reactions plays a large role in governing the course of treatment with hypnosis.

The same forces that activate resistance in psychotherapy are also operative when hypnosis is used. Patients' fears, ambivalences, and dynamic conflicts influence their responses to hypnotic treatment, as do considerations such as secondary gain. Brown and Fromm (1986) presented the following illustrative example:

> Using the Theatre Technique, I suggested, when the patient was in a rather deep trance, that we would go to a theater, sit down in our seats, and see a play that in some ways was connected with his problem. I described the beautiful red velvet curtain that was now being pulled up. As it was going up, the patient suddenly said, "Uh-uh, the rope broke. The curtain has fallen down." I tacitly recognized this as a defense. The patient was not yet ready to look more deeply at his problem. I explained that he could relax some more while the curtain was being repaired, a process I described in elaborate imagistic detail. A little later I said that the rope was now repaired, the play could begin, and the curtain again was being pulled up. When the curtain was halfway up, the patient informed me that the rope had broken again. Not only that, he said, but now a gold-colored metal curtain had come down, too, totally shutting the stage off from vision. Thus, through imagery, the patient told me in unmistakable terms that he still needed to protect himself from finding out more about the roots of his problem, that he was not yet ready for such uncovering. (p. 208)

The use of hypnosis does not render the usual mechanisms of defense inoperative, although it does provide unique opportunities for their creative expression.

Finally, the more general factors that have been identified as affecting therapy outcome, variables such as those described by Frank (1974), do not lose their potency when hypnosis is used. The patient's confidence in the therapist's skill as a healer, the social sanctions provided the help-giver by society, the therapist's rationale or myth that accounts for the patient's illness and provides hope for recovery, the emotional arousal that seems inherent to attitude and behavior change, the patient's sense of self-efficacy and mastery—all of these factors continue to play a part in determining the outcome when hypnosis is integrated into therapy. In sum, the extent to which the therapist addresses the general issues common to all psychotherapy, problems of transference, resistance, and secondary gain accounts to a considerable degree for the individual differences in the way patients respond to hypnotic treatment.

INDIVIDUAL DIFFERENCES IN RESPONSE TO HYPNOSIS PER SE

Although the integration of hypnosis into treatment does not change the essential nature of therapy, it does, of course, introduce a new feature, and patients differ markedly in their experience of hypnosis per se. Some individuals require little in the way of induction and are able to experience hypnosis rapidly and profoundly. They may have hypnotic dreams that are dramatically vivid or profound alterations in mood or memory; some may be able to experience age regression or even compelling hallucinations. Other patients will require considerable practice before experiencing these sorts of events, and some will have great difficulty altering their perceptions in the least. Although certain clients favor authoritarian and direct communications during hypnosis, others respond more positively to permissive and nondirect styles. Thus, although the outcome of hypnotic treatment is influenced by the sorts of variables general to psychotherapy, individual differences in response to the procedure of hypnosis itself also play a pivotal role in determining the course of treatment.

Differences in response to hypnosis have been recognized since the time of Mesmer (e.g., d'Eslon, 1784/1965), but it was not until the turn of the century that individual differences became a topic of central concern. Much like practitioners today, many clinicians using hypnosis in the 1800s tended to understand hypnotic responsiveness as a relatively stable trait that varied across patients. Braid, an English physician during the 19th century and originator of the term *hypnosis*, noted that "there is a remarkable difference in the degree of susceptibility of different individuals to the hypnotic influence, some becoming rapidly and intensely affected, others slowly and feebly so" (1843/1960, p. 72). Although the trait view is not the only way to conceptualize individual differences in hypnotic responding, it has been responsible for much of the systematic work aimed at measuring hypnotic behavior. Alternatives to the trait paradigm exist, and several are considered later in this chapter.

19th-Century Attempts to Assess Hypnotizability

Differences in hypnotic ability were recognized not only by 19th-century experimentalists (e.g., James, 1890/1950) but also by clinicians (e.g., Freud, 1891/1966) who wanted a method to predict which patients would be the most responsive to hypnotic treatment. Unfortunately, attempts to link hypnotic susceptibility to sex, diagnosis, muscular weakness, introversion, extraversion, social position, intelligence, willpower, and even nationality all met with disappointment. Early efforts to understand hypnotic ability in terms of personality, in particular hysteria, also failed for the most part. In 1891, Freud noted what most investigators recognized: "We can never tell in advance whether it will be possible to hypnotize a patient or not, and the only way we have of discovering is by the attempt itself" (1891/1966, p. 106). More recent studies have demonstrated that hypnotizability is not the same thing as compliance, conformity, gullibility, or persuadability and that it is not reliably associated with the personality traits measured by modern psychological tests, such as the Minnesota Multiphasic Personality Inventory and the Rorschach (e.g., E. R. Hilgard, 1965).

As it became evident that hypnosis must actually be attempted in order to estimate a patient's hypnotizability, investigators developed scales to directly measure the hypnotic responses of different individuals. Early scales, such as those designed by Liebault and Bernheim, outlined several stages of hypnosis and assumed that a person who showed responses characteristic of a greater degree of trance would always show the symptoms of lesser degree (E. R. Hilgard, 1967). Stages of hypnosis were not defined by specific tests, and inductions were unstandardized, so there was a good deal of uncertainty regarding classification. It is especially intriguing, then, to learn that the susceptibility estimates made by early clinicians are fairly consistent with the results of more systematic investigations during the past 50 years. As Table 1 illustrates, the consensus of 19th-century practitioners was that just over one third of their patients were minimally hypnotizable, another one third possessed moderate hypnotic talent, and close to one quarter were highly susceptible to hypnosis.

Modern Attempts to Measure Hypnotizability

The 20th century has witnessed a great deal of progress in the endeavor to systematically measure hypnotizability. The foundation for this enterprise was established at Stanford University in the 1950s and 1960s through the programmatic work of Ernest Hilgard and Andre Weitzenhoffer. Modeled after an earlier scale developed by Friedlander and Sarbin (1938), the Stanford Scales of Hypnotic Susceptibility, Forms A, B, and C (Weitzenhoffer & Hilgard, 1959, 1962) were carefully standardized, ensuring that each recipient receives the same hypnotic induction and the same set of 12 suggestions. Each suggestion calls for an observable response, enabling hypnotic ability to be defined in behavioral terms: Susceptibility is calculated by summing the number of suggestions to which the appropriate overt response is made. The use of psychometrically sound measurement instruments and the reliance on observable behavior has resulted in hypnotizability scores that are reliable, and has facilitated the acceptance of hypnosis research by scientists in related fields. The emphasis on overt behavior should not be understood to mean that Weitzenhoffer and Hilgard were uninterested in subjective experience. On the contrary, the Stanford scales are premised on the assumption that behavioral responses are reliable indicators of phenomenological experience.

It is worth highlighting that although Weitzenhoffer and Hilgard's (1959, 1962) conceptualization of hypnosis led to one approach to measuring hypnotic talent, other prominent investigators adopted somewhat different strategies according to their particular theoretical orientations. Tart (1970), for instance, emphasized subjective experience, and as a result

TABLE 1
Distribution of Susceptibility to Hypnosis: 19th-Century Studies

Investigator	Date	No. of cases	Distribution of susceptibility (%)			
			Refractory	Light	Moderate	Deep
Peronnet	ante-1900	467	25	10	20	45
Forel	ante-1898	275	17	23	37	23
Lloyd-Tukey	ante-1900	220	14	49	28	9
Bramwell	ante-1900	200	11	24	26	39
Von Schrenck-Notzing	ante-1900	240	12	17	42	29
Mosing	1889–1893	594	12	42	17	29
Hilger	ante-1900	351	6	20	42	32
Von Schrenck-Notzing (pooling of 15 reports)	1892	8,705	6	29	50	15
Liebault	1884–1889	2,654	5	22	62	11
Von Eeden & von Renterghem	1887–1893	1,089	5	43	41	11
von Renterghem	ante-1900	414	4	52	33	11
Wetterstrand	1890	3,209	3	36	48	13
Velander	ante-1900	1,000	2	32	54	12
Vogt	ante-1900	116	0	2	13	85
Total cases		19,534				
Range of percents			0–25	2–52	13–62	9–85
Mean of percents			9	29	36	26

Note: Adapted from "The Distribution of Susceptibility to Hypnosis in a Student Population: A Study Using the Stanford Hypnotic Susceptibility Scale," by E. R. Hilgard, A. M. Weitzenhoffer, J. Landes, and R. K. Moore, 1961, *Psychological Monographs, 75*(8, Whole No. 512), p. 4. In the public domain.

his scales assess moment-to-moment self-reports of hypnotic depth. Spanos, on the other hand, defines hypnosis in social psychological terms, and his scale (e.g., Spanos, Radtke, Hodgins, Stam, & Bertrand, 1983), in its construction and wording, reflects his eschewal of trance and his focus on cooperation, compliance, and conformity. Beginning with a more clinical perspective, Orne and O'Connell (1967) described a diagnostic system that assigns patients a score of 1 (*no response*) to 5 (*amnesia and true posthypnotic response*) and is based on an hypnotic evaluation using whatever inductions and suggestions seem best suited to the individual. What this approach loses in psychometric rigor it attempts to make up for in clinical sensitivity; it is more concerned with establishing a patient's maximum hypnotic potential than with obtaining a work sample under standard conditions. Spiegel and Spiegel (1978) took a much different approach with their Hypnotic Induction Profile (HIP), which is intended to provide typological information about personality in addition to data regarding hypnotic talent. The HIP also includes an eye-roll test that the Spiegels believe to reflect a physiological basis for hypnotizability. The differences in emphasis across experimenters are reflected in the fact that correlations between these various hypnotizability scales are far from perfect, indicating that they do not measure precisely the same thing (e.g., E. R. Hilgard, 1978–1979; Kihlstrom, 1985). Even among empirically minded researchers, then, there is room for disagreement about how to understand hypnosis and how to measure individual differences in hypnotic ability.

Despite this diversity, each of the various hypnotizability scales has provided empirical evidence in support of clinicians' observations of individual differences in hypnotic responding. Because the Stanford scales are generally accepted as the benchmark within the field, I outline data collected with these instruments. Those interested in a more detailed discussion of these scales should refer to E. R. Hilgard's (1965) book, *Hypnotic Susceptibility*. Stanford Forms A and B are parallel forms and are considered general-purpose scales because they are easily administered, require little equipment, and contain no provocative suggestions (e.g., age regression) that could be experienced as threatening to some subjects. Of the 12 suggestions making up each scale, 1 is a prehypnotic suggestion (e.g., postural sway); 3 call for an ideomotor response (e.g., hand lowering); 5 challenge the subject to overcome a suggested paralysis (e.g., finger lock); 1 asks the subject to hallucinate (e.g., a fly); 1 calls for a posthypnotic response (e.g., changing chairs at the hypnotist's signal); and 1 calls for amnesia for the events during hypnosis. Each suggestion is associated with a specific behavioral criterion (e.g., the hand must lower by 6 in. within 10 s), and the response to each is scored on a pass–fail basis. The total number of passes is calculated, so that each subject's hypnotizability score can range from 0 to 12.

The distribution of scores for college students completing either Form

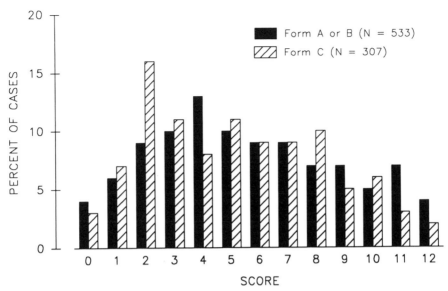

Figure 1: Distribution of scores on the Stanford Scales of Hypnotic Susceptibility, Form A or B and Form C. From *Hypnotic Susceptibility* (p. 237) by E. R. Hilgard, 1965, New York: Harcourt, Brace & World. Copyright 1965 by E. R. Hilgard. Adapted by permission.

A or B for the first time is presented in Figure 1. The bars above each number of the *x* axis represent the percentage of subjects obtaining that particular score. Hence, 4% of subjects failed to pass any item, whereas 13% passed exactly 4 suggestions, and another 4% passed all 12 suggestions. For my purposes, the most important feature about the distribution of scores is that students show marked differences in their responses to the standard set of suggestions. Hypnotizability scores from 0 to 4 are typically considered low, whereas scores of 5–7 are considered medium, and scores of 8 or above are considered high. Using this classification scheme, approximately 40% of the students score in the low range, whereas another 30% obtain medium scores, and a final 30% post high scores.

Like Forms A and B, Form C of the Stanford scales consists of 12 suggestions, each with a specific behavioral criterion. However, Form C is a graded-difficulty scale, meaning that suggestions are given in order of difficulty, from easiest to most difficult. Form C also includes fewer ideomotor and challenge suggestions while incorporating more items calling for fantasy and cognitive distortion. For instance, Form C includes suggestions for age regression, a dream, and anosmia to ammonia, along with three items calling for positive hallucinations and one suggested negative hallucination. Many of these suggestions are difficult and are experienced by relatively few individuals during hypnosis, providing Form C with more "top" than Forms A or B. As a consequence, the distribution of scores for Form C is skewed somewhat, with the modal score being 2 rather than 4 (see Figure 1). Nearly half of the subjects score in the low range on Form C, another 30% score in the medium range, and just more than 20% post high scores.

Although Forms A, B, and C of the Stanford scales were designed to measure general hypnotic ability, the Stanford Profile Scales of Hypnotic Susceptibility, Forms I and II (Weitzenhoffer & Hilgard, 1963, 1967) were created to assess particular areas of special hypnotic talent, as well as to identify the few individuals who are rightly considered "hypnotic virtuosos." The Stanford Profile Scales are intended to be administered following either Form A or B and produce a profile rather than a single summary score. Two illustrative profiles appear in Figure 2. Notice that there are six sub-scales listed along the bottom, with each reflecting a class of suggestion and consisting of several individual items. For instance, the Positive Hallucination subscale consists of suggestions to hallucinate music, a light, heat, and ammonia. The upper profile in Figure 2 reflects an individual who is particularly talented at experiencing suggestions for positive hallucinations, dreams or regressions, and loss of motor control, but not especially good at experiencing suggestions for amnesia or posthypnotic responses. The lower profile reflects an individual whose hypnotic talent is limited primarily to loss of motor control. Of the various instruments available to assess hypnotic ability, the Stanford Profile Scales are the most sensitive to differences in particular hypnotic aptitudes.

In an attempt to encourage the use of hypnotizability scales by clinicians, several shortened instruments have been designed by researchers at Stanford University. Perhaps the most useful is the Stanford Hypnotic Clinical Scale (Morgan & Hilgard, 1978–1979a), which requires approximately 20 min to complete and includes suggestions for hands moving together (or arm lowering), a dream, age regression, a posthypnotic response (clearing throat), and amnesia for events during hypnosis. The scores for the adult Clinical scale distribute normally and correlate .72 with scores on the Stanford scale, Form C. Because it includes a variety of hypnotic phenomena yet is rapidly administered, the Stanford Hypnotic Clinical Scale may be the best choice for busy clinicians who nevertheless want an estimate of their patients' hypnotic abilities. For research purposes, however, the longer and more psychometrically rigorous hypnosis scales should be used.

Contemporary investigations of the hypnotic responses of children have also been conducted at the University of Illinois by London (1963) and later at Stanford University by Morgan and Hilgard (1978–1979b). In 1889, Bernheim noted that "as soon as they are able to pay attention and understand, children are as a rule very quickly and very easily hypnotized" (1889/1947, p. 2). Bernheim's observations anticipated what was the general consensus among clinicians by the beginning of the 20th century and have been largely confirmed by recent experimental findings. Children do,

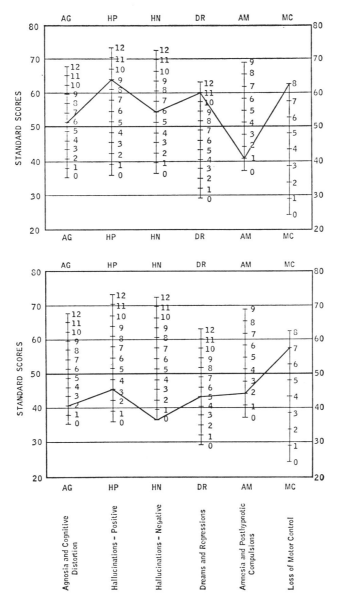

Figure 2: Specimen profiles from the Stanford Profile Scales, Forms I and II. From *Hypnotic Susceptibility* (p. 259) by E. R. Hilgard, 1965, New York: Harcourt, Brace & World. Copyright 1965 by E. R. Hilgard. Reprinted by permission.

in fact, seem to be particularly adept at experiencing hypnosis, especially those between 8 and 12 years of age. There is, however, little systematic information regarding hypnotizability for children below the age of 5. Gardner and Olness (1981) provided a thoughtful discussion of this matter in their book, *Hypnosis and Hypnotherapy with Children,* in which they suggested that the domain of hypnotic behaviors may be somewhat different for children and adults, especially for very young children. If this view is correct, then we may need to devote special attention to the behaviors that accompany hypnosis for younger children, and measurement scales may require some revision.

With regard to older adults, two studies have found that hypnosis scores for middle-aged individuals were significantly lower than those for younger adults (Gordon, 1972; Morgan & Hilgard, 1973). These two investigations relied on a cross-sectional design in which different individuals make up the comparison groups at each age level. A more recent study, using a longitudinal design in which the same set of subjects is followed over several years, failed to document any age-related decrement in hypnotic susceptibility (Piccione, Hilgard, & Zimbardo, 1989). Instead, these investigators observed remarkable stability in hypnotic performance across time: The correlation of .71 between hypnosis scores in middle adulthood and those obtained 25 years earlier is, in fact, comparable in magnitude to correlations reported for intelligence. As with the study of intelligence, it is possible that the conflicting pattern of results is an artifact of the methodological shortcomings of cross-sectional research. More specifically, older subjects in the cross-sectional studies might have scored lower on the hypnosis scales because their scores were always relatively low, not because their scores declined with age. The longitudinal findings, coupled with the possibility that hypnotic aptitude may be inherited to some extent (Morgan, 1973), support the view that hypnotizability is a fairly enduring characteristic of individuals.

RELATION OF HYPNOTIZABILITY TO TREATMENT OUTCOME

Contemporary research has identified several instances in which hypnotizability is reliably associated with treatment outcome when hypnosis is used. In these cases, patients with considerable hypnotic talent generally profit more from hypnotic intervention than patients with limited susceptibility. For instance, there is now a wealth of evidence, both laboratory (e.g., E. R. Hilgard, 1975) and clinical (e.g., E. R. Hilgard & Hilgard, 1975), that hypnosis affords pain relief roughly in proportion to hypnotizability. Figure 3 illustrates the relative degree of pain reduction achieved by experimental subjects of differing hypnotic ability. For the most hypnotizable individuals, hypnosis can provide more analgesic benefit than morphine (Stern, Brown, Ulett, & Sletten, 1977). As a consequence of its analgesic power, hypnosis has been used as the sole anesthetic during surgeries of all kinds, ranging from tooth extraction to cardiac surgery; has been a valuable tool in obstetrics and dentistry; is often used to reduce the intense pain caused by the redressing and debridement of burn wounds; and

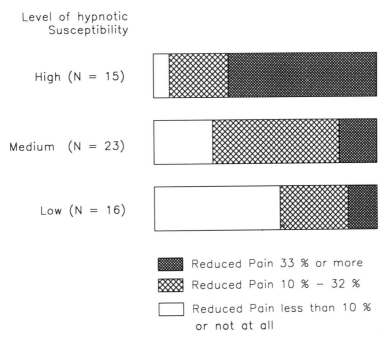

Figure 3: Pain reduction through hypnotically suggested analgesia as related to hypnotizability. From *Hypnosis in the Relief of Pain* (p. 69) by E. R. Hilgard and J. R. Hilgard, 1975, Los Altos, CA: Kaufmann. Copyright 1975 by William Kaufmann, Inc. Adapted by permission.

has been used to successfully treat migraine headaches (Orne & Dinges, 1984).

Recent work by J. R. Hilgard and LeBaron (1984) illustrates the relation between hypnotic ability and pain reduction while also serving as a model for how well-conducted clinical research can contribute to psychiatric treatment. Working with children and adolescents with cancer, primarily leukemia, Hilgard and LeBaron taught these patients how to use hypnosis to decrease the pain and anxiety caused by the frequent bone marrow aspirations that must be undergone during active phases of the disease. During an initial aspiration, baseline levels of pain and anxiety were rated by independent observers as well as by the patients themselves using 10-point scales. Hypnotic susceptibility was then carefully assessed, after which an individualized hypnotic treatment was provided in conjunction with rehearsal of the aspiration process. Of the 19 high-susceptible children, 10 were able to reduce their pain by at least 3 points during the subsequent aspiration, and another 5 experienced comparable success at the time of the next aspiration. These 15 patients were able to decrease their experience of pain relative to baseline by an average of 60%. On the other hand, *none* of the low-susceptible children were able to reduce their pain by 3 points or more. Findings for anxiety paralleled those for pain, confirming that although hypnotizability is no guarantee of significant relief, it seems to be a necessary prerequisite when the treatment is primarily hypnotic.

J. R. Hilgard and LeBaron (1984) provided the following example of a low-hypnotizable 6-year-old who had undergone 27 aspirations prior to his participation in the study. The case illustrates that some individuals who are unable to derive relief using hypnosis despite incredibly strong motivations for doing so may be better served by nonhypnotic procedures.

During the baseline, Jeff resisted vigorously as he was lifted onto the treatment table where three people restrained him throughout the procedure. His crying, which began as soon as he could no longer resist, persisted to the end. Because the needle had to be twisted and turned in order to obtain the aspirate, the session was a long one. Repeatedly, when gasping for breath, Jeff screamed, "Help me, Mommie." Using the picture scale, he rated his "hurt" at the top.

During the first hypnotic rehearsal of a bone marrow aspiration in the office, Jeff's attention span was very short and his interactions with the therapist quite brief. During the actual bone marrow procedure when hypnosis was attempted, neither his behavior nor his self-report differed from the evaluation made at the baseline observation.

At the time of the second bone marrow aspiration, the hypnotic rehearsal session was described in the therapist's words: "Jeff was friendly and playful, though he seemed so full of energy that it was very difficult to practice with him. He was reluctant to relax on the table, preferring to giggle and avoid the practice." Finally, he became involved in a game such as blowing out candles on a birthday cake, after first protesting that this could not be done because there were no real candles there. He was finally persuaded to pet his (imaginary) kitty. After this active rehearsal, Jeff went cheerfully to the treatment room, offered no resistance to getting on the treatment table, needed no restraint to keep him there, and remained calm until the sterile wash started the bone marrow procedure. Thereafter he ignored suggestions related to candles and kittens. He cried and screamed almost constantly. Between sobs he asked how soon it would all be over.

At the time of the third bone marrow aspiration six weeks later, Jeff again was a bundle of energetic activity. According to the therapist, "During rehearsal it was difficult to focus his attention on anything for more than a moment. He was interested only in rough physical play." For this reason, an alternative strategy of therapy was introduced. The decision was made to keep Jeff energetically occupied with one task after another. During the procedure, he followed signals for accelerated action, such as squeezing the therapist's hand, blowing big breaths, moving his head, and so forth, crying almost constantly as he continued to watch what was going on and listen carefully to instructions. This nonhypnotic strategy proved successful. Jeff rated the "hurt" at 1, saying that he hadn't really felt anything. The disease process accelerated, so this was the last bone marrow aspiration before his death. (J. R. Hilgard & LeBaron, 1984, pp. 76–77)

Other conditions that are effectively treated with hypnosis and for which treatment outcome appears to be positively related to hypnotic talent include asthma and various dermatologic diseases, especially warts. Work completed in Australia by Collison (1978) provides another example of how clinical research can be individualized and patient-centered while also being systematic. Over the course of 10 years, 121 asthmatic patients were referred by their primary physician, either because the physician suspected that psychological issues contributed to the asthma or because it had become necessary to decrease the dosage of steroid medication. Treatment included hypnotic suggestions that varied greatly across patients but were always directed at instilling a sense of calm and relaxation. In addition, psychotherapy within the context of hypnosis was frequently conducted, using phenomena such as age regression and posthypnotic suggestion, to help patients deal more confidently with their environment and to overcome the feelings of inferiority that are often experienced by asthmatics. Results for each patient were analyzed retrospectively at the end of the 10 years. Of the 90 patients who were judged to possess at least moderate hypnotic talent, 63 (70%) had either an excellent or good response to therapy, whereas only 2 of the 31 (6%) low-susceptible patients responded positively. Collison (1978) noted that "the use of these facts to assist in better patient selection for hypnotherapy in the management of asthma has been used in an on-going way by the author with even better results than those reported" (p. 272).

Although response to hypnotic treatment can be predicted on the basis of hypnotizability for a number of disorders, this relation does not hold for several other conditions. Hence, hypnosis is no more effective than other forms of treatment when used to help individuals stop smoking, and the patients who do stop do not differ in terms of hypnotic talent from those who fail. Similarly, investigations of hypnosis in the treatment of alcoholism and obesity have typically not shown any relation between hypnotic ability and either sobriety or weight loss (e.g., Wadden & Anderton, 1982).

Why does hypnotizability predict response to hypnotic treatment in some circumstances but not in others? One view focuses on fundamental differences between the conditions being treated (e.g., Perry, Gelfand, & Marcovitch, 1979). Disorders such as pain, asthma, and warts are regulated by bodily functions that operate outside of awareness and are typically treated hypnotically by helping patients alter their perceptions of the pain, tension, or area of affected skin. Addictions, on the other hand, are viewed as disorders of self-control, for which the fundamental problem is one of behavior rather than subjective experience. Presumably, hypnosis is more useful for treating the former conditions because, although it is an effective tool for altering perception, it is not a particularly effective behavior-control technique. Other theorists have observed that the nonvoluntary conditions usually involve immediate suffering, whereas the addictive disorders are hedonically rewarding in the short run (Wadden & Anderton, 1982). Whereas patients with the former conditions are likely to be highly motivated to change, those with disorders of self-control may experience more ambivalence about giving up their symptoms. The hedonic theory is consistent with the fact that hypnosis is highly effective in providing pain relief for conditions that are organic in nature but that it is much less helpful when the pain is functional or when secondary gain is present (Orne & Dinges, 1984).

The manner in which hypnosis is incorporated into treatment may also influence the relation between outcome and hypnotizability. When treatment consists of standardized protocols involving generic suggestions and few treatment sessions, hypnotic talent may not be an important factor. Hypnotizability may be more relevant when therapy is individualized, when suggestions are tailored to each patient, when hypnotic techniques are integral to treatment, and when therapy is longer term. Recent work completed by Andersen (1985) with overweight patients illustrates the point that hypnotic susceptibility may influence outcome only to the extent that hypnotic techniques are emphasized. The weight-loss program consisted of a single orientation session followed by 8 weekly individual hypnosis sessions and 3 months of self-hypnosis treatment. Unlike most "hypnosis" programs, which actually rely heavily on behavioral procedures such as stimulus control, Andersen's approach stressed hypnotic techniques such as visualization, age regression, glove anesthesia, time distortion, and posthypnotic suggestion. Although most investigations have not shown a sizable correlation between hypnotizability and weight loss, Andersen observed a correlation of .67. At the end of treatment, low-susceptible patients had lost an average of 10 lb, whereas those with moderate talent had lost 16 lb, and high-susceptible patients had lost an average of 32 lb. It is worth noting that of the 8 patients who discontinued treatment during the first 8 weeks, 6 were low hypnotizable, underscoring the fact that patients with limited hypnotic ability may be better served by treatments that are nonhypnotic in nature. Andersen's findings have the potential to help clarify the role of hypnotizability in hypnotic treatment, although they still await confirmation by other investigators.

CLINICAL IMPLICATIONS OF INDIVIDUAL DIFFERENCES IN HYPNOTIC RESPONDING

The scientific work that has just been reviewed confirms clinicians' observations of individual differences in hypnotic responding and provides an empirical foundation for the use of hypnosis in psychotherapy, medicine, dentistry, and social work. Any recommendation regarding the therapeutic use of hypnotic techniques should make sense in light of these fundamental observations. However, there are different viewpoints concerning the clinical implications of this information. Th way in which trait theorists understand the available evidence is much different, for instance, from the views expressed by social learning, psychoanalytic, and Ericksonian adherents. I briefly summarize these orientations in order to illustrate their diversity and outline the way each conceptualizes the experimental data concerning individual differences in hypnotizability.

The Trait View

As discussed earlier, one way of conceptualizing individual differences in response to hypnosis is by assuming that they reflect essential differences in hypnotic ability (e.g., Brown & Fromm, 1986; Frankel, 1976; E. R. Hilgard, 1965; Kihlstrom, 1985; Orne & Dinges, 1989; Spiegel & Spiegel, 1978). According to this view, people vary in their capacity for experiencing hypnosis, and this aptitude tends to remain stable throughout one's lifetime. Whereas some practitioners have maintained that the key to hypnosis is held by the hypnotist and that virtually anyone can become hypnotized if the operator is skilled enough and exerts sufficient effort (e.g., Bandler & Grinder, 1979), the trait view places the power of hypnosis squarely with the subject. The therapist can provide only an environment that minimizes the factors that prevent hypnosis in patients capable of responding. Although it is easy enough to create conditions that block a person from experiencing hypnosis, the trait view holds that little can be done to enable a truly low-susceptible patient to have profound hypnotic experiences.

A corollary of the trait position is that practitioners using hypnosis should have a reliable estimate of the hypnotic abilities of their patients (e.g., J. R. Hilgard & Hilgard, 1979; Kihlstrom, 1985). The Spiegels, for instance, as well as Frankel and his associates, regularly administer standardized hypnotizability scales in their clinical work. In addition to generating a wealth of data regarding hypnotizability and treatment, clients with little hypnotic talent can, when appropriate, be offered alternative, nonhypnotic treatment. However, the formal assessment of patients' hypnotizability concerns many clinicians, who believe that it is superfluous at best, and fear that it may be countertherapeutic for some clients (see Spinhoven, 1990, for a review of this issue). Indeed, Weitzenhoffer (1989), an experienced clinician as well as the first author of the Stanford scales, recommends against the routine assessment of hypnotic ability with patients. A survey of experienced hypnotherapists teaching workshops at the 1981 annual meeting of the American Society of Clinical Hypnosis revealed that approximately two thirds did not currently use any scale of hypnotizability and that none of the respondents routinely used any of the Stanford scales (Cohen, 1989). This state of affairs is disheartening to many trait theorists:

> The characteristic of an unscientific therapy is that there is only one disease and only one cure: such therapies imply that everyone can profit from the favored therapy regardless of the presenting problem. A scientific therapy is based on a diagnosis, which in psychotherapy means selecting the therapy of choice appropriate to fit the patient and the patient's complaints. Hypnosis is only one of these choices, and its choice and the manner of its use can profit from some estimate of the individual's hypnotic responsiveness. (E. R. Hilgard, 1982, p. 400)

Therapists who elect to conduct formal hypnotizability evaluations should recognize that their own attitudes about the process will influence patients' reactions to it, as will the manner in which assessment is introduced. If it has been determined that hypnosis is appropriate for a given client, Frankel and Orne (1976) suggested that the following instructions are likely to facilitate acceptance of the assessment procedure:

> In order for us to plan the strategy of your treatment with hypnosis more effectively, we need to know how you respond to suggestions in hypnosis. We use the same standardized measurement scale with all our patients. This enables us to know how your responses compare with others, and helps us to assess more accurately how hypnotizable you are. No matter what your responses during this assessment are, we will still be able to use the hypnosis technique in your treatment. Knowing *how* you respond will enable us to modify the technique so that it can fit in with the needs of *your* treatment. (pp. 1259–1260)

Patients with reservations about hypnosis can be acquainted with hypnoticlike responding through the use of prehypnotic experiences such as the Chevreul pendulum or Kohnstamm phenomenon (see Orne & Dinges, 1989) or by giving direct suggestions for arm heaviness or hand separation outside of hypnosis. These preliminary techniques help many patients appreciate that they can respond to suggestion, thereby facilitating subsequent hypnosis while also alerting the therapist to individuals who may have difficulty experiencing hypnotic effects. Any of the standardized hypnosis scales can then be used to measure hypnotic talent in a clinical setting. Alternatively, a formal evaluation can be conducted without the use of a standard scale if therapists strongly prefer to carefully design their own hypnotic procedures tailored to each individual patient (see Brown & Fromm, 1986, pp. 113–148).

According to the trait position, patients who lack the ability to experience hypnosis can often be expected to respond poorly to hypnotic therapy, particularly when the condition for which the patient is receiving treatment is one for which outcome correlates significantly with hypnotizability. In such circumstances, the therapist may decide against using a hypnotic technique or, at the very least, elect to supplement hypnosis with ancilliary procedures that are nonhypnotic in nature (e.g., Kihlstrom, 1985). The latter alternative may be indicated, for instance, when a low-susceptible patient expresses a particularly strong interest in hypnosis and the therapist believes that there is an opportunity to capitalize on the placebo value of the intervention.

Notice, however, that if a low-hypnotizable patient responds positively to hypnotic treatment, the trait view maintains that hypnosis per se had little to do with the favorable outcome. How could hypnosis effect a cure when it cannot be experienced by the patient? Instead, the therapeutic success is attributed to the nonspecific factors that are common to psychotherapy in general, features including the patient's attitude toward therapy and motivation for change, the healing power of a therapeutic relationship, the manner in which the therapist handles transference and resistance, and so on. The trait view holds that if hypnosis is responsible for therapeutic success with a particular disorder, then hypnotizability must correlate with response to treatment (e.g., Bowers & Kelly, 1979), as it generally does for conditions such as pain, asthma, and warts. Although hypnosis can be used with disorders for which such a correlation does not exist, the influence of nonspecific treatment factors should not be mistaken for the effect of hypnosis. According to many trait theorists, it is the failure to distinguish between these two sources of therapeutic influence that leads many clinicians to assert that hypnotic susceptibility is unrelated to treatment success. E. R. Hilgard (1982), for instance, conjectured that "the main source of the belief held by many practicing clinicians is that everyone is hypnotizable is a confusion between the success of their psychotherapy and the role of hypnosis in it" (p. 398).

The Social Learning View

Social learning, defined broadly to include both cognitive and behavioral dimensions, provides another way in which to conceptualize hypnosis and to understand individual differences in hypnotic responding. According to this perspective, hypnotizability does not reflect an underlying trait but instead is a function of learning history and environmental influence. In his landmark treatise titled *Hypnosis: A Scientific Approach*, T. X. Barber (1969) provided a basic framework within which hypnotic responding was viewed as a dependent variable, functionally related to antecedent stimuli. The contextual factors and subject characteristics that he found to be the most relevant included individuals' attitudes toward hypnosis and expectations about their own performance, the precise wording and intonation of suggestions, subjects' motivation to respond hypnotically, definition of the situation as hypnotic, suggestions for relaxation, the prestige and personality of the experimenter, and the experimenter–subject relationship.

The importance of expectations has long been recognized by practitioners interested in hypnosis regardless of their theoretical orientation (e.g., Bernheim, 1889/1947; Moll, 1889/1958; Orne, 1959). As a consequence, a variety of expectancy-management techniques have been devised. Patients' perceptions of hypnosis and expectations concerning treatment should be thoroughly explored so that inductions and hypnotic techniques that match their expectancies can be used. Alternatively, hypnotic responding can be modeled for initially refractory patients, a strategy that dates back to Liebault's work in Nancy, France. Hypnosis can be described as similar to ordinary awareness, so that patients do not begin with exaggerated expectations that, when unfulfilled, leave them convinced of their inability to experience hypnosis. Inductions that include suggestions for naturally occurring phenomena (e.g., eyelid heaviness during eye fixation) can be selected so that patients will interpret their perceptual changes as being responses to suggestion. Easy suggestions typically precede those that are more difficult, as they do on most standardized hypnotizability scales, because passing early items may strengthen patients' expectations for passing subsequent suggestions.

Irving Kirsch recently proposed an especially strong version of the expectancy theory that maintains that expectations may be the most important determinant of hypnotic responding. This view holds that individual differences in hypnotizability are primarily the result of differences in expectations and that the temporal stability of hypnotic performance reflects enduring response expectancies rather than a fixed personality trait. According to Kirsch, "it is possible that, with sufficiently strong response expectancies, *all* individuals would show high levels of hypnotic response" (1985, p. 1196).

Other proponents of the social learning view have emphasized various cognitive processes that are presumably initiated by subjects during hypnosis. Diamond (1989), for instance, suggested the following:

> It may be most fruitful to think of hypnotizability as a set of cognitive skills rather than as a stable trait. Thus, it is conceivable that the so-called "insusceptible" or refractory S [subject] is simply less adept at creating, implementing, or utilizing the requisite cognitive skills in hypnotic test situations. Similarly, what makes for a highly responsive or "virtuoso" S may very well be precisely the ability or skill to generate those cognitive processes within the context of a unique relationship with a hypnotist. (p. 382)

Some investigators have likened the pertinent mental skills to those involved with becoming so deeply engrossed in a book or movie that awareness of external reality fades. The cognitive processes responsible for such a condition have been variously referred to as "thinking with" (T. X. Barber, Spanos, & Chaves, 1974), "role enactment" (Sarbin & Coe, 1972), and "goal-directed fantasy" (Spanos, 1971). Interestingly, proponents of views other than social learning have also focused on cognitive activities, including "imaginative involvement" (J. R. Hilgard, 1970), "absorption" (Tellegen & Atkinson, 1974), "primary process" (Fromm, 1977), and "generalized reality-orientation" and "archaic involvement" (Shor, 1962).

According to the social learning paradigm, the often-observed correlation between clinical outcome and hypnotizability is misleading, both because it implies the existence of a trait for hypnosis and because hypnotic talent is presumed to directly influence treatment response. With regard to pain, for instance, social learning theorists have argued that factors such as attitudes, expectancies, and cognitive strategies mediate patients' responses to hypnotic analgesia (e.g., Spanos, Kennedy, & Gwynn, 1984). If high-hypnotizable individuals obtain more pain reduction from hypnosis than do low-hypnotizable patients, it is presumably because they are more favorably disposed toward hypnosis, have higher expectations, and use more effective cognitive strategies, not because they possess more "hypnotic ability."

An important clinical implication of the social learning perspective is that hypnotizability is modifiable and that therapists can enhance the hypnotic capacity of initially refractory patients. Clinicians, in fact, often observe that their patients' hypnotic experiences improve noticeably over the course of several preliminary sessions as initial apprehensions are overcome and rapport is strengthened. Social learning advocates maintain that even larger gains can be produced if patients receive systematic training. Some early practitioners expressed comparable views, including Wolberg (1948), who noted the following:

> Approximately one out of ten patients will, with very little training, be capable of entering a somnambulistic trance with posthypnotic amnesia. As many as five out of ten patients can, with proper training, be taught to enter a deep trance with varying degrees of posthypnotic amnesia. (Vol. 1, p. 153)

Experimental approaches toward enhancing hypnotic susceptibility have included sensory isolation, hallucinogenic drugs, biofeedback, encounter groups, extended practice, modeling, operant conditioning, expectancy management, and cognitive-skills training. Although some believe that the available information demonstrates the modifiability of hypnotic talent (e.g., Spanos, 1986; Diamond, 1977), others contend that such a conclusion is premature (e.g., Perry, 1977). Of the many thorny methodological problems that plague most of these studies, perhaps the most serious concerns their clinical relevance because few have involved patients. Modification research typically involves students whose participation is motivated by a general curiosity, a desire to contribute to science, and an interest in fulfilling academic requirements. In stark contrast, psychotherapy patients seek professional help in the hope of preventing or reducing overwhelming psychological and emotional distress. It is one thing for an undergraduate to obtain a high score on a standardized hypnosis scale after completing a training program; it is something altogether different when a woman undergoes childbirth with hypnosis as the sole anesthetic and then elects to do the same during her next pregnancy. Until there is evidence that modification findings generalize to the clinic or translate into more effective hypnotic treatment, these results are of limited consequence (e.g., Wadden & Anderton, 1982).

The Psychoanalytic View

Psychoanalysis represents still another vantage point from which to view individual differences in hypnotizability. Although psychoanalytic interest in studying hypnosis has waxed and waned over the past two decades, the views expressed by Merton Gill and Margaret Brenman during the 1950s and 1960s are generally acknowledged by contemporary analytical theorists. This perspective resembles that of the social learning approach in that it, too, incorporates hypnotic phenomena into a more general context. In this instance, hypnosis is explained in terms of general psychoanalytic theory as an adaptive regression that occurs in the context of a transferential relationship (Gill & Brenman, 1961). Regression is understood to be a process in which the ego relaxes control over defensive barriers, enabling earlier modes of perception and cognition to be activated and previously repressed feelings, memories, and experiences to be accessed. Hypnosis is an *adaptive* regression because the process is under voluntary control; although a subsystem of the ego regresses, "the overall ego remains in a nonhypnotic, reality-oriented relationship with the hypnotist, allowing him only temporary and tentative control over the subsystem and retaining the option of yielding to him greater or lesser control" (Gruenewald, 1982, p. 188). Although regression is considered a ubiquitous feature of psychoanalysis, the introduction of hypnosis is thought to greatly intensify it.

According to Schilder (1921/1956), "If the assumption is correct that hypnosis is based upon regression, it must be possible to induce this state in every person" (p. 41). Gill and Brenman (1961), in fact, reported a limited number of cases in which refractory individuals later had profound hypnotic experiences following a change in their "total psychological situation." It is doubtful, however, that most contemporary analysts would agree with Schilder's assumption that individuals are uniformly capable of regression, particularly adaptive regression. Indeed, analytical practitioners have generally recognized the existence of stable individual differences in hypnotizability (e.g., Freud, 1891/1966). Intensive analytical treatment, even when focused on the analysand's ability to experience hypnosis, rarely results in meaningful changes in hypnotic ability (Gill & Brenman, 1961).

Although the psychoanalytic view acknowledges a general capacity for hypnosis, analysts have typically been more interested in moment-to-moment changes in hypnotic depth that occur throughout the course of each therapy hour. These spontaneous depth changes are believed to reflect parallel changes occurring in the patient's ego functioning and relationship with the therapist.

> It is as if the established hypnotic relationship is itself a compromise formation like a dream or a symptom, and that the main function of a spontaneous change in depth is that it is one of a number of possible ways of attempting to deal with the anxiety which is released by a temporary breakdown in the existing equilibrium. If, in a given sample of material, there is evidence that a forbidden impulse *is* being adequately defended against by one or more of the usual mechanisms of defense, we do not expect a change in the depth of hypnosis. It is economically unnecessary. If, on the other hand, there are indications that an intense need or a hostile wish is breaking through, we expect a change in depth as a spontaneous effort to re-establish an equilibrium, an equilibrium which will provide a maximum of gratification and a minimum of anxiety. (Brenman, Gill, & Knight, 1952, p. 24)

The question of whether a particular ego threat will deepen or lighten hypnosis must be answered on an individual basis, and the answer will depend on the particular patient's psychological makeup. For instance, patients who experience a feeling of hostility toward the therapist may go deeper into hypnosis in order to deny the aggressive impulse by exaggerating their passive submission. Other patients may defend against the same anxiety by disrupting the hypnosis. Alternatively, patients who are able to tolerate the anxiety, and perhaps reflect on it with humor, may not evidence any change in depth.

A fundamental implication of the analytical approach is that the issue of individual differences in hypnotic responding transcends the experimental evidence gathered with standardized susceptibility scales. The Stanford scales measure general hypnotic talent, yet high scorers do not always achieve deep hypnosis, and even low scorers occasionally will. Although the scales help to establish a baseline level of performance, a fine-grained analysis reveals a very complicated picture in which patients' experiences of hypnosis are continuously changing. Moreover, these dynamic variations in depth are considered more meaningful within the context of therapy than overall hypnotizability.

The psychoanalytic model resembles other paradigms in its recognition of hypnotic responding as a multidetermined process, influenced by ongoing internal and external factors. Yet, the analytical approach focuses on the unconscious rather than the conscious, the irrational instead of the rational, and dynamic conflict rather than learning history, expectancies, or cognitive skills. Like both the trait and social learning viewpoints, the analytical approach places the power of hypnosis within the patient rather than the hypnotist. Each individual's particular hypnotic ability is recognized, and attention is not focused on developing innovative induction techniques.

The Ericksonian View

The theoretical approach elaborated by Milton Erickson, and now advanced by his followers, serves as another model of individual differences in hypnotic responding. According to this paradigm, all individuals possess hypnotic potential; however, each patient responds to different hypnotic techniques. Results from standardized hypnosis scales are considered misleading because the scales themselves are inflexible and fail to tap the full hypnotic capacity of most subjects.

Erickson's viewpoint was anticipated by several early practitioners (e.g., Bernheim, 1889/1947; Forel, 1906), including Moll (1889/1958):

> I lay stress on the fact that in individual cases persons appear refractory
> to one method while another succeeds. I have found persons insuscep-
> tible to the use of fixed attention, or to the method of Nancy, while
> I obtained results by mesmeric passes. (p. 35)

Indeed, inspection of Table 1 reveals a handful of 19th-century clinicians, Oskar Vogt in particular, who claimed to attain deep hypnosis with nearly all of their patients.

It was Erickson, however, who managed to transform this general maxim into an international movement. Apparently motivated by a desire to use hypnosis with initially refractory patients, Erickson developed an array of indirect induction techniques that he believed to facilitate hypnosis for these individuals. Presumably, these more individualized procedures circumvent or "depotentiate" unconscious resistances to hypnosis. Erickson introduced his naturalistic approach to hypnotherapy in a lead article for his newly founded *American Journal of Clinical Hypnosis* in 1958:

> One of the most important of all considerations in inducing hypnosis
> is meeting adequately the patient as a personality and his needs as an
> individual. Too often the effort is made to fit the patient to an accepted
> formal technique of suggestion, rather than adapting the technique to
> the patient in accord with his actual personality situation. In any such
> adaptation, there is an imperative need to accept and to utilize those
> psychological states, understandings and attitudes that the patient
> brings into the situation. To ignore those factors in favor of some ritual
> of procedure may and often does delay, impede, limit or even prevent
> the desired results. The acceptance and utilization of those factors, on
> the other hand, promotes more rapid trance induction, the develop-
> ment of more profound trance states, the more ready acceptance of

therapy and greater ease for the handling of the total therapeutic situation. (pp. 7–8)

The essential implication is that therapists must be more flexible in their use of hypnosis. Some advocates have even suggested that whenever patients evidence resistance, it is a reflection only of therapist inflexibility (Bandler & Grinder, 1979).

The subtle ingenuity of Erickson's work can perhaps be best illustrated with an example rather than with a laundry list of specialized techniques. Weitzenhoffer (1989) offered the following anecdote of Erickson from a 1958 meeting in Philadelphia involving himself, Erickson, Jay Haley, and Bernard Gorton:

> After introductions were made, MHE [Erickson] began to work with Joan. She readily developed a hypnotic state, but seemed unable to produce much phenomena. Undaunted, and knowing that she was usually a "good" subject, Erickson continued to work with her in a conversational manner. While he was doing this, I observed him nonchalantly picking up a sheet of paper that was lying near him on a coffee table. While still talking to the subject, and without looking at the paper, he rolled it into a cylinder, as if absent-mindedly playing with it. He then let it unroll, and then once again made a cylinder out of it. Holding it in his right hand near the middle, he had one end point toward the subject; then he rotated it counterclockwise so that this end now pointed toward his left, and he slowly introduced one finger of his left hand into that end, withdrew it, and then allowed the paper to unroll and fall to the floor. He appeared to have lost interest in it. With this last act, the subject's inability to perform vanished, and Erickson proceeded to give a noteworthy demonstration. When I questioned Erickson about the above incident, he explained what had happened. He had recognized Joan as a former medical student or intern who had attended a lecture and demonstration of his a year or so earlier and who had participated as a subject. Although nothing had been said about this earlier encounter during the introductions, Joan must have remembered it, too. On that first encounter, MHE had noticed that Joan had an engagement ring; she was no longer wearing it on this second meeting, nor was she wearing a wedding band. He hypothesized that Joan's relative refractoriness was due to resistance caused by anxiety that the failure of her engagement would somehow be revealed during the session. Erickson had therefore cleverly communicated to her non-verbally while conversing with her that he remembered the ring, was aware there was no ring now, and that he was not interested in pursuing the matter. With this reassurance, Joan's resistance had vanished. (Vol. 2, p. 187)

Without confirmation, it remains possible that Erickson's interpretation of the situation is mistaken. Nevertheless, the example showcases his incomparable ability to devise impromptu interventions. Presumably, the subject's hypnotizability would have been greatly underestimated by a standardized hypnosis scale because, without Erickson's highly personalized technique, she would have resisted all efforts at hypnosis.

This example also illustrates a second fundamental implication of the Ericksonian perspective, namely, that the traditional domain of hypnosis is too limited. Consider, for instance, the nonverbal message evidently conveyed with the rolled-up paper. According to the Ericksonian paradigm, this maneuver can be understood as an indirect hypnotic technique. Yet, it is fair to ask whether this intervention *should* be considered as falling within the realm of hypnosis. Why not classify it as a form of nonverbal communication that can occur within or outside of a hypnotic context and hence is entirely independent of hypnosis? The same question can be asked about many of the indirect procedures fashioned by Erickson and his followers. For instance, by what definitional criteria do anecdotes, allegorical stories, and metaphors qualify as hypnotic methods? Consider also the following case material intended to illustrate a utilization technique for inducing hypnotic analgesia:

> Seven year old Allan fell on a broken bottle and severely lacerated his leg . . . . All the way to the surgeon's office careful explanation was given him that his injury was really not large enough to warrant as many stitches as his sister had had at the time of her hand injury. However, he was urgently counselled and exhorted that it would be his responsibility entirely to see to it that the surgeon put in as many stitches as possible, and he was thoroughly coached all the way there on how to demand emphatically his full rights . . . . As Allan entered the room, he announced to the surgeon, "I want 100 stitches. See!" Whipping off the towel, he pointed at his leg and declared, "Right there, 100 stitches. That's a lot more than Betty Alice had." . . . While the surgeon performed his task in puzzled silence, Allan counted the sutures and rechecked his counting, demanded that the sutures be placed closer together and complainingly lamented that he would not have as many as his sister. His parting statement to the surgeon was to the effect that, with a little more effort, the surgeon could have given him more sutures . . . . No mention of pain or anesthesia was made to Allan at any time nor were any "comforting reassurances" offered. Neither was there any formal effort to induce a trance. Instead, various aspects of the total situation were utilized to distract his attention completely away from the painful considerations and to focus it upon values of importance to a seven year old boy and to secure his full, active cooperation and intense participation in dealing with the entire problem adequately. In situations such as this, the patient experiences as a personality a tremendously urgent need to have something done. Recognition of this need and a readiness to utilize it by doing something in direct relationship to the origin of the need constitutes a most effective type of suggestion. (Erickson, 1959, pp. 13–14)

Despite Erickson's recognition that this procedure relies primarily on distraction, he conceptualized it as an informal hypnotic induction that includes indirect suggestions for analgesia. Many other theorists, however, draw a clear distinction between analgesia achieved via attention diversion and via hypnosis. Recall that when J. R. Hilgard and LeBaron (1984) outlined their distraction-based treatment of Jeff, the energetic 6-year-old with leukemia, they were explicit that this constituted a "nonhypnotic strategy." According to what definition of hypnosis did Erickson categorize his use of distraction as hypnotic?

Although Erickson was an intrepid explorer, he was a poor cartographer. In his search to enlarge the domain of hypnosis, he left it to those who would follow to map the boundaries of his newly discovered territory. As a clinician, he might have felt that it is irrelevant whether a particular technique is actually hypnotic or not, as long as it works. However, the manner in which we define the domain of hypnosis has far-reaching implications for our understanding of this phenomenon. For instance, the Ericksonian claim that all individuals are hypnotizable may stand or fall according to how narrowly we define the realm of hypnotic responses. Similarly, the issue of whether hypnosis per se is responsible for a patient's recovery will depend in part on which interventions are deemed to be hypnotic. Using liberal standards, it may be possible to demonstrate that everyone is able to experience hypnosis and benefit from hypnotic treatment, whereas clear individual differences will emerge if more stringent criteria are adopted. Erickson's willingness to expand the domain of hypnosis is precisely what makes his approach exciting. However, the absence within the Ericksonian model of unambiguous criteria for determining where hypnosis begins and ends renders many of this paradigm's basic tenets untestable and, as a result, unverifiable.

A corollary of the Ericksonian view is that most existing research underestimates the clinical utility of hypnosis because the interventions are overly standardized and the suggestions are too direct. Indeed, J. Barber (1977) reported that 99 of 100 dental patients were able to complete their procedures comfortably without chemical anesthetic when administered a hypnotic treatment that was flexible, indirect, and permissive. Yet, this provocative finding has proved difficult to confirm (e.g., van Gorp, Meyer, & Dunbar, 1985). Unfortunately, few other proponents of the Ericksonian view have shown an interest in conducting experimental research. Some traditional theorists (e.g., Baker, 1987; Fromm, 1987) consider the Ericksonian movement as sensationalistic and irresponsible and fear that it will remystify hypnosis. Even among adherents, there is growing concern that the movement has become something of a cult, marked by "overzealous proselytizing of an Ericksonian approach as the 'one true light' " (Hammond, 1984, p. 236). Just as there is much about Erickson's work that deserves careful study, there is a tremendous need for his theoretical contributions to be subjected to the rigors of science.

CONCLUSION

In sum, patients' responses to hypnotic therapy are influenced by nonspecific treatment variables, including their attitudes toward therapy and motivation for change, rapport with the therapist, issues of primary and secondary gain, and the manner in which the practitioner handles transference and resistance. As a consequence, therapists using hypnosis should have extensive training in general psychotherapy and should not treat conditions with hypnosis that they would not treat without it.

Differential treatment outcome is also the result of individual differences in the way patients respond to hypnosis per se. That individuals vary in their particular hypnotic talents has been recognized by practitioners for several centuries. Recent experimental work obtained with standardized hypnosis scales has confirmed this fundamental observation, revealing that the majority of individuals score in the moderate range, whereas approximately a quarter lie at either end of the continuum. Despite this wealth of clinical and empirical evidence, there has been considerable disagreement about how to best conceptualize this information. Four diverse perspectives have been discussed, all with roots extending back through the 19th century. Each paradigm offers a unique viewpoint concerning individual differences in hypnotic responding and is associated with its own set of therapeutic implications for contemporary clinicians using hypnosis in their practice.

REFERENCES

Andersen, M. S. (1985). Hypnotizability as a factor in the hypnotic treatment of obesity. *International Journal of Clinical and Experimental Hypnosis, 33,* 150–159.

Baker, E. L. (1987). The state of the art of clinical hypnosis. *International Journal of Clinical and Experimental Hypnosis, 35,* 203–214.

Bandler, R., & Grinder, J. (1979). *Frogs into princes: Neuro linguistic programming.* Moab, Jordan: Real People Press.

Barber, J. (1977). Rapid induction analgesia: A clinical report. *American Journal of Clinical Hypnosis, 19,* 138–147.

Barber, T. X. (1969). *Hypnosis: A scientific approach.* New York: Van Nostrand Reinhold.

Barber, T. X., Spanos, N. P., & Chaves, J. F. (1974). *Hypnotism, imagination, and human potentialities.* Elmsford, NY: Pergamon Press.

Bernheim, H. (1947). *Suggestive therapeutics: A treatise on the nature and uses of hypnotism* (C. H. Herter, Trans.). New York: London Book Company. (Original work published 1889)

Bowers, K. S., & Kelly, P. (1979). Stress, disease, psychotherapy, and hypnosis. *Journal of Abnormal Psychology, 88,* 490–505.

Braid, J. (1960). *Braid on hypnotism: The beginnings of modern hypnosis* (rev. ed. by A. E. Waite). New York: Julian Press. (Original work, titled *Neurypnology or the rationale of nervous sleep considered in relation with animal magnetism,* published 1843)

Brenman, M., Gill, M., & Knight, R. P. (1952). Spontaneous fluctuations in depth of hypnosis and their implications for ego-function. *International Journal of Psychoanalysis, 33,* 22–33.

Brown, D. P., & Fromm, E. (1986). *Hypnotherapy and hypnoanalysis.* Hillsdale, NJ: Erlbaum.

Cohen, S. B. (1989). Clinical uses of measures of hypnotizability. *American Journal of Clinical Hypnosis, 32,* 4–9.

Collison, D. R. (1978). Hypnotherapy in asthmatic patients and the importance of trance depth. In F. H. Frankel & H. S. Zamansky (Eds.), *Hypnosis at its bicentennial: Selected papers* (pp. 261–274). New York: Plenum Press.

d'Eslon, C. (1965). Observations on the two reports of the commissioners named by the king to investigate animal magnetism (D. Chval, Trans.). In R. E. Shor & M. T. Orne (Eds.), *The nature of hypnosis: Selected basic readings* (pp. 8–20). New York: Holt, Rinehart & Winston. (Original work published 1784)

Diamond, M. J. (1977). Hypnotizability is modifiable: An alternative approach. *International Journal of Clinical and Experimental Hypnosis, 25,* 147–166.

Diamond, M. J. (1989). The cognitive skills model: An emerging paradigm for investigating hypnotic phenomena. In N. P. Spanos & J. F. Chaves (Eds.), *Hypnosis: The cognitive-behavioral perspective* (pp. 380–399). New York: Prometheus Books.

Erickson, M. H. (1958). Naturalistic techniques of hypnosis. *American Journal of Clinical Hypnosis, 1,* 3–8.

Erickson, M. H. (1959). Further clinical techniques of hypnosis: Utilization techniques. *American Journal of Clinical and Experimental Hypnosis, 2,* 3–21.

Forel, A. H. (1906). *Hypnotism or suggestion and psychotherapy: A study of the psychological, psychophysiological, and therapeutic aspects of hypnotism* (5th ed., H. W. Armit, Trans.). London: Rebman.

Frank, J. D. (1974). *Persuasion and healing: A comparative study of psychotherapy* (rev. ed.). New York: Schocken Books.

Frankel, F. H. (1976). *Hypnosis: Trance as a coping mechanism.* New York: Plenum Press.

Frankel, F. H., & Orne, M. T. (1976). Hypnotizability and phobic behavior. *Archives of General Psychiatry, 33,* 1259–1261.

Freud, S. (1966). Hypnosis. In J. Strachery (Ed. and Trans.), *The standard edition of the complete psychological works of Sigmund Freud* (Vol. 1, pp. 103–114). London: Hogarth Press. (Original work published 1891)

Friedlander, J. W., & Sarbin, T. R. (1938). The depth of hypnosis. *Journal of Abnormal and Social Psychology, 33,* 453–475.

Fromm, E. (1977). An ego-psychological theory of altered states of consciousness. *International Journal of Clinical and Experimental Hypnosis, 25,* 372–387.

Fromm, E. (1987). Significant developments in clinial hypnosis during the past 25 years. *International Journal of Clinical Hypnosis, 35,* 215–230.

Gardner, G. G., & Olness, K. (1981). *Hypnosis and hypnotherapy with children.* New York: Grune & Stratton.

Gill, M. M., & Brenman, M. (1961). *Hypnosis and related states: Psychoanalytic studies in regression.* Madison, CT: International Universities Press.

Gordon, M. C. (1972). Age and performance differences of male patients on modified Stanford Hypnotic Susceptibility Scales. *International Journal of Clinical and Experimental Hypnosis, 20,* 152–155.

Gruenewald, D. (1982). A psychoanalytic view of hypnosis. *American Journal of Clinical Hypnosis, 24,* 185–190.

Hammond, D. C. (1984). Myths about Erickson and Ericksonian hypnosis. *American Journal of Clinical Hypnosis, 26,* 236–245.

Hilgard, E. R. (1965). *Hypnotic susceptibility.* New York: Harcourt, Brace & World.

Hilgard, E. R. (1967). Individual differences in hypnotizability. In R. E. Gordon (Ed.), *Handbook of clinical and experimental hypnosis* (pp. 391–443). New York: Macmillan.

Hilgard, E. R. (1975). The alleviation of pain by hypnosis. *Pain, 1,* 213–231.

Hilgard, E. R. (1978–1979). The Stanford Hypnotic Susceptibility Scales as related to other measures of hypnotic responsiveness. *American Journal of Clinical Hypnosis, 21,* 68–82.

Hilgard, E. R. (1982). Hypnotic susceptibility and implications for measurement. *International Journal of Clinical and Experimental Hypnosis, 30,* 394–403.

Hilgard, E. R., & Hilgard, J. R. (1975). *Hypnosis in the relief of pain.* Los Altos, CA: Kaufmann.

Hilgard, J. R. (1970). *Personality and hypnosis: A study of imaginative involvement.* Chicago: University of Chicago Press.

Hilgard, J. R., & Hilgard, E. R. (1979). Assessing hypnotic responsiveness in a clinical setting: A multi-item clinical scale and its advantages over single-item scales. *International Journal of Clinical and Experimental Hypnosis, 27,* 134–150.

Hilgard, J. R., & LeBaron, S. (1984). *Hypnotherapy of pain in children with cancer.* Los Altos, CA: Kaufmann.

James, W. (1950). *The principles of psychology.* New York: Dover. (Original work published 1890)

Kihlstrom, J. F. (1985). Hypnosis. *Annual Review of Psychology, 36,* 385–418.

Kirsch, I. (1985). Response expectancy as a determinant of experience and behavior. *American Psychologist, 40,* 1189–1202.

London, P. (1963). *Children's Hypnotic Susceptibility Scale.* Palo Alto, CA: Consulting Psychologists Press.

Moll, A. (1958). *The study of hypnosis: Historical, clinical and experimental research in the techniques of hypnotic induction.* New York: Julian. (Original work, titled *Hypnotism,* published 1889)

Morgan, A. H. (1973). The heritability of hypnotic susceptibility in twins. *Journal of Abnormal Psychology, 82,* 55–61.

Morgan, A. H., & Hilgard, E. R. (1973). Age differences in susceptibility to hypnosis. *International Journal of Clinical and Experimental Hypnosis, 21,* 78–85.

Morgan, A. H., & Hilgard, J. R. (1978–1979a). The Stanford Hypnotic Clinical Scale for Adults. *American Journal of Clinical Hypnosis, 21,* 134–147.

Morgan, A. H., & Hilgard, J. R. (1978–1979b). The Stanford Hypnotic Clinical Scale for Children. *American Journal of Clinical Hypnosis, 21,* 148–169.

Orne, M. T. (1959). Hypnosis: Artifact and essence. *Journal of Abnormal and Social Psychology, 58,* 277–299.

Orne, M. T., & Dinges, D. F. (1984). Hypnosis. In P. D. Wall & R. Melzack (Eds.), *Textbook of pain* (pp. 806–816). New York: Churchill Livingstone.

Orne, M. T., & Dinges, D. F. (1989). Hypnosis. In H. I. Kaplan & B. J. Sadock (Eds.), *Comprehensive textbook of psychiatry* (5th ed., pp. 1501–1516). Baltimore, MD: Williams & Wilkens.

Orne, M. T., & O'Connell, D. N. (1967). Diagnostic ratings of hypnotizability. *International Journal of Clinical and Experimental Hypnosis, 15,* 125–133.

Perry, C. (1977). Is hypnotizability modifiable? *International Journal of Clinical and Experimental Hypnosis, 25,* 125–146.

Perry, C., Gelfand, R., & Marcovitch, P. (1979). The relevance of hypnotic susceptibility in the clinical context. *Journal of Abnormal Psychology, 88,* 592–603.

Piccione, C., Hilgard, E. R., & Zimbardo, P. G. (1989). On the degree of stability of measured hypnotizability over a 25-year period. *Journal of Personality and Social Psychology, 56,* 289–295.

Sarbin, T. R., & Coe, W. (1972). *Hypnosis: A social psychological analysis of influence communication.* New York: Holt, Rinehart & Winston.

Schilder, P. (1956). *The nature of hypnosis* (G. Corvin, Trans.). Madison, CT: International Universities Press. (Original work published 1921)

Shor, R. E. (1962). Three dimensions of hypnotic depth. *International Journal of Clinical and Experimental Hypnosis, 10,* 23–38.

Spanos, N. P. (1971). Goal-directed fantasy and the performance of hypnotic test suggestions. *Psychiatry, 34,* 86–96.

Spanos, N. P. (1986). Hypnosis and the modification of hypnotic susceptibility: A social psychological perspective. In P. L. N. Naish (Ed.), *What is hypnosis?*

Current theories and research (pp. 85–120). Philadelphia: Open University Press.

Spanos, N. P., Kennedy, S. K., & Gwynn, M. I. (1984). Moderating effects of contextual variables on the relationship between hypnotic susceptibility and suggested analgesia. *Journal of Abnormal Psychology, 93,* 285–294.

Spanos, N. P., Radtke, H. L., Hodgins, D. C., Stam, H. J., & Bertrand, L. (1983). The Carleton University Responsiveness to Suggestion Scale: Normative data and psychometric properties. *Psychological Reports, 53,* 523–535.

Spiegel, H., & Spiegel, D. (1978). *Trance and treatment: Clinical uses of hypnosis.* New York: Basic Books.

Spinhoven, P. (1990). The clinical relevance of hypnotic susceptibility. In M. L. Fass & D. Brown (Eds.), *Creative mastery in hypnosis and hypnoanalysis* (pp. 107–124). Hillsdale, NJ: Erlbaum.

Stern, J. A., Brown, M., Ulett, G. A., & Sletten, I. (1977). A comparison of hypnosis, acupuncture, morphine, valium, aspirin, and placebo in the management of experimentally induced pain. *Annals of the New York Academy of Science, 296,* 175–193.

Tart, C. T. (1970). Self-report scales of hypnotic depth. *International Journal of Clinical and Experimental Hypnosis, 18,* 105–125.

Tellegen, A., & Atkinson, G. (1974). Openness to absorbing and self-altering experiences ("absorption"), a trait related to hypnotic susceptibility. *Journal of Abnormal Psychology, 83,* 268–277.

van Gorp, W. G., Meyer, R. G., & Dunbar, K. D. (1985). The efficacy of direct versus indirect hypnotic induction techniques on reduction of experimental pain. *International Journal of Clinical and Experimental Hypnosis, 33,* 319–328.

Wadden, T. A., & Anderton, C. H. (1982). The clinical use of hypnosis. *Psychological Bulletin, 91,* 215–243.

Weitzenhoffer, A. M. (1957). *General techniques of hypnotism.* New York: Grune & Stratton.

Weitzenhoffer, A. M. (1989). *The practice of hypnotism* (Vols. 1–2). New York: Wiley.

Weitzenhoffer, A. M., & Hilgard, E. R. (1959). *Stanford Hypnotic Susceptibility Scale, Forms A and B.* Palo Alto, CA: Consulting Psychologists Press.

Weitzenhoffer, A. M., & Hilgard, E. R. (1962). *Stanford Hypnotic Susceptibility Scale, Form C.* Palo Alto, CA: Consulting Psychologists Press.

Weitzenhoffer, A. M., & Hilgard, E. R. (1963). *Stanford Profile Scales of Hypnotic Susceptibility: Forms I and II.* Palo Alto, CA: Consulting Psychologists Press.

Weitzenhoffer, A. M., & Hilgard, E. R. (1967). *Revised Stanford Profile Scales of Hypnotic Susceptibility: Forms I and II.* Palo Alto, CA: Consulting Psychologists Press.

Wolberg, L. R. (1948). *Medical hypnosis* (Vols. 1–2). New York: Grune & Stratton.

3

OPERATOR VARIABLES IN HYPNOTHERAPY

BILLIE S. STRAUSS

Although much has been written about technique and strategy, patient characteristics, and outcomes of hypnotherapy, relatively little has been written about the characteristics of successful hypnotherapists (Lazar & Dempster, 1984). Whereas successful hypnotherapists have all of the qualities of successful psychotherapists, they also have a number of distinguishing qualities relevant to the practice of hypnosis. In this chapter I identify therapist variables that contribute to successful hypnotherapy. Before I consider characteristics of particular relevance to hypnotherapy, I first consider the literature pertinent to the characteristics of successful psychotherapists in general. To illustrate the importance of therapist flexibility, realistically appraising the patient and the situation and assuming a goal-directed yet stepwise approach to the practice of hypnotherapy, I present two cases relevant to the training and general clinical context. Finally, a review of the research on operator variables in hypnotherapy, along with concluding comments, are presented.

THERAPIST CHARACTERISTICS

A number of therapist characteristics have been identified as conducive to the practice of successful psychotherapy. Wolberg (1977) noted that psychotherapists should be sensitive, flexible, objective, and empathic and have little emotional pathology or character problems. Traits such as integrity, respect for other people, a capacity for communicating warmth, and adequate communication skills have also been viewed as useful in producing positive therapeutic outcomes (Linehan, 1980; Strupp, 1960; Wolberg, 1977). The therapeutic self (Watkins, 1978) is empathic with the patient, although it retains its own identity.

The view that effective therapists must have specific traits is derived from Rogers's (1957) client-centered therapy model. The acquisition of the traits and skills just noted are goals of many therapist training programs (Alberts & Edelstein, 1990). Precisely how these therapist traits are related to the efficacy of therapy has not, however, been determined (Lambert, DeJulio, & Stein, 1978). Nevertheless, the evidence suggests that the skills and abilities that have traditionally been associated with successful psychotherapy are indeed associated with positive therapeutic outcomes. For example, Bergin and Lambert (1978) analyzed scores of studies and concluded that although the largest proportion of variation in therapy outcome is accounted for by preexisting client factors (e.g., motivation for change), therapist personal factors account for the second largest proportion of change. A more recent review by Raskin (1985) essentially echoed these conclusions.

In addition to personality characteristics or traits, the training and technical competence of the therapist have been viewed as important variables (Wolberg, 1977). Wolberg suggested that if psychotherapists have what he called "therapeutic personality qualities" such as sensitivity, flexibility, and empathy, then therapists who are well trained should achieve better treatment outcomes than therapists who are not as well trained. However, the relationships among treatment efficacy, training, and therapist competence have not yet been adequately validated (Alberts & Edelstein, 1990).

Alberts and Edelstein (1990) noted that Ford (1979) found that because most of the training studies published between 1960 and 1978 involved "skill acquisition" of specific behaviors, the trainees often were undergraduate students, and the interventions typically were brief, findings could not be generalized to an actual clinical situation. In their 1990 review of training studies published after Ford's (1979) review, Alberts and Edelstein (1990) considered studies that used professional therapists, often in the laboratory part of a clinical graduate course and often in an analog situation. Those studies showed that although some training helped therapists to acquire knowledge and the therapy process skills related to empathy and communication, the research did not show that trainees applied these skills in an effective way in actual clinical situations or after the training was completed.

The available research is limited, and firm conclusions cannot yet be drawn. Whether training plays a prominent role in psychotherapy outcome and significantly augments therapists' preexisting "natural" clinical abilities has yet to be documented. What is needed are additional studies that examine different types of training programs, that target a variety of clinical abilities measured in both the laboratory and natural clinical settings, and that relate skill acquisition to treatment outcome.

HYPNOTHERAPIST CHARACTERISTICS

In addition to general qualities viewed as useful for all therapists, therapists who practice hypnotherapy may have additional characteristics. One approach to examining these attributes is to consider what qualities are associated with a therapist's use of or failure to use hypnotic techniques. Finegold and Edelstien (1986) discussed five reasons that novice therapists may have for not using hypnosis: fear of failure, fear of power, the belief that others have better techniques, fear of the unexpected, and fear of colleagues' disapproval. Failures with hypnotic and hypnotherapeutic techniques often become apparent more quickly than with nonhypnotic techniques; hence, therapists who have concerns about their competence or about their status with colleagues or patients may fear failure with hypnotic techniques more than failure with nonhypnotic techniques.

Similarly, although hypnosis is a recognized treatment modality, many professionals are skeptical about it; therapists who are sensitive to colleagues' criticisms may be uncomfortable incorporating hypnosis into their clinical practice. Hypnosis has an aura of magic and power; therapists who have unresolved issues about control may mistakenly believe that hypnotic techniques can effect undue power over others. This belief may engender conflict or anxiety about using hypnosis and may thus lead therapists to shy away from using hypnotic interventions. Concern about the intricacies of technique, or depth of trance achieved by patients, stems from overfocusing on the production of a hypnotic state, even to the point of reifying hypnosis. This preoccupation may lead the therapist to devote less attention to the therapeutic implications of hypnotic interventions. Issues about competition with others may result in therapists' comparing their techniques with those used by other therapists. Finally, the use of hypnosis may result in the unexpected occurring: Therapists who are unsure of themselves, either about the use of hypnosis or about their competence in general, may not want to use techniques that may lead to unexpected responses.

Given these considerations, it is apparent that successful hypnotherapists must have personal qualities that do not result in their sidestepping the use of hypnotic techniques. Although hypnosis can be highly successful, it also can result in failure (Lazar & Dempster, 1981). Hence, hypnotherapists must have sufficient confidence in their ability to tolerate the failures that may occur. Similarly, hypnotherapists must abandon their concerns about whether the patient is or is not hypnotized and instead focus on the therapeutic implications of what transpires. Enjoyment of the unexpected and curiosity about what will happen is conducive to the use of hypnosis. Similarly, achieving a balance between comfort and confidence in one's own abilities to devise therapeutic strategies and a willingness to consider feedback from colleagues is helpful in deriving maximum benefit from hypnotic procedures.

Another approach to thinking about hypnotherapist characteristics is a task analysis. This involves examining the components of hypnotherapy and ascertaining what traits are required for their successful implementation. In hypnotherapy, as compared with psychotherapy that does not involve hypnosis, several aspects of the treatment may be accentuated. That is, the therapist may be more active, transference and countertransference reactions can be intensified, the attachment between therapist and patient may be greater and more variable, and hypnotherapy may work more quickly (Lazar & Dempster, 1984). The hypnotherapist therefore needs to respond to the patient sensitively, quickly, and flexibly to adapt to shifts in the patient and the therapeutic relationship. In addition, the hypnotherapist must carefully word suggestions and astutely observe the patient's response to these suggestions (Brown & Fromm, 1986). In short, the therapist needs a greater degree of concentration and imagination, as well as an ability to quickly synthesize and use a great deal of information on a variety of levels in order to be optimally responsive and open to the patient.

For example, I used permissive suggestions to produce an age regression in a highly intelligent professional male. I then asked the patient, "How old are you?" He replied in a clearly adult voice, "I feel like I'm 4, but I know I'm 32." I replied, "It's okay to know you're 32, but it's good to feel 4, focus on feeling 4, it's good to feel 4." The patient's voice shifted, sounded more like that of a child, and the age regression was continued. The question "How old are you?" evoked in the patient more reality-based perceptions and conflict between intellect and feelings, which might have reflected some ambivalence about the age regression. The response affirmed the patient's thoughts as well as his feelings but implicitly directed the subject to focus more on feelings.

To practice effectively, hypnotherapists need a mature personality structure that is capable of tolerating rapid shifts and even regressive reactions. That is, therapists must have achieved object constancy and be able to maintain internal equilibrium, stability, and a sense of competence regardless of the patient's affect or behavior. Therapists must also be able to accept patients' regression or shifts in attachment, yet not be drawn into their experiential world to the extent that they respond in a similar way or become angry at or disenchanted with the patient. At the same time, therapists must be able to deeply empathize with their patients.

For example, a patient with severe character pathology was referred to me by her individual therapist for hypnosis to help with panic reactions, which resulted in an almost catatonic state and occurred both during therapy sessions as well as in her daily life in response to stimuli that are benign for most people. Hypnosis was geared toward helping her feel comfortable, with no suggestions to evoke dissociative feelings or loss of control. Predictably, the patient did panic and feel overwhelmed during hypnosis. I worked toward mollifying and abating the panic attacks, with the goal of helping the patient to learn similar control. A strategy, for example, was to help the patient to focus on real or imagined concrete objects such as her get-well cards, her cat, or even her own hands.

In discussing therapist characteristics, hypnosis textbooks (e.g., Crasilneck & Hall, 1985; Weitzenhoffer, 1989) focus on the dimension of training and competence. Although particular competencies, skills, and training requirements are not clearly specified, Crasilneck and Hall (1985) suggested that knowledge of personality, management of transference and countertransference reactions, and a variety of approaches and techniques is necessary in order to practice with competence. Weitzenhoffer (1989) outlined detailed steps to help operators learn to hypnotize, including reviewing material, arranging props, role playing, listening to tape recordings of sessions, and practice with different subjects. Brown and Fromm (1986) suggested that an introductory hypnosis course should include theories of hypnosis, induction and deepening techniques, demonstration, practice, and methods of treatment and that further training should include practice and supervision of cases. In summary, because the hypnotherapist is viewed as a therapist who uses hypnosis, the hypnotherapist should be competent as a psychotherapist and in the use of hypnosis.

CLINICAL APPLICATIONS

In this section I examine how operator variables influence the hypnotherapeutic process. Hypnosis is not a unitary treatment; rather, it is a tool that spans a variety of treatment strategies and approaches. For example, hypnoanalytic techniques go well beyond those of classical analysis. These techniques and objectives include, but are not limited to, the following: enhancing vividness of associations; producing free association, imagery, and dream material; facilitating age regression to explore or reexperience genetic material; administering posthypnotic suggestions to produce dreams or affect behavior; suggesting permissive amnesia of material produced during a particular session and positive motivation needed to continue treatment (e.g., hope or curiosity); and facilitating understanding and insight at the patient's own pace.

Using hypnosis, therapists foster patients' trust by creating a safe relationship through the use of nurturing and positive imagery as well as by encouraging patients to develop their own inner resources (Eisen & Fromm, 1983). Hypnosis may also intensify infantile patterns of object relations that are reestablished with the therapist (Smith, 1984). Smith noted that issues that afford understanding of what happens in the hypnotic relationship include elements of developmental arrest and symptom formation, a capacity to create good self- and object representations, facilitating a maternal response matrix, the nature of transitional object relatedness, and the use of bad internal objects as a defense against abandonment.

In the regression that many believe (Gill & Brenman, 1959; Shor, 1979) ensues in hypnosis, the therapist may respond "as if" the patient were not an adult. A responsive therapist can relate to the regressed patient as he or she would relate to a child. Some therapists experience a "regressive pull" when their own dependency needs are reevoked by the patient's regression (Lazar & Dempster, 1984). Depending on the therapist's individual personality organization, the therapist may respond in a playful way that enhances the patient's growth or in a defensive way that may inhibit such growth.

An example of a playful way of responding is illustrated by work with a patient who was seen for hypnotherapy to relieve pain of sickle cell disease (Lazar & Dempster, 1984). The patient was in pain, moaned and rocked, and did not respond to direct or indirect suggestion. Because the patient previously had attended college in a desert region and in response to the patient's childlike demeanor, the therapist asked, "Remember the desert?" The patient smiled, and the therapist continued to talk about the desert, interspersing suggestions of warm and good feelings. When the patient stopped moaning, the therapist said, "Look, a desert animal, see it. . . . Look at it play, running, . . ." In giving these suggestions, the therapist experienced a childlike playfulness, which helped her respond to the regressed part of the patient. An example of a defensive way of responding would be for the therapist to remain serious, disparage the patient for being "too dependent" and "too resistant to treatment," and avoid engaging in childlike imagery.

It is frequently the case that in hypnotherapy, the therapist takes a more active approach than in nonhypnotic therapy. This activity, as well as many patients' wish for a magical cure (Eisen, 1990), may lead both patient and therapist to believe that the responsibility for treatment lies with the therapist rather than with the patient (Gill & Brenman, 1959). Gill and Brenman further noted that novice hypnotherapists often experience anxiety, probably because both patient and therapist attribute the responsibility of hypnosis to the therapist. If therapists do not have a realistic view of their own competence and limitations and of the efficacy and limitations of hypnotherapy, and if they also lack respect for patients as active participants in their own treatment, then this shift in attribution of responsibility may evoke therapist reactions such as grandiosity or self-focus. The sense of "doing something" to the patient also may detract from both the therapist and patient seeing the patient as active in the therapeutic process.

In contrast to grandiosity, a healthy amount of confidence is useful. Grandiosity is an unrealistic self-aggrandizement in which therapists are overly concerned about their performance and with how others view their presentation; hence, therapists focus less on the patient than on themselves. A healthy amount of confidence involves therapists' realistic, positive self-appraisals so that they need not be overly concerned with their performance or with how others view their presentation. Given this, therapists can focus on their patients. In a popular book, Wolberg (1982) noted that the operator's confidence, rather than the method of induction, is important in having subjects respond. For example, if therapists lose poise and become excited at the perceived "power" they wield when using hypnosis, they would, of necessity, be unable to respond empathically to their patients.

With hypnosis, countertransferential reactions tend to be intensified (Brown & Fromm, 1986). The nature of the type of countertransference evoked depends on the therapist's personality structure and the stimulus of the patient and therapy situation. For example, pregential parental countertransference in which therapists believe that patients know all that the therapist is thinking may stem from therapists' never having given up their belief in the omniscience of their parents. Alternatively, oedipal sexual countertransference, in which therapists believe they are worthless or, in grandiose fashion, believe that they can cure all patients quickly, may stem from therapists' never having worked through the oedipal phase of playing at being an adult. Yet another possibility is that sibling countertransference, in which therapists are competitive with their patients, may stem from unresolved competitive feelings with parents or siblings. Other kinds of countertransference may have their roots in unresolved dependency needs, unconscious conflicts about aggression, and need for control (Gruenewald, 1971).

Because hypnosis works rapidly, both successes and failures may be dramatic (Lazar & Dempster, 1981). For example, a man with severe itching secondary to liver cancer but exacerbated by family stress responded within seconds to hypnotic suggestions for imagery of "coolness"; the itching abated for the first time in several months. Rescue fantasies as well as competition with the patient, self-doubt, or a sense that the patient knows what the therapist is thinking may be evoked. Some hypnotherapists report experiencing great joy or disappointment depending on whether hypnosis succeeds or fails (Gill & Brenman, 1959). Although hypnosis does not create countertransferential issues, it may exacerbate concerns that otherwise might not have surfaced. To minimize and analyze the countertransference that may emerge, hypnotherapists should have the capacity for self-observation as well as the willingness to look honestly at their own reactions. That is, therapists must have sufficient ego resources as well as motivation to assess their reactions and attitudes toward patients and the therapeutic context.

Because of the variations in intimacy and attachment between patient and therapist (Baker, 1983), the hypnotherapist also experiences these shifts. To maintain empathy and intimacy, to avoid competition with the patient, and to maintain a sense of objectivity and self-identity, the therapist should have achieved a level of personality development that includes the ability to maintain object constancy, stability, and sense of competence regardless of the patient's affect or behavior. Increased observation of the subject results in greater sensitivity to the patient. Hypnosis also may be viewed as a talent or capacity, and the therapist should be able to enjoy the patient's success.

Hypnotherapy requires flexibility on the therapist's part. Shifts during the process, such as shifts between hypnosis and the waking state, require the ability to alter techniques and strategy according to the patient's requirements. For example, the therapist observes that the patient who is exploring conflictual material spontaneously moves from hypnosis to the waking state; that the patient's breathing becomes more rapid, eyes flutter and then open; and that the content of speech pertains to the therapy room rather than to the conflictual material. The therapist could then focus on the process of therapy and address what has happened (i.e., the patient has awakened from hypnosis and may explore why the patient awoke rather than continue to explore the conflictual material).

For the patient, the capacity for imaginative involvement (Hilgard, 1979) is an important trait. For the hypnotherapist, imagination and a capacity to tap the patient's talent for hypnosis is necessary. The hypnotherapist must be able to shift between providing sufficient structure for the hypnotic process, including use of meaningful imagery and metaphor, and allowing the patient's own creative process to unfold.

Teaching hypnotherapy may require personal characteristics that differ from teaching nonhypnotic psychotherapy. "Nonhypnosis" therapy courses may have a hands-on demonstration component or role playing with normal suggestions. In teaching hypnotherapy, more demonstrations are given with a greater chance for the unexpected to occur. The teacher is more on display, both in having students observe his or her technique and in handling problematic situations in a way that is appropriate, because subjects often are students in the class. For example, in a nonhypnosis therapy class, free association can be demonstrated by having students write associations; however, in a hypnotherapy course, age regression is best demonstrated when it is performed or enacted. The likelihood of having others witness one's errors is greater in teaching hypnotherapy, and the instructor must have self-confidence and a high level of competence and ability to respond flexibly to changing situational demands.

CASE MATERIAL

Throughout this chapter I have emphasized the importance of realistic appraisal of the patient, responsivity to the patient, and the need to maintain a flexible stance. The cases that follow illustrate the dilemmas of realistic appraisal of the patient and the importance of flexibility in the clinical context. The first case is a vignette about teaching hypnotherapy.

Case 1

The events portrayed in this case occurred in a class in which psychiatric residents and psychology interns practiced age regression. In addition to didactic material and demonstration, they previously had administered the Stanford Hypnotic Clinical Scale, Form A (Morgan & Hilgard, 1975), which includes an age regression item. Students were divided into four groups of 3 or 4 each, and I consulted with each group in turn.

In one group, the subject, another student in the class, reported that she was 4 years old and was with her grandfather. Her voice revealed some apprehension. She next indicated that she was alone and felt very lonely and sad. The operator was unsure of what to do and looked to me for assistance. Attempts to give suggestions to the operator did not work. I spoke to the subject and told her that sometimes people are sad, and that is okay, but that now it is time to return to the present and she could make use of this experience to help her with her own work personally and in becoming a psychologist. Following the age regression, I suggested that the operator could continue to work with her.

When I joined the practice group, I did not have a good sense of what was going on, but because this was a student and practice subject in a group situation rather than a patient, further exploration was not indicated. On the basis of my knowledge of the subject as a trainee in our program, I chose to normalize the situation. The suggestion that she make use of this experience had the connotation that this exploration was for future work, not for the present class. I was unsuccessful in communicating suggestions to the operator. The operator later said she was relieved when I took over, although my considerations included moving away from difficulties that the subject might have been having and helping the operator to maintain self-esteem.

During the practice session, the instructor had to synthesize a large amount of information, often incomplete and secondhand, and make judgments that considered the subject's well-being, the operator's knowledge, and the overall class time frame. Flexibility, the ability to empathize with the subject and the operator, the ability to maintain objectivity in evaluating what had happened, and creativity in formulating suggestions that are meaningful and ego syntonic were needed.

The importance of the operator's need to realistically appraise the subject, to respond on a continuous basis to the shifting demands of the situation, and to maintain a flexible, stepwise approach to treatment are also illustrated in the case that follows. Dealing with resistance to hypnotic suggestions sometimes demands a creative, spontaneous approach molded to the needs of the patient. The example that follows also highlights the fact that even in the case of a hospitalized patient, hypnosis and self-hypnosis can be used to increase autonomy and feelings of control.

Case 2

A woman in her 30s, who discovered she was pregnant several weeks earlier, was hospitalized for depression. She had many somatic complaints. She had been treated as an outpatient for about 10 years, and her therapist recently was unavailable because of his own illness. She felt her depression had been triggered several years earlier by an allergist who gave her a variety of medications. Several weeks before the hospitalization, after treatment at a fertility clinic, she discovered she was pregnant. She was highly ambivalent about having children.

The patient had a family history of affective disorder. She reported that she was nervous, had body tremors, could not sleep, felt like she was losing control, and had muscle spasm. Because of the pregnancy, antidepressant medication was contraindicated, and she was referred for hypnosis to help her regain a sense of control.

The treatment plan was to teach her self-hypnosis in order to reduce anxiety and somatic complaints, increase her sense of control, and help her to be more amenable to the therapy and milieu the hospital had to offer. An exercise of having her imagine an apple (Strauss, 1991) indicated she was resisting suggestions, and my approach was to focus on her controlling the sessions. In the second session, the patient was taught to use self-hypnosis for relaxation.

At the third session, the patient seemed less depressed and said her sleep had improved. She noted that hypnosis works "sometimes." She seemed interested when I inquired whether she would like to use hypnosis prophylactically. I told the patient to hypnotize herself and to signal me when she was comfortably hypnotized so I could give her additional suggestions. After the patient signaled that she was hypnotized, I gave her a "control stick" and told her that by "fiddling" with this stick, she could experience a greater sense of control. I suggested that she play with this stick. Because the patient previously had used Valium, I suggested that she imagine that she was given some Valium and spent some time eliciting descriptions of the pills and letting her decide the dose and with what she would take them. She decided to take three 2-mg white round pills with cold mineral water with ice cubes. At the end of her trance, the patient reported that she liked the hallucinated Valium and the control stick and that she felt some increased energy. During the following session, she was given hallucinated Elavil, which she had not previously taken but had heard about and wished she could take; she reported afterward that she felt "nice, mellow."

During subsequent sessions, the patient told me at the beginning of the session what she wished to work on. The issues and goals she delineated included relaxation, improved sleep, coping with stress, feeling more energetic, and handling anger. The therapist and staff reported that the patient was more amenable to treatment. She was discharged from the hospital. In a note sent after the birth of her child, she said she had practiced relaxation and was happy with her child.

The primary therapist and ward staff requested that the hypnotherapist "do something"; this had the potential to evoke rescue fantasies. What was important here was the therapist's realistic appraisal of what hypnosis could achieve. The therapist proceeded in stepwise fashion. The goal was not to have dramatic improvement to soothe a frustrated staff but to set the stage for the patient to become less depressed and more self-directed.

The therapist attempted to use the patient's background and interests in developing imagery. At times imagery was suggested and, at other times, it was initiated by the patient. It was particularly important to accede to the patient and encourage her to initiate and frame her activities as self-hypnosis when resistance surfaced, as perceptions of increased self-control, rather than operator control, were desirable. Indications that the hypnosis "worked" were used to move to another stage of therapy in which hypnosis was used for prophylactic purposes and in which imagery that was personally relevant and meaningful to the patient was exploited. At all times, the therapist was vigilant to cues about the patient's readiness to move forward in treatment, take risks, and respond to suggestions.

Indeed, the therapist tried to be flexible and focus on issues that were meaningful to the patient, although there was not always continuity from session to session. The therapist further conveyed to the ward staff that the patient was using self-hypnosis for herself so that they could facilitate her practicing but also allow her autonomy in deciding when to practice. This example also illustrates how a relatively brief and focused intervention that fosters a sense of personal control and autonomy can initiate a positive "ripple effect" or cycle in which heightened motivation and involvement in psychotherapy in turn leads to increasing perceptions of control and treatment gains in a recursive fashion.

RESEARCH AND APPRAISAL

The literature abounds with anecdotal reports about hypnotherapists that are useful for generating ideas, programs, and research. I could find only one report that supplied survey data. Lazar and Dempster (1984) reported on a survey of 21 practice subjects in two university hypnosis classes. Subjects were asked to evaluate operator characteristics. They reported that hypnotists with whom they had good experiences were sensitive, warm, friendly, competent, confident, relaxed, flexible, and creative. Traits of hypnotists with whom subjects had unpleasant experiences included insensitive, unsure, anxious, and rigid. These findings of "good" and "bad" hypnotist traits are similar to those reported by Truax and Carkhuff (1967) for therapists who did not use hypnosis.

Areas for future research include determining whether hypnotherapists differ from other therapists, whether hypnotherapist behaviors and characteristics are related to the patient's hypnotic and therapeutic experience and to the specific techniques and strategies used, and whether operator variables are related to the outcome of therapy.

The scope of hypnotherapy research is limited. Therefore, it is important to examine research on therapist variables in psychotherapy in nonhypnotic contexts because it is likely that these variables are equally important in hypnotherapy.

Therapist variables may be related to client satisfaction with the therapist or to outcome of therapy more generally (i.e., reduction of symptoms or whether the patient feels better). Assessment of competence of therapists is complex but important in maintaining professional standards (i.e., see Bernstein, 1982; Berven, 1987; Matarazzo, 1978; Stevenson & Norcross, 1987). Stevenson and Norcross noted that the vagueness of the term *competence* has resulted in a lack of clarity and poor construct validity. They reviewed four ways in which competence has been defined: (a) in the Rogerian tradition, which emphasizes the importance of interpersonal skills in creating a facilitative interpersonal relationship; (b) according to the behavioral approach, in which specific therapist behaviors are taught; (c) according to a psychodynamic perspective, in which supervisory ratings of global competence or of tactics such as "deals effectively with negative transference" are used; and (d) according to a cognitive information-processing perspective, which assesses one's ability to arrive at correct decisions. Measures of competence differ in terms of content (e.g., knowledge, personality characteristics), scoring method (e.g., rating scales, frequency of behavior), and source of scoring (e.g., observer, self-ratings, client).

Strategies for evaluating clinical skills include evaluation of work samples, evaluation of practice in a simulated clinical situation, and client ratings of the clinician. Berven (1987) also conceptualized competence in terms of knowledge (what one knows), skills (what one can do), and affect (personality characteristics including attitudes, values, beliefs, and motives). He discussed various paradigms of using simulation as an evaluation method. Matarazzo (1978) noted that student acquisition of skill must be related to patient improvement. She concluded that the ultimate criteria for evaluating therapists are patient satisfaction and outcome, but she also considered the facilitation of communication skills, relationship variables, personality variables, and technical skills and knowledge to be important criteria. Bernstein (1982) discussed issues in skill acquisition and generalization in relation to client behavior.

Research on the personality characteristics of therapists stems from the work of Roger's group (Rogers & Dymond, 1954; Rogers, Gendlin, Kiesler, & Truax, 1967; Truax & Carkhuff, 1967; Truax & Mitchell, 1972). These studies suggested that the therapist traits necessary for successful psychotherapy include empathy, positive regard for patients, and being in touch with one's own feelings. Other studies have related successful therapy to the therapist's degree of experience and self-confidence rather than to personality traits (Fiedler, 1950).

In a study by Hazler and Hipple (1981), new therapists were trained in empathy communication using mental imagery. Following a lecture format, one group used mental imagery practice, whereas a control group used discussion with no imagery. The two groups did not differ in empathic communication during a subsequent role-playing interview. Another study (Robinson & Cabianca, 1985) showed that the number of role-playing practice sessions was related to the acquisition of reflection of feeling responses.

Various programs have trained graduate students to implement a variety of therapeutic strategies (Brown, Kratochwill, & Bergan, 1982; Isaacs, Embry, & Baer, 1982; Iwata, Wong, Riordan, Dorsey, & Lau, 1982; Peters, Cormier, & Cormier, 1978; Scott, Cormier, & Cormier, 1980). In those studies, characteristics of trainees were not considered as a variable. For example, Peters et al. evaluated the four components of a microcounseling training model to teach counseling skills: written and video models, role-playing practice, observer feedback, and remediation practice. Graduate students were assigned to one of four groups, each of which used one of the aforementioned components of this training model. After 2 weeks of training, graduate students were evaluated using a written measure and a role-playing measure. No differences were found among the four groups, although students in each group evidenced learning. Unfortunately, this study did not evaluate long-term gains or treatment with actual patients.

Iwata et al. (1982) reported on two studies that assessed the training of clinical interviewing skills. Graduate students were trained on interviewing skills through the use of written material, classroom instruction and practice, and quizzes. In the first study, these graduate students were audiotaped while conducting interviews with role played or volunteer "clients"; in the second study, therapists interviewed parents of children with behavior problems. A 4-month follow-up was conducted. Results from both studies showed that these techniques were effective in training therapists to interview according to criteria and that changes in client behavior were related to changes in interviewer behavior. Isaacs et al. (1982) also used a training program that consisted of a written manual, videotaped models, rehearsal, role playing, and performance feedback to teach therapists instructing, informing, and praising skills in working with preschool children and their parents. Following the training program, therapists increased their rates of the target behaviors; parents increased attention to the children's compliance, decreased attention to children's noncompliance, and increased their praise to the children; and children increased their compliance and noncompliance.

Although these studies did not teach hypnosis or hypnotic techniques, the teaching methods that include role playing, rehearsal, use of written material, feedback, and practice certainly have been applied to the teaching of hypnosis. In addition, in teaching hypnosis, instructors evaluate the subject's response in evaluating the efficacy of the operator. For example, an operator who uses magnificent visual imagery with a subject who cannot successfully visualize or exploit such imagery would be viewed as using poor technique.

Because hypnotherapy involves many judgments, decisions, and a wide repertoire of skills and abilities on the therapist's part, research that examines this complex mix of variables will need to be carefully conducted and methodologically sophisticated. At the same time, even the most basic controlled investigations are presently lacking. Hypnosis research has focused more on the subjects' hypnotizability and imagery skills to the detriment of examining the influence of operator variables. The time is ripe for researchers and theoreticians to investigate the nature of the hypnotic proceedings with full recognition of their true diversity and complexity.

CONCLUSION

Knowledge of operator variables that contribute to the success of hypnotherapy is primarily derived from conceptual speculation, anecdotal reports, and research on the characteristics of therapists who do not use hypnosis. The one survey report (Lazar & Dempster, 1984) involved novice hypnotists in a practice setting rather than hypnotherapists in the clinical setting.

Conceptions of therapist characteristics are, for the most part, grounded in Rogers's (1957) model and seem "obvious" in a clinical context. In an informal way, clinicians evaluate the traits and skills of colleagues and students in reading case reports, making referrals, or inviting colleagues to teach. In examining hypnotherapy sessions, clinicians note the therapist's sensitivity in picking up on metaphor or in using suggestions that fit the patient's needs in an elegant but subtle way. Yet, the state of knowledge about characteristics of successful hypnotherapists leaves many questions unanswered, and there is a need for systematic empirical research in this area. For example, because hypnosis is a tool that can be used with a variety of treatment strategies, do therapists who use hypnoanalytic techniques differ from those who use behavioral techniques or a blend of techniques? Further research would be needed to determine whether specific traits of the hypnotherapist are related to effective hypnotherapy. If so, do colleagues develop such traits as the result of hypnosis training or is there a self-selection mechanism such that colleagues who exemplify these traits are most likely to gravitate toward using hypnosis in psychotherapy?

In addition to the traits of hypnotherapists, the level of personality development of hypnotherapists should be considered. A sufficiently high level is needed to allow the therapist to have mature judgment, a capacity for intimacy and uncertainty, flexibility and assertiveness in setting limits, objectivity, empathy, and sensitivity. Similarly, having a realistic self-concept and sense of confidence and an ability to manage countertransference related to issues such as power and intimacy are needed. As the training literature in nonhypnotic therapy receives more attention, training and competence of hypnotherapists should be considered.

The view that hypnotherapy, regardless of treatment strategy, involves the patient as an active participant in treatment suggests that patient variables are of primary importance in therapy, followed by therapeutic strategy, hypnotic technique, and therapist variables. Because of the importance of the relationship between the patient and therapist, therapist variables, including personality structure, style, and experience, should not be overlooked or underemphasized.

REFERENCES

Alberts, G., & Edelstein B. (1990). Therapist training: A critical review of skill training studies. *Clinical Psychology Review, 10,* 497–511.

Baker, E. L. (1983). Resistance in hypnotherapy of primitive states: Its meaning and management. *International Journal of Clinical and Experimental Hypnosis, 31,* 82–89.

Bergin, A. E., & Lambert, M. L. (1978). The evaluation of therapeutic outcome. In S. L. Garfield & A. E. Bergin (Eds.), *Handbook of psychotherapy and behavior change: An empirical analysis* (2nd ed., pp. 139–189). New York: Wiley.

Bernstein, G. S. (1982). Training behavior change agents: A conceptual review. *Behavior Therapy, 13,* 1–23.

Berven, N. L. (1987). Improving evaluation in counselor training and credentialing through standardized simulations. In B. A. Edelstein & E. S. Berler (Eds.), *Evaluation and accountability in clinical training* (pp. 203–229). New York: Plenum Press.

Brown, D., & Fromm, E. (1986). *Hypnotherapy and hypnoanalysis.* Hillsdale, NJ: Erlbaum.

Brown, D. K., Kratochwill, T. R., & Bergan, J. R. (1982). Teaching interview skills for problem identification: An analogue study. *Behavioral Assessment, 4,* 63–73.

Crasilneck, H. B., & Hall, J. A. (1985). *Clinical hypnosis: Principles and applications* (2nd ed.). New York: Grune & Stratton.

Eisen, M. R. (1990). From the magical wish to the belief in the self. In M. L. Fass & D. Brown (Eds.), *Creative mastery in hypnosis and hypnoanalysis* (pp. 147–157). Hillsdale, NJ: Erlbaum.

Eisen, M. R., & Fromm, E. (1983). The clinical use of self-hypnosis in hypnotherapy: Tapping the functions of imagery and adaptive regression. *International Journal of Clinical and Experimental Hypnosis, 31,* 243–255.

Fiedler, F. E. (1950). A comparison of therapeutic relationships in psychoanalytic, non-directive, and Adlerian therapy. *Journal of Consulting Psychology, 14,* 436–445.

Finegold, M., & Edelstien, M. G. (1986). Concern about practicing on patients. In B. Zilbergeld, M. G. Edelstien, & D. L. Araoz (Eds.), *Hypnosis: Questions and answers* (pp. 477–480). New York: Norton.

Ford, J. D. (1979). Research on training counselors and clinicians. *Review of Educational Research, 69,* 87–130.

Gill, M. M., & Brenman, M. (1959). *Hypnosis and related states.* New York: International Universities Press.

Gruenewald, D. (1971). Transference and countertransference in hypnosis. *International Journal of Clinical and Experimental Hypnosis, 19,* 71–82.

Hazler, R. J., & Hipple, T. E. (1981). The effects of mental practice on counselor behavior. *Counselor Education and Supervision, 20,* 211–218.

Hilgard, J. (1979). *Personality and hypnosis: A study of imaginative involvement* (rev. ed.) Chicago: University of Chicago Press.

Isaacs, C. D., Embry, L. H., & Baer, D. M. (1982). Training family therapists: An experimental analysis. *Journal of Applied Behavior Analysis, 15,* 505–520.

Iwata, B. A., Wong, W. E., Riordan, M. M., Dorsey, M. F., & Lau, M. M. (1982). Assessment and training of clinical interviewing skills: Analogue analysis and field replication. *Journal of Applied Behavioral Analysis, 15,* 191–204.

Lambert, M. J., DeJulio, S. S., & Stein, D. M. (1978). Therapist interpersonal skills: Process, outcome, methodological considerations, and recommendations for future research. *Psychological Bulletin, 85,* 467–489.

Lazar, B. S., & Dempster, C. R. (1981). Failures in hypnosis and hypnotherapy: A review. *American Journal of Clinical Hypnosis, 24,* 48–54.

Lazar, B. S., & Dempster, C. R. (1984). Operator variables in successful hypnotherapy. *International Journal of Clinical and Experimental Hypnosis, 32*, 28–40.

Linehan, M. M. (1980). Supervision of behavior therapy. In A. K. Hess (Ed.), *Psychotherapy supervision: Theory, research and practice* (pp. 148–180). New York: Wiley.

Matarazzo, R. G. (1978). Research on the teaching and learning of psychotherapeutic skills. In A. E. Bergin & S. L. Garfield (Eds.), *Handbook of psychotherapy and behavioral change* (pp. 895–924). New York: Wiley.

Morgan, A. H., & Hilgard, J. R. (1975). Stanford Hypnotic Clinical Scale. In E. R. Hilgard & J. R. Hilgard (Eds.), *Hypnosis in the relief of pain* (pp. 209–221). Los Altos, CA: Kaufmann.

Peters, G. A., Cormier, L. S., & Cormier, W. H. (1978). Effects of modeling, rehearsal, feedback, and remediation on acquisition of a counseling strategy. *Journal of Counseling Psychology, 25*, 231–237.

Raskin, N. (1985). Client-centered therapy. In S. J. Lynn & J. P. Garske (Eds.), *Contemporary psychotherapies: Models and methods* (pp. 155–190). Columbus, OH: Charles E. Merrill.

Robinson, S., & Cabianca, W. (1985). Effects of counselor's ordinal position when involved in role play practice in triads. *Counselor Education and Supervision, 24*, 365–371.

Rogers, C. R. (1957). The necessary and sufficient conditions of therapeutic personality change. *Journal of Consulting Psychology, 21*, 425–434.

Rogers, C. R., & Dymond, R. F. (Eds.). (1954). *Psychotherapy and personality change coordinated studies in the client-centered approach.* Chicago: University of Chicago Press.

Rogers, C. R., Gendlin, E. I., Kiesler, D. J., & Truax, C. B. (1967). *The therapeutic relationship and its impact: A study of psychotherapy with schizophrenics.* Madison: University of Wisconsin Press.

Scott, A., Cormier, W., & Cormier, L. (1980). Effects of covert modeling and written material on the acquisition of a counseling strategy. *Counselor Education and Supervision, 19*, 259–268.

Shor, R. E. (1979). A phenomenological method for the measurement of variables important to an understanding of the nature of hypnosis. In E. Fromm & R. E. Shor (Eds.), *Hypnosis: Developments in research and new perspectives* (2nd rev. ed., pp. 105–135). New York: Aldine.

Smith, A. H., Jr. (1984). Sources of efficacy in the hypnotic relationship: An object relations approach. In W. C. Wester II & A. H. Smith, Jr. (Eds.), *Clinical hypnosis: A multidisciplinary approach* (pp. 85–114). Philadelphia: Lippincott.

Stevenson, J., & Norcross, J. (1987). Current status of training evaluation in clinical psychology. In B. Edelstein & E. Berler (Eds.), *Evaluation and accountability in clinical training* (pp. 77–115). New York: Plenum Press.

Strauss, B. S. (1991). The use of a multimodal image, the apple technique, to facilitate clinical hypnosis: A brief communication. *International Journal of Clinical and Experimental Hypnosis, 39,* 1–5.

Strupp, H. H. (1960). *Psychologists in action.* New York: Grune & Stratton.

Truax, C. B., & Carkhuff, R. R. (1967). *Toward effective counseling and psychotherapy: Training and practice.* Chicago: Aldine.

Truax, C. B., & Mitchell, K. M. (1972). Research on certain therapist interpersonal skills in relation to process and outcome. In A. E. Bergin & S. L. Garfield (Eds.), *Handbook of psychotherapy and behavioral change* (pp. 299–344). New York: Wiley.

Watkins, J. G. (1978). *The therapeutic self.* New York: Human Sciences Press.

Weitzenhoffer, A. M. (1989). *The practice of hypnotism* (Vol. 2). New York: Wiley.

Wolberg, L. R. (1977). *The technique of psychotherapy* (3rd ed.). New York: Grune & Stratton.

Wolberg, L. R. (1982). *Hypnosis: Is it for you?* New York: Dembner Books.

4

EXPECTATIONS AND HYPNOTHERAPY

WILLIAM C. COE

The task in this chapter is to clarify the role that expectation plays in enhancing positive change and to demonstrate its use in hypnotic and suggestive techniques. Although hypnosis and suggestion are examples of where expectancy is used in psychotherapy, other therapeutic techniques could also be used as examples.

The importance of expectations to the outcome of treatment has long been recognized. Similarities among healers from many persuasions, including witchdoctors and psychotherapists, have been pointed out (e.g., Torrey, 1972). The importance of expectations may in fact overshadow the effects of the specific treatments that one claims to have administered. Drugs, for example, appear at times to be no more effective than the patient's faith in the treatment. Such curative effects are often called "placebo" effects, meaning that they are not specific to the treatment effects or purposely created. They exist nevertheless, sometimes to a remarkable degree, and should therefore be considered in administering helping procedures.

Torrey (1972) suggested that a patient's faith and motivation for improvement are determined by several factors: (a) the degree to which the therapist's ability to name the disease and its cause agrees with the views of the patient; (b) the degree to which the therapeutic techniques used are considered by the patient to be of value in helping; and (c) the degree to which the therapist's personal qualities match the patient's expectations of what a therapist should be.

Each principle encompasses strong cultural and subcultural value components for both the therapist and patient. Therapists need to be aware of the effects that these factors may have, adjusting their approach in order to maximize their therapeutic potential.

Naming the disease may in and of itself be effective in alleviating many of the client's problems. It indicates to the client that there is someone who understands; it also implies that something can be done to alleviate the suffering. However, when the healer's label does not agree with the client's view of "mental illness" (or psychological maladjustment), further therapeutic contact is less likely to be helpful. If, for example, the client views psychological problems as being related to unconscious repression of traumatic childhood experiences, a therapist who shares these views is much more likely to be perceived as competent and to enhance the client's faith.

Therapists' treatment procedures follow logically from their views of causation. Behavioral therapists use techniques for learning and unlearning habits, psychoanalysts use techniques for discovering unconscious conflicts, and so on. Likewise, clients, depending on their beliefs about why they are suffering, have expectations for the kinds of techniques from which they will benefit. A client's cultural or subcultural milieu is often important in determining such beliefs.

People have their own views on how a psychologist or psychiatrist should look and behave. Views vary greatly, ranging from "They're all crazy!" to "They're all wise, knowledgeable, and helpful." In general, people who contact therapists do so on the assumption that they are authorities who hold competencies that will be helpful. This expectation in itself may enhance the resolution of their problems. The therapist's office may also have an effect. Diplomas, certificates of membership in prestigious professional organizations, licenses, and other emblems establishing the therapist as a legitimate healer in American culture enhance the client's expectancies of being helped (Frank, 1961). The location of the office may also be a factor. Clients who hold common middle-class values may be impressed by a "plush" office because it suggests financial success and, by association, professional success. Clients who are less conformist may have an opposite reaction, categorizing the therapist as "straight" and as someone who is unable to understand their views (Bloom, Weigel, & Trautt, 1977). The dress and grooming of the therapist may have similar effects. Long hair, styled hair, casual clothing or business suits, among other characteristics, will tend initially to label the therapist for the client, and these early impressions may help or hinder therapy. Clearly, the physical surroundings and the therapist's appearance can have important effects. Alert therapists will recognize these effects and work to arrange (or rearrange) them in their favor.

The therapist qualities of warmth, genuineness, and understanding have long been emphasized by Rogers (1951) and more recently by Lazarus (1981), among others. As a general rule, these qualities seem desirable regardless of the therapist's theoretical orientation. People differ, however, in the degree of activity they expect of therapists, how directive or passive they should be, and the relative amount of time they should spend talking during the session. For example, business people who expect to unload their tensions through cathartic sessions would probably expect and desire traditional, listening therapists as opposed to therapists who are active. It is up to individual therapists to be alert to their clients' expectations and to use them advantageously.

Perhaps one of the most important variables is the therapist's belief that a client can be helped. Lerner and Fiske (1973) showed that the therapist's belief that he or she could help was a better predictor of outcome than client attributes that previously have been claimed to predict outcome. It seems likely that therapists subtly communicate their optimism or pessimism to their clients and thereby affect their clients' expectations of a positive or negative outcome.

Finally, the plausibility of the therapist's techniques to the client can be important. If clients can be convinced that a particular procedure will alleviate their suffering, the probability of success is substantially raised (e.g., McReynolds, Barnes, Brooks, & Rehagen, 1973).

CLINICAL APPLICATIONS

Techniques for Enhancing Expectation Effects

All of the variables just described may be important in enhancing client expectations of being helped. Torrey (1972) discussed three suggestive techniques that are widely used in American culture for enhancing expectations: direct suggestion, symbolism, and magical formulas.

Direct suggestion may be intentionally or unintentionally used by physicians and psychotherapists in their contacts with clients. For example, while writing a drug prescription, physicians may say, "Take this and you will feel better," a direct suggestion that the drug is effective, thereby raising the client's expectations. Or, as behavior therapists outline programs for change, they may add something like, "This program will help you accomplish your goals" or "You will find this program easy to follow and effective in _____." The antithesis of these positive suggestions would be something like, "Well, we might as well try such and such, what have we got to lose?"

As Americans become more familiar with Eastern cultures and religions, the use of *symbolism* is gaining importance. Symbolism exists in the form of rituals that are believed to bring about certain desired end states, such as relaxation, symptom removal, or contact with God. Hypnosis and relaxation training are common forms of symbolism used in American psychotherapy and are discussed more extensively later. Meditation approaches also include symbolic rituals, which are becoming more widely accepted. However, it is probably accurate to say that many if not all therapeutic schools also include rituals (Fish, 1973).

Symbolic rituals may be highly important to some people. The performance of the hypnotic induction, for example, is a signal that something profound and important may occur. Rituals not only enhance the client's expectations but therapists are often equally as convinced of their effectiveness, further enhancing the effect for the client. Rituals are effective, however, only when they are consistent with other client expectations and beliefs. When they are counter to their beliefs, they can have negative effects.

Magical formulas exist in American society mainly in the form of psychoactive, prescription drugs. For example, there are overworked people who will attest to the effectiveness of tranquilizers, even when they are actually sugar pills (placebos). The pills help them through the drudgery of their work and to be more patient with their associates. Mental health propaganda has convinced them that their stress is caused by a "nervous condition," and their physicians have confirmed the diagnosis. Physicians have also prescribed an acceptable cure in American culture, a pill, accompanied by the statement, "Almost without exception, these conditions are helped by taking one of these tablets each morning." Many Americans accept the prescription of medications as solutions to their problems.

Hypnosis and Hypnotic Techniques

Hypnosis has characteristically been associated with the mystical, the strange, the unusual, and the dramatic. The mass media and popular literature nearly always report hypnotic experiences as the ultimate of wonderment: the dramatic cure, the multiple personality, or the powerful influence of the hypnotist. From the mesmerizer of the 18th century to the stage hypnotist of today, the lay public has been exposed to hypnosis as a phenomenon of power and influence. The more conservative views of hypnosis, although present since its beginnings, have been given scant attention. In recent times, hypnosis has been viewed increasingly as a legitimate therapeutic tool in medicine, dentistry, and psychotherapy. Less dramatic expectations are replacing the overstated ones, but an aura of mystery and sensationalism remains. Unfortunately, the image of hypnosis as mysterious has caused some practitioners to avoid its use and people who could benefit from it to shy away. On the other hand, this same aura opens its practice to otherwise unqualified people who take advantage of those looking for the instant cure.

A satisfactory, scientific explanation of the nature of hypnosis has not yet been offered. Although many questions remain, most of the earlier notions about a trance state, the excessive power of the hypnotist, and so on, are being replaced by less exaggerated and more naturalistic explanations based on psychological and social psychological concepts (see, e.g., Barber, 1979; Barber, Spanos, & Chaves, 1974; Coe, 1978; Coe & Sarbin, 1977, 1991; Hilgard, 1977; Orne, 1977; Sarbin & Coe, 1972; Spanos & Chaves, 1989; Spanos & Coe, 1992).

The uses of hypnosis and autosuggestion have been expanded and refined, but in many instances they are still similar to those used a hundred years ago. It often seems that independent investigators have simply redis-covered the usefulness of self-suggestions, or interactive suggestions, only to relabel them so that they fit within a preferred theoretical framework.

Considerations for Enhancing Expectancy Effects

Almost everyone has some ideas about hypnosis and the behaviors that occur in the hypnotic setting: The more their expectations are in agreement with the hypnotist's, the more likely it is that they will be good hypnotic subjects. It behooves hypnotists to clarify what they expect. How-ever, if a person is unwilling to cooperate, he or she cannot be hypnotized; the potential hypnotic subject must be motivated to enter the relationship. The closer that subjects' expectations for their conduct match the requests of the hypnotist, the more likely they are to be responsive. Coupled with motivational factors are certain abilities that appear to be useful in hypnosis (i.e., concentration and absorbed imagining). It is also clear, however, that some individuals will simply comply with the hypnotist's instructions and not really experience their conduct as unusual.

The conditions of the environment and the characteristics of the hypnotist can make a difference in the level of responsiveness as well. Usually, both the setting and the hypnotist's appearance are designed to encourage the subject's cooperation. Style of dress, age, general professional manner, and office decor all add to the perception that the hypnotist is a competent, trustworthy person. Before the hypnotic induction has begun, these factors have entered into the relationship and have the potential for modifying the subject's response.

Inductions of Hypnosis

The wording of most inductions is aimed at increasing subjects' mo-tivations by providing cues that indicate what is expected of them. Initial suggestions are usually easy to follow and usually center around body relaxation, closing of the eyes, and heaviness of the body. Suggestions gradually progress toward behaviors that require higher levels of imaginal ability and concentration and are more difficult to perform. There are many ways of inducing hypnosis, and it is not clear whether one is more effective than another. It is probably a good idea for therapists to be familiar with several techniques. Weitzenhoffer (1989) and Kroger (1977) offered numerous methods. All of them provide expectations of how subjects are to respond.

There is also evidence that the usual inductions of hypnosis are not necessary to bring about increased responsiveness to suggestions. Barber (1965, 1979; Barber et al., 1974) has shown that instructions to imagine and instructions that motivate subjects (task-motivating instructions) result in increased responsiveness to many of the usual kinds of hypnotic suggestions. These sorts of instructions, as opposed to calling the procedure "hypnosis," may be potentially useful when subjects appear to have negative attitudes toward or expectations about hypnosis.

Barber and Wilson (1977) and Wilson and Barber (1978) developed a nonauthoritarian technique wherein responses are measured with their Creative Imagination Scale. Their technique is to use "think-with" instructions that are meant (a) to demonstrate how subjects can use their imaginations creatively to experience certain events and (b) to create positive attitudes and expectations that they will be able to do so. Think-with instructions are introduced by giving examples of what to do ("Think of the scene and become involved in it") and what not to do ("Do not take the negative attitude that you cannot do it"). Positive attitudes toward being able to imagine creatively, along with examples, precede the actual administration of the scale. (Verbatim instructions can be found in Barber & Wilson, 1977, p. 46.) If Barber's findings are stable, think-with instructions may be more effective for many people than are techniques that have been historically used to induce hypnosis (Barber & Wilson, 1979; Barber, Wilson, & Scott, 1980).

The study of hypnosis has been greatly facilitated by the development of standard measuring instruments that operationally define hypnosis. The items on these scales have typically been associated with hypnotic behavior since Mesmer's time. The most commonly used scales are the Stanford Hypnotic Susceptibility Scale, Forms A, B, and C (Weitzenhoffer & Hilgard, 1959, 1962) and the Harvard Group Scale of Hypnotic Susceptibility (Shor & Orne, 1962). Subjects are hypnotized and their responses to typical hypnotic suggestions are recorded. Administration requires approximately 45–50 min, with the hypnotist reading the instructions verbatim. Because these scales are highly structured, they are especially useful for novice hypnotists who are still unsure of themselves when using induction procedures.

Milton H. Erickson has been one of the major proponents of the use of hypnosis in psychotherapy and has made many contributions in the form of unique induction and therapeutic techniques. Erickson (1964; Erickson, Rossi, & Rossi, 1976; Haley, 1967) described a confusion technique that has been reported to be effective for a variety of purposes, especially with resistant subjects who try to analyze what is happening during the induction and therefore do not concentrate and respond well. A flow of words that is difficult to understand and to follow is presented in a serious, intent manner. Erickson incorporated irrelevant material, verb tenses, and so on, to create confusion in subjects until they were ready to accept any clear path of understanding, a presumed change in their expectations, and consequently respond to the hypnotist's suggestions. Although most of Erickson's work was based on clinical reports, his examples are usually convincing and offer new ideas for more stringent testing.

A technique called "pacing" (Bandler & Grinder, 1975) may be useful as a transition to other induction techniques because it leads subjects to expect that they will respond to future suggestions. The hypnotist provides overt feedback, covert feedback, or both on any part of the client's ongoing experience, which presumably creates client expectations that he or she is responding to the hypnotist's words. Examples of *overt pacing* are verbal comments on what the client is doing (e.g., "As you sit there in the chair, listening to my voice, with your feet resting on the floor . . ."). *Covert pacing* includes feedback from the hypnotist that does not appear to be consciously intended (e.g., mirroring the client's posture or hand placements, assuming the client's verbal tone and speed, or breathing in rhythm with the client).

The termination of hypnosis again usually provides clear instructions that subjects can expect a shift in roles back to those of the experimental subject or nonhypnotized client. In fact, subjects who respond well may be trained to enter hypnosis with a brief signal that eliminates the need to repeat time-consuming induction procedures in later sessions.

Increasing Responsiveness to Hypnosis

A question related to induction procedures has to do with increasing a person's responsiveness to hypnotic (or nonhypnotic) suggestions. It was believed earlier that hypnotic responsiveness was a stable trait of the person (e.g., Bowers, 1976; Hilgard, 1965). Repeated administrations of hypnosis resulted in shorter induction times but little or no increase in responsiveness to suggestions. Also, in support of a stable trait explanation, longitudinal studies over a period of years showed high positive correlations for hypnotic responsiveness.

Various techniques have been tested more recently that suggest that responsiveness can be increased, especially in moderately low and moderately susceptible subjects (Bertrand, 1989; Diamond, 1974, 1977a, 1977b, 1982). Studies that have demonstrated increases in responsiveness have used specific procedures other than the usual hypnotic induction. Diamond (1977a) outlined what he considered to be the three core components of these procedures:

1. *Optimal learning factors.* Included here are procedures that (a) increase subjects' motivations to experience hypnosis; (b) increase attention to the hypnotist and the training procedures; (c) use successive approximations to the desired response (shaping); (d) provide practice of newly learned responses; (e) offer reinforcement for successful experiences; and (f) provide feedback on the appropriateness of subjects' responses.

2. *Attitudes and set.* These procedures include methods that increase subjects' motivations and positive acceptance of hypnosis before the actual experience begins. They include relaxation; reduction of fears, attitudes, or expectations that interfere; building of interpersonal trust; and demonstrations of receptive perception.

3. *Cognitive strategy.* Diamond (1977a) believed that this factor was the most important of the three. Procedures are aimed at teaching subjects optimal ways of responding internally to hypnotic instructions in order to experience them. Included are (a) suspending reality concerns, (b) controlling imaginations in accord with the aims of the suggestions, and (c) focusing thought and attention on the suggestions.

More recently, a standardized modification procedure was developed by Gorassini and Spanos (1986): the Carleton Skill Training Package. It has been shown to increase hypnotic responsiveness significantly. All three of the aforementioned components are included; in addition, subjects are made aware of the ambiguities in many hypnotic suggestions and that they must be actively involved in making the responses occur.

As far as therapy is concerned, it is not clear whether high levels of hypnotic responsiveness are necessary for most purposes or whether hypnotic imagery is more useful than nonhypnotic imagery. It is possible that the expectations that clients have for hypnosis are the most important aspects for therapeutic outcome. Nevertheless, the procedures just outlined should offer helpful guidelines for clinicians who wish to increase hypnotic responsiveness in their clients.

CASE MATERIAL

Teaching Relaxation and Absorbed Concentration

I describe in detail a technique that I have found helpful in introducing clients to the use of imagination and concentration. The points where expectations are included are emphasized.

The technique is presented as one that will help to reduce general tension and to apply self-suggestions in the most effective way. It begins with a demonstration that shows clients that they can be successful in taking suggestions, in giving them to themselves, and in bringing about positive changes.

Clients are told that what they are about to learn is best viewed as a skill and that, as with other skills, they can become more adept at it with practice. Expectations of an instant cure or dramatic effects are downplayed. Rather, clients are encouraged to use certain natural abilities not normally used by people and led to *expect* that they can do so.

I begin by telling the client that I wish to explain the most effective way to use suggestions. For example,

> There are several things I would like to explain about taking suggestions, or giving them to yourself, so that they *will be most effective*. To begin with, there are a couple of things you should try to avoid. The first is trying to work too hard at the task. It is an easy-feeling sort of task, not one requiring what we ordinarily think of as hard concentration or hard work. If you take the attitude that you must work hard, you will find that thoughts about working, instead of the suggestions, will become the dominant thoughts. A second common problem is that when suggestions begin to have their effects, especially when you are first learning, it may seem a bit unusual, or interesting. The tendency is to try and analyze what is going on—to figure it out—but when you do, the suggestions are broken up, and their effects cease. If you will think of your mind as a river that flows along at a steady pace, allowing your thoughts to progress at the same pace, over and over again—easy, not forced, just flowing along at a nice, easy pace—your suggestions *will become* the dominant thing of interest and *will have their greatest effects*. The whole thing is really a rather easy, relaxed technique. If you should become distracted, that's all right, just go back to your thoughts, letting them flow through, over and over, so that they become the only thing of importance for that time. Don't worry about distractions. They are likely to occur, especially when you are first learning. *Simply recognize that you have been distracted and redirect your attention* back to the slow, easy flow of suggestion you were giving to yourself.

At this point, any questions the client may have should be answered by reiterating what has already been said.

The next step is to introduce a suggestive task to which almost everyone will respond. By so doing, the chances are maximized for clients to be successful in their first experience with suggestions and therefore expect to be successful later on.

The suggestion I use is called the "Chevreul pendulum." A thread or light string that is approximately the length from one's elbow to one's fingertips, with a moderately heavy bob of some sort attached, like a small key, is the only equipment needed. The client rests his or her elbow on the desk (or chair arm) and holds the loose end of the thread between the thumb and forefinger with the wrist bent at approximately a right angle. The bob then hangs straight down and away from the arm, an inch or so above the surface. I suggest that the client focus on the bob and think of it doing different things, such as making circles, swinging back and forth in predetermined directions, and so on. The following is a verbatim example:

> I want you to hold this little bob just the way I do. [Demonstrate the proper way to hold the thread.] That's it, just hold it so you can sit there comfortably and relax. Now I want you to take the attitude just for a moment or so that that little bob is the only thing of importance to you. That's it, look at it carefully, trace all around its outline, notice any geometric shapes that may be on it, like circles—squares—perhaps you can even find rectangles if you look carefully. Just try to learn everything you can about that little bob, think of it as a new and different experience, something unique, something you would like to know everything about. Notice its colors—notice how this varies from spot to spot and how it changes—as you become more interested in the bob; you notice that in fact it becomes more the center of your attention. Your vision narrows, things in the side of your vision tend to gray out, to become less important. The bob in fact becomes the center of your attention—now watch it very closely because in a moment it is going to begin doing something—it will begin moving back and forth, back and forth, back and forth.

At this point the bob may be naturally moving in one direction or another. It is helpful and encouraging to the subject to increase the natural movement that is occurring. Continue with the same suggestions, trying to time the suggestion to the tempo of the bob's movement:

> Back and forth, back and forth, more and more, farther each time, back and forth, back and forth, freer and freer, freer and freer, back and forth, back and forth, etc. (Once the movement is well established you are ready to change to a new movement.) Now the bob will change its direction—it's going to begin making a round, round circle. Round and round, round and round, round and round. There, it's beginning to go now. Round and round—rounder and rounder, rounder and

rounder. You can imagine a circle below it, and it's tracing right around that circle, rounder and rounder, rounder and rounder, etc.

Subjects vary greatly in the magnitude of their responses. However, even a small response in the suggested direction can be a *convincing experience*. At this point it has been *demonstrated* that the client is able to take suggestions. The next step is to show them that they can give suggestions to themselves (i.e., have them *think* about the bob moving in certain ways, and it does). A few people seem to be unable to respond to this task, but it is usually apparent that they are breaking their train of thought, often indicated by jerky movements of the bob. If this happens, it is good to stop and ask what they are doing and what they are thinking. Usually, they are committing one of the errors that they have already been cautioned about. A brief discussion of the problem before returning to the task may be enough. If the difficulty is still not overcome, the therapist can start the bob in the direction suggested, letting clients follow the swing with their throughts in order to grasp the tempo. As their thoughts fall into the rhythm of the bob, suggestions for change of direction are usually effective, and clients will have found that they can in fact take suggestions.

Because clients vary in the degree to which they report being aware of their fingers moving, the therapist can explain the following:

> There is *nothing really so unusual* about this. You did not notice your fingers moving for two reasons. First, your attention was very focused on the bob; therefore, you did not notice the small movements in your fingers. Had you focused on your fingers, you would have noticed the movements. Focusing on the suggestions rather than your fingers is an example of being able to take suggestions well. Your attention becomes focused on the suggestions and then other things are less likely to be noticed. Second, the small movements in your fingers were exaggerated by the length of the string, such that the movement of the bob would seem quite large compared with the very small muscle movement necessary to create it. The movement of the bob demonstrates *how your thoughts can affect your muscles or other organs* of your body. Your nervous system sends a message to the proper places in the body, in this case the muscles of your hand and fingers, and the appropriate actions result. At any rate, you have had a chance to see how you can take suggestions and the effects they might have. You have also seen that *you can give yourself suggestions* with the same results.

Inducing Hypnosis

At this point I have the client move to a comfortable chair (if not already in one); a recliner or couch that completely supports the client's body is the most appropriate. Once seated, I explain that it is always important to practice relaxing in a position in which all of the muscles are able to relax. I caution against crossing legs or resting hands on the stomach, a normal practice for many people when they sit or lie down, because the weight of one part of the body on another makes some muscle tension necessary in order to support the part on top.

I begin by demonstrating a suggestion that is easy to follow, explaining that I want them to start with an easy suggestion because their response to it tends to *increase their responsiveness to additional suggestions*. I often refer back to the way that they became more adept at following suggestions to the bob once they had started.

An easy suggestion is to ask them to look at a spot between their eyes, at hairline level. This forces them to roll their eyes up and back so that strain is created. Touch the spot on their forehead and tell them to remember it; then explain that they are to try and see the spot as an X and to focus on it. Be certain that they demonstrate by rolling their eyes up into the proper position. Explain that by looking at the spot, the natural strain created in their eyes becomes an easy thing to focus on. Their eyes will become tired, their eyelids will become heavy, and soon their eyes will feel like closing. Caution them not to fight the suggestion and to let their eyes close as the suggestions have their effects. Proceed as follows:

> I want you to look right at that spot, keep your attention right on the spot—notice the strain in your eyes, how it seems to grow and grow—straining more and more, the strain in your eyes is becoming greater and greater, more and more strain, more and more strain, your eyes become more and more tired, more and more tired, more and more tired. [If you notice that the client's eyes are beginning to blink slightly, suggestions of blinking can be included also.] Your eyes are blinking, becoming heavier and heavier—eyes tired, tired from straining, straining more and more, greater and greater strain—eyelids becoming heavier now, heavier and heavier, heavier and heavier, wanting to close, feeling heavier and heavier, etc.

Most people will close their eyes within a few minutes. If the therapist notices that they are looking away, or blinking excessively as if to reduce the strain, they should be cautioned not to fight the response. A few clients seem not to respond well to this suggestion. They constantly look away, blink frequently, and tend to stop their eyes from closing naturally. I often stop the procedure with these people and tell them that responding to this suggestion is *not really necessary* for our purposes. Simply have them close their eyes and go on. As the client's eyes close, the therapist continues as follows:

> Fine, now leave your eyes closed and let your eyes roll forward. Feel the strain going out of your eyes, and as you feel the strain going out of your eyes, think of the strain going out of your entire body—your body just letting go, dropping into the chair, going limp, limp, heavy

and relaxed. As your eyes close and roll forward, and you feel the strain going out of your eyes, that is a cue for the strain to begin going out of your entire body. Think of the strain as flowing right out of your body—from your eyes, throughout your body, right out of your toes. Your body is loosening, dropping into the chair—relaxing.

A procedure for progressive relaxation training then follows. Have clients focus on relaxing small muscle groups first (e.g., right toes, right foot, right calf, upper right leg), then larger groups (e.g., the entire right leg). The point is to show them the type of progress *they can expect*. As they become more adept at relaxing, they should be able to relax increasingly larger groups of muscles at the same time—suggest that to them. The eventual goal is for them to be able to sit down, close their eyes, and relax their entire body in a matter of seconds. I usually proceed as follows:

> left foot; lower left leg; upper left leg; entire left leg and left foot; same with right leg, then both legs and both feet; right hand; right forearm; upper right arm; right shoulder; entire right shoulder, arm, and hand; left hand; left forearm; upper left arm; left shoulder; entire left shoulder, arm, and hand; area across both shoulders; both shoulders, arms, and hands; chest; stomach; hips; lower back; middle back; upper back; entire body from shoulders to the feet; neck; jaw; lips; nose, right cheek; left cheek; eyelids; eyebrows; forehead; entire face; scalp and ears; entire head and neck; entire body. It is helpful if you simultaneously experience these muscles loosening because your own feelings can act as a guide in saying the proper words, such as "dropping," and "letting go."

The next step is to show clients how to deepen their concentration. The basic technique is to have them imagine going downward, having everything "come in" around them so that their thoughts and the therapist's words become the center of importance. There are a number of ways to suggest deepening (e.g., going down an elevator or a stairway, floating down on a cloud). Presenting a neutral suggestion may be best (e.g., "You are floating down"). Some clients are afraid of elevators, stairways, or other things; it is difficult to predict what could be negative for a particular person. I usually suggest something similar to the following:

> Now that you have relaxed your entire body, part by part, I want you to imagine that you are just moving out of your body, standing off, as if watching your body just relaxing in the chair, taking care of itself, breathing easily and relaxing. With each breath your body loosens a little bit more, becomes more and more relaxed, and you begin to float downward—downward, deeper and deeper. With each breath you are moving down, down—deeper and deeper—more and more attention to your thoughts and to my words. Your body is taking care of itself. Your muscles are completely relaxed. All the tension is flowing out and you are able to attend more and more to your thoughts. Attending more and more to your thoughts and my voice so that suggestions you

give to yourself, or that I give to you, will have maximum effects. Down, deeper and deeper, deeper and deeper, more and more relaxed, more and more concentrated on your thoughts. I am now going to count from 1 to 10 and with each count you will go deeper and deeper, and your thoughts will become more and more the center of your attention so that what you suggest for yourself will have its maximal effect.

After reaching 10, suggest that they will *be able to practice on their own* and have no difficulty in arousing themselves whenever they wish. Once aroused, ask what the experience was like. Were there any difficulties at particular points or in relaxing particular muscles? Are there any questions? Discuss ways that should help overcome any difficulties that might have been experienced. Reiterate the technique, including the purpose of starting with small groups of muscles and progressively moving to larger ones until, in a short time, they should be able to easily imagine their entire body relaxing and their concentration deepening. The technique should be practiced twice a day if possible. I tell clients to contact me if they run into any problems before seeing me the next time.

Once a person has learned to relax and to focus on thoughts, the groundwork has been laid for the application of many procedures that involve imagining. There is the initial benefit of relaxation itself, and the client will soon be ready to participate in other techniques.

By itself, learning to relax can make clients more confident that they have control over tenseness specifically and themselves more generally. They begin to expect that they can deal with problems; they begin to view themselves as more than victims of their bodies and their surroundings. Being able to relax can also bring physical comfort to clients who have been generally tense, and, for some, poor sleep patterns are overcome just by relaxing when going to bed. Also, if clients have learned to relax spontaneously to their mental signal, "relax," they may be able to reduce their general level of tenseness significantly when they are confronted with situations that are potentially tension arousing.

Being able to relax and focus on one's thoughts and images are the bases of many imagery rehearsal techniques. For example, systematic desensitization of fears requires clients to remain relaxed as they gradually imagine increasingly fearful images (fear hierarchy). The hoped-for result, of course, is the reduction or elimination of phobias (Wolpe, 1958; Wolpe & Lazarus, 1966). I have frequently had people who wanted to quit smoking imagine themselves in circumstances in which they would normally desire a cigarette but instead had them imagine themselves thinking "relax," reduce their tension, and feel pleased that they had not smoked. Other imagery techniques can be used for many purposes, such as imagining someone one admires dealing effectively with a problem situation that causes him or her difficulty, or imagining being assertive in difficult situations before they are encountered (e.g., Lazarus, 1977, 1981).

RESEARCH AND APPRAISAL

Using the results from published case studies, Barrios (1970) pointed out that psychoanalysis resulted in a 38% recovery rate after an average of 600 sessions, Wolpean behavior therapy a 72% recovery rate after an average of 22 sessions, and hypnotherapy a 93% recovery rate after an average of 6 sessions. Therapists cannot, of course, simply accept these figures as valid comparisons among the three therapies, but they can at least alert them to the positive potential of including hypnotic techniques among other therapeutic skills.

In keeping with the concept of expectancy, Barrios (1970) viewed the hypnotic induction as an effective method for establishing confidence and belief in the therapist. In turn, a strong personal relationship should develop wherein the therapist's words should be more effective in bringing about constructive change.

The Role of Expectations

Spinhoven (1988), in his review of headache treatments, concluded that nonspecific factors such as therapist credibility, attention, and support are probably the effective factors. According to him, they may lead to cognitive changes, especially self-efficacy expectations of pain control. He viewed such nonspecific factors as a "general nonhypnotic component of the two component model of hypnotic analgesia of Hilgard (1977)" (Spinhoven, 1988, p. 190).

Spanos, Williams, and Gwynn (1990) more recently confirmed the success of hypnotic treatment on wart regression compared with placebo and salicylic acid treatments. However, they did not find that subjects' expectations of success was an important factor for success. Instead, they indicated that hypnotic subjects reported more intense suggested sensations, a finding consistent with the hypothesis that vivid suggested imagery facilitates wart loss.

Prioleau, Murdock, and Brody (1983) performed a meta-analysis on 32 psychotherapy outcome studies in which placebo groups had been included as a comparison to the treated groups. They reached the conclusion that for actual outpatients and inpatients (versus fictitious patient subjects), the outcomes of the placebo treatments were just as effective as the outcomes of the actual treatments. In other words, they found that the *expectation* of being treated was by itself as effective as actually being treated.

Kirsch (1990, pp. 16–17) reviewed placebo studies on pain reduction, concluding that placebos can be effective. More important, the effectiveness of a particular placebo appeared to be related to its "believed effectiveness;" therefore, enhancing the credibility of a placebo will also enhance its effectiveness. The way one packages a placebo changes its effectiveness apparently by changing *patients' expectancies* of its effectiveness.

Kirsch (1990; Kirsch & Council, 1989) has become a leader in evaluating and analyzing the role that expectations play in people's lives. In particular, he focused on "response expectancies," peoples' beliefs about their own reactions, especially nonvolitional, emotional reactions to specific events. Kirsch differentiated between intentions and response expectancies. Intentions indicate how a person believes he or she will respond voluntarily; response expectancies indicate how a person believes he or she will respond nonvolitionally.

Response expectancies are important because they are self-confirming and can start vicious cycles of anticipating negative events by self-confirming that they will occur in the future. For example, the belief that one will soon have a panic attack can produce intense fear. Kirsch (1990) postulated that three cognitions interact and combine to determine a person's *hypnotic response expectancies:* (a) situational perceptions (e.g.,"Is this a hypnosis appropriate situation?"); (b) role expectancies (e.g., "my beliefs about the effects of hypnosis"); and (c) self-perceptions (e.g., "my beliefs about my susceptibility to hypnosis"). Subjects who have never been hypnotized may think of hypnosis as something much different or not much different from anything they have experienced. They are also unlikely to have strong hypnotic response expectancies. Therefore, the induction, as an entrance ritual, can easily act to change their response expectancies. For example, Council, Kirsch, and Hafner (1986) had subjects predict *before* the induction how many of 10 suggestions they would be able to experience. After the induction, they were asked to rate their trance depth on a 1–5 scale and to predict again how many of the 10 suggestions they would experience. The preinduction expectancies were only moderately correlated with subsequent responsiveness, but the postinduction expectancies were highly correlated with their responsiveness.

Kirsch (1990, pp. 157–158) offered further evidence that many of the subjects who had believed hypnosis to be a dramatically altered state before being hypnotized tended to end up as low responders, whereas subjects with only moderate beliefs turned out to be high and medium responders. His interpretation of that finding was that subjects who are expecting a great deal of change decide that they are not hypnotized and, therefore, they no longer expect to experience the suggestions that follow. On the other hand, subjects who believe that hypnosis is not so different may experience the same moderate alterations in consciousness as the other subjects, but they interpret the evidence as indicating they are hypnotized and thereby expect to be responsive to the suggestions that follow. In either case, according to Kirsch, the outcome is determined by the response expectancies generated during the induction.

A final experimental example supports Kirsch's position that response expectancies are important causal variables in hypnotic responding. Wickless and Kirsch (1989) used two procedures to convince people that they were good hypnotic subjects. A verbal expectancy manipulation misinformed subjects that personality tests they had taken earlier showed that they had a special talent for hypnosis. An experiential expectancy manipulation consisted of creating perceptual effects that were suggested (not hypnotic) such that subjects believed they had in fact experienced the effect. For example, after the suggestion that a subject would see the color *red*, a faint red tinge was created in the room from a hidden red bulb. Standard hypnotizability tests were administered after these manipulations.

Four groups were tested: (a) control, no prior expectancies; (b) verbal expectancy only; (c) experiential feedback only; and (d) both verbal and experiential feedback. The results showed that the verbal manipulation alone produced a small increase in responsiveness, the experiential manipulation alone produced a large increase, and the combined manipulations produced *no* low-susceptible and 73% high-susceptible subjects. Kirsch (1990) interpreted the results as suggesting "quite convincingly that with sufficiently strong expectations, everyone is hypnotizable" (p. 159). Even after the subjects had been called back for debriefing and shown how their expectations had been manipulated, they maintained their high level of responsiveness on a second hypnotic scale, a finding not surprising to Kirsch. As he explained, because they had actually experienced suggested effects, their positive response expectancies for hypnosis should remain intact.

CONCLUSION

In this chapter I have focused on the role of expectations in therapeutic change, with an emphasis on the ways that clinicians who use hypnosis can take advantage of what may be strong, positive effects for their clients. I have discussed ways in which others have incorporated expectation effects into their approaches and have presented some of the techniques that I have found helpful in my own practice. I also included case reports and verbatim transcripts in order to illustrate the clinical "feel" along with the theoretical ideas.

In the latter part of the chapter I examined research on the usefulness of expectancies in hypnosis as a therapeutic modality and what features about it contribute to its effectiveness. Its effectiveness has been found to vary depending on the type of problem, the type of client, and the context in which it is administered. Finally, I examined Irving Kirsch's research and theorizing on the importance of people's response expectancies. He presented a fairly convincing case that how people believe that they will respond involuntarily to a given situation in large part determines how they in fact do respond. His work clearly demonstrates how important expectations may be for therapists and their clients. Therapists should be more alert to the critical role that expectations may be playing in their practices.

REFERENCES

Bandler, R., & Grinder, J. (1975). *Patterns of the hypnotic techniques of Milton H. Erickson* (Vol. 1). Cupertino, CA: Meta Publications.

Barber, T. X. (1965). Measuring "hypnotic-like" suggestibility with and without "hypnotic induction": Psychometric properties, norms and variables influencing response to the Barber Suggestibility Scale (BSS). *Psychological Reports, 16,* 809–844.

Barber, T. X. (1979). Suggested ("hypnotic") behavior: The trance paradigm versus an alternative paradigm. In E. Fromm & K. E. Shor (Eds.), *Hypnosis: Research developments and perspectives* (2nd ed., pp. 217–271). Chicago: Aldine.

Barber, T. X., Spanos, N. P., & Chaves, J. F. (1974). *Hypnosis, imagination and human potentialities.* Elmsford, NY: Pergamon Press.

Barber, T. X., & Wilson, S. C. (1977). Hypnosis, suggestions, and altered states of consciousness: Experimental evaluation of the new cognitive-behavioral theory and the traditional trance-state theory of "hypnosis." *Annals of the New York Academy of Sciences, 296,* 34–74.

Barber, T. X., & Wilson, S. C. (1979). The Barber Suggestibility Scale and the Creative Imagination Scale: Experimental and clinical applications. *American Journal of Clinical Hypnosis, 21,* 84–108.

Barber, T. X., Wilson, S. C., & Scott, D. S. (1980). Effects of a traditional trance induction on response to "hypnotist-centered" vs "subject-centered" test suggestions. *International Journal of Clinical and Experimental Hypnosis, 28,* 114–126.

Barrios, A. (1970). Hypnotherapy: A reappraisal. *Psychotherapy: Theory, Research and Practice, 7,* 2–7.

Bertrand, L. D. (1989). The assessment and modification of hypnotic susceptibility. In N. P. Spanos and J. F. Chaves (Eds.), *Hypnosis: The cognitive behavioral perspective* (pp. 18–31). Buffalo, NY: Prometheus Books.

Bloom, L. J., Weigel, R. G., & Trautt, G. M. (1977). "Therapeugenic" factors in psychotherapy: Effects of office decor and subject-therapist sex pairing on the perception of credibility. *Journal of Consulting and Clinical Psychology, 45,* 867–873.

Bowers, K. S. (1976). *Hypnosis for the seriously curious.* Monterey, CA: Brooks/Cole.

Coe, W. C. (1978). The credibility of posthypnotic amnesia: A contextualist's view. *International Journal of Clinical and Experimental Hypnosis, 26*, 218–245.

Coe, W. C., & Sarbin, T. R. (1977). Hypnosis from the standpoint of a contextualist. *Annals of the New York Academy of Sciences, 296*, 2–13.

Coe, W. C., & Sarbin, T. R. (1991). Role theory: Hypnosis from a dramaturgical and narrative perspective. In S. J. Lynn & J. W. Rhue (Eds.), *Theories of hypnosis: Current models and perspectives* (pp. 303–313). New York: Guilford Press.

Council, J. R., Kirsch, I., & Hafner, L. P. (1986). Expectancy versus absorption in the prediction of hypnotic responsiveness. *Journal of Personality and Social Psychology, 50*, 182–189.

Diamond, M. J. (1974). Modification of hypnotizability: A review. *Psychological Bulletin, 81*, 180–193.

Diamond, M. J. (1977a). Issues and methods for modifying responsivity to hypnosis. *Annals of the New York Academy of Sciences, 296*, 119–128.

Diamond, M. J. (1977b). Hypnotizability is modifiable: An alternative approach. *International Journal of Clinical and Experimental Hypnosis, 25*, 147–166.

Diamond, M. J. (1982). Modifying hypnotic experience by means of indirect hypnosis and hypnotic skill training: An update (1981). *Research Communications in Psychology, Psychiatry, and Behavior, 7*, 233–239.

Erickson, M. H. (1964). The confusion technique in hypnosis. *American Journal of Clinical Hypnosis, 6*, 183–207.

Erickson, M. H., Rossi, E. L., & Rossi, S. H. (1976). *Hypnotic realities: The induction of clinical hypnosis and the indirect forms of suggestion.* New York: Irvington.

Fish, J. (1973). *Placebo therapy.* San Francisco: Jossey-Bass.

Frank, J. (1961). *Persuasion and healing.* Baltimore, MD: Johns Hopkins University Press.

Gorassini, D. R., & Spanos, N. P. (1986). A social cognitive skills training program for the successful modification of hypnotic susceptibility. *Journal of Personality and Social Psychology, 50*, 1004–1012.

Haley, J. (Ed.). (1967). *Advanced techniques of hypnosis and therapy: Selected papers of Milton H. Erickson, M.D.* New York: Grune & Stratton.

Hilgard, E. R. (1965). *Hypnotic susceptibility.* New York: Harcourt, Brace & World.

Hilgard, E. R. (1977). *Divided consciousness: Multiple controls in human thought and action.* New York: Wiley-Interscience.

Kirsch, I. (1990). *Changing expectations: A key to effective psychotherapy.* Pacific Grove, CA: Brooks/Cole.

Kirsch, I., & Council, J. R. (1989). Response expectancy as a determinant of hypnotic behavior. In N. P. Spanos & J. F. Chaves (Eds.), *Hypnosis: The cognitive behavioral perspective* (pp. 360–379). Buffalo, NY: Prometheus Books.

Kroger, W. S. (1977). *Clinical and experimental hypnosis* (2nd ed.). Philadelphia: Lippincott.

Lazarus, A. A. (1977). *In the mind's eye*. New York: Rawson.

Lazarus, A. A. (1981). *The practice of multimodal therapy*. New York: McGraw-Hill.

Lerner, B., & Fiske, D. W. (1973). Client attributes and the eye of the beholder. *Journal of Consulting and Clinical Psychology, 40*, 272–277.

McReynolds, W. T., Barnes, A. R., Brooks, S., & Rehagen, N. J. (1973). The role of attention-placebo influences in the efficacy of systematic desensitization. *Journal of Consulting and Clinical Psychology, 41*, 86–92.

Orne, M. T. (1977). The construct of hypnosis: Implications of the definition for research and practice. *Annals of the New York Academy of Sciences, 296*, 14–33.

Prioleau, L., Murdock, M., & Brody, N. (1983). An analysis of psychotherapy versus placebo studies. *Behavioral and Brain Sciences, 6*, 275–310.

Rogers, C. (1951). *Client-centered therapy*. Boston: Houghton Mifflin.

Sarbin, T. R., & Coe, W. C. (1972). *Hypnosis: A social psychological analysis of influence communication*. New York: Holt, Rinehart & Winston.

Shor, R. E., & Orne, E. C. (1962). *The Harvard Group Scale of Hypnotic Susceptibility, Form A*. Palo Alto, CA: Consulting Psychologists Press.

Spanos, N. P., & Chaves, J. F. (Eds.). (1989). *Hypnosis: The cognitive behavioral perspective*. Buffalo, NY: Prometheus Books.

Spanos, N. P., & Coe, W. C. (1992). A social–psychological approach to hypnosis. In E. Fromm & M. R. Nash (Eds.), *Contemporary hypnosis research*. New York: Guilford Press.

Spanos, N. P., Williams, V., & Gwynn, M. I. (1990). Effects of hypnotic, placebo, and salicylic acid treatments on wart regression. *Psychosomatic Medicine, 52*, 109–114.

Spinhoven, P. (1988). Similarities and dissimilarities in hypnotic and nonhypnotic procedures for headache control: A review. *American Journal of Clinical Hypnosis, 30*, 183–194.

Torrey, E. F. (1972). *The mind game: Witchdoctors and psychiatrists*. New York: Emerson Hall.

Weitzenhoffer, A. M. (1989). *The practice of hypnotism* (Vols. 1–2). New York: Wiley.

Weitzenhoffer, A. M., & Hilgard, E. R. (1959). *Stanford Hypnotic Susceptibility Scale, Forms A and B*. Palo Alto, CA: Consulting Psychologists Press.

Weitzenhoffer, A. M., & Hilgard, E. R. (1962). *Stanford Hypnotic Susceptibility Scale, Form C*. Palo Alto, CA: Consulting Psychologists Press.

Wickless, C., & Kirsch, I. (1989). The effects of verbal and experiential expectancy manipulations on hypnotic susceptibility. *Journal of Personality and Social Psychology, 57*, 762–768.

Wilson, S. C., & Barber, T. X. (1978). The Creative Imagination Scale as a measure of hypnotic responsiveness: Applications to experimental and clinical hypnosis. *American Journal of Clinical Hypnosis, 20,* 235–249.

Wolpe, J. (1958). *Psychotherapy by reciprocal inhibition.* Stanford, CA: Stanford University Press.

Wolpe, J., & Lazarus, A. A. (1966). *Behavior therapy techniques.* Elmsford, NY: Pergamon Press.

5

PREVENTION AND THERAPEUTIC MANAGEMENT OF "NEGATIVE EFFECTS" IN HYPNOTHERAPY

DAVID C. FRAUMAN, STEVEN JAY LYNN, and JOHN P. BRENTAR

For more than half a century of hypnosis research (MacHovec, 1988b; Schultz, 1922), there have been disquieting reports of so-called "negative effects" during and after hypnosis: unwanted or untoward reactions that degrade hypnotic involvement or eventuate in deleterious psychological sequelae. The spectrum of reported negative effects has encompassed minor complaints such as headaches, dizziness, or nausea (Coe & Ryken, 1979); serious reactions such as psychosis (Kleinhauz, Dreyfuss, Beran, Goldberg, & Azikri, 1979) or suicide (West & Deckert, 1965); transient symptoms lasting only a few minutes (MacHovec, 1987); and chronic conditions lasting for months (Kleinhauz & Beran, 1984). The range of negative effects includes physical pain or discomfort (Hilgard, 1974); anxiety or panic (Judd, Burrows, & Dennerstein, 1985); depression (Kleinhauz & Eli, 1987); difficulties in awakening from hypnosis (Orne, 1965); and unexpected reactions to an inadvertently given suggestion (Levitt & Hershman, 1963). MacHovec (1988a) suggested the following definition of hypnosis "complications": "unexpected, unwanted thoughts, feelings or behaviors during or after hypnosis which are inconsistent with agreed [*sic*] goals and interfere with the hypnotic process" (p. 46).

In the first half of this chapter, we critically examine the research literature with respect to both the incidence and nature of negative effects in hypnotherapy. More specifically, we address two questions: (a) What is the incidence of negative effects with respect to student versus clinical populations and clinical versus experimental settings? and (b) What is the nature and characteristics (i.e., hypnotist, client, procedural) of the most commonly reported negative effects? In the second half of the chapter, we draw on our literature review to provide a rationale for instituting strategies and techniques to prevent and manage negative effects. We attempt to answer the following questions: Under what circumstances and conditions are negative effects most likely to occur? and How can negative effects be most avoided or therapeutically managed? Because hypnosis is neither a precisely defined nor a universally agreed-on set of operations, we use the term *hypnosis* to refer to procedures mutually understood by the therapist-experimenter and the client-subject to be "hypnotic" in nature. Finally, we provide suggestions for future research on the nature and determinants of negative effects in hypnotherapy.

LITERATURE REVIEW

Experimental Versus Clinical Hypnosis

There is a consensus that hypnosis applied in experimental versus clinical settings can be distinguished in meaningful respects (Coe & Ryken, 1979; Crawford, Hilgard, & Macdonald, 1982; Orne, 1965). Coe and Ryken (1979) cited four critical differences between experimental and clinical hypnosis. In experimental hypnosis (a) the subjects are more likely to be emotionally stable; (b) the relationship between the subject and the hypnotist is more likely to be of circumscribed duration and characterized by scientific objectivity (cf. Orne, 1965); (c) the primary goal is usually the elicitation of cognitive or motoric as opposed to affective responses; and (d) the induction precedure tends to be more structured and emotionally neutral. Given that the hypnotic setting can have a bearing on the incidence and nature of negative effects, we report findings obtained in the experimental context separately from those obtained in the clinic.

Experimental Research With Hypnotic Samples

Orne (1965) reported that minor complications occurred following experimental hypnosis. On the basis of subjects tested in his laboratory over several years, he estimated that approximately 2%–3% of subjects complained of mild transient headaches, drowsiness, nausea, or dizziness on awakening. However, because most subjects rated hypnosis as pleasant, Orne concluded that it was, for the most part, a positive experience.

The frequency of negative effects in experimental settings has been examined following the administration of standardized hypnotizability scales. Hilgard, Hilgard, and Newman (1961) administered the Stanford Hypnotic Susceptibility Scale, Forms A and B (SHSS:A and SHSS:B) and interviewed subjects following the session. They found that 8% of the 220 subjects reported transient experiences consisting of headaches, dizziness, and confusion lasting 1 hr or longer. Hilgard et al. (1961) also found that subjects who experienced early childhood trauma with chemical anesthesia reported an increased frequency of negative effects. However, Hilgard (1974) failed to replicate this finding, and Orne (1965) confirmed this relationship in only some of his subjects.

Hilgard (1974) studied the frequency of negative effects in 120 subjects who were administered the SHSS:A followed by the administration of the Stanford Hypnotic Susceptibility Scale, Form C (SHSS:C; Weitzenhoffer & Hilgard, 1962). Subjects were interviewed about their experiences during hypnosis and enduring aftereffects. Hilgard found that 31% of the subjects reported negative effects (e.g., headaches, dizziness, nausea), 16% of the subjects reported short-term aftereffects lasting from 5 min to 1 hr, and 15% of the subjects reported that these effects lasted more than 1 hr. However, Hilgard also found that 60% of the subjects reported feeling relaxed and rested after hypnosis. Because Hilgard failed to use a nonhypnotized control group and did not counterbalance the administration of the hypnotic scales (Form C always followed Form A), order effects of scale presentation might have affected the obtained results. In comparing her data to earlier findings (Hilgard et al., 1961), Hilgard reasoned that a larger proportion of subjects reported negative effects following the administration of Form C, as compared with Forms A or B, because it contains more "cognitive" items that require more profound perceptual–kinesthetic distortions and have a more personalized meaning, such as asking subjects to "dream" about hypnosis and to age regress during hypnosis.

Crawford et al. (1982) contrasted the differences in negative effects following the group-administered Harvard Group Scale of Hypnotic Susceptibility, Form A (HGSHS:A; Shor & Orne, 1962) and the individually administered SHSS:C. A majority (72%) of the 107 subjects interviewed about their experiences after hypnosis reported feeling relaxed and rested. Following the group-administered Form A, 5% of their subjects reported some type of negative effect (e.g., headaches, nausea, confusion, dizziness, etc.); 4% of these experiences lasted 5 min to 1 hr, and 1% lasted more than 1 hr. By contrast, following the individually administered Form C, 29% of the subjects reported an aftereffect; 17% reported a duration of 5 min to 1 hr, and 12% reported a duration of more than 1 hr. Crawford et al. (1982) also found that subjects who reported cognitive distortions (confusion or disorientation) following hypnosis were significantly more hypnotizable than were subjects who experienced drowsiness, headaches, and nausea. The authors concluded that responsive subjects are more likely to experience cognitive distortions. Because Hilgard et al. (1961) found a similar small percentage (8%) following the individually administered SHSS:A and SHSS:B scales, which have items similar to those of the group-administered HGSHS:A, Crawford et al. (1982) agreed with Hilgard (1974) that the increased frequency of negative effects following administration of the SHSS:C was caused by its more "cognitive" content.

The "cognitive content hypothesis" has received support from studies showing that subjects occasionally experience transient anxiety in response to cognitive suggestions to have a hypnotic dream (Barrett, 1979), to age regress to 7 years of age (Lynn & Hamel, 1987), and to experience mind–body dissociation (Nash, Lynn, & Stanley, 1984). However, hypnotized subjects' responses to exclusively cognitive versus exclusively motoric-test suggestions have not been compared. Furthermore, the responses of subjects who received nonhypnotic cognitive tasks (e.g. dream analysis, the Rorschach) have not been compared with the responses of hypnotized subjects who received cognitive items as tasks.

A rival hypothesis is that negative effects arise not from some intrinsic quality of cognitive tasks but as a function of the greater difficulty of cognitive items. Perceived "failure" may engender feelings of anxiety, inadequacy, and dysphoria. For example, Lynn and Hamel (1987) demonstrated that compared with subjects who passed an age regression suggestion (to age 7), a slightly greater percentage of subjects who failed to age regress reported that the experience was negative (failed = 8.49% vs. passed = 2.48%). Negative ratings were largely attributable to frustration about being unable to have the suggested experiences. Interestingly, even when subjects reported anxiety, they generally rated their overall experience as positive and expressed a willingness to be rehypnotized.

A study by Lynn, Brentar, Carlson, Kurzhals, and Green (1991) suggested that hypnotizability is not associated with negative effects. The investigators administered the Posthypnotic Experience Questionnaire (PEQ) to 240 subjects, which asked them to rate their hypnotic and posthypnotic experiences (HGSHS:A; Shor & Orne, 1962). The PEQ included items that tapped positive experiences (e.g., feeling relaxed), negative experiences based on common complaints reported in the literature (e.g., headache), and unusual experiences (e.g., perceptual–kinesthetic; Gill & Brenman, 1959). The results indicated that measures of hypnotic responsiveness and rapport were associated with subjects' reports of their positive and unusual hypnotic experiences. By contrast, negative experiences were not associated with hypnotizability.

Brentar, Lynn, and Carlson (1992) developed the reliable and valid Posthypnotic Experience Scale (PES) as part of an attempt to develop a posthypnotic scale that would be empirically rather than rationally based, similar to the PEQ. The authors' findings were consistent with Brentar and Lynn's (1989) study, insofar as the scales that measured pleasant and somatic–kinesthetic experiences were correlated with hypnotizability and with subjects' overall ratings of their hypnotic experience. However, a scale that measured anxiety was also correlated with hypnotizability, although an anger–irritability scale was not associated with hypnotizability. Interestingly, the anxiety scale was not correlated with subjects' overall ratings of their hypnotic experience. Unlike Brentar and Lynn's (1989) earlier study, questions that tapped unambiguously negative experiences (e.g., headaches) were not included on any of the factor-analytically derived scales because of their relatively low base rates in the population.

Faw, Sellers, and Wilcox (1968) studied the psychopathological effects of hypnosis on college students in terms of differences in Minnesota Multiphasic Personality Inventory scores (preexperiment vs. postexperiment) and in terms of frequency of visits to the college counseling center and infirmary during a 90-day period following the experiment. Using a modified version of the SHSS:A, subjects were hypnotized three times over 3 successive weeks. No detrimental effects were observed following hypnosis; the authors concluded that hypnosis is a safe procedure when used with a normal college population.

Comparison Samples

To our knowledge, only one study (Coe & Ryken, 1979) has compared the negative effects associated with hypnosis with negative effects associated with other college activities. Coe and Ryken (1979) compared the experiences of a group of students taking part in a hypnosis experiment with that of four other groups of students in the following conditions: after a verbal learning experiment, attending a college class, taking a college examination, and college life in general. Using a self-report questionnaire, they found that 49% of the subjects in the hypnosis group reported some negative effect following the administration of the SHSS:C. However, they found that hypnosis did not have a higher frequency of negative effects when compared with other experiences in college life, such as attending a class or participating in a verbal learning experiment. In fact, subjects experienced more negative effects following a college examination than did students taking part in a hypnosis experiment. Additionally, hypnosis was consistently rated as the most pleasant experience when compared with those other activities. As a result, Coe and Ryken concluded that the experience of hypnosis is at least as positive an experience as other routine college activities, if not more so, and that the administration of a standardized scale of hypnotic susceptibility causes few or no harmful aftereffects when compared with other common experiences in college life.

Brentar, Lynn, Carlson, and Kurzhals (1992) administered the PEQ to subjects in hypnotic and nonhypnotic settings. In the latter case, all references to hypnosis were removed. In one group, subjects received the questionnaire following an introductory psychology class examination. A second group of subjects received the questionnaire following a "body sensation" experiment in which they were informed that the experiment was designed to study their awareness of bodily sensations and experiences when they were sitting quietly with their eyes closed. Subjects were told to focus on the sensations in different parts of the body corresponding to the body parts that are the focus of hypnotic suggestions. A third control group of subjects received the questionnaire after sitting quietly in a classroom for 20 min with no special instructions. In the fourth group, subjects were hypnotized in a situation defined as "hypnosis."

The researchers found that in no case did the positive experiences reported by hypnotized subjects significantly exceed the frequency of positive experiences reported by the sensation and control groups, whereas the examination group reported the lowest frequency of positive experiences. The frequencies of negative experiences were not significantly different across all four groups. They also found that unusual experiences were not specific to hypnosis. In no instance did the reports of unusual experiences after hypnosis exceed the reports of subjects in a control condition by more than 1 percentage point.

Summary

Most subjects experience hypnosis as a positive, satisfying, and relaxing experience (Lynn et al., 1991) that is no more stressful than mundane activities (Brentar, Lynn, & Carlson, 1992; Coe & Ryken, 1979). A small fraction, typically less than 20%, of subjects experience negative effects after hypnosis. The lack of association with hypnotizability, along with the finding that these effects are equally likely following mundane nonhypnotic procedures, suggests that they are not produced by or limited to hypnosis. However, the timing of their occurrence may lead subjects and experimenters to misattribute them to hypnosis. Most of these aftereffects are transitory, although some last longer than 1 hr. The most commonly reported aftereffects are physical complaints (e.g., headaches, dizziness, drowsiness, nausea, anxiety, and cognitive distortions such as confusion, disorientation, and distortion of perceptions). More difficult or personally meaningful tasks, such as asking subjects to "dream" about hypnosis or to age regress during hypnosis, may be associated with a higher incidence of reported negative effects, but hypnotizability does not seem to be reliably linked to negative sequelae.

Clinical Hypnosis

Survey Data

Averback (1962) surveyed 828 psychiatrists (414 returned questionnaires), and 120 reported knowledge of 210 negative reactions presumably associated with hypnosis. More than half of the cases ($n = 119$) involved psychotic decompensation, a number that widely exceeds the incidence reported by other investigators. Indeed, as MacHovec (1988a) has noted, more recent studies signify that anxiety is a much more frequent concomitant or aftereffect of hypnosis.

Levitt and Hershman (1963) reported that 27% of the 301 clinical hypnotists who responded to a questionnaire observed some unusual or unexpected reaction (e.g., anxiety, panic, depression) following hypnosis. In ordinal rank, the most commonly reported reactions were anxiety, panic, depression, headache, vomiting, fainting, dizziness, crying, loss of rapport, overt psychosis, difficulties involving sex, excessive dependency, and difficulties resulting from inadvertently given suggestions. A problem in interpreting these data resides in the fact that many of the hypnotists who reported negative reactions used hypnosis in obstetrical cases or in surgeries, in combination with chemical anesthetics. The most frequently reported negative effects (i.e., anxiety, panic, depression) could thus be attributable to concerns about surgery or to the effects of anesthetics rather than to hypnosis per se.

A survey (Judd, Burrows, & Dennerstein, 1986) of 202 Australian therapists indicated that 43.5% of the therapists reported adverse effects arising from the use of hypnosis during their career, whereas 24.2% reported a negative effect associated with one or more patients during the preceding year. Echterling and Emmerling (1987) surveyed college students who had attended a stage hypnosis show on campus. Eighteen of 94 attendees agreed to be interviewed; of these, 7 were "enthusiastically positive," 7 were both positive and negative, and 4 were "essentially negative" about their hypnotic experiences.

Interpretation of this survey-based data is problematic insofar as the reference samples were probably far from representative. With response rates that were typically less than 20%, it is impossible to generalize the survey findings to the broader population. For example, the possibility exists that subjects who experience negative effects, or clinicians who witness them, are more likely to respond to surveys, thereby inflating report rates of negative sequelae. In the next part of this chapter, we examine a number of possible determinants of negative effects.

Client Characteristics

Several authors (Kleinhauz et al., 1979; MacHovec, 1986) have argued that possible hazards of hypnosis are attributable largely to personality or attitudinal factors residing within the client. Complications are reported consistently in the case of either incipient–borderline psychotic clients who decompensate during hypnosis (Gill & Brenman, 1959) or paranoid clients who experience an intensification of hostile feelings about being controlled following hypnosis (Rosen, 1960; Speigel, 1978).

MacHovec (1987) highlighted the importance of client beliefs and perceptions in mediating negative effects in hypnotherapy. Clients who are afraid of experiencing hypnosis (Hilgard, 1974), who believe that they will lose control during hypnosis (Orne, 1965), or who feel a need to comply with or please the hypnotist (Milne, 1986; Overholser, 1988) may be at increased risk for complications.

Orne (1965) cautioned that symptoms may represent adaptive functions or defenses that the client is hesitant to abandon. If the client perceives that hypnosis will necessitate the forsaking of an entrenched and ego-syntonic adjustment pattern, then problems may ensue with the use of hypnosis. Similarly, it has been argued (Fromm, 1980; Meares, 1961) that hypnosis may short-circuit the client's normal repressive and censuring mechanisms, thereby increasing the conscious accessibility of affect, lowering the threshold for anxiety reactions, and facilitating the emergence of intolerable or traumatic insight.

Hypnotist Characteristics

Kost (1965) contended that dangers associated with hypnosis lie with the hypnotist as opposed to the client. Kost cited the hypnotist's ignorance, overzealousness, and a lack of understanding of interpersonal relationships as reasons why hypnosis may go awry. The clinical literature is replete with case studies implicating poorly trained or incompetent hypnotherapists in the incidence of negative reactions (Haberman, 1987; Judd et al., 1985, Kluft, 1982; MacHovec, 1987, 1988a; Milne, 1986). These reports tend to focus on the hypnotist's lack of training or judgment (e.g., the failure to recognize a potentially dangerous situation and the limits of one's competence) or on the hypnotist's tendency to gratify his or her own rather than the client's needs. Orne (1965) noted that hypnosis can accentuate hypnotist countertransference problems, such as the inability to keep a therapeutic distance from the client (Lindner, 1960), to be unaware of one's own reactions, and to mistime interpretations to be unhelpful and unpalatable to the client. In contradistinction to these findings, Janet

(1925) felt that "even in bad hands, suggestion and hypnotism do not seem to be able to do much harm" (p. 34).

Fromm (1980) focused on the values of the hypnotist, stating that an authoritarian, coercive, or omnipotent stance toward the client is likely to result in negative reactions. By contrast, a permissive, respectful, and collaborative hypnotist is unlikely to encounter complications.

Procedural Aspects

Occasionally, hypnotized clients fail to terminate hypnosis at the therapist's suggestion; they experience difficulty in awakening following hypnosis (Judd et al., 1985; MacHovec, 1988a; Williams, 1953). Kleinhauz and Eli (1987) contended that special attention ought to be given to the dehypnotization process in order to diminish the likelihood of this occurring. According to Orne (1965), this behavior may signify a passive–aggressive maneuver that veils hostility toward the hypnotist. When the hypnotist attempts to awaken the client, he or she becomes less rather than more responsive. An inexperienced hypnotist may become anxious and communicate anxiety to the client, thereby reinforcing the client's behavior. One approach to dealing with this problem is to change the client's motivation to remain in hypnosis by informing her that she can wake up whenever she wishes (Meares, 1961).

Meares (1961) believed that a greater danger is that the client may be allowed to leave the consulting room before being fully alert. Gravitz, Mallet, Munyon, and Gerton (1982) urged that "precautions should be taken to avoid the premature departure of a subject after hypnosis" (p. 306). Gravitz et al. advocated conversation with the client to combat drowsiness and ensure wakefulness. Crawford et al. (1982) tested this potential danger in the laboratory but did not confirm it. That is, experimental subjects who received special termination procedures following administration of the SHSS:C (Weitzenhoffer & Hilgard, 1962), including a stretching exercise and a conversation to ensure normal alertness, reported just as many posthypnotic transient effects as did subjects who received no special termination procedures.

Meares (1961) warned that specific posthypnotic suggestions that inform clients that they will respond to a suggestion after hypnosis, on presentation of a predetermined cue, should be used sparingly. Unfulfilled posthypnotic suggestions occur when a client does not respond to the suggestion because of external environmental or internal psychological factors. Effects ranging from transitory anxiety to a severe anxiety reaction purportedly ensue because clients equate an unfulfilled posthypnotic suggestion with "failure." To decrease the likelihood of clients experiencing a sense of failure when they are unable to fulfill the suggestion, Meares (1961) advocated the use of suggestions expressed in nonspecific terms.

Specific hypnotic procedures have been cited in the literature as having increased potential for negative effects. Weitzenhoffer (1957) described age regression as "potentially the most risky hypnosis phenomena" [*sic*] because of "inadvertently regressing a subject to a traumatic experience" (p. 105). Fromm (1980) decried the use of age progression except "only in connection with ego integrative suggestions of healthy growth and coping" (p. 429). Rosen (1960) warned against suggesting away a symptom "unless there are [other] symptoms to fall back on" (p. 142). Similarly, Orne (1965) speculated that directly suggesting the removal of a symptom during hypnosis may exacerbate symptoms or create symptom substitution, particularly if the client experiences an alarming loss of control.

Serious Reactions

Serious negative reactions following hypnosis such as psychosis (Kleinhauz et al., 1979), grave depression or suicide (Rosen, 1960; Seitz, 1951; West & Deckert, 1965), spontaneous age regression (Miller, 1983), and paranoid delusions (Hall, 1984) have been reported, although such cases are apparently rare. It is also difficult to parcel out the contribution, if any, of prior psychopathology in these cases. Meares (1961) and Conn (1972) pointed to a prepsychotic condition, rather than to any unique contribution of hypnotic procedures, in explaining serious negative reactions. Other studies either have failed to document negative effects with psychotic patients (Green, 1979) or have noted improvement in psychotic patients after hypnosis (Faw et al., 1968).

Summary

A small but unknown percentage of clients experience unexpected and untoward reactions during hypnotherapy. This percentage may be somewhat higher than that obtained by experimental hypnosis subjects. Whereas clients undergo hypnosis for symptom relief, experimental subjects participate because they are intrinsically motivated to do so or for credit or compensation. Moreover, experimental subjects are likely to have a more structured, formalized and objective relationship with the hypnotist than is the case with psychotherapy clients. Negative reactions in the clinic have been ascribed to client characteristics such as prehypnotic psychopathology or negative attitudes about hypnosis, hypnotist characteristics such as authoritarianism or a lack of awareness of countertransference feelings, and procedural problems such as inadvertent regression to a repressed trauma or overuse of posthypnotic suggestions.

Given the absence of comparative data with clinical samples, one cannot attribute these effects specifically to hypnosis. Just as the rate of negative effects occurring during and after experimental hypnosis does not differ from that occurring in conjunction with various control procedures

(Brentar, Lynn, Carlson, & Kurzhals, 1992; Coe & Ryken, 1979), it is possible that the effects reported by hypnotherapists would have occurred at the same rate even if hypnosis had not been used. Conflictual, anxiety-arousing, and traumatic material is dealt with in all forms of therapy; indeed, it is typically the focus of treatment to reduce discomfort regardless of whether it occurred in a hypnotic context.

Our literature review indicates that clinicians and researchers need to be as wary of unexpected negative reactions to hypnosis as they are of negative reactions to nonhypnotic procedures. Conversely, they need be no more wary of hypnotic procedures than they are of their nonhypnotic counterparts. In the following section, we enumerate a number of circumstances that require heightened vigilance, particularly on the part of the clinician, to circumvent or manage negative effects.

CLINICAL APPLICATIONS

Situations Requiring Heightened Vigilance

Regardless of whether hypnosis is used (e.g., systematic desensitization, relaxation, imagery-based procedures), there are a number of situations in the clinic, and occasionally in the experimental setting, that demand particular care and vigilance in order for the therapist to minimize or manage negative reactions. These circumstances, alone or in combination, account for a preponderance of reported negative effects. Familiarity with these situations will help the therapist to comprehend an otherwise puzzling or alarming client reaction and to intervene in a calm and reassuring manner.

A History of Dissociative Reactions

A client with a history of unusual experiences following the use of chemical anesthetics and analgesics (Hilgard et al., 1961) or a history of dissociative episodes of any type (e.g., depersonalization, derealization, fugue) requires particular attention. The subject may equate or confuse feelings of relaxation and perceptual alterations that commonly occur during hypnosis (see Brentar, Lynn, & Carlson, 1992) and nonhypnotic relaxation training with anesthesia-related sensations, resulting in the recapitulation of a prior aversive reaction to anesthesia. Because a discontinuity or disruption in the flow of mental associations and feelings of "unreality" may accompany hypnosis, relaxation training, and various imagery procedures (e.g., systematic desensitization), dissociative tendencies may be exacerbated or a dissociative reaction may be precipitated in reactive individuals. Dissociative experiences and somatic and perceptual alterations result from the fact that hypnotic inductions typically contain suggestions for eye closure, for perceptual and somatic alterations, and for imagery and fantasy consistent with suggested rather than reality-based events. For example, one of the authors (David C. Frauman) worked with a client referred for hypnosis for weight control. She exhibited a spontaneous age regression following seemingly innocuous suggestions for relaxation and serenity. Following termination of the hypnosis and a more thorough questioning of the client, she remembered two episodes of fugue as a teenager, once flying to Alaska to visit a grandparent who had lived there but who had been deceased for several years at the time of the flight.

Increased Psychopathology

Clients who are vulnerable to psychotic decompensation (Meares, 1961), those with a paranoid level of resistance to being influenced or controlled (Orne, 1965), and those with borderline character structure for whom hypnosis may be experienced as a sudden, intrusive, and unwanted intimacy may all be poor candidates for hypnosis. These clients may misconstrue the purpose of hypnosis or the intent of the hypnotist, resulting in a recrudescence or exacerbation of symptoms. A secure working alliance with these clients is therefore a prerequisite for hypnotic work. To illustrate, a psychiatric inpatient with a history of schizophrenia and debilitating anxiety was referred to a therapy group in which unit patients were given systematic relaxation and hypnosis suggestions in a group format. During the relaxation process, the patient began hearing insistent and threatening auditory hallucinations, became agitated and anxious, and had to be restrained in his room. The patient was subsequently calmed by a unit nurse through repeated reassuring comments and assurances as to the safety of the hospital.

Negative Transference

Some clients' histories with parents, authority figures, or helping professionals predispose them to view the hypnotist with mistrust, anger, and fear. Given the cultural associations of the hypnotist as having control, power, and authority over the client, the hypnotic situation may accentuate clients' negative reaction tendencies (Fromm, 1980) in situations imbued with connotations of personal dominance and control. If hypnosis is so perceived, involvement may be attenuated and hypnosis may be experienced as an emotionally charged, aversive event.

A client with a history of early childhood sexual abuse became unexpectedly enraged at her hypnotist, a man whom she admired and trusted on the conscious level. When the hypnotist was able to reassure the client that he was in fact a much different person from the perpetrator of abuse and that his purpose was indeed diametrically opposed to that of her abuser, she was able to relax and allow the events of hypnosis to unfold.

Misconceptions About Hypnosis

Misconceptions about hypnosis may hamper the subject's ability to trust the hypnotist and to participate fully in the events of hypnosis. Not uncommonly, perceptions about hypnosis are shaped by exposure to stage hypnosis and by sensationalized media coverages, including TV talk shows. It is therefore imperative to assess the person's ideas and feelings about hypnosis and to disabuse him or her of erroneous or threatening perceptions before initiating hypnosis. Some misconceptions that inhibit earnest participation in hypnosis are the following: (a) Hypnosis means losing control of one's behavior or losing consciousness or awareness of the environment; (b) hypnosis is "mind control," "brainwashing," or an "X-ray of the mind"; (c) hypnosis will mean giving away secrets or being coerced into performing silly or embarrassing actions; and (d) hypnosis requires and promotes passivity and dependency. Given these popular misconceptions, many hypnotic subjects are at least initially ambivalent about hypnosis; this ambivalence needs to be acknowledged and respected before it can be transformed into a cooperative working alliance with the client.

Negative Contemporary Reactions

Sometimes, the roots of a client's negative reaction to hypnosis lie not so much in a historic, transference-based association, as in a more contemporary, reality-based discomfort with the hypnotist or the hypnotic environment (Orne, 1965). A previous unpleasant experience with hypnosis is one such example. Usually, a frank discussion of the perceived problem, along with the hypnotist's sincere effort to correct the situation, will minimize the likelihood of a negative reaction: One client became irritated with her hypnotist for what she perceived as her tendency to rapidly terminate the induction and to rush her out of the consulting room at the end of the hour. The client was able to confront the hypnotist about her brusque manner, and changes in the pace of the session were arranged: The client was able to resume her therapeutic task.

Suggestions May Instigate or Reveal Unexpected Affect

Hypnotic suggestions may impinge on a person's current concerns or conflicts, trigger painful memories, and provide an avenue for the expression of suppressed or repressed affect (Fromm, 1980). Certain suggestions, such as for age regression or for hypnotic dreams about particular events or issues, delve into the client's archive of life experiences, imply that access to forgotten or repressed events can be achieved, and that insight into important psychological dynamics can be gained. Given this focus and the demands on the client, it is not surprising that unexpectedly intense abreactions can ensue following such suggestions: One hypnotic client, when asked to have "a dream about hypnosis" (SHSS:C), began to sob deeply. The client was reassured and asked to talk about his feelings. After hypnosis was terminated, the client was able to recall a distressing dream he had several nights previously in which he had seen his deceased father as still being alive.

As part of a hypnosis workshop skill practice sesson, one of the participants "age regressed" another participant to her 10th birthday. The latter participant began to breathe heavily and described, with intense emotion, how she was sexually molested by her uncle, who placed her hand on his penis during her birthday party.

Of course, these sorts of reactions are not unique to hypnosis and may be therapeutic rather than unwanted. For example, in psychodynamic therapies there is often an outpouring of affect in response to the exploration of conflict-laden issues. Indeed, the working through and integration of what is uncovered may be therapeutic. Nevertheless, the clinician needs to be prepared and trained to manage such reactions when they occur.

At times, suggestions that appear to be innocuous, and place few demands on the client, have unintended and unexpected repercussions. Consider the following examples:

1. At a workshop on "self-hypnosis" at a mental health facility, one of the authors (Steven J. Lynn) invited the mental health professionals to "focus on your thoughts" as part of a non-hypnotic experiential exercise. One of the workshop participants sat bolt-upright and asked to be excused from the room. It was learned that the man experienced an intense panic reaction when he thought of murdering his girlfriend, an obsessive thought that he had been struggling with for some time. The following week, he recognized the need for psychological treatment and voluntarily admitted himself to a mental hospital.

2. When one of the authors (Steven J. Lynn) was a neophyte hypnotist, he invited a hypnotized subject to "take a walk near the beach and count each wave" as part of "deepening" the hypnotic induction. Little care and time was taken to get to know the subject before hypnosis. After she "counted" two waves by lifting her index finger, her chest began to heave and she began to sob. The simple suggestion to walk near the beach triggered a memory of her walking to the water's edge during the past week while contemplating suicide.

Difficult or Inappropriate Suggestions

Suggestions vary in the cognitive, affective, and perceptual demands they place on the subject. Simple motoric suggestions, such as for hand levitation, are relatively easy and are passed by the majority of hypnotized subjects. By contrast, suggestions that involve posthypnotic directives, age regression, and out-of-body experiences are passed by 50% or fewer of the subject population. Perceived failure to comply with these suggestions may engender feelings of inadequacy, anxiety, or dysphoria (Lynn & Hamel, 1987). Negative reactions, stimulated by failure, may occur in the absence of a robust therapeutic rapport and prior success with more difficult hypnotic tasks. Finally, evidence (Nash et al., 1984) indicates that suggestions that invite the subject to experience perceptual alterations, even if they are experienced successfully, may engender dysphoria.

Direct Suggestions to Relinquish Symptoms

Because symptoms may represent coping or adaptive mechanisms that are associated with potent yet unconscious secondary gains, forceful directives to abandon symptoms may engender significant conflict in the client. Torn between having to disobey the hypnotist or relinquish a valued psychic strategy (Fromm, 1980), such a forced choice may result in anxiety or passive resistance on the client's part.

Countertransference Reactions

Although countertransference difficulties occur during and after hypnosis as they do in psychotherapy, Orne (1965) noted that the hypnotist-directive nature of hypnosis may accentuate countertransference problems. Orne (1965) observed the following:

> Acting as a hypnotist, the therapist may find it hard to maintain the therapeutic distance that is necessary if he is to be aware of his own reactions . . . . All too frequently, the use of hypnosis is primarily in the service of the therapist's needs. (p. 235)

Negative reactions in clients may ensue if they sense that their own needs or goals are somehow of secondary importance to the hypnotist. Consider this example: A physician faculty member at a university medical school asked a virtuoso hypnosis client of his to appear with him at a hypnosis demonstration for the assembled faculty at Grand Rounds. The client agreed and seemed to be looking forward to her part in the demonstration of hypnotic techniques. During the demonstration, the physician seemed to derive great satisfaction from impressing his colleagues with dramatic hypnotic effects, but the client appeared worried and distracted. After the demonstration, the client expressed anger at the physician for "putting me on display" and "caring more about how you looked to the faculty."

Inadequate Training in Psychology and Psychotherapy

Hypnotists lacking broad knowledge, training, and experience pertinent to the assessment and treatment of psychopathology may be vulnerable to a disproportionate number of negative effects (Fromm, 1980). By contrast, hypnotists with a substantial background in psychotherapy may be better able to anticipate the impact of diverse hypnotic techniques on their clients and may be better able to select and implement interventions to address their clients' needs. Moreover, adequately trained psychotherapists may also be able to identify and intervene appropriately in the case of an incipient negative reaction, thereby mitigating its significance and potential for harm to the client.

In a hypnosis class taught by one of the authors (Steven J. Lynn) during a practice session one team of neophyte graduate student hypnotists defied the instructor's directive not to practice suggestions they had not seen demonstrated by the instructor. During the time period that the instructor briefly stepped out of the room to supervise another team of students, the "renegade" hypnotists suggested to an anxious subject that her consciousness would be "dissociated" from her body and would float above her "self" and be able to observe the hypnotic proceedings. The high-hypnotizable subject, who had previously tested at the extreme of hypnotizability, complied with the suggestion but experienced an almost immediate panic reaction that was alleviated when the instructor returned and gave her suggestions for relaxation and mind–body integration.

Strategies for Limiting Negative Effects

In the next section, we enumerate strategies and techniques that we have used in our clinical practice to avoid or mitigate negative effects. Some of the strategies entail observing client anxiety and discomfort so as to minimize the likelihood of a negative reaction, whereas other strategies entail curtailing anxiety as it emerges so that a negative reaction can be attenuated.

Robust Working Alliance

A robust and resilient working alliance is a formidable deterrent against a negative effect in hypnotherapy. For the hypnotist, this means sincere caring for the client's well-being, respect for the client, honest self-evaluation, awareness of the limits of competence, and ongoing examination of countertransference feelings (Mays & Franks, 1985). A history of mutual respect, frank communication about problems, and effective solutions to problems is emblematic of a healthy working alliance.

Thorough Assessment of Client

To sidestep negative reactions, it is necessary to carefully assess the client's history of hypnotic experiences and attitudes about hypnosis. We begin with open-ended questions about the client's feelings about hypnosis and related phenomena (e.g., relaxation tapes, guided imagery). If a client recounts a prior hypnotic experience, we ask for details about it, including the client's perception of hypnotic "depth" (e.g., How deeply were you hypnotized, what did you feel at that time, and what suggestions were given?); how the client reacted to various suggestions (e.g., what was particularly pleasant or helpful, what was not; what types of sensations and perceptual alterations were experienced); and we listen carefully to the words that the client uses to describe the flow of hypnotic events.

What "worked" for the client in the past can be incorporated into a hypnotic intervention. However, we also listen for words or descriptors that connote potential problems or resistance to hypnotic procedures (e.g., feelings of excessive tiredness, feelings of loss of control), and we work to reframe certain experiences, such as tiredness or fatigue, as signifying that the client was able to experience hypnosis. At the same time, we inform the client that we will administer suggestions to counter undue fatigue during or after the present hypnosis session.

We also invite the client to have a fantasy about the upcoming hypnosis session, to imagine what it will be like and what suggestions would be the most helpful to enhance the overall experience and meet specific treatment objectives. The fantasy about hypnosis often reveals fears and misconceptions that inhibit full participation and that can be disabused by the therapist. Suggestions can be devised, with the cooperation of the client, to fortify perceived control during hypnosis. This procedure is particularly useful with clients who have never experienced hypnosis.

We also inquire about the client's previous experience with psychotherapy or counseling as a means of assessing attitudes about the interpersonal change process and as a means of assessing the client's level of overall adaptive functioning. An informal mental status, which includes an assessment of mood and cognitive functioning, can also pinpoint potential problem areas and provide indications for suggestions that are particularly relevant to the client's current concerns. Questions about the client's early childhood experiences and significant relationships may provide a tentative picture of potential transference feelings, as well as the client's ability to maintain a working therapeutic alliance. It is also important to pay particular attention to any history of dissociative experiences. Finally, we inquire about experiences with chemical anesthetics (Hilgard et al., 1961) and whether they were perceived as pleasant or aversive. Knowledge of these experiences can provide indications of the direction a negative reaction may take if it occurs.

Informed Consent

Hypnotic procedures should be administered only with the client's explicit consent. Obtaining informed consent provides the hypnotist with an opportunity to describe the procedures to the client and to create realistic expectations as to the likely outcome. Because the great majority of clients experience hypnosis as pleasant and relaxing (Brentar & Lynn, 1988), the hypnotist can confidently convey this message to the client, creating a positive expectation for enjoyment and success. The hypnotist can also clear up misconceptions about hypnosis and underscore the seriousness of purpose of hypnosis used in the clinic or laboratory. Consent should then be obtained from the client.

Client in Control

Client anxiety about hypnosis can be moderated by demystifying the procedures, thereby helping the client to feel more tangibly in control of the process. Explaining the procedures in a straightforward manner boosts client cooperation and reduces the likelihood of a negative reaction (Overholser, 1988). Procedures can be explained by analogy with familiar sensations ("similar to being very relaxed," "just like when you can concentrate easily") and introduced as "self-hypnosis" or "relaxation." These maneuvers militate against negative reactions without a sacrifice of treatment potency or confidence in the hypnotist (Fromm, 1980; Overholser, 1988).

Other techniques can reinforce the client's feelings of being in control. For a client fearful of losing consciousness, hypnosis can be described as "full alert consciousness" or a "state of awareness." For a client who requires reassurance from the hypnotist, the procedure can be described as follows: "You will be fully in contact with me at all times. You will be able to talk with me when you wish and open your eyes at any time to see that I am still here." Clients can also be comforted by the knowledge that research (Lynn, Weekes, & Milano, 1989) indicates that even deeply hypnotized subjects do not lose contact with their surroundings and retain an ability to monitor their environment. For a fearful client, a signal such as opening the eyes or lifting an index finger can be arranged beforehand, denoting some discomfort and a request for hypnotist intervention. Finally, in the induction itself, suggestions can be proferred that emphasize control and mastery, mental and physical relaxation, comfort and security, a sense of well-being, and a relaxed kind of "controlled spontaneity."

Collaborative Hypnosis

A therapeutic climate marked by permissiveness, collaboration, and respect for the client's goals is the most conducive to circumventing negative therapeutic effects (Fromm, 1980; Overholser, 1988). The client who feels coerced or commanded to respond is more likely to rebel either directly or indirectly, whereas the client who feels invited to participate is more likely to participate enthusiastically (Fromm, 1980). We ordinarily begin with the least authoritarian suggestions that can be devised and solicit the client's suggestions and feelings as hypnosis progresses.

Fromm (1980) suggested that collaborative hypnosis means giving something to the client rather than taking something away from the client. For example, instead of suggesting to an obese client that sweets and fatty foods will make him or her nauseous, the hypnotist may suggest that not enough enjoyment of eating is occurring because the client is not giving his or her taste buds an opportunity to savor the food. Henceforth, the client may wish to slowly savor each bite of food until the taste buds have optimized the client's enjoyment. These suggestions do not prohibit gratification but instead hint at another, possibly healthier gratification. Fromm (1980) noted that another benefit of this approach is strengthened client autonomy and self-pride in mastering a challenging problem or situation.

Reduced Difficulty and Threat

To foster a successful experience, the order and pace of hypnotic suggestions can be adjusted so that clients first respond successfully to easily complied with suggestions before more difficult suggestions are introduced when the client's confidence is high. An approach that we have outlined elsewhere (Lynn, Rhue, Kvaal, & Mare, in press) involves a graded series of suggestions that range from relatively low to high difficulty, personal and interpersonal focus, complexity, degree of structure imposed by the therapist, affectivity, conflict-evoking potential, and imaginative versus behavioral rehearsal. The therapist can thus titrate the demands placed upon the client by moving from suggestion to suggestion at a pace that permits exposure to anxiety and affect-eliciting stimuli in a safe, controlled manner, and the experience of self-efficacy through the mastery of successive steps and graduated rehearsals.

Age Regression

Age regression may result in a painful awareness of a forgotten or repressed memory (Fromm, 1980). To ensure that affect can be contained and eventually processed in a manner consistent with therapeutic objectives, special care should be taken when using these procedures. For example, we always establish a nonverbal cue (e.g., touch the right hand) for the person to feel alert, awake, and no longer hypnotized. We also may take additional precautions such as informing clients that they will be able to terminate their experience of "being a child" and comment on their childhood experiences from an adult perspective *during* the age regression, when the therapist contacts (e.g., by way of a tap on the right shoulder) a "part" of the client that retains an adult awareness during even the most compelling age regression.

Before hypnosis, age regression suggestions can be framed in terms of self-hypnosis in such a way as to deemphasize the dissociative aspects of hypnosis. Clients can simply be informed that they will be able to respond to the therapist's questions, even to the extent that they will be able to comment on their experiences from an adult perspective. We explain to the client that this is possible because they actively create their own experiences during hypnosis and have the capacity to view and review their actions and reactions from multiple vantage points during hypnosis without it disrupting their involvement in the experience.

Clients can also be protected from the full impact of painful memories by introducing the age regression as an autobiographical videotape, which appears on a viewing screen that the client can control (e.g., stop action, fast forward). Alternatively, the age regression can be introduced as a hypnotic dream about the client's childhood, with provisions for awakening from the dream on cue.

Although some clinicians advocate waking the client during a negative reaction (Gill & Brenman, 1959), another strategy is to talk to the client while he or she remains hypnotized (Orne, 1965). This latter strategy may be preferable because awakening the client may signify that the hypnotist is unable to manage the reaction within the bounds of hypnosis, diluting the client's trust in the hypnotist and increasing resistance to hypnosis (Orne, 1965). Nevertheless, the clinician should always establish nonverbal signals to reorient the client during age regression if, for some reason, the reaction is difficult to manage during hypnosis.

Clients may be conflicted about whether to attend to or suppress memories that are elicited during age regression. For example, during a clinical demonstration, one of the authors (Steven J. Lynn) hypnotized a woman who spontaneously relived a traumatic event of being sexually abused by her father when she was 7 years old. Afterward, she was told that she could "remember what she wanted to remember and forget what she wanted to forget." The woman remembered everything after hypnosis because she told herself prior to hypnosis that she wanted to remember everything. Nevertheless, she was visibly shaken and disturbed by her recall of an event that continued to recur and precipitated her seeking psychotherapy. Thus, following a negative reaction during age regression, clients' defenses may not be adequate to comply with a suggestion that indicates that they will be able to remember the memories that they want to and that will help them to understand and forget the memories that they do not want to remember.

We have found that a preferable strategy is to discuss with clients *during hypnosis* what they would like to remember and what they would like to forget, to discuss the reasons for their decision, and then to devise strategies that will facilitate the experience of amnesia, if indicated. At the same time, we recognize the necessity of adequate client follow-up, and we are prepared for the penetration of the memories or their derivatives into consciousness. That is, simply suggesting amnesia is no guarantee that this will happen in all clients. The key here is to respect the clients' defenses and to use good clinical judgment to pace hypnotherapy or uncovering work.

Incipient Negative Effects

The hypnotist must continuously monitor the client's reactions during hypnosis. Any sign of resistance or discomfort (e.g., frowning, agitation, physical pain, or a lack of interest) may signal a need for care and attention (Orne, 1965) or for relief from an "uncomfortable" suggestion. When a client seems anxious or uncomfortable during hypnosis, the first step is to ask for information. It is imperative to understand what the client feels and the cause of those feelings. A hesitant client can be reassured by saying, "Even though it may seem a little difficult at first, you can talk to me with no problem and tell me what you think and feel." For the client who appears to be unable to talk, the hypnotist may want to offer a suggestion about what is happening and await confirmation from the client.

The therapist should be prepared to discontinue a suggestion that causes apparent distress and to switch to an easier alternative suggestion or strategy. However, it is often helpful to permit or even encourage the client to ventilate feelings. As Orne (1965) noted, some clients have a need to talk about their experience before waking. Reassuring comments concerning the helpfulness of sharing feelings and "not keeping things locked up inside" can facilitate this process. Indeed, negative affect elicited by a suggestion may be either mitigated or encouraged depending on the needs of the client and the therapist's theory of psychology, therapeutic orientation, or both.

Continuing Follow-Up

Some negative reactions become apparent only after time has passed (MacHovec, 1988a). Remaining available for consultation for several days after a hypnosis session is ethical practice. It is wise to notify all clients (and experimental subjects) about the availability of continuing follow-up if a problem arises. Negative reactions that occur during the session should be discussed before the client departs in order to understand their cause and to devise a strategy to avoid future problems.

CONCLUSION

Research can contribute a great deal to the understanding of negative effects, particularly with respect to clinical populations. First, as our review suggests, survey studies have been limited by inadequate return rates and by questions about the representativeness of the therapist and client samples. Carefully done survey studies are therefore a priority.

An important caveat concerning the interpretation of the clinic-based data is that hypnosis is confounded with psychotherapy (Brentar & Lynn, 1989). In the case of hypnotherapy, the dynamics of hypnosis are superimposed on the dynamics of psychotherapy, rendering it difficult to determine whether negative effects are attributable to hypnosis, psychotherapy, nonspecific interpersonal factors, or a combination of these factors. Because negative sequelae in response to psychotherapeutic procedures have been documented (Hadley & Strupp, 1976; Smith, Glass, & Miller, 1980), it is possible that negative effects in hypnotherapy arise as a function of idiosyncratic client reactions or misapplications of the more inclusive and encompassing practice of psychotherapy. The Smith et al. (1980) meta-analysis of psychotherapy effectiveness showed that about 9% of the effect-size measures were negative; similarly, Jacobson and Edinger (1982) reported that about 5% of their patients experienced adverse effects following relaxation training. These statistics are a reasonable estimate of the frequency of negative effects during and after hypnosis. Hypnosis is neither more nor less hazardous than other psychotherapeutic procedures that are used because of their potential to influence and treat clients.

Second, it may not be prudent to assume that unanticipated or even unwanted experiences are necesarily perceived by the client as "negative." For example, the clinician would thus do well to elicit information from the client before assuming that an affect-laden experience of age regression is "negative" rather than cathartic. Nevertheless, clinicians, regardless of whether they function as hypnotists, would do well to be ever alert to potential deleterious concomitants or consequences of treatment interventions.

Third, the clinician who considers hypnosis as a treatment option should not be deterred by the idea that hypnosis poses unique or special risks to the client. That is, controlled research does not indicate that hypnosis per se is responsible for the changes commonly associated with it. Indeed, there is insufficient evidence to ascribe negative effects specifically to hypnosis, whether they arise in the context of an experiment or psychotherapy. Evidence is also lacking to suggest that hypnosis is any more stressful or anxiety provoking than other common experiences encountered by subjects or clients in psychotherapy. Nevertheless, reasonable precautions and strategies to avert or defuse negative effects should be instituted by the clinician committed to providing the most professional treatment of the client.

Brentar and Lynn (1989) have outlined a number of areas of further inquiry into negative effects during and after hypnosis. Much needs to be learned about the nature and structure of suggestions (e.g., direct vs. indirect, permissive vs. authoritative); the subjects' personality characteristics, expectancies, beliefs, and attitudes about hypnosis; and the nature of the therapeutic alliance in accounting for hypnotic and posthypnotic experiences. To ascertain whether negative effects are a function of hypnotic procedures, subjects' prehypnotic mood, physical condition (e.g., headache), and personality attributes (e.g., trait anxiety) should be evaluated. This is important because hypnotic experiences may be wrongly attributed to hypnosis rather than to a preexisting condition. The time frame and persistence of negative effects have not been adequately investigated, nor have phenomenological analyses, such as the "experiential analysis technique" (Sheehan & McConkey, 1982), been applied to negative effects. In this chapter we have elucidated the potential relevance of a number of variables (e.g., therapist training, client-subject attitude modification, preinduction talks) in reducing the frequency and severity of negative effects. Controlled clinical studies, comparable to the Coe and Ryken (1979) and Brentar, Lynn, Carlson, and Kurzhals (1992) experimental studies, are needed to study the impact of these factors, alone and in combination, on negative therapeutic effects in hypnotic and nonhypnotic contexts. The continued development and refinement of hypnotic and posthypnotic experience scales will abet the investigative process.

Because negative effects occasionally occur during or after hypnosis, the conscientious therapist must be prepared to recognize deleterious sequelae and to intervene accordingly. An awareness of the situations in which negative reactions are most likely to occur, as well as familiarity with strategies for obviating and limiting negative reactions, will allow the therapist to practice with safety and efficacy.

REFERENCES

Averback, A. (1962). Attitudes of psychiatrists to the use of hypnosis. *Journal of the American Medical Association, 180,* 917–921.

Barrett, D. (1979). The hypnotic dream: Its relation to nocturnal dreams and waking fantasies. *Journal of Abnormal Psychology, 88,* 584–591.

Brentar, J., & Lynn, S. J. (1988). "Negative" effects and hypnosis: A critical examination. *British Journal of Experimental and Clinical Hypnosis, 6,* 75–84.

Brentar, J., Lynn, S. J., & Carlson, B. (1992, August). *The Posthypnotic Experience Scale: Validity and reliability studies.* Paper presented at the 100th Annual Convention of the American Psychological Association, Washington, DC.

Brentar, J., Lynn, S. J., Carlson, B., & Kurzhals, R. (1992). Controlled research on hypnotic aftereffects: The post-hypnotic experience questionnaire. In W. Bongartz (Ed.), *Hypnosis: 175 years after Mesmer* (pp. 179–201). Konstanz, Germany: University of Konstanz Press.

Coe, W. C., & Ryken, K. (1979). Hypnosis and risks to human subjects. *American Psychologist, 34,* 673–681.

Conn, J. H. (1972). Is hypnosis really dangerous? *International Journal of Clinical and Experimental Hypnosis, 20,* 61–79.

Crawford, H. J., Hilgard, J. R., & Macdonald, H. (1982). Transient experiences following hypnotic testing and special termination procedures. *International Journal of Clinical and Experimental Hypnosis, 30,* 117–126.

Echterling, L. G., & Emmerling, D. A. (1987). Impact of stage hypnosis. *American Journal of Clinical Hypnosis, 29,* 149–154.

Faw, V., Sellers, D. J., & Wilcox, W. W. (1968). Psychopathological effects of hypnosis. *International Journal of Clinical and Experimental Hypnosis, 16,* 23–37.

Fromm, E. (1980). Values in hypnotherapy. *Psychotherapy: Theory, Research and Practice, 17,* 425–430.

Gill, M. M., & Brenman, M. (1959). *Hypnosis and related states: Psychoanalytical studies in regression.* Madison, CT: International Universities Press.

Gravitz, M. A., Mallet, J. E., Munyon, P., & Gerton, M. I. (1982). Ethical considerations in the professional applications of hypnosis. In M. Rosenbaum (Ed.), *Ethics and values in psychotherapy* (pp. 297–312). New York: Free Press.

Green, J. T. (1979). Hypnotizability and hospitalized psychotics. *International Journal of Clinical and Experimental Hypnosis, 27,* 103–108.

Haberman, M. (1987). Complications following hypnosis in a psychotic patient with sexual dysfunction treated by a lay hypnotist. *American Journal of Clinical Hypnosis, 29,* 166–170.

Hadley, S. W., & Strupp, H. H. (1976). Contemporary views of negative effects in psychotherapy: An integrated account. *Archives of General Psychiatry, 33,* 1291–1302.

Hall, J. A. (1984). Toward a psycho-structural theory: Hypnosis and the structure of dreams. *American Journal of Clinical Hypnosis, 26,* 159–165.

Hilgard, J. R. (1974). Sequelae to hypnosis. *International Journal of Clinical and Experimental Hypnosis, 22,* 281–298.

Hilgard, J. R., Hilgard, E. R., & Newman, M. R. (1961). Sequelae to hypnotic induction with special reference to earlier chemical anesthesia. *Journal of Nervous and Mental Disease, 133,* 461–478.

Jacobson, R., & Edinger, J. D. (1982). Side effects of relaxation training. *American Journal of Psychiatry, 139,* 952–953.

Janet, P. (1925). *Psychological healing: A historical and clinical study* (Vol. 1). London: Allen & Unwin.

Judd, F. K., Burrows, G. D., & Dennerstein, L. (1985). The dangers of hypnosis: A review. *Australian Journal of Clinical and Experimental Hypnosis, 13,* 1–15.

Judd, F. K., Burrows, G. D., & Dennerstein, L. (1986). Clinicians' perceptions of the adverse effects of hypnosis: A preliminary study. *Australian Journal of Clinical and Experimental Hypnosis, 14,* 49–60.

Kleinhauz, M., & Beran, B. (1984). Misuse of hypnosis: A factor in psychopathology. *American Journal of Clinical Hypnosis, 26,* 283–290.

Kleinhauz, M., & Eli, I. (1987). Potential deleterious effects of hypnosis in the clinical setting. *American Journal of Clinical Hypnosis, 29,* 155–159.

Kleinhauz, M., Dreyfuss, D. A., Beran, B., Goldberg, G., & Azikri, D. (1979). Some after-effects of stage hypnosis: A case study of psychopathological manifestations. *International Journal of Clinical and Experimental Hypnosis, 3,* 219–226.

Kluft, R. P. (1982). Varieties of hypnotic intervention in the treatment of multiple personality. *American Journal of Clinical Hypnosis, 24,* 230–240.

Kost, P. F. (1965). Dangers of hypnosis. *International Journal of Clinical and Experimental Hypnosis, 13,* 220–225.

Levitt, E. E., & Hershman, S. (1963). The clinical practice of hypnosis in the United States: A preliminary survey. *International Journal of Clinical and Experimental Hypnosis, 11,* 55–65.

Lindner, H. (1960). The shared neurosis: Hypnotist and subject. *International Journal of Clinical and Experimental Hypnosis, 7,* 61–70.

Lynn, S. J., Brentar, J., Carlson, B., Kurzhals, R., & Green, J. (1991, August). *Posthypnotic experiences: A controlled investigation.* Paper presented at the 99th Annual Convention of the American Psychological Association, San Francisco.

Lynn, S. J., & Hamel, J. (1987). *Hypnosis, age regression and "negative effects."* Unpublished manuscript, Ohio University, Athens, OH.

Lynn, S. J., Rhue, J. W., Kvaal, S., & Mare, C. (in press). Hypnosuggestive procedures in the treatment of anorexia nervosa. *Contemporary Hypnosis.*

Lynn, S. J., Weekes, J. R., & Milano, M. (1989). Reality versus suggestion: Pseudomemory in hypnotizable and simulating subjects. *Journal of Abnormal Psychology, 98,* 75–79.

MacHovec, F. J. (1986). *Hypnosis complications: Prevention and risk management.* Springfield, IL: Charles C Thomas.

MacHovec, F. J. (1987). Hypnosis complications: Six cases. *American Journal of Clinical Hypnosis, 29,* 160–165.

MacHovec, F. J. (1988a). Hypnosis complications, risk factors and prevention. *American Journal of Clinical Hypnosis, 31,* 40–49.

MacHovec, F. J. (1988b). Minimizing hypnosis risk. *Psychotherapy in Private Practice, 6,* 59–67.

Mays, D. T., & Franks, C. M. (1985). *Negative outcome in psychotherapy and what to do about it.* New York: Springer.

Meares, A. (1961). An evaluation of the dangers of medical hypnosis. *American Journal of Clinical Hypnosis, 4,* 90–97.

Miller, J. (1983). "Spontaneous" age regression: A clinical report. *American Journal of Clinical Hypnosis, 26,* 53–55.

Milne, G. (1986). Hypnotic compliance and other hazards. *Australian Journal of Clinical and Experimental Hypnosis, 14,* 15–29.

Nash, M. R., Lynn, S. J., & Stanley, S. (1984). The direct suggestion of altered mind/body perception. *American Journal of Clinical Hypnosis, 27,* 95–102.

Orne, M. T. (1965). Undesirable effects of hypnosis: The determinants and management. *International Journal of Clinical and Experimental Hypnosis, 13,* 226–237.

Overholser, J. C. (1988). Applied psychological hypnosis: Management of problematic situations. *Professional Psychology: Research and Practice, 19,* 409–415.

Rosen, H. (1960). Hypnosis: Applications and misapplications. *Journal of the American Medical Association, 172,* 683–687.

Schultz, J. (1922). *Gesundheitsschaedigungen nach hypnose* [Mental health after hypnosis]. Halle, Germany: C. Morhold.

Seitz, P. F. D. (1951). Symbolism and organ choice in conversion reactions. *Psychosomatic Medicine, 13,* 255–259.

Sheehan, P. W., & McConkey, K. M. (1982). *Hypnosis and experience: Phenomena and processes.* Hillsdale, NJ: Erlbaum.

Shor, R. E., & Orne, W. C. (1962). *The Harvard Group Scale of Hypnotic Susceptibility, Form A.* Palo Alto, CA: Consulting Psychologists Press.

Smith, M. L., Glass, G. V., & Miller, T. I. (1980). *The benefits of psychotherapy.* Baltimore, MD: Johns Hopkins University Press.

Speigel, H. (1978). *Trance and treatment.* New York: Basic Books.

Weitzenhoffer, A. M. (1957). *General techniques of hypnotism.* New York: Grune & Stratton.

Weitzenhoffer, A. M., & Hilgard, E. R. (1962). *Stanford Hypnotic Susceptibility Scale, Form C.* Palo Alto, CA: Consulting Psychologists Press.

West, L. J., & Deckert, G. H. (1965). Dangers of hypnosis. *Journal of the American Medical Association, 192,* 9–12.

Williams, G. W. (1953). Difficulty in dehypnotizing. *International Journal of Clinical and Experimental Hypnosis, 1,* 3–12.

II

MODELS OF HYPNOTHERAPY

6

PSYCHOANALYTIC AND PSYCHODYNAMIC MODELS OF HYPNOANALYSIS

MARLENE R. EISEN

There is a strong historical precedent for the use of hypnosis as a therapeutic modality. Freud studied with two early hypnosis practitioners, Charcot and Breuer, and used this art in his practice. In discussing the idealization of the object (i.e., the image of the significant person in the mind of the individual), Freud (1905/1953b) was impressed by hypnotized subjects' credulous submissiveness to the hypnotist. Comparing hypnosis to being in love, Freud pointed out that just as the loved object often stands in the place of the idealized aspect of the self, the essence of hypnosis resides in an unconscious fixation of the subject's libido to the hypnotist as an ego ideal.

Schilder and Kauders (1927/1956) agreed with Freud that hypnosis and suggestion have an erotic root. Submission to authority has an erotic–masochistic component. Subjects project their desires for magical powers onto the hypnotist and, subsequently, by the process of identification, attain those powers that they would not otherwise be able to ascribe to themselves.

Ferenczi (1965) proposed that the hypnotic relationship represents a reactivation of the Oedipus complex, with the subject standing in a child–parent relationship with the hypnotist. He differentiated between maternal (based on love) and paternal (based on fear) forms of hypnosis. In contemporary terms, maternal hypnosis would be defined as nondirective hypnosis, whereas paternal hypnosis would be defined as directive hypnosis.

These concepts are important insofar as the patient's various perceptions of the therapist (e.g., maternal or paternal figure, ego ideal, magician, and healer) represent manifestations of the cornerstone of psychoanalytic therapy: transference. In psychoanalysis, transference is thought to be a basically regressive phenomenon in which the patient's feelings, attitudes, and expectations, which were once directed at significant people in the patient's past, are projected or "transferred" onto the therapist. Transference is considered to be a fundamental tool for helping the patient (Brown & Fromm, 1986). It is in the interpretation of the meaning of the transferential relationship with the patient that conflicts are resolved and personality integration ultimately occurs. Later in this chapter I discuss transference in greater depth and present research that buttresses the claim that hypnosis potentiates transference phenomena.

PRIMARY AND SECONDARY PROCESS THOUGHT

Freud (1900/1953a) identified two distinct modes of mental functioning: primary process functioning, typical of early childhood thinking, and secondary process functioning, a more mature, cognitively based mode of thinking. The main format of primary process thinking is preverbal imagery that is highly mobile, fluid, and undifferentiated. In this mode, anything is possible, even the impossible. Logical thinking and critical, analytical abilities are dramatically reduced, if evident at all, and several ideas may be condensed into a single image. Dreams and hypnosis share this primitive, regressive mode of thinking (see Nash, 1991): the "stuff that dreams are made of." By contrast, secondary process thinking is logical and sequential. It functions by way of language rather than images, and it is reality oriented, guided by the critical and analytical functions of the ego.

Although primary process thinking precedes secondary process thinking in the developmental sequence, it does not disappear with age. Instead, it takes other forms, including imagery and the illogical characteristics of playful activities, jokes, and dreams that persist through adulthood. Furthermore, according to Brown and Fromm (1986), the full range of mental experience, from strictly reality-oriented cognition to the more fluid and undifferentiated primary process thought, continue to interact in adulthood. Various states of consciousness can be described as existing on a continuum from primary to secondary process as one moves from fantasy to reality;

from nocturnal dreams to full wakefulness; and from unfocused, free-floating attention to focused attention.

Even in adulthood, play and creativity (mind play) use regression in service of the ego, a rich reservoir that hypnosis taps for healing purposes. It was Hartmann (1936/1958) who first referred to *adaptive regression*. This concept was derived from his belief that the ego and id were relatively autonomous, a hypothesis that established the theoretical base for ego psychological psychotherapy. Kris (1934/1952) termed the same process *regression in the service of the ego* and described how the creative artist experiences a more or less intentional return to or resumption of irrational, archaic modes of imagination, thought, and sensibility. Fenichel (1945) described how adaptive regression enables the hypnotist to take over the function of the patient's superego and even parts of the ego, thus allowing for regression within a safe milieu.

Nash (1987) suggested that this form of regression common to hypnosis is topological rather than temporal (i.e., patients do not exhibit truly childlike behavior during hypnosis) and is related to alternative modes of mature thought rather than to immature thought patterns. According to Loewald (1981)

> regression in service of the ego is not simply a means for increased ability to make the irrational rational, for extending the range of rationality. It frees the ego from the excessive domination of rationality and increases the dimensions and range, not of rationality, but of the ego as an organization encompassing the totality of human experience, including the irrational. (p. 40)

ACTIVITY, PASSIVITY, AND RECEPTIVITY LEVELS OF EGO FUNCTION

The psychoanalytic theory of ego activity and passivity was introduced by Rapaport (1953/1967) and Hart (1961) and was extended by Fromm (1972). The concept of ego receptivity was developed by Deikman (1971) and was discussed in the context of hypnosis by Fromm and Shor (1979). The ego is active or autonomous when the individual can make an ego-syntonic choice (i.e., a choice that is consciously or implicitly consistent with the individual's goals and objectives). It is passive when the person is overwhelmed by instinctual drives or demands from the environment or superego. Ego activity and passivity are related to coping. The ego may cope in a masterful or defensive mode. In hypnotherapy, ego activity may be represented by resistance or by the patient's countertherapeutic self-suggestions taking precedence over the therapist's suggestions (Fromm & Shor, 1979). Ego passivity manifests itself when the patient feels overwhelmed by the therapist or by the perceived demand characteristics of the therapeutic situation. When this occurs, the results are usually ego dystonic and associated with subjective discomfort.

In ego receptivity, critical judgments, a strict adherence to the demands of reality, and active, goal-oriented thinking are minimal. Receptive in this manner, patients experience a free-flowing stream of consciousness characterized by the emergence of unconscious and preconscious material. In hypnotherapy the patient becomes more receptive both to the therapist's suggestions and to a clearer awareness of the internal flow of images and thoughts. This mode in which experience is organized around taking in and letting things happen, can be contrasted with the ego-active mode in which the individual makes things happen and actively manipulates the environment.

A fourth mode of ego function, often reported in certain forms of meditation, is ego inactivity. The individual reports experiencing nothing and coming away from the experience refreshed and relaxed. Meares (1960), working with severely ill patients in Australia, found that a nonverbal induction of a deep state of calm had a remarkably curative effect on many patients. Of course, much more research needs to be done in the area of defining and differentiating between the different levels of ego function in hypnotic and nonhypnotic situations.

TRANCE DEPTH AS A DIMENSION OF THERAPY

The hypnotic experience can be characterized by the capacity to sustain a state of attentive, receptive, intensely focused concentration with diminished peripheral awareness. In this chapter I refer to this state as *trance*, which fluctuates on a continuum between focal and peripheral awareness (H. Spiegel & Spiegel, 1978). The degree to which peripheral awareness, or general reality orientation, fades in relation to focused attention determines trance depth.

Although there is no direct correlation between the depth of trance and the degree of primary process thought, in general it has been found that the deeper the altered state of consciousness, the more likely one is to experience vivid, often free-floating attention; diminished critical thought; and increased ego receptivity (Fromm & Kahn, 1990). Under these circumstances, cognition is less likely to be reality oriented and more likely to be idiosyncratic or influenced by suggestions from a strong environmental stimulus (i.e., the therapist).

For the most part, the patient's depth of trance is not a crucial issue in hypnotherapy. A light or moderate trance is sufficient to achieve the major goals of psychodynamic hypnotherapy: uncovering, reframing, and reintegrating repressed or disowned aspects of the personality. If the trance is not deep, the patient is more likely to be able to interact verbally with the therapist. Many patients who go into deep trance states have difficulty with verbal communications, and the therapist may need to resort to ideo-motor signaling. This is not an insurmountable problem, but if the patient can carry on a dialogue with either the therapist or other ego states within the self (i.e., the "inner child"), the work of therapy proceeds much more satisfactorily.

The traditional psychoanalytic goals of uncovering of drives and de-fenses, working through affects, and achieving new levels of personality integration can be effectively realized by way of psychodynamic hypno-therapy or hypnoanalysis. The characteristics of hypnosis discussed in this section—the preponderance of primary process thinking stimulated by regression in the service of the ego and the patient's receptivity to the emerging mental representations of neurotic defenses and areas of conflict—facilitate achieving these goals quickly and effectively. Hypnosis enhances the process of uncovering dynamically relevant material by stimulating increased awareness of symbolic processes, memories, and affective states (Nash, 1987). Hypnosis can also provide opportunities for cognitive and perceptual changes that lead to new opportunities for insight and conflict resolution (Frankel, 1976). In the next section I discuss the use of hypnosis as a tool in the clinical setting and how its distinctive qualities facilitate and enrich the therapeutic experience.

DOUBLE CONSCIOUSNESS: THE PARTICIPATING AND OBSERVING EGO

E. R. Hilgard (1977), Fromm and Shor (1979), and others have distinguished between two levels of ego function common to the hypnotic experience: (a) the "participating ego," which relinquishes the critical func-tion (reality testing) to the control of the hypnotist or to self-directives in self-hypnosis; and (b) "the observing ego," which maintains the critical function and monitors the level of involvement of the participating ego. Nash (1991) referred to this phenomenon as an experienced separation between intent to comply and awareness of that intent.

Hypnotized subjects are not automatons, and they clearly demonstrate will and volition in refusing to comply with ego-dystonic suggestions (Lynn, Rhue, & Weekes, 1990). It is this capacity of the observing ego or "hidden observer" (the volitional aspect) that makes the hypnotic experience feel safe enough to allow the ego to move into a more regressed state. It is also the hidden observer that is able to interpret the symbolic representations of imagery and dreams because of its access to information dissociated from or split off from conscious experience (E. R. Hilgard, 1973, 1974).

HOMEOSTASIS: ADAPTIVE SYNCHRONY

The human being constantly strives for a state of adaptive synchrony, or homeostasis in time and space. According to Restak (1979), the brain has the primary responsibility for maintaining itself and the body; it succeeds in this task largely through an automatic set of regulating mechanisms that serve to maintain body integrity. Restak referred to this process as a "feedback loop."

This feedback loop process can be viewed from a psychodynamic perspective. In wakeful states of consciousness, the ego is cognizant of messages from both the id and the environment, which it processes, evaluates, and responds to on the basis of relevance, urgency, or both. During waking moments, the senses are busy gathering volumes of information from the environment, whereas physical and emotional states are pervasive and inescapable. The mind selects environmental features that are the most salient (i.e., most likely to reduce physical and emotional tension levels and attain balance or homeostasis).

When environmental information is restricted, as in the trance state, mental or physical inner processes take precedence. The perception of the environment is restructured through internal, primary process functioning. Becoming involved in a TV show, a book, music, deep breathing, or any activity in which the focus of attention is so intense that elements of the environment fade or are gated out of awareness alters customary cognitive processing.

Fenichel (1945) declared that hypnosis represents a nostalgic reversion to the phase of life when "passive–receptive" mastery represented the primary means of coping with the world. Security was achieved by participating in or encompassing a greater unit, the all-powerful parent. The hypnotist comes to represent the powerful parent who both guides and protects, and who promises or is believed to promise, surcease from pain or displeasure. It often becomes apparent that the patient's greatest satisfaction derives from the giving over of the troubled aspects of self to the powerful, well-controlled adult in a permissive setting.

Hypnosis satisfies that universal infantile core in each person that longs for wholesale abdication of his or her usual powers and responsibilities (Gill & Brenman, 1959). In my experience, "good hypnotic subjects" may present with intense unconscious needs to be both passive and aggressively demanding, much like the infant. In everyday life these people relentlessly defend against such feelings, both through denial and reaction formation, to such an extent that the manifest personality is frequently that of a self-sufficient "high achiever."

TRANCE AND AFFECT

Clinical experience suggests that during hypnosis, intense absorption and involvement leads to much greater affect intensity, particularly in highly hypnotizable subjects. Changes in the nature and quality of affect such as outbursts of weeping, intense expressions of rage, anxiety, fear, and despair are not uncommon. It is as if the trance state itself represents a generalized amplification of affect (Brown & Fromm, 1986). A dramatic aspect of the subject's affective response is the abruptness with which it can be turned off when trance is terminated.

THE "ILLOGIC" OF TRANCE LOGIC

Because the ego releases the critical function in hypnotic trance and regresses to more primary thought processes, subjects can visualize anger in concrete form and speak to it or act on it without regard for the irrationality of the act. For example, they can simultaneously visualize the angry "self" sitting in one place and the contented self in another place, representing different affective states. Subjects in a trance state may find nothing unusual about visualizing someone sitting beside them and also standing across the room. This phenomenon has been referred to as "trance logic" (Orne, 1959).

NURTURING IMAGES: THE INNER CHILD

A powerful image used to reinforce self-nurturing is the adult caring for his or her inner child. Typically, the patient spontaneously evokes in the trance the image of himself or herself as a sad, lonely little child. The therapist can suggest that the adult patient provide the child with the kind of parenting the child needs and desires. Patients often use this image to their advantage in self-hypnosis, becoming self-nurturing, giving the inner child loving, accepting messages (Eisen & Fromm, 1983). Nurtured until it becomes more content, the child ego state can then experience joy and liberate creativity. Of course, the caring and accepting therapist serves as a model for such patient behavior.

THE USE OF DREAMS

Using dreams in hypnoanalysis provides valuable insights. When a patient brings in dream material, the hypnotherapist can suggest that the patient reexperience the dream in trance, this time with a clear understanding of the meaning of the images. Dreams may also be induced in the heterohypnotic hour. The focus can be on a particular conflict or issue raised in therapy. The patient may be encouraged to redream the dream once or several times with different, perhaps more effective, resolutions.

A posthypnotic suggestion that the patient will have dreams that foster understanding and problem resolution and that these dreams will be readily recalled and comprehended can stimulate a spate of dreaming, as can recording dreams in a journal.

DEFENSES AND RESISTANCES

Interpretation of defenses and resistances should be handled carefully, gently, and respectfully. Defenses should not be attacked prematurely but need to be acknowledged and understood in the context of their unique and personal meaning. Resistance also serves an adaptive function that must be understood and respected.

A common form of resistance in hypnoanalysis is refusal to go into a trance. Rather than interpreting this maneuver as a resistance, the therapist would do well to note the issues being worked with at the time and find different or safer ways of approaching the subject, or simply defer exploring the particular topic to a more appropriate time. Resistance can also be manifested when a patient's communications in relation to a particular issue are ambiguous. Interpreting this communication style as resistance can, on occasion, be helpful and move the therapy forward. Finally, there are occasions when acknowledging the resistance will be sufficient to overcome it.

TRANSFERENCE

Transference is a term that indicates the patient's distorted perceptions, feelings, or behaviors toward the therapist, who comes to represent a significant figure from childhood such as a parent or sibling. When there is a positive transference, the therapist is loved and idealized. However, when the transference is negative, the therapist is hated or feared. Hypnosis intensifies transference, bringing conflicts and repressed affects associated with internal representations into focus more rapidly and intensely.

Most frequently, three types of neurotic transferences are encountered. Infantile dependency transferences are the most common in hypnotherapy, especially at the beginning of treatment, when the patient comes to be taken care of and wants the therapist to solve all of the patient's problems for him or her. Like the small child, the patient hopes that the therapist is omniscient, possessing the healing power of the perfect parent. Often, significant others and referring professionals share this unrealistic fantasy or wish. Not infrequently, magical thinking accompanies this positive transference. For example, one patient may say, "I carry your voice and the image of your couch, and I feel the healing power."

Transferences can also take the form of seduction or competition. A patient who falsely accuses the therapist of attempting to seduce him or her may actually be acting out an old fantasy of wishing to be seduced by the opposite-sex parent. A patient's attempt to outdo or to compete with the therapist, rooted in early sibling rivalry, may be expressed by statements such as, "I get much better imagery in self-hypnosis," or by regaling the therapist with stories of personal successes while finding fault with the current therapy or therapist.

Using such transferential feelings may be more effective than interpreting them. For instance, patients who attempt to outshine the therapist can be praised for their excellent abilities. It can be demonstrated that outdoing is not destroying and that such special abilities allow for greater success in using trance states.

There are also specific transference reactions related to idiosyncratic experiences. For example, a patient whose analyst had committed suicide wanted to use trance work but feared it would increase her dependence on the current therapist, reenacting her great loss when the analyst on whom she had become so dependent abandoned her. The former analyst had assured her that he would not die after having made a previous attempt. Therefore, even if her current therapist said she was not planning to kill herself it would do little to relieve the patient's distress. Instead, her fears of dependency were acknowledged, and the ways in which this therapist was different from the former one were consistently pointed out.

EGO STATES: RELEVANCE IN TREATMENT

Watkins and Watkins (1981) have modified and expanded the ego-state theories of Federn (1952) and Weiss (1952), who described a continuum of permeability and flexibility of ego-state boundaries within each individual. Healthy ego states with fluid boundaries occur in everyday life as people move from one situational context or role to another (e.g., student, daughter, date). As ego-state boundaries become more rigid and impermeable, they become increasingly maladaptive until, at the opposite end of the continuum, there are dissociative states, manifesting in some cases as multiple personality disorders.

When significant figures are internalized or acknowledged in the form of consistent, ongoing mental representations, they are originally recognized as "not self" or as "other." In object relations theory, they are referred to as "objects." Eventually, the individual may identify so strongly with this internalized other that it begins to feel like part of the "self" and ultimately to become part of the self.

The concepts of "object" and "self" ego states have important implications for understanding hypnosis and for dealing with transferences (Watkins & Watkins, 1990). Hypnosis can be used to manipulate the patient's perceptions of ego states. For example, during hypnosis, suggestions can be given for the "frightened child" ego state to be protected by the "competent adult" ego state. In dealing with transference, it is important to understand that it may not be the "whole patient" who has projected the abusing parental figure onto the therapist but a particular ego state that has done so, which represents a relatively vulnerable fragment of the whole.

In working with ego states, it is important not to cast out those that appear to be flawed. They are, after all, still part of the self, often internalizations of significant others. Rather, these "shadow selves" need to be acknowledged and integrated (Watkins & Watkins, 1979).

NARCISSISTIC AND BORDERLINE PATIENTS

Narcissistic patients respond strongly to therapists' failures of empathy. The mildly narcissistic may express anger or disappointment to the therapist during the therapy hour. By contrast, the highly narcissistic patient reacts with rage and disillusionment by missing appointments, making suicide threats or gestures, or making midnight phone calls to the therapist. In such instances, the hypnoanalyst must actively play the role of the good parent, fulfilling the hitherto unmet needs of the patient for admiration and unconditional positive regard.

Borderline patients are unable to form stable self- and object transferences. Instead, the transference is characterized by boundary diffusion and splitting, panic states, and transient loss of self- and object representations. To counter these tendencies, the therapist must provide a "holding environment" (Winnicott, 1975). The environment must be safe, all nurturing, and all accepting, with clear boundaries delineated. Distinctions must be made between reality and fantasy as a step toward integration. First, however, it may be necessary for the therapist to join the patient in a fantasy world, together exploring the meaning of the patient's inner life. The therapist becomes an internalized good object by being all giving within the context of firm limits. It is in the relationship with the therapist that the patient begins to build an integrated sense of self.

In working with borderline patients, the value of hypnosis rests with the power of imagery to provide "as if" situations or imaginative scenarios, in which the patient can "try out" different ways of being and relating to others. Much like the sociodramatic play of young children, hypnosis can be used by borderline patients to regress to an early stage of life when psychological development was truncated and to begin to build a new, healthier personality structure.

COUNTERTRANSFERENCE

When an attitude or behavior on the patient's part calls forth feelings in the therapist that are not appropriate to the therapeutic relationship, this is referred to as *countertransference*. Borderline patients are particularly likely to evoke intense feelings because of their insatiable demands on the therapist's time and attention. Traumatized patients' stories of their horrific past may provoke countertransference feelings, whereas patients' problems that trigger unresolved issues from the therapist's past may also engender countertransference reactions.

It is important for the therapist to recognize countertransference issues so that they do not contaminate the therapeutic alliance. When therapists recognize that they may be acting out feelings on the basis of countertransference (i.e., forgetting appointments with a particular patient, being late, using up time on superficial issues to avoid the hypnotic work), it is a good idea to seek consultation. If the relationship with the patient is resilient enough, direct discussion may prove to be the most beneficial.

HYPNOANALYTIC TECHNIQUES

Hypnotic techniques particularly suited to hypnoanalysis include age regression for tracing early developmental stages of personality organization, for identifying life themes, and for recovery of repressed memories and affects. Metaphors, automatic writing or drawing, and guided and spontaneous imagery can all be used to access emotional states and personal myths and to resolve emotional traumata. Hypnosis can be used to stimulate dissociation of the observing ego from the participating ego (Fromm & Shor, 1979), to integrate dissociated ego states (Watkins & Watkins, 1979), and to differentiate the body self from the mind self to facilitate healing (Eisen, 1990).

The purpose of hypnoanalysis is to help the patient achieve insight, conflict resolution, and mastery (Fromm, 1992). Whereas symbolic fantasy or imagery can help uncover repressed material, reality testing, fantasy, or imagery rehearsal techniques can help integrate new insights into novel behavior patterns. Working with a supportive therapist who promotes insight, the patient can safely practice different coping strategies and visualize the successful implementation of one or another. Regressing into the inner world of fantasy and practicing more successful adaptations allows the patient to return to a state of greater active consciousness feeling stronger and more competent.

Some tools of hypnotherapy, in particular imagery and primary process thought, give patients a creative way to use their inner potential for problem solving and growth. Both fantastic imagery and reality-based imagery can be used in treatment to access the inner world of the mind. Often, the ritual of trance, the "excuse" of the altered state, facilitates the patient's adaptive regression.

In hypnoanalysis, the "ego ideal" can be used to help the patient to identify with the healthier, stronger parts of the self. The therapist can suggest the presence of a strong, positive figure that has achieved what the patient wants to achieve and with whom the patient can have a dialogue. This can be done by having the patient imagine a split screen, or a couch with the "self" at one end and the "ideal self" at the other end. As they interact, the two "selves" can come closer together and finally meld into one. The therapist can then suggest that the patient look out at the world through the eyes of the ideal, or competent, self.

THE HEALER WITHIN

The therapist can suggest that a "spirit guide" or "inner healer" lives in the quiet, calm center of the mind and knows all that the patient needs to know about himself or herself and all that can be known about human experience. For cancer patients this inner spirit is a healer. For others, it becomes a creative force to unblock higher functioning or a good mother from a previous life who can provide warmth and nurturing. Each patient finds the image needed to promote healing. This power within the self, like the ego ideal, can be an excellent source of mastery and fuels a sense of personal power. It mitigates against the helpless feeling engendered by the vulnerability of serious illness.

CASE MATERIAL

A number of hypnotic techniques have been described, and various issues germane to hypnotherapy have been discussed. Case material provides another dimension to illuminate and understand the concepts presented in the previous discussion of therapeutic modalities.

Healing Images: The Mask

My discussion indicates that hypnosis can promote primary process thinking that can be used to advantage in hypnoanalysis. Certain images have a historical precedent, a mythic power to evoke intense affective states. One such image is the "mask." I begin with two cases in which the mask became a healing metaphor.

The first is a narcissistic patient who feared self-exploration but also sought it out with great intensity (Eisen & Fromm, 1983). He had created a "living myth" for himself comprised of a perfect family, a loving wife, two beautiful, accomplished children, and a successful career. In truth, he avoided all sexual contact with his wife, his daughter was showing signs of becoming anorexic at age 11, the son was withdrawn and depressed at age 5, and the patient was having difficulties with his job. He came into hypnotherapy because of persistent severe headaches and insisted that this was his only problem.

In a trance, this patient felt compelled to create strong images of power. He envisioned himself as an armored knight on a great horse and used this image in hypnotherapy and also in self-hypnotic episodes at home. As he became more comfortable with his capacity for self-soothing through hypnosis and his headaches abated, he was given the suggestion that perhaps he was wearing a mask that he could remove when he was ready. It took some months before he could risk removing the mask, which had eventually expanded to cover his whole body. What he found behind the mask was not an empty shell as he had feared but a humanly flawed yet acceptable self, with some ambivalence about his sexual orientation.

The second patient was the healthier of twin girls who felt that she had been "punished" by her parents because of her crippled sister. She came into therapy to deal with profuse sweating under her arms that was a constant source of embarrassment. She was always fearful that she would not perform well enough to please her parents, her teachers, and her employers.

Once she learned to use self-hypnosis to control her tension and sweating, she was able to use her vivid imagination to work on more dynamic issues. In imagery she found herself trapped behind a masklike gate. Sitting on a stool, she manipulated strings that allowed the mask to maintain adultlike features. Behind her on a hill, a castle full of treasure beckoned. Once she could accept her "childlike" need to engage in spontaneous activities without feeling she would be punished, she was able to drop the strings, destroying the mask of adulthood (the false self), and to let her whole being respond to the "treasures" life offered. Note that she not only hid behind the mask of adulthood but distanced herself from it. As a gate, it not only protected her but kept the world out. When she could acknowledge the child within (her dependency needs) she could become her true adult self.

Ego States: The Inner Child and The Nurturing Adult

Hypnosis not only provides ample opportunities to use adaptive regression and primary process thinking to advantage, but it also provides a context for using metaphors relevant to altering the relation between and among the patient's ego states and promoting personal integration. For instance, the adult who nurtures the child self, or inner child, is a powerful metaphor. It gives the patient permission to acknowledge the needy, dependent part of the self.

A patient who needed to give up smoking for health reasons but found herself "sneaking" cigarettes whenever she could was enraged with herself. A tough professional woman who lived alone, she began questioning her mental stability when she experienced a childlike glee each time she "got away with" another quick puff. When she was given the suggestion that her adult self begin a dialogue with her child self, she found that the little girl within felt unacknowledged. "She," the child, needed to have some fun in this woman's demanding, superresponsible life. Smoking became the "child's" outlet. When this woman began actively acknowledging this "little kid" ("My friends think I'm nuts, but my nephews love it!") and finding other ways to "play," it was relatively easy for her to decrease and finally give up the cigarettes.

Hypnotic Dreams

When dreams are reexperienced in trance, the results can be therapeutically powerful. A devoutly religious cancer patient dreamed of a surgical amphitheater with many patients lying on tables. An audience sat in a surrounding chamber behind windows. Three hooded figures stood silently at the door. Calm pervaded the scene. He realized that all the patients were, in fact, himself. The hooded figures (his brother-in-law, a priest, and the surgeon) and the patient himself embodied the cornerstones of his life (family, church, and his own responsibility), along with the professional healer. He "knew" that with this structure firmly in place the surgery would be successful. There was no place for death in his vision, although he was aware that death lurked just beyond. His initial fear of looking under the hoods was that one of them would be death itself.

A male victim of paternal incest had a recurrent dream that he lived in a strange, scary house that his father had built. He wandered through that house trying to "find his way," seeking help from his father who remained hidden. Several months into therapy, he dreamed that he was in a house that he was building himself. It was not finished yet, but it felt safe and was brightly lit. His wife and friends were helping him with the construction.

In the redreaming he saw this as a metaphor for working on himself, with help from others. He realized that the old dream represented his hopeless efforts as an adult to connect with his abusive, abandoning father and to find a safe home or haven. His new dream symbolized his efforts to construct a healthier self in a safer world with the help of people he could trust and depend on.

Defenses and Resistances

Interpretation of defenses and resistances is an important aspect of hypnoanalysis. Interpretation should be handled carefully, gently, and respectfully. Defenses should not be broken down prematurely. A patient suffering from global amnesia (Eisen, 1989) had seen two psychiatrists prior to her current therapy. Both had focused on reviving memories, as her mother had demanded. Terrified of what this had felt like, she entered therapy with fear and trepidation. It was clear that she was using enormous energy to maintain the "not knowing" because her ego was too fragile to "know" the "unknowable."

First, my patient and I worked with images to build ego strength. The consistent message was, "You will begin to know what you need to know when you are ready to know." With this fragile patient each step brought new resistances. As her memories began to emerge, she fled periodically into not knowing, fearful that she would be deluged with a flood of nightmare images. Providing her with the image of a large book on a pedestal with a lock on it, and pictures as well as words, allowed her to titrate her awareness at her own pace. She could unlock the book, glance briefly at a picture, or focus on reading a page of words. It took more than a year for memories to return with any historical validity, by which time she was ready to let down her defensive walls and return to the world.

An interesting aftermath of this case is that this woman, healthy now and living a fully functional life, went back to school and became a librarian. The image of a book, her own personal history, brought her back to life, and she now finds great satisfaction in encouraging others to read.

I noted earlier that a common form of resistance in hypnoanalysis is refusal to go into a trance. This is the most typical of patients who want to explore past trauma but have some ambivalence about reliving painful and hitherto repressed experiences. An incest victim, terrified of what would be revealed in the trance, avoided the hypnosis she had originally requested by talking excessively from the moment she entered the office. It was suggested that she allow herself to just relax at home and let her left hand (not her writing hand) write freely, perhaps a short story, poem, or thoughts. She appeared at the following session with her writing—a frightening story of incest and cult abuse. Horrified by what had surfaced, she was now willing to work with trance states. Her argument was, "At least in trance I know what's coming, and I am not alone!"

This patient often uses trance states to activate her creativity and then writes poems and stories that reflect her affective states. She has joined a computer poetry group and shares her poems with others whom she will never meet in person yet who are supportive and encouraging. Through this long-distance sharing, she is learning to trust people again.

Narcissistic patients find creative ways to respond to what they perceive as "failure of empathy" on the part of the therapist. A young woman came for therapy because she felt a sense of isolation even though she was seemingly well accepted in the academic program she was pursuing. She identified herself as the adult child of alcoholic parents. She was the only girl in a large Irish Catholic family and was the family caretaker. She kept a journal beautifully detailed in calligraphy. In it she recorded her anger and disappointment as well as her idealizations in pictures, prose, and poetry, which she shared regularly with her therapist.

Initially, the primary theme was idealization of the therapist. With the inevitable failures of empathy came anger and despair. As therapy progressed her responses became more benign. Recognizing her transference issues she wrote of the therapist, "She reminded me of my mother today, sitting there looking smug and self righteous . . . but of course she isn't my mother." Eventually, this young woman was able to separate herself from her family and develop a loving relationship with a mentoring older woman. She has found success and satisfaction in her work and is growing more comfortable with a broader range of social relationships.

A woman diagnosed as suffering from a borderline personality disorder had difficulty recognizing when her feelings were "real" and when they were "made up." She had been hospitalized several times in the past and was in an outpatient program at a local hospital when we started working together. She had had numerous jobs that included actress, waitress, computer analyst, and boutique salesperson. She did each job well initially, then became obsessively immersed in the work. She was unable to leave at night when the job was over, but she was also unable to get herself together to arrive at work at the appropriate time. Eventually, she lost each job. She was also totally obsessed about the workings of her body and harbored a pervasive feeling that others were trying to control her, notably her mother or anyone she worked for.

One of our first tasks in working together was to give her a sense of her autonomy in the therapeutic alliance. Because she felt that only her physical sensations were real, we started with that awareness, using ideomotor actions. She was free to ask for exactly what she needed in the experience of hypnosis, which she did before the trance was induced. Some days she wanted to breathe and stretch, and other days she wanted a hand on her forehead or her solar plexus applying light, rhythmic pressure. Eventually, she asked for more complex body work in the trance, asking for the therapist to pull her arms up or press down on her shoulders, during which violent feelings of anger, fear, and grief emerged in deeply regressed form. She kicked and pounded and screamed blood-curdling screams, rolling up in a fetal position.

She dissociated these feeling states to a little girl aged 5. When this little girl state became more firmly established, she began taking over the therapy sessions. She and the therapist together developed outrageous stories of attack rabbits and protective armor while the patient was in the trance, with humor occasionally replacing the negative feelings. The "little girl" and the "adult" sometimes competed for the therapist's attention, often in the form of demands for more. The patient, whose financial resources were extremely limited, began to complain about having to pay for her sessions, claiming that if the therapist really cared for her this would not be an issue. The therapist firmly maintained boundaries and insisted on regular but much reduced payments.

Slowly, this previously semifunctional patient became more adept at relationships. She has been able to live independently for about 1½ years and has not had to be hospitalized since therapy began. She is aware of her limitations but is also learning to capitalize on her strengths. She is now working for her mother, using her computer skills to organize her mother's business, working on her own time schedule, and, because her mother had recently become ill, assuming caretaking functions she never thought herself capable of.

She has come to recognize and differentiate the real and the unreal. Fearing both the loss of self in the other and abandonment by the much-needed other, this woman has learned that she can control the level of intimacy in a relationship without losing herself or the other (the therapist). She can become angry without being abandoned or destructive and be her damaged child self without relinquishing her fragile adult self. Doing this through hypnosis also gives her a feeling for her power to use her mind and control her world in a self-guided way.

The Healer Within

For certain patients, getting in touch with an internal spirit guide, or healer within, constitutes a powerful symbol. A bright, creative artist—a weaver—was going through chemotherapy for breast cancer. Determined not to experience debilitating side effects, she needed a way to take control and therefore chose hypnosis. An excellent, highly motivated subject, she quickly got in touch with her inner spirit guide (the original suggestion by the therapist was that there may be a wise inner spirit who lives in the quiet place in the center of her mind). Her spirit guide was an elderly Indian woman, a healer and a weaver, who not only helped her remain symptom-free during the full course of chemotherapy but imparted ancient weaving skills. The patient's skills improved greatly, her work is now enthusiastically sought by collectors, and she feels healed in body and in spirit.

Transference

Positive transference can be an important ally in the healing process, which sometimes takes an unexpected form. The fact that the patient views the therapist as the good parent with magical abilities may be a logical extension of the fact that hypnosis (and psychotherapy) has an aura of mystery surrounding it.

One woman consulted me in the midst of a long analysis for the amelioration of a specific symptom. It soon became clear that she was using her male analyst and me as surrogate parents to work through unresolved issues. On occasion, she would attempt to manipulate the feelings of one therapist against the other, watching carefully for a response. After 18 months of hypnotherapy, during which time the problem for which she sought hypnotherapy was alleviated, she and I agreed that our work together was completed. She spent several weeks working through termination. In the end, she reported that she could tell me and her mother (who had died several years before) goodbye and move on. Her mother had never given her permission to leave, as I had, but our parting also made it possible for her to see herself as an adult separate from her mother. In her rich trance fantasies, she was always surrounded by three protective figures: her analyst, me, and her husband, in that order. Eventually, her husband took over the protecting role in her fantasies, and the therapists faded into the background. A favorable outcome of therapy was a closer, more spontaneous relationship with her husband and the final termination of her 20-year analysis.

These cases exemplify some of the seminal issues dealt with in psychodynamic hypnotherapy. One can see the broad diversity in the type of patient, in the form the therapy takes, and in the kind of therapeutic relationship established. The one common theme is the ultimate goal: autonomy for the patient, the sense that healing comes from within so that when therapy is terminated, the individual leaves with a strong belief in the power of the internal healer, the spirit of the self.

RESEARCH AND APPRAISAL

Psychoanalysis and psychodynamic therapy are rich clinical traditions. In recent years, research inspired by these traditions has made valuable contributions to understanding psychoanalytic and ego psychology constructs as they pertain to the hypnotic situation.

Psychoanalytic and psychodynamic theorists (e.g., Fromm, 1992; Gill & Brenman, 1959; Nash, 1991, 1992) are in agreement that "regression in service of the ego" is a central psychotherapeutic mechanism that is intimately related to manifestations of primary process thinking in hypnotic and nonhypnotic contexts. One interesting question is, "What is the nature of the regression that occurs in hypnosis?"

On the basis of a literature review of more than 100 studies, Nash (1987) concluded that hypnotized subjects neither truly function in a childlike manner nor do they literally relive childhood experiences in response to suggestions for age regression. Instead of a literal regression, what occurs is a topographic regression that has the following characteristics: an increase in primary process material, the experience of nonvolition, unusual body sensations, more spontaneous and intense emotion, and the tendency to displace core attributes of important others onto the hypnotist and to be receptive to inner and outer experience. These hypnotized features of topographic regression constitute a useful framework of psychoanalytically derived hypotheses.

There is a great deal of support for the idea that during hypnosis, there is an increased availability of primary process thinking. Research indicates that fantasy, imagery, and imaginative involvement are modestly correlated with hypnotizability (see J. R. Hilgard, 1970; Kirsch & Council, 1992; Lynn and Rhue, 1988; Roche & McConkey, 1990), although the relationship may be partly moderated by expectations and situational influences (see Kirsch & Council, 1992). However, several studies (Hammer, Walker, & Diment, 1978; Wiseman & Reyher, 1973) have suggested that increased primary process mentation cannot be fully accounted for in terms of compliance with role demands.

Consistent with the idea that primary process thought is a frequent accompaniment of certain altered states of consciousness, Fromm and Kahn's (1990) research has shown that imagery is a prominent characteristic of self-hypnosis as well as heterohypnosis. This research also indicated that the more spontaneous, self-actualized, and open to internal impulses the subject is, the more likely he or she is to have a rich, satisfying hypnotic experience. A particularly fascinating aspect of this study was an exploration of journals kept by self-hypnosis subjects, which dramatized the impact of personality characteristics on the nature of the self-hypnotic experience for each individual. Additional studies are needed to determine whether the changes in cognitive processing during hypnosis and self-hypnosis are attributable to specific or unique characteristics of hypnosis rather than to general concomitants of hypnotic suggestions for eye closure and relaxation, for example.

Research comparing hypnotic and nonhypnotic control groups is important in evaluating several other psychoanalytic hypotheses. Consistent with Fromm's (1992) view of "ego receptivity," a great deal of research (see Lynn et al., 1990) supports the hypothesis that many hypnotized subjects relinquish a consciously directed, task-oriented mode of ego functioning during hypnosis. Instead, they respond to the tacit demands of the hypnotic situation and experience suggestion-related movements, for example, as having an effortless, automatic, and involuntary quality.

Although hypnotized subjects often report that their responses are involuntary occurrences rather than goal-directed actions, many *nonhypnotized* subjects who receive passively worded suggestions with imagery that encourages them to attribute their responses to an external agency (e.g., "your hand will rise higher and higher, lift right off the resting surface as the balloons that are attached to that wrist of yours lift it higher and higher") also report that their responses are involuntary (see Lynn & Sivec, 1992, for a review). This implies that the suggestions that subjects receive, along with their interpretation of the suggestions that are administered, play an important role in how subjects come to experience hypnosis. Of course, this by no means disqualifies the psychoanalytic hypothesis; it simply suggests that a variety of stimulus conditions and situational factors may be involved in instigating primary process thinking and automatized experiences associated with the topographic regression hypothesized by psychoanalytic theorists.

Research (see Brentar & Lynn, 1989, for a review; Crawford, Hilgard, & Macdonald, 1982) is generally supportive of the psychoanalytic hypothesis that hypnosis results in shifts in body experience from the baseline of body awareness during mundane task-oriented activities and cognitive processes. However, several experimental studies (Brentar, Lynn, Carlson, Kurzhals, & Green, 1992; Kirsch, Mobayed, Council, & Kenny, 1990) have shown that hypnotized subjects' subjective experiences, including bodily experiences, cannot be reliably distinguished from nonhypnotized subjects who are relaxed, asked to imagine suggested activities, or invited to focus on body parts that parallel the focus of hypnotic suggestions. To provide a more definitive answer to the question of whether body experience is a marker of topographic regression, studies in clinical contexts in which regressive experiences are *cultivated* are required.

Although hypnotized subjects report a wide variety of altered body and perceptual experiences (Brentar & Lynn, 1989; Gill & Brenman, 1959), the evidence is mixed regarding the ability of hypnosis to enhance affect. Whereas several studies (Nash, Johnson, & Tipton, 1979; Nash, Lynn, Stanley, Frauman, & Rhue, 1985) have shown that age-regressed subjects have greater access to intense emotions than simulating control subjects, other studies have shown that simulating subjects can mimic the nature (Bryant & McConkey, 1989) and intensity (Mare, Lynn, Kvaal, & Segal, 1992) of hypnotized subjects' emotions. Additional studies with subtle measures conducive to eliciting affect will be necessary to delineate the conditions in which hypnosis may enhance the expression of affect.

One of the cornerstones of psychoanalytic thinking is that transference is a fundamental psychotherapeutic process. Research (see Sheehan, 1991, for a summary) supports the hypothesis that certain hypnotized subjects evidence an especially motivated involvement with the hypnotist and a cognitive commitment to the task of responding to hypnotic suggestions. This research also indicates that hypnotized subjects' investment in the hypnotist and the hypnotic relationship cannot be duplicated by nonhypnotized simulating and task-motivated subjects instructed to do their best to respond to suggested events.

Recent developments in this area of inquiry include the study of the intricate and sometimes subtle nature of the hypnotist and subject's *interaction* (see Banyai, 1991) and the development of reliable and valid instruments (Nash & Spinler, 1989) to measure transference and archaic involvement with the hypnotist (Shor, 1979, defined archaic involvement as "the extent to which there occurred a temporary displacement or 'transference' onto the . . . hypnotist of core personality emotive attitudes . . . most typically in regard to parents," p. 133). This research promises to advance understanding of the nature of hypnotic rapport, transference, and subjects' motivations to respond to hypnotic suggestions.

In addition to the experimental tradition, the use of psychodynamic hypnotherapy is a rich source of data, providing a strong base for increased understanding of this mode of therapy in relation to a wide variety of cases. Baker (1981) and Brown (1985) have written extensively on the use of hypnosis with severely disturbed patients. Adler (1981, 1985), among others, discussed borderline and narcissistic personalities and their responses to hypnotherapeutic intervention. A large number of clinicians have described their work with veterans suffering from posttraumatic stress disorders (e.g., Kingsbury, 1988; Peebles, 1989; D. Spiegel, 1981, 1984), and there also is a growing body of clinical literature on hypnotherapy with victims of sexual abuse and with multiple personality disorders (Bliss, 1986; Kluft, 1984).

To my knowledge, there are no studies in which hypnoanalytic treatments were compared with other psychotherapeutic interventions. Controlled outcome studies are obviously a high priority. Ideally, clinical research will supplement more rigorous laboratory investigations of psychoanalytic and ego psychology constructs to enrich the understanding of relevant constructs, treatment mechanisms, and the effectiveness of hypnoanalytic psychotherapy relative to alternative therapeutic approaches.

CONCLUSION

I have touched on a number of key concepts related to hypnosis as a therapeutic tool. As the literature review indicates, there is empirical support for a number of constructs pivotal to psychodynamic and psychoanalytic therapy, including hypnoanalysis. I have viewed hypnosis as an altered state of consciousness, during which the subject experiences his or her physical, cognitive, emotional self in a dissociated manner. The body sense changes, parts of the body appear to function as separate entities, sensory experiences become a function of inner processes rather than external stimuli, and movement or lack of it seems to be under a different control system.

Cognitively, there is a clear split between the experiencing and the observing ego. This means that at one level, the critical function is set aside and the subject can accept mutually exclusive possibilities as natural (trance logic), which is a function of the participating ego, while on another level, the observing ego maintains its integrity and monitors the proceedings from a steadfast reality orientation. Emotionally, the subject is capable of strong responses that can be evoked or terminated at will and do not necessarily seem connected to ongoing, logical thought processes.

I have also conceptualized hypnosis as a regression in the service of the ego, during which the subject may revert to a more intuitive, imaginative, free-flowing mode of functioning (primary process), allowing for archaic involvement with the hypnotist and with elements of the self. In pathological regression, the ego is helplessly inundated with a sense of uncontrollable feelings and unmet needs. However, in regression in the service of the ego, it initiates, lends itself to, and uses regressive mental activity as a healing process.

The experience of involvement with the therapeutic process over time, and the eventual conscious understanding and integration which is called "working through," potentiates structural change in intensive psychoanalytic treatment. Hypnosis can help to direct the experience, contain and modulate the process, and facilitate internal representation and integration in a direct and efficient manner not usually possible in more traditional psychotherapy (Baker, 1990).

Finally, hypnosis can be viewed as a ritual that provides a framework for working through grief and mourning, unresolved relationship conflicts, and developmental discontinuities. Many patients use the special therapeutic relationship hypnotherapy provides to engage in magical thinking and experience strong emotional abreactions they could not allow themselves in more cognitively or intellectually oriented therapy settings. It is not only the regressive nature of hypnosis but the implied "magic" connected historically to hypnosis that gives it this special power.

The hypnotherapist needs to remain cognizant of the "demand characteristics" of this interaction and to respect the patient's dual need for a safely dependent relationship and autonomy. The patient must be allowed to create the therapeutic agenda and not bow to the agenda of the therapist.

Psychodynamic hypnotherapy provides a technique for uncovering repressed material, reworking the meaning of that material into the fabric of one's present life, and reintegrating one's history with a contemporary sense of self. The therapist serves as a benign guide on this journey through the shadows. Hypnoanalysis adds a new dimension to psychoanalysis because of its unique and special tools: imagery, primary process, age regression, hypermnesia, dissociation, and automatic writing. The hypnoanalyst attempts to help patients achieve new levels of mastery as they sort out and come to terms with conflicts, fears, painful memories, and destructive habits. Patients can acquire more mature levels of object constancy and more benign, growth-promoting object representations that help in the development of more integrated, healthier self-representations.

As researchers explore the dynamics of hypnoanalysis, they also learn more about the primary and secondary process operations, the various ego states, the function and process of memory, and the way human beings use mental "playfulness" to achieve more joyful, mature, fully functioning levels of self.

REFERENCES

Adler, G. (1981). The borderline-narcissistic personality disorder continuum. *American Journal of Psychiatry, 138,* 46–50.

Adler, G. (1985). *Borderline psychopathology and its treatment.* Northvale, NJ: Jason Aronson.

Baker, E. L. (1981). An hypnotherapeutic approach to enhance object relatedness in psychotic patients. *International Journal of Clinical and Experimental Hypnosis, 124,* 136–147.

Baker, E. L. (1990). Hypnoanalysis for structural pathology: Impairments of self-representation and capacity for object involvement. In M. Fass & D. Brown (Eds.), *Creative mastery in hypnosis and hypnoanalysis* (pp. 255–262). Hillsdale, NJ: Erlbaum.

Banyai, E. (1991). Towards a social-psychobiological model of hypnosis. In S. J. Lynn & J. W. Rhue (Eds.), *Theories of hypnosis: Current models and perspectives* (pp. 564–600). New York: Guilford Press.

Bliss, E. L. (1986). *Multiple personality, allied disorders, and hypnosis.* New York: Oxford University Press.

Brentar, J. P., & Lynn, S. J. (1989). Negative effects and hypnosis: A critical examination. *British Journal of Experimental and Clinical Hypnosis, 6,* 75–84.

Brentar, J. P., Lynn, S. J., Carlson, B., Kurzhals, R., & Green, J. P. (1992, August). *The Posthypnotic Experiences Scale: Reliability and validity studies.* Paper presented at the 100th Annual Convention of the American Psychological Association, Washington, DC.

Brown, D. P. (1985). Hypnosis as an adjunct to the psychotherapy of the severely disturbed patient: An affective development approach. *International Journal of Clinical and Experimental Hypnosis, 33,* 281–301.

Brown, D. P., & Fromm, E. (1986). *Hypnotherapy and hypnoanalysis.* Hillsdale, NJ: Erlbaum.

Bryant, R. A., & McConkey, K. M. (1989). Hypnotic blindness: A behavioral and experiential analysis. *Journal of Abnormal Psychology, 98,* 71–77.

Crawford, H. J., Hilgard, J. R., & Macdonald, H. (1982). Transient experiences following hypnotic testing and special termination procedures. *International Journal of Clinical and Experimental Hypnosis, 30,* 117–126.

Deikman, A. J. (1971). Bimodal consciousness. *Archives of General Psychiatry, 25,* 481–489.

Eisen, M. (1989). Return of the repressed: Hypnoanalysis of a case of total amnesia. *International Journal of Clinical and Experimental Hypnosis, 37,* 107–119.

Eisen, M. (1990). From the magical wish to the belief in the self. In M. L. Fass & D. Brown (Eds.), *Creative mastery in hypnosis and hypnoanalysis* (pp. 147–157). Hillsdale, NJ: Erlbaum.

Eisen, M. R., & Fromm, E. (1983). The clinical uses of self hypnosis in hypnotherapy: Tapping the functions of imagery and adaptive regression. *International Journal of Clinical and Experimental Hypnosis, 31,* 243–255.

Federn, P. (1952). *Ego psychology and the psychoses.* New York: Basic Books.

Fenichel, O. (1945). *The psychoanalytic theory of the neuroses.* New York: Norton.

Ferenczi, S. (1965). Comments on hypnosis. In R. Shor & M. T. Orne (Eds.), *The nature of hypnosis: Selected basic readings* (pp. 177–182). New York: Holt, Rinehart & Winston.

Frankel, F. H. (1976). *Hypnosis: Trance as a coping mechanism.* New York: Plenum Press.

Freud, S. (1953a). The interpretation of dreams. In J. Strachey (Ed. and Trans.), *The standard edition of the complete psychological works of Sigmund Freud.* London: Hogarth Press. (Original work published 1900)

Freud, S. (1953b). Three essays on the theory of sexuality. In J. Strachey (Ed. and Trans.), *The standard edition of the complete psychological works of Sigmund Freud* (Vol. 7, pp. 125–245). London: Hogarth Press. (Original work published 1905)

Fromm, E. (1972). Ego activity and ego passivity in hypnosis. *International Journal of Clinical and Experimental Hypnosis, 18,* 79–88.

Fromm, E. (1992). An ego-psychological theory of hypnosis. In E. Fromm & M. R. Nash (Eds.), *Contemporary hypnosis research.* New York: Guilford Press.

Fromm, E., & Kahn, S. (1990). *Self-hypnosis: The Chicago paradigm.* New York: Guilford Press.

Fromm, E., & Shor, R. E. (1979). *Hypnosis: Developments in research and new perspectives* (2nd ed.). Chicago: Aldine.

Gill, M. M., & Brenman, M. (1959). *Hypnosis and related states.* Madison, CT: International Universities Press.

Hammer, A. G., Walker, W., & Diment, A. D. (1978). A nonsuggested effect of trance induction. In F. H. Frankel & H. S. Zamansky (Eds.), *Hypnosis at its bicentennial: Selected papers* (pp. 91–100). New York: Plenum Press.

Hart, H. H. (1961). A review of the psychoanalytic literature on passivity. *Psychiatric Quarterly, 35,* 331–352.

Hartmann, H. (1958). *Ego psychology and the problem of adaptation* (D. Rapaport, Trans.). Madison, CT: International Universities Press. (Original work published 1936)

Hilgard, E. R. (1973). A neodissociation interpretation of pain reduction in hypnosis. *Psychological Review, 80,* 396–411.

Hilgard, E. R. (1974). Toward a neodissociation theory: Multiple cognitive controls in human functioning. *Perspectives in Biology and Medicine, 17,* 301–316.

Hilgard, E. R. (1977). *Divided consciousness: Multiple controls in human thought and action.* New York: Wiley.

Hilgard, J. R. (1970). *Personality and hypnosis: A study of imaginative involvement.* Chicago: University of Chicago Press.

Kingsbury, S. J. (1988). Hypnosis in the treatment of posttraumatic stress disorder: An isomorphic intervention. *American Journal of Clinical Hypnosis, 31,* 81–90.

Kirsch, I., & Council, J. R. (1992). Situational and personality correlates of hypnotic responsiveness. In E. Fromm & M. R. Nash (Eds.), *Contemporary hypnosis research.* New York: Guilford Press.

Kirsch, I., Mobayed, C. P., Council, J. R., & Kenny, D. A. (1990, August). State of the state debate: Can experts detect hypnosis? In R. St. Jean (Chair), *Social and cognitive aspects of hypnosis: Papers honoring W. C. Coe.* Symposium conducted at the 98th Annual Convention of the American Psychological Association, Boston.

Kluft, R. P. (1984). Treatment of multiple personality disorder. *Psychiatric Clinics of North America, 7,* 9–29.

Kris, E. (1952). *Psychoanalytic explorations in art.* Madison, CT: International Universities Press. (Original work published in 1934)

Loewald, H. W. (1981). Regression: Some general considerations. *Psychoanalytic Quarterly, 50,* 22–43.

Lynn, S. J., & Rhue, J. W. (1988). Fantasy proneness: Hypnosis, developmental antecedents, and psychopathology. *American Psychologist, 43,* 35–44.

Lynn, S. J., Rhue, J. W., & Weekes, J. R. (1990). Hypnotic responsiveness: A social cognitive analysis. *Psychological Review, 97,* 169–184.

Lynn, S. J., & Sivec, H. (1992). The hypnotizable subject as creative problem-solving agent. In E. Fromm & M. R. Nash (Eds.), *Contemporary hypnosis research* (pp. 292–333). New York: Guilford Press.

Mare, C., Lynn, S. J., Kvaal, S., & Segal, D. (1992). *The dream hidden observer: Primary process and demand characteristics.* Manuscript submitted for publication.

Meares, A. (1960). *A system of medical hypnosis.* Philadelphia: W. B. Saunders.

Nash, M. R. (1987). What, if anything, is regressed about hypnotic age regression? A review of the empirical literature. *Psychological Bulletin, 102,* 42–52.

Nash, M. R. (1991). Hypnosis as a special case of psychological regression. In S. J. Lynn & J. W. Rhue (Eds.), *Theories of hypnosis: Current models and perspectives* (pp. 171–194). New York: Guilford Press.

Nash, M. R. (1992). Hypnosis, psychopathology, and psychological regression. In E. Fromm & M. R. Nash (Eds.), *Contemporary hypnosis research* (pp. 149–169). New York: Guilford Press.

Nash, M. R., Johnson, L. S., & Tipton, R. D. (1979). Hypnotic age regression and the occurrence of transitional object relationships. *Journal of Abnormal Psychology, 88,* 547–555.

Nash, M. R., Lynn, S. J., Stanley, S. M., Frauman, D., & Rhue, J. W. (1985). Hypnotic age regression and the importance of assessing interpersonally relevant affect. *International Journal of Clinical and Experimental Hypnosis, 33,* 224–235.

Nash, M. R., & Spinler, D. (1989). Hypnosis and transference: A measure of archaic involvement with the hypnotist. *International Journal of Clinical and Experimental Hypnosis, 37,* 129–144.

Orne, M. (1959). The nature of hypnosis: Artifact and essence. *Journal of Abnormal and Social Psychology, 58,* 277–299.

Peebles, M. J. (1989). Through a glass darkly: The psychoanalytic use of hypnosis with post-traumatic stress disorder. *International Journal of Clinical and Experimental Hypnosis, 37,* 192–206.

Rapaport, D. (1967). Metaphysical considerations concerning activity and passivity. In M. M. Gill (Ed.), *The collected papers of David Rapaport* (pp. 530–568). New York: Basic Books. (Original work published 1953)

Restak, R. M. (1979). *The brain: The last frontier.* New York: Doubleday.

Roche, S. M., & McConkey, K. M. (1990). Absorption: Nature, assessment, and correlates. *Journal of Personality and Social Psychology, 59,* 91–101.

Schilder, P. F., & Kauders, O. (1927). Hypnosis. (S. Rosenberg, Trans.). Nervous and Mental Disease Monographs #46. (Reissued in P. F. Schilder (Ed.), *The nature of hypnosis* (pp. 43–184). New Translation by Gerda Corvin. Madison, CT: International Universities Press, 1956.)

Sheehan, P. W. (1991). Hypnosis, context and commitment. In S. J. Lynn & J. W. Rhue (Eds.), *Hypnosis: Current models and perspectives* (pp. 520–541). New York: Guilford Press.

Shor, R. E. (1979). A phenomenological method for the measurement of variables important to an understanding of the nature of hypnosis. In E. Fromm & R. E. Shor (Eds.), *Hypnosis: Developments in research and new perspectives* (2nd ed., pp. 105–135). Chicago: Aldine.

Spiegel, D. (1981). Vietnam grief work using hypnosis. *American Journal of Clinical Hypnosis, 24,* 33–40.

Spiegel, D. (1984). Multiple personality as a posttraumatic stress disorder. *Psychiatric Clinics of North America, 7,* 101–110.

Spiegel, H., & Spiegel, D. (1978). *Trance and treatment: Clinical uses of hypnosis.* New York: Basic Books.

Watkins, J. G., & Watkins, H. (1979). The theory and practice of ego state therapy. In H. Grayson (Ed.), *Short term approaches to psychotherapy* (pp. 176–220). New York: National Institute for the Psychotherapies and Human Sciences Press.

Watkins, J. G., & Watkins, H. H. (1981). Ego-state therapy. In R. J. Corsini (Ed.), *Handbook of innovative therapies* (pp. 252–270). New York: Wiley.

Watkins, J. G., & Watkins, H. H. (1990). Ego-state transferences in the hypnoanalytic treatment of dissociative reactions. In M. Fass & D. Brown (Eds.), *Creative mastery in hypnosis and hypnoanalysis* (pp. 255–261). Hillsdale, NJ: Erlbaum.

Weiss, E. (Ed.). (1952). *Ego psychology and the psychoses.* New York: Basic Books.

Winnicott, D. W. (1975). *Through pediatrics to psychoanalysis.* New York: Basic Books.

Wiseman, R. J., & Reyher, J. (1973). Hypnotically induced dreams using the Rorschach inkblots as stimuli: A test of Freud's theory of dreams. *Journal of Personality and Social Psychology, 27,* 329–336.

7

COGNITIVE–BEHAVIORAL HYPNOTHERAPY

IRVING KIRSCH

Cognitive–behavioral therapy is a set of treatment procedures that has been developed by cognitive therapists and behavior therapists since the 1950s. Many of these procedures were derived from experimental psychology, and their use is based on a conception of psychological problems as learned maladaptive responses sustained by dysfunctional cognitions. Cognitive–behavioral hypnotherapy refers to the use of hypnotic inductions to enhance the effectiveness of cognitive–behavioral interventions.

THE DEVELOPMENT OF COGNITIVE–BEHAVIORAL THERAPY

The development of behavior therapy in the 1950s and 1960s (Eysenck, 1960; Wolpe, 1958) represented a radical departure in the conceptualization and treatment of behavioral and emotional problems. Instead of viewing presenting problems as symptoms of underlying disorders, behavior therapists saw them as maladaptive learned responses that were to be the direct targets of therapeutic interventions. Assuming that operant conditioning and classical conditioning were the mechanisms by which learning occurred, early behavior therapists developed treatments in which conditioning procedures were used to teach clients more adaptive responses.

The term *cognitive therapy* is generally used to designate the treatment techniques described by Beck (1976) and his colleagues (Beck, Rush, Shaw, & Emery, 1979). However, the "rational–emotive therapy" developed by Ellis (1962) should be recognized as the first contemporary cognitive therapy. According to cognitive therapists, emotional problems are not caused by the stimulus events themselves but by the ways in which those events are interpreted. Emotional disturbance is seen as a consequence of unwarranted assumptions and illogical thinking. The strategy of cognitive therapy is to alleviate emotional distress by teaching clients to interpret events in a more rational and adaptive manner.

Although cognitive and behavioral therapies were initially distinct schools, a number of developments have brought about a convergence between the two. First, Bandura (1969) presented an influential overview of behavior therapy that emphasized the role of cognitive factors in human learning. Two years later, Lazarus (1971), who a decade earlier had been one of the pioneers of behavior therapy, added Ellis's (1962) "cognitive restructuring" to the broad spectrum of techniques used by behavior therapists. Conversely, virtually all of the methods of behavior therapy have been incorporated into cognitive therapy (Beck et al., 1979; Ellis & Grieger, 1977). In 1974, Meichenbaum (1974) presented "cognitive–behavior modification," a formal integration of cognitive and behavioral psychotherapy. Finally, although once regarded as behavioral mechanisms, classical conditioning and operant conditioning are now more widely viewed as procedures that change behavior via their effects on cognitions (Bolles, 1972; Rescorla, 1988, 1991).

With this much convergence, the distinction between cognitive therapy and behavior therapy is no longer useful, and the appellation *cognitive–behavioral*, which is seen with increasing frequency, is the most accurate characterization of these treatment procedures. Indeed, the label *behavior therapy* has always been somewhat problematic, given that some of the earliest and most widely studied "behavioral" procedures were based on the use of imagery (Wolpe, 1958).

THE COGNITIVE–BEHAVIORAL VIEW OF HYPNOSIS

Hypnosis is traditionally defined as a sleeplike state in which people are more suggestible than they are in the normal waking state. Cognitive–behavioral theorists have challenged the hypothesis that hypnotic phenomena are attributable to an altered state of consciousness (Barber, 1969; Kirsch, 1990; Sarbin & Coe, 1972; Spanos & Chaves, 1989). In their view, hypnotic phenomena can be explained by the same variables that account for nonhypnotic behavior. This rejection of the altered state construct is based on the following data:

1. No physiological markers of the hypothesized hypnotic states have been found (Sarbin & Slagle, 1979).
2. All of the phenomena produced by suggestion following a hypnotic induction can also be produced without a hypnotic induction (Barber, 1969; Hilgard, 1965; Hull, 1933).
3. The increases in suggestibility that are produced by hypnotic induction are small (Hilgard, 1965) and can be duplicated or even surpassed by a variety of other procedures, including placebo pills (Glass & Barber, 1961) and imagination training (Katz, 1979; Vickery, Kirsch, Council, & Sirkin, 1985).
4. Rather than describing their experience as an altered state, most hypnotized subjects describe hypnosis as a "normal state of consciousness that simply involves the focusing of attention [and] thinking along with and imagining the suggestions given by the hypnotist" (McConkey, 1986, p. 314). These descriptions of the hypnotic experience are especially common among highly responsive subjects.
5. Descriptions of the state of consciousness produced by typical hypnotic inductions appear to be indistinguishable from those produced by progressive relaxation training (Kirsch, Mobayed, Council, & Kenny, 1992).

Because hypnosis was traditionally defined as an altered state, the nonstate position seemed to challenge the very concept of *hypnosis*. As a result, cognitive–behavioral theory was sometimes misinterpreted as a denial of the reality or importance of hypnotic phenomena. Fortunately, hypnosis is now defined by many scholars as a particular kind of social interaction in which various changes in experience and behavior are suggested (Kihlstrom, 1985). Cognitive–behavioral theorists and psychodynamic theorists agree that a person's experience may be altered during hypnosis (Lynn & Rhue, 1991), but they disagree about whether the concept of a hypnotic "trance" is useful in explaining those changes in experience.

The use of hypnosis in cognitive–behavioral therapy is as old as behavior therapy itself. Wolpe and Lazarus (1966), for example, reported using hypnotic inductions instead of progressive relaxation with about one third of their systematic desensitization patients. From a cognitive–behavioral perspective, hypnosis provides a context in which the effects of cognitive–behavioral interventions can be potentiated for some clients. Specifically, hypnosis is likely to enhance the effects of cognitive–behavioral therapy among clients with positive attitudes and expectancies toward hypnosis (Kirsch, 1990). Conversely, it is likely to degrade the effects of treatment among clients who view hypnosis with fear or derision. Hypnosis can also provide a disinhibiting context, allowing clients to exhibit responses that they do not realize they are capable of making. Finally, hypnosis can disinhibit therapists by providing a context for therapeutic behaviors that may seem inappropriate in other settings (Barber, 1985). For example, the hypnotic context permits the therapist to repeat statements over and over again, thereby enhancing their forcefulness and salience. Outside of the hypnotic context, this style of communication would seem strange and inappropriate.

CLINICAL APPLICATIONS

Cognitive–behavioral interventions are best known as treatments for phobic anxiety and depression. However, there are also cognitive–behavioral therapies for personality disorders, autism, stuttering, enuresis, encopresis, Gilles de la Tourette's syndrome, marital distress, hypertension, asthma, obsessive–compulsive disorders, sexual dysfunctions and deviations, pain, addictions, obesity, and so forth (Bellack, Hersen, & Kazdin, 1990; Freeman, Pretzer, Fleming, & Simon, 1990). Some of these dysfunctions are the focus of behavioral medicine, which is generally regarded as a subspecialty of cognitive–behavioral therapy. The application of hypnosis to the treatment of specific problems is discussed in other chapters of this book. This chapter focuses on the cognitive–behavioral procedures that are common to these various applications.

Relaxation

Relaxation training is a component of many cognitive–behavioral treatments. It is frequently taught as a coping skill with which anxiety and stress can be countered. It may be paired with stressful imagery, as in systematic desensitization, or clients may be instructed to generate relaxation as a way of reducing anxiety and tension when it is encountered in daily life. Relaxation training is often used in treating phobias, hypertension, cardiac arrhythmias, asthma, chronic diarrhea, irritable bowel syndrome, pain, headaches, epilepsy, and insomnia (Taylor, 1982).

The traditional method of teaching relaxation is to instruct clients to alternately tense and relax various groups of muscles until the whole body is relaxed (Jacobson, 1929). However, many therapists omit the instructions for muscle tension and instead maintain a consistent focus on relaxation. In either case, the requests to relax particular muscle groups are interspersed with suggestions for general relaxation, such as "deeply relaxed . . . more and more relaxed . . . all the tension is draining from your body."

The striking similarity between relaxation training and typical hypnotic inductions is easily recognized. In fact, all that is needed to transform relaxation training into a hypnotic induction is the addition of the word *hypnosis*. Thus, whenever relaxation training seems indicated in treatment, a hypnotic induction can be used in its place. Similarly, relaxation exercises at home can be replaced by training in "self-hypnosis," the essential difference being the label.

The use of the relaxation response in real-life settings can be encourged by a posthypnotic suggestion to the effect that one will become better and better at producing relaxation at will. For example, the client can be told the following:

> Whenever you find yourself experiencing stress or anxiety, you can relax the tension away. All you need do is take a deep breath, think the word *relax* as you exhale, and let the tension drain from your body. As you practice self-hypnosis, you will find this easier and easier to do, and you may be surprised at how easy it becomes to just let yourself relax.

Imagery

Relaxation is often paired with guided imagery of stressful encounters, with the aim of enabling the client to experience the stressor with reduced anxiety. In traditional systematic desensitization, client and therapist work together to construct a hierarchy of anxiety-related scenes. Clients are then instructed to relax and to begin imagining the least anxiety-provoking scene from their hierarchies. When anxiety is experienced, they are instructed to discontinue the imagined stressful encounter. Brief relaxation instructions are given until relaxation is regained, at which point the anxiety imagery is resumed. Once the image can be tolerated without eliciting anxiety, the next scene on the hierarchy is imagined.

Desensitization is a robust treatment, in that it retains its effectiveness over a remarkably wide range of variations in procedure (Kirsch, 1990). For example, rather than discontinuing stress-related imagery when anxiety is experienced, clients can be instructed to stay with the imagined scene while breathing slowly, relaxing away their anxiety, and imagining themselves applying these coping strategies in the anxiety-provoking situation. Another variation in procedure is to condense or even eliminate the hierarchy entirely, so that the client begins by imagining a relatively stressful scene.

Imagery can also be used without relaxation. This is particularly useful in practicing assertive interpersonal behavior, which could be inhibited by relaxation. Here, too, imagery can be preceded by a hypnotic induction; however, in this case, an "alert induction" (e.g., Gibbons, 1974) may be better than the more traditional relaxation induction. Instead of suggesting relaxation, the therapist induces hypnosis with suggestions for increased energy and focused attention, using phrases similar to the following: "With each breath you take, you can feel yourself becoming more and more alive and vital. Feel the energy flow through your body . . . through your feet . . . your legs . . . your thighs."

Behavioral Practice

In most applications, practice in imagination is followed by real-life practice. In the treatment of phobias, this is termed *exposure*. Phobic clients are instructed to enter the feared situation while making use of the coping strategies they have learned during hypnosis sessions. Clients with panic disorders practice slow, shallow breathing to counteract the tendency to hyperventilate. For depressed clients, the aim of behavioral practice may be to (a) increase activity levels, (b) provide pleasurable experiences that have the potential to change affect and convince clients that pleasure is possible, and (c) provide experiences of mastery and success that can enhance self-esteem and generalized self-efficacy.

Real-life practice is also a part of traditional psychotherapy (Freud, 1919/1959), but it is initiated sooner and emphasized more in cognitive–behavioral therapy. This is because of consistent research findings indicating that experiential learning may be more effective than vicarious learning in producing behavior change (e.g., Barlow, Leitenberg, Agras, & Wincze, 1969; Fazio & Zanna, 1981; Wickless & Kirsch, 1989). In fact, imagery practice may add little if anything to the final outcome of treatment. However, the use of imagery as a preparation for behavioral practice is a "kinder and gentler" therapy. It makes real practice easier to tolerate and may thereby decrease the likelihood of premature termination.

Successive Approximation

The reinforcement of successive approximations of a desired response is termed *shaping*. It is through shaping that animal performers are taught the complex behaviors they display in movies and public exhibitions, and it is through shaping that autistic children have been taught to speak (Lovaas, 1969).

The principle of graduated practice is a ubiquitous aspect of cognitive–behavioral treatments. It can be seen, for example, in the hierarchy of anxiety-provoking scenes that is constructed during systematic desensitization. Similarly, behavioral exposure to anxiety situations typically involves progressively longer exposures to increasingly difficult situations. Depressed clients may initially be asked for only modest increases in behavior, and it is wise to choose initial mastery exercises that are easy enough so that success is virtually guaranteed. The usefulness of successive approximation in hypnosis is implicitly recognized in the structure of hypnosis scales, which begin with relatively easy suggestions and progress to more difficult items. Successive approximation has also been reported in the cognitive–behavioral treatment of multiple personality disorders (Kirsch & Barton, 1988).

Cognitive Restructuring

The object of cognitive restructuring is to identify and modify the dysfunctional cognitions that may contribute to emotional and behavioral disorders. The nature of these cognitions varies from disorder to disorder and from person to person. People suffering from panic disorders, for example, often believe that their attacks are caused by a fatal physical condition (e.g., cardiac arrest) or that they are in danger of "going crazy." Depressed individuals may hold negative beliefs about themselves, their world, and the future, a set of beliefs that Beck (1976) termed a "negative cognitive triad." Clients with multiple personality disorders often believe that the personas they have created really are different people who exist physically outside of themselves.

Maladaptive beliefs may be maintained against disconfirming evidence because of distortions in the logical processing of information. These distortions include attending to confirmatory information and ignoring disconfirmatory information (selective abstraction), drawing arbitrary inferences in the absence of supportive data, overgeneralizing, magnifying the significance of some events and minimizing the significance of others, personalizing external events without any factual basis for making such a connection, and thinking in dichotomous black–white terms (Beck et al., 1979; Lazarus, 1971).

When dysfunctional thoughts or beliefs are identified, they are evaluated through Socratic questioning. Clients are urged to treat them as hypotheses rather than facts. These hypotheses are then tested by mutual examination of available data. If the data are insufficient for a conclusion to be drawn, behavioral homework may be assigned as a means of testing the validity of old beliefs and potential alternatives. When the client reaches the conclusion that a particular thought or belief is invalid, it is replaced by a more adaptive alternative that is to be integrated into the client's belief system.

It is at this point that hypnosis and self-hypnosis can be particularly useful. New adaptive beliefs that the client has accepted as valid are given as hypnotic suggestions to facilitate their full incorporation into the client's cognitive structure. Without hypnosis, some clients may feel foolish or silly intentionally repeating sentences to themselves, despite the fact that the content of those sentences is accepted as valid and important. The purpose of hypnosis in this process is to provide a special context in which clients can feel comfortable practicing their new cognitions.

Hypnosis

One of the premises of the cognitive–behavioral perspective is that whatever can be done with hypnosis can also be done without it. This is one implication of the hypothesis that hypnosis is not a special state or condition. Conversely, anything that can be done without hypnosis may also be done in a hypnotic context. Given these premises, how is one to decide whether to augment an intervention by establishing a hypnotic context?

Some clients come to therapy requesting hypnosis or are referred for hypnotic treatment by another therapist. The latter occurs with increasing frequency as a therapist gains a reputation as a hypnotherapist. These clients almost invariably hold positive attitudes and expectations about hypnosis, and this makes them good candidates for hypnotic interventions. The danger in these cases is that the client's expectations may be too positive. They may think of hypnosis as a powerful procedure that will do the work for them, so that little effort on their part is required. This, of course, is a setup for failure, and hypnotic treatment should not be started without first educating the client about the real nature of hypnosis.

Although some clients come to a therapist requesting hypnosis, most come asking for help because of a particular set of problems they are facing, and they look to the therapist to suggest the treatment procedures that will be used. One way that therapists sometimes evaluate the suitability of clients for hypnotic treatment is to assess their hypnotizability. However, treatment outcome is not always correlated with hypnotizability (Wadden & Anderton, 1982), and even when it is, the correlation is modest. Baker and Kirsch (in press), for example, reported a correlation of .25 between hypnotizability and hypnotic analgesia. In my experience, many clients who are only moderately hypnotizable benefit from the use of a hypnotic induction. This tends to be the case for clients who have positive attitudes toward hypnosis and for whom the use of hypnosis makes therapy more credible.

Self-Regulation Therapy

An innovative approach to cognitive–behavioral hypnotherapy, termed *self-regulation therapy*, was developed in Spain by Amigó (1992). Self-regulation therapy combines conventional cognitive–behavioral treatment techniques with procedures originally developed to increase people's responsiveness to hypnosis (Sachs & Anderson, 1967). First, the client is presented with stimuli that will automatically produce particular sensations (e.g., a heavy book is placed in the person's hand to produce a sensation of arm heaviness). The patient is then asked to associate the sensation with some internal or external stimulus (e.g., a thought, image, or word). Next, the client practices generating the sensation without the aid of the stimulus, with the aim of learning to produce it effortlessly in response to suggestion. This process is repeated with a number of suggestions, thus enhancing the person's response expectancies. Once this occurs, therapeutic suggestions appropriate to the presenting problem are given.

Although it is based on hypnotic procedures and uses typical hypnotic suggestions, self-regulation therapy is conducted without any trance induction, with the client's eyes open and in a normal conversational style. No mention of hypnosis is made. Thus, it is a procedure that may be especially useful with clients who hold negative attitudes and expectations about hypnosis.

CASE MATERIAL

Deciding to Use Hypnosis

Rather than assessing hypnotizability, an excellent way of determining whether to use hypnosis is to ask the client. This is illustrated in the following excerpt. The client had presented with a fear of flying and had disclosed, during the assessment interview, that she also experienced a fear of heights and tunnels. Intentional hyperventilation produced sensations similar to those she experienced in these situations, leading to the supposition that stress-cued hyperventilation might have been contributing to feelings of panic she experienced. The choice of procedures was presented to her as follows:

Therapist: There are two procedures that we can use to help you with your fear. One of these is hypnosis. We would use hypnosis here in the office, and I would also teach you to use self-hypnosis at home. A second possibility is to use a desensitization procedure that involves relaxation training and imagery. In either case, once you achieve some initial fear reduction, either through hypnosis or through the relaxation and imagery exercises, I'll ask you to begin practicing these skills in real-life settings, probably beginning with heights, since airplane trips are rather expensive. Do you have any initial reactions about whether to use hypnosis or muscle relaxation as a method of coping with your fears?

Client: Well, I'd want to use whatever works best. Does one work better than the other?

Therapist: Hypnosis and the imagery/relaxation procedures seem to be about equally effective. But some people find hypnosis more helpful, whereas others benefit more from relaxation training. What it really depends on is how comfortable you are with one method or the other. Since you know yourself much better than I do, you're probably the best judge of which method would work better for you. What do you think?

Client: I don't really know. But, I have a pretty strong will, so I don't think I would be able to be hypnotized. I want to do whatever will work best.

Therapist: Well, based on what you've told me, my sense is that relaxation training may be the best way to begin.

This client's comments indicated that she held some fairly common misconceptions about hypnosis and that these led her to have negative expectations about her hypnotizability. An alternate response might have been to educate her about the nature of hypnosis in an effort to change her attitude. There are a number of reasons for thinking that accepting the client's judgment was a better tactic. First, regardless of the therapist's educational efforts, the client could still hold the suspicion that responding to hypnosis was an indication of a weak will. Second, the actual procedures that would be used once the choice was made are virtually identical. Third, research indicates that allowing clients to choose between therapeutic alternatives enhances treatment outcome (Devine & Fernald, 1973; Kanfer & Grimm, 1978; Lazarus, 1973).

Hypnosis can also be indicated when problems are encountered in the use of nonhypnotic procedures. For example, some people respond to relaxation training with a paradoxical anxiety reaction. The switch to hypnosis in such a case is illustrated in the following vignette. After a few minutes of relaxation instructions, a 17-year-old client suddenly sat upright with eyes wide open.

Client: This is stupid. I can't do it. It just makes me feel more uptight and nervous.

Therapist: What happened?

Client: I don't know. I tried to relax. But the more I tried, the more antsy I got. I just can't do it.

Therapist: Okay, it's clear that the relaxation exercise is not working for you. Perhaps we should try something else. I wonder what you think about hypnosis. It might be an alternative that we could try.

Client (with evident excitement): Do you do hypnosis?

Therapist: Yes, I sometimes use it in therapy. You seem pretty interested in the idea. I wonder what you know about hypnosis or what ideas you have about it.

After discussing the nature of hypnosis from a cognitive–behavioral perspective, a muscle-relaxation, eye-closure induction was begun. In the hypnotic context, the client responded to relaxation suggestions with relaxation instead of discomfort.

Finally, hypnosis can be useful in working with clients who are unreflective and tend to give quick "I don't know" answers to questions rather than working on finding an answer. With these clients, the following suggestion is often helpful:

> We all have hidden wisdom of which we are unaware, parts of us that know more than we think we know. In a moment, I'm going to ask you a question. But I don't want you to answer it right away. Instead, I want you to repeat the question to that hidden, wise part of yourself that knows more than you know. And when you've asked the question, I'd like you to wait. Just wait quietly until you become aware of an answer.

From a psychodynamic perspective, instructions of this sort may be seen as a way of accessing unconscious material. Neodissociation theorists (e.g., Hilgard, 1986) may view it as a means of accessing dissociated cognitive structures. From a cognitive–behavioral perspective, however, it is a method of interrupting a habitual response, slowing the client down, and encouraging reflective thought.

Hypnotic Skills Training

Considerable effort is often devoted by hypnotherapists to sharpening their skills at administering hypnotic inductions. Workshops are given in which indirect inductions, double inductions, special deepening techniques, and other procedures of this sort are taught. In contrast to the amount of attention devoted to teaching and learning these procedures, relatively little effort has been expended in evaluating their efficacy, and that which has been done indicates that they are not particularly effective (Lynn, Neufeld, & Matyi, 1987; Mathews, Kirsh, & Mosher, 1985).

Instead of devoting energy to fancy inductions, cognitive–behavioral hypnotherapists emphasize adequate preparation of clients for hypnosis. This consists of explaining the cognitive–behavioral view of hypnosis and demonstrating how hypnotic experiences can be produced even without a hypnotic induction. The following is a condensed example of a cognitive–behavioral approach to hypnotic skills training:

> Many people think of hypnosis as a mysterious altered state of consciousness, in which the person goes into a trance and loses control over his or her behavior. Hypnosis really isn't like that at all. Most people describe hypnosis as just a normal state of focused attention. When you are hypnotized, you remain awake and in full control of your behavior, and after hypnosis, you can remember everything that happened while you were hypnotized.
>
> Hypnosis isn't something that I do to you. Instead, it's something that you do to yourself. In fact, it's sometimes said that all hypnosis is really self-hypnosis. My job isn't to hypnotize you. It's to show you how to hypnotize yourself.

The purpose of using hypnosis is to make it easier for you to experience suggestions. When I suggest something to you, whether in or out of hypnosis, my suggestion doesn't make the experience happen. You have to decide whether you want to accept the suggestion, and if you do, it's you who makes the suggestion happen. If you don't like a suggestion I make, you can ignore it, just as you can outside of hypnosis. Or you can change it into a suggestion that you *would* like to experience. But if you want to experience the suggestion, hypnosis may make it easier for you to do so.

Let me give you an example of what I mean. [The therapist holds up a pendulum.] Now, when I show you this pendulum, it probably makes you think of those old movies in which the hypnotist says, "Watch the watch! Watch the watch!" Well, I'm not going to use this to hypnotize you. What I want to do with it is show you how you can experience hypnotic suggestions without hypnosis. Let me show you what I mean. If I hold the pendulum between my thumb and forefinger, and if I concentrate on the pendulum moving in a particular direction, let's say clockwise, just by imagining it moving, I can get it to move that way. [The pendulum begins to move.] As I concentrate on it, it begins to move in wider and wider circles, and I can get it to change direction, to back and forth, let's say, just by imagining it. [The pendulum changes direction.] It happens pretty quickly for me, because I've done this a lot. For a lot of people, it happens more slowly. But most people can do it, if they try.

Now I could easily just swing the pendulum intentionally, but that would be meaningless. Or I could focus my attention on keeping my hand still, and then the pendulum probably wouldn't move at all. But I don't do any of those things. Instead, I ignore my hand and focus all of my attention on the pendulum and on the way I want it to move. And a funny thing happens. It seems as if the pendulum were moving all by itself, as if the thought went right from my head to the pendulum, bypassing my hand and arm altogether. Now that couldn't really be happening. Somehow, my imagination is causing my hand to move, and those movements are being amplified by the pendulum. But I'm not aware of moving my hand at all. It feels as if the pendulum is moving all by itself. Why don't you try it? [The therapist hands the pendulum to the client.]

In what direction would you like the pendulum to move? [Client answers "clockwise."] Alright, now just concentrate on the pendulum. But stay awake. I don't want you to be hypnotized yet. Just picture the pendulum moving in a clockwise direction . . . round and round . . . round and round . . . [the pendulum begins to move] . . . making wider and wider circles . . . wider and wider. Why not make it change directions now? How about making it move sideways? Back and forth . . . back and forth.

Okay! Now here's what I'd like you to notice. First of all, you weren't hypnotized, were you? You weren't in some kind of trance. Second, I didn't make the suggestion happen. You did! You could have ignored what I said. You could have made it move in any direction you wanted to, right? That's just what hypnosis is like. In hypnosis, I make a suggestion, and you decide whether you want to experience it. And if you do, you have to make it happen. You have to concentrate on the suggestion and imagine along with it. If I ask you to hold out your arm and to imagine it becoming heavy, and if you want to experience that, then you have to imagine something that would make your arm feel very heavy, and you have to imagine the feeling of heaviness. If you concentrate on it, you can probably generate a feeling of heaviness and make it feel like your arm is being dragged down all by itself. But I can't make your arm feel heavy or move down. That's something that you have to do.

Most clients feel comfortable with this description and demonstration. They often express amazement when the pendulum starts to move, smiling and exclaiming, "This is weird!" Their fears about giving up control are assuaged. They have learned that taking an active role as a hypnotic subject will make it easier for them to respond to suggestion. More important, they have learned that they must take an active role as client rather than wait passively for the therapist to "cure" them.

Successive Approximations With Hypnosis

Elsewhere, a colleague and I reported on the use of successive approximations in the treatment of multiple personality disorders (Kirsch & Barton, 1988). Instead of reifying the personas presented by the client as "personalities" in the traditional sense of the term, we conceptualized them as believed-in persons who had been created by the client as a way of coping with extreme stress. The therapeutic task was to gradually weaken and eliminate the imaginary separation she had constructed between these personas. Hypnosis was used as a ritual that allowed the client to do things of which she was capable but that she believed herself to be incapable of doing without hypnosis. Posthypnotic suggestions were then used to enable her to accomplish the same tasks outside of hypnosis.

First, a dialogue between two personas was suggested during hypnosis, with the therapist cuing switches between one persona and the other. Next, the therapist suggested that the client take over the cuing function. When she was finished speaking as one persona, she would call the name of the other, just as the therapist had done in the previous conversation. The therapist then suggested that she would be able to do this outside of hypnosis. Next, speech was replaced by subvocal communication, first during hypnosis and then outside of hypnosis. Memories were then shared so that one persona would be able to remember experiences that had occurred in the role of the other persona. Once this was done, the believed-in separation between the two roles had been weakened to the point that role integration was a relatively small final step. A more detailed presentation of these procedures can be found in Kirsch and Barton (1988).

Hypnosis and Cognitive Restructuring

When a dysfunctional interpretation, thought, or belief has been evaluated, and the client has accepted the conclusion that it is illogical or unwarranted, it is replaced by an alternate, more adaptive cognition. However, old thought patterns may not disappear automatically once their fallacy has been demonstrated. Clients often report thinking maladaptive thoughts that they know to be erroneous. They report knowing one thing in their heads but feeling another in their hearts. Clients prone to panic attacks, for instance, may know intellectually that their attacks are not dangerous. However, the irrational thought that it is the beginning of a heart attack may occur nevertheless, and it may occur with enough conviction to generate panic. I sometimes refer to this as a "head–heart split."

Hypnosis and self-hypnosis are useful techniques for helping the head convince the heart of what the head knows to be true. Hypnosis is particularly useful in this process because it allows the therapist to speak in ways that would be inappropriate in other contexts. It is normal, during hypnosis, for the therapist to speak slowly and forcefully, put more emphasis than usual on particular words or phrases, and to repeat the same idea many times. The following is an example of a repetitive message that sounds normal in a hypnotic context, even when spoken in a slow, deliberate, and emphatic manner:

> Even though the thought sometimes occurs that feelings of anxiety might be the beginning of a heart attack, you know that they are not. They are a normal response to stress . . . a normal response . . . and they are not dangerous. And when the thought that they may be dangerous occurs, you can think, "I know . . . that this is only my anxiety . . . It cannot hurt me . . . . It cannot hurt me . . . . All I need to do is slow my breathing and relax . . . . Breathe slowly and relax . . . slowly and relax." Whenever you feel anxious, you can tell yourself that you know that it is only anxiety and that it cannot hurt you, and you will know that you are safe. You will remember to relax your muscles and to breathe slowly . . . relax and breathe slowly. And even if a scary thought occurs, you will know that it is just a thought and that it isn't true. Anxiety may be scary, but it can't hurt you. It isn't a heart attack, and you're not going crazy. It's not a heart attack, and you're not going crazy. And as you practice these new thoughts during your self-hypnosis sessions at home, the old thoughts will come less and less often . . . less and less often . . . and you'll know in your heart that they aren't true.

It is important to remember that suggestions such as these are only given *after* maladaptive thoughts have been evaluated and the client has intellectually concluded that they are wrong. This is not the way to convince the client of the truth of alternative beliefs; it is a way to help the client become more confident of his or her changed beliefs, so that the old thoughts lose their force and the new thoughts surface more automatically.

Converting adaptive cognitions into hypnotic and self-hypnotic suggestions is also useful as a means of countering rationalization. Smokers trying to quit, for example, often relapse because they rationalize that they can have one cigarette without becoming addicted again. This is reinforced when they do not feel especially strong cravings following that one cigarette. However, these lapses then occur with greater and greater frequency, until the person concludes that he or she has become a smoker again. The likelihood of relapse may be decreased by frequent forceful repetition of the following self-suggestion: "This is a rationalization! It is how I fooled myself into failing in the past. If I give in now, it will only be harder to resist the next time I'm tempted. This time I won't give in." The client is instructed to use this suggestion during self-hypnotic practice at home and also whenever a temptation to smoke is experienced. Once again, it is important that the client has accepted the validity of this conclusion before it is assigned for use as a self-hypnotic suggestion.

RESEARCH AND APPRAISAL

More than any other approach to treatment, cognitive–behavioral therapy is closely linked to empirical research. Many of the treatment techniques were derived from experimental research, and their efficacy has been tested in an exceptionally large number of therapy outcome studies (Bellack et al., 1990). Similarly, the cognitive–behavioral approach to hypnosis is backed by an extensive body of research (Spanos & Chaves, 1989). In this section, I review data on the effectiveness of hypnotic skills training, the efficacy of cognitive–behavioral therapy compared with other forms of treatment, and the effects of adding hypnosis to cognitive–behavioral interventions.

Effects of Hypnotic Skills Training

Research on the effects of hypnotic skills training similar to that described earlier in this chapter indicates that it produces modest but significant increases in responsiveness to suggestion (Katz, 1979; Vickery et al., 1985). More substantial increases have been demonstrated with the Carleton Skill Training Package (CSTP), which adds to these procedures instructions for enacting the physical components of suggested responses

(Gorassini & Spanos, 1986). However, these instructions may lead some subjects to fake their responses by responding behaviorally even when they do not experience the suggested phenomena (Bates, 1990). On the other hand, there are data indicating that the CSTP retains full effectiveness even when these instructions are deleted (Gearan, Schoenberger, & Kirsch, 1992).

Comparative Effectiveness of Cognitive–Behavioral Therapy

It is often claimed that therapy outcome data reveal all methods of psychological treatment to be equally effective. However, meta-analyses of these studies indicate a different conclusion. Meta-analysis allows a numerical comparison of the magnitude of outcomes across disparate studies. This is done by calculating effect sizes, which are the mean of the experimental group minus the mean of the control group divided by the standard deviation of the control group.

Table 1 summarizes data from two meta-analyses of the outcomes of different psychotherapies. The effect sizes in the first column were derived from a meta-analysis reported by Smith, Glass, and Miller (1980), which included analogue studies with college student volunteers, as well as outcome studies with genuine psychotherapy clients. Concerned that the results of analogue studies might not generalize to clinical settings, Andrews and Harvey (1981) restricted their meta-analysis to studies with real patients diagnosed with neurotic, phobic, depressive, and psychosomatic disorders, "the type of patients who usually seek psychotherapy" (p. 1204). The results of this analysis are summarized in the second column of Table 1.

The results of these two meta-analyses were the same: Cognitive–behavioral therapy was significantly more effective than psychodynamic therapy, which in turn produced better outcomes than placebo treatment,

TABLE 1
Comparative Effectiveness of Different Psychotherapies

Type of therapy	Mean effect size	
	Analog and real clients[a]	Real clients only[b]
Cognitive–behavioral	1.03[c]	0.97
Psychodynamic	0.78	0.72
Placebo	0.56	0.55
Humanistic	0.63	0.39
Counseling	0.42	0.31

[a]Smith, Glass, and Miller (1980). [b]Andrews and Harvey (1981). [c]Includes therapies categorized by Smith et al. (1980) as behavioral, cognitive, and cognitive–behavioral.

counseling, or client-centered therapy (Andrews & Harvey, 1981; Smith et al., 1980).

Hypnotic Versus Nonhypnotic Cognitive–Behavioral Therapy

My colleagues and I have located 18 published studies in which the effects of a cognitive–behavioral treatment were compared with the effects of the same treatment supplemented by hypnosis (Sapirstein, Montgomery, & Kirsch, 1992). In all but two of the studies, sufficient data were reported to calculate effect sizes. We analyzed these data by treating the groups receiving nonhypnotic treatment as control groups and those receiving hypnotic treatment as experimental groups. This resulted in a mean effect size of 0.87 standard deviations, and a t test revealed that the difference between hypnotic and nonhypnotic treatment was significant. An effect size of this magnitude indicates that the average client receiving cognitive–behavioral hypnotherapy is better off at the end of it than more than 80% of the clients who receive the same treatment in a nonhypnotic context.

Hypnosis is not for everyone. Some people are frightened by the loss of control that they mistakenly associate with hypnosis. Others think that hypnotizability is an indication of a weakness in will or that hypnotizable people are gullible. For clients with negative attitudes toward hypnosis, the hypnotic context is likely to diminish rather than enhance the effectiveness of treatment. Therefore, a modest overall effect is the most that would be expected when subjects are assigned to conditions randomly.

For these reasons, we found the size of the effect surprising. It is about the same magnitude as the effect size for psychotherapy in general compared with no treatment at all (Smith et al. 1980). An effect of this magnitude may be expected if clients were selected for inclusion in studies only if they preferred hypnotherapy. However, this does not seem to be the case in most of the studies we found (see Lazarus, 1973, for a notable exception). Perhaps the settings in which some of these studies were conducted attracted individuals who were particularly interested in hypnotherapy. Alternately, it is possible that hypnosis is currently viewed in a sufficiently positive light as to generate these results among a representative selection of patients. In any case, these data indicate that the question of whether hypnosis enhances treatment effects deserves far more attention among cognitive–behavioral researchers than it has been given to date.

CONCLUSION

Cognitive–behavioral hypnotherapy is the addition of hypnosis to the treatment procedures currently used by cognitive–behavioral therapists. These procedures have demonstrated effectiveness for a wide variety of dysfunctions, and meta-analyses indicate that they are significantly more effective than other psychotherapeutic methods. Although relatively sparse, research on the addition of hypnosis to these procedures indicates that the hypnotic context can enhance the efficacy of cognitive–behavioral therapy, especially for clients who are positively disposed to hypnosis.

Because hypnotic inductions and suggestions are similar to standard cognitive–behavioral procedures, a competent cognitive–behavioral therapist needs little additional training to incorporate hypnosis into treatment. In fact, cognitive–behavioral relaxation and imagery procedures can be thought of as hypnotic inductions and suggestions without the hypnotic label. Thus, for the cognitive–behavioral therapist, *hypnosis* is merely a new label for what is already being practiced. However, it is a label that can potentiate treatment for many clients. Unlike a rose, a therapy by a different name may not be experienced as the same.

REFERENCES

Amigó, S. (1992). *Manual de terapia de autorregulación.* Valencia, Spain: Promolibro.

Andrews, G., & Harvey, R. (1981). Does psychotherapy benefit neurotic patients? A reanalysis of the Smith, Glass, and Miller data. *Archives of General Psychiatry, 36,* 1203–1208.

Baker, S., & Kirsch, I. (in press). Hypnotic and placebo analgesia: Order effects and the placebo label. *Contemporary Hypnosis.*

Bandura, A. (1969). *Principles of behavior modification.* New York: Holt, Rinehart & Winston.

Barber, T. X. (1969). *Hypnosis: A scientific approach.* New York: Van Nostrand Reinhold.

Barber, T. X. (1985). Hypnosuggestive procedures as catalysts for psychotherapies. In S. J. Lynn & J. P. Garske (Eds.), *Contemporary psychotherapies: Models and methods* (pp. 333–375). Columbus, OH: Charles E. Merrill.

Barlow, D. H., Leitenberg, H., Agras, W. S., & Wincze, J. P. (1969). The transfer gap in systematic desensitization: An analogue study. *Behaviour Research and Therapy, 7,* 191–196.

Bates, B. L. (1990). Compliance and the Carleton Skill Training Program. *British Journal of Experimental and Clinical Psychology, 7,* 159–164.

Beck, A. T. (1976). *Cognitive therapy and the emotional disorders.* Madison, CT: International Universities Press.

Beck, A. T., Rush, A. J., Shaw, B. F., & Emery, G. (1979). *Cognitive therapy of depression.* New York: Guilford Press.

Bellack, A. S., Hersen, M., & Kazdin, A. E. (Eds.). (1990). *International handbook of behavior modification and therapy* (2nd ed.). New York: Plenum Press.

Bolles, R. C. (1972). Reinforcement, expectancy, and learning. *Psychological Review, 79,* 394–409.

Devine, D. A., & Fernald, P. S. (1973). Outcome effects of receiving a preferred, randomly assigned or nonpreferred therapy. *Journal of Consulting and Clinical Psychology, 41,* 104–107.

Ellis, A. (1962). *Reason and emotion in psychotherapy.* Secaucus, NJ: Lyle Stuart.

Ellis, A., & Grieger, R. (Eds.). (1977). *Handbook of rational-emotive therapy.* New York: Springer.

Eysenck, H. J. (Ed.). (1960). *Behavior therapy and the neuroses.* Elmsford, NY: Pergamon Press.

Fazio, R. H., & Zanna, M. P. (1981). Direct experience and attitude-behavior consistency. *Advances in Experimental Social Psychology, 14,* 161–202.

Freeman, A., Pretzer, J., Fleming, B., & Simon, K. M. (1990). *Clinical applications of cognitive therapy.* New York: Plenum Press.

Freud, S. (1959). Turnings in the ways of psycho-analytic therapy. In E. Jones (Ed.), *Sigmund Freud: Collected papers* (Vol. 2, pp. 392–402). New York: Basic Books. (Original work published 1919)

Gearan, P., Schoenberger, N. E., & Kirsch, I. (1992, August). *Modifying hypnotic responsiveness: A new component analysis.* Paper presented at the 100th Annual Convention of the American Psychological Association, Washington, DC.

Gibbons, D. E. (1974). Hyperempiria, a new "altered state of consciousness" induced by suggestion. *Perceptual and Motor Skills, 39,* 47–53.

Glass, L. B., & Barber, T. X. (1961). A note on hypnotic behavior, the definition of the situation, and the placebo effect. *Journal of Nervous and Mental Diseases, 132,* 539–541.

Gorassini, D. R., & Spanos, N. P. (1986). A social-cognitive skills approach to the successful modification of hypnotic susceptibility. *Journal of Personality and Social Psychology, 50,* 1004–1012.

Hilgard, E. R. (1965). *Hypnotic susceptibility.* New York: Harcourt, Brace & World.

Hilgard, E. R. (1986). *Divided consciousness: Multiple controls in human thought and action* (expanded ed.). New York: Wiley.

Hull, C. L. (1933). *Hypnosis and suggestibility: An experimental approach.* New York: Appleton-Century-Crofts.

Jacobson, E. (1929). *Progressive relaxation.* Chicago: University of Chicago Press.

Kanfer, F. H., & Grimm, L. G. (1978). Freedom of choice and behavioral change. *Journal of Consulting and Clinical Psychology, 46,* 873–878.

Katz, N. (1979). Comparative efficacy of behavioral training, training plus relaxation, and a sleep/trance induction in increasing hypnotic susceptibility. *Journal of Consulting and Clinical Psychology, 47,* 119–127.

Kihlstrom, J. F. (1985). Hypnosis. *Annual Review of Psychology, 36,* 385–418.

Kirsch, I. (1990). *Changing expectations: A key to effective psychotherapy.* Pacific Grove, CA: Brooks/Cole.

Kirsch, I., & Barton, R. D. (1988). Hypnosis in the treatment of multiple personality: A cognitive-behavioural approach. *British Journal of Experimental and
Clinical Hypnosis, 5,* 131–137.

Kirsch, I., Mobayed, C. P., Council, J. R., & Kenny, D. A. (1992). Expert
judgments of hypnosis from subjective state reports. *Journal of Abnormal Psychology, 101,* 657–662.

Lazarus, A. A. (1971). *Behavior therapy and beyond.* New York: McGraw-Hill.

Lazarus, A. A. (1973). "Hypnosis" as a facilitator in behavior therapy. *International
Journal of Clinical and Experimental Hypnosis, 21,* 25–31.

Lovaas, O. I. (1969). *Behavior modification: Teaching language to psychotic children*
[Film]. New York: Appleton-Century-Crofts.

Lynn, S. J., Neufeld, V., & Matyi, C. L. (1987). Inductions versus suggestions:
Effects of direct and indirect wording on hypnotic responding and experience.
Journal of Abnormal Psychology, 96, 76–79.

Lynn, S. J., & Rhue, J. W. (Eds.). (1991). *Theories of hypnosis: Current models
and perspectives.* New York: Guilford Press.

Mathews, W. J., Kirsch, I., & Mosher, D. (1985). The "double" hypnotic induction: An initial empirical test. *Journal of Abnormal Psychology, 94,* 92–95.

McConkey, K. M. (1986). Opinions about hypnosis and self-hypnosis before and
after hypnotic testing. *International Journal of Clinical and Experimental Hypnosis, 34,* 311–319.

Meichenbaum, D. (1974). *Cognitive behavior modification.* Morristown, NJ: General
Learning Press.

Rescorla, R. A. (1988). Pavlovian conditioning: It's not what you think it is.
American Psychologist, 43, 151–160.

Rescorla, A. (1991). Associative relations in instrumental learning: The 18th
Bartlett Memorial Lecture. *Quarterly Journal of Experimental Psychology, 43B,*
1–23.

Sachs, L. B., & Anderson, W. L. (1967). Modification of hypnotic susceptibility.
International Journal of Clinical and Experimental Hypnosis, 15, 172–180.

Sapirstein, G., Montgomery, G., & Kirsch, I. (1992). [Hypnosis as an adjunct to
cognitive behavior therapy]. Unpublished raw data.

Sarbin, T. R., & Coe, W. C. (1972). *Hypnosis: A social psychological analysis of
influence communication.* New York: Holt, Rinehart & Winston.

Sarbin, T. R., & Slagle, R. W. (1979). Hypnosis and psychophysiological outcomes. In E. Fromm & R. E. Shor (Eds.), *Hypnosis: Developments in research
and new perspectives* (rev. ed., pp. 81–103). Chicago: Aldine.

Smith, M. L., Glass, G. V., & Miller, T. I. (1980). *The benefits of psychotherapy.*
Baltimore, MD: Johns Hopkins University Press.

Spanos, N. P., & Chaves, J. F. (Eds.). (1989). *Hypnosis: The cognitive-behavioral
perspective* (pp. 360–379). Buffalo, NY: Prometheus Books.

Taylor, C. B. (1982). Adult medical disorders. In A. S. Bellack, M. Hersen, & A. E. Kazdin (Eds.), *International handbook of behavior modification and therapy* (pp. 467–500). New York: Plenum Press.

Vickery, A. R., Kirsch, I., Council, J. R., & Sirkin, M. I. (1985). Cognitive skill and traditional trance hypnotic inductions: A within-subjects comparison. *Journal of Consulting and Clinical Psychology, 53,* 131–133.

Wadden, T. A., & Anderton, C. H. (1982). The clinical use of hypnosis. *Psychological Bulletin, 91,* 215–243.

Wickless, C., & Kirsch, I. (1989). The effects of verbal and experiential expectancy manipulations on hypnotic susceptibility. *Journal of Personality and Social Psychology, 57,* 762–768.

Wolpe, J. (1958). *Psychotherapy by reciprocal inhibition.* Stanford, CA: Stanford University Press.

Wolpe, J., & Lazarus, A. A. (1966). *Behavior therapy techniques.* Elmsford, NY: Pergamon Press.

8

RATIONAL–EMOTIVE THERAPY AND HYPNOSIS

ALBERT ELLIS

Rational–emotive therapy (RET) is closely related to hypnosis and is consequently used by many hypnotherapists. It was originated in 1955 as the first of modern cognitive–behavioral therapies, and three surveys have shown it to be the most popular form of psychological treatment (Heesacker, Heppner, & Rogers, 1982; Smith, 1982; Warner, 1991). In its well-known ABC theory of neurosis, following ancient philosophers (e.g., Epictetus, Marcus Aurelius) and early cognitive psychologists (e.g., Alfred Adler, Robert Woodworth, Edward Tolman), the stimulus–response and conditioning theories of the psychoanalysts and radical behaviorists are revised. According to RET, individuals are not viewed as mere products of their early environment and social conditioning but as constructivists who actively *create* much of their reactions to others and to the world and who consequently *construct* their own disturbances by vitally *interacting* with their environment (Ellis, 1990).

In RET terms, unfortunate As (Activating Events) *seem* to cause Cs (disturbed emotional and behavioral Consequences) and thereby create people's neurotic reactions. More accurately, however, their Bs (Belief Systems) *about* their As strongly interact with these As and significantly affect their disturbed Cs. Moreover, according to RET, if people want to change their neurotic reactions at C, they can do so by changing the unfortunate As that occur in their lives; however, because these are often difficult or impossible to change, they can more efficiently change their Bs about their As and thereby become significantly less neurotic. Because people's As, Bs, and Cs are never pure but significantly interact with each other, and because their thoughts, feelings, and behaviors are also not disparate but integrally overlap, people had better change their Bs by using a number of powerful and persistent cognitive, emotional, and behavioral methods (Bernard, 1991; Ellis, 1957, 1962, 1985, 1988, 1991, 1992; Ellis & Dryden, 1987, 1990; Ellis & Grieger, 1977, 1986; Ellis & Harper, 1975; Ellis & Velten, 1992; Tosi, 1974; Tosi, Judah, & Murphy, 1989).

Although RET is always cognitive–behavioral, it stresses the active Disputing (D) of disturbed people's irrational (i.e., rigid, dogmatic, and "musturbatory") beliefs, more so than other systems of psychotherapy. Its methods of disputing include scientific debating, persuasion, suggestion, and positive thinking (Ellis, 1988, 1990); it also builds on and goes further than hypnotists such as Hippolyte Bernheim and Emile Coué in this respect. Bernheim (1886–1947) realized that hypnotism partly works through the hypnotist's strong suggestion (1947); Coué (1923) went a step further and realized that people use the hypnotist's suggestions and make them into self-suggestions or autosuggestions, thus enhancing the original suggestions. RET goes further still and holds that people use self-suggestion as one of the main modes by which they disturb themselves and thereby create and maintain their main irrational, dysfunctional beliefs. Because their disturbances are largely (not completely) self-created by conscious and unconscious self-suggestions, they almost always have the *choice* or *power* of telling themselves more functional or rational coping statements. They can do this by (a) listening to the suggestions of a hypnotist and *adopting* his or her health-producing ideas or (b) using autosuggestions or self-hypnosis independently (Ellis, 1958, 1962, 1984, 1986; Ellis & Dryden, 1987; Stanton, 1977, 1989).

RET practitioners do not favor hypnosis but instead favor teaching clients to consciously look for their own self-defeating beliefs, to discover and figure out what they are, and to actively dispute and challenge them (cognitively and behaviorally) until they explicitly acquire a new Effective Philosophy (E). This new philosophy, if it is achieved, tends to permanently change their dysfunctional, absolutist musts, shoulds, demands, and commands to flexible, alternative-seeking preferences. According to RET, people construct or adopt scores of dysfunctional or Irrational Beliefs (IBs), about 30 of which are common. For psychotherapeutic purposes, these can be categorized under three major headings: (a) "I *must* do well and win approval for my performances or else I am an inadequate, undeserving person." (b) "Other people *must* treat me considerately and fairly, and if they don't they should be severely damned and viewed as rotten, undeserving people." (c) "My life conditions and my environment *must* be arranged so that I easily and comfortably get all the important things I need and avoid all serious pain and frustration" (Ellis, 1957, 1991; Ellis & Harper, 1975; Ellis & Velten, 1992).

These basic self-sabotaging and socially destructive IBs, according to RET, are consciously and unconsciously (explicitly and implicitly) held by most people when they are feeling severely anxious, depressed, self-hating, and self-pitying, and when they neurotically behave against their own interests. The main objective of RET is to help clients consciously see and understand their IBs, fully realize that they mainly upset themselves by strongly and rigidly holding them, and steadily work and practice to give up their absolutist shoulds and musts and (fairly permanently) replace them with healthy, nonimperative preferences, desires, goals, and values (Ellis, 1962, 1988, 1991; Ellis & Dryden, 1987, 1990; Ellis & Harper, 1975).

Because a purpose of RET is to help clients effect a profound, highly conscious philosophic change, RET differs from many other kinds of hypnotic therapies. Thus, in psychoanalytic-oriented hypnosis, attempts are made to reveal clients' unconscious, presumably repressed experiences, and, by bringing them to consciousness, give them insight into the origins of their disturbances and release them to change. Ericksonian hypnosis presumably uses indirect suggestion to subtly help clients with little awareness to overcome their unconscious resistance to change. Behavioral hypnosis uses strong persuasion to help clients act more effectively but often gives them little awareness of what they are telling themselves to make themselves function poorly and how they can change their self-statements. Cognitive–behavioral hypnosis is largely derived from RET, but it tends to be less active–directive, less philosophical, and less forcefully emotive (Golden, 1985; Golden, Dowd, & Friedberg, 1987).

Although I have practiced hypnosis since 1950 and have been a Diplomate in Clinical Hypnosis since my early use of RET in the mid-1950s, I actually *discourage* most of my clients from persuading me to combine RET with hypnosis in their treatment. I tell them that we had better first use regular RET without hypnosis and that if that does not work, we will probably use it with hypnosis later. When they agree and we have had several sessions of regular RET first, almost all of them never get back to asking for hypnotic sessions. So we proceed without them.

My main reasons for *not* using hypnosis except in special instances are the following: (a) RET espouses that people should think for themselves and not to unthinkingly adopt the suggestions of a hypnotist (or of anyone else). Suggestion is a low-level form of thinking and not high-level falsification practiced by good scientists. (b) RET holds that people must be fully conscious of their dysfunctional beliefs and not merely cover them up with more productive rational beliefs that they tend to parrot (as in Emile

Coué's and Norman Vincent Peale's positive thinking) but not really firmly hold and follow. (c) Clients often want to be hypnotized because, having low-frustration tolerance, they view hypnotism as an easy and magical way of changing themselves. However, RET emphasizes that people almost always have to work hard and consistently practice new ways of thinking, feeling, and behaving, until—after some time—they semiautomatically begin to become self-conditioned to them. (d) RET aims to show clients how to be on their own and independently construct self-helping methods for the rest of their lives, whereas hypnosis often implies that they need an authoritative (or even authoritarian) hypnotist's help (Deltito & Baer, 1986).

In spite of these disadvantages, when my clients persist in asking me to use hypnosis combined with RET, I usually do so; in some cases I even suggest that we use it. The advantages of using hypnosis include the following: (a) Clients often believe in the power (or magic) of hypnosis and therefore are more likely to work at using RET when it is combined with hypnotism. (b) As indicated in the case presented later, I usually conduct RET hypnotherapy by recording the hypnosis session and having the clients listen to this recording 20 or 30 times. As they do so, they keep hearing the RET messages on the tape over and over and keep getting urged to do RET homework. They therefore are likely to respond to the rational self-statements that are on the tape and to keep doing their RET homework. (c) Each hypnotic taped session usually includes working with one or two of the client's main problems and helps the client concentrate on solving this neurotic problem before going on to other issues. (d) The general philosophy of RET—that people largely upset themselves and can therefore choose to "unupset" themselves—is repetitively shown to clients, so that they can adopt it and keep experimenting with applying it. (e) RET hypnotherapy is rarely used by itself but is combined with regular RET nonhypnotic individual or group therapy, so that clients are fully encouraged to think for themselves and not to merely unthinkingly follow the suggestions of the hypnotist.

CLINICAL APPLICATIONS

When I first used RET hypnotherapy, I put my clients in a light or heavy trance several times and gave them RET education and homework assignments for a number of sessions. However, I discovered that the depth of their trance did not seem to make much difference because when I gave them posthypnotic suggestions to work at using RET in their regular lives, they usually did so regardless of whether they achieved any deep trance state. In the 1970s, when most clients had cassette recorders, and when I found that having them tape their therapy sessions (which we encourage at the Institute for Rational–Emotive Therapy in New York) and listen to them in between sessions often helped them learn RET better, I decided to change my hypnotic procedure.

I first have at least one session—and frequently several sessions—of regular RET with my clients and ask them to go over with me one or two major problems that they want to deal with during our hypnotic session. They usually pick a problem such as social anxiety, depression over loss of a loved person, or overeating. I tell each of them to bring a blank cassette for recording our session.

At the beginning of the hypnotic session, I review the main problem we are going to work on. I tell them to lie down comfortably on a sofa in my office, with their shoes off, and with their hands and arms at their sides. They are not to say anything to me during the session but to just listen carefully to everything I say. I then put their blank cassette into one of my recorders and begin to record the session. For the first 8 or 10 min of the session, I try to put them into a light trance state by using Jacobson's (1938) progressive relaxation technique and getting them to go deeper and deeper into a state of hypnotic relaxation. Almost all of them report that they become exceptionally relaxed, but few of them become deeply hypnotized.

After 10 min, at most, of deep relaxation, I spend the next 10 min telling them how to use RET posthypnotically to work on their problem. Thus, if a man has social anxiety and is afraid to approach women at a dance or party, I will instruct him under hypnosis: (a) "Look for the irrational beliefs you are holding when you fail to approach a woman and keep looking until you find them." (b) "Particularly discover your dogmatic *shoulds* and *musts,* such as 'I *have* to succeed with her and I'm an *inadequate person* when I don't!' " (c) "Vigorously dispute your grandiose demands. Keep challenging them with questions such as 'Why do I *have to* succeed? How do I become a totally *inadequate person* if I don't?' " (d) "Tell yourself many times, very strong rational coping statements such as, 'It's uncomfortable to get rejected, but it's not *awful*! I don't like it but I definitely *can* stand it!' " (e) "Use rational–emotive imagery by imagining the worst thing that can happen to you—such as being rejected several times at a dance or party—let yourself feel very upset about this—such as feeling very anxious or depressed—and then work on your feelings to make yourself feel *only* appropriately sorry and disappointed but *not* anxious or depressed." (f) Practice this same rational–emotive imagery everyday for 20 or 30 days in a row, until you automatically begin to feel appropriately disappointed instead of inappropriately depressed about rejection." (g) "Make sure that at least a few times every week you do in vivo desensitization by risking getting rejected by suitable women you talk to." (h) "Begin to see that just about all your neurotic problems stem from your rigid *shoulds* and *musts* and that you can always choose to change these to *desires* and *preferences.*"

After 10 min of RET instructions for posthypnotic use, I end the hypnotic session by telling the clients that they will have no bad effects after the session and will have a subsequent good, happy day. I then give them the cassette to take home with them, with instructions to listen to it at least once a day for the next 30–60 days. I also see them for (usually a few) subsequent sessions to see whether they are listening to the tape, whether they are following its instructions, and what good or bad results they are getting. If they are doing well with the problem addressed on the hypnotic tape, we may have other sessions dealing mainly with their other problems, and especially with their self-denigration, which is usually their greatest neurotic hangup. We may also return to regular RET, with occasional reliance on special hypnotic sessions.

I have not done any detailed follow-up studies with the clients with whom I use RET hypnotherapy, but, on the basis of their informal reports I estimate that about 15% of them get unusually good results and 50% get fairly good results compared with nonhypnotic RET. About 5% get little or poor results, and about 30% get the same kind of results they get with regular RET. All told, the use of this method produces favorable findings, but this may be because I generally use it with clients who ask for it, who are prejudiced in favor of it, and who may therefore do their RET homework more consistently and forcefully because they favor hypnosis.

CASE MATERIAL

Because it would require too much space to include a transcript of a complete session of RET hypnotherapy in this chapter, I provide excerpts from a case that I have published in full elsewhere (Ellis, 1986). The client was a 33-year-old unmarried borderline woman who had been in therapy since the age of 13 for severe anxiety about her school, work, and love and sex performance; she was especially anxious about her anxiety and was afraid that it would make her go crazy and wind up in a mental hospital. Although she was attractive and did well as a sales manager, she was terrified about becoming homeless without any friends, lovers, or money.

After 13 sessions of RET, the client was using RET to notably decrease her terrors of failing, but she would tend to fall back (as borderlines often do) to feeling panicked again—and, especially, to feeling panicked about her panic. Hearing that one of her friends stopped smoking by using hypnotherapy, she asked me if I would use it with her, and I agreed to do so and had a single hypnotic session with her.

As usual, I spent the first 10 min of our session putting her in a light hypnotic trance using Jacobson's (1938) progressive relaxation procedure. As the following verbatim transcript shows, I then continued as follows:

> You're only focusing on my voice and you're going to listen carefully
> to what I'm telling you. You're going to remember everything I tell

you. And after you awake from this relaxed, hypnotic state, you're going to feel very good. Because you're going to remember everything and use what you hear—use it for you. Use it to put away all your anxiety and all your anxiety *about* your anxiety. You're going to remember what I tell you and use it every day. Whenever you feel anxious about anything, you're going to remember what I'm telling you now, in this relaxed state, and you're going to fully focus on it, concentrate on it very well, and do exactly what we're talking about—relax and get rid of your anxiety, relax and get rid of your anxiety.

Whenever you get anxious about anything, you're going to realize that the reason you're anxious is because you are saying to yourself, telling yourself, "I *must* succeed! I *must* succeed! I *must* do this, or I *must* do that!" You will clearly see and fully accept that your anxiety comes from your self-statements. It doesn't come from without. It doesn't come from other people. *You* make yourself anxious, by demanding that something *must* go well or *must* not exist. It's *your* demand that makes you anxious. It's always you and your self-talk; and therefore *you* control it and *you* can change it.

You're going to realize, "*I* make myself anxious. I don't *have* to keep making myself anxious, if I give up my demands, my musts, my shoulds, my oughts. If I really accept what is, accept things they way they are, then I won't be anxious. I can always make myself unanxious and less tense by giving up my musts, by relaxing—by wanting and wishing for things, but not *needing*, not *insisting*, not *demanding*, not *mus*turbating about them."

You're going to keep telling yourself, "I can *ask* for things, I can *wish*. But I do not *need* what I want, I never *need* what I want! There is nothing I *must* have; and there is nothing I *must* avoid, including my anxiety. I'd *like* to get rid of this anxiety. I *can* get rid of it. I'm *going* to get rid of it. But if I tell myself, 'I *must* not be anxious! I *must* not be anxious!' then I'll be anxious.

"Nothing will kill me. Anxiety won't kill me. Lack of sex won't kill me. There are lots of unpleasant things in the world that I don't like, but I can *stand* them, I don't *have* to get rid of them. If I'm anxious, I'm anxious—too damn bad! Because *I* control my emotional destiny— as long as I don't feel that I *have* to do anything, that I *have to* succeed at anything. That's what destroys me—the idea that I *have* to be sexy or I have to succeed at sex. Or that I *have* to get rid of my anxiety."

In your regular life, after listening to this tape regularly, you're going to think and to keep thinking these things. Whenever you're anxious, you'll look at what you're doing to *make* yourself anxious, and you'll give up your demands and your musts. You'll dispute your ideas that "I *must* do well! I *must* get people to like me! They *must* not criticize me! It's terrible when they criticize me!" You'll keep asking yourself, "Why *must* I do well? Why do I *have* to be a great sex partner? It would be *nice* if people liked me, but they don't *have* to. I do not *need* their approval. If they criticize me, if they blame me, or they think I'm too sexy or too little sexy, too damn bad! I do not *need* their approval. I'd *like* it, but I don't *need* it. I'd also *like* to be unanxious but there's no reason why I *must* be. Yes, there's no reason why I *must* be. It's just *preferable*. None of these things I fail at are going to kill me!

"And when I die, as I eventually will, so I die! Death is not horrible. It's a state of *no* feeling. It's exactly the same state as before I was born. I won't feel *anything*. So I certainly need not be afraid of that!

"And even if I get very anxious and go crazy, that too isn't terrible. If I tell myself, 'I *must* not go crazy! I *must* not go crazy!' then I'll make myself crazy! But even if I'm crazy, so I'm crazy! I can *live* with it even if I'm in a mental hospital. I can *live* and not depress myself about it. *Nothing* is terrible—even when people don't like me, even when I'm acting stupidly, even when I'm very anxious! *Nothing* is terrible! I *can* stand it! It's only a pain in the ass!"

Now that is what you're going to think about in your everyday life. Whenever you get anxious about anything, you're going to see what you're anxious about, you're going to realize that you are demanding something, saying "It *must* be so! I *must* get well! I *must* not do the wrong thing! I *must* not be anxious!" And you're going to stop and say, "You know—I don't need that nonsense. If these things happen, they happen. It's not the end of the world! I'd *like* to be unanxious, I'd *like* to get along with people, I'd *like* to have good sex. But if I don't, I *don't*! Tough! It's not the end of everything. I can always be a happy human *in spite of* failures and hassles. If I don't *demand*, if I don't insist, if I don't say, 'I must, I must!' Musts are crazy. My *desires* are all right. But, again, I don't *need* what I *want!*"

Now this is what you're going to keep working at in your everyday life. You're going to keep using your head, your thinking ability, to focus, to concentrate on ridding yourself of your anxiety—just as you're listening and concentrating right now. Your concentration will get better and better. You're going to be more and more in control of your thoughts and your feelings. You will keep realizing that *you* create your anxiety, *you* make yourself upset, and *you* don't have to, you never have to keep doing so. You can always give your anxiety up. You can always change. You can always relax, and relax, and relax, and not take *anyone*, not take *anything* too seriously.

This is what you're going to remember and work at when you get out of this relaxed state. This idea is what you're going to take with you all day, every day: "*I* control me. I don't *have* to upset myself about anything. If I do upset myself, too bad. I may feel upset for a while but it won't ruin my life or kill me. And I can be anxious without putting myself down, without saying, 'I must not be anxious!' At times I will make myself anxious, but I can give up my anxiety if I don't *demand* that I be unanxious."

And you're going to get better and better about thinking this rational way. You'll become more in control of you. Never *totally* in control because nobody ever is totally unanxious. But you'll make yourself much less anxious and able to live with it when you are anxious. And if you live with it, it will go away. If you live with it, it will go away. Nothing is terrible, not even anxiety. That's what you're going to realize and to keep thinking about it until you really, really believe it.

Now you feel nice and free and warm and fully relaxed. In a few minutes I'm going to tell you to come out of this relaxed, hypnotic state. You will then have a good day. You will feel fine when you come out of this state. You will experience no ill effects of hypnosis. You will remember everything I just said to you and will keep working at using it. And you will play this tape every day for the next 30 days. You will listen to it every day until you really believe it and follow it. Eventually you will be able to follow its directions and to think your way out of anxiety and out of anxiety *about* being anxious without the tape.

You will then be able to release yourself from anxiety by yourself. You can always relax and use the antianxiety technique you will learn by listening to the tape. You can always accept yourself *with* your anxiety and can stop telling yourself, "I must not be anxious! I must not be anxious!" Just tell yourself, "I don't *like* my anxiety, I'll work to give it up. I'll conquer it. I'll control myself, control my own emotional destiny. I can always relax, make myself feel easy and free and nice, just as I feel now, get away from cares for a while and then feel un-anxious. But I can more elegantly accept myself first with my anxiety, stop fighting it desperately, and stop telling myself it's awful to be anxious. Then I can go back to the original anxiety and get rid of it by refusing to awfulize about failing and vigorously disputing my irrational beliefs, 'I must do well! I must not be disapproved.' "

Now you feel good, you feel relaxed, and in a couple of minutes I'm going to count to three and when I count to three you will awake and feel quite alive, have a good day, and experience no bad effects, no headaches, no physical discomfort! Everything is going to be fine and you'll have a good day. You will remember all this and, as I said, you will listen to this tape whenever you possibly can, at least once a day. And you will think and act more and more on its message. You'll be able to control yourself and reduce your anxiety appreciably. And when you do feel anxious you'll live with the anxiety, accept it, and refuse to panic yourself about it. All right, I'm going to count to three and when I say *three* you'll wake and be fully alive and alert and feel great for the rest of the day. One, two, three! (Ellis, 1986, pp. 5–10)

This client replayed the recording of her hypnotic RET session at least once a day for 45 days and said that her anxiety, and especially her anxiety about her anxiety, had significantly decreased. She was no longer phrenophobic, mainly because she convinced herself that she probably would never go to a mental hospital but that if she did it would be extremely inconvenient but not horrible. She also worked on her fears of sex and other failures, conquered them for a while, and when they partially reappeared was able to cope with them.

I saw her for regular, nonhypnotic RET sessions for 14 months more but had only eighteen 30-min sessions with her during that period. I see her occasionally now, not as a client but as a participant in my regular Friday night workshops at the Institute for Rational–Emotive Therapy in New York, where I do public demonstrations of RET with volunteer participants. She has largely maintained her nonanxious demeanor, with a few setbacks when a crisis occurs in her life, and is now happily married and highly productive. Once in a while, she still listens to the original hypnotic tape and feels that it is helpful and that it was instrumental in her making greater progress than she had previously made with RET.

RESEARCH

A number of articles, case studies, and books have been published that show the effectiveness of combining RET with hypnosis, including those by Araoz (1982), Boutin (1989), Ellis (1958, 1984, 1986), Golden (1983, 1985), Golden et al. (1987), Greene (1973), Grossack (1974), Hartman (1967), Hoellen (1988), Johnson (1980), Levitzky (1968), Tosi (1974), and Tosi & Baisden (1984).

A number of research studies have been done comparing the effects of using RET combined with hypnosis with the effects of non-RET treatment. Donald J. Tosi, of Ohio State University, has created rational state-directed hypnotherapy, which (like regular RET) includes cognitive restructuring, experiential and behavioral methods, and hypnosis. He and his students have found that his integration of RET and hypnosis has shown considerable effectiveness for a number of psychological disorders, including guilt (Tosi & Marsella, 1977; Tosi & Reardon, 1976); depression (Fuller & Tosi, 1980; Reardon, Tosi, & Gwynne, 1977); test anxiety (Boutin & Tosi, 1983); nonassertiveness (Gwynne, Tosi, & Howard, 1978; Howard & Tosi, 1978); learning disabilities (Tosi, Fuller, & Gwynne, 1980); academic underachievement (Corley & Tosi, 1980); hypertension (Rudy & Tosi, 1980); migraine headache (Howard, Reardon, & Tosi, 1982); chronic pain (Murphy, Tosi, & Parisser, in press); adolescent delinquency (Reardon & Tosi, 1977); and duodenal ulcer (Tosi et al., 1989).

Stanton (1977, 1989) has also reported two studies in which RET combined with hypnosis produced significantly better therapeutic results than did a control group using other therapy procedures when used with anxious individuals. As I have also suggested (Ellis, 1986), a useful study may be done using the rational suggestions included in the tape recording described in the previous section of this chapter, with and without hypnosis, to determine whether hypnosis adds anything to RET used by itself.

CONCLUSION

The RET theory of neurosis holds that people largely upset themselves by strongly thinking and suggesting to themselves dogmatic, rigid musts and demands about their more flexible, healthy desires and preferences. They consciously and unconsciously often create, and powerfully suggest to themselves, absolutist shoulds and musts, especially (a) "I *must* perform well and be lovable!" (b) "You *must* treat me fairly and nicely!" (c) "Conditions *must* be the way I really want them to be!" People can ameliorate or surrender these self-defeating irrational beliefs by scientifically disputing them, by changing the feelings that accompany them, and by persistently acting against them.

This can perhaps best be done if people are taught, through RET, to become less suggestible to others and more prone to independent thinking, feeling, and acting for themselves. Hypnosis is often achieved mainly through other-suggestion rather than through self-suggestion and is therefore by no means an elegant form of therapy. RET can be combined with hypnosis, however, and can significantly help many clients, particularly those who resist using its cognitive, emotive, and behavioral methods to change themselves. A number of studies have shown that RET combined with hypnosis is more effective than with a control that does not use RET. The question still to be studied is whether RET combined with hypnosis is more effective than similar RET used by itself.

REFERENCES

Araoz, D. L. (1982). *Hypnosis and sex therapy*. New York: Brunner/Mazel.

Bernard, M. E. (Ed.). (1991). *Using rational–emotive therapy effectively*. New York: Plenum Press.

Bernheim, H. (1947). *Suggestive therapeutics*. New York: London Book Company. (Original work published 1886)

Boutin, G. E. (1989). Treatment of test anxiety by rational stage directed hypnotherapy: A case study. *Australian Journal of Hypnotherapy and Hypnosis, 10*(2), 65–72.

Boutin, G. E., & Tosi, D. J. (1983). Modification of irrational ideas and test anxiety through rational stage directed hypnotherapy (RSDH). *Journal of Clinical Psychology, 39*, 382–391.

Corley, D., & Tosi, D. J. (1980, June). *The treatment of academic underachievement through rational stage directed imagery (RSDI)*. Paper presented at the Third Annual Conference on Rational–Emotive Therapy, New York.

Coué, E. (1923). *My method*. New York: Doubleday.

Deltito, J., & Baer, L. (1986). Hypnosis in the treatment of depression. *Psychological Reports, 58,* 923–929.

Ellis, A. (1957). *How to live with a neurotic: At home and at work.* New York: Crown.

Ellis, A. (1958). Hypnotherapy with borderline psychotics. *Journal of General Psychology, 59,* 245–253.

Ellis, A. (1962). *Reason and emotion in psychotherapy.* Secaucus, NJ: Citadel.

Ellis, A. (1984). The use of hypnosis with rational emotive therapy. *International Journal of Eclectic Psychotherapy, 3*(2), 15–22.

Ellis, A. (1985). *Overcoming resistance.* New York: Springer.

Ellis, A. (1986). Anxiety about anxiety: The use of hypnosis with rational–emotive therapy. In E. T. Dowd & J. M. Healy (Eds.), *Case studies in hypnotherapy* (pp. 3–11). New York: Guilford Press.

Ellis, A. (1988). *How to stubbornly refuse to make yourself miserable about anything— Yes, anything!* Secaucus, NJ: Lyle Stuart.

Ellis, A. (1990). Is rational–emotive therapy rationalist or constructivist? In A. Ellis & W. Dryden (Eds.), *The essential Albert Ellis* (pp. 114–141). New York: Springer.

Ellis, A. (1991). The revised ABCs of rational–emotive therapy. *Journal of Rational–Emotive and Cognitive Behavior Therapy, 9,* 139–172.

Ellis, A. (1992). *Brief therapy: The rational–emotive method.* In S. H. Budman, M. F. Hoyt, & S. Friedman (Eds.), *The first session in brief therapy* (pp. 36–58). New York: Guilford Press.

Ellis, A., & Dryden, W. (1987). *The practice of rational–emotive therapy.* New York: Springer.

Ellis, A., & Dryden, W. (1990). *The essential Albert Ellis.* New York: Springer.

Ellis, A., & Grieger, R. (Eds.). (1977). *Handbook of rational–emotive therapy* (Vol. 1). New York: Springer.

Ellis, A., & Grieger, R. (Eds.). (1986). *Handbook of rational–emotive therapy* (Vol. 2). New York: Springer.

Ellis, A., & Harper, R. A. (1975). *A new guide to rational living.* North Hollywood, CA: Wilshire Books.

Ellis, A., & Velten, E. (1992). *When AA doesn't work for you: Rational steps to quitting alcohol.* New York: Barricade Books.

Fuller, J., & Tosi, D. J. (1980, June). *The treatment of hysterical depression through rational stage directed hypnotherapy.* Paper presented at the Third Annual Conference on Rational–Emotive Therapy, New York.

Golden, W. L. (1983). Rational–emotive hypnotherapy: Principles and practice. *British Journal of Cognitive Psychotherapy, 1*(1), 47–56.

Golden, W. L. (1985). Commonalities between cognitive-behavior therapy and hypnotherapy. *Cognitive Behaviorist, 7*(2), 2–4.

Golden, W. L., Dowd, E. T., & Friedberg, F. (1987). *Hypnotherapy: A modern approach.* Elmsford, NY: Pergamon Press.

Greene, J. (1973). Combining rational–emotive and hypnotic techniques: Treating depression. *Psychotherapy, 10,* 72–73.

Grossack, M. (1974). *Hypnosis and self hypnosis for rational living.* Boston: Branden Press.

Gwynne, P. H., Tosi, D., & Howard, L. (1978). Treatment of nonassertion through rational stage directed therapy (RSDH) and behavior rehearsal. *American Journal of Clinical Hypnosis, 20,* 263–271.

Hartman, B. J. (1967). Applied rational therapy. *Rational Living, 2*(2), 25.

Heesacker, M., Heppner, P., & Rogers, M. (1982). Classics and emerging classics in counseling psychology. *Journal of Counseling Psychology, 29,* 400–405.

Hoellen, B. (1988). Hypnosverfahren im Rahmen der RET. In J. Laux & H.-J. Shchubert (Eds.), *Klinische hypnose* (pp. 73–80). Pfaffenweiler, Federal Republic of Germany: Centaurus-Verlag.

Howard, L., Reardon, J. P., & Tosi, D. (1982). Modifying migraine headache through rational stage directed hypnotherapy: A cognitive experimental perspective. *International Journal of Clinical and Experimental Hypnosis, 30,* 257–269.

Howard, L., & Tosi, D. (1978). Effects of rational stage directed imagery and behavioral rehearsal on assertiveness. *Rational Living, 13,* 3–8.

Jacobson, E. (1938). *You must relax.* New York: McGraw-Hill.

Johnson, W. R. (1980). Hypnotherapy and cognitive therapy in a case of secondary impotence. In H. G. Beigel & W. R. Johnson (Eds.), *Application of hypnosis in sex therapy.* Springfield, IL: Charles C Thomas.

Levitsky, A. (1968). Guilt, self-criticism and hypnotic induction. *American Journal of Clinical Hypnosis, 15,* 127–130.

Murphy, M. A., Tosi, D. J., & Parisser, R. R. (in press). Psychological coping and the management of pain with rational stage directed therapy and biofeedback. *Psychological Reports.*

Reardon, J., & Tosi, D. (1977). The effects of rational stage directed imagery on self-concept and reduction of stress in adolescent delinquent males. *Journal of Clinical Psychology, 33,* 1084–1092.

Reardon, J., Tosi, D., & Gwynne, P. (1977). The treatment of depression through rational stage directed hypnotherapy (RDH): A case study. *Psychotherapy, 14,* 95–103.

Rudy, D. R., & Tosi, D. J. (1980, June). *Rational–emotive therapy in the family program.* Paper presented at the Third Annual Conference on Rational–Emotive Therapy, New York.

Smith, D. (1982). Trends in counseling and psychotherapy. *American Psychologist, 37,* 802–809.

Stanton, H. E. (1977). The utilization of suggestions derived from rational–emotive therapy. *International Journal of Clinical and Experimental Hypnosis, 25,* 18–26.

Stanton, H. E. (1989). Hypnosis and rational–emotive therapy: A de-stressing combination. *International Journal of Clinical and Experimental Hypnosis, 37,* 95–99.

Tosi, D. J. (1974). *Youth: Toward personal growth, a rational–emotive approach.* Columbus, OH: Charles E. Merrill.

Tosi, D. J., & Baisden, B. S. (1984). Cognitive experiential therapy and hypnosis. In W. Wester & J. Smith (Eds.), *Clinical hypnosis* (pp. 155–178). Philadelphia: Lippincott.

Tosi, D. J., Fuller, J., & Gwynne, P. (1980, June). *The treatment of hyperactivity and learning disabilities through RSDH.* Paper presented at the Third Annual Conference on Rational–Emotive Therapy, New York.

Tosi, D. J., Judah, S. M., & Murphy, M. M. (1989). The effects of a cognitive experiential therapy utilizing hypnosis, cognitive restructuring, and developmental staging on psychological factors associated with duodenal ulcer. *Journal of Cognitive Psychotherapy, 3,* 273–290.

Tosi, D., & Marzella, J. N. (1977). The treatment of guilt through rational stage directed therapy. In J. L. Wolfe & E. Brand (Eds.), *Twenty years of rational therapy* (pp. 234–240). New York: Institute for Rational Emotive Therapy.

Tosi, D., & Reardon, J. P. (1976). The treatment of guilt through rational stage directed therapy. *Rational Living, 11*(1), 8–11.

Warner, R. E. (1991). A survey of theoretical orientations of Canadian clinical psychologists. *Canadian Psychology, 32,* 525–528.

9

AN ERICKSONIAN MODEL OF HYPNOTHERAPY

WILLIAM J. MATTHEWS, STEPHEN LANKTON, and
CAROL LANKTON

Milton Erickson (1901–1980) was generally acknowledged to be the world's leading practitioner of medical hypnosis. He had a life-long dedication to exploring hypnotic phenomena and published more than 100 papers on a variety of subjects related to his interest during his professional life. Erickson was an innovator in his approach to therapeutic change who often used hypnosis to help bring about change in his clients. He thought of therapy as a way of helping people to extend their self-perceived limits. Although such a perspective seems reasonable to therapists today, this notion was at odds with traditional psychiatry during much of Erickson's professional life.

Few people have had more need to extend their limits than Erickson. In 1919, Erickson contracted polio and was told he would never walk again. He spent hours learning to discover feelings and sensations in the muscles not completely destroyed by polio. Within a year he was walking with crutches. He once remarked that these physical limitations made him more observant. The skills that he developed for his own survival he used in his observations of others. He believed that the minute muscle movements people use would be revealing if one would only learn to observe them (Haley, 1967). For example, because he was tone-deaf, he learned to tell the quality of a pianist by the range of touch he or she used. High-level playing requires many different types of touch. Erickson said,

> My tone deafness has forced me to pay attention to inflections in the voice. This means I'm less distracted by the content of what people say. Many patterns of behavior are reflected in the way a person says something rather than in what he says. (quoted in Haley, 1967, p. 2)

One particular experience in Erickson's early life seems particularly influential in creating a context for his professional contributions. After contracting polio at age 17, he overheard three doctors tell his parents that their son would be dead in the morning. He indicated that he felt intense anger that a mother should be told such a thing about her son. When his mother came into his room after meeting with the doctors, he instructed her to arrange the furniture in a particular way. The rearranged furniture allowed him to see out of the west window. Erickson said that he would be "damned if I would die without seeing one more sunset" (quoted in Rossi, Ryan, & Sharp, 1983, p. 10). This experience was powerful in forming Erickson's worldview of overcoming one's real or perceived limitations. Erickson, of course, lived to see many more sunsets, during which time he overcame many of his limitations and helped thousands of clients overcome theirs.

Prior to presenting an Ericksonian approach to hypnosis followed by a case example, we discuss the philosophical underpinnings of Erickson's work, which can provide an important context in which to understand his interventions.

RATIONALE AND PHILOSOPHY

One can see in Erickson's articles a constant effort to challenge the limitations of most schools of psychotherapy. In the development of most approaches to psychotherapy, there has been considerable effort to elaborate a theory that would guide clinical procedure. Although practice needs to be informed by theory, the clinical interventions developed seem fairly restrictive in the range of behaviors proscribed for the therapist. This appears to be particularly true for most psychoanalytically oriented therapies, which continue to hold a position of dominance in the medical and psychological communities.

Rossi (Erickson & Rossi, 1980) suggested that the limitations of these therapies arise from three general assumptions: (a) Therapy based on observable behavior and related to the present and future circumstances of the client is often viewed as superficial and lacking depth when compared with therapies that seek to restructure clients' understanding of the distant past. (b) The same approach to therapy (e.g., classical analysis, Gestalt therapy, transactional analysis, nondirective therapy) is appropriate for all clients in all circumstances. This assumption denies the context of the problem, the unique learning, experiences, and resources of clients and the type of symptom presented. (c) Effective therapy occurs through an interpretation and explanation of a client's inner life on the basis of assumptions of the given theory. Change, from this perspective, occurs mainly through insight by a client into his or her own behavior.

Rossi (Erickson & Rossi, 1980), in his introduction to Erickson's approach, indicated that the elaborate and involved theoretical interpretations of human behavior in conjunction with rigid therapeutic procedures have made the process of psychotherapy longer and more expensive than it need be and thus unavailable to many people. Most therapies require, at least indirectly, that clients adapt to the therapist's worldview when it may not be in their best interests to do so. From early in his life, Erickson began to challenge traditional notions, expectations, and limitations placed on him.

The Importance of the Client's Daily Life in Therapy

Focusing on history to the exclusion of the client's daily life contradicts basic experience. Events in daily life can have a profound influence in the development of character or personality. These events can occur completely out of the immediate situation and dramatically affect the client's present and future. As Rossi (Erickson & Rossi, 1980) correctly pointed out, these events do not need to be considered extensions of earlier unresolved infantile traumata in order to be understood.

Although people have memories, perceptions, and feelings regarding their past, current realities impinge on them and affect their daily and future interactions in the world. Preoccupation with the past and a disregard of present and future needs unnecessarily prolong and complicate the process of therapy. Certainly a hallmark of an Ericksonian approach is an emphasis on current interpersonal relationships and their influence on the development and resolution of problems. Although an individual might have developed a symptomatic behavior in the distant past, the Ericksonian view focuses on how the problem is maintained in the present. Thus, in this approach, the unique interpersonal interactions in the client's daily life are more important than relying on the application of a rigid theory and techniques.

Although past events and traumata can be the basis for psychotherapy, they need not be its exclusive focus. Ericksonian therapy is based on identifying client strengths and increasing the possibility of new learning and experiences that can be used in solving a given problem in the client's present life. In addition, this work focuses on orienting a given solution toward future developmental changes. A more detailed discussion on assessment and intervention follows.

ERICKSONIAN APPROACHES TO HYPNOSIS

There is not total agreement among experts on the meaning of the word *hypnosis*. *Hypnosis* means *sleep* in Greek, and many hypnotherapists at one time or another have probably used the expressions "going to sleep" or "waking up" when doing hypnosis. However, the act of sleeping seems to have little connection to the process of hypnosis. Thus, as Araoz (1982) indicated, hypnosis is a construct that can mean a special state of mental functioning, the technique to create that state, the experience of oneself in that special state of mental functioning, or all of these.

A view held by much of the scientific community regarding hypnosis is that it is a particular state of consciousness (Bowers, 1966; Gill & Brenman, 1959; Hilgard, 1966; Orne, 1959) that can be experienced only by those with the personality trait of "hypnotizability" (Hilgard, 1965, 1975; Hilgard, Weitzenhoffer, Landes, & Moore, 1961). Hypnotizability as a trait has often been measured by classical scales of hypnotizability (Shor & Orne, 1962; Weitzenhoffer & Hilgard, 1959, 1962). The trance state is assumed to exist because of the behaviors manifested by hypnotized people. Because these behaviors do not usually occur in the normal waking state, it is assumed that inducing hypnotizable people puts them in this special state of mental functioning. This model is an approach common to most psychological research (i.e., the influence of the independent variable (hypnotic induction) on the dependent variable (hypnotic behaviors; Araoz, 1982).

Ericksonian approaches to hypnosis emphasize the intervening variables of the inner processes of the individual. It is these mediational variables of both the conscious and unconscious mind (that which is outside of conscious awareness) that allow the individual to experience hypnosis. In the traditional approach, it is accepted that hypnosis will not occur with uncooperative individuals. Embedded in this position is the notion that hypnosis can occur when the person allows it to occur. The notions of trait and hypnotizability, constructs viewed as being in the individual, become significantly less relevant when the hypnotist–client context is considered. The essence of the Ericksonian approach is creating the context that will allow hypnosis to occur.

Hallmarks of the Ericksonian Approach

Rossi (Erickson & Rossi, 1980; S. Lankton & Lankton, 1983, 1986; Matthews, 1985a, 1985b; O'Hanlon, 1987; Zieg, 1980, 1982), among others, has identified four basic principles to Erickson's work. Rossi (Erickson & Rossi, 1980) has indicated that these principles represent a paradigmatic shift to an entirely different way of using hypnotherapy. These principles are as follows:

1. The unconscious need not be made conscious. Unconscious processes can be facilitated such that they can remain outside of conscious awareness and be used for problem solving.

For Erickson, the unconscious was considered to be a complex set of associations that covered a broad range of human experience. It is the unconscious patterns of the individual that regulate, control, and guide the moment-to-moment conduct of an individual. These patterns are resources that can be used in hypnotherapy to create different perceptions, experiences, and behaviors by the individual. For Erickson, the unconscious was a repository of positive resources and skills that could be used for positive therapeutic change. This conscious–unconscious splitting or differentiation provides for the possibility of multiple levels of communication between the hypnotherapist and client. S. Lankton and Lankton (1983) stated that everything done by, to, or for the body at an unconscious level is done either for maintaining health, prohibiting it, or promoting it (p. 9). Thus, it is at the unconscious level that stories, double binds, and paradoxes are directed. Rossi (Erickson & Rossi, 1979) suggested that if the metaphor of "conscious" and "unconscious" could be translated to the metaphor of "dominant" and "nondominant" hemispheres, there may be a neuropsychological basis for describing a new hypnotherapeutic approach (p. 247).

2. Mental mechanisms and personality characteristics need not be analyzed for the client. They can be used as processes for facilitating therapeutic goals.

One of Erickson's major contributions to the process of hypnotherapy specifically and to therapy in general is this notion of utilizing the client's ongoing behavior, perceptions, and attitudes for therapeutic change. Clients are not asked to conform to the therapist's mode of interaction; rather, their behavior is accepted and utilized in the treatment process. Haley (1967) provided a dramatic example of utilization in the client who could not stop pacing in Erickson's office. Rather than trying to force the man to sit in the chair and relax in order to begin, which might have resulted in an escalation of wills between Erickson and the client and perhaps a termination of therapy, Erickson asked the individual if he were willing to cooperate with him by continuing to pace the floor. The man replied that he must continue to pace the floor in order to remain in the office. In accepting this behavior, Erickson then proceeded to make fairly direct and simple suggestions that coincided with the man's pacing. Over a period of time, suggestions of relaxation and the desire to eventually sit in a particular chair were embedded in Erickson's offerings. Erickson offered suggestions in such a manner that anything the client did was construed as a positive response. Over a period of time, the client was able to sit in the chair and develop a therapeutic trance. Thus, behaviors that might have been viewed as antithetical to therapeutic success were considered to be a part of the process of therapy and were used to increase the expectation for a positive therapeutic outcome by both therapist and client.

> 3. Suggestions need not be direct. Indirect suggestion permits (a) the subject's individuality, previous life experience, and unique potentials to become manifest; (b) the classical psychodynamics of learning with processes such as association, contiguity, similarity, and contrast are all involved on a more or less unconscious level so that (c) the client's conscious limitations and criticism can be bypassed and therefore increase therapeutic effectiveness (Erickson & Rossi, 1980, p. 455).

Direct suggestion occurs when the hypnotherapist makes a clear, direct request for a certain response. With indirect suggestion, the relation between the hypnotherapist's request and the client's response is less clear. For example, using direct suggestion in trance induction, the therapist may say to the client, "Close your eyes, and become more and more relaxed." In using a more indirect approach, the same suggestion could be, "As you develop a level of comfort necessary for your own learning, perhaps you will notice your eyes closing, closing part way or remaining as they are, as you go deeper into trance." Here, the client is given a wide range of options in developing a trance state that is unique to him or her.

As S. Lankton and Lankton (1983) and Hammond (1984) have indicated, Erickson certainly used direct suggestion. In the early part of his career, he relied greatly on direct suggestion and repetition. However, in the latter part of his life, he utilized indirection more heavily. He observed that indirection allowed him to show respect for clients by not directly challenging them to do what their conscious mind, for whatever reason, would not do. Indirection is the basis for the therapeutic use of metaphors, stories, paradox, binds, and so forth, because they allow clients to make meaning relevant for them and to explore their potential to facilitate new responses.

> 4. Hypnotic suggestion is not a process of programming the client with the therapist's point of view but a creation of new meanings, attitudes, or beliefs that can lead to different behaviors.

Hypnosis itself is not a curative force. No serious student of hypnosis believes hypnosis can transcend one's normal capabilities and bring about a dramatic change. Erickson (Erickson & Rossi, 1980) was clear that in all of his years of clinical experience, he never found any validity to such claims of miraculous healing by some unusual power arising out of hypnosis. He simply maintained that people have more potential and resources than they realize. For Ericksonians, the value of hypnosis lies in its ability to evoke and utilize the client's vast storehouse of hidden potential. The evocation and utilization of the client's potential is a process unique to the individual and seems less likely to occur with a purely direct, rigid, or programmed approach.

Therapeutic Trance

Within the Ericksonian framework, hypnotic trance is a time when the client's conscious limitations are at least partially suspended so that the individual can be receptive to alternative associations and ways of mental functioning that are supportive of problem solving. Rossi (Erickson & Rossi, 1979) conceptualized the dynamics of trance into a five-stage process. Stage 1 is the *fixation of attention,* which seeks to utilize the client's beliefs and behaviors for focusing on inner realities. Stage 2 *appends* the client's typical frames of reference and belief systems. The use of distraction, surprise, shock, metaphor, and doubt will disrupt the client's typical conscious functioning and create the possibility for Stage 3, an *unconscious search* for new meanings or experiences that may lead to problem resolution. This unconscious search leads to, and overlaps with, Stage 4, an *unconscious process* that is the activation of personal associations and mechanisms whereby a reorganization of one's experience can take place. Finally, Stage 5 is the *hypnotic behavior* in which the individual often reports or shows a behavior as seemingly being independent of his or her typical conscious control. The so-called "Eureka" experience is a naturalistic example of unconscious search and process that often happens without formal trance induction. Hand levitation as the result of hypnotic induction is a more typical example of unconscious search and process leading to a behavior that the client often reports as spontaneous. In the following section we present a conceptual model of assessment and intervention in conjunction with a case study. One should note that there is no one Ericksonian method or approach. The following material was developed from Erickson's work based on the interpretation of C. Lankton and Lankton (1989), S. Lankton and Lankton (1983, 1986), S. Lankton, Lankton, and Matthews (1991), Matthews (1985a, 1985b), and Matthews & Dardeck (1985).

CLINICAL APPLICATIONS

Seemingly dramatic Ericksonian interventions such as hypnosis, symptom prescription, paradox, and metaphors cannot be used in the absence of an understanding of client functioning within his or her social system. Any form of assessment needs to be related to intervention, and intervention needs to connect back to assessment.

Figure 1 (Matthews, 1985b) is a conceptual cybernetic model of assessment, intervention, and termination within an Ericksonian framework. The central notion is that the therapist is a part of the system he or she observes rather than being separate from or hierarchical to it. The therapist–client system and interaction becomes primary as opposed to the therapist acting independently on the passive client.

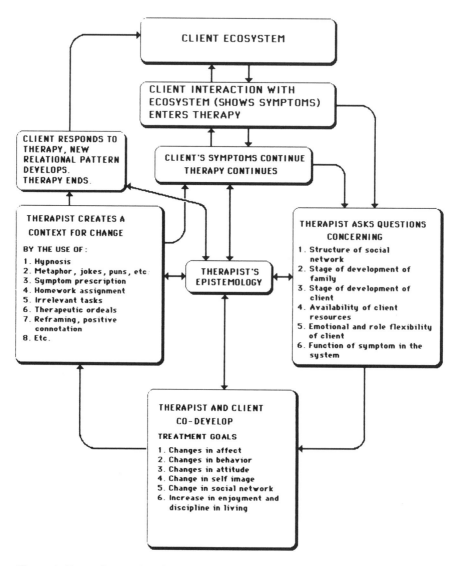

Figure 1: Recursive model of Ericksonian therapy. Reprinted with permission from Matthews, 1985b, p. 55.

Client Ecosystem

The client enters therapy as part of a larger system consisting of family, ethnic, and cultural influences. Each person has a personal history, world-view, and particular roles within his or her family. The therapist, even if seeing only the individual client, needs to consider how the client's behavior (symptoms) fit within the larger systemic framework. One needs to consider that problematic behavior at one level within the system may contribute to stability at another level within the system. However, an escalation (in symptomatic behavior) has occurred that has resulted in a client or the family seeking help outside of their present system.

Diagnostic Parameters

S. Lankton and Lankton (1983) suggested six categories from which to assess the client's levels of functioning. They are as follows: (a) What is the structure of the client's social network? Who is in it? Does the client have friends, family? Who talks to whom? Who is most and least aware or concerned about the client's concerns? What kind of work does the client do? How is that related to the presenting issue? Questions such as these place the client within his or her social context. (b) What is the stage of development of the client's family? Is the client an adolescent leaving home? The first in his or her family of origin to get married? Are the client's parents facing retirement, illness, divorce, death? Is the client facing the birth of a first child, divorce, remarriage, the empty nest, and so on? Questions of this nature place the client in the context of his or her nuclear and family of origin and place the presenting issue in a developmental life span framework. (c) What is the developmental age and task of the client? Given the client's age, certain developmental tasks seem reasonable to consider. For example, is the client an adolescent dealing with his or her first intimate relationship? A college student about to graduate and enter the job market? A person about to become a first-time parent? An elder shifting from work to leisure activities? However, a person's developmental age may not fit his or her chronological age. For example, does a 35-year-old man who complains of no intimate relationships with women continue to treat women as he did when he was a 16-year-old? What does it mean for a 32-year-old woman to leave her parents' home and live on her own for the first time? Determining the relation between developmental age and tasks will aid the therapist in designing treatment interventions that fit the client's needs. (d) What is the availability of resources of the client? Does the client have the ability to relate to others in a friendly, intimate, and assertive manner? What range of problem-solving skills does the client have? The intention here is to build on the client's strengths rather than focus only on his or her weaknesses. (e) What is the emotional and role flexibility of the client? Can the client show a wide range of emotional behaviors in various settings? Does the client have the ability to show a wide range of roles in various settings? Is the client cast by his or her social network into one role (e.g., scapegoat, incompetent, depressive, peacemaker, etc.) in all situations? Thus, to the extent that the client can experience a range of different emotions and roles, he or she has a higher probability of achieving satisfaction in interpersonal relationships. (f) What is the function or meaning of the symptom within the system? What will happen within the larger system when the client changes his or her behavior? Thus, assessment will always, to some degree, involve a larger system context even when a single client seeks therapy.

Treatment Goals

Goals for treatment need not be fixed ideas imposed on the client but can be mutually agreed on by the client and therapist. On the basis of the assessment, treatment goals may cover any one or all of the categories listed in Figure 1, which are as follows: changes in affect, behavior, attitudes, beliefs, self-image, and social network, as well as an increase in enjoyment and discipline in living. The latter goal is particularly Ericksonian, as Erickson held the view that life was to be enjoyed and that enjoyment was closely connected to discipline in daily living.

Therapeutic Interventions

Following Figure 1, the therapist and client can then decide on what interventions may be used to cocreate the desired and agreed-on goals. Interventions within this framework have a connection to assessment and continuous process of evaluation. Although the focus of this chapter is on hypnotherapy, one should note that the interventions listed can occur with or without the use of formal hypnosis.

As Figure 1 indicates, if the client's symptoms continue, then the therapist needs to cycle back for reassessment of the diagnostic parameters, treatment goals, and treatment interventions. If, however, the client develops new patterns of interaction relative to the presenting issue, then therapy is terminated. Embedded in the middle of this chart is the therapist's epistemological stance, a stance that is part of the client–therapist system and not only influences this system but is simultaneously influenced by it. Here, the therapist seeks to positively connote the client's behavior and to recognize that the presenting behavior has some ecological fit for the client. Important in this frame is the idea that the map created about the client is invented by the therapist on the basis of his or her worldview, not an absolute representation of reality.

CASE MATERIAL

The following case of a 42-year-old woman (S. Lankton, 1989; reprinted by permission) was a demonstration given in Phoenix, Arizona, in December 1988 (and followed for 8 months thereafter). "Linda" had a history of physical and sexual abuse in her home. She was unmarried and living alone at the time of the therapy. Her presenting complaint was that she avoided others because of self-imposed criticisms and thoughts that she was not acceptable to others. Linda specifically requested therapy to help her accept compliments. The following material in small type is part of the actual transcript with Linda (S. Lankton, 1989; reprinted with permission), followed by commentary by the senior author (William J. Matthews).

> Lankton: Would you be willing to tell us your age?

A simple question, but in asking it Lankton implies that she has control of the information she decides to share and what she has the right to withhold. Linda then explains that she engages in a lot of negative and self-deprecating thoughts that she would like to stop.

> Lankton: I would like to change it, if it were me. I'm not quite sure what your motivation is for changing it. Why do you want to? Woody Allen does fine with it.
> Linda: It is really unhelpful for me!
> Lankton: But what is your motivation for getting rid of this self-effacement? How do you imagine your life would be improved somehow if you did?
> Linda: I wouldn't be, um, I would be able to be less afraid about being in groups and more able to receive credit when people try to give it to me. I would be able to teach easier without it being traumatic. I mean those are the things that I am doing.

In this exchange about what reason Linda has for changing her behavior and how specifically her life would be improved by this change, Lankton sought to determine (a) the context and logic of this behavior in her life, (b) what behaviors would indicate positive identifiable change, and (c) what the cost of change would be. Perhaps in changing the self-effacing behavior, she would be more unhappy if, for example, by being more self-assured Linda were challenging a family rule of communication or some notion of how a woman is supposed to be in interpersonal relationships.

> Lankton: . . . . We remember the past for the ways we are doing this stuff, or we credit them for the ways we are doing it. What do you blame or credit for how come you are self-effacing? In some ways I reckon it's a real strength that helped: kept you somehow from getting more punishment that you expect you might have gotten. And by keeping yourself self-critical, you've anticipated punishment

and maybe removed some of the actual punishment that you would have gotten; so in a way it's been real handy, and it's sort of survival strength. But why did you do it in the first place?

Lankton offers the possibility of reframing a perceived limitation (self-effacing behavior) as a strength. In doing so, the meaning of this behavior for Linda can dramatically change. Linda responds to Lankton's last question with uncertainty as to why she learned this behavior. Lankton reiterated his reframe with the notion that given the unpleasantness of her home life rather than being self-critical she could have said to herself, "I survived another day!" (which is also an indirect suggestion for future positive self-talk). Following this suggestion, Lankton introduces the idea of hypnosis.

> Lankton: . . . . We might/could talk for two hours and really get something accomplished that would be useful just by talking. I wonder what we could accomplish that would be useful in trance. That's what I would like to attempt to do. And I know you will seek further help and so on afterward to the extent you need it, and you are capable of doing that.

This brief introduction is a good example of the use of indirect suggestion. Lankton says much could be accomplished in just talking, but his wondering about what would be accomplished in trance is an indirect suggestion to Linda to experience trance in order to find out. He also reminds her that she has the ability to seek additional therapy after this demonstration if it is in her best interest.

> Lankton: You go into trance in your own way, of course, and in your own time into the depth that is appropriate for you. And although you may have your eyes open in trance, you may begin by closing them. Sooner or later the sense of concentrating your attention and becoming comfortable, by letting your conscious mind focus "in" on certain thoughts that are least distressing for you, so that your unconscious can have some freedom to play with other thoughts, entertain other ideas, investigate experiences. You can lean back in the chair all right, or is that a problem.
> Linda: (leans back in chair).

In this interaction, Lankton offers Linda a range of ideas and opportunities to develop her own trance experience that will be valuable to her. He suggests that although she can experience a trance with her eyes open, she may begin by closing them. The implication is that with her eyes open or closed, she can experience a trance that is useful for her. In his next offering to Linda, Lankton suggests that although her conscious mind has a specific task to focus on relaxing thoughts, her unconscious mind can begin to investigate new possibilities that, by definition, will be outside of her conscious awareness. He creates, with Linda, the possibility for new ideas and associations to occur, although her conscious mind may have doubts and concerns.

> Lankton: One of the things that I sometimes ask people to do in trance is to dissociate their experience in trance from everything else—to never have the generalization of the successful experience in the trance—not to anticipate having it, not to worry about having it. Just let the experience be all by itself, like standing on the observation deck of the Eiffel Tower. Thinking about all that history, and you're not part of it.

Linda's presenting issue is self-effacing behavior in which she examines her ongoing experience and criticizes herself for not doing "better" regardless of what she is doing. In order to circumvent her critical conscious mind, Lankton suggests that this trance experience need not be generalizable. Instead, she can learn to dissociate from her experience and perhaps develop a different understanding. He then proceeds to offer her a number of anecdotes of how one dissociates.

As we discussed at the beginning of this chapter, metaphor and anecdote are important means of communicating at multiple levels with the client. Lankton suggests the importance of Linda learning to dissociate from her experience in order to develop a different perspective and then proceeds to tell a story that demonstrates a natural, everyday dissociative experience that he has had. Although one cannot assume that Linda is having exactly the experiences Lankton is describing, we do assume that Linda is making some meaning related to comfort, relaxation, and dissociation. Her nonverbal behavior was consistent with a relaxed state. At the end of the story, Lankton states that his job in this trance experience with Linda is to help stimulate conscious and unconscious thinking in ways that can be useful to her. Following this story, Lankton gives Linda feedback about her physical state that ratifies a trance experience (i.e., her cheek muscles are relaxed, rapid eye movement has decreased, swallow reflex has slowed, breathing is deeper and slower, etc.).

Lankton again reiterates that this trance experience can be valuable in and of itself and need not have generalizability in her daily life. He then proceeds to tell another story about a woman with whom he worked who had chronic back pain that was significantly diminished in their trance work. Lankton suggests that the woman make sure that the pain comes back after the trance and that this experience need not influence her daily life in any way unless she wanted it to. Lankton continues with the value of metaphor.

> Lankton: There's another problem in telling metaphors to people in trance, and that is: Who will the person identify with? I think it would be perfectly legitimate for you to identify with everybody I talk about in the metaphor. I might talk about my daughter and my

conduct with my daughter. After all you can't really understand the situation that occurs to people in the metaphor unless you have projected into it. I don't know if you have ever thought of holding yourself as a little girl. Everyone sooner or later has the idea. Your conscious mind may have flirted with the idea and allowed your unconscious mind to have the experience a little bit. Maybe your conscious mind has had the experience a little bit and allowed your unconscious mind to flirt with the idea.

Lankton is now ready to help Linda re-create or invent some pleasant childhood experiences but, prior to doing so, he directly suggests to Linda the importance of identifying with all of the characters in the metaphors he may tell, specifically with the idea of having the feelings and experiences of a little girl. Lankton is fully aware that Linda's childhood experiences were not predominantly positive, so he tells her that she can identify with his daughter and her experiences. This creates the likelihood that she will have the positive experiences that Lankton soon details.

Lankton proceeds with a series of stories about the tender relationship between him and his own daughter and between his daughter and her mother. In these stories he details the tender physical and emotional connections with his own daughter. The intention here is to have Linda identify with and have these tender feelings as she projects herself into the story Lankton tells. In order to enhance this learning for Linda, Lankton offers a description of the physical feelings his daughter has during these tender interactions. However, rather than refer to his daughter by name or as "she," as one would typically do when speaking with a third person (i.e., Linda), he repeatedly uses the pronoun *you*, which may serve to confuse Linda about whom he is talking (i.e., his daughter) or her [Linda], thereby becoming a suggestion for Linda to identify with the positive feelings being discussed.

> Lankton: . . . . And I wonder how it makes a child feel, where you'd feel it on your face. What would happen with regard to your heart rate, your breathing rate, your feelings of your musculature, your sense of self? You learn it, it becomes a part of you. You bring it with you the next time you walk into the living room.

Lankton seeks to have Linda's physiological experience in trance coincide with her psychological state, thus enhancing the positive connection between the two. He then continues with the importance of having feelings of mastery in one's life. He offers a series of anecdotes of how children achieve mastery by pretending.

> Lankton: And there is no harm in pretending, it is very good rehearsal to make space somewhere inside for that new feeling to develop.

In the midst of the anecdotes of how children pretend, Lankton offers a statement about the value and importance of pretending. Lankton then becomes more direct with Linda and suggests how she can use the experience she is having in trance.

> Lankton: Then you can think about my daughter and you can have those experiences. What is memory anyway except imagination? So go into trance to a depth necessary to allow you to have the imagination of the memory. Feeling that degree of safety and comfort with the agreement that if you have it now, it's disconnected from everything. It's a trial period. It has no meaning. There is no threat it will generalize into the rest of your life. Just like an ant digging a little bitty tunnel down into the sand and making a great big hole in which he can live, or a little rabbit that makes a little burrow, down a little thin hole up to the earth. But inside the burrow who knows what the rabbit is doing? Maybe just storing jars of honey before Pooh Bear comes to visit.

Lankton directs Linda to have a memory and imagine having feelings like his daughter, but she need not worry about having to generalize those feelings to her everyday life with references like those to Pooh Bear; he probed for associations to a deeper sense of hope and childhood dreams. Like the rabbit in the burrow, who knows what positive experiences she is storing in her unconscious for use at a later time.

> Lankton: And let the feeling of safety be something that you feel more now than you ever felt before. Know what it's like for your little finger to feel it, for your ankle. Feel the skin temperatures change with it. And know that your conscious mind needn't even remember it, but that you have made an agreement that you are going to the depth of the trance necessary to have the experience now more than you have ever had it. Let it radiate to the tips of your fingers. Let it radiate out your fingers and toes. Ooze safety, security, belonging, in a way you most imagined that my daughter probably does. And then I want you to keep it constant for the next five minutes, with the agreement that if there is any difficulty for you having that experience, you can be fully assured that you won't have it again after the trance is over. It's just a little experiment. Now memorize it and hold on to it. Does it feel good?
> Linda: (slight head nod and smile).

Lankton continues to emphasize that this experience for Linda should be considered only as an experiment with no lasting effects. She has the control to make such a decision. In response to his question about whether the experience she is having feels good, she answers affirmatively. He then asks her to open her eyes while having these positive feelings and know that she is able to open her eyes while holding onto these feelings. Linda is able to do so. He then asks her to look at the group (audience) while holding onto the feelings. Linda is able to look at the audience while holding onto the positive feelings. In order to further stabilize her desirable state of consciousness, he subsequently checked whether she was able to project her current emotional state onto the audience and verify that she believed the audience to be accepting of her. After establishing that Linda can have her eyes open and look at the audience while holding onto these feelings, Lankton then asks her to try to have self-effacing thoughts while she is holding onto the positive feelings. He exhorts her to try to have negative memories from her childhood while maintaining these positive feelings and images looking at the audience. Lankton comments to the audience and indirectly to Linda that this is a form of reciprocal inhibition that floods a person's negative experience with positive feelings rather than the reverse.

> Lankton: Sometimes I work with people and I mention that they will do an experience in trance and they'll gain an idea that they just won't be able to shake when the trance is over. Something will seize their mind as a useful concept or an idea and it will stay with them.

Lankton offers, indirectly, the possibility that Linda may want to keep this positive experience without challenging her with a direct posthypnotic suggestion that she will continue to have this experience. Thus, there is no chance of Linda failing regardless of what she does. At this point, Lankton continues his challenge of Linda to try to have negative memories of experiences that in the past had served to prove she is wrong and should be self-effacing.

> Lankton: So I would like you to try really hard to feel bad while you are holding this feeling and looking at the group that you become aware that you failed at feeling bad. And maybe criticize yourself for that.
> Linda: (laughs).

To help reduce her performance anxiety, Lankton uses a paradox with Linda in that he challenges her to feel bad and when she fails at this task, to criticize herself for failing at failing. Prescribing the symptom creates the possibility of new meaning (e.g., as taking conscious control of what was thought to be involuntary) for the symptom. While in the trance, Lankton asks Linda how this experience worked. She is clear that this experience is new to her (i.e., to look at others without thinking they are criticizing her). She indicates that she feels relaxed and comfortable with this new learning.

Lankton then asks Linda, who continues in the trance, to close her eyes and appreciate what she has just done. He explicitly reminds her of her accomplishment and the fact that this experience can have many different meanings for her. To illustrate his point metaphorically, he then proceeds to tell Linda a series of short anecdotes about his own learning experiences as a child in which he learned significant things such as riding a bike and swimming almost as if by accident. He reminds her that there are many things that one does by accident that have important connections to the rest of one's life. This interaction is a direct attempt to strengthen the significant experience that Linda has just had while in the trance and to create the possibility that she will take this experience with her into her everyday life.

Lankton then begins a 5-min metaphoric story about a fictitious youth who lived "before the age of technology."

> Lankton: . . . . And he had lived kind of in isolation with a wall around him for a long time, in a city with a wall around it. It seemed perfectly reasonable. It was all he knew. He had very few possessions, and he carried them with him most of the time: a key [that] didn't open any lock, a feather that he pretended was an eagle feather (which actually just came from a seagull that had gotten lost in the desert), a whistle that he hardly ever used because when he blew it it didn't make any sound, and a crystal.

In the story, the young man then left his town to explore the desert, only to return to find that his beloved town was gone. Not knowing what to do, he went to see the region's magistrate, who listened to his story.

> Lankton: The Magistrate said, "Well, it's always different in each case. And this one of course, is unique. But one thing that is certain to me is that sometimes it's a matter of trust and sometimes it's a matter of wit, and sometimes it's a matter of courage and sometimes it's a matter of the heart. And the tests that you have will be a test of your heart."

Clearly, the intention here is for Linda to identify with the protagonist of the story and to follow his quest with the parallels in her own life. Lankton proceeds to take his protagonist through a series of trials in which he needed courage, heart, trust, and wit to overcome. In each of the trials, the protagonist used one of his possessions (the key, feather, whistle, or crystal) to solve his dilemma. In doing so, however, he lost each possession. For instance, he found himself locked in a cage for which he used his key to free himself, but the key became lodged in the lock. In each trial, a different emotion and character trait were emphasized. However, the protagonist thought he was a failure and was certain that the magistrate would think the same. However, in the end, the magistrate reviewed each of the trials that the protagonist had to overcome.

> Lankton: . . . . The Magistrate congratulated him on a job well done. He passed the test! . . . . The Magistrate said you have a heart filled with *truth* and you saw it. And you could have thought that the beast was evil and malicious, but to you it was humorous, and your heart passed the test of being a *light heart*. And you saw that the cage had come undone, and you could have thought that it was evil

and malicious, but you decided it was an accident and proved you have the *capricious and forgiving heart*. And when the animals threatened you, you could have tried to be brave and pretend, but you have the *trusting* heart and you asked for help . . . . Go back to where you came from now, and you will find, I think, free of delusion, that the home you look for is there.

Remembering that the overall contract is to reduce her debilitating self-criticism, the story offers Linda a way to draw conclusions for herself about herself. A story of this structure invites the listener to reevaluate isolated experiences previously thought to be failures in light of a larger context of one's growth and life accomplishments. This act of maturing is one of the natural ways in which people learn to forgive themselves and perhaps others.

Lankton then offers the idea of amnesia for what they had done in this session and reminds her that she does not need to change anything if she chooses not to. Again, he attempts to relieve any pressure on Linda to have immediate success with this experience. He then returns to his initial story about the client with back pain. He reports that her pain had gone.

> Lankton: . . . . because you can use those unconscious accidental experiences that occur to you, in your own unconscious way, at your own speed, and let your unconscious discover just how or if you'll use what you've done here today.

Case Follow-Up

Within 4 months after this initial therapy session, Linda reported being surprised to find that she sought out and engaged in more social contact, including allowing others to touch her for the first time. Interestingly, the increased social contact occurred simultaneously with a great deal of criticism from a co-worker who was in disagreement or in competition with her. She stated that she was more aware of incidents in her past and that she was not self-critical as a result of this increased awareness. She subsequently engaged in additional therapy to resolve important aspects of her past that she had refused to share with others before this session.

In this session, Lankton emphasized three different areas that focused on Linda's major presenting issues: (a) the method of dealing with social avoidance and posttraumatic stress in which a secure reality was created and Linda was given the opportunity to experience others as noncritical; (b) the repeated paradoxical restraint from change in order to reduce Linda's anxiety and inhibit her self-critical faculties from undercutting the potential of change; and (c) the emphasis in the final metaphor on reevaluating her life as that of a person with a "good heart." The implication in this metaphor was that perhaps Linda may begin to reevaluate her life and to appreciate her qualities and strengths.

These three aspects of the treatment in the case of Linda emphasize key elements of an Ericksonian approach, which are (a) a focus on the present and future with an opportunity to reexperience previously negative stimuli from a different perspective; (b) the therapeutic use of reframing in which any response the client makes can be considered to be positive and a part of the therapeutic process; and (c) the challenging and shifting of negative attitudes about the self that have created limitations in the client's worldview and subsequent experience.

RESEARCH AND APPRAISAL

Most of the Ericksonian interventions reported in the literature are either clinical case studies or anecdotes, not systematic investigations of clinical claims. Although clinical case studies are both fascinating and informative to practitioners, this method, however, has well-known weaknesses in terms of making causal connections between treatment and outcome. More univariate, multivariate, and multiple-baseline research designs need to be used to further investigate the important observations made by clinicians. Over the past decade, an increasing amount of research has been conducted concerning Erickson's ideas. The following is a brief overview of some of the initial research on Ericksonian techniques and principles.

Bandler and Grinder (1975, 1979) developed a neurolinguistic programming (NLP) model of psychotherapeutic practice primarily on the basis of their view of Erickson's patterns of communication. NLP hypothesizes that individuals make mental maps of the world by processing sensory data through idiosyncratic frames of reference on the basis of auditory, visual, and kinesthetic input. Their model predicts that individuals have a primary system or preferred way (e.g., auditory) of making such reality maps. Therapy that uses, changes, or broadens the client's primary representational system was hypothesized to be more effective in developing rapport and increasing the possibility of change.

Dowd and Petty (1982), Gumm, Walker, and Day (1982), Dowd and Hingst (1983), Henry (1984), and Coe and Scharcoff (1985) found no support for a preferred modality in clinical or laboratory settings. Falzett (1981), however, found that therapists who matched clients' primary representational system were reported to be more trustworthy than therapists who did not. Yapko (1981) reported mixed findings in that subjects showed more physical relaxation when the primary representational system was used to induce hypnosis; however, their self-reports of relaxation failed to match the wording of the primary representational system with the wording of the relaxation instructions. The research on NLP is at best mixed in support of the theory and demands more empirical validation to support the claims of its practitioners.

Bandler and Grinder (1975) also called attention to a double hypnotic induction procedure that is based on Erickson's notion of two-level communication; in such a procedure, one would offer one set of suggestions with one tone of voice while interspersing another set of suggestions in a different tone of voice. Bandler and Grinder (1975) used two separate hypnotists speaking simultaneously to the subject and hypothesized that this induction procedure would be particularly effective. Matthews, Kirsch, and Mosher (1985), in comparing a standard induction (Stanford Hypnotic Susceptibility Scale, Form C; Weitzenhoffer & Hilgard, 1963) with a double hypnotic induction, found no significant differences between the two inductions in terms of depth of trance (as measured by behavioral responses to suggestion). Additionally, they reported that the double hypnotic induction might have actually decreased hypnotic responsiveness. Their data raised questions about the claims of greater trance depth with the double induction made by Bandler and Grinder (1975).

An important element of the Ericksonian approach both in the induction of trance and in treatment intervention is the use of indirect suggestion (Erickson & Rossi, 1979, 1980; Haley, 1973; S. Lankton & Lankton, 1983; Matthews, 1985b). Indirect suggestions are defined as suggestions that have a degree of ambiguity and allow for increased latitude in responding on the subject's part. By contrast, direct suggestion is a clear request for a particular response by the hypnotist to the subject. Alman and Carney (1980), using audiotaped inductions of direct and indirect suggestions, compared male and female subjects on their responsiveness to posthypnotic suggestions. They reported that indirect suggestions were more successful in producing posthypnotic behavior than were direct suggestions.

McConkey (1984) used direct and indirect suggestions with real and simulating hypnotic subjects. He found that although all of the simulating subjects recognized the expectation for a positive hallucination, half of the real subjects responded to the indirect suggestions and half did not. McConkey (1984) concluded that "indirection may not be the clinically important notion as much as the creation of a motivational context where the overall suggestion is acceptable such as making the ideas congruent with the other aims and hopes of a patient" (p. 312).

Van Gorp, Meyer, and Dunbar (1985), in comparing direct and indirect suggestions for analgesia in the reduction of experimentally induced pain, found direct suggestion to be more effective as measured by verbal self-reports and autonomic lability scores. Stone and Lundy (1985) investigated the effectiveness of indirect and direct suggestions in eliciting body movements following suggestions. They reported that indirect suggestions were more effective than direct suggestions in eliciting the target behaviors.

Mosher and Matthews (1985) investigated the claim by S. Lankton and Lankton (1983) that embedding a series of metaphors will create a natural structure for amnesia for material presented in the middle of the metaphoric material. The authors compared treatment groups who received multiply embedded stories with indirect suggestion for amnesia with control groups who received multiple embedded metaphor without indirect suggestions for amnesia. They found support for the structural effect of embedding metaphors on amnesia but also reported that indirect suggestion did not enhance the effect of amnesia.

Matthews, Bennett, Bean, and Gallagher (1985) compared subjects' responses on the Stanford Hypnotic Clinical Scale (Morgan & Hilgard, 1978) to subjects' responses on the same scale rewritten to include only indirect suggestions. They found no significant behavioral differences between the two scales. However, they did report that individuals who received the indirect suggestions perceived themselves to be more hypnotized than those who received the Stanford Hypnotic Clinical Scale.

In a follow-up study, Matthews and Mosher (1988) sought to compare direct and indirect hypnotic induction and direct and indirect suggestions. Thus, one quarter of the subjects received direct induction followed by direct suggestions, one quarter received indirect induction followed by indirect suggestion, and the remaining half of the subjects received a mixed procedure. The results did not support the efficacy of indirect induction and suggestion over direct induction and suggestion. Contrary to expectations, the data also revealed that subjects who received indirect induction and suggestions reported feeling more resistant to the hypnotist than did subjects who received direct induction and suggestion.

Weekes and Lynn (1990) also compared direct and indirect suggestions for a range of hypnotic behaviors and found no significant behavioral differences; however, they did find that subjects who received direct suggestions perceived their hypnotic responses to be more involuntary than did those who received indirect suggestions. Weekes and Lynn also found that subjects who received indirect suggestions reported a greater fear of negative appraisal by the experimenter than did subjects who received direct suggestions. This latter result may be similar to the earlier finding by Matthews and Mosher (1988) of an increase in resistance to the hypnotist by subjects who received indirect suggestions. The research to date would appear to be mixed at best in support of indirect suggestion as compared with direct suggestion in producing trance depth and a range of hypnotic and posthypnotic behaviors.

In most of this research, the reader should remember that the tests were done with audiotaping to standardize the intervention and that it was therefore not possible to tailor the suggestions (whether direct or indirect) and stories to the individual. As a result, they do not emphasize the importance Erickson attached to adapting and using the unique responses of the individual. Similarly, and perhaps more important, these tests were not designed in a context that attempted to address the relevant goals of each individual. Therefore, in this regard, the research may not represent an accurate picture of how a clinical client would experience the interventions.

Systematic study of Erickson's ideas in the clinical setting may provide more useful information with regard to process and efficacy than the more limited analogue studies previously mentioned. For example, Bank (1985) reported positive results over a 22-month period when hypnotic suggestions (both direct and indirect) were used for the control of bleeding that occurs in patients following the insertion and removal of the angiographic catheter. During this time period, an ABA design was used out of medical necessity with a particular patient who was given suggestions to stop his bleeding, which he did. The patient was then told that in order to find out what was bleeding, he needed to undo the previous suggestion and start bleeding, which he did. Bank concluded that although a causal connection was not established beyond any possible doubt, he believed that the use of hypnotic suggestion was highly effective in the control of this type of bleeding. Bank's study underscores the importance of a context in which certain suggestions have a significant relevance not often found in the analogue study.

Matthews and Langdell (1989) used S. Lankton and Lankton's (1983) multiple embedded metaphor procedure with 6 clients who had a range of presenting issues on three separate occasions over eight treatment sessions. The purpose of the study was to simply ask the clients what meaning they made about the treatment they were receiving. The assumption in the use of metaphor was that effectiveness was most likely when clients were amnesic for the metaphoric experience. Clients were shown video presentations of their hypnotic inductions and metaphors and were asked a series of structured questions about their experience. Five of the 6 clients believed that they were completely aware and nonamnesic of the meaning and purpose of the metaphors at the time of the clinical session.

They indicated that although the stories seemed obvious to them, they trusted and liked the therapist and as such chose to go along with the treatment. Each reported thinking about the meaning of the therapeutic stories told to them during the intervening week and how they could act differently with regard to the presenting issue. Each of the 5 clients reported a positive change in the presenting problem. The 6th client reported almost total amnesia for each of the metaphor sessions. He also indicated his dislike of the treatment process and reported no therapeutic change.

Nugent (1989a) attempted to show a causal connection between symptomatic improvement and Erickson's notion of "unconscious thinking without conscious awareness." In a series of seven independent case studies with a range of presenting problems (e.g., fear of injections, performance anxiety, claustrophobia), he used the same methodological procedure and treatment intervention (i.e., orientation, induction, Ericksonian suggestions for change, trance ratification). A pretreatment baseline response, the most recent onset of the problem, and therapeutic change relative to the intervention were all systematically assessed by Nugent. In all seven cases, each client reported a clear, sustained positive change with respect to the presenting problem. Although the individual case study has certain methodological limitations, Nugent's use of seven independent cases with a carefully followed treatment protocol makes his conclusion of causality more convincing.

In a related study, Nugent (1989b) used a multiple-baseline design to investigate the impact of an Ericksonian hypnotic intervention. The Ericksonian interventions used were the "pseudo-orientation in time" technique (Erickson & Rossi, 1980) and the "unconscious thinking without consciousness awareness" directive (Erickson & Rossi, 1979). The target behaviors were two athletic skills performed by a collegiate athlete and her level of confidence to perform those behaviors adequately. The data indicated that the target behaviors changed as a result of the treatment intervention. Each of the Nugent (1989a, 1989b) studies, in addition to the Matthews and Langdell (1989) study, have methodological weaknesses but represent a legitimate attempt to systematically investigate the clinical validity of Ericksonian interventions.

With the exception of the aforementioned clinically oriented studies, this research review has focused on Ericksonian techniques and has an important contribution to make to scientific knowledge. However, it is perhaps easier to discuss Erickson's techniques than to discuss the subtle but more important contributions of his overall approach. With an overemphasis on technique, novice therapists have frequently been guilty of applying a technique without an adequate sense of how such techniques develop a natural interaction with clients. The effective application of Ericksonian techniques relies heavily on the principles of use and cooperation that emerge in the clinical context. The same criticism may be applied to researchers who attempt to study a particular technique separate from the therapeutic context.

For the future, research that may have more bearing on Erickson's approach is that which examines the differences between pathological and nonpathological models (i.e., Ericksonian). For that, researchers may need to look beyond traditional hypnosis research, such as the frequently cited Rosenthal and Jacobson (1968) study in which randomly selected students were described to their teachers as having exceptional intelligence and could be expected to perform better than their peers, which they did. When retested 9 months later, these students continued to outperform their peers simply as a function of teacher expectations (positive, nonpathological). The recent work of Kirsch (1985, 1990) on the importance of expectancy and its relation to behavior may capture more of the essence of Erickson's approach, which was to create a context with the client in which an expectancy for change will occur. Thus, the gestalt of the therapist epistemology, beliefs, attitudes, and expectancies create the context in which a given technique may have meaning for clients. Future research must not focus on techniques to the exclusion of the context in which they occur.

CONCLUSION

Fisch (1990) stated that perhaps Erickson's greatest contribution to psychotherapy was not his innovative techniques of metaphor and paradox but his ability to "depathologize" people. Instead of considering a client's problematic behavior as indicative of an underlying personality deficit, he viewed people as making the best choice they can in an unfolding life cycle. Family therapist Lynn Hoffman once described Erickson as "a human dialysis machine" (personal communication, 1987). He filtered out people's negative self-perceptions and focused on what clients could do, not what they could not.

Erickson's approach to therapeutic change was to help the client access the resources needed to solve a given problem. If the resources needed were not fully developed, Erickson would create opportunities within and outside of the hypnotic session for the client to develop and use the needed resources for problem resolution. One is reminded of the time when an inpatient at a state hospital kept insisting that he was Jesus Christ. The more the staff confronted the patient on the falseness of his belief, the more insistent he became. Erickson simply said to the man, "I hear you are a carpenter" and then asked him to make some bookcases (Haley, 1973). The process of change had begun.

Ericksonian hypnotherapy is solution focused. The therapeutic orientation is to identify what is of concern to the client, what solutions have been used to date, and what is the desired outcome. These questions are considered within a developmental and systemic framework. The essence of this approach is the reassociation of positive resources to the needed situation such that the client has an increased sense of agency. The client is always considered within some interpersonal context. The ultimate goal of therapy is to promote more adaptive and satisfying interpersonal relationships.

Erickson developed many techniques to help create the desired therapeutic change. His use of paradox, symptom prescription, metaphor, jokes, and puns with and without a hypnotic trance have become legend. Underlying these interventions is the importance of using the client's behavior to promote change. Ericksonian work also places emphasis on indirect use of suggestions to bypass conscious resistance and access unconscious resources and associations. Of equal importance is the metaphor of the splitting of the conscious mind, where the stuckness of the presenting problem resides from the unconscious mind, where the necessary tools and resource experiences can emerge. Ericksonian hypnotherapy, because of its focus on solution, tends to be brief with the focus on present and future functioning over various developmental stages.

The research on concepts such as indirect suggestion, metaphor, and Ericksonian hypnotherapy as causal to therapeutic change is relatively new. The data reviewed in this chapter is mixed in its support for the importance of indirect suggestion and the necessity for amnesia for a given metaphor. However, two studies did reveal preliminary support for the effectiveness of Ericksonian hypnosis as a clinical intervention. More research on this approach and its various claims needs to be conducted and to be used as part of a feedback loop to inform both clinicians and future research. Although Erickson has become a legendary figure, those who use his clinical principles need to have more than anecdotal evidence to support their belief systems. Researchers, on the other hand, need to develop methodologies that accurately reflect the clinical setting.

Finally, as has been stated, there is no one Ericksonian approach. The essence of this work is to help the client to develop creative ways of being. The range of behaviors used by therapists in helping clients to achieve this creativity should not be limited by the tyranny of clinical orthodoxy. Each client offers the therapist a unique opportunity to create a positive climate for change. The legacy of Milton Erickson is not to use clever techniques arbitrarily but to stimulate each therapist to act as creatively as possible for the client's benefit.

REFERENCES

Araoz, D. (1982). *Hypnosis and sex therapy*. New York: Brunner/Mazel.

Alman, B., & Carney, R. (1980). Consequences of direct and indirect suggestion on success of posthypnotic behaviour. *American Journal of Clinical Hypnosis, 23*, 112–118.

Bank, W. O. (1985). Hypnotic suggestion for the control of bleeding in the angiography suite. *Ericksonian Monographs, 1*, 76–89.

Bandler, R., & Grinder, R. (1975). *Patterns of the hypnotic techniques of Milton H. Erickson, M.D.* Cupertino, CA: Meta Publications.

Bandler, R., & Grinder, J. (1979). *Frogs into princes*. Moab, UT: Real People Press.

Bowers, K. S. (1966). Hypnotic behavior: The differentiation of trance and demand characteristic variables. *Journal of Abnormal Psychology, 71*, 42–51.

Coe, W., & Scharcoff, J. (1985). An empirical evaluation of the neurolinguistic programming model. *International Journal of Clinical and Experimental Hypnosis, 23*, 310–319.

Dowd, E. T., & Petty, J. (1982). Effect of counselor predicate matching on perceived social influence and client satisfaction. *Journal of Counseling Psychology, 29*, 206–209.

Dowd, E. T., & Hingst, A. G. (1983). Matching therapists' predicates: An in vivo test of effectiveness. *Perceptual Motor Skills, 57,* 207–210.

Erickson, M. H., & Rossi, E. (1979). *Hypnotherapy: An exploratory casebook.* New York: Irvington.

Erickson, M. H., & Rossi, E. L. (Eds.). (1980). *The collected papers of Milton H. Erickson on hypnosis: Vol. 1. The nature of hypnosis and suggestion.* New York: Irvington.

Falzett, W. C. (1981). Matched versus unmatched primary representational systems and their relationship to perceived trustworthiness in a counseling analogue. *Journal of Counseling Psychology, 28,* 305–308.

Fisch, R. (1990). The broader implications of Milton H. Erickson's work. *Ericksonian Monographs, 7,* 1–6.

Gill, M. M., & Brenman, M. (1959). *Hypnosis and related states: Psychoanalytic studies in regression.* Madison, CT: International Universities Press.

Gumm, W. B., Walker, M. K., & Day, H. D. (1982). Neurolinguistic programming: Method or myth? *Journal of Counseling Psychology, 29,* 327–330.

Haley, J. (Ed.). (1967). *Advanced techniques of hypnosis and therapy: Selected papers of Milton H. Erickson, M.D.* New York: Grune & Stratton.

Haley, J. (1973). *Uncommon therapy: The psychiatric techniques of Milton H. Erickson, M.D.* New York: Norton.

Hammond, D. (1984). Myths about Erickson and Ericksonian hypnosis. *American Journal of Clinical Hypnosis, 26,* 236–245.

Henry, D. (1984). *The neurolinguistic programming construct of the primary representational system: A multitrait multi-method validational study.* Unpublished master's thesis, University of Connecticut, Storrs, CT.

Hilgard, E. R. (1965). *Hypnotic susceptibility.* New York: Harcourt, Brace & World.

Hilgard, E. R. (1966). Posthypnotic amnesia: Experiments and theory. *International Journal of Clinical and Experimental Hypnosis, 14,* 104–111.

Hilgard, E. R. (1975). Hypnosis. *Annual Review of Psychology, 26,* 19–44.

Hilgard, E. R., Weitzenhoffer, A., Landes, J., & Moore, R. (1961). The distribution of susceptibility to hypnosis in a student population: A study using the Stanford Hypnotic Susceptibility Scale. *Psychology Monographs, 75,* 1–22.

Kirsch, I. (1985). Response expectancy as a determinant of experience and behavior. *American Psychologist, 40,* 1189–1202.

Kirsch, I. (1990). *Changing expectations: A key to effective psychotherapy.* Pacific Grove, CA: Brooks/Cole.

Lankton, C., & Lankton, S. (1989). *Tales of enchantment: Goal-oriented metaphors for adults and children in therapy.* New York: Brunner/Mazel.

Lankton, S. (1989). Motivating action with hypnotherapy for a client with a history of early family violence. *Ericksonian Monographs, 6,* 43–61.

Lankton, S., & Lankton, C. (1983). *The answer within: A clinical framework of Ericksonian hypnotherapy.* New York: Brunner/Mazel.

Lankton, S., & Lankton, C. (1986). *Enchantment and intervention in family therapy: Training in Ericksonian approaches*. New York: Brunner/Mazel.

Lankton, S., Lankton, C., & Matthews, W. (1991). Ericksonian family therapy. In A. Gurman & D. Kniskern (Eds.), *Handbook of family therapy* (pp. 239–283). New York: Brunner/Mazel.

Matthews, W. (1985a). Ericksonian and Milan therapy: An intersection between circular questioning and therapeutic metaphor. *Journal of Strategic and Systemic Therapy, 3,* 16–26.

Matthews, W. (1985b). A cybernetic model of Ericksonian hypnotherapy: One hand draws the other. *Ericksonian Monographs, 1,* 42–60.

Matthews, W., Bennett, H., Bean, W., & Gallagher, M. (1985). Indirect versus direct hypnotic suggestions—An initial investigation: A brief communication. *International Journal of Clinical and Experimental Hypnosis, 33,* 219–223.

Matthews, W., & Dardeck, K. (1985). The use and construction of therapeutic metaphor. *American Mental Health Counselors Association Journal, 7,* 11–24.

Matthews, W., Kirsch, I., & Mosher, D. (1985). Double hypnotic induction: An initial empirical test. *Journal of Abnormal Psychology, 94,* 92–95.

Matthews, W., & Langdell, S. (1989). What do clients think about the metaphors they receive? *American Journal of Clinical Hypnosis, 31,* 242–251.

Matthews, W., & Mosher, D. (1988). Direct and indirect hypnotic suggestion in a laboratory setting. *British Journal of Experimental and Clinical Hypnosis, 5*(2), 63–71.

McConkey, K. (1984). The impact of indirect suggestion. *International Journal of Clinical and Experimental Hypnosis, 32,* 307–314.

Morgan, A., & Hilgard, J. (1978). The Stanford Hypnotic Susceptibility Scale for Adults. *American Journal of Clinical Hypnosis, 21,* 148–169.

Mosher, D., & Matthews, W. (1985, August). *Multiple embedded metaphor and structured amnesia.* Paper presented at the 93rd Annual Convention of the American Psychological Association, San Diego, CA.

Nugent, W. (1989a). Evidence concerning the causal effect of an Ericksonian hypnotic intervention. *Ericksonian Monographs, 5,* 35–55.

Nugent, W. (1989b). A multiple baseline investigation of an Ericksonian hypnotic approach. *Ericksonian Monographs, 5,* 69–85.

O'Hanlon, W. (1987). *Taproots.* New York: Norton.

Orne, M. (1959). The nature of hypnosis: Artifact and essence. *Journal of Abnormal and Social Psychology, 58,* 277–299.

Rosenthal, R., & Jacobson, L. (1968). *Pygmalion in the classroom.* New York: Holt, Rinehart & Winston.

Rossi, E., Ryan, M., & Sharp, F. (Eds.). (1983). *Healing in hypnosis by Milton H. Erickson.* New York: Irvington.

Shor, R. E., & Orne, E. C. (1962). *The Harvard Group Scale of Hypnotic Susceptibility, Form A.* Palo Alto, CA: Consulting Psychologists Press.

Stone, J. A., & Lundy, R. M. (1985). Behavioral compliance with direct and indirect body movement suggestions. *Journal of Abnormal Psychology, 3,* 256–263.

Van Gorp, W. G., Meyer, R. G., & Dunbar, K. D. (1985). The efficacy of direct versus indirect hypnotic induction techniques on reduction of experimental pain. *International Journal of Clinical and Experimental Hypnosis, 4,* 319–328.

Weekes, J. R., & Lynn, S. J. (1990). Hypnosis, suggestion type and subjective experience: The order effects hypothesis revisited. *International Journal of Clinical and Experimental Hypnosis, 38,* 95–101.

Weitzenhoffer, A. M., & Hilgard, E. R. (1959). *Stanford Hypnotic Susceptibility Scale, Forms A and B.* Palo Alto, CA: Consulting Psychologists Press.

Weitzenhoffer, A. M., & Hilgard, E. R. (1962). *Stanford Hypnotic Susceptibility Scale, Form C.* Palo Alto, CA: Consulting Psychologists Press.

Weitzenhoffer, A. M., & Hilgard, E. R. (1963). *Stanford Hypnotic Susceptibility Scale, Form C.* Palo Alto, CA: Consulting Psychologists Press.

Yapko, M. D. (1981). The effect of matching primary representational system predicates on hypnotic relaxation. *American Journal of Clinical Hypnosis, 23,* 169–175.

Zeig, J. (Ed.). (1980). *A teaching seminar with Milton H. Erickson.* New York: Brunner/Mazel.

Zeig, J. (Ed.). (1982). *Ericksonian approaches to hypnosis and psychotherapy.* New York: Brunner/Mazel.

10

COGNITIVE–DEVELOPMENTAL HYPNOTHERAPY

E. THOMAS DOWD

Cognitive therapy has, in its relatively short life, undergone a significant metamorphosis. It was originally developed by Aaron T. Beck, Albert Ellis, and Donald Meichenbaum as a way of modifying distorted thought patterns that were presumed to underlie emotional disorders. Beck (1976) emphasized the role of dysfunctional automatic thoughts and maladaptive rules in the development of psychological problems. He noted that these automatic thoughts were idiosyncratic to the person, even to those with the same disorder. Ellis (1977), on the other hand, stressed the role of irrational beliefs in the development of emotional problems and developed a list of typical irrational beliefs engaged in by disturbed individuals. Meichenbaum (1977) emphasized the role of the internal dialogue, or negative self-statements, in the development of psychological problems. Indeed, Meichenbaum's negative self-statements seem to function as negative verbal conditioning.

These three systems of cognitive therapy share four underlying assumptions. First, it is assumed that emotional disorders have in common a set of negative cognitions regarding one's abilities, worth, or activities. Although it is incorrect to say that these negative cognitions directly *cause* psychological disorders, they do appear to interact with environmental events, which results in dysfunctional behavioral and emotional patterns. Thus, a history of negative cognitions may predispose the individual, under stressful conditions, to develop emotional problems. However, without the existence of a stress-inducing situation, these individuals may function adequately. Second, these negative cognitions tend to be ahistorical in nature (i.e., it is what the individuals tell themselves *now* that really matters). Thus, there is an assumption that if current dysfunctional thinking can be corrected, the emotional problems will diminish. Therefore, there is a third similarity among these systems of cognitive therapy: the emphasis on directly disputing (Ellis), presenting evidence against (Beck), or counteracting by coping strategies (Meichenbaum) the negative cognitions existing in the present. Replacing these with more adaptive cognitions is assumed to result in less emotional distress. Fourth, there seems to be a tacit assumption that these negative cognitions are more or less accessible to consciousness. Therefore, it is the task of the therapist to help the client to identify them so that they can be disputed and corrected.

There is a recent development within cognitive therapy, however, that deviates from some of these assumptions. I refer to the cognitive–developmental approach. In some ways, this approach represents a significant departure from previous cognitive therapy models.

In the cognitive–developmental approach, above all, cognitive activity is seen as being developmental in nature; that is, over time the cognitive organizational structure is progressively elaborated and differentiated by interaction with the environment, especially the environment of other people (Guidano & Liotti, 1983). These environmental interactions result in a set of cognitive assumptions or rules that guide the individual's further interactions with the environment. In particular, individuals acquire knowledge about themselves (self-knowledge or self-concept) through interactions with other people. Thus, cognitive assumptions both cause and are the result of the individual's interaction with the environment.

The cognitive–developmental model also distinguishes between tacit and explicit knowledge, including self-knowledge (Guidano & Liotti, 1983). Tacit knowledge, by its nature, is developed prior to the acquisition of formal language structures and, as a result, it is largely nonaccessible verbally. Rather, it tends to be accessed through images and feelings (Guidano, 1987). From a cognitive science perspective, Tataryn, Nadel, and Jacobs (1989) made the same point when they referred to nonconscious mental processing. Explicit knowledge, on the other hand, is that which is acquired by means of language processes and is therefore much more accessible verbally. It is also much more amenable to change via verbal psychotherapy. Tacit knowledge, precisely because it is nonaccessible verbally, is also much more difficult to modify by traditional verbal psychotherapy. These two types of knowing processes should not be seen as two polarities, however, but as two processes in constant interaction (Guidano, 1987). Thus, tacit knowledge, as well as explicit knowledge, is constantly being elaborated and differentiated over the individual's life span.

One important implication of the cognitive–developmental model for psychotherapy is that resistance to change is not necessarily an annoying by-product of human cussedness but a natural and necessary self-protective mechanism (Mahoney, 1988). Sudden and massive changes in core cognitive constructs that are part of tacit knowledge are deeply unsettling and frightening because they threaten the individual's personal meaning structure and therefore implicate personal identity (Dowd & Seibel, 1990; Liotti, 1987). Precisely because these core constructs are embedded within the tacit knowledge system and are not verbally accessible, they are therefore highly resistant to change via verbal psychotherapy. Cognitive constructs contained within the explicit knowledge system, however, should be considerably easier to change using language.

It follows from the aforementioned that verbal psychotherapy, as traditionally practiced, should be much more useful in changing cognitive constructs that are part of the explicit knowledge system than those that are contained within the tacit knowledge system. Indeed, that has been the clinical intuition of generations of practicing psychologists. Peripheral attitudes and behaviors are often readily modifiable, whereas core constructs involving issues of personal identity and self-concept change only slowly over time. In addition, one implication of the previous discussion is that verbal interaction may be of limited help in changing tacit cognitive constructs at all because it relies primarily on the use of language. Rather, tacit constructs may best be changed by recourse to interventions involving images and emotions. This, too, has been part of clinical lore. Interventions that engage the "head" only, without emotional involvement, do not appear to have the same power to cause "deep" change. This, indeed, was the basis of the "corrective emotional experience" (Alexander, 1963), wherein psychological change was predicated on emotional reinvolvement with a previously problematical situation. Tataryn et al. (1989) likewise have stated that maladaptive behavior is governed largely by tacit schemata.

CHARACTERISTICS OF HYPNOSIS

There have been a number of different definitions of hypnosis, with several aspects appearing common to most. First, hypnosis is characterized by a heightened suggestibility and receptivity to suggestions. Second, the individual's perceptual and cognitive focus is both narrowed and intensified. Indeed, one form of hypnosis has been called "alert hypnosis" (Golden,

Dowd, & Friedberg, 1987). Third, the hypnotic trance state tends to rely more on imagery and intuitive cognitive processes than on the formal use of language. In this regard, certain descriptions of hypnotic phenomena consider them to be dissociative in nature (Kihlstrom, 1984). Fourth, the Ericksonian hypnotherapists in particular (Erickson & Rossi, 1979, 1981) argue that their indirect hypnotic techniques are particularly useful in bypassing, discharging, or displacing resistance.

It is important to assess the hypnotic ability of the individual. Although almost anyone can enter at least a light trance, people vary greatly in their ability to achieve a moderate or deep trance. Indeed, Bowers (1984) went so far as to state that "the effects of a treatment intervention are *not* due to suggestion *unless* treatment outcome is correlated with hypnotic ability" (p. 444). Hypnotic ability seems to be distributed among the population on a normal curve and is highly stable over time (Bowers, 1976; Udolf, 1981). Therefore, the ability to enter a trance readily and to benefit from hypnosis differs considerably among individuals. Hypnotic ability can be assessed in a number of ways. Preinduction hypnotic ability tests, such as arm levitation, hand clasping, and the postural sway, are discussed in a variety of sources (e.g., Crasilneck & Hall, 1985; Udolf, 1981). However, Crasilneck and Hall (1985) considered them to be of little use in the clinical situation and even to involve some risk (p. 58). Standardized tests, such as the Stanford Hypnotic Susceptibility Scale or the Harvard Group Scale of Hypnotic Susceptibility, can also be used. However, these instruments are laborious to administer in a clinical situation and are used primarily for research. Perhaps, as Crasilneck and Hall (1985) stated, "There is, after all, no better test for susceptibility to hypnosis than a trial induction of hypnosis itself" (p. 58). Several signs can be observed that indicate moderate to good hypnotic ability. These include eyelid fluttering, spontaneous eye closure, deep relaxation and flaccid facial muscles, deep and slow breathing, and changes in the swallow reflex (Crasilneck & Hall, 1985; Udolf, 1981).

Given this, one can see how hypnosis can be useful in modifying the disordered tacit schemata that underlie emotional disorders from a cognitive–developmental viewpoint. The resistance that is aroused naturally by the threat to existing core cognitive schemata may be reduced by indirect hypnotic suggestions. The concentrated perceptual and cognitive focus and increased receptivity to influence and suggestions from the hypnotherapist likewise may increase the probability of psychological change of any kind, particularly core cognitive change that is tacit in nature. The reliance of hypnosis on imagery and intuitive cognitive processing also may provide the type of intervention that is most helpful in facilitating changes in tacit cognitive schemata. Thus, hypnosis may be an especially useful intervention both in accessing and modifying tacit knowledge.

CLINICAL APPLICATIONS

There is probably no psychological disorder that someone, somewhere, sometime has not attempted to cure using hypnosis. Although almost any hypnotherapeutic intervention can succeed on occasion, often for reasons unrelated to hypnosis, certain kinds of disorders in general seem more amenable to change via hypnosis than others. Wadden and Anderton (1982), in a comprehensive review of the experimental literature, concluded that hypnosis is more effective with nonvoluntary disorders (e.g., pain, warts, asthma) than with self-initiated behavior (e.g., obesity, smoking, alcoholism). They speculated that one reason for that situation is that the latter problems are rewarding, at least in the short run, whereas the former are not. My own experience has led me to similar conclusions. In addition to the clinical problems discussed by Wadden and Anderton, I have found hypnosis to be useful in treating depression, anxiety, and stress-related disorders. It can also be useful in overcoming client resistance (Golden et al., 1987). However, I have been approached by numerous individuals who wanted me to hypnotize them to "get me to stop smoking" or "to make me lose 5 or 10 lb." I have rarely found that hypnosis is particularly useful with these problems in that context. The issue seems to be lack of motivation. These individuals appear to view hypnosis as a quasi-magical technique that will remove their problem without any effort on their part. When I encounter such a person, I ask, "do you want to eliminate your problem or do you want to want to?" When put like that, they generally admit sheepishly that it is the latter.

A major point of this chapter, however, is that hypnosis can also be useful in cognitive restructuring, especially the restructuring of tacit cognitive schemata. Cognitive restructuring has been extensively described by Marvin Goldfried (Goldfried, Decenteceo, & Weinberg, 1974), but it underlies other cognitive therapies, such as those of Beck (1976), Ellis (1977), and Meichenbaum (1977). As a hypnotherapeutic technique, it has been described by Golden et al. (1987) and Spiegel and Spiegel (1978).

Cognitive Restructuring

Originally, this technique referred to the replacement of negative self-statements by more adaptive or positive self-statements. These statements, such as "I must be perfect in everything I do" or "everyone must approve of me," could be readily accessed, either directly by the individual or with the help of a therapist. Golden et al. (1987) provided several examples of cognitive restructuring of specific and accessible statements and their replacement by more adaptive self-statements within a hypnotherapeutic framework. For example, the negative thought "I'm hopeless, I'll never change, I don't do anything right" can be replaced by "I used to do many things well before I became depressed and I can do so again." These more adaptive statements can be said to the client while in a trance by the therapist and eventually by the client. Self-statements pertaining to a wide variety of psychological problems can thus be corrected while the client is in a hypnotic trance. Cognitions such as these have been described by Meichenbaum and Gilmore (1984) as cognitive events.

It has been increasingly noticed, however, that some cognitions are not directly accessible to the client, even with the assistance of a therapist, and are not necessarily in the form of self-statements. Rather, they are in the form of tacit assumptions, schemata, or implicit rules for living that form the bedrock of human cognition. These schemata are laid down early in life by the interaction of the individual with the environment. Because they are formed at a preverbal developmental stage, they are highly resistant to subsequent modification. Once formed, however, these schemata act as templates to filter and channel future environmental stimuli, so that they also constrain the ability of the individual to modify these schemata on the basis of new information. Thus, the structure of the existing cognitive framework tends to be preserved. Meichenbaum and Gilmore (1984) referred to these schemata as "cognitive structures."

A particularly important cognitive structure is the self-schema (Markus, 1977), which refers to cognitive generalizations about the self that are based on the individual's past social experience. New information that is congruent with one's self-schema tends to be processed easily, whereas information that is discrepant tends to be processed more slowly, if at all. This may be the source of much therapeutic resistance and the finding that low-interpretation discrepancy in the therapeutic situation tends to be more effective than high-interpretation discrepancy in causing immediate client attitudinal or behavioral change (e.g., Claiborn & Dowd, 1985). *Interpretation discrepancy* refers to the difference between the therapist's interpretation of an event or a behavior and the client's interpretation. In a similar vein, Mahoney (1988) argued that core cognitive structures are appropriately resistant to massive change in order to protect the self-identity. In many instances, however, it is precisely the self-schema that is appropriately the target of change. If so, hypnotherapy can be useful both in modifying these self-schemata and in bypassing the resistance that generally accompanies attempts to change these schemata.

Hypnotherapeutic Cognitive Restructuring

Because of the resistance that can be aroused by direct change attempts on core cognitive schemata, the indirect approach used by Ericksonian hypnotherapists can be useful. Golden et al. (1987) described two ways that the indirect techniques of Milton Erickson can be used to bypass resistance. First, Erickson used therapeutic binds, or the "illusion of alternatives" (p. 112), wherein the therapist offers only alternatives that will help to overcome the problem. Second, he used implications or implied directives, wherein the therapist implies a particular change without directly suggesting it. These techniques tend to discharge client resistance because they do not directly challenge an existing client attitude or belief.

There are two types of hypnotherapeutic cognitive restructuring: restructuring cognitive events and restructuring core cognitive structures.

Restructuring Cognitive Events

Initially, it is important to understand the negative self-statements that underlie the individual's presenting problem. Because these are cognitive events, they are generally accessible to the client with the help of the therapist. The first task is to identify these negative self-statements, to test the reality of these negative assumptions, and to develop alternative adaptive self-statements. The cognitive psychotherapy techniques of Beck (1976) and Ellis (1977), as well as other more recent writings, provide numerous examples. Especially valuable is the two-column technique (Golden et al., 1987), in which negative self-statements are written down one vertical column and corresponding adaptive self-statements are written down the other.

The second task is to assist the client in entering a hypnotic trance. For those with moderate to good hypnotic ability, standard inductions available in most textbooks (e.g., Udolf, 1981) should suffice. For clients with little hypnotic ability, repeated inductions may be necessary. Fortunately, most hypnotic cognitive restructuring of cognitive events can be accomplished with a light trance. Moderate or deep trances are not needed.

The third task is to replace the negative self-statements with more adaptive coping statements while the individual is in the trance. It is helpful if the therapist first says the negative self-statement to the client, then replaces it with the adaptive statement. After repeated practice with this, the client is asked to state aloud the negative and adaptive statements. After more practice, the client can do the exercise silently and outside of the therapeutic situation. It is important that the therapist monitor the activity to ensure that it is practiced diligently.

Restructuring Core Cognitive Structures

Because these are not accessible to the client and only by inference to the therapist, they are much more difficult to change. The Ericksonian indirect hypnotherapeutic methods have been claimed to be especially useful here because they do not tend to arouse the client's resistance and may implicitly suggest new perceptions and new ways of looking at problematic situations, often without the client being aware that these are being suggested. However, this position has been challenged. Bowers (1990) discussed laboratory studies indicating that subtle and indirect hypnotic suggestions were *not* more effective than direct suggestion in reducing pain and causing positive hallucinations and that they might have actually aroused *more* resistance. The dependent measures used in these studies, however, have consisted of relatively straightforward phenomena, in which the subjects presumably had little hedonic investment. Tacit cognitive schemata, on the other hand, are much less accessible to conscious awareness and much more central to an individual's sense of identity. It is therefore likely that changes in these cognitive structures would be much less amenable to direct suggestion. Therefore, in accordance with past clinical practice, indirect suggestions were used in these cases.

There are several tasks that the hypnotherapist must complete in attempting to restructure core cognitive structures. The first task is to identify the major themes and assumptions that underlie the client's core cognitive structure. Effective therapists of all persuasions often do this as part of the therapeutic work, although it generally extends over several sessions and often continues intermittently throughout the course of therapy. Indeed, the explicit identification of these themes to the client forms the basis of interpretation and is at the heart of psychodynamic psychotherapy. However, client resistance is often aroused and therefore interpretations, especially of core assumptions, are often challenged or not processed by the client. Indirect suggestion can facilitate the acceptance of these challenges to core assumptions.

The second task, as in the previous description of restructuring cognitive events, is to assist the client in entering a hypnotic trance. Often, more indirect methods are used, such as a conversational induction (Erickson & Rossi, 1979). Although Ericksonian hypnotherapists downplay the importance of good hypnotic ability, I think that it is important for the ultimate therapeutic outcome even in Ericksonian hypnotherapy. However, even individuals who can achieve only a light trance can benefit somewhat from hypnotherapeutic interventions. In addition, hypnotic ability can often be increased to some extent as the individual becomes more comfortable with the hypnotist and the situation.

The third task is the creation and use of an indirect hypnotic routine designed to address the client's core cognitive assumptions. Examples of such routines are available in many books on Ericksonian hypnotherapy. However, the construction of these routines is not as easy as it appears, and the nascent hypnotherapist is well advised to enroll in skill-building workshops sponsored by the Erickson Foundation or other hypnosis societies. As I illustrate shortly, indirect hypnotherapeutic routines make use of techniques such as embedded suggestions, multiple levels of meaning, and implicit reframing of meaning to address the core cognitive assumptions and facilitate new learning, as well as open-ended suggestions, truisms, and the "yes set" to bypass resistance.

In attempting to restructure either cognitive events or cognitive structures, it is important that the hypnotherapist rely on repetition of constructed routines. Using a hypnotic routine once or twice is, except in rare instances, not likely to result in permanent change. This is especially true in attempting to change core assumptions. Unfortunately, some of the clinical anecdotes have fostered the image of hypnosis as a quick and mysterious cure.

CASE MATERIAL

Detailed examples of the clinical application of hypnosis abound in the literature (e.g., Dowd & Healy, 1986). In order to illustrate the specific applications of hypnosis to cognitive restructuring, I provide excerpts of cases. It is important to emphasize that the hypnotherapist be creative in devising hypnotic inductions and routines and not rely on a "cookbook approach." These cases should therefore be used for their heuristic potential.

Restructuring Cognitive Events: The Case of John

"John" sought assistance in order to cope with anxiety regarding being successful in his new job. Initially, the therapist helped John to identify the negative self-statements that he had concerning his job performance. This was accomplished partly by skilled therapist questioning and partly by asking John to self-monitor his cognitions during times of self-doubt. The following negative self-statements were uncovered:

1. I will never be able to succeed at this job!
2. I got this job only because I was able to hide my incompetence.
3. If I lose this job, I'll never get another!
4. My wife will leave me if I lose this job.

The therapist then helped John generate adaptive coping statements to match the negative statements. The following were generated:

1. There is no reason to think I won't succeed at this job, since I've succeeded at every other I've held.
2. I got this job because I had demonstrated competence on previous jobs.
3. Even if I lost this job, I have more than enough skills to get another.
4. My wife has stuck with me through worse than job losses before, and I'm sure she will again.

The therapist's next step was to assist John in entering a trance. An initial trance induction, using eye fixation and muscle relaxation, indicated that John may have moderate hypnotic ability. However, he was highly anxious about "doing a good job" and was able to enter into a light trance only after two practice sessions. While he was in a trance, the therapist then used the following hypnotic routine.

> You have constantly been hypnotizing yourself with negative thoughts. Now, I'd like to help you hypnotize yourself with positive thoughts. As I explained, all hypnosis is really self-hypnosis, so that you can learn to do what I teach you . . . . Now, say to yourself, "I've succeeded at every job I've ever had, so there's no reason to think I won't succeed at this one." That's right . . . . Now, say to yourself, "I've shown competence on every other job, which is why I got this one!" That's right, very good . . . . Now, say to yourself, "Even if I lose a job, I have the skills to get another one." Very good! . . . Now, say to yourself, "My wife has shown her loyalty to me many times and has stuck with me, and I'm sure she'll do it again." That's right . . . . Now, notice how good you feel after having said those things. Notice how warm, peaceful, and comfortable you feel . . . . And you can recapture this feeling anytime you want, just by entering a trance and saying the same things to yourself, letting those thoughts gently roll around in your mind.

The therapist practiced this kind of hypnotic routine (expanded) with John for parts of several sessions and then asked him to practice it at home. The therapist then discussed the results of the home practice with John and suggested modifications. After several sessions, John reported that his job anxiety had diminished and that he was able to function better at work.

It is important to remember that this example is only a guide. Hypnotic routines should be constructed only after some information about the client has been collected, although preliminary trance inductions can be done almost immediately.

Restructuring Cognitive Structures: The Case of Joan

"Joan" entered therapy because of an intense fear of the dark. She had been in therapy previously for a number of issues, which had been generally resolved to her satisfaction. However, her fear of the dark was proving inconvenient because she experienced intense anxiety when home alone at night and when walking alone in the evening. She felt that easy mobility was restricted to daylight hours.

After two sessions, the therapist suspected that Joan had an unusually strong need to be in control of herself and situations that involved her. This need extended to control of the therapy sessions, which hampered the development of the therapeutic alliance and led her to resist therapist interventions. Such an expectation of, and need for, control has been hypothesized to be a core cognitive assumption for many people, especially in the individualistic North American and Western European cultures (Dowd, 1989). The therapist likewise suspected that this core assumption of the desirability of a high level of control was an exacerbating factor in her earlier problems and therefore decided to intervene hypnotically at the tacit level.

An initial hypnotic induction, including eye closure and a subsequent arm levitation, indicated that Joan had good hypnotic ability. She reported that her arm had appeared to rise nonvolitionally, and the therapist observed that it dropped abruptly into her lap after it touched her forehead. This level of hypnotic ability made it more likely that a hypnotic intervention would be successful. After Joan had entered a trance, the therapist used the following hypnotic routine. This routine had been developed in outline form earlier and was fleshed out in detail on the basis of Joan's responses while in the trance. Commentary on the routine appears in brackets.

> You have learned many things recently [referring to previous sessions] about yourself and your relations to others. Now you can, if you wish, learn more about your fear of the dark and other things [open-ended invitation to relax and absorb suggestions, with an implication to search cognitively]. It has been important to remain in control, hasn't it, in many ways [introduction of tacit assumption and facilitation of yes set]? It is important to be *right* now [multiple levels of meaning; "right" is used simultaneously in two senses]. And this control has been good in many ways, hasn't it [reframing and yes set]? But perhaps you have learned that control may not always be good [a truism; few things are!]. Perhaps you have longed to relax, to relinquish control [implicitly tying together two concepts] . . . to find peace and relaxation. And perhaps you have discovered an important thing [raises client's interest level, focuses attention] . . . that **only those people who are truly in control can afford to give up control temporarily** [words in italic boldface indicate that they were vocally emphasized]! So, the more control you really have, the more comfortable you can feel giving it up temporarily . . . knowing that you can take it back whenever you want [paradoxical reframing]. And, you can practice being truly in control at a deeper, more profound level by relinquishing control briefly, for as long as you feel comfortable, knowing that you can take the control back whenever you want [future paradoxical prescription]. It's just like right now, isn't it? You can comfortably allow yourself to be relaxed here [note earlier pairing with relaxation and relinquishing control], knowing that you could leave the trance any time you wanted [I had earlier mentioned that all hypnosis is self-hypnosis]. But you really don't want to right now, do you [yes set]? You feel so relaxed and comfortable just being in a trance. And you can have this feeling anytime you want by relaxing and letting go, feeling increasingly comfortable in relaxing and letting go, finding peace and happiness in so doing. And the more you

practice relaxing, letting go, you, Joan, can begin to find increasing relaxation and less control [the underlined words identify an embedded suggestion], the more you can feel truly in control . . . and the more you feel truly in control, the more you can allow yourself to relinquish control longer [setting up an adaptive spiral], and you can allow yourself to learn many new things about yourself [open-ended future invitation].

This routine, with variations, was repeated during each session for several more sessions. The vocally emphasized sentence was used repeatedly because this was a key area for this client. The following hypnotic routine was then used as the client entered a trance:

> Now imagine yourself walking alone at night but in a lighted area. As you begin to feel anxious, allow yourself to let go and to relax all over . . . . That's right! . . . Now imagine yourself at home alone at night. As you begin to feel anxious, just allow yourself to let go and to relax all over . . . . That's right! And you can let go, relax, and relinquish control whenever you feel anxious, knowing that you do not have to be in control at all times to have ultimate control, that you can achieve control by relaxing because then you have control of your reactions [introducing by implication the concept of personal control as being distinct from environmental control] . . . . So that the more you relax, the more you can achieve personal control. You don't even have to do anything [introducing the concept of obtaining control by not trying to]. And every time you feel anxious in the dark, you can find increasing personal control by relaxing and letting go.

In order to further test Joan's level of hypnotic ability, I asked her not to remember all or most of what I had said (posthypnotic amnesia). After awakening from the trance, she did indeed remember little, thereby further validating her high level of hypnotic ability. We discussed relaxation exercises she could practice when anxious, and her fear of the dark had diminished markedly within a few weeks.

RESEARCH AND APPRAISAL

The therapeutic effectiveness of cognitive restructuring, compared with control conditions and other treatments, has been investigated for some time. Studies have almost universally shown that cognitive restructuring is more effective than a no-treatment control. However, research has not clearly shown the superiority of cognitive restructuring to alternative treatments or in conjunction with other treatments for a variety of psychological disorders. Biran and Wilson (1981) found that guided exposure was superior to cognitive restructuring on most measures in the treatment of phobic disorders. Baucom, Sayers, and Sher (1990) found that the addition of cognitive restructuring or emotional expressiveness training did not increase the effectiveness of behavioral marital training with maritally distressed couples. However, Mattick and Peters (1988) found that cognitive restructuring and guided exposure were more effective than guided exposure alone in treating social phobia. Pecsok and Fremouw (1988) found that cognitive restructuring was more effective than self-monitoring in overcoming binge eating. However, Franklin (1989) found that cognitive restructuring was less effective than respiratory retraining but more effective than a placebo in treating agoraphobia. De Jong, Trieber, and Henrich (1985) found that cognitive restructuring alone was as effective as a combination of activity scheduling, social competence training, and cognitive restructuring in the treatment of severe and chronic depression; both treatments were more effective than a waiting-list control condition. Patsiokas and Clum (1985) found that cognitive restructuring was equally as effective as problem-solving training and a nondirective control condition in reducing feelings of hopelessness among suicide attempters, although problem-solving training was significantly more effective than the nondirective condition.

These mixed and inconclusive results are characteristic of the literature. Cognitive restructuring sometimes adds significantly to a treatment package, but it is not generally more effective than alternative treatments. That these results may be attributable to individual differences was suggested by Frank and Noble (1984), who found that field-independent individuals were more efficient in their use of cognitive restructuring skills than were field-dependent individuals.

There have been a few studies on the effectiveness of cognitive restructuring with hypnosis. Tosi, Judah, and Murphy (1989) found that a combination of hypnosis and cognitive restructuring (called *rational stage-directed hypnotherapy* [*RSDH*]) was generally more effective than cognitive restructuring and hypnosis alone in the treatment of psychological factors (e.g., locus of control, irrational beliefs, personality coping styles) associated with duodenal ulcers. Boutin and Tosi (1983) compared RSDH with hypnosis only, a placebo condition, and a no-treatment control condition on the modification of irrational ideas and test anxiety in nursing students. They found that RSDH and hypnosis were both effective in ameliorating these problems but that RSDH was significantly more effective than hypnosis alone. Howard and Reardon (1986) found that a cognitive hypnotic imagery approach was more effective than cognitive restructuring or hypnosis alone in the immediate and long-term reduction of anxiety and enhancement of self-concept in male weight lifters. Edelson and Fitzpatrick (1989) compared hypnosis, cognitive–behavioral, and attention-control interventions in the treatment of chronic pain. They found that both procedures reduced pain intensity (as measured by the McGill Pain Questionnaire) but that only the cognitive–behavioral treatment led to a significant increase in the overt motor behavior element of chronic pain. Wall and

Womack (1989) compared standard hypnotic instructions with an active cognitive coping strategy in the treatment of procedurally induced pain and anxiety. Both interventions proved equally effective in reducing pain, but neither was effective in reducing anxiety. No studies were found regarding the effectiveness of cognitive–developmental hypnotherapy, as described and illustrated in this chapter.

Thus, there is tentative evidence that hypnosis may add to the efficacy of cognitive restructuring in the treatment of a variety of cognitively based phenomena. However, to my knowledge, no study appears to have investigated the utility of hypnosis in the modification of tacit cognitive schemata. It is there that future research should be directed.

CONCLUSION

Cognitive–developmental hypnotherapy is in its infancy. Although the theoretical and conceptual foundations for its practice are being laid down, and interventions are being developed, there has been no research evidence directly bearing on its effectiveness. Indirectly, however, it tentatively appears that hypnotherapeutic cognitive restructuring may be effective beyond that demonstrated by cognitive restructuring alone. Theoretically, cognitive–developmental hypnotherapy derives from the developmental and constructivistic movements within cognitive therapy and epistemologically from the distinction between tacit and explicit knowing systems. The interventions have been developed in part from the writings and practice of Milton Erickson and his successors, who seem to operate at the level of tacit knowledge. In this chapter I have outlined the theoretical structure underlying cognitive–developmental hypnotherapy and illustrated how its principles may be applied to actual case examples. Although it has not been demonstrated fully, it is my contention that tacit cognitive restructuring can best be used with individuals who have good hypnotic ability.

REFERENCES

Alexander, F. (1963). *Fundamentals of psychoanalysis.* New York: Norton.

Baucom, D. H., Sayers, S. L., & Sher, T. G. (1990). Supplementing behavioral marital therapy with cognitive restructuring and emotional expressiveness training: An outcome investigation. *Journal of Consulting and Clinical Psychology, 50,* 636–645.

Beck, A. T. (1976). *Cognitive therapy and the emotional disorders.* Madison, CT: International Universities Press.

Biran, M., & Wilson, G. T. (1981). Treatment of phobic disorders using cognitive and exposure methods: A self-efficacy analysis. *Journal of Consulting and Clinical Psychology, 49,* 885–899.

Bowers, K. S. (1976). *Hypnosis for the seriously curious.* New York: Norton.

Bowers, K. S. (1984). Hypnosis. In N. S. Endler & J. M. Hunt (Eds.), *Personality and the behavioral disorders* (2nd ed., pp. 439–475). New York: Wiley.

Bowers, K. S. (1990). Unconscious influences and hypnosis. In J. L. Singer (Ed.), *Repression and dissociation* (pp. 143–179). Chicago: University of Chicago Press.

Boutin, G. E., & Tosi, D. J. (1983). Modification of irrational ideas and test anxiety through rational stage directed hypnotherapy (RSDH). *Journal of Clinical Psychology, 39,* 382–391.

Claiborn, C. D., & Dowd, E. T. (1985). Attributional interpretations in counseling: Content versus discrepancy. *Journal of Counseling Psychology, 32,* 188–196.

Crasilneck, H. B., & Hall, J. A. (1985). *Clinical hypnosis: Principles and applications.* New York: Grune & Stratton.

de Jong, R., Treiber, R., & Henrich, G. (1985). Effectiveness of two psychological treatments for inpatients with severe and chronic depressions. *Cognitive Therapy and Research, 10,* 545–553.

Dowd, E. T. (1989). Stasis and change in cognitive psychotherapy: Client resistance and reactance as mediating variables. In W. Dryden & P. Trower (Eds.), *Cognitive psychotherapy: Stasis and change* (pp. 139–158). London: Cassel & Collier Macmillan.

Dowd, E. T., & Healy, J. M. (1986). *Case studies in hypnotherapy.* New York: Guilford Press.

Dowd, E. T., & Seibel, C. A. (1990). A cognitive theory of resistance and reactance: Implications for treatment. *Journal of Mental Health Counseling, 12,* 458–469.

Edelson, J., & Fitzpatrick, J. L. (1989). A comparison of cognitive-behavioral and hypnotic treatments of chronic pain. *Journal of Clinical Psychology, 45,* 316–323.

Ellis, A. (1977). The basic clinical theory of rational-emotive therapy. In A. Ellis & R. Grieger (Eds.), *Handbook of rational-emotive therapy* (pp. 3–34). New York: Springer.

Erickson, M. H., & Rossi, E. L. (1979). *Hypnotherapy: An exploratory casebook.* New York: Irvington.

Erickson, M. H., & Rossi, E. L. (1981). *Experiencing hypnosis: Therapeutic approaches to altered states.* New York: Irvington.

Frank, B. M., & Noble, J. P. (1984). Field independence-dependence and cognitive restructuring. *Journal of Personality and Social Psychology, 47,* 1129–1135.

Franklin, J. A. (1989). A 5-year followup of the effectiveness of respiratory retraining, in-situ isometric relaxation, and cognitive modification in the treatment of agoraphobia. *Behavior Modification, 13,* 139–167.

Golden, W. L., Dowd, E. T., & Friedberg, F. (1987). *Hypnotherapy: A modern approach*. Elmsford, NY: Pergamon Press.

Goldfried, M. R., Decenteceo, E. T., & Weinberg, L. (1974). Systematic rational restructuring as a self-control technique. *Behavior Therapy, 5,* 247–254.

Guidano, V. F. (1987). *Complexity of the self: A developmental approach to psychopathology and therapy*. New York: Guilford Press.

Guidano, V. F., & Liotti, G. (1983). *Cognitive processes and emotional disorders*. New York: Guilford Press.

Howard, W. L., & Reardon, J. P. (1986). Changes in the self-concept and athletic performance of weight lifters through a cognitive-hypnotic approach: An empirical study. *American Journal of Clinical Hypnosis, 28,* 248–257.

Kihlstrom, J. F. (1984). Conscious, subconscious, unconscious: A cognitive perspective. In K. S. Bowers & D. Meichenbaum (Eds.), *The unconscious reconsidered* (pp. 149–211). New York: Wiley.

Liotti, G. (1987). The resistance to change of cognitive structures: A counterproposal to psychoanalytic metapsychology. *Journal of Cognitive Psychotherapy: An International Quarterly, 1,* 87–104.

Mahoney, M. J. (1988). Constructive metatheory: II. Implications for psychotherapy. *International Journal of Personal Construct Psychology, 1,* 299–316.

Markus, H. (1977). Self-schemata and processing information about the self. *Journal of Personality and Social Psychology, 35,* 63–78.

Mattick, R. P., & Peters, L. (1988). Treatment of severe social phobia: Effects of guided exposure with and without cognitive restructuring. *Journal of Consulting and Clinical Psychology, 55,* 251–260.

Meichenbaum, D. (1977). *Cognitive behavior modification: An integrative approach*. New York: Plenum Press.

Meichenbaum, D., & Gilmore, J. B. (1984). The nature of unconscious processes: A cognitive behavioral perspective. In K. S. Bowers & D. Meichenbaum (Eds.), *The unconscious reconsidered* (pp. 273–298). New York: Wiley.

Patsiokas, A. T., & Clum, G. A. (1985). Effects of psychotherapeutic strategies in the treatment of suicide attempters. *Psychotherapy, 22,* 281–290.

Pecsok, E. H., & Fremouw, W. J. (1988). Controlling laboratory binging among restrained eaters through self-monitoring and cognitive restructuring procedures. *Addictive Behaviors, 13,* 37–44.

Spiegel, H., & Spiegel, D. (1978). *Trance and treatment: Clinical uses of hypnosis*. New York: Basic Books.

Tataryn, D. J., Nadel, L., & Jacobs, W. J. (1989). Cognitive therapy and cognitive science. In A. Freeman, K. M. Simon, L. E. Beutler, & H. Arkowitz (Eds.), *Comprehensive handbook of cognitive therapy* (pp. 83–98). New York: Plenum Press.

Tosi, D. J., Judah, S. M., & Murphy, M. A. (1989). The effects of a cognitive experiential therapy utilizing hypnosis, cognitive restructuring, and developmental staging on psychological factors associated with duodenal ulcer disease: A multivariate experimental study. *Journal of Cognitive Psychotherapy: An International Quarterly, 3*, 273–290.

Wadden, T. A., & Anderton, C. H. (1982). The clinical use of hypnosis. *Psychological Bulletin, 91*, 215–243.

Wall, V. J., & Womack, W. (1989). Hypnotic versus active cognitive strategies for alleviation of procedural distress in pediatric oncology patients. *American Journal of Clinical Hypnosis, 31*, 181–191.

Udolf, R. (1981). *Handbook of hypnosis for professionals.* New York: Van Nostrand Reinhold.

III

HYPNOTIC TECHNIQUES

11

ENHANCING HYPNOTIZABILITY AND TREATMENT RESPONSIVENESS

JEFFREY D. GFELLER

Within the context of hypnosis, some people vividly experience perceptual changes and enact behavioral suggestions, whereas others experience little or no success in responding to suggestions. Hypnotizability is the construct most frequently cited as being responsible for these individual differences (Lynn & Rhue, 1991). Although there is a consensus that individuals vary widely with regard to their hypnotizability, the extent to which hypnotic responsiveness can be modified continues to be vigorously debated (Bertrand, 1989; Diamond, 1977; Perry, 1977).

In this chapter I assert that hypnotizability can be substantially enhanced and that increased hypnotic ability can lead to more successful treatment of certain disorders. Approaches and strategies that facilitate optimal hypnotic responding are presented and discussed, with particular reference to the treatment of dysfunctional pain. Case material is used to illustrate these principles and bring the ideas to life for the practitioner who uses hypnotic approaches. Before presenting this information, I briefly discuss alternative perspectives regarding the enhancement of hypnotic responsiveness and whether hypnotizability is relevant to clinical outcome.

There is still considerable debate among proponents of two alternative paradigms regarding the extent to which hypnotic responsivity can be enhanced. One perspective, termed the *special process view* (Hilgard, 1977, 1979), conceptualizes hypnotic responsiveness as reflecting the ability to passively experience dissociation among various cognitive subsystems. This dissociative ability is purported to account for most hypnotic phenomena, including hypnotic analgesia, hypnotic amnesia, and the sense of involuntariness that often accompanies responses to ideomotor suggestions. This dissociative capacity, particularly evident in highly hypnotizable people, is viewed as an enduring trait that resides in the individual and is not amenable to substantial modification.

An alternative perspective, termed the *cognitive skills model* (Spanos, 1982), views hypnotic responding as the by-product of an ability that is determined by numerous interrelated factors. These include expectancies and attitudes toward hypnosis, various cognitive skills such as vividness of imagery and absorption in imaginings, and interpersonal variables such as the degree of trust and rapport with the hypnotist. Each factor is viewed as potentially modifiable, at least to a limited extent. The cognitive skills model contends that hypnotizability can be substantially enhanced when subjects are given facilitative information and training that addresses these factors.

Interestingly, Coe (1989) has reported that clinicians who use hypnosis tend to embrace the special process view, whereas hypnosis researchers are more likely to use social psychological and cognitive skills constructs to understand hypnotic phenomena. This is unfortunate because the cognitive skills perspective provides a descriptive account of the various attitudinal, cognitive, and interpersonal factors that affect hypnotic responsivity. This perspective may be useful for clinicians who are not comfortable using special process constructs to conceptualize hypnosis in their work with patients. The cognitive skills model is particularly appealing to cognitive–behavioral clinicians who view hypnosis as an active coping skill that the patient learns in the context of a collaborative relationship with the therapist. The focus on practice and the enhancement of hypnotic skills moves the patient toward independent practice with the technique. Thus, once the patient has been given facilitative information and coaching, the process can, for the most part, be thought of as a self-hypnotic approach.

The strategies and techniques presented in this chapter are based largely on the principles derived from the cognitive skills model of hypnosis. (For a more comprehensive discussion of this model and its comparison to the special process view, see Diamond, 1989.)

Before presenting strategies to enhance hypnotizability, the issue of whether the level of hypnotic responsiveness matters significantly with regard to treatment outcome for various conditions deserves consideration. Hypnosis has been used as a means of treatment for many conditions, including anxiety disorders (Clarke & Jackson, 1983), impotence (Crasilneck, 1982), addictive disorders such as cigarette smoking (Holroyd, 1980) and alcoholism (Granone, 1971), obesity (Wadden & Flaxman, 1981), psychophysiological disorders including asthma (Neinstein & Dash, 1982), dermatological conditions such as warts (Tasini & Hackett, 1977), and as a treatment for intractable pain stemming from various etiologies (Barber, 1986).

Intuitively, one surmises that a patient's level of hypnotizability does not equally affect clinical outcome for each of the conditions noted earlier. Wadden and Anderton (1982) and others (Soskis, 1986) have noted that hypnotizability is the most relevant to the conditions in which successful intervention can be achieved through altering the patient's subjective experience. Conditions in which the alteration of perception and subjective experience can bring about positive outcome include those involving traumatic memories, psychophysiological conditions such as asthma, anxiety disorders, and dysfunctional pain.

In conditions in which successful outcome requires behavioral change (e.g., smoking cessation or weight reduction), hypnotizability appears to be less important insofar as significant alteration of subjective experience by itself does not guarantee alteration of behavior.

Indeed, although clinical reports of the successful hypnotic treatment of conditions requiring behavioral change abound, most experimental studies have showed that successful treatment of such conditions is likely to be a function of nonspecific factors (Wadden & Anderton, 1982). Therefore, although hypnosis may serve as a useful component in the treatment of conditions requiring behavioral change, the use of adjunctive cognitive and behavioral approaches is clearly warranted.

From a common-factors view of treatment (Frank, 1974), the level of hypnotizability may nevertheless influence outcome when hypnosis is used as an adjunct to other approaches to effect behavior change. More specifically, a patient's experience of significant perceptual alterations during the hypnotic induction enhances the credibility of the "therapeutic myth" that facilitative suggestions provided during hypnosis result in expected behavioral transformations.

An example is a multicomponent smoking cessation treatment that uses a variety of self-regulatory approaches, including self-hypnosis as a cognitive strategy, to help the patient cope with the inevitable desire for a cigarette. In this situation, a patient who has successfully responded to an ideomotor suggestion such as hand levitation will be far more likely to believe that "hypnotic ability" will assist him or her in successfully resisting the urge to smoke during the initial days of abstinence. The successful implementation of self-hypnosis to cope with smoking urges may give the patient a sense of mastery and self-efficacy (Bandura, 1977) that will facilitate a successful outcome.

CLINICAL APPLICATIONS

The evidence summarized earlier suggests that hypnotic responsiveness is most relevant with respect to conditions in which successful outcome can be achieved by altering the patient's subjective experience and perceptions. This guideline is clearly applicable with respect to the hypnotic treatment of dysfunctional pain. Dysfunctional pain may be defined as pain that has lost its "signal value," meaning that the discomfort experienced by the patient should no longer be perceived as a cue that requires immediate medical attention (Soskis, 1986).

The experimental and clinical studies relating hypnotizability to the extent of pain reduction have documented a reasonably strong and positive relationship between these variables (Friedman & Taub, 1984; Hilgard, MacDonald, Morgan, & Johnson, 1978; Hilgard & Morgan, 1975; Spanos, Radke-Bodorik, Ferguson, & Jones, 1979). Therefore, facilitating hypnotizability among people experiencing dysfunctional pain should enhance their ability to decrease their discomfort with hypnotic interventions.

As noted previously, the cognitive skills model provides a descriptive account of the salient attitudinal, cognitive, and interpersonal factors that facilitate optimal hypnotic responding. For illustrative purposes, I discuss these factors primarily within the context of enhancing hypnotizability among individuals experiencing dysfunctional pain. Nevertheless, the scheme for enhancing hypnotic responsiveness, described shortly, is applicable to a wide range of psychological and psychophysiological disorders.

Attitudes and Expectancies

Discussing patients' general attitudes and expectancies about hypnosis, as well as any past hypnotic experience, is an important component of facilitating hypnotic responsiveness and behavior change (Kirsch, 1985; Kirsch & Council, 1989). Common negative expectancies about hypnosis such as fearing a loss of control or a belief that people are gullible or weakwilled if they are hypnotizable should be explored. One useful instrument to evaluate general beliefs about hypnosis is the Hypnotic Attitudes Questionnaire (Spanos, Brett, Menary, & Cross, 1987). Examination of the patient's responses to this questionnaire provides a point of departure for discussing misconceptions about hypnosis that inhibit hypnotic ability.

Negative expectancies specific to the hypnotic treatment of a particular disorder should be explored before initiating hypnosis. Asking patients what they expect to experience during hypnosis and how hypnosis may affect their situation often will provide information regarding inhibitory beliefs. Table 1 lists a number of inhibitory expectancies frequently encountered with patients with dysfunctional pain. Beliefs that can potentially limit hypnotic responding merit attention.

TABLE 1
Negative Expectancies of Patients With Dysfunctional Pain

1. The use of hypnosis implies that the pain problem is psychological in nature and not caused by a medical condition.
2. Hypnosis represents an ineffective technique when compared with prescription medication.
3. The use of hypnosis to attenuate pain will result in a loss of attention from family or a loss of compensation resulting from the pain condition.
4. There is a fear of being unable to discern when one's pain level has increased, resulting in further injury.

The expectation that the effective use of hypnosis implies that a pain problem is primarily psychological in nature can severely limit a patient's willingness to use hypnosis to attenuate pain. Therefore, patients often need reassurance that the hypnotist believes that their pain condition is genuine and not psychological in origin. At the same time, the hypnotist can provide a model for understanding how hypnosis can successfully reduce "organic" pain. The gate-control theory of pain (Melzack & Wall, 1982) is a useful model that provides a credible account of how physiological, emotional, and cognitive factors interact to influence pain perception.

The belief that the successful use of hypnosis may result in a loss of family attention or a loss of compensation stemming from the pain condition may also inhibit optimal hypnotic responding. Accepting patients' reports of pain as genuine does not mean that their expression of pain is nonresponsive to external factors such as attention and support from those around them. Addressing this operant component of pain (Fordyce, 1976) by educating family members is often an important means of influencing the social reinforcement of the patient's verbal and behavioral expression of pain. Failure to address these social contingencies certainly limits patients' ability to acquire hypnotic skills as a means of managing their pain.

Some patients may be reluctant to experiment with hypnosis because of their belief that its use would impair their ability to discern increases in pain, resulting in further injury or discomfort. This is a genuine concern among pain patients who have overused some form of cognitive distraction in the past to cope with pain that is exacerbated with physical activity. Therefore, it is important to frame hypnosis as a means of coping with pain increases resulting from activities such as exercise or a family outing, not as a means of allowing the person to overdo an activity. Discussing the previously mentioned concept of the signal value of pain and situations in which patients need to attend to increases in discomfort is helpful in this regard.

It is neither necessary nor feasible to address every negative attitude that may limit patients' hypnotic ability before exposing them to hypnosis. However, the clinician should be ready to explore inhibitory beliefs with patients who experience limited success with hypnotic interventions.

Cognitive Skills Factors

The cognitive skills model emphasizes facilitating a number of cognitive processes in order to enhance patients' ability to use hypnosis as a means of ameliorating their symptoms or condition. Pertinent cognitive strategies for optimal hypnotic responding are listed in Table 2.

Portraying hypnosis as an experience not far removed from many everyday phenomena provides patients with a sense of what to expect during hypnosis. Using examples such as maintaining focused attention while reading a novel and imaginative involvement while daydreaming are helpful in this regard.

The role of goal-directed fantasy (Spanos & Barber, 1974) or involvement in imaginings consistent with symptom reduction is another important concept to explore with patients. With regard to the treatment of dysfunctional pain, Chaves (1989) noted the value of eliciting a detailed description of patients' phenomenological experience of their pain (e.g., "My leg feels like it is burning," "My back feels like it is in knots"). This information often suggests particular imagery or metaphors that can be readily used by the patient.

Elaborating on the role of absorption, or "staying focused," on imaginings in order to facilitate optimal hypnotic responding is also important insofar as the failure to remain focused on images that attenuate pain impedes patients' success with hypnosis. The theatrical concept of the "willing suspension of disbelief" provides a useful metaphor to assist patients with appreciating the suspension of reality orientation necessary to attain optimal hypnotic skills.

TABLE 2
Cognitive Skills Factors and The Enhancement of Hypnotizability

1. Portraying hypnosis as a cognitive experience not far removed from many everyday life phenomena.

2. Discussing the concept of goal-directed fantasy or imaginative involvement and its role in hypnotic experience.

3. Elaborating on the importance of absorption and suspension of reality orientation for facilitating optimal hypnotic responsiveness.

4. Explaining hypnosis as an active process to be learned by the patient as a coping skill.

Presenting hypnosis as an active process that can be mastered to better manage their condition is an essential component in enhancing hypnotizability (Spanos, Robertson, Menary, & Brett, 1986). For example, patients with dysfunctional pain should understand the importance of actively interpreting suggestions for analgesia rather than passively waiting for the analgesia to occur. Thus, if a patient is given a hypnotic suggestion that ice is being applied to the site of pain, the patient should actively focus on imagery consistent with this suggestion in order to maximize its effectiveness.

The modeling of these cognitive strategies by the hypnotist is a particularly effective means of imparting skills that facilitate optimal hypnotic responding. For example, the hypnotist may demonstrate an ideomotor response such as arm levitation and verbally report his or her goal-directed imaginings that facilitate a sense of lightness or movement in the arm. Similarly, the hypnotist may verbally report his or her subjective experience during attentional focusing and describe how this process results in a diminution of other sensory experiences in the body. The modeling of cognitive strategies by the hypnotist also conveys an implicit message that the hypnotist "practices what he or she preaches." This message usually has a positive effect on rapport between the patient and therapist.

Patients undoubtedly have limits on the extent to which they can acquire and enhance cognitive skills such as goal-directed fantasy and absorption in imaginings. However, initial lack of success should not be taken as proof of limited hypnotic ability. Positive changes can occur with facilitative information and practice. Lazarus (1977) provided a number of structured exercises for enhancing imagery skills. One imagery enhancement exercise that can be readily applied to pain reduction involves creating the image of a black board on which patients picture themselves printing or writing letters of the alphabet and erasing the letters to conclude the exercise. With several attempts, patients usually report increased clarity of the imagined board and letters. At this point, patients can be given a permissive suggestion to imagine a drawing of their pain on this board using whatevery imagery they choose. Erasing this image of their pain from the blackboard often results in a significant decrease in discomfort for a period of time.

This imagery exercise can be easily adapted for other applications ranging from defusing traumatic memories to decreasing the urge to smoke. For example, during hypnosis, an ex-smoker who is craving a cigarette may draw a picture of a cigarette on the imaginary blackboard and then "mentally erase" this drawing, resulting in a diminished urge to smoke.

Interpersonal Factors

As in all therapeutic contexts, establishing a positive therapeutic alliance is necessary in order to assist patients in enhancing their hypnotic abilities (Gfeller, Lynn, & Pribble, 1987). The cognitive skills perspective views the therapeutic relationship as a collaborative process in which the hypnotist is a participant-observer who assists patients in understanding the nature of hypnosis and exploring the limits of their hypnotic ability. Patients must perceive the hypnotist as trustworthy and genuine in order to achieve these goals. Therefore, a hypnotic intervention should not be implemented until there is a clear sense that some degree of positive rapport has been established. With receptive patients, simply encountering a clinician who demonstrates an understanding of their condition and expresses a desire to improve their situation is sufficient. However, less receptive patients, who express skepticism and inhibitory beliefs regarding hypnosis, require additional attention from the hypnotist in order to establish an interpersonal climate in which they feel safe to develop their hypnotic abilities. Exploring patients' inhibitory beliefs is one means of increasing receptiveness to hypnosis. The modeling of hypnotic responding by the therapist also conveys a sense of genuineness that facilitates rapport. Whatever approach taken should be advanced in the spirit of providing information to the patient, not as a "hard sell" intended to portray hypnosis as a panacea.

Although hypnotizability is portrayed as a skill that can be enhanced with instruction and practice, nothing facilitates rapport more effectively than a positive first encounter with hypnosis. Thus, clinicians must balance optimizing patients' first experience of hypnosis with the hazard of excessively delaying this initial experience by overpreparing them.

CASE MATERIAL

The case of "John" clearly illustrates the application of the various strategies for facilitating hypnotic ability and treatment outcome.

John was a 43-year-old physician who was referred for pain management related to abdominal pain resulting from pancreatic cancer. In addition to abdominal pain, he experienced nausea and anorexia, which resulted in significant weight loss. He had undergone both chemotherapy and radiation therapy, which caused a minimal remission of the progression of cancer. His oncologist had informed him there was little else that could be done to medically treat his condition.

Because John was requiring increasingly large doses of narcotic medication to reduce his abdominal pain, both he and his physician were interested in exploring psychological means to reduce his discomfort. John's personal interest in using alternative methods of pain control stemmed from his displeasure with the sedation he experienced from the analgesic medications. The sedation compromised the quality of time he spent with his wife and their young son. Although he was no longer regularly seeing patients, he continued to consult with colleagues on selected cases from his home and took great pride in maintaining this activity, which was limited when he felt excessively drowsy or fatigued.

During our initial meeting, John briefly summarized his medical treatment for the pancreatic cancer as well as the adverse symptoms he was currently experiencing. When asked to describe his abdominal pain in detail, he reported the pain to be "gnawing" and "relentless" in nature. When asked if he used any mental strategies to reduce his discomfort, he acknowledged that his pain sometimes decreased when he was reading or talking with his wife.

Although John indicated that he had never experienced hypnosis, he was somewhat pessimistic that he could be hypnotized because he was "too inquisitive and scientifically minded." I replied that he may initially experience limited success with hypnosis for a variety of reasons, including his scientific mode of thinking and his lack of understanding of what was required of him. However, I had confidence in his ability to use hypnosis once we attended to his inquisitive nature by providing him with information about the nature of hypnosis and how to optimize his hypnotic ability. At this point, I gave John the following information:

> Hypnosis is difficult to define, but one thing I know for certain is that the ability to be hypnotized lies within you; it is not a power that I possess. Successful hypnosis seems to involve the ability to focus your mental attention on a particular sight, sound, or image that you create in your mind's eye. This ability is something akin to the absorption you have experienced when reading or when engrossed in conversation with your wife, experiences you mentioned earlier that resulted in some pain reduction.
>
> People differ in their ability to experience hypnosis. Some take to it like a duckling to water; others seem initially uncomfortable with the process and demonstrate limited hypnotic ability. However, a person's degree of hypnotizability is not etched in stone. While you may not take to hypnosis like a duck to water, you can certainly become more proficient with hypnosis, just as you can learn to be proficient at swimming.

In order to determine whether John held beliefs that would impede his responsiveness to hypnosis, I explored his expectations about what hypnosis would be like as well as his perception about how this experience may affect his level of pain. John's comments indicated that he had few misconceptions about hypnosis and that he was not fearful of experiencing a loss of control during hypnosis. However, he expressed two beliefs that could limit his hypnotizability. First, he conveyed the expectation that somehow the experience of hypnosis would just happen and would not require effort on his part. Second, he was concerned that hypnotic analgesia would be minimal and transient compared with that produced from the potent medications he was taking.

To address the first concern, we discussed the nonvolitional nature of hypnosis, with me demonstrating an ideomotor response (arm levitation). As I responded, I reported my imaginings that facilitated movement in the arm. Following the demonstration, I elaborated on the experience, noting that although it was clear that I had raised my own arm, I experienced a sense of the arm rising by itself because I was so engrossed in imagining a rope and pulley that was being used to hoist my arm into the air.

John required little prompting in order to try responding to a similar suggestion. I provided a less difficult suggestion for arm lowering that he performed with ease, indicating afterward that he had imagined someone placing increasingly heavier amounts of weight on his hand that caused it to move downward. Following this, I indicated that his experience of hypnosis would be a similar process that would require his active participation. Hypnosis was not something that I would do *to* him; rather, being hypnotized was an experience that he would initially create with my assistance and later create entirely on his own.

With regard to John's expectation that hypnotic analgesia would be limited and transient in nature, I indicated that some people are able to use hypnosis to markedly reduce their level of discomfort. Because he was a man of science, I asked that he keep an open mind about how effective hypnosis might be in reducing his pain. I also indicated that just as there were a number of medications one could take for pain, there were also a number of available hypnotic strategies to reduce the experience of pain. We reviewed several possible approaches, including imagined anesthesia, direct diminution of pain, reinterpretation of painful sensations, and dissociation from pain through the use of vivid imagery (see Barber, 1986). John expressed a fondness for the dissociative approach, indicating he wanted to "get as far away from my pain as possible." Therefore, we discussed possible scenes or images that would provide such an escape. John indicated that he loved to scuba dive and that he had very vivid memories of tropical fish and coral he had encountered while diving. We agreed to use these images during his initial experience with hypnosis.

Although John would benefit from additional information to facilitate hypnotic responding, these benefits had to be balanced against the importance of initiating hypnosis and assisting him in reducing his pain. Because we had addressed the identified barriers to hypnotic responding and he had positively responded to an ideomotor suggestion, I believed he was ready to experience hypnosis and suggestions for pain reduction.

I asked John to rate the severity of his abdominal pain on a 1–5 scale of increasing discomfort. He reported that his pain level had been a 3 throughout our meeting. I then guided him through a 20-min hypnotic exercise with suggestions for relaxation and attentional focusing. I suggested that he picture himself slowly descending in scuba gear toward a reef teeming with marine life in order to deepen his absorption in the imagery he was experiencing. After spending several minutes describing this reef in great detail, I ended the exercise with the suggestion that he would soon be successful at mentally traveling to this setting on his own.

John's response to hypnosis was highly positive. He reported experiencing the reef and marine life with vividness and clarity. Most important, he indicated that his pain level had decreased to a 1.5 on the 5-point scale. I asked him to note his pain level over the next few hours to help determine how long this relief lasted. I then scheduled John for an appointment several days later.

At the start of the next session, John indicated that the reduction in pain had lasted only several hours, and he expressed pessimism that hypnosis could result in more lasting relief. I reassured him that the duration of relief would likely increase as his experience with hypnosis increased. Moreover, he would soon be able to reduce his pain without my assistance. I again guided him through a hypnotic exercise and re-created the imagery of the reef he had visited in his mind's eye several days earlier. However, this time, we tape-recorded the procedure, and John used the tape to experience hypnosis at home during the next week.

At our third session, John indicated that with the benefit of the tape-recorded exercise at home, he had successfully reduced his pain. Additionally, the analgesia was lasting up to 5 or 6 hr. At this time, I recommended that John begin alternating between using the tape-recorded procedure and self-initiating hypnosis, including the imagined setting.

At the next session, John was visibly pleased. He indicated that he had been successful in reducing his pain using his own "induction." Moreover, he reported that he was using less medication to control his pain. His wife indicated that he was more interactive and seemed less focused on his discomfort.

I continued to see John periodically to assist him with refining his hypnotic abilities and to explore other hypnotic approaches to attenuate his pain. For example, we attempted to use hypnosis to counter the anorexia caused by the cancer or radiation therapy he had received. Although we had little success in affecting this symptom, his wife reported that John had continued to use hypnosis to reduce his pain until shortly before his death.

RESEARCH AND APPRAISAL

The efficacy of the strategies presented for enhancing hypnotizability, derived largely from the cognitive skills model of hypnosis, is supported by numerous studies that have documented appreciable gains in hypnotic responding when subjects have been provided with the facilitative information and cognitive skills training (Diamond, 1972; Gfeller et al., 1987; Gorassini & Spanos, 1986; Katz, 1979; Spanos & Flynn, 1989; Spanos et al., 1986).

Proponents of the special process view (Bates, 1990; Bowers & Davidson, 1991) have frequently questioned the genuine nature of these increments, suggesting that enhanced hypnotizability represents artificial compliance with experimental demands on the subjects' part.

However, in several studies (e.g., Gfeller et al., 1987; Gorassini & Spanos, 1986), subjects' enhanced hypnotic abilities generalized to novel suggestions, and their subjective reports were not distinguishable from "natural high" susceptible subjects who did not have cognitive skills training. These findings place some burden of proof on proponents of the special process view to identify characteristics that differentiate natural hypnotic talents from those enhanced through cognitive skills training. Conversely, proponents of the cognitive skills model should venture beyond studies with undergraduate student populations and formally investigate whether hypnotic modification techniques are effective in clinical contexts with different disorders and patient populations.

CONCLUSION

The strategies outlined in this chapter can facilitate the successful use of hypnosis, particularly with patients who are viewed as being unlikely candidates for hypnotic intervention because of limited hypnotizability. The approaches are believed to improve clinical outcome, especially in the treatment of disorders that are ameliorated by altering patients' sensory and perceptual experiences. The strategies should be used flexibly and tailored to address idiosyncratic factors that limit hypnotic responsivity with individual patients.

More generally, the cognitive skills model, from which the strategies are derived, provides an alternative perspective for conceptualizing hypnotic phenomena that may appeal to clinicians who are not comfortable using constructs associated with the special process view of hypnosis. The model may be particularly appealing to cognitive–behavioral clinicians in that hypnosis is viewed as an active coping skill that patients learn to use independently through a collaborative relationship with the therapist.

It should be stated that these techniques have their limitations. Some people, for a variety of reasons, have limited success in using facilitative information and cognitive skills training to enhance their hypnotic responsiveness. Those who study hypnotic phenomena will continue to search for factors that constrain and enhance patients' hypnotic skills. This search will undoubtedly shed additional light on the nature of hypnotizability and how to best use hypnotic interventions to help patients.

REFERENCES

Bandura, A. (1977). *Social learning theory*. Englewood Cliffs, NJ: Prentice-Hall.

Barber, J. (1986). Hypnotic analgesia. In A. D. Holzman & D. C. Turk (Eds.), *Pain management: A handbook of psychological treatment approaches* (pp. 151–167). Elmsford, NY: Pergamon Press.

Bates, B. L. (1990). Compliance and the Carleton Skills Training Program. *British Journal of Experimental and Clinical Hypnosis, 7,* 159–164.

Bertrand, L. D. (1989). The assessment and modification of hypnotic susceptibility. In N. P. Spanos & J. F. Chaves (Eds.), *Hypnosis: The cognitive-behavioral perspective* (pp. 18–31). Buffalo, NY: Prometheus Books.

Bowers, K. S., & Davidson, T. M. (1991). A neo-dissociation critique of Spanos's social–psychological model of hypnosis. In S. J. Lynn & J. W. Rhue (Eds.), *Theories of hypnosis: Current models and perspectives* (pp. 105–143). New York: Guilford Press.

Chaves, J. F. (1989). Hypnotic control of clinical pain. In N. P. Spanos & J. F. Chaves (Eds.), *Hypnosis: The cognitive-behavioral perspective* (pp. 242–272). Buffalo, NY: Prometheus Books.

Clarke, J. H., & Jackson, J. A. (1983). *Hypnosis and behavior therapy: The treatment of anxiety and phobias*. New York: Springer.

Coe, W. C. (1989). Hypnosis: The role of sociopolitical factors. In N. P. Spanos & J. F. Chaves (Eds.), *Hypnosis: The cognitive-behavioral perspective* (pp. 418–436). Buffalo, NY: Prometheus Books.

Crasilneck, H. B. (1982). A follow-up study in the use of hypnotherapy in the treatment of psychogenic impotence. *American Journal of Clinical Hypnosis, 25,* 52–61.

Diamond, M. J. (1972). The use of observationally presented information to modify hypnotic susceptibility. *Journal of Abnormal Psychology, 79,* 174–180.

Diamond, M. J. (1977). Hypnotizability is modifiable: An alternative approach. *International Journal of Clinical and Experimental Hypnosis, 25,* 147–165.

Diamond, M. J. (1989). The cognitive skills model: An emerging paradigm for investigating hypnotic phenomena. In N. P. Spanos and J. F. Chaves, (Eds.), *Hypnosis: The cognitive-behavioral perspective* (pp. 380–399). Buffalo, NY: Prometheus Books.

Fordyce, W. E. (1976). *Behavioral methods for chronic pain and illness*. St. Louis, MO: Mosby.

Friedman, H., & Taub, H. A. (1984). An evaluation of hypnotic susceptibility and peripheral temperature elevation in the treatment of migraine. *American Journal of Clinical Hypnosis, 24,* 172–182.

Frank, J. D. (1974). *Persuasion and healing*. New York: Schocken Books.

Gfeller, J. D., Lynn, S. J., & Pribble, W. E. (1987). Enhancing hypnotic suscep-tibility: Interpersonal and rapport factors. *Journal of Personality and Social Psychology, 52,* 586–595.

Gorassini, D. R., & Spanos, N. P. (1986). A social-cognitive skills approach to the successful modification of hypnotic susceptibility. *Journal of Personality and Social Psychology, 50,* 1004–1012.

Granone, F. (1971). Hypnotism in the treatment of chronic alcoholism. *Journal of the American Institute of Hypnosis, 12,* 32–40.

Hilgard, E. R. (1977). *Divided consciousness: Multiple controls in human thought and action.* New York: Wiley-Interscience.

Hilgard, E. R. (1979). Divided consciousness in hypnosis: The implications of the hidden observer. In E. Fromm & R. E. Shor (Eds.), *Hypnosis: Developments in research and new perspectives* (pp. 45–85). Chicago: Aldine.

Hilgard, E. R., MacDonald, H., Morgan, A. H., & Johnson, L. S. (1978). The reality of hypnotic analgesia: A comparison of highly hypnotizables and sim-ulators. *Journal of Abnormal Psychology, 87,* 239–246.

Hilgard, E. R., & Morgan, A. H. (1975). Heart rate and blood pressure in the study of laboratory pain in man under normal conditions and as influenced by hypnosis. *Acta Neurobiologia Experimentalis, 35,* 741–759.

Holroyd, J. (1980). Hypnosis treatment for smoking: An evaluative review. *In-ternational Journal of Clinical and Experimental Hypnosis, 28,* 341–357.

Katz, N. W. (1979). Comparative efficacy of behavioral training, training plus relaxation, and a sleep/trance hypnotic induction in increasing hypnotic sus-ceptibility. *Journal of Consulting and Clinical Psychology, 47,* 119–127.

Kirsch, I. (1985). Response expectancy as a determinant of experience and be-havior. *American Psychologist, 40,* 1189–1202.

Kirsch, I., & Council, J. R. (1989). Response expectancy as a determinant of hypnotic behavior. In N. P. Spanos & J. F. Chaves (Eds.), *Hypnosis: The cognitive-behavioral perspective* (pp. 360–379). Buffalo, NY: Prometheus Books.

Lazarus, A. (1977). *In the mind's eye: The power of imagery for personal enrichment.* New York: Guilford Press.

Lynn, S. J., & Rhue, J. (1991). An integrative model of hypnosis. In S. J. Lynn & J. W. Rhue (Eds.), *Hypnosis theories: Current models and perspectives* (pp. 397–438). New York: Guilford Press.

Melzack, R., & Wall, P. D. (1982). *The challenge of pain.* New York: Basic Books.

Neinstein, L. S., & Dash, J. (1982). Hypnosis as an adjunct therapy for asthma: Case report. *Journal of Adolescent Health Care, 3,* 45–48.

Perry, C. (1977). Is hypnotizability modifiable? *International Journal of Clinical and Experimental Hypnosis, 25,* 125–146.

Soskis, D. A. (1986). *Teaching self-hypnosis: An introductory guide for clinicians.* New York: Norton.

Spanos, N. P. (1982). Hypnotic behavior: A cognitive social psychological perspective. *Research Communications in Psychology, Psychiatry, and Behavior, 1,* 199–213.

Spanos, N. P., & Barber, T. X. (1974). Toward a convergence in hypnosis research. *American Psychologist, 29,* 500–511.

Spanos, N. P., Brett, P. J., Menary, E. P., & Cross, W. P. (1987). A measure of attitudes toward hypnosis: Relationships with absorption and hypnotic susceptibility. *American Journal of Clinical Hypnosis, 30,* 139–150.

Spanos, N. P., & Flynn, D. M. (1989). Simulation, compliance and skill training in the enhancement of hypnotizability. *British Journal of Experimental and Clinical Hypnosis, 6,* 1–8.

Spanos, N. P., Radke-Bodorik, H. L., Ferguson, J. D., & Jones, B. (1979). The effects of hypnotic susceptibility, suggestions for analgesia, and the utilization of cognitive strategies on the reduction of pain. *Journal of Abnormal Psychology, 88,* 282–292.

Spanos, N. P., Robertson, L. A., Menary, E. P., & Brett, P. J. (1986). Component analysis of cognitive skill training for the enhancement of hypnotic susceptibility. *Journal of Abnormal Psychology, 95,* 350–357.

Tasini, M. F., & Hackett, T. P. (1977). Hypnosis in the treatment of warts in immunodeficient children. *American Journal of Clinical Hypnosis, 19,* 152–154.

Wadden, T. A., & Anderton, C. H. (1982). The clinical use of hypnosis. *Psychological Bulletin, 91,* 215–243.

Wadden, T. A., & Flaxman, J. (1981). Hypnosis and weight loss: A preliminary study. *International Journal of Clinical and Experimental Hypnosis, 29,* 162–163.

12

CLINICAL SELF-HYPNOSIS: TRANSFORMATION AND SUBJECTIVITY

SHIRLEY SANDERS

In recent years, clinical self-hypnosis has become an important adjunct to psychotherapy (Sanders, 1991). Because there is great diversity in the way that self-hypnosis is implemented, conceptualized, and taught, the potential of self-hypnosis can be realized most fully when the therapist samples its varied applications in clinical situations (Sanders, 1991). No one approach is universally hailed as being superior to others, nor is there one that is consistently taught as the best self-hypnosis method (Crasilneck & Hall, 1985; Erickson, 1980; Kroger, 1977).

The dimensions of self-hypnosis are complex and include therapist variables, patient variables, therapeutic contexts, the variety of self-hypnotic procedures, and the target of treatment. The interactions among these factors contribute to the patient's experiencing a truly unique and creative response to self-hypnosis. In this chapter I introduce readers to clinical self-hypnosis by discussing relevant applications, procedures, clinical examples, and research.

I think that the purpose of teaching the patient self-hypnosis is three-fold: First, self-hypnosis provides a vehicle for the patient to participate actively in the treatment process. Second, self-hypnosis is a way to reinforce self-mastery. By encouraging patients to participate actively in their treatment, in the context of an emotionally safe environment, the therapist fortifies patients' coping abilities and sense of power and efficacy. By suggesting helpful words, images, and imaginary alternatives and possibilities, which patients imbue with meaning and significance, the therapist encourages psychological health. Finally, self-hypnosis extends hypnotherapy beyond the consultation room and into patients' homes.

These facilitative aspects of self-hypnosis enrich and enliven psychotherapy. Rather than being a treatment in and of itself or providing an alternative to a particular type of psychotherapy, self-hypnosis adds an interactive dimension to the treatment process that is mutually and dynamically shaped by the therapist and patient. For example, the therapist may describe a relaxing beach scene, which the patient then elaborates on with personal associations, memories, and accompanying affect that are unique to the patient and resonate in meaningful ways with the patient's current and past life circumstances. Thus, in response to the suggested beach scenario, the patient could respond, "Yes, I am at Hilton Head. It is beautiful, just as it was when I was there last. I feel so at peace with myself, so one with nature." This description does more than mirror the therapist's bare-bones sketch of the suggested scene; it reflects emotions evoked by the patient's memory. The therapist can in turn access, embellish, and use these feelings at the appropriate therapeutic moment. Such team work generates a shared inner space similar to that described by Winnicott (1953). Of course, interactions of this sort occur in heterohypnosis as well. However, they are more likely to occur when patients are given a more active role, as they are in self-hypnosis.

If questions or fears arise, the therapist must remain emotionally available to patients. The therapist can clarify issues and procedures and reassure, validate, and support patients during the session, at the next session, or, if more urgent and pressing, by telephone. Thus, clinical self-hypnosis is part of a mutual, ongoing treatment endeavor rather than being restricted to a single meeting.

Before discussing clinical applications of self-hypnosis, I distinguish between self-hypnosis and heterohypnosis. Heterohypnosis and self-hypnosis are comparable in that both are thought to facilitate access to the unconscious (Johnson, 1979) and are associated with imagery and fantasy production and a variety of alterations in subjective experience (Fromm et al., 1981). However, heterohypnosis and self-hypnosis can be clearly differentiated on a structural or contextual basis. According to Fromm et al. (1981), self-hypnosis is a self-directed, self-induced state, whereas heterohypnosis is a dyadic situation in which the hypnotherapist provides the patient's induction. As I have noted elsewhere (Sanders, 1991), "the essence of self-hypnosis appears to involve the patient initiating the self-hypnotic state and self-directing it by choosing to do it" (p. 211).

CLINICAL APPLICATIONS

Indications and Counterindications

What are the indications and counterindications of using clinical self-hypnosis? In this section I discuss patient motivation, therapist availability, presenting problems, and hypnosis as a means of resistance.

Patient Motivation

There are two factors that affect patients' motivation: (a) their desire for improvement, which can be conceptualized as the resolve to develop and pursue a therapeutic agenda; and (b) their willingness to use self-hypnosis as a tool in the treatment process. For example, patients may want to use hypnosis as a way to avoid awareness of painful memories, but they may not be truly motivated to make difficult life changes. On the other hand, patients may be motivated to make life changes, but they may be so fearful of hypnosis that they are unable to use or exploit hypnotic procedures to their advantage, leading to resistance and counterproductive thoughts and behaviors.

Because motivation is multidimensional and necessary for successful treatment, it is wise to assess it in the initial interview or in the early stages of therapy by exploring patients' attitudes toward, interest in, and expectations about hypnosis. Some patients may believe that hypnosis is somehow harmful or dangerous, whereas other patients may believe that the suggestion to use hypnosis represents a "discounting" of their problems. These attitudes and beliefs are important to identify and discuss with patients before hypnosis is begun. If these issues are not successfully resolved, a power struggle between the patient and therapist may ensue, which may disrupt the therapeutic alliance, provoke resistance, produce counterproductive reactions (Bliss, 1983; Shengold, 1978), and negate the benefits of potentially useful suggestions. This destructive and consuming power struggle may provide an avenue of escape, or at least a diversion, from the work of the therapy (Bliss, 1986).

Inadequate motivation or outright resistance to hypnosis may be the result of low hypnotizability or past failures to experience hypnosis in a therapeutic context. If patients have fears of relinquishing control to the hypnotist, or if heterohypnosis has not been successful in the past, the therapist can differentiate it from self-hypnosis in salient respects, such as patients' heightened self-control in self-hypnosis.

It is important to assess whether patients view hypnosis as being integral to the therapeutic endeavor and to identify sources of resistance to pursuing the treatment agenda. One way this can be done is by asking patients directly about how important it is to change various aspects of their life and what impediments they anticipate in their struggle to achieve therapeutic objectives. If they are not interested or motivated to use self-hypnosis and to make significant life changes in keeping with treatment goals, patients may resist attempts to learn self-hypnosis, subvert the therapist's best efforts to devise therapeutic suggestions, and fail to practice self-hypnotic techniques.

Therapist Availability

When self-hypnosis is used, the therapist must remain available to the patient between sessions. The therapist uses a variety of skills and interventions that include validating the patient; identifying, clarifying, and interpreting problems, issues, and conflicts; empathizing with the patient's struggles; and challenging and confronting the patient at appropriate times. For the most part, these skills and interventions are used during the therapy session. However, the therapist must be available and ready to intervene between sessions when the patient is overwhelmed by affect or imagery stimulated by the work of therapy or by the use of self-hypnosis at home.

In addition to being available for consultation between sessions, the therapist should use treatment sessions to monitor the patient's self-hypnotic practice. One of the therapist's tasks is to provide a platform for the patient to discuss questions and concerns, as well as words and images generated during self-hypnosis. Therapist monitoring is advisable in order to ensure that helpful suggestions are identified and used to the patient's advantage. Patients often enter treatment because they feel out of control and have not been able to take command of their lives. A measure of self-control can be reinstated when the therapist provides a safe and comfortable therapeutic haven in which patients' cognitive and affective experiences, generated during self-hypnosis, can be examined and monitored. During each session, patients have an opportunity to describe their use of self-hypnosis. Patients' experiences can be reviewed either by direct verbal feedback to the therapist or by way of a personal journal. For example, the patient records his or her experiences and reads the experiences to the therapist.

The Presenting Problem

There are some situations and problems for which self-hypnosis is contraindicated. In particular, a thorough medical examination or evaluation should be conducted before hypnosis is used in a medical context. For example, it would be unwise to administer suggestions for diminished pain when pain serves the important function of "signaling" a serious or potentially lethal medical condition. Although hypnosis is helpful in situations in which the patient is anxious, hypnotic procedures, including self-hypnosis, are not indicated when the patient is experiencing the pain of appendicitis. In this instance, removal of the signal pain could lead to a ruptured appendix and even death. What are indicated are medical diagnosis and surgical intervention.

Hypnosis as a Means of Resistance

Hypnosis and self-hypnosis must not provide an escape from useful work or interfere with ongoing treatment. The use of hypnosis is advantageous only if it facilitates the achievement of therapeutic goals (e.g., reduces anxiety, heightens imagery, provides opportunity for exploration). If it is a deterrent to therapeutic goals, then it is contraindicated. A useful hypnotic intervention will reduce a tense patient's anxiety by teaching active relaxation skills such as deep breathing. The relaxation that occurs permits the patient to explore situational triggers that generate the anxiety response. However, on occasion, the hypnotic experience itself can be used as a defense mechanism or source of resistance that deters exploration or change in therapy. For example, when a patient who is trying to quit smoking falls asleep and snores during hypnosis, hypnosis itself becomes a resistance to be overcome.

Therapeutic Applications

Self-hypnosis reflects the individual's subjective encounter with the self in that what is experienced during hypnosis is the by-product of personal attributes and life experiences. Focusing attention inward while focusing relatively less attention on the external world permits the patient to experience helpful self-suggestions and imagery effortlessly. This self-directed practice may be based on imagery that was generated during a heterohypnotic session or that was spontaneously generated during self-hypnosis.

A goal of such practice may be to facilitate the automatized experience of feelings of mastery and comfort. To accomplish this, the patient may enter self-hypnosis via deep breathing and relaxation and imagine himself or herself feeling safe and comfortable, with an awareness of concomitant body sensations and perceptions. With repeated practice, these feelings have an increasingly automatic, effortless, and spontaneous quality. Similar feelings can be engendered by suggesting that an anxious patient "relax on the beach" while watching an imaginary movie about new places and new activities. This open-ended imagery task encourages the individual to contemplate novel or untested possibilities.

Self-hypnosis can also be used as a means of facilitating self-mastery and autonomy. The patient may use self-hypnosis to master a fear of failure while simultaneously nurturing a belief in his or her own ability. For example, by permitting herself to take an objective view of her reluctance to write her dissertation, one patient was enabled to imagine the future when she had completed her dissertation. The emotions connected with this goal were joy and fear. During self-hypnosis she was able to relax, discriminate between the emotions of joy and fear, and use her joy to energize herself. As she succeeded in moving toward her goal, she needed less reassurance from me, and her independent, goal-directed behavior increased. Ultimately, she was able to successfully complete her dissertation.

One consequence of using self-hypnosis is that alterations of a patient's personal reality orientation may occur, so that internal and external events are viewed in novel ways. A patient's fear of verbally asserting himself (or herself), for example, may be altered so that he views himself differently. His reality orientation is transformed, and he is able to assert himself effectively in a variety of situations. For example, one patient who was given the task of imaginatively rehearsing "speaking up" during self-hypnosis and enacting this with respect to a classroom situation not only succeeded in creating relevant imagery during self-hypnosis but also experienced feelings of mastery following in vivo practice. It is notable that the patient's sense of self-efficacy was not directly suggested or "willed" by the patient; rather, it was spurred by the transformation of meaning via words and images that were spontaneously generated during self-hypnosis. Not infrequently, transformations of this sort are set in motion by self-hypnotic tasks that involve alterations in imagery, affect, cognition, and behavior. The patient is, paradoxically, both the operator who devises self-suggestions during hypnosis and the respondent who reacts to the self-suggestions, thereby creating, shaping, and transforming experience and behavior in manifold ways.

Self-hypnosis has many other applications. Among its major uses are the following: It can be used as a means of changing behavioral patterns. Thus, a pain patient may exhibit increases in activity and decreases in medication after using self-hypnosis to foster hypnoanesthesia. Self-hypnosis can also provide a way of "being with" the therapist. The self-hypnosis induction, when repeated at home, may be associated with calming, soothing mental images or representations of the therapist that serve much the same function as a transitional object (Copeland, 1986). Self-hypnosis can be used in conjunction with and to reinforce the therapist's posthypnotic suggestions designed to spur personal growth. It can also provide a means for tapping imagery and adaptive regressions. Finally, self-hypnosis can stimulate imagery and sensory and perceptual alterations that may be associated with or actuate primitive thought processes and fantasies (e.g., spontaneous age regressions; Fromm & Kahn, 1990) that are normally inaccessible to conscious awareness. Holroyd (1987) discussed a number of ways that hypnosis may facilitate psychotherapy.

TECHNIQUES AND PROCEDURES

There are many potential applications of self-hypnotic procedures, and the selection of specific techniques will vary according to the needs of the patient, the style of the therapist, and the nature of the problem. Whatever procedures are used, they encompass the creative work of psychotherapy. According to Fromm (1947), humans' main task in life is to give birth to themselves. Because humans are social animals who learn language, meanings, and realities through social interactions, self-hypnosis in therapy is best learned by way of therapeutic interactions with a trained hypnotherapist who validates patients' unique, meaningful, and creative experiences.

One way that the hypnotherapist can validate the patient's experience is by mirroring it (i.e., by reflecting the patient's unique experience back to him or her). Another way is for the therapist to respond empathically to the patient, who may, for the first time, feel liberated from emotional constraint and no longer feel that he or she is programmed to experience a certain emotion. Permission to feel spontaneously and to have those feelings shared by another human being may be savored and remembered as a climactic moment in the hypnotherapy situation.

Teaching Self-Hypnosis

To optimize the therapeutic potential of clinical self-hypnosis, it is best for the therapist to begin working with the patient by administering suggestions in the dyadic situation and then to progressively transfer the responsibility for self-induction and self-direction to the patient. Consequently, the therapist is in a position to alter as many ego functions as the patient is able to tolerate (e.g., changes in attention, concentration, perception, affect, and cognition) and to help the patient to implement self-hypnotic procedures; there is the added benefit that the therapist can observe the patient's reactions to suggestions administered in a more traditional context. As Orne and McConkey (1981) observed, the clinical use of heterohypnosis generally establishes the protocol for the use of self-hypnosis. Patients then use self-hypnosis to refresh or reinforce the suggestions given to them by the clinician (Gardner, 1981; Sacerdote, 1967).

During heterohypnosis, the therapist can suggest to patients that they can experience self-hypnosis by initiating a cue or signal such as taking a deep breath. Patients can thus use a straightforward, unobtrusive behavioral prompt to set the stage for what the therapist and patient mutually define as "self-hypnosis." Many different inductions, instructions, and cues can be used. The following is a procedure that I have used successfully to teach self-hypnosis to patients.

The initial induction includes three components: (a) visualization of a beach scene; (b) the imagery of enjoying the beach and feeling the sun on one's skin and the gentle, cooling breeze; and (c) deep breathing combined with progressive relaxation. Patients then learn to do these exercises alone and are instructed to practice them daily for 3–10 min depending on perceived need. The goal of the exercise is to establish and maintain a sense of calm and self-control, as well as to reduce the overall level of negative affect. Verbatim instructions are as follows:

> Just imagine that you are at a pleasant beach, one that you have enjoyed before. Just allow yourself to see the beach; hear the sounds at the beach; feel the warm, comfortable sun; and feel the pleasant breeze. Let me know when you are there. Good. And as you allow yourself to experience the beach, looking at the blue sky, feeling the warmth, allowing yourself to relax more and more . . . just let me know when you are comfortably relaxed.
>
> Good. You are now in your comfortable place, and you feel very, very relaxed. And whenever you feel tense, it is perfectly all right for you to relax . . . to become just as relaxed as you are now. You can begin by taking long, slow, deep breaths, relaxing every muscle of your body, and going to your comfortable place . . . allowing yourself to see the beach, hear its sounds, and feel the warmth and the breeze, just as you are doing now.
>
> You will find that you can relax on your own more and more deeply as you practice more, so that self-hypnosis becomes a daily part of your life. This practice will permit you to enter self-hypnosis easily, when you want, where you want, and how you want.
>
> It is important to do this at least 3 times a day and whenever you are aware that you are becoming tense. Also, it is important to practice self-hypnosis everyday. You can easily go into self-hypnosis by visualizing the beach and taking long slow deep breaths, just as you did here. Now I am going to ask you to return to the here and now by counting backward from 5 to 1 and opening your eyes to the here and now.

Another useful suggestion is to take long, slow, deep breaths when angry. This suggestion may be initially administered during heterohypnosis. However, the therapist may also suggest that the patient use it in everyday life to manage anger and to put these feelings into words to promote effective communication. By teaching and reinforcing new coping behaviors that are framed as posthypnotic suggestions, and by encouraging discussion about the patient's conscious awareness of new coping behaviors, progress toward therapeutic goals can be monitored. Reinforcing the patient's progress also facilitates feelings of mastery and self-confidence (Crasilneck & Hall, 1985; Spiegel & Spiegel, 1978).

There is variability in the ease with which patients use self-hypnosis. Ideally, patients will be sufficiently comfortable with self-hypnosis to practice appropriate techniques in a self-directed, yet free-flowing, manner. Of course, not everyone is a good candidate for self-hypnosis. As noted earlier, some individuals lack hypnotic ability, whereas others lack trust in the therapist and the motivation to respond to suggestions. Moreover, not every candidate is sufficiently comfortable with clinical self-hypnosis to use it on an intensive, daily basis. Individuals who wish to use self-hypnosis but find it difficult to do so may require certain modifications in the technique (Baker, 1983; Murray-Jobsis, 1984; Scagnelli, 1980).

For example, a schizophrenic patient who becomes terrified by eye closure during hypnosis may be instructed to focus on a book in the bookcase, maintaining eye fixation during the entire procedure. Another patient may be able to tolerate only a brief hypnotic trance. In this instance, the patient may experience a series of brief hypnotic experiences lasting from seconds to minutes. Thus, one patient, "Jennifer," was asked to remember her puppy from many years ago and to imagine that she was with the puppy again. This experience was terminated after 30 s and repeated later for 1 min. By successive approximations over time, Jennifer was gradually able to learn to remain in hypnosis for longer and longer periods.

Self-Hypnotic Phenomena in the Clinical Situation

With clinical self-hypnosis, a variety of phenomena can be used to benefit the patient. These phenomena include relaxation, imagery, rehearsal in fantasy, age regression and progression, hypnotic dreams and metaphors, and physiological changes, all of which also occur within heterohypnosis but may be subjectively experienced differently during self-hypnosis. Theoretically, both hypnosis and self-hypnosis involve a reduction of the generalized reality orientation (Shor, 1979) and increased receptivity to and absorption in internal experiences (Tellegen & Atkinson, 1974). In addition, fantasy and free-floating imagery may be augmented. In short, the patient's typical way of perceiving the world may be altered during self-hypnosis.

Alterations of the self and the body are also commonly experienced. Changes in body perception include alterations in the sensations of heaviness, lightness, warmth, and coolness. Perceived changes in body size and voluntary control may also occur. These experiences are certainly not universal, and patients may describe a variety of idiosyncratic experiences. Nevertheless, the perceptual alterations achieved during self-hypnosis may be used to the therapist's advantage to reinforce the idea that the patient is capable of responding not only to hypnosis but also to therapeutic directives.

The key to success lies not in the hypnotic phenomena that are elicited but in the meaning the patient ascribes to the thoughts, feelings, images, and altered bodily perceptions that arise during hypnosis. Patients in turn share their impressions of, interpretations of, and associations to this material with the therapist. Both the patient and the therapist integrate this expanding and evolving understanding of the patient into subsequent interventions that involve self-suggestion, heterohypnosis, or both. Clinical self-hypnosis can thus provide the foundation for a new awareness of the self as the patient accesses new perceptions, feelings, and behaviors that facilitate creative expression and feelings of security, confidence, and mastery. Clinical self-hypnosis enables the patient to open the doors to the unconscious and the unspoken, to new ways of experiencing, and to new and more adaptive possibilities of living.

CASE MATERIAL

Because of space constraints, I cannot exhaustively discuss the many ways that self-hypnosis can be used in therapy and experienced by patients. Instead, I present two illustrative examples from my clinical practice.

Case 1

A job or career change in midlife can be an important transition that requires individuals to take charge of their life circumstances and master the feelings that emerge in response to this transition. In the example that follows, the patient experiencing this life passage wanted to change his infantile acting-out of primitive feelings to more mature, modulated, and appropriate feelings. According to Gould (1978), it is during midlife that the individual strives for a genuineness in experience and expression of feelings. Thus, the defensive barriers erected to prevent the emergence of pain crumble. The goal of personal development is to integrate personality and self-knowledge. The patient's wish for mastery of his or her emotions lead to the completion and realization of the developmental process in an honest, undistorted way.

Mr. Z., a 55-year-old retired professor embarking on a new career path, was referred for hypnotherapy by his ex-psychoanalyst for biting his nails, fingers, and knuckles. Mr. Z. had undergone a lengthy psychoanalysis for depression and was able to gain important insights about himself from this. However, this one symptom continued to trouble him and eluded transformation. In times of stress, such as being evaluated for a job position, he inevitably began to bite himself. At age 55, he was embarrassed and ashamed of this symptom, just as he had been at age 5.

Tapping into his abilities, strengths, and positive motivation, Mr. Z. used self-hypnosis to transform and manage his feelings of anxiety, anger, and frustration regarding his difficulty in finding suitable employment. He learned to express his anger and frustration in a genuine and assertive way, with people close to him, freeing him to perform new tasks and face new challenges. From the stagnant biting behaviors rooted in his past, he moved along developmentally appropriate lines to become increasingly able to contain and express his feelings during self-hypnosis and later in real-life situations.

Mr. Z. achieved self-hypnosis by taking long, slow, deep breaths, breathing in quiet and breathing out the perceived inner storm. He was able to use these techniques to move from the physically turbulent state of agitation to the mental state of contemplation. He noticed how, as the emotional storm subsided, he experienced himself in a more comfortable way. The quiet feeling was a good feeling. It was related to mastery. As the storm continued to subside, he felt increasingly in control.

This example illustrates how self-hypnosis can act as a catalyst that triggers transformation from one type of experience (stormy) to another type of experience (calm). As Mr. Z. became able to regulate his internal experience, he was better able to control his behavior, including his reactions to job-related stress and the habit of biting himself.

Case 2

A second patient's experience with self-hypnosis illustrates how affect can be contained and modulated in a borderline patient with concurrent dissociative symptoms.

Rita was a 36-year-old paraprofessional who had been diagnosed as having a borderline personality with dissociative defenses. The early causes of dissociation appeared to have been related to childhood abuse, which has been reported to occur in 95% of the patients diagnosed with multiple personality disorder (Kluft, 1984). Rita entered therapy to lose weight. For 6 months she resisted reaching her goal. During that time, she did not trust me and believed that I would betray her. Beginning treatment initiated inner disequilibrium. As she began to feel more comfortable with me, she seemed to show inconsistencies. First, she experienced anxiety attacks and found herself in precarious, life-threatening situations without knowing how she had gotten there. Second, she reported that she could not account for large amounts of time, sometimes as much as half a day. She had no awareness that her life roles were split into specialized alter personalities, each with the specific function of carrying and coping with a particular emotion. The alter egos consisted of remembered histories of important people in her life, fantasies based on other people she knew, and fantasies based on reading. Over time, these internalized fantasies became elaborated and acted out overtly. The fantasized person's attributes consolidated and took a name. Each time the fantasy was enacted, it was reinforced.

Each alter ego expressed a specific sensory function or affect that was part of a whole, more continuous personality. At each occurrence, the alter ego's experience was reinforced in that it progressively established a memory bank of roles, experiences, and life functions. Furthermore, each alter ego experience was preceded by deep breathing and a spontaneous eye roll, leading to a self-hypnotic trance with a particular set of conflicts and affects. Alternations or switches from one role to another occurred when overwhelming feelings and conflicts were present. The self-hypnosis permitted each alter ego to dominate the body in turn.

Each "switch" permitted the learning of experiences that occurred with respect to that particular personality and that one alone. Thus, learning was state dependent and amnesia existed between and among the different personalities. Amnesia protected Rita from the trauma of knowing pain. Switching also gave her control over the environment because others around her became confused in the face of her "mood changes." Switching also became a negative defense against therapy in that she prevented herself from gaining insight and understanding by switching.

Rita continued to prefer pain and reliving the terrors of the past to remembering and vanquishing her fears. This preference led to self-destructive behaviors that required hospitalization. In the hospital, Rita learned to use self-hypnosis intentionally and appropriately to soothe and calm herself. One technique she practiced was imagining a quiet, safe place to control tension and anxiety. When Rita remembered her anger at her mother, she felt guilty and embarrassed. These feelings escalated until they were perceived as being "out of control." By focusing on comforting images from the safety of her quiet place, she was able to watch a storm, with tidal waves and strong winds, much like Hurricane Andrew, abate. She felt the warmth of the sun and the freshness of the air. She allowed the tension to dissipate as the water receded back into the ocean. In this manner she learned to recognize, contain, and reduce affect. With the ability to master affect, Rita increasingly recognized her anger, differentiated it from other feelings, discussed it with her therapist, and integrated it into her present life. In so doing, she gradually unfroze herself from her past, which was marked by the expression of immature and primitive feelings.

Cognition, like affect, was transformed as well. Rita became able to interpret her feelings from a present-centered adult vantage point rather than from a childlike, global, and undifferentiated perspective tied to earlier experiences and reexperiences of the trauma of childhood abuse. Self-hypnosis served the important function of enabling Rita to attach words to feelings, which, in turn, facilitated communication of her feelings to me. In time, Rita learned to recognize, label, and communicate feelings and to engage in problem-solving activity instead of acting out her impulses.

Finally, her self-esteem was transformed. With her newfound ability to adopt a realistic and age-appropriate perspective, Rita began to discover new and better solutions to life's problems that bolstered her self-esteem. During self-hypnosis, Rita used imagery rehearsal to rerun interpersonal situations and try out new ways of relating to other people. When she felt comfortable and safe, she experimented with her newly acquired interpersonal skills and techniques in real-life situations.

Rita was pleased with the outcome of her efforts. Self-hypnosis enabled her to use covert imagery to her advantage, which ultimately led to in vivo success and enhanced well-being and self-esteem during hypnosis and in real life. Over time, Rita became more comfortable, less emotional and reactive, and more solution focused. These transformations, which involved the synthesis of feelings, cognitions, and enhanced self-esteem, constituted powerful evidence of personal change. Rita sorted through many sensations, perceptions, memories, and images that engendered a unique experience that was, in its richness and complexity, apparent only to her. Rita knew that her experience was changing.

RESEARCH AND APPRAISAL

In their landmark book on self-hypnosis, Fromm and Kahn (1990) presented a comprehensive study of self-hypnosis and personality factors that underlined the multidimensional nature of self-hypnotic phenomena. Indeed, as is the case with other areas of human performance and cognition, hypnosis (Kumar & Pekala, 1987) and self-hypnosis may be viewed as being the result of the interactions among complex variables.

A number of processes and variables can be identified that contribute to the understanding of the way that self-hypnosis can be exploited in the clinical situation and the manner in which it interacts with other aspects of the treatment situation. First, self-hypnosis can engender an altered state of consciousness that involves changes in cognition that include increased primary process thinking and alterations in memory. According to Fromm and Kahn (1990), self-hypnotic imagery consists of both reality-oriented fantasy and primary process fantasy. Useful therapeutic work, based on imagery and fantasy but not entirely divorced from the patient's analytical abilities, can be accomplished using self-hypnosis. Moreover, the ability to translate insight into action is enhanced when a flexible relationship exists between primary process thinking and ego activity.

Second, individual differences in personality structure, hypnotic susceptibility (Fromm et al., 1981), and fantasy proneness or creative imagination (Lynn & Rhue, 1986) may affect the patient's experience of self-hypnosis. For example, Fromm et al. found that deeply involved self-hypnotic subjects were less likely to be in conflict with their environment, were more emotionally stable, and reported fewer unusual thoughts and experiences than less involved subjects. However, because these findings may be characteristic of normal, highly hypnotizable subjects, the results cannot be generalized to the patient population. Additional studies are needed that identify personality correlates of self-hypnotic susceptibility and that clarify how self-hypnosis mediates or effects changes in cognition and affect (Sanders, 1991).

Third, dissociative processes (Hilgard, 1979) and nonconscious involvement play some role in creating the self-hypnotic experience. During self-hypnosis, patients may describe their awareness as being divided between a directing and an experiencing mode while imagery unfolds in a seamless and effortless manner (Fromm et al., 1981; Hilgard, 1979; Singer & Pope, 1981). Furthermore, during self-hypnosis, time may be experienced in a distorted way (Crasilneck & Hall, 1985; Erickson & Cooper, 1954/1959; Fromm et al., 1981; Kroger, 1977). With a reduction in self-monitoring and a division of executive functioning, the subject may have greater difficulty monitoring the passage of time.

Fourth, individual differences in physiological functions, including differences in recurrent rhythmic patterns such as ultradian rhythms (Rossi, 1986), are also important subject variables. Rossi (personal communication, March 12, 1990) has maintained that the therapeutic potential of self-hypnosis can be maximized by tapping into the individual's ultradian cycle.

These variables alone and in combination shape the rich, complex, and ultimately multidimensional quality of self-hypnosis. Of course, research is needed to disambiguate these variables and to assess their unique and interactive contribution to the patient's self-hypnotic experience.

In self-hypnosis research, it is important to take contextual factors into consideration. For instance, there are problems in generalizing findings from the laboratory to the clinical context. Fromm et al. (1981) made important strides in delineating the cognitive processes associated with self-hypnosis, including the increased availability of imagery as well as expansive and free-floating attention and ego receptivity to stimuli coming from within the unconscious. Johnson and Weight (1976) found that self-hypnosis generated more vivid and frequent experiences of time distortion, disorientation, active direction, and trance variability than did heterohypnosis.

However, what is needed is research that determines whether the preliminary findings secured in the experimental situation generalize to the clinical context. For example, viewing attention as a continuum, as described by Fromm et al. (1981), would suggest that self-hypnosis can be used to both expand and focus attention. Although it may be more difficult to focus attention in self-hypnosis than in heterohypnosis, it is nevertheless possible to focus attention during self-hypnosis. In the clinical situation, patients are able to focus their attention in an effortless way after adaptation to self-hypnosis (Sanders, 1991).

According to Gruenewald, Fromm, and Oberlander (1979), hypnotic susceptibility involves a regression in the service of the ego. Those researchers found that significant psychopathology may interfere with adaptive regression because regressed patients have greater difficulty in regulating ego functions. Significant psychopathology may thus interfere with the patient's receptivity to self-hypnosis and his or her ability to capitalize on self-hypnotic procedures. Nevertheless, Baker (1983) and Murray-Jobsis (1984) believed that severely disturbed individuals can learn to use self-hypnosis with appropriate modifications, slowly learning to control images, feelings, and experiences. Research comparing the use of self-hypnosis with different clinical populations and patients varying in their degree of psychopathology is a priority.

Clinical anecdotes prevail in the literature, although increasing numbers of clinical studies are being conducted. Brown and Fromm (1986, 1987) provided particularly good reviews of the literature. Studies of patient motivation to master problems have been reported by Von Dedenroth (1962) and Estabrooks and May (1965), and the need for therapist availability has been emphasized by Carrington (1977) and Sanders (1991). Crasilneck and Hall (1985) advocated the use of self-hypnosis as a way to reinforce posthypnotic suggestion. The use of self-control strategies has been frequently reported (Brown, 1977; Glucksman, 1981; Holroyd, Neuchterlein, Shapiro, & Ward, 1982; Shapiro, 1982), as have techniques such as imagery rehearsal (Cautela, 1967; Fromm et al., 1981; Leuner, 1969). The use of self-hypnosis to reduce pain has been documented by a variety of theorists (Barber, 1982; Crasilneck & Hall, 1985; Hilgard & Hilgard, 1975; Sacerdote, 1982).

Finally, the use of tapes as an adjunct to self-hypnosis has been evaluated, with equivocal results (Hammond, 1987; Lieberman, Fishers, Thomas, & King, 1968; Paul & Trimble, 1970). The effectiveness of tapes has been confounded by the use of a variety of other techniques and procedures. A cautious use of tapes may be helpful, but there is no evidence that these techniques are effective in their own right, separate from the methods of hypnotherapy and psychotherapy with which they have been combined (Sanders, 1991). Research in this area would profit from greater clarity of description of the methods and procedures used by clinicians and researchers.

CONCLUSION

Clinical self-hypnosis presents methodological and conceptual challenges to the researcher and creative challenges to the clinician. One level of complexity in interpreting the effects of self-hypnosis rests with the therapist's theoretical orientation. Because the hypnotherapist's theory of hypnosis is superimposed on his or her theory of psychotherapy (Sanders, 1991), it is difficult to disentangle the effects of these theoretical positions. Furthermore, it may be tempting to attribute changes that occur following hypnotherapy to self-hypnosis, when the changes that occur following therapy may in fact have little or nothing to do with self-hypnosis (Gruenewald, 1982).

Self-hypnosis is a paradox (Johnson, 1979) because it requires patients to simultaneously observe their experience of suggestions while they create and respond to suggestions. Traditional experimental methodology fails to capture patients' subjective experiences and responses. Thus, the development of descriptive observational methods are necessary to advance inquiry in this area. Methodologies that could prove useful in future research include the phenomenological approach described by Shor (1979); clinical interviews, including Sheehan and McConkey's (1982) experiential analysis technique; and subject-maintained journals.

The need for sophisticated, theoretically grounded, and well-controlled research aside, self-hypnosis has many useful clinical applications. Although the patients described in this chapter had different diagnoses, they successfully used self-hypnosis to learn self-soothing behavior via quieting, each in his and her own way. The use of self-hypnosis also permitted them to develop autonomy, maintain their individuality, and transform themselves in a unique way so that they became more comfortable while they achieved greater personal control and mastery.

Because of space limitations, it was not possible to provide an exhaustive review of the multiplicity of ways that self-hypnosis can be used in psychotherapy. Nonetheless, it appears that self-hypnosis facilitates multifaceted personal changes, not only at the behavioral and affective levels, but at the level of self-perception as well: The way that a person experiences himself or herself is altered by self-hypnosis. For example, Mr. Z., the hand biter, learned to experience anger as anger aimed outward in the here and now rather than as a primitive, involuntary behavior frozen in time, bringing the distant past into the present.

The important dimension of human potential that is tapped by self-hypnosis is an increased range of personal experience. For the most part, the scientific method focuses on behavior in controlled situations or on cognitions and feelings within a limited range of controlled conditions. However, a person responds simultaneously to both external and internal stimuli. The challenge to science is to measure and study these synchronous occurrences (i.e., to study behavior in response to environmental stimuli and the person's internal reactions, such as heightened self-esteem). Self-hypnosis is a truly unique context, which facilitates personal transformation, because the hypnotized patient reacts to external stimulation and also acts in a way that affects his or her subjective and life situations. The two-edged sword of the person as subject and actor has been largely neglected by psychology and psychiatry, although it has been examined by the existential and phenomenological schools of philosophy (Kierkegaard, 1853/1954; Merleau-Ponty, 1963). Fromm and Kahn (1990) made a significant step in this direction by focusing on the interaction between personality variables and variables unique to the hypnotic context. However, more emphasis must be placed on the self-perception and internal stimulation that empower the individual to paradoxically go beyond where he or she is.

REFERENCES

Baker, E. L. (1983). The use of hypnotic techniques with psychotics. *American Journal of Clinical Hypnosis, 25*, 283–288.

Barber, J. (1982). Incorporating hypnosis in the management of chronic pain. In J. Barber & C. Adrian (Eds.), *Psychological approaches to the management of pain* (pp. 40–59). New York: Brunner/Mazel.

Bliss, E. L. (1983). Multiple personalities, related disorders and hypnosis. *American Journal of Clinical Hypnosis, 26*, 114–123.

Bliss, E. L. (1986). *Multiple personality, allied disorders, and hypnosis.* New York: Oxford University Press.

Brown, D. P. (1977). A model for the levels of concentrative meditation. *International Journal of Clinical and Experimental Hypnosis, 25*, 236–273.

Brown, D. P., & Fromm, E. (1986). *Hypnotherapy and hypnoanalysis.* Hillsdale, NJ: Erlbaum.

Brown, D. P., & Fromm, E. (1987). *Hypnosis and behavioral medicine.* Hillsdale, NJ: Erlbaum.

Carrington, P. (1977). *Freedom in meditation.* New York: Doubleday.

Cautela, J. R. (1967). Covert sensitization. *Psychological Reports, 20*, 459.

Copeland, D. (1986). The application of object relations theory to the hypnotherapy of developmental arrests: The borderline patient. *International Journal of Clinical and Experimental Hypnosis, 34*, 157–168.

Crasilneck, H., & Hall, J. (1985). *Clinical hypnosis: Principles and applications* (2nd ed.). New York: Grune & Stratton.

Erickson, M. H. (1980). Hypnotic alteration of sensory, perceptual and psychophysical process. In E. L. Rossi (Ed.), *The collected papers of Milton H. Erickson on hypnosis* (Vol. 2). New York: Irvington.

Erickson, M. H., & Cooper, L. F. (1959). *Time distortion in hypnosis.* Baltimore: Williams & Wilkins. (Original work published 1954)

Estabrooks, G. H., & May, J. A. (1965). Hypnosis in integrative motivation. *American Journal of Clinical Hypnosis, 4*, 346–352.

Fromm, E. (1947). *Man from himself: An inquiry into the psychology of ethics.* New York: Holt.

Fromm, E., Brown, D. P., Hurt, S. W., Oberlander, J. Z., Boxer, A. M., & Pfeifer, G. (1981). The phenomena and characteristics of self-hypnosis. *International Journal of Clinical and Experimental Hypnosis, 29*, 189–246.

Fromm, E., & Kahn, S. (1990). *Self-hypnosis: The Chicago paradigm.* New York: Guilford Press.

Gardner, G. G. (1981). Teaching self-hypnosis to children. *International Journal of Clinical and Experimental Hypnosis, 29,* 300–312.

Glucksman, M. L. (1981). Physiological measures and feedback during psychotherapy. *Psychotherapy and Psychosomatics, 36,* 165–199.

Gould, R. (1978). *Transformations.* New York: Simon & Schuster.

Gruenewald, D. (1982). Problems of relevance in the application of laboratory data to clinical situations. *International Journal of Clinical and Experimental Hypnosis, 30,* 345–353.

Gruenewald, D. F., Fromm, E., & Oberlander, O. (1979). Hypnosis and adaptive regression: An ego psychological inquiry. In E. Fromm & R. Shor (Eds.), *Hypnosis: Research developments and perspectives* (pp. 619–635). Chicago: Aldine.

Hammond, C. D. (1987). The use of fractionation in self-hypnosis. *American Journal of Clinical Hypnosis, 30,* 119–124.

Hilgard, E. R. (1979). Divided consciousness in hypnosis: The implications of the hidden observer. In E. Fromm & R. E. Shor (Eds.), *Hypnosis: Developments in research and new perspectives* (2nd ed., pp. 45–80). Chicago: Aldine.

Hilgard, E., & Hilgard, J. (1975). *Hypnosis in the relief of pain.* Los Altos, CA: Kaufmann.

Holroyd, J. (1987). How hypnosis may potentiate psychotherapy. *American Journal of Clinical Hypnosis, 29,* 194–200.

Holroyd, J. C., Nuechterlein, K. H., Shapiro, D., & Ward, F. (1982). Individual differences in hypnotizability and effectiveness of hypnosis or biofeedback. *International Journal of Clinical and Experimental Hypnosis, 30,* 45–65.

Johnson, L. S. (1979). Self-hypnosis: Behavioral and phenomenological comparisons with heterohypnosis. *International Journal of Clinical and Experimental Hypnosis, 27,* 240–264.

Johnson, L. S., & Weight, D. G. (1976). Short report self-hypnosis versus heterohypnosis: Experiential and behavioral comparisons. *Journal of Abnormal Psychology, 85,* 523–526.

Kierkegaard, S. (1954). *Fear and trembling* (W. Lowrie, Trans.). New York: Doubleday. (Original work published 1853).

Kluft, R. P. (1984). Multiple personality in childhood. *Psychiatric Clinics of North America, 7,* 121–134.

Kroger, W. S. (1977). *Clinical and experimental hypnosis* (2nd ed.). Philadelphia: Lippincott.

Kumar, V. K., & Pekala, R. J. (1987). Hypnotizability, absorption and individual differences in phenomenological experience. *International Journal of Clinical and Experimental Hypnosis, 36,* 80–95.

Leuner, H. (1969). Guided affective imagery. *American Journal of Psychotherapy, 23,* 4–22.

Lieberman, L. R., Fishers, J. R., Thomas, R., & King, W. (1968). Use of tape recorded suggestions as an aid to probationary students. *American Journal of Clinical Hypnosis, 11*, 35–41.

Lynn, S. J., & Rhue, J. W. (1986). The fantasy-prone person: Hypnosis, imagination, and creativity. *Journal of Personality and Social Psychology, 51*, 404–408.

Merleau-Ponty, M. (1963). *The structure of behavior* (A. Fisher, Trans.). Boston: Beacon Press.

Murray-Jobsis, J. (1984). Hypnosis with severely disturbed patients. In W. C. Wester & A. H. Smith, Jr. (Eds.), *Clinical hypnosis: A multidisciplinary approach* (pp. 368–404). Cincinnati, OH: Behavior Sciences Center.

Orne, M. T., & McConkey, K. M. (1981). Toward convergent inquiry into self-hypnosis. *International Journal of Clinical and Experimental Hypnosis, 29*, 313–323.

Paul, G. L., & Trimble, R. W. (1970). Recorded vs. live relaxation training and hypnotic suggestion: Comparative effectiveness for reducing physiological arousal and inhibiting stress response. *Behavior Therapy, 3*, 285–302.

Rossi, E. L. (1986). *The psychobiology of mind-body healing: New concepts of therapeutic hypnosis.* New York: Norton.

Sacerdote, P. (1967). *Induced dreams* (2nd ed.). New York: Gaus.

Sacerdote, P. (1982). Techniques of hypnotic intervention with pain patients. In J. Barber & C. Adrian (Eds.), *Psychological approaches to the management of pain* (pp. 60–83). New York: Brunner/Mazel.

Sanders, S. (1991). *Clinical self-hypnosis: The power of words and images.* New York: Guilford Press.

Scagnelli, J. (1980). Hypnotherapy with schizophrenic and borderline patients: The use of trance. *American Journal of Clinical Hypnosis, 22*, 164–169.

Shapiro, D. H. (1982). Overview: Clinical and physiological comparison of meditation with other self-control strategies. *American Journal of Psychiatry, 139*, 267–274.

Sheehan, P. W., & McConkey, K. (1982). *Hypnosis and experience: Phenomena and processes.* Hillsdale, NJ: Erlbaum.

Shengold, L. (1978). Autohypnotic watchfulness. *Psychoanalytic Quarterly, 47*, 113–115.

Shor, R. (1979). Hypnosis and the concept of the generalized reality-orientation. *American Journal of Psychotherapy, 13*, 582–602.

Singer, J. L., & Pope, K. S. (1981). Daydreaming and imagery skills as predisposing capacities for self-hypnosis. *International Journal of Clinical and Experimental Hypnosis, 29*, 271–281.

Spiegel, H., & Spiegel, D. (1978). *Trance and treatment: Clinical uses of hypnosis.* New York: Basic Books.

Tellegen, A., & Atkinson, G. (1974). Openness to absorbing and self-altering experiences ("absorption"): A trait related to hypnotic susceptibility. *Journal of Abnormal Psychology, 83,* 268–277.

Von Dedenroth, T. E. A. (1962). Trance depth: An independent variable in therapeutic results. *American Journal of Clinical Hypnosis, 4,* 174–176.

Winnicott, D. W. (1953). Transitional objects and transitional phenomena. *International Journal of Psychoanalysis, 34,* 89–97.

13

ACTIVE–ALERT HYPNOSIS IN PSYCHOTHERAPY

ÉVA I. BÁNYAI, ANNAMÁRIA ZSENI, and FERENC TÚRY

Since the time of ancient Egypt, hypnosis and hypnotic-like suggestive techniques have been used as effective psychotherapeutic procedures. These techniques typically contain methods such as suggestions for relaxation, sleep, and drowsiness for decreasing activity level. Although current hypnosis theories no longer conceptualize hypnosis as a form of sleep, the metaphor of sleep is still part and parcel of traditional relaxation-based hypnotic inductions.

Because modern schools of psychotherapy emphasize the necessity of patients' actively participating in the healing process (e.g., Rogers, 1970), it is not surprising that hypnosis has been criticized for promoting passivity

We would like to express our gratitude to psychologist Gabriella Szemes, M.A., member of the Section of Active–Alert Hypnosis of the Hungarian Hypnosis Association, for her courtesy of providing us with the case material of Case 4 before publication.

We wish to express our gratitude to Anna Csilla Gősi-Greguss for her invaluable help in the preparation of this chapter. We also thank the members of the Section of Active–Alert Hypnosis of the Hungarian Hypnosis Association for sharing their experiences in active–alert hypnotherapy with us.

The preparation of this chapter was supported in part by a grant from OTKA I/3 (Grant No. 2168/91) to Éva I. Bányai.

rather than active involvement in psychotherapy. This criticism may have merit. Physical passivity may increase the likelihood that patients will erroneously attribute treatment gains to the activity (and even magical power) of the hypnotist. Thus, the role of patients' inner resources and active coping efforts to better their lives may be ignored or minimized. To counter this tendency, it is important that patients recognize the contribution of their own activity and effort to achieving therapeutic objectives, particularly when their problem involves an inhibition of physical and mental activity in stressful or anxiety-evoking situations. In these cases, it would be beneficial to exploit the advantages of hypnotherapy without the inhibitory effects of traditional relaxation-based induction techniques.

A large body of evidence (see Bányai & Hilgard, 1976), dating back to ancient times, has shown that trance states can be induced not only by decreasing activity level, but also by maneuvers that increase tension, alertness, and physical activity. A parallel can be drawn between the induction of these sorts of trance states and shamanistic healing rituals (Eliade, 1964; Halifax, 1980).

Relying on these naturalistic observations, Bányai and Hilgard (1976) introduced the active–alert hypnosis procedure to the arsenal of modern hypnotic techniques. In this method, the hypnotic subject rides a bicycle ergometer set to a resistance, with the eyes open throughout the entire hypnotic session. While the subject exercises in this manner, verbal suggestions are administered to enhance his or her alertness, attentiveness, and feelings of freshness. No mention is ever made of passive relaxation, sleepiness, or eye closure. Throughout the procedure, the room remains illuminated at its customary level.

Laboratory studies (Bányai, 1976, 1980, 1987; Bányai & Hilgard, 1976; Bányai, Mészáros & Greguss, 1981, 1983; Cikurel & Gruzelier, 1990) with nonclinical volunteers have documented the fact that active–alert hypnosis represents a genuinely altered state of consciousness, with features both similar and dissimilar to a relaxation-based hypnotic state. Features shared by active–alert and traditional hypnosis include heightened responsiveness to suggestions, feelings of relinquishing the planning function of the ego, lack of reality testing, a sense that attention is highly focused, and a lateral shift in favor of the facilitation of right hemispheric processing. The differences between the two types of hypnosis can be summarized as follows: increased alertness, enhancement of positive emotional tone, and perceptions of more active participation in active-alert hypnosis as compared with traditional hypnosis.

On the basis of the characteristics of active–alert hypnosis, Bányai (1977) suggested that this type of hypnosis can serve as a useful therapeutic intervention. Indeed, some subjects express a preference for active–alert hypnotic procedures, suggesting that these techniques may be particularly beneficial for some patients. Furthermore, when the patient's emotional tone is negative or marked by depressive cognitions, active–alert hypnosis may be more advantageous than traditional hypnosis. The feelings of increased involvement in the psychotherapeutic process that come from active–alert methods make it especially well suited to patients who can benefit from ego strengthening and enhanced self-esteem.

CLINICAL APPLICATIONS

Because the original active–alert hypnosis procedure was developed for research purposes, the induction was standardized. However, for therapeutic purposes, it is wise to tailor the script to each patient's unique needs and characteristics. The general features of the clinical application of active–alert hypnosis, which serve as the basis of the clinician's creative elaboration, are described below:

- The resistance against which the patients have to pedal the bicycle is always set by the patients themselves. The instruction is to set the resistance as if the patient were riding the bicycle uphill. As therapy progresses, the resistance is generally increased spontaneously, which demonstrates to patients that their productivity is increasing.
- In the induction phase, verbal feedback is given about patients' increased activity pedaling the bicycle.
- Patients are informed that because of the vigorous physical activity, they can experience bodily sensations more keenly than usual, and thus exhibit greater control over their experiences.
- To enhance patients' active participation in the therapeutic process, emphasis is placed on maintaining control of the speed and rhythm of pedaling.
- Suggestions are administered that are designed to engender positive emotions, feelings of power, energy, satisfaction, and pleasure associated with activity. In this way, energy blocked by patients' symptoms can be released and steered in a creative and productive direction.

Therapeutic Active–Alert Hypnotic Induction, Deepening, Suggestions, and Dehypnosis

Although in actual practice inductions and suggestions are individually tailored to the patient, an example of a typical active–alert induction, taken from a patient's hypnosis session, is presented below:

> Please start pedaling, and from now on pedal continuously. Pedal steadily, while listening to what I say. Concentrate deeply on my words.

Try to concentrate your attention much more deeply than usual. Try to detach yourself from everything that may disturb you in this state of concentration.

Let the disturbing effects of the outer world and the disturbing thoughts and worries become distant for a while. Don't pay attention to anything but what I call your attention to. Please pedal continuously, steadily, as you've been doing so far. Concentrate on cycling, and try to observe exactly what you feel in your legs. Observe everything you feel in your legs very carefully while cycling. Pay attention to the rhythmic movement of the muscles, to the contraction and relaxation of the muscles. Pay close attention to the kinds of changes arising in your muscles as a result of active muscle activity. If you can concentrate your attention totally on this process, then you will notice that your muscles will move more and more automatically. Just pay attention to your legs. Perhaps you can already feel your muscles become alive, as they become less and less stiff. As a result, it becomes easier to pedal, cycling becomes easier. If you pedal for a sufficient period of time you will reach that pleasant state in which your legs can perform this motion more and more easily, and more and more automatically. Just pay attention to your legs. Probably you have to exert great effort to work against the resistance of the pedal. After a while, however, the movements will be so well trained that you will be able to pedal the bicycle very easily, without any feeling of tiredness, and automatically. Your legs will learn this movement. Soon your legs will move by themselves, almost automatically. The muscles of your legs become more alive and full of energy with each turn of the pedals. Cycling is more and more easy. Your legs do not get more tired, in fact they become more and more fresh from pedaling. The blood circulates in your vessels vigorously, from which a nice warm feeling spreads over your legs . . . your arms . . . over your whole body. Pay close attention to when the second wind starts. From that point on, cycling will require no effort. Your legs move very easily, automatically. As if they became independent from your body. Your whole body becomes more and more fresh and alive. The more you cycle, the stronger these feelings become. A feeling of pleasant warmth and energy and freshness spreads over your body. Every muscle of your body moves. Blood freely flows in your dilated vessels. Even your head feels light and clear, you can concentrate more and more easily. You pedal the bicycle easily, automatically, without tension and effort. You feel you could continue pedaling for any period. Your whole body feels the pleasant activity. Let yourself feel the joy of movement as fully as possible. You are filled with energy. Your body gradually gets used to the increasingly active tempo. Just pay attention to it. Your breathing and heartbeat are somewhat faster than usual so that they can meet the increased demands of your body. It's a rhythmic, strong, and reassuring feeling. Your muscles, your internal organs, your whole body is in activity and in a balance. You are able to perceive the functioning of your body correctly. You are able to observe everything that takes place inside your body. You don't have to pay attention to the bike any more, you can safely rely on your legs. Your legs continue to pedal easily and effortlessly and without fatigue, while you can pay attention to your feelings more and more easily, too. You need to learn how you can direct your energy toward a goal. For this, try to pay close attention to yourself, and find an internal spot. A spot where hidden tension accumulates. Maybe you'll find that spot where your symptoms appear usually, but it can be anywhere else, too. You can find that spot, you are able to find it. When you find it, concentrate deeply on this spot. Just notice how much accumulated and blocked energy strains this spot. You are able to release your blocked energies. You are able to dissolve this source of tension. Just let this released energy spread over your body, just pay attention to it as it gets transformed into useful energy. It's very good to feel that you are able to create peace and active harmony in yourself. Just let yourself experience yourself as fully as possible, let yourself feel your newfound feelings and the joy of activity.

In addition to commonly used deepening techniques like counting and imagery, direct deepening suggestions in active–alert hypnosis are based on activity increases. Phrases like "As your legs pedal more and more automatically, you'll go into deeper and deeper hypnosis," "As your breathing becomes sufficiently frequent and regular, you'll become more and more alert and attentive," and "Feel the effortless pedaling, which helps you to turn your attention to and find your inner resources" are repeated and paraphrased whenever necessary.

After active–alert hypnosis has been sufficiently deepened and stabilized, patients receive suggestions consistent with therapeutic objectives. The structure and wording of the suggestions may resemble that of traditional hypnosis procedures, with the exception that attention is not directed toward relaxation, but instead toward patients' ability to cope with problems actively and, in this way, to get closer to the "real inner self." In our experience, suggestions that require imaginal activity have proved to be more useful than motor suggestions because the constant motor activity required by the active–alert procedure may interfere with the performance of other movements.

In the course of dehypnosis, decreasing pedal speed is a useful way of orienting patients to mundane reality. For instance, counting or another verbal rhythm can be used to help the patient gradually decrease the speed of pedaling until a full stop is made. Another useful method, which facilitates patients' return to normal wakefulness in their own rhythm, involves inviting the patient to imagine a slope or a downhill road ending on a level surface, where the cyclist can come to rest.

The suggestions given during hypnosis are reinforced by posthypnotic suggestions. Finally, we suggest that the active, creative coping mechanisms learned during hypnosis will become an integral part of the patient's everyday life. After active–alert hypnosis is terminated, it is essential that the hypnotist discuss the patient's experience of hypnosis and ensure that no untoward posthypnotic reactions or aftereffects are experienced.

Self-Hypnotic Active–Alert Technique

To help patients mobilize their inner resources and self-healing mechanisms, self-hypnosis is often used during the later phases of hypnotherapy. Active–alert hypnosis is suited for self-hypnotic purposes, with the same provisos and cautions as in traditional hypnosis, discussed in Sanders's chapter (Chapter 12, this volume). That is, active–alert self-hypnosis should always follow initial heterohypnotic exposure, and it should be conducted under the direct supervision of the therapist, before the therapist moves to a more indirect supervisory role with the patient. Furthermore, the therapist may give the patient an audiocassette with a recording of a hypnotic session, complete with verbal induction and suggestions, or appropriate rhythmic sounds or musical pieces to facilitate active–alert hypnosis.

A fortunate accident spurred the development of nonverbal forms of active–alert self-hypnosis: In one of the sessions to be recorded for self-hypnotic purposes, the microphone failed to record the hypnotist's voice; only the sounds of the speeding bicycle could be heard. To our great surprise, the patient reported that he achieved just as deep a level of hypnosis as when the hypnotist was present. It was apparent that the sounds of increasing bicycle speed served to cue recall of the suggestions previously given by the hypnotherapist. The monotonous but increasing rhythm had apparently assumed the role of verbal suggestions, analogous to the monotonous and increasingly fast drum play of shamans in tribal ceremonies that produces subjective alterations in consciousness in receptive individuals.

After this serendipitous discovery, we identified musical pieces whose rhythm was characterized by monotony and acceleration. Of the several musical compositions we located, Ravel's "Bolero" proved to be the most useful in inducing an active–alert hypnotic state. The refreshing and energizing effect of this music appears to be comparable to the relaxing effects of autogenic training, progressive relaxation, or "neutral," traditional hypnosis.

The positive features of nonverbal active–alert hypnosis notwithstanding, therapists must use caution in administering and monitoring these, and all, hypnotic procedures. For example, patients' emotionally positive subjective experiences—the ecstatic "high" that is sometimes achieved with active–alert hypnosis—can be so pleasant that a danger looms that certain patients will use the cassette more often than indicated by the hypnotherapist. This misuse of the cassette may result in physical overexertion or, as occurred on one occasion, may even precipitate psychotic episodes in borderline patients. This latter outcome is no doubt an extremely rare negative sequela of active–alert hypnosis, but it is noted to underscore the need for careful evaluation of the patient and supervision of all aspects of hypnotherapy.

Group Application

If a sufficient number of exercise bikes are available, then active–alert hypnosis can be administered in a group context, much like traditional hypnosis. To treat patients who share similar problems and concerns in a group situation when appropriate equipment is unavailable, we developed alternative means of engendering the increased activity that is prerequisite to active–alert hypnosis. We found that an adequate substitute for exercise bicycles was to simply ask patients to move freely and to experience the joy of moving.

We first administer a verbal induction and suggestions to help reduce inhibitions about moving and to increase awareness of the coparticipants. The structure and wording of these suggestions are similar to individually administered active–alert hypnotic communications. However, music then replaces the verbal communications, to capitalize on its refreshing and energizing effects in a group situation.

Experiences With Therapeutic Active–Alert Hypnosis

Although active–alert hypnosis was implemented on an irregular and sporadic basis after its introduction as a clinical method in 1977, within 6 years its therapeutic potential was recognized by an increasing number of clinicians in Hungary. Hypnotherapists trained themselves in the technique in case discussion groups organized according to Michael Bálint's principles (Bálint, 1957). In 1983, the most active group participants founded the Section of Active–Alert Hypnosis within the Hungarian Hypnosis Association. What we have learned about the clinical utility of active–alert hypnosis, along with its range of application and the case material presented below, is based largely on knowledge from Section members.

Behavioral Effects

In the initial active–alert therapeutic sessions, patients generally set the resistance of the bicycle to 60–120 W, although they often spontaneously increase this resistance by 10–20 W from one session to the next. The duration of one session usually varies between 30 and 60 minutes. Although patients pedal the bicycle steadily, at least at the initial speed, they ultimately attain a speed that is sometimes two or three times faster than their speed at the beginning of induction. Nevertheless, they only occasionally complain about getting tired and, afterwards, never report that they feel muscular stiffness. Temporary slowdowns that occur during imagination and verbalization are not atypical.

About 70% of the patients choose to close their eyes during the procedure (as opposed to less than 50% of the healthy, nonpatient volunteers), noting that their concentration is improved when visual input is curtailed. In the patient population, a vacant, "trancelike" expression and, in case of open eyes, an unfocused gaze are observed, similar to that of the nonpatient volunteers.

We have observed that a long-term behavioral effect of active–alert hypnosis is that patients become more self-assured, active, and future-oriented. With exposure to active–alert hypnosis, they increasingly prefer to use active coping mechanisms when they confront their problems.

Subjective Experiences

Like nonclinical volunteers, patients report a feeling of freshness, even in the face of increasing pedal speed and workload. Some people report that they feel their legs are dissociated from their body. We also found that the experience of riding a bicycle is often expressed in imagery when an unspecified imagination suggestion (e.g., to imagine a pleasant scene) is administered. Compared with images conjured up during traditional hypnosis, the images associated with active–alert hypnosis are usually more lively, and the patients play a more active role in their imagined activities. During this activity, they often discover what they would like to do in real life. The following verbatim quotation from a patient's report illustrates this point: "A meadow, or rather the image of a garden occurred to me . . . the image of my own real piece of ground. I not only saw this ground . . . I worked on it . . . with a pleasant feeling. It was good to know that it was my garden. After a long period of time I have found a goal at last, which has been missing from my life. It was a joyful feeling to discover the reality of this goal, because my goals hitherto seemed to be rather illusory."

The extent of mood changes, and the feeling of energy release, vary from patient to patient and from session to session. Even if no change in mood is reported after the initial sessions, in the long run, the patient's mood generally improves, paralleling positive long-term behavioral changes.

The Range of Clinical Application

Before describing the range of clinical application of active–alert procedures, it should be noted that, like traditional hypnosis, active–alert hypnosis can be used as an adjuvant to psychotherapy; it is not designed to serve as an independent treatment method. As an adjuvant, however, it can be used as a catalyst to a variety of psychotherapeutic approaches. That is, active–alert hypnosis can be integrated in the behaviorally oriented, short-term symptomatic treatment of patients with neurotic, psychophysiological, and habit disorder problems; in supportive ego-strengthening hypnotherapy; in dynamically oriented hypnotherapy; and, with special care, even in the long-term hypnotherapy of developmental deficits (classification from Brown & Fromm, 1986).

On the basis of more than 200 cases treated by the therapists of the Section of Active–Alert Hypnosis of the Hungarian Hypnosis Association, active–alert hypnosis has an unequivocally beneficial effect in conditions in which the core problem is a lack of initiative and energy, generalized inhibition, depression, or an extremely withdrawn personality. Active–alert hypnosis is also useful in anxiety states that result in secondary inhibition.

We have found that active–alert hypnosis provides the fastest symptomatic relief in patients suffering from depressions that include neurotic depression, endogenous depression, and depressive reactions. We have noted that patients can achieve a significant breakthrough with active–alert hypnosis. Indeed, in some cases, a single active–alert hypnotic session is sufficient to relieve symptoms and hurdle a therapeutic impasse. By alleviating patient inhibition in this way, therapy can proceed more efficiently and can often be concluded in approximately 10 sessions.

Even in the presence of complex symptoms with a long-standing history, active–alert hypnosis has the potential to accelerate healing and promote treatment gains (see Case 1 below). Nevertheless, precautions should be taken to monitor and control any suicidal tendencies that are present. All in all, we have been impressed by the salutary effects of active–alert hypnosis, particularly given the fact that depression appears to be man's most common serious emotional complaint.

Active–alert hypnosis has also proven to be very effective in the treatment of different kinds of disorders that are commonly described in terms of the umbrella category "neurotic." These disorders include generalized anxiety, panic attacks, conversion reactions, dissociative hysteria, and phobias.

Active–alert hypnosis is also indicated in the treatment of psychophysiological disorders. However, its effectiveness depends on the nature of the problem. For example, whereas bulimic and anorexic patients respond favorably to active–alert hypnosis (see illustrative example Case 2), a paradoxical effect is sometimes apparent in obese patients. That is, the positive emotions that flow from active–alert procedures may induce hunger and weight gain in this population (Túry, 1992). Although the ego-strengthening effect of active–alert hypnosis holds promise for treating alcoholics and drug addicts, to date, active–alert hypnosis has not been uniformly successful in the treatment of drug and alcohol abusers (Zseni & Vadász, 1988).

Certain personality disorders have been amenable to treatment with active–alert hypnosis. For example, active–alert hypnosis can help to regulate the frequent acting out of impulses of patients with explosive personality disorder. The emotionally positive and soothing effects of active–alert hypnosis can also be useful in treating patients with asthenic personality features (e.g., tiredness, lack of energy).

In the case of performance problems, patients' ability to pedal the bicycle for a long time without experiencing fatigue may constitute irrefutable evidence that hidden inner resources are available for problem solving and performance enhancement. This applies not only to the treatment of pathological performance problems, but also to enhancing peak performance in sport competitions (Biró, 1989; Unestáhl, 1980).

The hypnotherapy of psychotic patients has gained acceptance in the last two decades (see Murray-Jobsis, 1984; Chapter 20, this volume). Although skill and care are required to work with psychotic patients, active–alert hypnosis has been successfully administered to inhibited schizophrenic patients. Active–alert hypnosis may be successful with psychotic patients because keeping the eyes open reduces feelings of defensiveness and vulnerability, compared with traditional hypnosis, which typically includes eye closure suggestions (see Case 3.).

Although traditional hypnosis can be widely used with children, they usually dislike or rebel against the request to maintain silence and eye closure. We have found that they often prefer active–alert hypnosis because it is compatible with their natural desire to move, and it instills a sense of self-mastery and competence. Beyond the usually successful treatment of typical children's problems (e.g., enuresis), active–alert hypnosis has been successfully used as an adjunct to a medical treatment in a case of autism (see Case 4).

Of course, active–alert hypnosis does not have a long history of clinical application and experimentation. Nevertheless, it could prove to be useful in a number of areas, such as the treatment of psychosexual disorders and post-heart-attack rehabilitation programs.

CASE MATERIAL

The following cases were selected to provide examples of effective applications of active–alert hypnosis (Cases 1, 2, and 3) and to illustrate the promise of active–alert hypnosis in a challenging case of childhood autism (Case 4).

Case 1

Patient B. B. was a 48-year-old man who was admitted as an inpatient to the Department of Psychiatric Rehabilitation after a long history of somatic diseases and psychological problems. B. B. was the elder of two sons in a family in which the mother played a very domineering role. He had had several organic diseases in his childhood (polio, frequent pulmonitis, etc.), and, as a consequence, he was declared unfit for army service. B. B. was enuretic until the age of 9, had sleeping problems, and in school and other performance-demand situations was anxious and performed well below his potential. At 18 years of age, he left his parents' home. Although his somatic problems remitted, his anxiety and sleeping disorders continued to trouble him. To reduce anxiety, he became a regular alcohol consumer. He later married, had children, and led a routine family life. His wife proved to be a domineering woman, just like his mother.

At age 35, the patient developed a condition involving dyspnea, compulsive sighing, and then dizziness in the street. He was hospitalized several times, but no organic cause was found. His complaints became constant, and he consumed an increasing amount of sedatives and sleeping pills to relieve his insomnia and dizziness. His constant feeling of insecurity resulted in phobic reactions, manifested as fears of leaving his home and traveling. In the course of subsequent psychiatric treatments, panic disorder was diagnosed. Two years later, this diagnosis was changed to neurotic depression. He became psychologically dependent on every medicine he received, and he occasionally developed a more serious physical dependence problem. He potentiated these drug effects by the concurrent use of alcohol. At the time of his hospitalization at age 48, his primary symptoms consisted of an agitated depressive reaction to alcohol deprivation, and phobic reactions.

The initial therapeutic intervention was to deprive B. B. of all medication. As a result, his depression deepened, and he slept only 1 to 2 hours a night. Because of his psychological and physical adynamia, he could walk only with help. At this point, active–alert hypnosis was instituted. The initial 4 sessions per week were later reduced to 2 sessions per week. Altogether, he participated in 12 symptom-oriented active–alert hypnotic sessions. After each hypnosis session, his mood improved dramatically, his somatic symptoms decreased then finally disappeared, and his physical strength increased. As a result of ego-strengthening suggestions, he experienced a release of energy blocked by his previous symptoms, and he felt the stirrings of a sense of inner harmony. After the fifth hypnotic treatment, he conquered his phobias and was released from the hospital to outpatient care. After 6 weeks of psychotherapy, he returned to work. He has been living without alcohol or medication for the past 2 years. His family life has improved to the point that he is able to face and resolve interpersonal conflicts and assume his share of household responsibilities.

In this case, active–alert hypnosis was so effective in releasing energy blocked by the patient's physical symptoms that a substantial strengthening of ego functions and a breakthrough in the direction of health was achieved.

Case 2

F. L. was a 22-year-old hospital nurse who was referred to an eating-disorder unit of a hospital with the *DSM–III–R* (American Psychiatric Association, 1987) diagnosis of anorexia nervosa and bulimia nervosa. Her gradual weight loss, binge episodes, and self-induced vomiting 2 to 3 times a day began after an abortion at the age of 18. Her unwanted pregnancy caused severe guilt feelings and proved to be a traumatic event. Before admission to the hospital, she was in psychoanalysis for two years. Unfortunately, although her self-awareness increased, her symptoms persisted.

On her admission to the hospital, she weighed 73 pounds (with a body height of 158 cm). One of her main problems was that she was very sensitive to the shape of her stomach. When she believed it was not flat enough, she became anxious and depressed and increased her maneuvers (e.g., fasting, self-induced vomiting, extreme physical activity) to lose weight.

Active–alert hypnosis was chosen as the primary psychotherapeutic intervention because it was suited to F. L.'s extreme need for physical activity. Because she scored 7 on the Stanford Hypnotic Susceptibility Scale, Form A (Weitzenhoffer & Hilgard, 1959), it was anticipated that hypnosis would maximize treatment effects. Elements of behavior therapy, ego-strengthening, and psychodynamic therapy were integrated into her active–alert hypnotherapeutic treatment.

On the psychodynamic level, her symptoms had a symbolic meaning of getting rid of the unwanted pregnancy; that is, the binge–purge cycles could be considered as symbolic manifestations of fertilization and abortion. Exposure plus response prevention, re-creation of the body image, and sensitization to inner cues of hunger and satiety were the main behavior-therapeutic elements applied in the context of active–alert hypnosis. Self-strengthening and age-progression suggestions were administered to create and stabilize a positive image of her future. Individually tailored suggestions helped F. L. to evaluate her life path and to canalize her repressed aggression.

After 6 weeks of treatment, consisting of two active–alert hypno-therapeutic sessions a week, the daily binge and purge episodes disappeared; they returned only during F. L.'s visits home. After 3 months in the hospital (27 active–alert hypnosis sessions), the patient gained 18 pounds, and her menstrual cycle normalized. She reported that she was very fond of active–

alert hypnosis because: "I feel free, powerful, full with energy. I can trust the future much better now than before."

After 43 active–alert hypnotherapeutic sessions, a repressed family memory came to light: Her father had had an illegitimate child, which was a taboo in the family. This memory explained F. L.'s severe guilt feelings after getting pregnant. After the recall of this memory, the focus of therapy was changed to future-oriented relaxation hypnosis (e.g., "visualize a future in which you are relaxed and content and how you arrive at that possible future"), group therapy, and working through issues pertinent to family dynamics. At this phase in her treatment, her parents were invited to attend therapy sessions. At the end of 9 months of inpatient treatment (a special pregnancy . . .), she reached a stable body weight of 99 pounds. At 1 year follow-up, she was symptom-free and emotionally stable.

Case 3

O. P., a 21-year-old male patient, was hospitalized because of anxiety and severe catatonic (i.e., schizophrenic) inhibition. After electroconvulsive therapy and the administration of neuroleptics, individual psychotherapy was initiated. After 4 months of treatment, O. P. was able to continue his university studies, but he exhibited retarded psychomotor activity, lack of initiative, and problems adjusting to university life.

To alleviate these residual symptoms, active–alert hypnosis was instituted. During the first session with active–alert hypnosis, he reported a pain in his penis; as a result, castration fears came closer to consciousness. Several verbal psychotherapeutic sessions were necessary to relieve these fears and enhance his sense of competence and efficacy. The second active–alert hypnosis session occurred 3 weeks after the first session. During the second session, guided imagery of a house was introduced. The house he imagined contained only two rooms and an attic; there was no kitchen, bathroom, or toilet. He visualized himself cleaning the dusty attic. In the subsequent session, during which he focused on this symbolic imagery, he became more emotional, brought rich dream material for discussion, and became livelier on the whole. In the next session of active–alert hypnosis, an age-progression suggestion was administered. In response to this suggestion to project himself into the future, he experienced himself as a married man and a father. After this session, he reported a marked improvement in his mood and activity level. As the examination period at the university approached, his learning problems were dealt with in two final therapeutic active–alert hypnosis sessions. He experienced significant benefits from suggestions for effective learning and from imaginative rehearsal of performing successfully on his examinations.

Three years after he terminated therapy, he is progressing with his studies; his academic achievement is comparable to his performance prior to his psychological problems. Although his overall adjustment is adequate, he does not have a romantic companion or marital partner. He has not taken medication for almost 2 years.

In summary, in this case active–alert hypnosis had two significant effects. First, its energizing effects appeared to play a role in alleviating the residual symptoms of schizophrenia. Second, it facilitated awareness of and working through fundamental fears and conflicts.

Case 4

P. X. was a 10-year-old autistic boy with a middle-class family background. He entered a medical research program in which the efficacy of naltrexone as a treatment for autism was evaluated. Part of this program involved twice-weekly intensive psychotherapy sessions. In the first 6 months, skin sensation mapping and the strong stimulation of body zones identified as pleasant, unpleasant, and neutral skin were undertaken. As a result of this phase of therapy, P. X. began to explore his own body and discover its functioning.

After these preliminary interventions, active–alert hypnosis was introduced to enhance his awareness of his muscle activity, to have him focus on sensations of different sensory modalities, and to help him experience and differentiate moods and emotions. Experiencing the monotonous motor activity, P. X. entered hypnosis easily and proved to be amenable to imagery techniques. His first task was to imagine and relive the experiences of body stimulation and to relate his sensations and feelings to one another. Next, he was to imagine himself participating in everyday life situations, prior to imagining scenes related to archetypal images (e.g., sea, sun, and countryside). In the course of active–alert hypnosis treatment, P. X. began to experience his body boundaries and personal space. Once, when the therapist bent too close to him during hypnotic induction, he said, "Don't come so close." This was the first time he indicated that he could differentiate himself and another person and that he perceived an intrusion into his personal space.

After 2 years of treatment, his therapy is still in progress. Initial results, however, are very encouraging.

In this therapy, the use of active–alert hypnosis was significant in that it appeared to enhance P. X.'s self-awareness, a process that was initiated by the combination of medication and stimulation therapy. These interventions helped P. X. to begin to differentiate himself from the world around him.

RESEARCH AND APPRAISAL

Our examples make it clear that active–alert hypnosis can be a useful tool in the treatment of a variety of conditions and disorders. Active–alert methods can be helpful when used alone or in combination with other treatment methods. However promising active–alert procedures appear to be, it is, nevertheless, premature to conclude that they are superior to any number of other hypnotherapeutic techniques. Furthermore, in the examples cited, it is difficult to isolate the specific role of active–alert methods in the treatment gains achieved. Controlled outcome research utilizing a variety of hypnotherapeutic strategies and approaches is therefore a high priority.

It is worth noting that the technique of active–alert hypnosis was developed less than 20 years ago (Bányai & Hilgard, 1976), and its clinical application has an even shorter history (Bányai, 1977; Zseni & Vadász, 1988). Nevertheless, research that compares active–alert hypnosis with traditional relaxation-based hypnosis, even if not conducted within a clinical setting, is relevant to the clinical application of active–alert hypnosis. In the remainder of this section, we will summarize the research that has been conducted on active–alert hypnosis, particularly where it is relevant to hypnotherapy.

Studying nonclinical volunteer subjects, Bányai and her colleagues have systematically analyzed the subjective experiences, behavioral manifestations, and physiological changes associated with active–alert hypnosis. In a series of five experimental studies, Bányai and her associates (Bányai, 1976, 1980, 1987; Bányai & Hilgard, 1976; Bányai et al., 1981, 1983) administered active–alert hypnosis to a total of 94 subjects. In these studies, the effects of active–alert methods were compared with relaxation-based hypnosis and waking control conditions (i.e., pedaling the bicycle without induction, and a waking, relaxed state). The main findings of this research program have been replicated and extended by other investigators (Cikurel & Gruzelier, 1990; Malott, 1984; Miller, Barabasz, & Barabasz, 1991).

Although systematic research has not been conducted in a clinical setting, the published data on clinical applications of active–alert hypnosis confirm the results obtained with nonclinical volunteer subjects (Túry, 1992; Zseni & Vadász, 1988).

Subjective Experiences in Active–Alert Hypnosis

Subjects exposed to traditional and active–alert procedures hold similar expectations about hypnosis. Likewise, after both procedures, subjects feel that they have achieved a genuinely altered state of consciousness. Across the entire sample of 94 subjects, only 2 subjects did not notice any difference between their usual waking state and their subjective state after the active–alert induction. Notably, both of these subjects also failed to experience an altered state of consciousness after the traditional induction.

Although subjects reported some differences between the two forms of induction, the altered state of consciousness achieved with both procedures was essentially comparable. The two states were similar insofar as they were characterized by reports of relinquishing the planning function of the personality (52% of subjects), a lack of reality-testing ability (55.32%), and a sense that attention could be highly focused (78%). In contrast, the two procedures could be distinguished in terms of reports of differences in the level of alertness (72.34% of subjects rated active–alert hypnosis as more alert), in the emotional tone of experiences (68% of subjects rated active–alert hypnosis as more joyous, often even ecstatic), and in the level of active involvement (32% of subjects rated participation as more active in active–alert hypnosis).

Ecstatic-like peak experiences were not frequently reported when active–alert hypnosis was used in psychotherapy. Nevertheless, patients reported differences in the level of alertness and active involvement between active–alert and traditional hypnotic treatments, similar to those reported by nonclinical volunteers (Túry, 1992; Zseni & Vadász, 1988).

Behavioral Manifestations of Active–Alert Hypnosis

Many of the behavioral concomitants or features of traditional hypnosis are also associated with active–alert methods. For example, after the active–alert induction, the subject's facial expression becomes vacant. Although the eyes generally remain open during the induction, the gaze seems unfocused, as though staring at some distant object. However, in response to the demands of the active–alert induction, the subject's posture generally becomes more tense, and movements are speeded up and often exaggerated. This is reflected in the significant increase (32%) of pedal speed in active–alert hypnosis above and beyond the pedal speed of waking control subjects (Bányai et al., 1981). Increases over baseline pedal speed have also been observed in active–alert hypnotherapy (Zseni & Vadász, 1988).

Heightened responsiveness to suggestions is considered to be the most important characteristic feature of the hypnotic state. Because patients' responsiveness to suggestions plays a prominent role in the therapeutic application of hypnotic techniques, it is important to compare patients' responsiveness to test suggestions in active–alert and relaxation-based hypnosis.

The application of active–alert hypnosis to a wide range of clinical situations is justified by repeated demonstrations that traditional and active–alert procedures produce equivalent behavioral responses to motor suggestions (Bányai, 1987; Bányai & Hilgard, 1976; Malott, 1984). However, even more germane to the clinical context is the fact that performance equivalence has been demonstrated across a range of suggestions (Bányai, 1980, 1987; Bányai & Hilgard, 1976; Malott, 1984; Miller et al., 1991), including posthypnotic and cognitive suggestions (e.g., suggestions that evoke imagery, dreams, hypermnesia, and analgesia). For example, active–

alert hypnosis has been found to be as effective in reducing cold-pressor pain as traditional hypnosis (Miller et al., 1991). With respect to only one suggestion, auditive hallucination, was performance found to be slightly better in traditional versus active–alert hypnosis conditions (Bányai, 1980).

It is also worth noting that this similarity between traditional and active–alert hypnosis extended to subjects' cognitive experiences and involvement in suggestions. That is, across induction types, similarities were observed in subjects' experiences of suggestion-related involuntariness and dissociation. Furthermore, clear, vivid, and dreamlike visual imagery accompanied suggestions; memory was improved without effort; and subjects devised rationalizations for suggestions performed posthypnotically, in both traditional and active–alert test conditions (Bányai, 1980, 1987; Miller et al., 1991).

One interesting finding relevant to clinical practice is that the hypnotic dream content of nonpatient volunteers who received an active–alert induction was more joyous than that of volunteers who received a traditional induction. If another person was introduced into the dream in the active–alert condition, he or she was perceived as a good person, a helping parent, friend, or lover. In active–alert hypnosis, the dream content often had sexual connotations (Bányai, 1980, 1987). In contrast, another person introduced into the dream in traditional hypnosis tended to be a respected, rather serious authority figure. Taken together, these findings suggest that active–alert hypnosis may prove to be helpful in mobilizing patients' dormant inner resources.

Preference for Induction Type

Also germane to the clinical utility of active–alert hypnosis is the fact that some people prefer the active–alert form of hypnosis to traditional hypnosis (Bányai, 1987; Bányai & Hilgard, 1976). Because subjects are more responsive to hypnosis when they are tested with an induction they prefer (Bányai & Hilgard, 1976), it may be wise to assess patients' preference for a variety of inductions before choosing to implement a hypnotic technique in therapy. This recommendation is supported by the fact that this preference effect was shown to be very robust in the clinical context: Eight patients who scored in the low hypnotizable range (0–2 on the Stanford Hypnotic Susceptibility Scale, Form A: Weitzenhoffer & Hilgard, 1959) and who indicated a preference for active–alert hypnosis were able to experience deep hypnosis in response to active–alert techniques (Zseni & Vadász, 1988).

Physiological Characteristics of Active–Alert Hypnosis

In active–alert hypnosis, central indices of arousal (background EEG and evoked potentials) have not been found to parallel increases in the general level of activation reflected in subjective reports and activity level. However, evidence for activation at the physiological level has been found (Bányai, 1987; Bányai et al., 1981, 1983) with peripheral indices (electromyographic activity).

Evoked potential and CNV (contingent negative variation) studies have provided data indicating that, in a manner similar to traditional hypnosis, it is the modification of selective attention that is associated with the characteristic subjective and behavioral changes in active–alert hypnosis (Bányai et al., 1981; Mészáros, Bányai, & Greguss, 1981). Cikurel and Gruzelier (1990) demonstrated that the modification of selective attention in active–alert hypnosis is accompanied by a shift to more right-hemispheric information processing. In fact, they found that in the case of haptic processing, the lateral shift in favor of a facilitation of right-hemispheric processing was significantly greater with the active–alert procedure than with relaxation-based hypnosis. This lateral shift is thought to facilitate the fading of the generalized reality orientation and to potentiate primary process thinking, imagery, and archaic involvement with the hypnotist. These positive accompaniments of active–alert hypnosis constitute a corrective for fixed, faulty patterns of functioning, rendering active–alert hypnosis of benefit in psychotherapy.

CONCLUSION

The results obtained with the use of active–alert hypnosis, both with nonclinical volunteers and with patients seeking therapy, show that active–alert hypnosis deserves a prominent place in the array of treatment options available to hypnotherapists. At the same time, controlled outcome research is necessary to further evaluate the nature and magnitude of treatment-related gains. The positive emotional state achieved by recipients of active–alert hypnosis is consistent with a shift in emphasis in contemporary psychology from a focus on negative emotional states to the induction of positive emotions such as love and happiness (Argyle, 1988; Fromm, 1956). Moreover, the active participation of people in active-alert hypnosis is in harmony with current trends in psychotherapy to cultivate competence (White, 1959), self-actualization (Maslow, 1962), the establishment of positive mental health based on mastery (Murphy, 1962), ego activity (Rapaport, 1967), and an internal locus of control (Rotter, 1966). By emphasizing positive goals in life and enhancing feelings of mastery, active–alert hypnotherapy can be a potent tool not only in correcting dysfunctions and in treating disorders, but also in enhancing self-development by actuating a cycle of growth-enhancing human potentials.

REFERENCES

American Psychiatric Association. (1987). *Diagnostic and statistical manual of mental disorders* (3rd ed., rev.). Washington, D.C.: Author.

Argyle, M. (1988). *The psychology of happiness.* New York: Penguin.

Bálint, M. (1957). *The doctor, his patient and the illness.* London: Pitman Medical. [American edition: New York: International Universities Press, 1957]

Bányai, É. I. (1976). A new way to increase suggestibility: Active–alert hypnotic induction. *International Journal of Clinical and Experimental Hypnosis, 24,* 358.

Bányai, É. I. (1977, October). *A possible new method for psychotherapy: Active–alert hypnosis.* Paper presented at the symposium "Theorie, Praxis and Leistung der Hypnose," Rostock, Germany.

Bányai, É. I. (1980). A new way to increase a hypnotic-like altered state of consciousness: Active–alert induction. In L. Kardos & C. Pléh (Eds.), *Problems of the regulation of activity* (pp. 261–273). Budapest, Hungary: Akadémiai Kiadó.

Bányai, É. I. (1987). *Aktivitás-fokozással létrehozható módosult tudatállapot: Aktívéber hipnózis* [Altered state of consciousness induced by increasing activity: Active–alert hypnosis]. Unpublished thesis for the degree of C.Sc., Eötvös Loránd University, Budapest, Hungary.

Bányai, É. I., & Hilgard, E. R. (1976). Comparison of active–alert hypnotic induction with traditional relaxation induction. *Journal of Abnormal Psychology, 85,* 218–224.

Bányai, É. I., Mészáros, I., & Greguss, A. C. (1981). Alteration of activity level: The essence of hypnosis or a byproduct of the type of induction? In G. Ádám, I. Mészáros, & É. I. Bányai (Eds.), *Advances in physiological sciences: Vol. 17. Brain and behaviour* (pp. 457–465). Budapest, Hungary: Pergamon Press/Akadémiai Kiadó.

Bányai, É. I., Mészáros, I., & Greguss, A. C. (1983). Psychophysiological comparison of active–alert and traditional relaxation hypnosis. In R. Sinz & M. R. Rosenzweig (Eds.), *Psychophysiology* (pp. 225–230). Jena, Germany, and Amsterdam, The Netherlands: VEB Gustav Fischer Verlag and Elsevier Biomedical Press.

Biró, G. (1989, May). *Video demonstration and discussion of training an athlete with active–alert hypnosis.* 1. Magyar Hipnózis Találkozó [1st Hungarian Hypnosis Meeting]. Miskolc, Hungary.

Brown, D. P., & Fromm, E. (1986). *Hypnotherapy and hypnoanalysis.* Hillsdale, NJ: Erlbaum.

Cikurel, K., & Gruzelier, J. (1990). The effects of active alert hypnotic induction on lateral haptic processing. *British Journal of Experimental and Clinical Hypnosis, 11,* 17–25.

Eliade, M. (1964). *Shamanism: Archaic techniques of ecstasy* (Willard R. Trask, Trans.; Bollingen Series 76). New York: Pantheon Books.

Fromm, E. (1956). *The art of loving.* New York: Harper & Row.

Halifax, J. (1980). *Shamanic voices: The shaman as seer, poet and healer.* Harmondsworth, Middlesex, England: Penguin Books.

Malott, J. M. (1984). Active–alert hypnosis: Replication and extension of previous research. *Journal of Abnormal Psychology, 93,* 246–249.

Maslow, A. (1962). *Toward a psychology of being.* New York: Van Nostrand.

Mészáros, I., Bányai, É. I., & Greguss, A. C. (1981). Evoked potential, reflecting hypnotically altered state of consciousness. In G. Ádám, I. Mészáros, & É. I. Bányai (Eds.), *Advances in physiological sciences: Vol. 17, Brain and behaviour* (pp. 467–475). Budapest, Hungary: Pergamon Press/Akadémiai Kiadó.

Miller, M. F., Barabasz, A. F., & Barabasz, M. (1991). Effects of active alert and relaxation hypnotic inductions on cold pressor pain. *Journal of Abnormal Psychology, 100,* 223–226.

Murphy, L. (1962). *The widening world of childhood: Paths toward mastery.* New York: Basic Books.

Murray-Jobsis, J. (1984). Hypnosis with severely disturbed patients. In W. C. Wester II, & A. H. Smith, Jr. (Eds.), *Clinical hypnosis: A multidisciplinary approach* (pp. 368–404). Philadelphia, PA: Lippincott.

Rapaport, D. (1967). Some metapsychological considerations concerning activity and passivity. In M. M. Gill (Ed.), *The collected papers of David Rapaport* (pp. 530–568). New York: Basic Books.

Rogers, C. R. (1970). *On becoming a person: A therapist's view of psychotherapy.* Boston: Houghton Mifflin.

Rotter, J. B. (1966). Generalized expectancies for internal versus external control of reinforcement. *Psychological Monographs, 80*(1, Whole No. 609).

Túry, F. (1992, July). *Dynamic or "active–alert" hypnosis in eating disorders.* Paper presented at the 12th International Congress of Hypnosis, Jerusalem, Israel. (Book of abstracts, p. 38)

Unestáhl, L.-E. (1980, May). *Comment on the use of active–alert hypnotic induction in training athletes.* Second European Congress of Hypnosis, Dubrovnik, Yugoslavia.

Weitzenhoffer, A. M., & Hilgard, E. R. (1959). *Stanford Hypnotic Susceptibility Scale, Forms A and B.* Palo Alto, CA: Consulting Psychologists Press.

White, R. W. (1959). Motivation reconsidered: The concept of competence. *Psychological Review, 66,* 297–333.

Zseni, A., & Vadász, J. (1988). Terápiás tapasztalatok egy új hipnózis indukciós eljárással. Az aktív-éber (dinamikus) hipnózis módszere [Experiences with the therapeutic application of a new hypnotic induction procedure: The method of active–alert (dynamic) hypnosis]. *Psychiatria Hungarica, 3,* 311–320.

14

HYPNOSIS AND METAPHOR

PETER BROWN

Listen closely to anything anyone says, and soon you will hear analogies. We speak of time in terms of space as like a fluid that's *running out;* we talk of our friends in physical terms, as in "*Mary and John are very close.*" All of our language is riddled and stitched with curious ways of portraying things as though they belong to alien realms. . . .

When such conceptions play important roles in our most productive forms of thought, we find it natural to ask, "*what is a metaphor?*" but we rarely notice how frequently we use the same techniques in ordinary thought.

What, then, *is* a metaphor? It might be easy to agree on functional definitions like "*a metaphor is that which allows us to replace one kind of thought with another.*" But when we ask for a structural definition of "metaphor," we find no unity, only an endless variety of processes and strategies. (Minsky, 1986, p. 299)

The study of the "processes and strategies" of metaphor has only recently achieved scientific legitimacy. Susan Langer (1957) demonstrated the prejudices of Western literacy for "secondary process" thinking, which neglects elements of metaphor, imagery, and emotion and overlooks the fundamentally intelligent and purposive nature of all brain function. Metaphor is an active, goal-directed process that is particularly important in situations where new meanings are being developed (Gerrig & Gibbs, 1988). This is most clearly seen in the face-to-face interaction in which two people play with language to create a mutually shared meaning. Metaphor allows these interactions to be open-ended and ambiguous, always ready to exploit new possibilities (P. Brown, 1991a).

The use of metaphor in hypnosis is best known through the work of Milton Erickson (Zeig, 1980). While drawing on an extensive stock of metaphoric structures that he used and reused, Erickson was able to alter his language dramatically in response to contextual demands. Ostensibly discussing stories drawn from previous case material, his own childhood, or the life of his family, Erickson integrated story, strategic interventions, and a flexible use of trance phenomena to create a structure that was analogous to that of the presenting problem and current life situation of the patient (Lankton & Lankton, 1983, 1989). A second stream that has influenced the clinical use of metaphor comes from the realm of child psychotherapy (Gardner, 1977). In attempting to develop therapeutic techniques with young children, creative therapists have used a variety of approaches, including encouraging children's fantasies, mutual storytelling, and the development of "therapeutic" stories, which give a coherent frame to the child's problems and suggest possible solutions (e.g., Aurela, 1987; Brooks, 1985; Davis, 1986; Kestenbaum, 1985; Lawson, 1987; Levine, 1980; Rhue & Lynn, 1991; Rhue, Lynn, Henry, Buhk, & Boyd, 1991). The influence of this work is now also being felt in adult hypnotherapy. This chapter will present a simple approach to the uses of metaphor in hypnosis and link these uses to current research on metaphor and cognition.

CLINICAL APPLICATIONS AND CASE MATERIAL

There are a number of methods for introducing metaphor (Table 1) into the clinical setting. Similarly, the uses of metaphor in hypnotherapy can be classified under four broad headings: (a) establishing a therapeutic context, (b) facilitating induction and hypnotic phenomena, (c) stimulating problem solving, and (d) linking therapeutic change to subsequent behavior (Table 2). Three extended clinical examples will illustrate possible applications of each of these categories.

Establishing a Therapeutic Context

The first stage of the use of therapeutic metaphor is to identify and develop the metaphors that the patient uses to describe his or her symptoms and predicament (Steckler, 1992). This involves asking detailed questions related to the structure, emotional associations, memories, and other aspects

TABLE 1
Clinical Methods of Metaphor

1. Establishing a therapeutic context
   a. Presenting problem in patient's own words
   b. Match therapeutic metaphor to patient's personal metaphors
   c. Prehypnotic suggestion

2. Facilitating induction and hypnotic phenomena
   a. Link personal metaphor to induction and suggestions
   b. Permissive language to encourage individual variation

3. Stimulating problem solving
   a. Identify heightened emotional response
   b. Explore associations, memories, or spontaneous images related to therapeutic interaction
   c. Incorporate spontaneous elaborations of metaphor and figures of speech into therapeutic process

4. Linking therapeutic change to subsequent behavior
   a. Ensure metaphors mesh with existing schemas
   b. Posthypnotic suggestion
   c. Linking hypnotic responses to cues from wider life context

TABLE 2
Clinical Uses of Metaphor

1. Establishing a therapeutic context
   a. Identify key issues
   b. Build rapport and shared expectancies
   c. Create common model
   d. Prepare future responses

2. Facilitating induction and hypnotic phenomena
   a. Absorb attention
   b. Provide "fail-safe" induction
   c. Progressive hypnotic skill training
   d. Enhancing self-esteem and confidence

3. Stimulating problem solving
   a. Emotional abreaction
   b. Encourage collaborative stance and active patient role
   c. Cognitive reorganization (reframing)
   d. Promote narrative drive for closure

4. Linking therapeutic change to subsequent behaviour
   a. Ensure gains made are effective in real life
   b. Encourage problem solving stance (generative change)

of the metaphor. Therapists focus on a metaphor for a number of purposes: to "short circuit" repression and facilitate the recovery of significant memories, to promote affective expression by connecting imagery with the appropriate emotions, to alter defenses or coping style, to modulate affect, and to increase control over unbidden imagery or overwhelming emotion (Horowitz, 1989). The contents of these metaphors are typically related to traumatic memories, emotional conflicts, or disavowed self-images. In a metaphoric context, patients are more likely to be able to talk about current concerns and/or painful or difficult areas from the past (McMullen, 1989).

Sensitive clinicians know that the patient's descriptive language provides a glimpse into how the problem, possible resources, solutions, and underlying life structure may all be linked. At the same time, the metaphors used to explain a therapeutic approach allow the patient to have a glimpse as to how he or she is perceived by the therapist. If the initial metaphors are built in a collaborative way, joining the initial descriptions of the patient with a framework that can be understood and accepted, these metaphors will not only enhance rapport but provide a cognitive structure that can begin to generate possible solutions.

Context-building metaphors can appear at a number of different times in hypnosis. They can appear either at the start of therapy or along the way to introduce new themes or recapitulate old ones. In a more traditionally organized hypnotherapy they usually follow a formal trance induction, relying on that induction to make the ideas more meaningful and easier to accept. Using a more naturalistic approach, the metaphors may precede other hypnotic techniques and provide an orientation that will influence the way in which hypnotic phenomena are experienced (sometimes described as "prehypnotic suggestion").

Contextual metaphors are not limited to what we tell the patient. Metaphor is also an important part of what we tell ourselves. Theoreticians of different schools have noted the metaphoric underpinnings of not only the language of therapy, but also of the diagnostic formulations and even the therapeutic context (Hillman, 1983; Spence, 1987). Every diagnosis or formulation, indeed every case history, is also a metaphoric creation aspiring to be what Hillman (1983) termed a "healing fiction."

Metaphor is well suited as a transitional step in conceptual understanding. Indeed, psychological symptoms can be conceptualized as "failed" or incomplete metaphors (Wright, 1976). Siegelman (1990) suggested that personally important metaphors are related to ongoing concerns, strong emotions, specific concrete images, and a creative stance. In this way, the language used by an individual to describe a problem can be viewed as part of a work in progress that can be used to develop personal understanding.

The following examples of initial metaphors are taken from the case histories of three women presenting with adjustment disorders in reaction to metastatic breast cancer. All of the women sought psychotherapy "to cope better," and all of them suffered from comparable levels of distress. However, each of these women had a clearly distinctive metaphoric description for her situation, which illustrates the marked individual differences in the way in which a similar predicament was conceptualized in a very different way by each.

1. The Script

"My mother died of breast cancer when she was my age. Now it's my turn. I'm living her script. I wish that she was here to tell me what to do." (In this case, current adjustment issues were secondary to an unresolved brief reaction to the death of her mother.)

2. A Time Bomb

"I did everything right: I looked after myself, exercised, and ate carefully. This is not fair. I feel like I have been assaulted. My body is a time bomb. I feel like I could die at any moment." (This patient demonstrated considerable but undirected anger that was associated with the strong feeling of the loss of control over the situation. The principle therapeutic direction was to restore a sense of self-efficacy and a sense of control over individual decisions.)

3. Not in the Picture

"I am a failure. I let my family down at a time when they really need me. I don't have a role any more. If I died my husband could remarry and he would have a real wife and my children would have a real mother. I'm not in the picture." (In this case, the patient saw herself as having failed at her principle roles, with resultant negative self-image that left her feeling devalued and emotionally isolated from her family. At the same time, she was irritable and resented their ability to get on without her. The goal of the therapy was to restore her sense of self-esteem and reconnect her to her emotional supports.)

Facilitating Induction and Hypnotic Phenomena

In the second stage of the use of therapeutic metaphor, the patient's own metaphors can be linked to a hypnotic induction trance and the development of hypnotic phenomena by extending that metaphor or using metaphors with overlapping entailments. Typically, the therapist also aims to (a) add more sensory description to increase the vividness and sense of involvement in the metaphor; (b) incorporate suggestions for greater control of imagery, changes in perspective, modulation of emotional response (encouraging and increasing emotional response when this is indicated, or dampening affective response in cases of overwhelming or intrusive emotions); and (c) include suggestions to link the problem metaphor with possible resources. This form of linking allows the original problem situation to become a cue in which the new and desired response can then be implemented. Hypnotic phenomena can then be seen as a link between the initial metaphor and the new response. Permissive wording of suggestions will also encourage the patient to develop personally relevant responses.

Metaphor can be part of a naturalistic and permissive orientation that encourages patients to respond in their own way and at their own speed (Lachnit, 1989). This result is a "fail-safe" approach in which progressively graded tasks are introduced to gradually improve hypnotic responsiveness without the risk of overt failure (Erickson, Rossi, & Rossi, 1976). Highly hypnotizable subjects do appear to be more sensitive to verbal nuance and more likely to respond automatically to structural verbal connections (Dixon, Brunet, & Laurence, 1990). These findings suggest that highly hypnotizable subjects are more likely to be able to use metaphor effectively. Indeed, this skill appears to allow highly hypnotizable subjects to respond equally well to direct and indirect inductions (Hammond, 1990). Perhaps the real value of metaphor is with subjects who have less hypnotic ability, because it can provide them with an external structure to assist them in doing what the subjects with greater ability can do spontaneously. A number of related approaches repeating the same theme in a number of different ways does serve to improve recall of related material, increase imagery, and develop rapport for the majority of subjects (Gibb & Wales, 1990; Kemper, 1989).

The following are examples:

1. The Script: Hypnotic Amplification of Memory

After a standard trance induction with instructions for relaxation, the patient was given the following suggestion: "You can let the story of your life reverse before your eyes: Allow yourself to drift back gradually drifting back through the weeks, months, and years. You may remember certain circumstances which are particularly relevant to your current situation. In your mind's eye this story can stop at a particularly significant moment. When you have reached it, allow yourself to observe and remember the situation as clearly as possible and then describe it to me." (After a few moments the patient described memories of the death of her mother as well as expressing her continued regret that she had not been able to talk to her mother and say goodbye in the way in which she would have liked.)

2. A Time Bomb: Arm Levitation

"There are a number of possible ways in which you can take an active role in reestablishing your sense of control over your body and, hopefully, to allow your body to fight back against your illness. Tune your attention internally and while doing that notice a growing sense of comfort and relaxation. As you become more aware of that comfort, your arm will begin to raise, as if by itself. You can be pleased and surprised as your arm raises to learn that there are many options which you are capable of which you have yet to consider." (The therapeutic goal was to provide the patient with a sense of realistic control, i.e., recognizing the inherent danger of the situation while developing a sense of control over those things that she was capable of controlling. Arm levitation was chosen as a simple hypnotic phenomena that allowed the patient to master a new skill that she had not thought she was capable of performing. In this way, she found that she had greater control over some aspects of her body and behavior than she had previously assumed.)

3. Not in the Picture: Initiating Hypnosis

"Sometimes you need to look at a picture more privately. You have been tired out by your illness and treatment and your emotional reserves have been depleted. Take this time right now to take a few deep, comfortable breaths, relax and gradually allow your eyes to become heavy and to close. (Pause.) That's right. As you do this you will find the relaxation that provides you with strength that you need to look after your family. Picture this as that small vacation you really need. The more you are able to relax right now the more you will have to give later. The more successful you are at relaxing deeply and comfortably now the better it is for your family. You will be able to find that you can best look after them by taking this time to look after yourself."

Stimulating Problem Solving

The goal of the third phase of metaphor use is to incorporate changes in the existing metaphor. Implicitly, every psychotherapeutic orientation has a particular way of doing this. In practice, this appears to evolve most consistently out of a collaborative therapeutic stance as the metaphors are developed by both therapist and patient. "Good imagery work is a kind of dialogue. . . . The role of the therapist is primarily to amplify the experience not to suggest it. . . . In each case, the therapist either stimulates exploration of what it immediately presented or encourages the patient to generate additional images, scenes, or fantasy productions. The objective is for the patient to continuously generate the imaginal experiences" (D. Brown & Fromm, 1986, p. 167). This shared work integrates images, affects, and verbal descriptions while a new perspective is achieved. Metaphor can also serve as a catalyst for emotional abreaction as feelings are connected to new images or ideas.

The use of metaphor to stimulate problem solving either can be done through a variety of predetermined scripts, such as the use of guided imagery, or can incorporate a more collaborative approach in which the patient's associations are elicited and used for further elaborations of the metaphoric themes. Metaphor may provide a new structure with which to organize experience or provide a means to express deeply personal or previously poorly understood aspects of experience.

Ongoing feedback is critical in identifying situations in which the therapeutic metaphor is not having its desired effect. Horowitz (1989) described a number of common situations in which patients may find it difficult to utilize metaphor. These typically involve situations in which there is a poor connection between imagery and verbal modes of representation: Patients may not be able to connect words with the images of the metaphor and may ignore or be inattentive to spontaneous associated imagery, feelings, or sensations. Such patients will require greater therapist involvement to develop an effective working model.

The qualities of vivid imagery, strong emotional valence, holistic thinking, and personal identification link metaphor to the therapeutic aspects of hypnosis (D. Brown & Fromm, 1986) as well as to spontaneous states of creativity or reverie (Rossi & Smith, 1990). Rothenberg (1988) has suggested that the metaphoric structure required for therapeutic change involves particular creative processes: the homospatial process, which involves the blending of two discrete images to produce a new metaphor that combines elements of each, and the janusian process, which combines two or more opposites simultaneously. In a series of studies, Rothenberg (1988) found that creative individuals were far more likely to use these processes when confronted with vivid images or new situations. The new metaphor that resulted was typically a transitional, unstable stage that stimulated further effort to seek out symmetry, balance, and integration. This drive to completion ultimately achieved a dramatic restructuring of previous models.

In summary, to achieve full therapeutic potency, metaphor must include significance (i.e., must have structural equivalence for both conscious and unconscious aspects of the task), vividness (i.e., must use strong perceptual involvement to absorb emotional and cognitive resources), and a drive toward resolution (i.e., must be open-ended so that the attempt to achieve closure becomes an immediate and important goal) (Beck, 1987). To achieve these goals, the metaphor must fit with the contextual cues and be sensitive to individual variability.

The following are examples:

1. The Script: Completion of Mourning

The patient reported an image of herself talking with her mother. Expressing a deep sadness, she was able to acknowledge how much she missed her mother and was able to gain some comfort in the memory of her mother that she carried within her. Through several imagined conversations, she and her mother were able to collaborate on a new script for her that involved her learning from her own and her mother's mistakes.

2. A Time Bomb: Abreaction

Drawing comfort and confidence from her ability to achieve arm levitation, the patient was able to visualize a time bomb lodged in her spine (the place where her recurrence had been discovered). On opening the panel on the front of the bomb, she suddenly felt terrified. She acknowledged that the fear that she had felt at the time of her original diagnosis had been put away in a box and that this was the emotional time bomb that she had been responding to. "Disarming" this time bomb by expressing and acknowledging her fear allowed her to reestablish a sense of control.

3. Not in the Picture: Reframing

In the course of relaxation the patient spontaneously reported the image of a photograph of her family in which her figure had been cropped out. It was suggested that she look more carefully at the photograph, and she noted how unhappy the faces of her family were. When she reinserted her own figure in the photograph, the colors were brighter and more vivid and her family wore happy expressions. She was able to see feelings of relaxation and comfort as a way of continuing her role in the family. She also recognized the need to let her family know how she was feeling and that this would be good not only for her but for them as well.

Linking Therapeutic Change to Subsequent Behavior

The therapeutic relationship can provide a safe environment where the patient can experiment with new ways of relating, rehearse alternative strategies, or respond more flexibly to contextual cues. This appears to be true whether we are talking about relatively simple hypnotic suggestions or more complex psychotherapeutic interactions. The collaborative process of metaphoric elaboration is a process that can provide meaning by building a coherent structure, develop rapport through the evolution of a common language, and encourage problem solving both by implying that a new resolution is possible and by stimulating a search for the appropriate strategies.

It has been suggested that the use of metaphor may increase the effectiveness of posthypnotic suggestion (Lankton & Lankton, 1983). The new patterns of behavior established in therapy can be linked to real-life situations. By linking metaphor to posthypnotic suggestion, a context may be created whereby therapeutic gains can be consolidated and extended beyond the immediate context. This implies that the goal of therapy need not be simple symptom relief but can extend to generative change: a more open-minded and creative orientation toward future problems (Rossi & Smith, 1990).

The following are examples:

1. The Script: Developing Analgesia

After using hypnosis to recover and amplify memories of her relationship with her mother and some expression of the sadness that she felt in missing having her mother with her at many important times, the patient was able to talk about some of the aspects of her mother's personality that could be helpful to her in controlling her pain and suffering. As part of the hypnotic training, the following suggestion was given: "It happens sometimes that you experience pain and that pain makes you feel lonely and frightened. Whenever you experience these feelings in the future you will be able to simply take a deep breath and relax as you do the hypnotic exercises that you have practiced. Once you have done this, you will find that it will be possible to continue the mental conversation with your mother: Perhaps you will want to tell her how upset you are or perhaps you will simply find yourself telling her about some unrelated things that you think she might want to hear. While this conversation is occurring it will absorb all of your attention and you will find that any part of your body that really needs to will feel more and more cool and relaxed and comfortable. You will still be able to tell your doctor about any concerns that you might have but you can focus on feeling as comfortable as possible once you have told her of these concerns." (The patient was able to develop effective pain relief from bony metastases using this technique. She particularly enjoyed "conversations" with her mother in which she let her know about her experiences in hypnosis and her success at pain relief. Sharing the experience with her mother in imagination allowed her to feel that her mother would have liked and approved of the resourceful woman that her daughter had become.)

2. A Time Bomb: Self-Hypnosis for Relaxation

The following suggestions were made with regard to controlling chemotherapy side effects: "It is a pleasant feeling to feel relaxed and in control. During treatment, you often end up in situations where you are told what to do and what time you must do it. In addition, the side effects you experience also give you a sense that your body is being invaded. However, just as you were pleased to learn that you can learn to do many things with hypnosis that you didn't think were possible, you can also use this experience to give yourself greater control during your treatments. You can use the experience to prepare yourself for your treatments, to arm yourself with a feeling of safety and comfort during the treatments, or to recover more quickly and more easily from the side effects once the treatment is completed. You can enjoy a growing sense of competence and self-protection as you are able to calm yourself and increase the feelings of safety with more and more practice."

3. Not in the Picture: Effective Communication

Following the completion of her chemotherapy, this patient focused on her difficulty in expressing emotional needs and desires to her family. These issues were incorporated into the metaphors that had been used in the previous sessions in order to facilitate self-hypnosis rehearsal of emotional expression: "There will be times when you need to take a break in order to clarify the picture of what is going on in your family. Whenever you recognize the need to do so you will be able to relax comfortably in order to ask yourself, 'what is it that I am really feeling right now?' You can then visualize a screen and allow yourself to run a movie of yourself talking with whoever it is in your family that you need to talk to. You can rehearse various versions and perhaps try simpler, more direct requests. You can monitor their reactions very carefully and you can work on it until you have formed the kind of picture that you would like to see. You will be able to see on their faces how much more relaxed and comfortable your family are when they know what it is that you are trying to say. You can rehearse these conversations as much as you like and then when you are ready you can approach the person and put it into practice. Each time you do this you will learn more about communicating and will be able to use that learning to get better and better at this." As was the case in the other examples, the patient found that this form of personalized image facilitated subsequent hypnotherapeutic work.

RESEARCH AND APPRAISAL

According to the new view of metaphor, the cognitive patterns that organize information are not objective but deeply personal. "Furthermore, their structures typically depend on the nature of the human body, especially on our perceptual capacities and motor skills" (Johnson, 1987, p. xi). In this way, cognition is fundamentally connected with our physical being and "we make use of patterns that obtain in our physical experience to organize our understanding" (Johnson, 1987, p. xv). Reality is actively constructed through the combination of our perceptions and the way that those perceptions are organized by our categories of thought. Using these patterns, we can extend our understanding to "domains of experience that do not have a pre-conceptual structure of their own" (Lakoff, 1987, p. 303).

Entailments are the specific consequences or rules of behavior that a particular metaphor suggests. The entailment structure allows the listener to extend systematically beyond the simple figure of speech. This is particularly true for ideas that are novel, ambiguous, or abstract (Glucksberg, 1989; Glucksberg & Keysar, 1990). Faced with novel situations, successful subjects typically use language flexibly, moving systematically from simple metaphors to more complex ones (Gerrig & Gibbs, 1988).

Language that makes use of imagery is better suited than is literal language for transmitting complicated information (Porush, 1987), stimulating more extensive attempts at problem solving (Yaniv & Meyer, 1987), or providing a conceptual structure that can be used for dealing with situations beyond the immediate context (Clement & Falmagne, 1986; Evans, 1988; Helstrup, 1988). Such metaphorical structures may also be more effective in integrating relevant information from immediate to long-term memory (Kosslyn, 1981).

Metaphor can influence cognition by heightening emotional response, enhancing the use of imagery, and increasing personal salience. By absorbing attention and promoting active involvement, metaphor may facilitate the efficient use of cognitive resources, increasing the levels on which the information is processed. Metaphor encourages holistic rather than analytic approaches (Bischofshausen, Makoid, & Cole, 1989). The use of metaphor also encourages cognitive flexibility and the use of alternative processing strategies (Weiner, 1985). The effective use of analogical reasoning correlates strongly with heightened situational sensitivity, cognitive flexibility, and the ability to identify and utilize the most effective cognitive strategy in a particular context (Klein, 1987). These attributes appear to be the same ones that are shown to be strongly associated with hypnotic ability (Crawford, 1990).

Metaphor also provides a link to unconscious learning (P. Brown, 1991a). Our basic metaphors and their entailments implicitly structure our experience and determine our responses to events, often without explicit conscious awareness (Kihlstrom, 1987). It has been suggested that conscious processes have evolved as a way of voluntarily selecting and controlling automatic unconscious processes, functioning in a permissive manner as a gate for the implementation of patterns that arise unconsciously (Libet, 1985). Metaphor can be seen in this light, as a bridge connecting conscious and unconscious processes (Fowler, Wolford, Slade, & Tasinary, 1981). This raises the possibility that changes in metaphoric structure can alter these relationships and restructure understanding (Olson, 1988).

Metaphoric comprehension can be increased in a number of ways. Related metaphors and metaphors that share similar structures tend to increase metaphoric comprehension, whereas contrasting metaphors or metaphors in which the structures clash tend to interfere with comprehension (Kemper, 1989). The context, the similarity (isomorphism), and the vividness of the imagery of a metaphor results in greater learning and retention. In this sense, the use of a number of structurally related metaphors may "prime" metaphoric understanding (McCabe, 1988). Subtle changes in context result in very different processing strategies being applied (Gregory & Mergler, 1990). Comprehension of metaphor is thus an interactive process with an ongoing development of understanding that depends on the metaphor, the context, and the ongoing interpretation of the individual listener (Gibbs & Gerrig, 1989; Vosniadou, 1989).

Although little work has been done on its role in hypnosis, there is a literature on metaphor in psychotherapy (e.g., Evans, 1988; Siegelman, 1990). Two recent studies in particular have illustrated how sensitivity to metaphor can facilitate psychotherapy. Angus and Rennie (1988) reviewed audiotapes of four therapy sessions, one from each of four therapeutic pairings, and identified 11 extended metaphor sequences. These were rated as to whether they revealed meaning conjunction (i.e., the pair had similar understandings of the metaphor) or meaning disjunction (i.e., the pair used the metaphor for different purposes).

Two of the pairs showed a collaborative and conjunctive style, whereas two showed a disjunctive style. In the conjunctive pairs, the therapists demonstrated attentive listening strategies, encouraging the patients to describe their individual associations and subjective experiences related to the metaphor. Furthermore, the therapists elaborated the metaphor in ways in which the patients found supportive and enlightening. These elaborations encouraged the patients to amplify their associations by incorporating the therapists' contribution. The patients described themselves as feeling understood, and they apprehended the therapists' elaborations as embodying and ratifying their own understandings.

In contrast, the noncollaborative or disjunctive metaphoric communications resembled interrogations. The therapists' assumptions led to questioning along a predetermined line, despite signals from the patients that they were not participating in the elaboration. The therapists saw the patients as resistant, whereas the patients reported feeling misunderstood or denigrated by the therapists' choice of images. Once this occurred, the misunderstandings tended to multiply with the patients' attempts to clarify their answers, which were interpreted as further resistances and attempts to deviate from the "true" meaning (i.e., the therapists' predetermined one).

Similarly, McMullen (1989) examined the relationship between metaphor use and the ultimate outcome of therapy. She compared the audiotapes of three successful and three unsuccessful cases of psychotherapy. The successful cases all revealed the progressive development of a single central metaphor that emerged out of the consolidation of figurative meanings produced by both therapist and patient. Both patient and therapist were more likely to make extensive use of the metaphors introduced by the other and, in turn, to agree with the elaborations that were made of their own language. These elaborations occurred in discrete "bursts," or creative moments, in which both patient and therapist appeared to be actively involved. Elaboration of these figures was related to a greater sense on the part of the patients that their perceptions of events and feelings were shared. In addition, patients in the successful cases consistently used figurative language to describe positive personal change. In contrast, unsuccessful cases showed little development of a central theme, no bursts of figurative language, and an absence of positive self-descriptions by the patients. Patients in the unsuccessful cases often used vivid language, but the metaphors were not picked up by the therapists. Figurative language describing self-image was largely negative and tended to show little change over time.

McMullen also pointed out that bursts of figurative language may be an important indicator of "good moments" of therapy, which are important for the therapist to encourage and utilize. At these times, patients may be more likely to explore and express thoughts that are usually painful or difficult to articulate. Such moments may also represent unique opportunities for introducing other hypnotic techniques to explore associated memories and emotions.

In summary, metaphor involves an active integration of perception and abstraction and is particularly important in expressing issues that are novel, complex, or emotionally charged. Hypnosis combines examples of all of these features: an extensive use of metaphoric language, an obvious and immediate embodiment of that language through the linking of ideas with physical contingencies (e.g., "and as you become more comfortable you can float more deeply into the trance"), and a sensitivity to context, which allows words to take on specific personal significance (P. Brown, 1991a, 1991b).

CONCLUSION

Although the use of metaphor is often associated with elaborate "indirect" approaches, direct and indirect styles of hypnotic communication appear to be equally effective in evoking hypnotic responses (P. Brown, 1991a; Hammond, 1990). Concern with metaphor does not imply the use of flowery, elaborate, or "mystifying" language or the adoption of a storytelling "once upon a time" tone of voice. Neither does it imply a passive patient for whom generic metaphors can be "programmed." In other words, sensitivity to metaphor and the use of metaphor in hypnotherapy does not imply any specific style or orientation. It is far more important that the *uses* of metaphor be novel and potent than that they be testaments of the therapist's creativity or aesthetic sense.

In Langer's (1970) memorable phrase, metaphor has the "symbolic equivalence of sensations—it motivates behavior as powerfully as do perceptions" (p. 230). The basis of this equivalence is the link between metaphor and vivid sensory-based language, with its foundation in individual experience. Much of children's play involves enactment of the metaphors that they use to structure and comprehend the things that are happening to them as they grow (Sweetser, 1990). By extension, for adults metaphor remains an opportunity for internal play, a framework for fantasy, a theater for exploring difficult situations, and a vehicle for creativity and exploration. Metaphor changes understanding by providing strong images that serve as a matrix for organizing experience and by revealing the limitations of current patterns of thinking, feeling, or behavior (Means, Wilson, & Dlugokinski, 1986–1987).

There are three major implications of our current understanding of metaphor. In the first place, regardless of whether we recognize it, we constantly use metaphors in psychotherapy. Second, improvisation and spontaneous creativity in the therapeutic context evolve from intense practice and familiarity with the best work of individuals from a variety of orientations (e.g., Hammond, 1990; Lankton & Lankton, 1989). Finally, and perhaps most critically, metaphor is most salient and effective if it is perceived by the patient as emerging organically from his or her particular situation and is generally congruent with the context of personal history and experience. Metaphor is an active and collaborative process that cannot succeed without the cooperation of therapist and patient.

REFERENCES

Angus, L. E., & Rennie, D. L. (1988). Therapist participation in metaphor generation: Collaborative and non-collaborative styles. *Psychotherapy, 25*(4): 552–560.

Aurela, A. A. (1987). A systematic storytelling therapy. *Psychiatria Fennica, 18*, 31–34.

Beck, B. E. F. (1987). Metaphors, cognition, and artificial intelligence. In R. E. Haskell (Ed.), *Cognition and symbolic structures: The psychology of metaphoric transformation* (pp. 9–30). Norwood, NJ: Ablex.

Bischofshausen, S., Makoid, L. A., & Cole, J. (1989). Effects of inference requirements on comprehension and recognition of metaphors. *Metaphor and Symbolic Activity, 4*(4): 227–246.

Brooks, R. B. (1985). The beginning sessions of child therapy: Of messages and metaphors. *Psychotherapy, 22*, 761–769.

Brown, D., & Fromm, E. (1986). *Hypnotherapy and hypnoanalysis.* Hillsdale, NJ: Erlbaum.

Brown, P. (1991a). *The hypnotic brain*. New Haven, CT: Yale University Press.

Brown, P. (1991b). Oral poetry. In S. Lankton (Ed.), *Ericksonian Monographs, Vol. 8*, 66–94.

Clement, C. A., & Falmagne, R. J. (1986). Logical reasoning, world knowledge, and mental imagery: Interconnections in cognitive processes. *Memory & Cognition, 14*, 299–307.

Crawford, H. J. (1990). Cognitive and psychophysiological correlates of hypnotic responsiveness and hypnosis. In M. L. Fass & D. Brown (Eds.), *Creative mastery in hypnosis and hypnoanalysis: A festschrift for Erika Fromm*. Hillsdale, NJ: Erlbaum.

Davis, J. M. (1986). Storytelling using the child as consultant. *Elementary School Guidance and Counseling, 21*, 89–94.

Dixon, M., Brunet, A., & Laurence, J. (1990). Hypnotizability and automaticity: Toward a parallel distributed processing model of hypnotic responding. *Journal of Abnormal Psychology, 99*, 336–343.

Erickson, M. H., Rossi, E. L., & Rossi, S. I. (1976). *Hypnotic realities: The indication of clinical hypnosis and forms of indirect suggestion*. New York: Irvington.

Evans, M. B. (1988). The role of metaphor in psychotherapy and personality change: A theoretical reformulation. *Psychotherapy, 25*, 543–551.

Fowler, C. A., Wolford, G., Slade, R., & Tasinary, L. (1981). Lexical access with and without awareness. *Journal of Experimental Psychology: General, 110*, 341–362.

Gardner, R. (1977). *Therapeutic communication with children: The mutual storytelling technique* (2nd ed.). New York: Aronson.

Gerrig, R. J., & Gibbs, R. W., Jr. (1988). Beyond the lexicon: Creativity in language production. *Metaphor and Symbolic Activity, 3*, 1–19.

Gibb, H., & Wales, R. (1990). Metaphor or simile: Psychological determinants of the differential use of each sentence form. *Metaphor and Symbolic Activity, 5*(4): 199–213.

Gibbs, R. W., Jr., & Gerrig, R. J. (1989). How context makes metaphor comprehension seem "special." *Metaphor and Symbolic Activity, 4*(3): 145–158.

Glucksberg, S. (1989). Metaphors in conversation: How are they understood? Why are they used? *Metaphor and Symbolic Activity, 4*(3): 125–143.

Glucksberg, S., & Keysar, B. (1990). Understanding metaphorical comparisons: Beyond similarity. *Psychological Review, 97*, 3–18.

Gregory, M. E., & Mergler, N. L. (1990). Metaphor comprehension: In search of literal truth, possible sense, and metaphoricity. *Metaphor and Symbolic Activity, 5*(3): 151–173.

Hammond, D. C. (1990). *Handbook of hypnotic suggestions and metaphors*. New York: Norton.

Helstrup, T. (1988). The influence of verbal and imagery strategies on processing figurative language. *Scandinavian Journal of Neurosurgery, 64*, 693–704.

Hillman, J. (1983). *Healing fiction*. New York: Station Hill.

Horowitz, M. J. (1989). *Nuances of technique in dynamic psychotherapy: Selected clinical papers*. Northvale, NJ: Aronson.

Johnson, M. (1987). *The body in the mind: The bodily basis of meaning, imagination, and reason*. Chicago: University of Chicago Press.

Kemper, S. (1989). Priming the comprehension of metaphors. *Metaphor and Symbolic Activity, 4*(1): 1–17.

Kestenbaum, C. (1985). The creative process in child psychotherapy. *American Journal of Psychotherapy, 39*, 479–489.

Kihlstrom, J. F. (1987). The cognitive unconscious. *Science, 237*, 1445–1452.

Klein, G. A. (1987). Applications of analogical reasoning. *Metaphor and Symbolic Activity, 2*, 201–218.

Kosslyn, S. M. (1981). The medium and the message in mental imagery: A computational approach. *Psychological Review, 94*, 148–175.

Lachnit, H. (1989). Indirect suggestion as a research tool. In V. A. Gheorghiu, P. Netter, J. Eysenck, & R. Rosenthal (Eds.), *Suggestion and suggestibility: Theory and research* (pp. 347–350). New York: Springer-Verlag.

Lakoff, G. (1987). *Women, fire, and dangerous things: What categories reveal about the mind*. Chicago: University of Chicago Press.

Langer, S. K. (1957). *Philosophy in a new key: The study in the symbolism of reason, rite and art*. London: Harvard University Press.

Langer, S. (1970). *Mind: An essay on human feeling* (Vol. 1). Baltimore: Johns Hopkins University Press.

Lankton, C. H., & Lankton, S. R. (1989). *Tales of enchantment: Goal-oriented metaphors for adults and children in therapy*. New York: Brunner/Mazel.

Lankton, S. R., & Lankton, C. H. (1983). *The answer within: A clinical framework of Ericksonian hypnotherapy*. New York: Brunner/Mazel.

Lawson, D. M. (1987). Using therapeutic stores in the counseling process. *Elementary School Guidance and Counseling, 12*, 134–141.

Levine, E. S. (1980). Indirect suggestions through personalized fairy tales for treatment of childhood insomnia. *American Journal of Clinical Hypnosis, 23*, 57–65.

Libet, B. (1985). Unconscious cerebral initiative and the role of conscious will in voluntary action. *Behavioral and Brain Sciences, 8*, 529–566.

McCabe, A. (1988). Effect of different contexts on memory for metaphor. *Metaphor and Symbolic Activity, 3*, 105–132.

McMullen, L. M. (1989). Use of figurative language in successful and unsuccessful cases of psychotherapy: Three comparisons. *Metaphor and Symbolic Activity, 4*, 203–225.

Means, J. R., Wilson, G. L., & Dlugokinski, L. J. (1986–1987). Self-initiated imaginal and cognitive components: Evaluation of differential effectiveness in altering unpleasant moods. *Imagination, Cognition and Personality, 6*, 219–230.

Minsky, M. (1986). *The society of mind*. New York: Simon & Schuster.

Olson, D. R. (1988). Or what's a metaphor for? *Metaphor and Symbolic Activity, 3*(4): 215–222.

Porush, D. (1987). What Homer can teach technical writers: The mnemonic value of poetic devices. *Journal of Technical Writing and Communication, 17,* 129–143.

Rhue, J. W., & Lynn, S. J. (1991). Storytelling, hypnosis and the treatment of sexually abused children. *International Journal of Clinical and Experimental Hypnosis, 39*(4), 198–214.

Rhue, J. W., Lynn, S. J., Henry, S., Buhk, K., & Boyd, P. (1991). Child abuse, imagination, and hypnotizability. *Imagery, Cognition, Personality, 10,* 53–62.

Rossi, E. L., & Smith, M. (1990). The eternal quest: Hidden rhythms of stress and healing in everyday life. *Psychological Perspectives, 21*(2), 6–23.

Rothenberg, A. (1988). *The creative process of psychotherapy.* New York: Norton.

Siegelman, E. Y. (1990). *Metaphor and meaning in psychotherapy.* New York: Guilford Press.

Spence, D. (1987). *The Freudian metaphor.* New York: Norton.

Steckler, J. (1992). The utilization of hypnosis in psychotherapy: Metaphor and transformation. *Psychiatric Medicine, 10*(1): 41–50.

Sweetser, E. (1990). *From etymology to pragmatics.* Cambridge, England: Cambridge University Press.

Vosniadou, S. (1989). Context and the development of metaphor comprehension. *Metaphor and Symbolic Activity, 4*(3): 159–171.

Weiner, B. (1985). "Spontaneous" causal thinking. *Psychological Bulletin, 97,* 74–84.

Wright, K. (1976). Metaphor and symptom: A study of integration and its failure. *International Review of Psychoanalysis, 3,* 97–109.

Yaniv, I., & Meyer, D. E. (1987). Activation and metacognition of inaccessible stored information: Potential bases for incubation effects in problem solving. *Journal of Experimental Psychology: Learning, Memory, and Cognition, 13,* 187–205.

Zeig, J. K. (1980). *Teaching seminar with Milton H. Erickson, M.D.* New York: Brunner/Mazel.

IV

TREATING PSYCHOLOGICAL DISORDERS

15

PHOBIAS AND INTENSE FEARS: FACILITATING THEIR TREATMENT WITH HYPNOSIS

HELEN J. CRAWFORD and ARREED F. BARABASZ

Most clinical and experimental psychologists have been acquainted with clients, students, or research subjects who have described irrational and debilitating fears of specific stimuli or situations. An understanding of phobias, both their etiology and maintenance, and the role of hypnosis in their treatment should help facilitate appropriate referrals and increase the probability of successful outcomes.

Several treatment approaches have been shown to be effective. This chapter concentrates on the use of hypnosis in the treatment of phobias as an adjunct to cognitive therapy, behavior therapy, insight therapy, and other approaches. We will review experimental research that finds that the effectiveness of hypnosis in the treatment of phobias seems to be related to the often high hypnotic responsivity of phobics and their unusual capacity for imagery vividness, focused attention, and flexibility in information-

We greatly appreciate the insightful comments and suggestions made by Thomas Ollendick and Fred Frankel to an earlier version of this chapter.

processing strategies. We will also review investigations of the relationship between hypnotizability and phobias that implicate cognitive skills such as imagery, absorption, and dissociative-like attention that may be used in the development and maintenance of phobias. These characteristics of highly hypnotizable persons may provide insight into the etiologies of phobias, as well as into the intricate expression of phobias in a complex interplay of affective, cognitive, and physiological reactions. Because hypnotizability has been shown to be related to therapeutic outcome when hypnosis is used, we will show how the standardized testing of hypnotic susceptibility level during clinical evaluations may facilitate the choice of the most appropriate therapeutic approach. Two case studies, a school-phobic child and a phobia of a single phase of airplane flight activity, are presented to illustrate the importance of the assessment of hypnotic susceptibility and the tailoring of the particular hypnotic intervention in a wider therapeutic context to fit the characteristics of the individual. The importance of concurrent psychophysiological evaluation as an index of the client's arousal to anxiety-producing stimuli prior to and during therapy is demonstrated in both cases. Finally, our review points out strengths and limitations of present theory and research. We hope to stimulate interest in further experimental and clinical research with normal and clinical populations.

CLINICAL APPLICATIONS

Overview of Phobias: Types and Prevalence

Phobias are thought to be on a continuum with intense fears (e.g., I. M. Marks, 1969, 1987). They are typically characterized by anxiety reactions to a stimulus or situation, which cannot be controlled voluntarily. They lead to an active or passive avoidance of the feared stimulus, which persists over an extended period of time. Phobias are classified among "anxiety disorders" in the revised third edition of the *Diagnostic and Statistical Manual of Mental Disorders* (American Psychiatric Association, 1987) and among "neurotic disorders" in the *International Classification of Diseases* (World Health Organization, 1992). There are a wide variety of specific or simple phobias (including animals, blood, tissue injury, closed spaces, and air travel), as well as social phobias and simple agoraphobia without panic attacks.

Similar factor structures of common fears are found in phobic and nonphobic psychiatric populations (e.g., Arrindell, 1980; Arrindell, Emmelkamp, & van der Ende, 1984; Arrindell et al., 1990; Tomlin et al., 1984), college student populations (e.g., Arrindell et al., 1984; A. M. Brown & Crawford, 1988), the elderly (A. M. Brown, 1987), and children (Ollendick, 1983; Ollendick, King, & Frary, 1989). The most frequently occurring factors are fears of interpersonal events (e.g., social evaluation or social interaction) and fears associated with death, physical pain, and surgery. Fears of animals and insects appear fairly consistently. A fear of environmental concerns sometimes occurs (Arrindell, 1980; A. M. Brown & Crawford, 1988). A general fear factor has not been found (e.g., Arrindell, 1980; Arrindell et al., 1984), suggesting possible etiological differences among these fear factors.

The frequency of phobias in clinical practice is probably not an accurate reflection of their prevalence in the general population. For instance, although agoraphobics constituted only 8% of all phobics in an interview survey in a Vermont community (Agras, Sylvester, & Oliveau, 1969), between 50% and 60% of all phobics under treatment are agoraphobic (for a review, see I. M. Marks, 1987). Phobias of natural events (e.g., thunderstorms or darkness) are underrepresented in psychiatric clinics (I. M. Marks, 1969).

Women and girls report experiencing intense fears and phobias more often than do men and boys (e.g., A. M. Brown & Crawford, 1988; I. M. Marks, 1969, 1987; Ollendick et al., 1989). Similarly, substantially more women seek therapy for phobias than do men (e.g., I. M. Marks, 1987). In a large college population (Brown & Crawford, 1988), one or more extremely intense fears on the Fear Survey Schedule (FSS–III; Wolpe & Lang, 1964) were reported by 59% of the men (range = 1–30; M = 4.21 intense fears) and 78% of the women (range = 1–40; M = 7.16). In light of these findings, it would seem important to assess whether or not additional phobic or anxiety sensitivities may be occurring in all phobic patients.

Clinical Treatment of Phobias

A plethora of therapeutic approaches have been attempted, and the effectiveness of interventions that emphasize imagery has been demonstrated (e.g., A. F. Barabasz, 1977; Habeck & Sheikh, 1984; McGuinness, 1984). Both common and uncommon phobias have been treated successfully with hypnosis as the focused attentional method with behavioral (including systematic desensitization, cognitive desensitization, emotive imagery, and flooding) or psychodynamic (including uncovering, abreaction, and insight) treatment strategies (for reviews, see A. F. Barabasz, 1977; Humphreys, 1986; Kluft, 1986; McGuinness, 1984).

Imagery can produce neurophysiological and affective response patterns similar or identical to those evoked by veridical phobia-producing stimuli (e.g., A. F. Barabasz & Barabasz, 1981; Cook, Melamed, Cuthbert, McNeil, & Lang, 1988). Behavior and cognitive therapies are concerned with how phobias may be acquired by learning. In contrast, psychodynamic approaches emphasize the use of imagery as a means to ascertain the symbolic meanings and, ultimately, the etiology of the phobia. Clinicians using these approaches have found that the introduction of hypnosis with moderately to highly hypnotically responsive individuals can often produce a state in which the client is more relaxed or attentively focused. These clients are open to presented suggestions to reduce the neurophysiological and affective responses to phobia-producing stimuli. Only recently have studies (reviewed below) explored the predictors of successful hypnotic intervention so that therapists can maximize effectiveness.

On the basis of the classical conditioning paradigm, systematic desensitization and in vivo exposure, both counterconditioning techniques, have been the primary approach in behavior therapy for the treatment of phobias (e.g., I. M. Marks, 1987; Wolpe, 1969; Wolpe & Lazarus, 1966). Systematic desensitization relies heavily on imagery to create a hierarchy of anxiety-provoking situations surrounding the phobia. The patient is asked to visualize hierarchical imagery from least to most anxiety producing in temporal contiguity, while experiencing a relaxed state antagonistic to anxiety in order to countercondition the phobic responses. Other related imagery-based therapies that have been used successfully to treat phobias include covert reinforcement, implosive therapy, covert modeling, guided imagining, paradoxical intention, and rational emotive therapy (for a review, see Habeck & Sheikh, 1984).

Behavior therapists have found that the introduction of hypnosis during systematic desensitization and other behavioral techniques can enhance the therapeutic effectiveness of the treatment. For instance, S. Wolpe and Lazarus (1966) noted, "In about one-third of our cases desensitization is performed under hypnosis. . . . In those who are difficult to hypnotize and in those who for any reason object to it, hypnosis is abandoned, and they are told instead to close eyes and relax according to instructions" (p. 79). The explicit use of authoritative, hypnoticlike suggestions abounds in systematic desensitization, although hypnosis per se is often not used (e.g., McGuinness, 1984).

Knowledge of the origin and development of phobias presented by patients may assist in choosing the most effective treatment approach. There are multiple pathways to fear, including direct conditioning, vicarious learning, and instruction/information (A. F. Barabasz, 1977; Rachman, 1977). Although it has often been assumed that most phobic patients experienced direct conditioning, "it is evident that one half to one third of such patients do not attribute their serious fears and phobias to such events. . . . Moreover, a majority of highly fearful nonphobic subjects also report indirect paths of fear acquisition" (Ollendick & King, 1991, p. 117). In large samples of American and Australian children (ages 9 to 14), fearful children "attributed the onset of their fears to vicarious and instructional factors (56% and 89%, respectively), rather than to direct conditioning events (36%)" (Ollendick & King, 1991, p. 121). These apparently alternate pathways of fear are most likely interactive rather than independent.

Assuming that direct conditioning of the phobia has occurred, some therapists advocate the uncovering of the origin of phobias, sometimes in a hypnotic context. Psychodynamically oriented therapists may use hypnotic age regression as a means to elicit memories about the origins of phobias and other childhood-produced traumas for subsequent exploration in hypnosis or waking (e.g., D. Brown & Fromm, 1986, 1987). However, it must be recognized that hypnotically recalled memories may be pseudomemories with no real basis, even though the individual recalling them feels extremely confident that they are actual memories (for a review, e.g., see Orne, Whitehouse, Dinges, & Orne, 1988). Because hypnotically recalled memories may be inaccurate reconstructions or completely false, they always need to be independently collaborated if used outside of the therapeutic context (e.g., forensic purposes).

Cognitive–behavioral therapy may attempt to restructure "cognitively" the original pathogenic situation in order to make the memory no longer anxiety producing (Meichenbaum, 1977). Again, the implicit assumption is that the recalled memory has, in fact, some basis. This recalled memory is then restructured through the use of suggestions and active imaginal rehearsals so that negative beliefs and affects related to it are altered. Such cognitive restructuring has been used under hypnosis, often with the use of guided imagery and hypnotic age regression as a presumed facilitator of memories, to relieve anxieties and eliminate phobic responding (e.g., Kossak, 1987; Lamb, 1985). Ellis (1984, 1987) also reports that hypnosis combined with rational emotive therapy can assist in disputing irrational belief systems.

Other closely related behavioral procedures are flooding done in vivo and implosion done imaginally, in which the client is encouraged to stay with the situation, real or imagined, until anxiety is decreased. Hypnosis combined with flooding has been found to facilitate the extinguishing of the phobic response (e.g., Bushnell & Barabasz, 1975; Scrignar, 1981).

Clinicians, when considering alternate therapeutic approaches, should evaluate whether presenting phobias occur alone, with other phobias or fears, or as part of a larger psychological problem (e.g., part of a depressive disorder, panic disorder, or posttraumatic stress syndrome). Many simple and complex phobias are prime candidates for the introduction of hypnosis as an adjunct in therapy.

CASE MATERIAL

The hypnosis literature is replete with reports of cases of highly hypnotizable persons treated successfully with hypnotic interventions. Little can be said about the specificity of hypnosis in, or for that matter about the scientific rigor of, case reports in which hypnotizability per se was not assessed (A. F. Barabasz & Barabasz, 1992). To be meaningful, assessment of hypnotizability must be by standardized tests with acceptable psychometric properties. Clinical conclusions about susceptibility and depth of hypnosis are meaningless without systematic testing data.

Two phobia cases presented below, a school-phobic child and a phobia of a single phase of flight activity in an airline transport pilot, were chosen from the clinical practice of Arreed F. Barabasz. Both cases met with failure in prior traditional, nonhypnotic treatment interventions and thus illustrate how subsequent hypnosis can serve as a successful treatment modality in difficult cases. Both cases illustrate the importance of the assessment of hypnotic susceptibility and the tailoring of the particular hypnotic intervention, in a wider therapeutic context, to fit the characteristics of the individual. The school-phobic child was highly hypnotizable, whereas the second case was unique in that the pilot initially plateaued at a very low level of hypnotizability but, through exposure to restricted environmental stimulation, an environmental manipulation that can easily be incorporated by clinicians with the use of a quiet, sound-attenuated room, became substantially more responsive to hypnotic suggestions. Additionally, the latter case introduces a new eyes-open, focused-attention form of hypnosis.

Each case emphasizes the importance of a psychophysiological evaluation of a client's skin conductance response (SCR) and peripheral pulse volume (PPV) response to imagined hierarchy stimuli prior to and during therapy. Silver/silver chloride electrodes are attached to the distal phalanges of the second and third digits of the client's left (nondominant) hand to measure SCR using standardized procedures (Lykken & Venables, 1971). A photoelectric phlethesmographic pulse transducer is attached to this hand's fifth digit to obtain heart rate and PPV data (A. F. Barabasz, 1977, pp. 127–134).

A clinician can be misled by the fact that a client's anxiety reactions are experienced in a specific context that represents only the occasion for the fear and not its actual source (A. F. Barabasz, 1977, p. 135). Because anxiety imagery has been shown to produce SCR and/or PPV arousal responses that resemble responses to actual stimuli (A. F. Barabasz & Barabasz, 1981), a psychophysiological evaluation serves to help order and reorder hierarchies and to identify anxiety-producing stimuli that might otherwise be missed as relevant (A. F. Barabasz, 1977, p. 137). The procedure also often serves to identify specific stimuli that can then be targeted by tailored hypnotic suggestions.

Incorporated during therapy, the psychophysiological measures provide the therapist with a continuous index of the client's arousal to various visualization stimuli. The scene need be repeated only until arousal has significantly diminished, and there is no need for the patient to be distracted by concerns as to whether he or she should raise a finger to signal anxiety to the therapist, as is required by traditional methodology. This continuous flow of physiological data can also help determine relative degrees of relaxation in response to initial instructions. The displaying of arousal by SCR or decreases in PPV may indicate mind wandering and disattention, something that can be addressed immediately by asking the patient to refocus his or her attention in the desired direction (A. F. Barabasz, 1977, p. 138). This physiological evaluation serves as an independent assessment of the success (or failure) of the therapeutic intervention and guides the therapist in tailoring subsequent interventions.

The Case of the School Phobic

Lynn was a school phobic. At age 11, she had missed the entire previous 5th-grade year, during which time she had been seen by a variety of counselors and clinical psychologists. Medication, client-centered, family therapy, and classical systematic desensitization interventions had been attempted without success.

Lynn claimed to be highly motivated to return to school, noting that she had "gotten close to getting back in with the system of desensitization." She had learned to respond to relaxation training and had constructed an elaborate, and apparently logical, school-related hierarchy with a previous psychologist. The hierarchy included items thought to be anxiety provoking, such as being asked to stand up in class and called on to recite multiplication tables, taking examinations, and being involved in group activities in front of a teacher. Her attempt at classical systematic desensitization included in vivo sessions but succeeded only in getting her to visit the school grounds after months of treatment.

Hypnosis was discussed and accepted by her as a way of improving the quality of the relaxation achieved in her previous therapy. Myths about hypnosis were debunked, and she was happy to learn that hypnosis had been shown to help make desensitization more successful. She readily participated in the administration of the Stanford Hypnotic Clinical Scale for Children (SHCSC; Morgan & Hilgard, 1978–1979), scoring 4 points out of a possible 5 and failing only the age-regression item.

The psychophysiological evaluation of Lynn's SCR and PPV response to imagined hierarchy stimuli (A. F. Barabasz, 1977) was extremely valuable. The evaluation revealed substantial inconsistencies in arousal produced by hierarchy stimuli, which invalidated the order of the hierarchy that had been produced previously in unsuccessful therapy using traditional methodology. For Lynn, the greatest physiologically arousal-producing item was opening the door to the school building on a regular school-day morning, a stimulus that had been placed near the bottom of the original hierarchy in earlier therapy.

Because a new school year had just begun and Lynn had already missed over a week of attendance, it was decided to conduct intensive therapy sessions on a daily basis, including Saturday and Sunday. The hierarchy was reordered to reflect correctly the psychophysiological arousal responses. After a SHCSC relaxation induction, densensitization sessions were conducted in hypnosis. SCR and PPV were monitored continuously during exposure to images of hierarchy stimuli with hypnotic instructions for calmness and deep relaxation. Rather than depending on the counterconditioning effects of the simple counterposing of relaxation with anxiety-producing imagery, direct hypnotic suggestions were given to accelerate progress through the hierarchy and to overcome anxiety-producing stimuli that failed to show psychophysiological arousal reductions upon repetition. For example, Lynn was told, "The next time I give you the scene, just as in real life, your anxiety level will be much, much lower; you will be able to relax throughout the visualization and when you do it for real. Now, once again, just imagine. . . ." The entire hierarchy was mastered in only four 50-minute sessions.

Because Lynn had demonstrated the capacity to respond to the SHCSC posthypnotic suggestion, she agreed to use hypnosis to establish a "special feeling of calmness" when opening the door to the school building (this had been revealed in the preliminary psychophysiological evaluation to be the most anxiety-producing stimulus). An appropriate physiological response to the suggestion was confirmed by both SCR and PPV. Arrangements were also made to enroll Lynn in a different school to avoid her concerns about being teased with regard to her missing school during the previous year. It was also agreed that the present therapist would provide transportation for Lynn for her first day in school so as not to rekindle her parents' previous patterns of apprehension. After a total of only six daily sessions, including her initial evaluation, Lynn entered the school building yawning as she opened the door.

A follow-up revealed that she had missed fewer than 6 school days in 3 years, carried a B average, and been active in intramural sporting activities. No other phobic reactions or other behavioral disorders were reported.

The Case of the Fearful Airline Pilot

Mr. M., a physically fit, 48-year-old airline pilot, had over 16,000 hours of flight experience, including 2 years of combat service during the Vietnam War and subsequently as an air transport pilot, with no history of stressful reactions. Suddenly, one night he became fearful: "I lost confidence three years ago, becoming afraid we'd [the flight crew] left something out [missed a checklist item] inside the marker [final descent path of a precision instrument approach] in some weather with minimum fuel." The landing was uneventful, but he reported he "felt palpitations . . . so weak [and] incapacitated." Paramedics rushed him to the emergency room and "days of hospital tests" revealed no abnormalities. He concluded he was a victim of food poisoning and vowed "never to eat harbor trout again."

Within a week, Mr. M. requested a workout on the airline's flight simulator, something routinely done by pilots, and reported he "felt great" and was told "I handled more emergencies in there than he'd [the check pilot] seen anyone do in a long time." A few days later he flew commercially again and reported that all went well until the approach to the third destination: "This time it was worse than before, cold and hot at the same time, weak and lightheaded, and afraid for no apparent reason." He turned the controls over to the first officer, who completed the approach and landing. On subsequent flights, all appeared normal until the approach to landing, when the symptoms returned "again and again" with increasing severity and accompanying further losses of confidence.

During the following 3 years, Mr. M. did not fly as a commercial pilot. He felt a strong responsibility to be "fully physically and mentally capable in the cockpit." His Federal Aviation Agency medical certificate was revoked. Convinced that he had an undiagnosed physical problem, he underwent over 20 workups (including extensive EEG and CAT scan, as well as neurological, abdominal, immunological, and allergy evaluations), all without any abnormal finding.

Psychological and psychiatric evaluations were completed independently at highly reputable institutions. Mild depression was diagnosed and treated with various antidepressant medications. All medications were abandoned because of severe side effects. Panic disorder was ruled out because the symptoms, which occurred even in flight simulator situations, were expected by him in response to a highly specific set of stimuli occurring in only a single phase of flight. Because the attack was precipitated solely by exposure to a circumscribed phobic stimulus, a *DSM–III–R* (American Psychiatric Association, 1987) diagnosis of a simple phobia (300.29) was agreed on. Systematic desensitization was attempted on different occasions by two independent psychologists, who both noted that Mr. M. was highly cooperative. No evidence of improvement occurred in the 18 to 20 desensitization sessions. Mr. M. concluded that he had learned another way to relax but noted that "the cockpit is no place to be relaxing with a hundred people sitting behind you . . . depending on you."

Next, Mr. M. was referred to Arreed F. Barabasz by a large eastern U.S. medical facility, and he flew to Washington state for 4 days of consecutive treatment lasting from 6 to 9 hours daily. Such intensive treatment over a few days can be quite effective and is used by Barabasz, as well as by Helen H. Watkins and John G. Watkins (J. G. Watkins, personal communication, October, 1990) in Montana, with clients traveling from other areas of the United States. Mr. M. presented himself as highly motivated to fly again because "this is what I want more than anything." Rapport seemed well established after 4 hours of discussion about his phobic symptomatology and psychological well-being and after introductory information about hypnosis, practice with simple imaginative activities, and observation of a moderately hypnotizable laboratory assistant being hypnotized in a demonstration. Mr. M. was intrigued to learn that hypnosis had been used to enhance instrument flight performance for military pilots (A. F. Barabasz, 1985). Recognizing its scientific basis, he was eager to undergo formal hypnosis testing. Rapport was enhanced by the psychologist's background as a commercial pilot and former flight instructor.

The administration of the Stanford Hypnotic Clinical Scale for Adults (SHCSA; Morgan & Hilgard, 1978–1979) resulted in a score of 1 out of 5, a demonstration of low hypnotizability that was disappointing to the patient.

To ascertain that physiological arousal actually accompanied his phobic experiences, SCR and PPV were measured during flight simulation. An instrument flight simulator capable of being "flown" through complex precision instrument flight regimes, including the full instrument landing system (ILS) approach (his phobia centered around this aspect of flight), was first flown by Barabasz to familiarize Mr. M. with its flight characteristics and reduce the potential of any surprise-related artifacts in the psychophysiological recording. In less than 15 minutes at the flight simulator, Mr. M. reported himself confident and ready to "shoot an ILS."

Mr. M. flew the simulator with exquisite precision from start to finish, including the ILS approach. When the blue panel light flashed to announce the beginning of the final descent path, Mr. M. showed anticipatory anxiety and stated, "I might need some help here." At this same point in time, his SCR, PPV, and heart rate measures showed intense arousal: 60%–100% or greater than his normal tonic levels. Yet he completed the "flight" quite safely and with remarkable accuracy. During each of four subsequent flights, Mr. M.'s physiological responses showed the same dramatic arousal, with no indications of reduced intensity upon repeated exposure to the anxiety-provoking stimulus. (Because of normal day-to-day variations in general SCR responsiveness, session-to-session data was evaluated using Lykken and Venables's [1971] startle response procedure at the start of each session.) There were no apparent habituation effects. At the point of flight in question, Mr. M. explained that he felt "light-headedness and loss of confidence. It makes no sense, does it?" Despite the safe laboratory situation, he showed dramatic physiological reactivity and fearful ideation. He viewed the reactions as identical to his in-flight problems.

It can be therapeutically useful for patients who are knowledgeable of the scientific approach to read relevant research as a means of reinforcing their understanding of and commitment to the intervention. Thus, Mr. M. read relevant studies of clinical and experimental hypnosis and restricted environmental stimulation (REST), both therapeutic techniques commonly used by Arreed F. Barabasz. After reading that instrument flight performance was significantly improved after exposure to flotation REST (Melchiori & Barabasz, 1990) and that REST (A. F. Barabasz, 1982) enhanced hypnotic performance, Mr. M. requested a flotation REST experience "before we do anything else . . . I think this could really help me and improve my hypnotic skills too."

Using the usual 1-hour duration, Mr. M. floated supine on a 20% (D = 1.30 g/cc) solution of tap water and epson salts (24 cm deep at 34.2 °C) in a sound-attenuated light-free fiberglass tank (Floatarium Model SWS) that resembled an enclosed bathtub. Upon leaving the tank, he was administered the Stanford Hypnotic Susceptibility Scale, Form C (SHSS:C; Weitzenhoffer & Hilgard, 1962) and given posthypnotic suggestions of calmness during subsequent flights, particularly during the crucial anxiety-producing part of the flight. He described himself as "more relaxed than I can remember," but again showed low hypnotizability (3 out of a possible 12 on the SHSS:C). He reported, "I think I felt a little hypnotized this time." Consistent with the literature (A. F. Barabasz & Kaplan, 1989; M. Barabasz, Barabasz, & O'Neill, 1991; Miller, Barabasz, & Barabasz, 1991) the demand characteristics of the intervention were not enough to produce a significant increase on the objective measure of hypnotizability. Enthusiastically, he flew the simulator again, demonstrating a virtually flawless instrument flight performance. At the outer marker point of the ILS approach, Mr. M. once again showed the same dramatic increases in autonomic arousal. The psychophysiological data and symptoms were then discussed.

On the third day, Mr. M. happily consented to experiencing REST in a sound-attenuated, double-doored chamber. Wax earplugs (20-db reduction) were worn in this light-free environment for the usual 6-hour period (A. F. Barabasz, 1982; A. F. Barabasz & Barabasz, 1989). It should be noted that any therapist can produce an excellent sound-attenuated REST chamber by simply adding inexpensive sound-proofing (costing a few hundred dollars at most) to existing facilities (see Suedfeld, 1980). Thus, similar environmental conditions can easily be achieved by clinicians through the use of a darkened, quiet room. Clients wear inexpensive earplugs and eye masks to achieve a sound-attenuated, light-free environment. Muted sounds that may come through do not disturb clients, and monitoring can easily be achieved using a simple intercom.

As in flotation REST, Mr. M. was monitored continuously using an audio intercommunications system. After exposure, Mr. M. scored 9 out of 12 points on the SHSS:C, a dramatic increase in hypnotizability to a moderately high level. Although chamber REST (A. F. Barabasz, 1982) is known to enhance hypnotic susceptibility, more recent research (A. F. Barabasz & Kaplan, 1989) has shown that flotation REST does not, as was also the case for Mr. M. However, flotation REST has been shown to provide an induction alternative for subjects of known high hypnotic capacity (A. F. Barabasz, 1990).

On the same day, after a discussion of the REST experience and its implications, relaxation instructions from the SHCSA were read. Mr. M. rated his depth of hypnosis as being quite deep. The following posthypnotic suggestion was then administered and repeated three times: "When you near the outer marker you will feel well, calm, confident, and alert. You have the power, the control, the confidence, and no outside force controls you." Mr. M. was taken out of hypnosis, and he commented positively about the suggestion.

The use of alternative forms of hypnosis helps to insure the maximization of responsiveness and serves to reinforce the posthypnotic suggestion. Therefore, Mr. M. was rehypnotized using the brief (30-s) eyeball set induction of rolling one's eyes up while they remain closed. The posthypnotic suggestion was then readministered, and additional alert focused attention suggestions emphasized his ability to reinforce the suggestions with self-hypnosis. Self-hypnosis procedures were introduced and taught at this time. Because of Mr. M.'s previously discussed concern about alertness while flying, the traditional relaxation hypnotic induction was contraindicated and, instead, a new eyes-open, focused attention form of self-hypnosis was introduced. This newly developed technique, used successfully with military pilots (A. F. Barabasz, 1985) to enhance sustained vigilance and attentional processing, is described below.

Subsequent to hypnosis, it was explained that the posthypnotic suggestion could be reinforced at any time by focused-attention self-hypnosis with eyes open, so that he could still maintain an especially alert state in the cockpit environment. Mr. M. was given the above posthypnotic suggestion and self-hypnosis instructions in writing to take with him as an additional reinforcer to ensure that self-hypnosis would be practiced (A. F. Barabasz, Baer, Sheehan, & Barabasz, 1986). At the end of the session he felt "quite sure I'm going into hypnosis, but the real test will be to see what happens to my symptoms at the marker (in simulated and actual flight)."

To promote transfer of the posthypnotic suggestion and self-hypnosis to the flying environment, Mr. M. once again flew in the flight instrument simulator. Before beginning, Mr. M. learned to (a) concentrate on his breathing for a moment, feeling the calm of breathing out; (b) brush his forehead with a hand as a sign for self-hypnotic responding; and (c) give the posthypnotic suggestions to himself while remaining alert. The first simulated flight was performed flawlessly, with a full ILS approach. In dramatic contrast with all previous simulated flights, Mr. M. showed no significant changes in physiological arousal on the laboratory measures. No symptoms of lightheadedness or fear were reported despite his expectations that they might occur. Subsequently, Mr. M. performed an actual flight with no debilitating fears or abnormal physiological arousal felt.

For the next 5 months, Mr. M. underwent extensive flight simulator training provided by his employer. He was also subjected to a variety of physical and psychological tests. He regained his Federal Aviation Agency first-class medical certificate and flight crew status. He once again began flying for his company.

Regular telephone follow-ups were conducted over a period of 18 months after his return to flight status. As is quite common in such phobic cases, Mr. M. reported that he continued to expect that he would not handle the approach well, and it took over 100 approaches before this expectation of symptoms finally disappeared. Other than a brief bout with influenza, Mr. M. remained on active flight status. He reported remaining symptom-free and using the focused attention self-hypnosis "every once in a while still, about once a week, just because it feels good." Mr. M. has been promoted to captain and retained for flight of larger jet aircraft.

Theoretical Implications of the School Phobia and Airline Phobia Case Studies

These case studies suggest that the success of traditional desensitization techniques may be greatly enhanced and expedited by their being administered during hypnosis to individuals responsive to hypnosis (A. F. Barabasz, 1977). Hypnosis provides a more focused attentional state in which an individual can often imagine environmental stimuli more intensely and with greater involvement (e.g., A. F. Barabasz, 1982; Crawford, 1989), thereby producing a much more realistic, in-vivo-like experience. In addition, greater responsiveness to suggestions, often those typically given in traditional desensitization, is found in hypnosis. Thus, we argue that direct suggestions given in hypnosis can accelerate progress through the hierarchy and help clients overcome anxiety arousal. Posthypnotic suggestions assist clients to confront once-anxiety-producing stimuli in the in vivo, once-phobic-producing environment with greater ease and calmness.

The psychophysiological evaluation of fear-producing stimuli prior to therapy provides the therapist with the entire hierarchy, often illuminating specific stimuli that would otherwise be missed. Such was the case in the school phobic. This physiological evaluation directs the order in which each stimulus is addressed in desensitization sessions. Concurrent physiological evaluations during therapy provide immediate feedback to the clinician as to whether or not the client is attending, as well as immediate feedback that arousal has significantly diminished for a certain scene, thereby eliminating the traditional distracting finger signal of anxiety reduction.

The airline phobia case illustrates the addition of several new aspects to the treatment of phobics with hypnosis, as well as the importance of a continuing rapport and the patient's complete understanding of all procedures. This case seems to support the notion, discussed below, that adequate hypnotic capability is essential to treatment success when hypnosis is used. Most important is the demonstration that a virtual nonresponder to hypnosis can become moderately to highly hypnotizable through the use of 6 hours of chamber REST. This finding is consistent with studies of REST in natural (e.g., A. F. Barabasz, 1980, 1984; A. F. Barabasz & Gregson, 1979; M. Barabasz, Barabasz, & Mullin, 1983), experimental laboratory (e.g., A. F. Barabasz, 1982; A. F. Barabasz & Barabasz, 1989; A. F. Barabasz & Kaplan, 1989), and other clinical (e.g., A. F. Barabasz et al., 1986; M. Barabasz, 1987) settings. Such findings have been conceptualized within Hilgard's (1986) neodissociation theory (e.g., A. F. Barabasz, 1982, 1993). The dramatic reduction of external stimuli during REST permits a possible re-organization of cognitive functioning (e.g., Tart, 1975) so that some individuals are subsequently open to experiencing hypnotic phenomena. Although much more research needs to be conducted in this area, it seems clear that the normally highly stable trait of hypnotizability can be modified by REST.

Finally, the airline phobia case introduces an alternative form of hypnosis. The eyes-open, focused-attention hypnotic induction seemed to fit the client's concerns about the inappropriateness of feeling relaxed in the cockpit. Closed eyes are not necessary for the induction of hypnosis and may in fact be counterindicated when self-hypnosis is used in the workplace. Similarly, a continuing alertness with focused and sustained attention is crucial in such conditions (A. F. Barabasz, 1985).

RESEARCH AND APPRAISAL

In the previous sections we have reviewed the prevalence and types of phobias, clinical applications for the treatment of phobias, with an emphasis on hypnosis, and finally two case studies. We now turn to the underlying question of why and when hypnosis potentiates therapeutic outcome in the treatment of phobias.

On the basis of an analysis of numerous case studies in the literature, as well as of his own patients, Frankel (1974) proposed that there may be a "similarity between phobic panic states and an experience of trance" (p. 263). This has led to more thorough conceptualizations, often within a neodissociation theoretical framework (e.g., Hilgard, 1986), of how certain cognitive abilities may play roles not only in the development of the ability for trance and hypnotic responsiveness, but also in the development and maintenance of intense fears and phobias.

Vivid imagery, absorption, and dissociative-like, extremely focused attentional skills have been hypothesized as playing roles in the development of the ability for hypnotic responsiveness and trance (e.g., Crawford, 1982, 1989, 1990; Crawford, Brown, & Moon, in press; Tellegen & Atkinson, 1974). Such skills may be responsible in part for reported relationships between hypnotizability and certain psychological disorders such as hysteria, fugue states, posttraumatic stress disorder (D. Spiegel & Cardeña, 1991;

D. Spiegel, Hunt, & Dondershine, 1988; Stutman & Bliss, 1985), multiple personalities (e.g., Bliss, 1986), bulimia (e.g., M. Barabasz, 1991; Pettinati, Horne, & Staats, 1985), and phobias and intense fears (A. Brown & Crawford, 1986; Crawford, Brown, & Heyman, 1991). A review of the literature finds that there is often a strongly significant relationship between hypnotizability and these disorders. Quite commonly, researchers finding positive relationships interpret them in terms of an underlying common dissociative-like capacity that may be used either adaptively, as in hypnosis, or maladaptively, as when used as a defense or coping mechanism.

Relationships Between Hypnotizability and Phobia Presence

Heightened hypnotic susceptibility has often been associated, albeit not consistently, with phobic disorders in case study reports (e.g., Frankel, 1974, 1976) and studies in clinical phobic populations (for a summary, see Table 1). Bushnell and Barabasz (1975) reported that 60% of a group of claustrophobics were highly hypnotizable. Frankel and Orne (1976) reported that in a group of 25 general phobics, 58% were highly hypnotizable and "not a single nonresponsive individual was seen" (p. 1260). Kelly (1984) found a higher than normal proportion of medium and high hypnotizables in a general population of phobic patients. General phobic patients referred to the Department of Psychiatry at the University of Melbourne, Australia, were almost all medium (48%) or high (48%) hypnotizables (Foenander, Burrows, Gerschman, & Horne, 1980). In a group of 20 Canadian women phobic to snakes, spiders, or rats, 55% were high hypnotizables, 20% medium, and 25% low hypnotizables (John, Hollander, & Perry, 1983). In Australia, dental phobics are apparently much more highly hypnotizable than the general population or other patients with chronic orofacial pain (Gerschman, Burrows, Reade, & Foenander, 1979; Gerschman, Burrows, & Reade, 1987). High hypnotizability in Vietnam veterans experiencing posttraumatic stress syndrome has been reported as well (D. Spiegel et al., 1988; Stutman & Bliss, 1985).

Three studies (Frischholz, Spiegel, Spiegel, Balma, & Markell, 1982; D. Spiegel, Frischholz, Maruffi, & Spiegel, 1981; Owens, Bliss, Koester, & Jeppsen, 1990) found phobics not to be higher in hypnotizability than the general population or other psychiatric groups. D. Spiegel et al. (1981) found no such relationship in a group of flying phobics, an environmentally based phobia, and concluded that a major confound of previous studies was a lack of control for age differences between phobia and comparison groups. Frischholz et al. (1982) found no relationships within various kinds of phobic groups, but their Ns were quite small. Most recently, Owens et al. (1990) observed no relationships when using a more cognitively oriented measure of hypnotizability. Although Owens et al. suggested that the previous studies may have been biased in some undetermined manner in their

TABLE 1
Clinical Studies That Evaluated the Hypnotizability Level of Phobics Under Treatment

Study	Patient population	N	Hypnotic scale*	Membership in hypnotic groups (%)		
				Low	Medium	High
Positive relationships found						
Bushnell & Barabasz (1975)	claustrophobics	20	SHCSA	10	30	60
Frankel & Orne (1976)	general phobics	24	HGSHS or SHSS:A	0	42	58
Foenander et al. (1980)	general phobics	33	HGSHS	6	48	45
Gerschman et al. (1979)	dental phobics	40	DRS	17.5	35	47.5
Gerschman et al. (1987)	dental phobics	130	DRS	5	47.5	47.5
Kelly (1984)	general phobics	19	SHCSA; HIP	0	21	79
John et al. (1983)	animal phobics	20	HGSHS	25	20	55
No relationships found						
Frischholz et al. (1982)	general phobics	95	HIP	not provided		
Owens et al. (1990)	general phobics	25	SHSS:C	68	20	12
D. Spiegel et al. (1981)	flying phobics	178	HIP	34	66	

Note: SHCSA = Stanford Hypnotic Clinical Scale for Adults (Morgan & Hilgard, 1978–1979); SHSS:A = Stanford Hypnotic Susceptibility Scale, Form A (Weitzenhoffer & Hilgard, 1959); SHSS:C = Stanford Hypnotic Susceptibility Scale, Form C (Weitzenhoffer & Hilgard, 1962); HGSHS = Harvard Group Scale of Hypnotic Susceptibility (Shor & Orne, 1962); HIP = Hypnotic Induction Profile (H. Spiegel, 1973); DRS = Diagnostic Rating Scale (Orne & O'Connell, 1967). Reprinted with permission from Crawford et al. (1991).

selection of phobics, their own sample was biased. Advertising on the radio and in the newspaper for individuals who had had phobias for over 1 year produced a sample of individuals 80% of which had received prior therapy. They may have been "therapeutic failures." If so, it would be interesting to investigate whether low hypnotizable individuals respond less positively to certain traditional interventions (see below for a further discussion). Further research should elucidate these fascinating, although conflicting, results and may lead to further insights.

It is not uncommon for individuals to possess more than one intense fear or phobia (e.g., Bushnell & Barabasz, 1975; A. M. Brown & Crawford, 1988). Those phobics who present multiple phobias have sometimes been found to be even more highly hypnotizable than those with only single phobias (Bushnell & Barabasz, 1975; Frankel & Orne, 1976; Gerschman et al., 1987; Kelly, 1984). By contrast, Foenander et al. (1980) found dental monophobics to be more hypnotizable than polyphobics, possibly because the single phobias were more severe. Thus, severity of the phobia may further moderate relationships with hypnotizability. Owens et al. (1990) reported a nearly significant correlation ($N = 25$, $r = .33$) between phobia severity and hypnotizability.

In a nonclinical college population, those women who reported intense fears on the FSS–III were significantly more likely to be highly hypnotizable than those without intense fears (A. Brown & Crawford, 1986; Crawford et al., 1991). This relationship was present for three of the four major FSS–III factors (fear of interpersonal events; fear of animals and insects; and fear of medical–surgical procedures and interventions, as well as of bodily insults). Like several clinical studies (e.g., Frankel & Orne, 1976; Kelly, 1984), Crawford et al. (1991) also found that women who reported many multiple, intense fears were significantly more hypnotizable than those reporting fewer intense fears, possibly because of greater dissociative, absorptive, and imagery vividness propensities.

Surprisingly, only one of these clinical studies addressed gender as a possible moderating factor, yet it is potentially important because women report substantially more phobias than do men. Frischholz et al. (1982) reported no gender differences within their clinically diagnosed phobic sample. Crawford et al. (1991) found the relationship between hypnotizability and intense fears significant for women but not for men in a nonclinical college population.

To evaluate the hypothesized relationships between certain cognitive abilities and intense phobias that have been discussed but not evaluated in the clinical literature, Crawford et al. (1991) compared college students reporting few (1–5), some (6–12), and many (13–44) intense fears on the FSS–III. Those individuals who reported more multiple intense fears were significantly more hypnotizable, higher in reported visual imagery as assessed by the Vividness of Visual Imagery Questionaire (D. F. Marks, 1973), more absorptive as assessed by the Tellegen Absorption Scale (Tellegen & Atkinson, 1974), and more extremely focused in attention as assessed by a subscale of the Differential Attentional Processes Inventory (Grumbles & Crawford, 1981).

Complementary to these findings, Cook et al. (1988) presented Sheehan's (1967) modification of Betts's (1909) Questionnaire Upon Mental Imagery (QMI) to various phobic subgroups. High imagers in every group produced stronger visceral responses to their imagery than did low imagers. Overall, simple phobics were more responsive physiologically to their own phobic imagery than were social phobics. McNeil, Vrana, Melamed, Cuthbert, and Lang (1993) found that heart rate acceleration to imagery of their own phobic content was positively related to QMI imagery vividness in multiphobic and dental phobic groups but not for speech phobics. Future research along the lines of these studies could profit by examining the additional cognitive skills of hypnotic susceptibility, absorption, and extremely focused attention.

The literature has sometimes (e.g., Frankel, 1974, 1990; Frankel & Orne, 1976) implied a causal relationship between hypnosis (hypnotizability) and phobias. For instance, Frankel (1974) proposed that "the trance or hypnotic experience is invoked spontaneously as a defense mechanism against intolerable anxiety, and the accompanying social situation, or important aspects of it are then perceived in a distorted manner" (p. 261). Frankel (1990) clarified this further by saying, "Clearly, what is implied in the case of phobic patients is that individuals who are able to enter hypnotic-like conditions spontaneously—the highly hypnotizable subjects reported in the literature—presumably do so under stress, thus creating symptoms, even though neither they nor unsuspecting observers are aware of it" (p. 826). Although some case studies have indicated that this may be the case (e.g., Frankel, 1974), we are unaware of any empirical studies demonstrating that phobics commonly go into a trance at the time that they are exposed to fear-producing stimuli or situations.

In addition, we suggest that a fear is often developed and rehearsed in complete awareness (e.g., A. F. Barabasz, 1977; Rachman, 1977) and may have even been primed prior to the initial exposure to the stimulus or situation. If an individual has extremely vivid imagery and highly absorptive skills, then the intensity and vividness of subsequent imagery of the fear-producing stimulus or situation may become so exacerbated that the fear is "blown out of proportion" and becomes an intense fear or phobia (e.g., Crawford et al., 1991). Accompanying physiological reactivity may further exacerbate and reinforce the fearful imagery.

Consistent with Hilgard's (1986) neodissociation theory, we would argue that, sometimes, the resulting memories of the fear may become dissociated from immediate awareness and eventually result in a cognitive subsystem that appears to exist involuntarily, without self-control or self-awareness. It is then that the stage is more likely set for the phobia to take on dissociative qualities. Interestingly, in a sizable clinical phobic population, Lazarus (1971) found that few could recall specific experiences that led to their fears. Thus, we propose that those phobics who are amnesic to the origins of their fears may more likely be the extremely highly hypnotizables who may be inclined to possess dissociative memory subsystems. These theoretical considerations are presently being investigated more systematically.

Relationships Between Hypnotizability and Therapeutic Outcome

Given the previous discussion, it would be anticipated that moderately to highly hypnotizable individuals would show more responsiveness to hypnotic approaches, as well as to nonhypnotic but imaginally based therapeutic approaches, because of their skills in imagery and absorption.

Horowitz (1970) found a significant relationship ($r = .39$) between hypnotizability and treatment outcome in snake phobics treated in hypnosis. Gerschman et al. (1979) found highly hypnotically responsive phobics to be more favorable to hypnotic treatment of their dental phobias. Gerschman et al. (1987) reported a substantially positive correlation ($r = .54$) between hypnotizability and reduced global dental anxiety after hypnotic treatment. In a population of 178 consecutive flying phobia patients, D. Spiegel et al. (1981) found that "hypnotizable patients were over two and one half times more likely to report some positive impact than those who were found to be nonhypnotizable" when treated in a single 45-minute session involving hypnosis and a problem restructuring strategy. In a related anxiety group of panickers treated in a Hungarian psychiatric clinic, those patients who demonstrated substantial improvements with nonhypnotic treatments were significantly more hypnotizable than those who demonstrated little or no improvement (Kopp, Skrabski, Mihaly, Buza, & Ratkoczi, 1988).

In summary, those studies that have examined the relationship between hypnotizability and therapeutic outcome with hypnosis as an adjunct in treatment have consistently reported the relationship to be positive. Given these findings, it would follow that clinicians should administer standardized hypnotic scales (our preference being the SHSS:C or the shorter SHCSC or SHCSA) as part of the initial evaluation to determine the appropriateness of the use of hypnosis. The scales can also identify specific hypnotic skills (e.g., age regression) that may be relevant to the patient's treatment. Treatment methods need to be tailored to the client's individual cognitive skills as well as to their fear response-profile (see also Hugdahl, 1981).

CONCLUSION

The theoretical rationale for the use of hypnosis in the treatment of phobias and intense fears has been reviewed in this chapter. Clearly, hypnosis is a successful therapeutic adjunct that can be used with behavioral or psychodynamic treatment strategies in the treatment of intense fears and phobias in hypnotically responsive individuals (A. F. Barabasz, 1977; Humphreys, 1986; Kluft, 1986; McGuinness, 1984). Hypnosis provides a focused attentional state in which an individual can imagine environmental stimuli more intensely with greater involvement. Although beyond the scope of this chapter, we note that Crawford and Gruzelier's (1992) neuropsychophysiological model of hypnosis provides an organizing framework for understanding brain functioning shifts that accompany hypnotic phenomena.

As demonstrated in our two case studies, direct suggestions given in hypnosis accelerate progress through the hierarchy and help individuals to overcome anxiety arousal. The advantages of using hypnosis with a primary treatment strategy when working with a moderately to highly hypnotizable individual may include reduced time; increased vivid imagery; increased relaxation, focused, alert attention, or both; greater immersion in the primary anxiety situation in imagery or in vivo; greater personal control and confidence; greater responsiveness to suggestion; and the opportunity to develop self-hypnosis skills to be applied when the therapist is no longer available.

The often-found relationship between hypnotizability and phobia presence is seen not as causal but rather as due to underlying extremely vivid imagery skills and highly absorptive skills found in both high hypnotizables and a substantial number of phobics (Crawford, 1989; Crawford et al., 1991). There is no experimental evidence that individuals enter a trance at the time of exposure to anxiety-producing stimuli and thus produce a phobia out of awareness. Rather, we present an argument that the intensity and vividness of subsequent imagery of the fear-producing stimulus or situation may become so exacerbated that the fear becomes intense and eventually a full-blown phobia. Such may also be the case in posttraumatic stress disorders (e.g., D. Spiegel et al., 1988). In line with Hilgard's (1986) neodissociation theory, the fear may become dissociated from immediate awareness so that it appears to exist involuntarily. Thus, further research on the underlying cognitive abilities that moderate the hypnotizability–phobia link and tie it to dissociative processing of information is needed.

The importance of a moderate to high hypnotic susceptibility level being positively related to therapeutic outcome in the treatment of phobias and related disorders has been demonstrated in several studies, as well as in the case of the phobic airline pilot, and needs to be investigated further.

It is evident from the literature that hypnotizability is not a universal characteristic of individuals who have intense fears and phobias. Therefore, as illustrated in the two presented case studies, the standardized screening for hypnotizability level, as well as for imagery production and extremely focused attentional skills, should be part of the initial evaluation to determine the appropriateness of the use of hypnosis as an adjunct to imagery-based approaches in the treatment of phobias. That an individual is not hypnotically responsive may indicate the need for alternative therapeutic approaches or the introduction of REST techniques prior to imagery-based therapeutic approaches.

The two case studies clearly demonstrate the importance of the psychophysiological evaluation of a client's SCR and PPV response to imagined hierarchy stimuli prior to and during therapy. A psychophysiological evaluation serves to help order and reorder hierarchies and to identify anxiety-producing stimuli. Such measurement also provides an ongoing, unobtrusive evaluation of the effectiveness of anxiety-reducing techniques during therapy.

The unique case of the phobic airline pilot demonstrates how hypnosis subsequent to REST brought about dramatic reductions in physiological and psychological reactivity surrounding the phobia-producing stimulus. In line with experimental research (e.g., A. F. Barabasz, 1982, 1993; A. F. Barabasz & Barabasz, 1989; A. F. Barabasz & Kaplan, 1989), it also demonstrates the use of REST for hypnotic responsiveness enhancement in originally hypnotically nonresponsive individuals to achieve therapeutic outcomes in the desired direction. REST, which shares some similarities with hypnosis (e.g., Crawford, 1993), can easily be incorporated into regular clinical and experimental settings (Suedfeld, 1980).

REFERENCES

Agras, S., Sylvester, D., & Oliveau, D. (1969). The epidemiology of common fears and phobias. *Comprehensive Psychiatry, 10,* 151–156.

American Psychiatric Association. (1987). *Diagnostic and statistical manual of mental disorders* (3rd ed., rev.). Washington, DC: Author.

Arrindell, W. A. (1980). Dimensional structures and psychopathology of the Fear Survey Schedule (FSS–III) in a phobic population: A factorial definition of agoraphobia. *Behavior Research and Therapy, 18,* 229–242.

Arrindell, W. A., Emmelkamp, P. M. G., & van der Ende, J. (1984). Phobic dimensions: I. Reliability and generalizability across samples, gender and nations. *Advances in Behavior Research, 6,* 207–254.

Arrindell, W. A., Solyom, C., Ledwidge, B., van der Ende, J., Hageman, W. J. J. M., Solyom, K., & Zaitman, A. (1990). Cross-national validation of the five-components model of self-assessed fears: Canadian psychiatric outpatients vs. Dutch target ratings on the Fear Survey Schedule III. *Advanced Behaviour Research and Therapy, 12,* 101–122.

Barabasz, A. F. (1977). *New techniques in behavior therapy and hypnosis.* Los Angeles: Borden.

Barabasz, A. F. (1980). EEG alpha, skin conductance, and hypnotizability in Antarctica. *International Journal of Clinical and Experimental Hypnosis, 28,* 63–74.

Barabasz, A. F. (1982). Restricted environmental stimulation and the enhancement of hypnotizability: EEG alpha, skin conductance and temperature responses. *International Journal of Clinical and Experimental Hypnosis, 30,* 147–166.

Barabasz, A. F. (1984). Antarctic isolation and imaginative involvement. *International Journal of Clinical and Experimental Hypnosis, 32,* 296–300.

Barabasz, A. F. (1985, March). Enhancement of military pilot reliability by hypnosis and psychophysiological monitoring: In-flight and simulator data. *Aviation, Space and Environmental Medicine,* pp. 248–250.

Barabasz, A. F. (1990). Eingeschranke stimulation durch die Umwelt ruft spontane Hypnose fur die Schmerzkontrolle beim cold pressor test hervor. *Experimentelle und Klinishe Hypnose, 4,* 95–105.

Barabasz, A. F. (1993). Neo-dissociation accounts for pain relief and hypnotic susceptibility findings: Flotation REST elicits hypnosis. In A. F. Barabasz & M. Barabasz (Eds.), *Clinical and experimental restricted environmental stimulation: New developments and perspectives* (pp. 41–52). New York: Springer-Verlag.

Barabasz, A. F., Baer, L., Sheehan, D. V., & Barabasz, M. (1986). A three year follow-up of hypnosis and restricted environmental stimulation therapy for smoking. *International Journal of Clinical and Experimental Hypnosis, 34,* 169–191.

Barabasz, A. F., & Barabasz, M. (1981). Effects of rational–emotive therapy on psychophysiological and reported measures of test anxiety arousal. *Journal of Clinical Psychology, 37,* 511–514.

Barabasz, A. F., & Barabasz, M. (1989). Effects of restricted environmental stimulation: Enhancement of hypnotizability for experimental and chronic pain control. *International Journal of Clinical and Experimental Hypnosis, 37,* 217–223.

Barabasz, A. F., & Barabasz, M. (1992). Research designs and considerations. In E. Fromm & M. R. Nast (Eds.), *Contemporary hypnosis research* (pp. 173–200). New York: Guilford Press.

Barabasz, A. F., & Gregson, R. A. M. (1979). Antarctic wintering-over, suggestion and transient olfactor stimulation: EEG evoked potential and electrodermal responses. *Journal of Biological Psychology, 9,* 285–295.

Barabasz, A. F., & Kaplan, G. M. (1989). Effects of restricted environmental stimulation (REST) on hypnotizability: A test of alternative techniques. In D. Waxman, D. Pedersen, I. Wilke, & P. Mellott (Eds.), *Hypnosis: The 4th European Congress at Oxford* (pp. 139–145). London: Whurr.

Barabasz, M. (1987). Trichotillomania: A new treatment. *International Journal of Clinical and Experimental Hypnosis, 35,* 146–154.

Barabasz, M. (1991). Hypnotizability and bulimia. *International Journal of Eating Disorders, 10,* 117–120.

Barabasz, M., Barabasz, A. F., & Mullin, C. (1983). Effects of brief Antarctic isolation on absorption and hypnotic susceptibility: Preliminary results and recommendations. *International Journal of Clinical and Experimental Hypnosis, 31,* 235–238.

Barabasz, M., Barabasz, A. F., & O'Neill, M. (1991). The effect of experimental context, demand characteristics and situational cues: New data. *Perceptual and Motor Skills, 73,* 83–93.

Betts, G. H. (1909). *The distribution and functions of mental imagery* (Contributions to Education Series, No. 26). New York: Columbia University Teachers College.

Bliss, E. L. (1986). *Multiple personality, allied disorders and hypnosis.* New York: Oxford University Press.

Brown, A. M. (1987). *Distribution of common fears in an elderly population*. Unpublished doctoral dissertation, University of Wyoming, Laramie.

Brown, A., & Crawford, H. J. (1986). Hypnotizability, intense fears and eating disorder patterns: Tapping similar underlying cognitive processes? *International Journal of Clinical and Experimental Hypnosis, 34,* 275.

Brown, A. M., & Crawford, H. J. (1988). Fear Survey Schedule—III: Oblique and orthogonal factorial structures in an American college population. *Personality and Individual Differences, 9,* 401–410.

Brown, D., & Fromm, E. (1986). *Hypnotherapy and hypnoanalysis*. Hillsdale, NJ: Erlbaum.

Brown, D., & Fromm, E. (1987). *Hypnosis and behavioral medicine*. Hillsdale, NJ: Erlbaum.

Bushnell, J., & Barabasz, A. (1975). *Effects of flooding on claustrophobia*. Unpublished Department of Psychology Research Report, University of Canterbury, New Zealand.

Cook, E. W., III, Melamed, B. G., Cuthbert, B. N., McNeil, D. N., & Lang, P. J. (1988). Emotional imagery and the differential diagnosis of anxiety. *Journal of Consulting and Clinical Psychology, 56,* 734–740.

Crawford, H. J. (1982). Hypnotizability, daydreaming styles, imagery vividness, and absorption: A multidimensional study. *Journal of Personality and Social Psychology, 42,* 915–926.

Crawford, H. J. (1989). Cognitive and physiological flexibility: Multiple pathways to hypnotic responsiveness. In V. Gheorghiu, P. Netter, H. Eysenck, & R. Rosenthal (Eds.), *Suggestion and suggestibility: Theory and research* (pp. 155–167). New York: Springer-Verlag.

Crawford, H. J. (1990). Cognitive and psychophysiological correlates of hypnotic responsiveness. In D. Brown & M. Fass (Eds.), *Creative mastery in hypnosis and hypnoanalysis: A festschrift for Erika Fromm* (pp. 47–54). Hillsdale, NJ: Erlbaum.

Crawford, H. J. (1993). Comparisons of Restricted Environmental Stimulation Techniques (REST) and hypnosis: Implications for future research. In A. F. Barabasz & M. Barabasz (Eds.), *Clinical and experimental restricted environmental stimulation: New developments and perspectives* (pp. 175–186). New York: Springer-Verlag.

Crawford, H. J., Brown, A. M., & Heyman, S. (1991). *Hypnotic responsiveness and development of intense fears: Tapping some similar underlying capacities*. Unpublished manuscript.

Crawford, H. J., Brown, A. M., & Moon, C. (in press). Sustained attentional and disattentional abilities: Differences between low and high hypnotizables. *Journal of Abnormal Psychology*.

Crawford, H. J., & Gruzelier, J. (1992). A midstream view of the neuropsychophysiology of hypnosis: Recent research and future directions. In E. Fromm & M. Nash (Eds.), *Contemporary perspectives in hypnosis research* (pp. 227–266). New York: Guilford Press.

Ellis, A. (1984). The use of hypnosis with Rational Emotive Therapy (RET). *International Journal of Eclectic Psychotherapy, 3,* 15–22.

Ellis, A. (1987). Angst vor der Angst: Die Verwendung von Hypnosemit Rational–Emotiver Therapie. *Hypnose und Kognition, 4,* 64–71.

Foenander, G., Burrows, G. D., Gerschman, J. A., & Horne, D. J. de L. (1980). Phobic behaviour and hypnotic susceptibility. *Australian Journal of Clinical and Experimental Hypnosis, 8,* 41–46.

Frankel, F. H. (1974). Trance capacity and the genesis of phobic behavior. *Archives of General Psychiatry, 31,* 261–263.

Frankel, F. H. (1976). *Hypnosis: Trance as a coping mechanism.* New York: Plenum Press.

Frankel, F. H. (1990). Hypnotizability and dissociation. *American Journal of Psychiatry, 147,* 823–829.

Frankel, F. H., & Orne, M. T. (1976). Hypnotizability and phobic behavior. *Archives of General Psychiatry, 33,* 1259–1261.

Frischholz, E. J., Spiegel, D., Spiegel, H., Balma, D. L., & Markell, C. S. (1982). Differential hypnotic responsivity of smokers, phobics and chronic pain control patients: A failure to confirm. *Journal of Abnormal Psychology, 91,* 266–272.

Gerschman, J., Burrows, G. D., Reade, P., & Foenander, G. (1979). Hypnotizability and the treatment of dental phobic behavior. In G. D. Burrows, G. D. R. Collison, & L. Dennerstein (Eds.), *Hypnosis 1979* (pp. 33–39). New York: Elsevier/North-Holland.

Gerschman, J. A., Burrows, G. D., & Reade, P. C. (1987). Hypnotizability and dental phobic disorders. *International Journal of Psychosomatics, 33,* 42–47.

Grumbles, D., & Crawford, H. J. (1981, October). *Differential attentional abilities and hypnotizability.* Paper presented at the Society for Clinical and Experimental Hypnosis, Portland, Oregon.

Habeck, B. K., & Sheikh, A. A. (1984). Imagery and the treatment of phobic disorders. In A. A. Sheikh (Ed.), *Imagination and healing* (pp. 171–196). Farmingdale, NY: Baywood.

Hilgard, E. R. (1986). *Divided consciousness: Multiple controls in human thought and action* (expanded ed.). New York: Wiley.

Horowitz, S. L. (1970). Strategies within hypnosis for reducing phobic behavior. *Journal of Abnormal Psychology, 75,* 104–122.

Hugdahl, K. (1981). The three-systems-model of fear and emotion: A critical examination. *Behavior Research and Therapy, 19,* 75–85.

Humphreys, A. (1986). Review of the literature on the adjunctive use of hypnosis in behaviour therapy: 1970–1980. *British Journal of Experimental and Clinical Hypnosis, 3,* 95–101.

John, R., Hollander, B., & Perry, C. (1983). Hypnotizability and phobic behavior: Further supporting data. *Journal of Abnormal Psychology, 92,* 390–392.

Kelly, S. F. (1984). Measured hypnotic response and phobic behavior: A brief communication. *International Journal of Clinical and Experimental Hypnosis, 32,* 1–5.

Kluft, R. P. (1986). Hypnosis in the treatment of phobias. *Psychiatric Annals, 16,* 96–101.

Kopp, M. S., Skrabski, A., Mihaly, K., Buza, K., & Ratkoczi, E. (1988, September). *Psychophysiological regulation treatment in two subgroups of panic patients.* Paper presented at the 5th International Congress of Psychophysiology, Prague, Czechoslovakia.

Kossak, H. C. (1987). Verhaltenstherapie generalisierter Sozialangste Kognitive Umstrukturierung unter Hypnose. *Experimentelle und Klinische Hypnose, 3,* 13–28.

Lamb, C. S. (1985). Hypnotically-induced deconditioning: Reconstruction of memories in the treatment of phobias. *American Journal of Clinical Hypnosis, 28,* 56–62.

Lazarus, A. A. (1971). *Behavior therapy and beyond.* New York: McGraw-Hill.

Lykken, D., & Venables, P. (1971). Direct measurement of skin conductance: A proposal for standardization. *Psychophysiology, 8,* 656–672.

Marks, D. F. (1973). Visual imagery differences in recall of pictures. *British Journal of Psychology, 64,* 17–24.

Marks, I. M. (1969). *Fears and phobias.* New York: Academic Press.

Marks, I. M. (1987). *Fears, phobias, and rituals: Panic, anxiety, and their disorders.* New York: Oxford University Press.

McGuinness, T. P. (1984). Hypnosis in the treatment of phobias: A review of the literature. *American Journal of Clinical Hypnosis, 26,* 261–272.

McNeil, D. W., Vrana, S. R., Melamed, B. G., Cuthbert, B. N., & Lang, P. J. (1993). Emotional imagery in simple and social phobia: Fear versus anxiety. *Journal of Abnormal Psychology, 102,* 212–225.

Meichenbaum, D. (1977). *Cognitive–behavior modification: An integrative approach.* New York: Plenum Press.

Melchiori, L., & Barabasz, A. (1990). Effects of restricted environmental stimulation on simulated flight performance. In P. Suedfeld, J. Turner, Jr., & T. Fine (Eds.), *Restricted environmental stimulation: Theoretical and empirical developments in flotation REST* (pp. 135–142). New York: Springer-Verlag.

Miller, M. F., Barabasz, A., & Barabasz, M. (1991). Effects of active alert and relaxation hypnotic inductions on cold pressor pain. *Journal of Abnormal Psychology, 100,* 223–228.

Morgan, A. H., & Hilgard, J. R. (1978–1979). The Stanford Hypnotic Clinical Scale for Adults. *American Journal of Clinical Hypnosis, 21,* 134–147.

Ollendick, T. H. (1983). Reliability and validity of the Revised Fear Survey Schedule for Children (FSSC–R). *Behaviour Research and Therapy, 21,* 685–692.

Ollendick, T. H., & King, N. J. (1991). Origins of childhood fears: An evaluation of Rachman's theory of fear acquisition. *Behaviour Research and Therapy, 29,* 117–123.

Ollendick, T. H., King, N. J., & Frary, R. B. (1989). Fears in children and adolescents: Reliability and generalizability across gender, age and nationality. *Behaviour Research and Therapy, 27,* 19–26.

Orne, M. T., & O'Connell, D. N. (1967). Diagnostic ratings of hypnotizability. *International Journal of Clinical and Experimental Hypnosis, 15,* 125–133.

Orne, M. T., Whitehouse, W. G., Dinges, D. F., & Orne, E. C. (1988). Reconstructing memory through hypnosis: Forensic and clinical implications. In H. M. Pettinati (Ed.), *Hypnosis and memory* (pp. 21–63). New York: Guilford Press.

Owens, M. E., Bliss, E. L., Koester, P., & Jeppsen, E. A. (1990). Phobias and hypnotizability: A reexamination. *International Journal of Clinical and Experimental Hypnosis, 37,* 207–216.

Pettinati, H. M., Horne, R. L., & Staats, J. M. (1985). Hypnotizability in patients with anorexia nervosa and bulimia. *Archives of General Psychiatry, 42,* 1014–1016.

Rachman, S. (1977). The conditioning theory of fear acquisition: A critical examination. *Behaviour Research and Therapy, 15,* 375–387.

Scrignar, C. B. (1981). Rapid treatment of contamination phobia with handwashing compulsion by flooding with hypnosis. *American Journal of Clinical Hypnosis, 23,* 252–257.

Sheehan, P. W. (1967). A shortened form of Bett's questionnaire upon mental imagery. *Journal of Clinical Psychology, 23,* 386–389.

Shor, R., & Orne, E. (1962). *Harvard Group Scale of Hypnotic Susceptibility.* Palo Alto, CA: Consulting Psychologists Press.

Spiegel, D., & Cardeña, E. (1991). Disintegrated experience: The dissociative disorders revisited. *Journal of Abnormal Psychology, 100,* 362–378.

Spiegel, D., Frischholtz, M. A., Maruffi, B., & Spiegel, H. (1981). Hypnotic responsiveness and the treatment of flying phobia. *American Journal of Clinical Hypnosis, 23,* 239–247.

Spiegel, D., Hunt, T., & Dondershine, H. E. (1988). Dissociation and hypnotizability in posttraumatic stress disorder. *American Journal of Psychiatry, 145,* 301–305.

Spiegel, H. (1973). *Manual for Hypnotic Induction Profile: Eye-Roll Levitation Method* (rev. ed.). New York: Soni Medica.

Stutman, R. K., & Bliss, E. L. (1985). Posttraumatic stress disorder, hypnotizability, and imagery. *American Journal of Psychiatry, 142,* 741–743.

Suedfeld, P. (1980). *Restricted environmental stimulation.* New York: Wiley Interscience.

Tart, C. T. (1975). *States of consciousness.* New York: Dutton.

Tellegen, A., & Atkinson, G. (1974). Openness to absorbing and self-altering experiences ("absorption"), a trait related to hypnotic susceptibility. *Journal of Abnormal Psychology, 83,* 268–277.

Tomlin, P., Thyer, B. A., Curtis, G. C., Nesse, R., Cameron, O., & Wright, P. (1984). Standardization of the Fear Survey Schedule based upon patients with DSM–III disorders. *Journal of Behavior Therapy and Experimental Psychiatry, 15,* 123–126.

Weitzenhoffer, A. M., & Hilgard, E. R. (1959). *Stanford Hypnotic Susceptibility Scale, Forms A and B.* Palo Alto, CA: Consulting Psychologists Press.

Weitzenhoffer, A. M., & Hilgard, E. R. (1962). *Stanford Hypnotic Susceptibility Scale, Form C.* Palo Alto, CA: Consulting Psychologists Press.

Wolpe, J. (1969). *The practice of behavior therapy.* New York: Pergamon Press.

Wolpe, J., & Lang, P. J. (1964). Fear Survey Schedule for use in behavior therapy. *Behaviour Research and Therapy, 2,* 27–30.

Wolpe, J., & Lazaras, A. (1966). *Behavior therapy technique.* New York: Pergamon Press.

World Health Organization. (1992). *ICD-10: The International statistical classification of diseases and related health problems* (10th ed., rev.). Geneva: Author.

16

HYPNOSIS AND DEPRESSION

MICHAEL D. YAPKO

There is a popular bumper sticker that says, "Life is a bitch and then you die." If one considers recent epidemiological data describing the prevalence of major depression in the United States, it is easy to understand why such a dark appraisal of life would become a commercial success. The fact is that clinical depression as a disorder is increasing steadily in all age groups, and in the so-called "baby boomer" generation (i.e., those born from 1945 to 1964), depression has increased by an astounding factor of nearly 10 (Robins et al., 1984). Such a huge increase in so specific an age group suggests a number of things immediately relevant both to the understanding of depression as a disorder and to the formation of effective treatment strategies.

First, the data strongly suggest a relatively small likelihood of biological factors (i.e., genetics or biochemistry) being the primary causal agent of this increase in depression. Gene pools and biochemical makeup simply do not change so dramatically in so short a span of time. This is not to suggest that there is no biological basis for or correlation with major depression, but it would seem that biologically caused depressions are likely to comprise

The author would like to thank Linda M. Griebel for her help in the preparation of this manuscript.

only a minority of cases. Second, the role of sociocultural influences on the prevalence of depression is highlighted by relating socialization factors to the increased rates of depression. Virtually no one escapes the influence of the omnipresent socialization process, and so individual life-style patterns (i.e., repetitive subjective responses that surface in the course of managing one's life) evolve in response to life experiences. These patterns can apparently predispose one to clinical depression. Third, the epidemiological data encourage cross-cultural comparisons to determine just how strong a role sociocultural factors play in predisposing individuals to depression. There are a number of studies that strongly implicate societal structure and degree of Westernization as major variables influencing the prevalence of depression (Schiefflin, 1985; Seligman, 1988).

It seems clear, then, that depression is largely a consequence of sociocultural influences that inculcate patterns of thought, behavior, and feeling that place individuals at risk for the disorder. These factors must necessarily be identified and treated at an individual level to successfully treat existing depression as well as to reduce the risk for later episodes. In this chapter, several key patterns related to depression will be presented and described. It should be understood that the complete treatment of depression encompasses many different focal points and many different patterns of intervention. However, this chapter has as its specific focus ways to utilize hypnosis in the treatment of depressed individuals within a larger treatment plan that includes a variety of approaches beyond hypnosis.

HYPNOSIS IN THE TREATMENT OF DEPRESSION

Historically, depression has been viewed as a disorder for which hypnosis was contraindicated (Burrows, 1980). Theorists expressed alarm over the potential for hypnosis to strip the depressed patient of what few inadequate defenses he or she had, perhaps precipitating suicidal behavior or thoughts in the patient. Furthermore, concern over the likelihood of symptom substitutions involving symptoms even more serious than depression was considered sufficient justification to espouse the "fact" that hypnosis was simply not an appropriate treatment modality for the depressed patient (Barnett, 1981; Crasilneck & Hall, 1985). Others have simply not found hypnosis to be useful in the treatment of depression (Weitzenhoffer, 1989).

Of course, times have changed, and so have views of depression as a disorder and hypnosis as a treatment modality. It is now understood that depression is a predictable consequence of some very specific intra- and interpersonal variables (some of which will be mentioned later). In regard to hypnosis, it is now recognized that sophisticated applications can meaningfully address underlying dynamic issues as well as symptoms, serving as a highly efficient therapeutic tool for establishing meaningful associations.

(For a more complete discussion of clinical hypnosis, see Yapko, 1990.) In that regard, hypnosis may be used in conjunction with any other therapy modality to facilitate a more rapid and deeply integrated establishment of the desired therapeutic associations.

A RATIONALE FOR USING HYPNOSIS WITH DEPRESSED INDIVIDUALS

The goal of any therapy, regardless of its emphasis, is to interrupt existing hurtful or limiting patterns of a person's experience and to build adaptive or functional patterns in their place. Historically, psychotherapists have focused on resolving abstract "issues" or "dynamics" as the target of therapy. The emphasis has been on "pathology," with a seemingly paradoxical attempt to encourage health. Recently, however, a shift in the practice of psychotherapy has been to focus on and amplify positive resources of the patient, to actively structure positive learning, and to encourage dormant positive capacities to develop.

Thus, hypnosis can be used to skillfully address the individual concerns and individual makeup of the patient. In particular, the emphasis of the "utilization approach" to hypnosis (Erickson & Rossi, 1979; Yapko, 1990) is on the patient's subjective reality; it involves identifying and using each patient's unique patterns to organize experience in a goal-directed fashion. Enhancing rapport (and the subsequent capacity for influence), organizing and mobilizing undeveloped or underdeveloped personal resources, and establishing new associations within the patient to familiar and unfamiliar contexts are some of the best reasons to use hypnosis in treatment. Even an induction as primitive as a countdown ("I'll count from 10 to 1 while you go deeply into hypnosis. . . 10. . . relax. . . 9. . . deeper. . ." etc.) can have a therapeutic impact because it interrupts the flow of the patient's negative ruminations, anxiety, and discomfort and provides some relaxation and a positive focus for a change. Although such a simplistic induction process is unlikely to generate any meaningful therapeutic gain in and of itself, it has great potential, if properly used, to establish in the patient's mind that his or her experience is changeable. For reasons more fully described later, the perception of changeability is vital to recovery from depression (Seligman, 1989).

The emphasis in this section has been on the use of hypnosis to both interrupt and build patterns, paralleling the general goals of therapy. Hypnosis, as an intervention tool, is able to amplify existing resources, reassociate dissociated aspects of experience, and facilitate the establishment of desirable associations on whatever level (i.e., cognitive, relational, physiological, etc.) the therapist deems appropriate. Hypnosis affords the therapist a greater opportunity to provide multidimensional interventions, in contrast with those interventions that focus exclusively on cognition, affect, or physiology.

RELATION TO OTHER VIEWS OF DEPRESSION

Currently, there are two prominent and well-researched models of depression that dominate the clinical field: the cognitive and interpersonal models. Both have substantial support in efficacy studies as effective and consistent methods of intervention (Beck, 1987; Klerman, Weissman, Rounsaville, & Chevron, 1984). Each will be considered in this section in relation to the implications for treating depression with hypnosis.

Cognitive models of depression take at least two forms. In the model developed primarily by Aaron Beck (1967, 1973, 1987), which is probably the best-researched treatment model, the emphasis is on the "cognitive distortions" evident in the patients' thinking. Simply put, the patient makes regular and predictable errors in thinking that fuel the negativity and despair of depression. In treatment, the patient is taught to identify and self-correct faulty patterns of thinking. Beck identified many of the most common categories of cognitive distortions and developed techniques for refuting and clarifying the patient's thoughts (Beck, Rush, Shaw, & Emery, 1979; Burns, 1980).

Martin Seligman (1989, 1990) developed another cognitive model that focuses on the "attributional style" of the patient. Seligman described attributional style as an explanatory style: a regular and predictable pattern for explaining to one's self or others why an event occurs or what it means. Seligman identified specific patterns of attributional style and encouraged the use of Beck's cognitive therapy techniques for refuting and clarifying the patient's depressogenic misattributions. The skills of flexible thinking, looking for multiple plausible explanations for an event, drawing clear and reasonable conclusions, and responding appropriately and effectively to the context at hand are all emphasized as desirable outcomes in the cognitive models.

The interpersonal model of depression, primarily developed by Klerman, Weissman, and others (Klerman, Weissman, Rounsaville, & Chevron, 1984), emphasizes depression as a consequence of dysfunctional interpersonal relationships. The treatment emphasis is on the building of effective relationship skills in order to establish mutual support, mutual respect, clarity of boundaries, open and honest communication, intimacy, and the other necessary and desirable skills for relating meaningfully to others.

It is enlightening to note that both cognitive and interpersonal views of depression focus on interrupting specific dysfunctional patterns and building functional ones, rather than on abstract dynamics. Neither view emphasizes history, focusing on concrete change in the present rather than abstract insight about the past. Both views emphasize that therapy should be brief, not long-term. Both require the therapist to be an active teacher and facilitator, not a passive support. Both emphasize that the role of therapy is to change the structure of *how* the patient thinks or relates, and not focus only on *what* the patient thinks or does. A key point is that when the structure of a patient's pattern changes, so must the associated content.

The points above are highly relevant to using hypnosis. Of course, hypnosis is not in and of itself a complete therapy; it is a tool compatible with other therapeutic tools. Hypnosis can be used to highlight to a patient his or her cognitive distortions, with suggestions for more "automatically" recognizing and refuting them. Although Beck and Seligman have not spoken of an "unconscious mind" in the way that practitioners of hypnosis might, they have described "automatic thoughts" that must be identified and refuted. Hypnosis can play a role in focusing an individual on any dimension of internal experience one chooses, including a cognitive one. Thus, if one wishes to make use of cognitive therapy techniques, hypnosis can be used to help establish associations in the patient for more readily identifying and clarifying his or her distorted thoughts and attributions (Yapko, 1992).

Similarly, if one chooses to focus on the relational dimension, using the interpersonal model as a conceptual and practical framework, hypnosis is also applicable. Identifying and relating to others' needs and values, establishing and consistently enforcing limits with others, and developing greater awareness of one's own needs and how they might best be met are obvious examples of target skills appropriate for one's hypnotic suggestions.

In essence, whatever the goal of a therapeutic intervention may be, the ability of hypnosis (either formally or informally) to build a strong link between a context and the response desired in that context is the main reason why it can be so easily related to nearly any model of treatment. I have focused here on the cognitive and interpersonal models simply because they have proven to be the most reliable in the treatment of depression.

CLINICAL APPLICATIONS

Thus far, I have described hypnosis as the use of influential communication to establish therapeutic associations in the depressed patient. In therapy, then, whether hypnotically based or otherwise, the key dysfunctional patterns must be interrupted and replaced with more adaptive ones.

The remainder of this chapter will focus on two specific patterns associated with depression that are viewed as so central to the treatment process that therapy cannot succeed if they are not addressed either directly or indirectly. These two patterns are (a) a stable attributional style (Seligman, 1989) and (b) perceptual and/or behavioral rigidity (Zeig, 1980). In the remainder of this section, I will describe what these two patterns are and how hypnosis may be used in addressing them.

Stable Attributional Style

Probably the single most important pattern to evaluate and address in the depressed patient is his or her degree of stable attributional style. A stable attributional style is the perception that hurtful life conditions are unchanging and even unchangeable—hence "stable." Beck (1967, 1973; Beck et al., 1979) described "negative expectations" as a fundamental component of depression, which is another way of describing the fact that the depressed patient is typically unable to project positive changes ahead into the future, thus restricting his or her vision of the future to either an undefined but negative impression or an interminable continuation of the currently deteriorating circumstances. I see this as a cognitive deficit that I have called a "disturbance of temporal orientation" (Yapko, 1985, 1989). The key point is that the depressed patient is immersed in the belief that his or her experience of depression and negative life circumstances is not changeable. Thus, it becomes a primary goal in the treatment process to address a patient's stable attributional style, for several important reasons. First, the relationship between a stable attributional style and one's level of motivation to attempt to change should be apparent. Why should a depressed person try to improve if he or she believes nothing can change? Second, why should depressed patients continue in therapy if there is no immediate experiential evidence that their condition can improve? Extensive history-taking by the therapist at the outset of treatment does nothing to change the patient's experience, and may unwittingly reinforce the patient's stable attributional style. This is the basis for the strong recommendation that hypnosis, specifically a trance process to build positive expectancy, be used early on in the treatment process, perhaps even in the first session (Yapko, 1988, 1992). This process will be described below. It should be apparent that unless the depressed patient is oriented to a concrete representation of the future that permits an experiential contact with positive and realistic possibilities, the likelihood of the person continuing in and participating fully in treatment is reduced.

Hypnosis may be used to build positive expectancy and to facilitate the development of an unstable attributional style. This is the reason for doing even a simple, positive induction process with a patient. It suggests that experience can change. The use of hypnosis to build positive expectancy in a particular area of the depressed patient's life can amplify the patient's motivation to change and guide it in a particular direction. Once hypnosis is performed, posthypnotic suggestions to help generalize the pos-

TABLE 1
A Hypnotic Process for Building Expectancy

1. Identify the patient's dominant temporal orientation (past, present, or future)
2. Identify the patient's primary representational system (preferred or most heavily relied on sensory system)
3. Identify the patient's cognitive style (degree of concrete or abstract style; degree of specific or global style)
4. Identify the goal (expectancy regarding what specifically?)
5. Induction, building a response set
6. Metaphors illustrating the inevitability of change
7. Accessing personal transitions from the patient's history
8. Identifying personal resources evident in past transitions
9. Identifying specific future contexts requiring new responses
10. Embedding the positive resources identified in No. 9 above
11. Rehearsal of new (behavioral, cognitive, affective) sequence
12. Generalization of positive resources to other selected contexts
13. Posthypnotic suggestions for integration
14. Disengagement, reorientation to waking state

itive expectations to other areas of the patient's life as well will need to be given; otherwise, the typically concrete cognitive style of the depressed patient will lead him or her to restrict the new learning to only the specific context considered.

Table 1 suggests a sequence for conducting a hypnosis session designed to interrupt the negative expectations for the future. The goal is to impart the messages, at an experiential level, that "the future is not simply more of the past" and "you already have resources that you can use to resolve your current difficulties."

Clearly, the trance phenomenon of age progression plays a clear and pivotal role in building expectancy. Age progression techniques are approaches that experientially orient the patient to the future (Erickson, 1954; Yapko, 1990). In the sequence outlined in Table 1, age progression is used to extend personal resources identified in the past into future contexts where they will be needed or wanted. In essence, the hypnotized patient is encouraged to experience positive future consequences now that arise from implementing new changes and decisions. At a stage of treatment as early as the first session, the expected changes need not even be specified, but can be described in a general way that only sounds specific, such as in the following example:

> You've described the discomfort that has led you to seek help. . . and
> you want to feel differently. . . and you really don't know yet that you

can. . . but you'll discover quickly what you've known all along. . . that when you do something differently than you used to. . . the result will also be different. . . and so you can go forward in time. . . so that it's been a while since our work together. . . and you can take a moment. . . to be fully there. . . able to review decisions that you've recently made. . . differently. . . and you can review the positive consequences of those decisions. . . on *all* dimensions within you. . . and what a pleasure to discover that you're so capable. . . of shifting thoughts and feelings. . . and that you can enjoy the relief you worked so hard for. . . and why not look forward to even more changes. . . that feel good. . . as you discover more and more ways of using what you've learned to continue growing stronger. . . .

A second age progression strategy involves orienting the client to the negative consequences of continuing current patterns (i.e., experiencing the effects of remaining ambivalent or immobilized regarding self-help decisions). Considering the degree of ambivalence often found in the depressed individual, hypnotically facilitating a concrete experience of the negative patterns can provide the client with the momentum needed to make positive decisions. Age progression can move distant consequences into the realm of immediate experience.

Age progression as a basic trance phenomenon involves the manipulation of the mechanism of "self-fulfilling prophecy." More important, however, the chief depressogenic pattern of stable attributional style can be meaningfully addressed in the therapy; little else is likely to have an impact on the depressed patient if this pattern is not skillfully dealt with.

Perceptual and Behavioral Rigidity

Related to but distinguishable from a stable attributional style is the rigidity of the depressed person's patterns of responding to life experiences. The reason that depression is recurrent in afflicted individuals is not solely or even primarily because of the nature of depression. Rather, it is because of the patterned way in which all people respond to life's challenges. If one has a broad array of resources to use to respond flexibly to the great diversity of experiences life throws at us, effectively handling each situation according to its own merits, depression is less likely. If one responds rigidly to circumstances, usually by applying patterns developed in similar past circumstances to current but different circumstances, one is likely to get hurt and, depending on where blame is placed for the hurt, depressed. Rigidities in thinking, feeling, or behaving can be viewed as the basis for pathology in general and depression in particular.

Once the seeds of recognition that change is possible have been planted, the patient is likely to experience a shift in perception, initiating a hope that there will be a way to effectively resolve the problems that led to therapy in the first place. Certainly, the patient is likely to have thought that way before, but viable solutions were either never discovered or were dismissed as too demanding in some way (with the demand exceeding the perceived supply of ability to meet it). With the help of the clinician, the patient can arrive at a state of willingness to entertain the possibility of developing meaningful alternatives. Table 2 describes a hypnotic process for facilitating flexibility in some aspect of the depressed patient's experience.

The use of hypnosis to facilitate flexibility is a means to impart several key messages: (a) There are many right ways to accomplish a goal; (b) if you fail, try another approach; (c) familiarity aside, find the best response; and (d) change is inevitable.

It should be pointed out that even the use of hypnosis itself is a potentially powerful statement from the therapist because it models flexibility in the therapeutic relationship; the boundaries of how the therapist and the patient interact are enlarged in the process.

The patient's beliefs and values are among the most potent factors dictating his or her range of responses. Ultimately, this is why the cognitive elements of the patient's world will need to be addressed. When a patient feels "stuck," it is most likely an indication of subjective perceptions and not objective possibilities. Direct hypnotic suggestions to seek alternative interpretations or solutions whenever feeling stuck is one obvious application of hypnosis; however, the use of metaphorical approaches with the hypnotized patient is a valuable means of providing important messages in memorable contexts.

TABLE 2
Facilitating Flexibility: Hypnotic Structure

1. Induction
2. Establish receptive mind-set
3. Introduce metaphors that reflect change
4. Introduce metaphors that reflect rigidity
5. Access personal ability to adapt ("change with changing times")
6. Identify adaptive resources in current and future contexts
7. Extend existing resources in current and future contexts
8. Anticipate, allow integration of adaptive skills
9. Posthypnotic suggestions for automatically using new responses in the appropriate context(s)
10. Disengagement
11. Reorientation to waking state

The ability of metaphors, or anecdotes, to impart perspective and build an identification has been well described in the literature (Lankton & Lankton, 1983; Zeig, 1980). In the early stages of treatment, in which facilitating flexibility is considered a preliminary goal preceding interventions more specifically focused on the patient's individual issues, metaphors may be used to build a momentum of acceptance for ideas and tactics relating to flexibility and the inevitability of change. Such metaphors may involve either universal life transitions or transitions unique to that particular patient taken from his or her own personal history (Yapko, 1988).

The general goal of facilitating flexibility is one that continues throughout the therapy, with the clinician continually imparting the message that change is possible as a new response set.

CASE MATERIAL: ROLAND

The use of hypnosis to facilitate experiential learning and build new adaptive associations can be a powerful tool in the overall therapy plan. In addition to the use of hypnosis in the therapist's office, teaching self-hypnosis and encouraging learning in "real-life" contexts with "experimental" behaviors (given by the therapist as behavioral task assignments to complete between therapy sessions) are also considered fundamental to the treatment of depression. Hypnotic interventions in particular are described in this section as they were used in the treatment of a depressed patient named Roland.

Roland was a 65-year-old man presenting with an incapacitating episode of depression. He reported sleep disturbance, constant anxiety, negative ruminations, withdrawal, and feelings of sadness. Roland was on disability, unable to continue his work as a city project engineer. This depressive episode had its onset 4 months earlier, near the time that he had had surgery for a hernia. Prior to the surgery, Roland had experienced a considerable amount of pain, which he catastrophized himself into thinking was cancer. The diagnosis of a hernia provided little relief for Roland, who by now had convinced himself that he was "officially old" and that the hernia was just the first step on the road of inevitably deteriorating health. Roland began to ruminate constantly about ill health, interpreting every physical sensation as evidence of something wrong. Roland reported that his depression was intense, immobilizing, and incurable because he "knew" he was old and deteriorating. He stated his view that his life was over, with nothing to look forward to other than deterioration and death. At the time of the hernia surgery, Roland had only 6 weeks to work before his retirement. Unless he could return to work and complete those 6 weeks, he would lose his retirement pension. He felt unable to return to work and could not foresee that changing, although it was an eventual goal.

Roland was married to a very loving, supportive woman who was seen in one joint session early in the treatment process. He had been seen previously for treatment by two psychotherapists: a psychiatrist who prescribed antidepressant medications to which Roland did not respond well, and a supportive psychologist who encouraged him to ventilate feelings of anger at losing his youth. Roland felt that this latter treatment depressed him more, and soon discontinued therapy. He was referred to me by a friend of his who was also a therapist. Roland's health was deemed well above average for his age, and posed no significant limits on what he was physically able to do.

In was immediately clear that Roland's highly intellectual and analytical demeanor was lending itself to the uncontestable ruminations about aging and deteriorating. It was also apparent that Roland expected nothing positive from his imminent retirement and, in fact, had made no plans at all for it. Although for some individuals spontaneity is a good thing, Roland's life was a highly structured, duty-bound one. The lack of a plan for retirement and of a sense of purpose, combined with the expectations of poor health, provided ample fuel for depression. The goals of therapy included the following:

1. Facilitating a positive future orientation (positive expectancy regarding the future)
2. Facilitating an unstable attributional style relative to personal circumstances
3. Facilitating a flexible and generative approach to daily living (expanding his narrow repertoire of activities and self-generating things to become involved in)
4. Facilitating a positive relationship with his body to interrupt the emerging hypochondriacal one
5. Facilitating a sense of personal value from activities other than work

Roland was seen for a total of 13 sessions; ten of these were concentrated over the first 4½ months of treatment, and the remaining 3 were conducted over the next 3 months. Hypnosis was used formally in 9 of the 13 sessions. Each of the hypnosis sessions was audiotaped, and the tapes were given to Roland to permit him to reinforce the relevant learning as often as he wished.

The hypnosis sessions each addressed either the theme of that particular session's content or a goal consistent with the larger aims of treatment. The hypnosis sessions are described below:

1. In the first session, hypnosis was used to promote general relaxation, both physically and mentally. A key idea was that "there are worthwhile experiences you are capable of having that are beyond logic or rationality." A goal of this session was to promote in Roland a recognition

that the things that would make a difference for him were things beyond what he already knew, and that his view of himself and his world was limited to what he knew, but that that was not all there was. This helped to destabilize his stable attributions about himself and his world while encouraging a legitimate basis for hopefulness. Also, by focusing him on physical sensations associated with the trance that were defined as comfortable and pleasant, the idea was seeded that he could experience his body in a positive manner.

2. In the next hypnosis session, an idea was elaborated that had been the focus of the previous session, namely that Roland could not fully control his own destiny—that some things were uncontrollable and could be comfortably accepted as such (e.g., the weather, the seasons, the phases of life, etc.). This trance session reframed therapeutically his negative focus on aging as a futile attempt to control the uncontrollable. These ideas were further developed in the third therapy session. Following this session, Roland went back to work half-time to begin his final 6 weeks. He was working full-time again within 2 weeks.

3. Self-exploration was encouraged in the next hypnosis session as a way of discovering what he enjoyed independently of others' expectations or their demands of him. Roland was encouraged to consider metaphors of people with public personas who, on a personal level, are not as they seem. A metaphor encouraging exploration at a deeper level was provided by describing ocean swimmers and surfers with a surface view of the ocean, in contrast with divers who submerge themselves in the deep ocean. This session paved the way for later learning to respond to personal preferences and interests. Following this fourth session, Roland signed up for a course in philosophy and begain taking walks on the beach.

4. In the following hypnosis sessions, the focus was on reinforcing the changes taking place that Roland was aware of, particularly physical ones. Roland reported a marked improvement in his sleep and attributed this to the self-hypnosis procedure he was taught, which he described as "a more satisfying process than just counting sheep." The hypnosis focused on the many physical sensations he was capable of experiencing that were very pleasant ("the loving touch of your wife. . . the feel of your bed supporting you at night. . . the soothing sensations of a hot shower. . ."). The goal was to redefine physical sensations as comfortable, not suspect. Sensations described in hypnosis went from external ones to internal ones ("the feeling of stretching your muscles. . . the feeling of pleasant hunger that precedes a wonderful meal. . . the comfort of being tired before a good night's sleep. . ."). This redefinition of physical sensations took place in the seventh session, directly following the previous several sessions' focus on developing more and varied interests. In addition, Roland was encouraged to do at least one spontaneous thing each day. He consistently chose

to approach strangers in contexts appropriate for making small talk. He enjoyed discovering his sense of humor.

5. In the next hypnosis session, which took place in the ninth therapy session, Roland was encouraged to associate retirement with feeling free to pursue personal interests that may have seemed too tangential or even trivial when he was working. Examples of things to absorb one's interest were provided by me but then immediately discounted by me as trivial. Roland's response was to emerge from the trance with an irritated statement that my judgments about the trivialities of peoples' hobbies seemed questionable because all that mattered was that *they* enjoyed them. Roland then defended being able to do as one wished, regardless of another person's judgment. This was important because it established the worth of things that are not explicitly purposeful or meaningful.

6. In the next hypnosis session, Roland was encouraged to review all of the changes he had experienced since beginning therapy: His sleep had normalized; he had returned to work, completed his 6 weeks, and formally retired; he had enrolled in and enjoyed a philosophy course; he had established a regular walking and exercise program; he had established social contact with others; he had developed greater spontaneity; and he focused on things he could do and make happen rather than on things he could not. The major learning was summarized, and posthypnotic suggestions for retrieving this learning as needed in the appropriate contexts were provided. This took place in the tenth session.

The subsequent hypnosis sessions each reinforced Roland's progress and emphasized remaining more flexible and responsive to balancing his internal needs with external realities. After these monthly follow-up sessions, therapy was terminated. A 1-year follow-up personal interview was conducted to establish that the therapeutic gains had been maintained, which they were.

DISCUSSION OF ROLAND'S CASE

The emphasis in this case narrative was on how the hypnosis sessions were distributed and conducted throughout a therapy, to illustrate the use of hypnosis in treating depression. Hypnosis was used as a tool to consolidate important learning and establish new and beneficial associations in the patient. Each of the goals of therapy was met by addressing Roland's concerns through a focus on the associated patterns maintaining his symptoms. Hypnosis played a significant role in mobilizing Roland's resources in the direction of positive and lasting change.

Two cornerstones of depression are hopelessness and helplessness. Roland had convinced himself that his future contained little more than progressive deterioration. His selective focus on such a negative expectation drained any motivation to try to go beyond his difficulties. To catalyze successful outcomes, it is essential to facilitate a motivating and compelling vision of the future in treatment. Research clearly indicates that expectancy plays a key role at every stage of treatment (Kirsch, 1991; Seligman, 1989).

Hypnosis, in and of itself, is not curative. Rather, it is the ability of hypnosis to stimulate the patient's subjective associations on cognitive, affective, and behavioral dimensions of experience. Thus, hypnosis can be used to correct cognitive distortions or change a behavior. In Roland's case, his distorted belief (i.e., overgeneralization), that a transient episode of pain related to a hernia was the harbinger of disasters to come, was a focus of treatment. Specifically, the first two sessions encouraged him to adopt a view of negative circumstances as transient, not permanent. This served to build hopefulness and a willingness to participate in the treatment process. Thus, hypnosis was used to facilitate the correction of an error in his thinking.

It should be apparent that I do not generally view hypnosis as the therapeutic agent, but rather as the catalyst for communicating therapeutic ideas or facilitating therapeutic experiences. The case of Roland highlights the use of hypnosis and directives in the active treatment of patterns of depression.

RESEARCH AND APPRAISAL

As stated earlier, the use of hypnosis in treating depression has been actively discouraged. Hypnosis has been viewed as a catalyst for suicide, psychosis, hysteria, and other undesirable outcomes in previous considerations of the hypnotic treatment of depression. These unfounded and obsolete views prevented any systematic study of hypnotic methods in the treatment of depression, so that meaningful research is sparse. However, there is research that indicates that hypnotized persons may have easier access to more intense emotions (Nash, 1992). Thus, the narrow focus on negative emotions typical of the depressive person may even be viewed as a "negative self-hypnosis" (Araoz, 1985).

Before any substantive research can be done, two important factors will need to be taken into account. First, because hypnosis is not in and of itself a therapy, it can be used as a tool only within the context of a structured therapeutic approach. How will the effects of hypnosis in particular be evaluated in relation to the therapy in general? Second, we can distinguish formal hypnotic procedures from the informal use of hypnotic suggestive patterns. How will we determine which aspects of hypnosis are the central elements of a meaningful therapeutic intervention?

If one uses a broader definition of hypnosis (see Yapko, 1990) that encompasses the patterns of influential communication evident in any psychotherapy, the necessity of defining undefinable trance experiences diminishes. The use of hypnosis to present important ideas and to structure important experiential learning can be better studied when hypnosis is not so narrowly defined as to be limited to a specific type of procedure. However, such a broad definition makes research considerably more difficult.

Despite the difficulties described above, research investigating the use of hypnosis with depressive patients clearly needs to be done if there is to be any legitimate basis for encouraging its use with such a population. There are at least two possible avenues of research: (a) investigating whether therapies using formal hypnosis sessions to teach specific skills or ideas show better results (e.g., more rapid symptom relief or less relapse) than the same therapies conducted without the use of formal hypnosis; and (b) investigating whether therapies using hypnotic communication patterns (e.g., therapeutic metaphors, reframings, or paradoxes) in the therapy to teach specific skills or ideas show better results than the same therapies conducted without such methods.

Only the most obvious and standardized of hypnotic methods will be researchable. The subtleties of nuance, nonverbal delivery, implication, and so forth will likely always evade objective scrutiny. However, the positive value of substantive research cannot be ignored, and such research holds the key to a more widespread acceptance and use of hypnosis in the treatment of depression.

CONCLUSION

With society's increasing emphasis on individualism, materialism, technology, speed, and other such sociocultural phenomena, it is predictable that the prevalence of depression will also increase. The role of the therapist is to focus on the patterns with which an individual has been socialized, identifying how those patterns create, maintain, or put the individual at risk for depression. The therapy process is one of pattern interruption and pattern building, differing from one treatment to the next only in the content of the patterns that are addressed and in the choice of therapy model.

There are a number of useful frameworks for conducting therapy with depressed patients. The cognitive and interpersonal approaches have demonstrated their efficacy and are thus often seen as strong allies of hypnosis. However, it bears repeating that hypnosis is a valuable therapeutic tool and not a therapy in itself.

There are many excellent reasons to use hypnosis in the treatment of depressed patients, some of which follow:

- Hypnosis facilitates active and experiential learning.
- Hypnosis catalyzes more rapid integration of relevant learning.
- Hypnosis establishes therapeutic associations in a more focused and concentrated way.
- Hypnosis interrputs one's usual experience of one's self, enhancing an unstable attributional style.
- Hypnosis models flexibility by encouraging experiences beyond one's usual parameters.

New understanding of both depression and hypnosis affords therapists the opportunity to approach the treatment of depressed patients in a more comprehensive way than ever before. Depression is a highly treatable problem with a high rate of recovery, and a therapist who is skilled in the use of hypnosis can play a powerful role not only in the recovery process, but in the prevention of relapses as well.

REFERENCES

Araoz, D. (1985). *The new hypnosis.* New York: Brunner/Mazel.

Barnett, E. (1981). *Analytical hypnotherapy: Principles and practice.* Kingston, Ontario: Junica.

Beck, A. (1967). *Depression: Causes and treatment.* Philadelphia: University of Pennyslvania Press.

Beck, A. (1973). *The diagnosis and management of depression.* Philadelphia: University of Pennyslvania Press.

Beck, A. (1987). Cognitive therapy. In J. Zeig (Ed.), *The evolution of psychotherapy* (pp. 149–163). New York: Brunner/Mazel.

Beck, A., Rush, J., Shaw, B., & Emery, G. (1979). *Cognitive therapy of depression.* New York: Guilford Press.

Burns, D. (1980). *Feeling good: The new mood therapy.* New York: Morrow.

Burrows, G. (1980). Affective disorders and hypnosis. In G. Burrows & L. Dennerstein (Eds.), *Handbook of hypnosis and psychosomatic medicine* (pp. 149–170). Amsterdam: Elsevier/North-Holland: Biomedical Press.

Crasilneck, H., & Hall, J. (1985). *Clinical hypnosis: Principles and applications* (2nd ed.). New York: Grune & Stratton.

Erickson, M. (1954). Pseudo-orientation in time as a hypnotherapeutic procedure. *Journal of Clinical and Experimental Hypnosis, 2,* 261–283.

Erickson, M., & Rossi, E. (1979). *Hypnotherapy: An exploratory casebook.* New York: Irvington.

Kirsch, I. (1991). The social learning theory of hypnosis. In S. Lynn & J. Rhue (Eds.), *Theories of hypnosis* (pp. 439–465). New York: Guilford Press.

Klerman, G., Weissman, M., Rounsaville, B., & Chevron, E. (1984). *Interpersonal psychotherapy of depression.* New York: Basic Books.

Lankton, S., & Lankton, C. (1983). *The answer within.* New York: Brunner/Mazel.

Nash, M. (1992). Hypnosis, psychopathology, and psychological regression. In E. Fromm & M. Nash (Eds.), *Contemporary hypnosis research* (pp. 149–169). New York: Guilford Press.

Robins, L., Helzer, J., Weissman, M., Orvaschel, H., Gruenberg, E., Burke, J., & Regier, D. (1984). Lifetime prevalence of specific psychiatric disorders in three sites. *Archives of general psychiatry, 41,* 949–958.

Schiefflin, E. (1985). The cultural analysis of depressive affect: An example from New Guinea. In A. Kleinman & B. Good (Eds.), *Culture and depression: Studies in anthropology and cross-cultural psychiatry of affect and disorder* (pp. 101–133). Berkeley: University of California Press.

Seligman, M. (1988, October). Boomer blues. *Psychology Today,* pp. 50–55.

Seligman, M. (1989). Explanatory style: Predicting depression, achievement, and health. In M. Yapko (Ed.), *Brief therapy approaches to treating anxiety and depression* (pp. 5–32). New York: Brunner/Mazel.

Seligman, M. (1990). *Learned optimism.* New York: Knopf.

Weitzenhoffer, A. (1989). *The practice of hypnotism* (Vol. 2). New York: Wiley.

Yapko, M. (1985). Therapeutic strategies for the treatment of depression. In S. Lankton (Ed.), *Ericksonian monographs* (No. 1, pp. 89–110). New York: Brunner/Mazel.

Yapko, M. (1988). *When living hurts: Directives for treating depression.* New York: Brunner/Mazel.

Yapko, M. (1989). Disturbances of temporal orientation as a feature of depression. In M. Yapko (Ed.), *Brief therapy approaches to treating anxiety and depression* (pp. 106–118). New York: Brunner/Mazel.

Yapko, M. (1990). *Trancework: An introduction to the practice of clinical hypnosis* (2nd ed.). New York: Brunner/Mazel.

Yapko, M. (1992). *Hypnosis and the treatment of depressions.* New York: Brunner/Mazel.

Zeig, J. (1980). *A teaching seminar with Milton H. Erickson, M.D.* New York: Brunner/Mazel.

17

HYPNOTHERAPY WITH CHILDREN

DANIEL P. KOHEN and KAREN OLNESS

The application of hypnotherapy and related techniques with children can be traced to Mesmer's era in the late 18th century. Prior to the availability of anesthesia, British surgeons described the successful use of hypnoanesthesia with many children. During the 19th century, there were several reports of clinical applications of child hypnotherapy. However, from 1900 to 1946, there were no English-language reports about hypnotherapy with children (Olness & Gardner, 1988). In fact, clinical reports documenting the successful use of hypnotherapy with children did not begin to appear in the American medical literature until the 1960s and 1970s, at which time pediatricians and pediatric psychologists reported that children readily learned self-hypnotic skills and applied them successfully. In the 1970s, several research groups buttressed these clinical observations with carefully conducted prospective studies.

In the 1960s and 1970s, there was also a proliferation of training workshops devoted to child hypnotherapy. These workshops stimulated a great deal of interest in the professional community and were instrumental in training hundreds of child health professionals in the use of hypnotic techniques with children. Today, most pediatric institutions in the United

States offer hypnotherapy for treating a variety of problem behaviors and disorders.

A number of other developments have occurred that have defined and expanded the boundaries of pediatric hypnosis. As the formal study of pain assessment and management in pediatrics progressed, hypnotherapeutic methods were included in pain-management programs and in individual treatment regimens. Over the years, pediatric hypnosis research has become a field of inquiry in its own right, as research has become increasingly sophisticated. For example, in 1987 Olness, MacDonald, and Uden published what is considered to be the first prospective study comparing a pharmacological treatment, a placebo control, and hypnotherapeutic methods for managing a common pediatric problem: juvenile migraine headaches. Tightly controlled, methodologically rigorous prospective studies are in progress that are examining the efficacy of hypnotherapeutic methodologies in great detail.

With these developments has come an appreciation that hypnotherapeutic methods can be used to instill a sense of mastery and competence in children. Successful methods include enhancing children's decision-making abilities and self-control and exploiting children's natural propensities to imagine and fantasize. Ongoing studies (Kosslyn, Margolis, Barrett, Goldknopf, & Daly, 1990) regarding the properties and characteristics of children's imagery will no doubt provide clinicians with more specific guidelines for individualizing hypnotherapeutic approaches to conform to the unique needs and imaginative styles of children with psychological and medical problems.

In this chapter we summarize the state of knowledge in this area in the early 1990s. During the next decade, geometric increases in research are anticipated that will provide guidance for child health professionals in choosing hypnotherapeutic interventions and in determining mechanisms underlying treatment success and failure.

CLINICAL APPLICATIONS

As most child clinicians complete their first workshop training in clinical hypnosis, they begin to think of ways to apply the seemingly "new" skills that they have acquired. In so doing, they often become aware of a number of realities about the techniques, phenomenology, and applicability of self-regulatory, or cyberphysiologic, skills and methods. In this chapter, we use the term *cyberphysiology* to refer to the self-regulatory nature of hypnosis and self-hypnotic skills. The term is derived from the Greek word *kyber*, meaning *helmsman*, and thus refers to steering and self-directing, or self-regulating, sought and cultivated by hypnotic strategies.

As group hypnosis demonstrations provide opportunities for learning and a forum for personal hypnosis experiences, and as small group practice sessions unfold, therapists often notice that they have already been using many of the techniques and so-called "hypnotic-like" language in their clinical work with children. Accordingly, many therapists realize that using hypnotic techniques in their practice will be easier and faster than they initially thought. That is, therapists learn that hypnosis involves adding relaxation and imagery techniques to the work that they are already doing, and refining already-established models and styles of effective therapeutic communication that are individually tailored and addressed to the needs of a given child–clinician relationship.

We define *hypnosis* functionally as an alternative state of awareness and alertness characterized by heightened and focused concentration that is achieved in order to actualize a particular goal or latent potential. This state may be achieved with or without relaxation. From this perspective, therapists might well have been "doing" hypnosis or hypnotic-like work when they engaged young patients in conversation in which the children were absorbed, paying attention, listening, or responding as requested. Indeed, most children move fluidly in and out of spontaneous hypnotic (alternative) states as they focus their concentration on TV, football, or other sports; listen to a story; enjoy puppet play; and engage in fantasy. As Kuttner (1988) noted, children—especially young children—lack distinct boundaries between fantasy and reality and move frequently, easily, and naturally from fantasy to reality-based cognitive activities.

Natural, spontaneous hypnotic states are usually positive in affective tone and are conducive to conversation, learning, and understanding. Like purposefully induced hypnotic states, they are characterized by absorption in fantasy and imagination, focused attention, and heightened suggestibility. As is the case with adults, children's hypnotic states may be marked or indexed by observable physiological indicators. These include the following characteristics: if the eyes are open, a fixed gaze and staring without blinking; if the eyes are closed, eyelid flutter followed by eye movement under closed eyelids; unsuggested stillness in the chair (with younger children under 5 or 6 years old, this may not be seen or may be more evident in small segments of time); and unsuggested or spontaneous slowing of the respiratory rate.

When therapists appreciate that they are already doing hypnosis-like work with children, it often increases their interpersonal sensitivity and their commitment to carefully selecting language and monitoring the timing and pacing of their communications and interventions with children. Therapists often come to respect that during hypnosis, whether it is spontaneous or induced, children are focused intensely on the therapists' communications and may interpret what is said in a literal manner. These realizations sharpen therapists' interpersonal and communication skills in hypnotic and nonhypnotic contexts alike.

Developmental Considerations

A question we have encountered is the following: "When does hypnosis start and finish?" Practitioners who are acquainted with self-hypnosis recognize the fluidity with which children move in and out of hypnosis and realize that formal "induction" techniques may not be as important as they first believed. Rather, what is probably most important is the therapists' careful, concerned, and continuing observation of children and the mutuality of their interactions with the clinician. What evolves from this process is positive rapport, the strong therapeutic alliance that is so critical to the development of therapeutic communication in the hypnotic relationship.

Hypnosis sometimes begins as early as when "the therapist" enters the waiting room and introduces himself or herself to the child. When the therapist says, "I'm looking for someone named Meghan" instead of methodically, formally, or routinely saying, "Mrs. Johnson please" or calling, "Larry Peterson?", Meghan will invariably identify herself, even if her parent does so first. The therapist can then approach Meghan and introduce himself or herself.

We maintain that this interaction can be thought of as "hypnosis" if it engages the child's interest, focuses the child's attention, and achieves the desired result of making a personal connection with the child. If it is the therapist's intent to capture the child's attention and to evoke curiosity about developing a communicative relationship, then such an approach may be effective, particularly because it is unusual for children to be greeted in a personal and direct manner by the doctor on a first visit. Of course, parents are ordinarily receptive to this informal, rapport-building approach.

At the same time, we maintain that it is also hypnosis if during the second or fifth visit, a more formal induction technique is taught and experienced by the child. We suggest that both experiences are potentially effective, valid hypnotic (or hypnotic-like) techniques. In short, formal and more naturalistic, even spontaneous approaches and techniques can be equally hypnotic in nature and produce desirable therapeutic outcomes.

What, when, how, and why child hypnotherapy is used depends on many clinician, child, family, and situational variables. We are often asked the question, "At what age can a child be hypnotized?" In actuality, age itself is of little consequence. Age is secondary to the child's level of maturation, which encompasses the child's ability to understand language, concentrate, and maintain an external focus of attention. Thus, the more appropriate question is not "Is the child 2 years old?" but "Is the child able to respond to hypnotic strategies that are useful for preschool-age children?"

Appropriate questions to assess the child's readiness to respond to hypnosis include whether the child has the ability to attend to and enjoy a pop-up book, to be engaged in a bedtime story, or to listen to and participate in a story on audio- or videotape.

Whereas children of the same age may be much different developmentally, children of different ages may be highly similar developmentally. Hypnotic techniques and approaches must therefore be individually tailored and adapted to meet children's needs at their particular developmental level. A child of 9 or 10 years of age who is developmentally delayed and functioning at a 5-year-old level should be approached hypnotically as one would approach a 5-year-old. Conversely, a precocious or bright 10-year-old could well be more appropriately treated the way a 12-, 13-, or 14-year-old would be treated. The child's personality, likes and dislikes, learning style, family constellation, prior experiences, and comprehensive clinical history can all contribute critical information in devising specific hypnotic techniques and strategies and in structuring therapeutic suggestions.

In relation to the question of *how* child hypnotherapy is used, we emphasize that we do not use the verb *hypnotize* except as a reflexive one. Our belief is that all hypnosis is, in actuality, self-hypnosis. Thus, the only person a therapist can truly "hypnotize" is himself or herself. We explain this during the first visit with a child or family if the words *hypnosis* or *hypnotize* are mentioned. This sets the tone for the family and the patient to understand our belief that nothing really "happens" unless the child is oriented toward learning, motivated to change, and has a reason to acquire self-hypnotic skills.

This latter belief is in accordance with our definition of hypnosis, which underlines its goal-directed nature (i.e., the orientation of suggested activities, feelings, and imaginings toward actualizing personal goals and human potentials). Because therapeutic suggestions are geared toward specific objectives, we always give patients a clear reason ("Because . . .") why they should carry out any suggestion we offer.

Hypnotic Induction Techniques

Helpful and successful hypnotic techniques are tendered confidently and competently by clinicians to help children to enjoy using their internal resources to solve problems, attain goals, and master situations. Metaphorically speaking, Milton Erickson noted that one must greet the patient where he or she is and go with the patient (Haley, 1973). What this means is that the skilled therapist strives to avoid imposing an agenda on the patient. Instead, the therapist exhibits empathy and respect for the patient's needs, wishes, decisions, and defenses while capitalizing on the patient's expectations and resources to work toward mastery and to achieve treatment goals. True in all hypnotherapeutic encounters, this is mandatory for success in child hypnotherapy.

Following the establishment of rapport and comfort in the relationship with the child, following agreement with the child about the nature of the problem, and following indications of the child's motivation to change, the clinician can introduce hypnotherapy. How this is accomplished is a matter of personal comfort and style within the framework of the therapist's practice. Nevertheless, whether the clinician meets with success or failure may depend on the manner in which the patient is introduced to whatever is about to occur. To avoid common pitfalls, including forging ahead too early, too quickly, or too slowly, the clinician must attempt to learn what the child's understanding is of why he or she has come for treatment and what he or she expects is going to happen at present and future visits. The therapist's rationale and explanation of the use of hypnosis will, of course, depend on the patient's response.

Whether it is the child's or someone else's idea to do hypnosis, in asking a child directly why he or she has come for treatment, one may learn within the first few moments of a first visit that "You are supposed to hypnotize me" or "I'm here to get rid of my headaches" or "I need to learn how to relax." As the clinician explores the reasons for the visit, he or she learns about the child's expectations and language and devises his or her response and explanation with an eye toward constructing later verbalizations.

As an example, the clinician may explore with children who have headaches what activities the children enjoy that they are unable to do when they have headaches and what situations they have been engaged in during which they have never had a headache. As the history unfolds, the clinician acquires critical information about what kinds of imagery the child may enjoy (e.g., "When you have a headache, just imagine that you are at your grandma's cabin where you feel so happy and comfortable and nothing bothers you") as well as about what sensory modalities (i.e., visual, auditory, kinesthetic, olfactory) may be particularly important, meaningful, and effective to weave suggestions around.

Refreshingly, some children have positive ideas about relaxation or about helping themselves because their parents have spoken positively about personal experiences that they have had with self-hypnosis, relaxation, biofeedback, or similar self-management strategies. Parents' experiences may center around a wide variety of problems such as pain control, smoking cessation, or stress management. However, for children, the value of their parents' experience is not so much the discussion of a particular problem or technique but their parents' often spontaneous and enthusiastic expression of positive attitudes or feelings about the process of hypnosis or related activity. Alternatively, children may have positive expectations and ideas about hypnosis on the basis of seeing a program describing Olympic or professional athletes successfully applying imagery or hypnosis.

Unfortunately, many children derive their knowledge of hypnosis from parents' or others' culturally based misconceptions of hypnosis, which were probably derived from exposure to the ubiquitous stage hypnotist or to images of the all-powerful and all-controlling hypnotist portrayed in cartoons and movies. To demystify hypnosis, and to maximize the child's potential to respond to hypnotic suggestions, it is essential that the therapist correct these and other misconceptions about hypnosis prior to initiating a hypnotic intervention.

It is at this early juncture in therapy that we underscore the point that all hypnosis is self-hypnosis. It is, of course, also helpful to teach children about the hypnotic relationship in terms that they can understand. Thus, we may proceed by saying something similar to the following: "I am a pretty good coach and can help kids to use their inside minds to help themselves with something like those headaches you were telling me about." Allowing time for questions, the therapist can then introduce a brief explanation of how the experience of being "hypnotized" or "being in hypnosis" is natural and similar to many everyday experiences and that "It's just like daydreaming or pretending." This introduction to hypnosis is highly effective because we have never encountered a child or adolescent who failed to admit that he or she had done some pretending, daydreaming, or imagining.

Sometimes, we will take the opportunity to conduct a very brief "experiment" with the parent and child. For example, we will say abruptly,

> Let's do an experiment, everyone close their eyes and just pretend you're not here . . . pretend maybe you're at home . . . or maybe somewhere else . . . where you are very happy and comfortable and be there for a few moments. Good. See who's there with you, hear what's going on, enjoy it . . . and you can either tell about it after or you don't have to because it's your imagining and your inside mind and your self-hypnotizing and you're the boss of it. And you have probably noticed already, in just these few moments, that you also changed a little. Your breathing became slower, you were sitting real still and it's like your body and brain were talking with each other. Your body knew that your brain was imagining and it got relaxed. . . . Isn't that interesting? . . . Nice going!

Following the experiment, the parents and child who were formerly anxious are often relieved and even excited. Seeds are then planted to facilitate future interventions by way of statements such as, "And next time you come, you and I will meet in private and do some more imagining and learn how to use this to help those tummyaches that used to bother you!"

If the patient does not mention the word *hypnosis* but instead uses the word *biofeedback*, we may talk about how the body is its own best biofeedback and how people get signals from the body when they have different feelings. We may ask each person in the room to talk briefly about how their body reacts if he or she is about to cross a street and then hears screeching tires coming near. Discussions of this sort not only allow children to hear their parents describe their own links between psyche and soma, but they also catalyze expectations that change will occur. We weave into the discussion that we see ourselves as a coach and teacher and that we "don't really care what we call this process; some people call this relaxation, some call it biofeedback, some call it self-hypnosis, some call it imagining—we call it relaxation and mental imagery because that seems to be what all the kids say is happening and because it works." Statements of this sort are presented in a deliberate way and in a timely fashion in order to be facilitative and reassuring and to elicit strong expectations of positive outcomes.

When a therapist in a general clinical practice setting is consulted by a patient who either does not know that the therapist practices hypno-therapy, or the patient does not know what hypnosis is, there are a variety of approaches that may be useful. What approach is adopted ultimately depends on the therapist's personal style and beliefs, the patient's history, and the therapist's knowledge of the patient's current learning and inter-actional style.

One approach that could be taken is for the therapist to first ask the parents and child if they have ever heard of hypnosis or imagery and then to proceed with an explanation. More often, however, we are inclined to include comments about the nature of the problem by making comments along the following lines: "Many children with this problem get great relief by learning how to use their mind to help their body" and noting that "Some call it biofeedback, some call it self-hypnosis, some call it imagining—we call it relaxation and mental imagery because that's what all kids say is happening, and it works." We may go on to explain that "Most kids say it's the same feeling they get as when they daydream or when they concentrate on a book or music and don't seem to hear or notice other things quite the same."

We also draw the distinction between such spontaneous hypnotic states and states we induce or cultivate for some purpose (e.g., working on pain control, a tic, or anxiety). Often, we will abruptly turn to the child during such a discussion and say matter of factly, "You know how to daydream, don't you?" The child, of course, will respond affirmatively.

In more urgent situations, such as an emergency room consultation, lengthy explanations are neither indicated nor useful. Instead, it is appro-priate to proceed to "do" hypnosis by offering positive therapeutic sugges-tions that work for patients who are already in spontaneous negative trances (Kohen, 1986b). In emergency situations, people—especially children—are often frightened and have experiences and act in a manner characteristic of the altered state of awareness that we call *hypnosis*. Typically, these experiences and behaviors include the following: a narrowed, focused concentration on the injured or painful part of the body, sometimes to the complete exclusion of awareness of another injured part (i.e., spontaneous hypnoanesthesia for the other part); a fixed gaze or stare reminiscent of, if not equivalent to that elicited by, a spontaneous eye-fixation induction technique; and spontaneous or selective inattention to the surroundings, as evidenced by apparently not hearing or seeing things in the environment. Although these behaviors, which are so familiar to emergency personnel, are analogous to patients' hypnotic behaviors, they can also be thought of as negative, self-perpetuating (like purposely induced hypnotic states), and counterproductive states.

Although many variations of hypnotic inductions exist, in reality they all are forms of personal imagery, regardless of whether physical relaxation is also used. Muscular relaxation, although often facilitative, is by no means a mandated or an essential characteristic of the hypnotic state (Thompson, 1979). The therapist who expects physical relaxation to accompany hypnosis is likely to be disappointed, particularly with preschool-age children. Most often, the key ingredient to a successful and enjoyable hypnotic experience is a positive therapeutic relationship (e.g., whether the therapist and child are "friends" yet) and knowledge of the child's favorite activities.

A therapist then only needs to invite the child to begin to daydream or pretend in order to "start." This is easily accomplished by saying the following:

> To start doing this, all you have to do is start pretending or daydreaming about something fun that you like. I don't know what it will be, but you'll find out when you get there in your inside thinking. Some kids like to close their eyes when they do this, and you can if you want or you can keep them open or until they close or whatever . . . cause you're the boss of this, I'm just the coach . . . good. . . . I don't know what you'll daydream or pretend about . . . maybe it will be [insert some of their favorite activities] or something else. Let your head nod [note that this dissociative suggestion is a different hypnotic suggestion or request than "nod your head"] when you can really feel inside like you are somewhere else.

For children who are skeptical or hesitant about experiencing hypnosis, more concrete or physical validation may be not only facilitative but fun. In such cases, the "fingers together" induction technique or the technique of a "pretend sandpail on one wrist and a bunch of helium balloons on the other" are often fun and easy (self-) inductions. After the induction, "deepening" can be accomplished easily through intensification of imagery through multisensory suggestions (e.g., "See who and what's there, smell the smells, hear the sounds"), along with interspersed suggestions for progressive relaxation.

Successful child clinicians using hypnotherapy will be those who (a) are competent and confident clinicians in their child health field; (b) are experienced with their own self-hypnosis and alternative states of awareness; (c) have had introductory workshop training in general and child clinical hypnosis and intermediate and advanced workshop training in child hypnosis and hypnotherapy; (d) understand and are knowledgeable about child development and developmental differences among children; (e) talk with and learn from other child clinicians about their successes and failures in the use of hypnotherapy; (f) review their own hypnotic sessions with children via audio- or videotapes to critique and continue to improve themselves; and (g) stay abreast of clinical and research literature and developments in the rapidly growing area of child cyberphysiology (self-regulation).

Clinical applications of child hypnosis can be broadly divided into seven categories. Although the categories are arbitrary, they afford a reasonable and useful way of formulating and thinking about applying hypnotic techniques in a variety of clinical practices of child health maintenance, supervision, and illness care.

1. Habit problems and disorders: thumb sucking, nail biting, hair pulling (trichotillomania), enuresis.
2. Behavioral problems and concerns: adjustment reaction, anger, sibling rivalry, ego strengthening as an adjunct to psychotherapy.
3. Biobehavioral disorders: asthma, migraine, Tourette syndrome, inflammatory bowel disease.
4. Pain
   a. Acute: injury, illness, procedural, recurrent acute
   b. Chronic and recurrent: illness, trauma, recurrent procedures.
5. Anxiety: performance (e.g., stage fright, tests, recitals, sports, new experiences)
   a. Acute: grief and bereavement
   b. Chronic: phobias.
6. Psychoneuroimmunological: warts, autoimmune disorders, cancer.
7. Chronic disease, multisystem disease, and terminal illness: hemophilia, acquired immunodeficiency syndrome (AIDS), cystic fibrosis, chronic renal disease (dialysis).

CASE MATERIAL

In our discussion of the management of disorders and conditions in each category, we note each briefly and focus on the manner in which hypnosis and hypnotherapy have been and can be useful in each arena. Because our discussion is not exhaustive, we present a fairly exhaustive reference list and urge the reader to review specific reference materials for a more detailed discussion of research, clinical strategies, and verbalizations pertinent to particular disorders or problems. The brief clinical vignettes that follow illustrate the specific applications, development of strategies, hypnotic techniques and language, and the outcomes of actual clinical encounters with patients from our practices.

Habit Problems

The treatment of habit problems is often one of the most gratifying areas for the application of relaxation and mental imagery (RMI) and the teaching of self-hypnotic skills (Gardner, 1978; Kohen, Olness, Colwell, & Heimel, 1984). With the presence of a habit problem and a definite indication that the patient (and not only the family) has a desire for the habit to end, the teaching and use of RMI skills can be presented as the approach of choice. In this case, the therapist and patient can focus their efforts on the complete disappearance of the problem.

In treating habit problems, hypnotic techniques and suggestions must be individualized. It is, of course, impossible to predict how quickly a particular child will be completely free of a troubling habit. However, therapists can instill positive expectations by informing patients and families that most well-motivated children are able to learn self-hypnosis RMI within one or two visits and achieve a degree of improvement within four or five visits (Kohen et al., 1984). Unlike the concern often noted in the hypnotherapeutic management of adult habit problems, symptom substitution is rarely seen in children when habit problems are treated with self-regulation techniques (Gardner, 1978; Olness & Gardner, 1988).

For habit problems, as with many children's problems, it often is critical to develop rapport with the child and to educate the child about how the body works. The explanation about how the "problem" has come about must be formulated in the child's language in terms that the child can readily comprehend. For example, because most kindergarten-level children have some familiarity with or at least awareness of computers, a computer analog metaphor can be highly useful in talking with children about what habits are and how they develop. We present two examples: The first is for the treatment of a "traditional" habit problem of thumb sucking; the second is for the treatment of nocturnal enuresis.

Thumb Sucking

The therapist initiates the following discussion with the child with or without the parent present (depending on the age of the child). Although it precedes more formal or "official" hypnosis training, the therapist's statements contain hypnoticlike language and suggestions and set the tone for the kinds of language, expectations, and suggestions offered later during hypnosis.

> Bobby, from what you've told me I guess that sometimes it seems like that thumb [the dissociation suggestion is *that* thumb, not *your* thumb] makes its way to your mouth without you even noticing it? [He agrees!] And . . . it's kind of amazing that sometimes you are so used to it that you don't even notice it sometimes until it's been in there awhile? You know what a habit is, don't you? It's like something that is automatic, that happens [no responsibility] without knowing it or thinking about it on purpose. Do you have any habits? [He agrees that thumb sucking is one little habit.] You know which is the best computer in the world? [After he finished guessing IBM, etc., I point to his head and he knows that the brain is in there.] One of the ways that the brain works well and so fast is by having habits—just like a computer does—so if you push "A" on the computer, it always types "A" or if you give some other direction it always does it the same way. And our brains are the same. But after you learn something you don't always have to think about it, do you? Like walking—do you think about walking, or talk about it out loud, or do you just do it? You just walk, don't you? Well, that's because your brain, the computer, knows how and it has a good habit, and now the feet and legs and back know how to walk, don't they? You don't have to say "Okay, feet now walk . . . ," but you did have to learn, didn't you?
>
> When you were just a little kid you learned a lot of good habits with your parents' help. And, sometimes, you learned some other habits that you then stopped using—like crawling. You don't still crawl most of the time, do you? Well, your brain still knows how, but it stopped using that habit that it used to need, didn't it? [pause] Well, that's right and when you were younger [this is a purposeful appeal to the developing ego and desire for growth, mastery, and development present in all children], you learned that other habit very well of sucking that thumb. Back then it was a good one to use but now you don't need it any more, do you? Well, it was such a good automatic one when you first started that it has kept going. Now that you don't need it anymore, you just have to reprogram that computer we call the brain to do it differently . . . and that's how daydreaming and imagination can help . . . and I'll be your coach/teacher/helper.

A discussion along these lines is often sufficient for younger children. However, for somewhat older schoolchildren and parents, it may be useful to explain how, because such automaticity is by definition "subconscious" and out of one's usual awareness, that that is what makes it a "habit." Conquering the habit, or "undoing it," is best accomplished through the use of subconscious maneuvers such as daydreaming, imagination, self-hypnosis, and RMI (Kohen, 1991).

Nocturnal Enuresis

Nocturnal enuresis may not be as true a habit disorder, as, for example, thumb sucking or nail biting. However, the therapist's presentation of nocturnal enuresis as a type of habit is not only legitimate and direct but is often effective in relieving a sense of guilt or responsibility, which in turn empowers and motivates the child to work to make a change. Prior to the introduction of hypnosis, it is mandatory that a comprehensive medical history, physical examination, and urinalysis have assured both the clinician and the family that no evident or easily remedied physical problem is responsible for the problem (Kohen, 1990; Olness, 1975).

In developing rapport and devising a clinical strategy, the clinician must understand the patient's and family's beliefs and attitudes regarding the origin of the problem, as well as their expectations for participation in the successful resolution of the problem. In this rapport-building and strategy development phase, it is particularly important for the clinician to present an easily understood explanation of normal genitourinary anatomy and physiology. In this context, and in the conversation that follows, enuresis may be presented as being analogous to a habit problem or disorder while also introducing RMI as a useful strategy for reversing or changing the habit.

"So, your accidents occur at night? Some or all nights?" If the answer is *all*, we move to the next idea. If it is *no*, we say something like, "Oh, so 2 nights a week your bladder and brain talk to each other just fine! Great! That makes it even easier to think about solving. And in the day you don't have any accidents? Never? Wow . . . how do you do that?" Of course, patients never know how they do it because it is unconscious, which is the thrust of the discussion. "So, when do you go to sleep at night and when do you wake up in the morning?"

By asking this, we wish to point out to the patient, if he or she is old enough to understand math and percentages, what percentage of the usually 24-hr day is "already solved," thus reframing the patient's understanding. Of course, most children even as young as 5 years of age who are having accidents only at night will find it "gross" that the therapist would even suggest the possibility that they might be wet in the daytime. This allows for ego-strengthening suggestions such as the following:

> Well, great, so you're growing up . . . but you didn't always know how to be dry in the day, how did you learn? [The implication is, of course, that they did learn, are capable of learning, and that it was automatic because they are unlikely to remember.] So, when you were younger, like around 2 or 3, your parents taught you and pretty soon you knew all by yourself. At first you probably had to think on purpose and maybe

even talk out loud about how to go to the bathroom, but now I bet you don't do that, do you? You don't say out loud "I have to pee" and then go to the bathroom. . . . Mostly you just go, right? Let's say you had to go right now, how would you know and what would you do? Well, your bladder would say to your brain, "Hey, brain, I'm full," and your brain would get the message and say back to your bladder, "Well, thanks for telling me, but keep the gate closed on the bladder because it wouldn't be nice to pee on the doctor's chair!" Would you say that or think that, or would it just happen that way in your inside mind and thinking? [Introduce and validate subconscious ideas and the concept of an "inside mind," which will be used during the hypnotic suggestions later.] And then, would you think out loud, "Okay, feet stand up and walk to the bathroom, hands open door, turn on light, take off pants, now bladder open gate and let pee out in the toilet?" Or would you just do it?

Of course, you'd just do it because your brain and your bladder know how to talk to each other because you taught them when you were younger, and now they have the good and automatic habit of doing it without even thinking about it. Because you know that, it'll be easy to remind them how to do it at night. Because at night they just accidentally [removal of blame] got into the accidental bad habit [again] of not talking to each other during the night even though they know how. . . . So, using your inside mind I can show you with your day-dreaming and imagining that you can help them get rid of that old habit and get a new habit going so you can wake up dry in the morning. [The suggestion "you can help" is an appeal to the growing ego helper in the child; the "them" as a reference to brain and bladder is a dissociative suggestion to distance them from responsibility and the shame or blame—as with thumb sucking. The "old habit" is a reframing to indicate its lack of continued usefulness.]

Such explanations of habits with the use of a computer analogy or metaphor serve several purposes: (a) initiating relief of guilt or shame associated with the problem; (b) providing a useful way of thinking about the problem; and (c) planting seeds of motivation and positive expectations for the resolution of the problem with hypnotic techniques.

Behavior Problems

RMI and hypnotic techniques can play an important adjunctive role in the treatment of the wide range of conditions called *behavioral problems*. Indeed, RMI can sometimes interrupt behavioral patterns or cycles sufficiently to facilitate change or enhance associated therapeutic interventions (e.g., counseling, psychotherapy, family therapy, behavioral modification). Reasonable objectives in approaching behavioral problems with the aid of self-hypnosis and RMI include enhancing coping abilities, allaying anxiety, and facilitating self-esteem and autonomy. As with any hypnotherapeutic approach with children, family members' cooperation and involvement is required to first "allow" and then facilitate children's ability to learn and apply hypnotic techniques.

An example of a common behavioral situation in which RMI can be an effective adjunct is the management of children's anger or temper tantrum responses. In addition to whatever counseling or family education therapy is used, teaching a self-hypnotic exercise often gives children something constructive, personal, and relaxing to do to interrupt the anger, helplessness, and loss of control that commonly accompany tantrum behavior.

Along with the easily accessed and demonstrated relaxation response, children can be taught that when they practice RMI and self-hypnosis (every day or night) when they are not having a tantrum, they can teach themselves how to establish control quickly "when you really need it" (e.g., "Change the VCR from the angry, upset Rachel movie to the happy, comfortable growing up Rachel movie of you playing" or "As soon as you notice that angry, mad feeling starting, notice what color it is, turn on the faucet in your mind, run the feeling out of your thinking, down your face, into your neck, down your shoulder, and into your arm and down into your hand. Roll it into a tight fist and then throw the angry mad feelings into the ocean or to outer space because you don't need them now that you are relaxing so well. Then see what color the angry feeling changed to because that is your color of feeling relaxed and comfortable and more controlled").

In an analogous fashion, self-hypnotic exercises focusing on control and relaxation can be an effective adjunct in managing adjustment reactions or sibling rivalry and in building self-esteem through ego strengthening and as a key feature in general stress-management treatments. With respect to more complex behavior problems and conditions, such as encopresis, RMI and self-hypnosis can play integral roles in a multimodal therapeutic plan.

Biobehavioral Disorders

In this category is a group of diseases or problems with clearly identified pathophysiological origins and effects, which traditionally have been thought or known to have emotional or psychological components. Examples include asthma, migraine headaches, Tourette syndrome, and inflammatory bowel disease, all of which are known to include emotional or psychological stress as a "trigger" that adversely affects or exacerbates the disease or symptoms associated with it. In working with children and teenagers with these problems, the goal is to teach RMI skills for the purpose of enhancing a sense of self-control along with the definitive reduction of clinical symptoms.

Our research and that of others has established the effectiveness of RMI as a tool through which children can regulate functions previously thought to be completely autonomic. These functions include the demonstration of the self-regulation of peripheral temperature (Dikel & Olness, 1980), brain stem audio-evoked responses (Hogan, Olness, & MacDonald, 1985), transcutaneous oxygen flux (Olness & Conroy, 1985), salivary immunoglobulin (Olness, Culbert, & Uden, 1989), migraine headaches (Olness et al., 1987), pulmonary function (Kohen, 1986a), and tics and Tourette syndrome (Kohen & Botts, 1987).

Clinical experience has repeatedly demonstrated the ability of children using self-hypnosis to modify and modulate an acute episode of wheezing with asthma (Kohen, 1986b, 1986c). Research (Kohen, 1986a) has also demonstrated that children with asthma who learn RMI have decreased functional morbidity, along with fewer emergency room visits, fewer missed school days, and an enhanced sense of control. Children and adolescents with juvenile migraines who have learned RMI demonstrate more effectiveness than control patients and patients using propranolol in reducing the intensity, frequency, and duration of their migraine headaches (Olness et al., 1987).

As with all hypnotherapy with children, the specific hypnotic suggestions administered depend on the child's favorite place or activity imagery, his or her formulation and understanding of the problem, and the imagery and feelings produced in association with the amelioration or disappearance of the problem. For example, as part of the initial history, an 11-year-old girl with migraine headaches was asked to describe and draw her image of a migraine and her image of comfort without a headache. For the former, she scribbled a chaotic mixture of red, black, and blue lines. For the latter, she methodically drew an ocean with a beach, a blanket, and a beach umbrella; on the blanket was a book, a "boom box" radio, and a drink with a carefully placed parasol. The choice of hypnotic imagery "where nothing bothers or disturbs you and where those headaches that used to be there are not even present or noticed" was obviously easy to identify.

Case History: Kevin

Kevin, age 14, was referred for training in self-hypnosis to control migraines. He had been hospitalized a year earlier for a migraine episode associated with neurological deficits, and he continued to have severe migraine episodes every 7–10 days while on propranolol. A review of his patient information questionnaire and an interview with Kevin revealed that he was an excellent student with many interests that included computer programming, classical music, soccer, and baseball.

Kevin was fascinated with the concept of viewing his autonomic responses portrayed on a computer screen as he learned relaxation and pain-control techniques. With respect to changes in mental processing, during the first visit it was apparent that his peripheral temperature was more labile than was his galvanic skin resistance (GSR). Kevin was intrigued when he observed his peripheral temperature change rapidly as he thought about scary or exciting memories or participated in relaxation practice. He enjoyed a simple progressive relaxation exercise cued to breathing and agreed to practice twice daily.

At the second visit, Kevin was in the throes of a migraine episode. After 30 min of participating in the progressive relaxation review, with suggestions to develop a mental computer program to control pain and nausea, he spontaneously said that his headache pain had moved from a self-rating of 10 down to a rating of 3.

Kevin's third visit was 3 weeks later, and he had no migraine episodes in the interim period. Now practicing for 10 min twice a day, he was encouraged to focus on soccer imagery, on being in control of his body as he played, and on enjoying the feeling of control. He was able to describe in detail his special computer code for reducing sensations of pain and nausea. Subsequently, he was followed by monthly phone calls for 6 months and every 2 months thereafter. In the ensuing year, Kevin had three mild migraine episodes, each of which ended quickly.

Case History: Terri

Terri, age 14, was referred by her primary physician with symptoms similar to those of Kevin. However, the initial evaluation revealed that she had documented learning disabilities and that her private school was highly stressful in spite of special classes and tutors. Her parents regarded her as coping well with her learning handicaps and as compensating successfully for her deficits. In casual conversation, her concrete thinking was evident, in contrast to Kevin's abstract reasoning skills.

At the time of the first visit, it was noted that Terri's baseline GSR was high (30) and did not decrease during several efforts to help her identify relaxing images. She had a severe math handicap and also said that she had difficulty with visualization. Nevertheless, she was able to elaborate vivid kinesthetic imagery (e.g., the comfortable feeling of a whirlpool bath). She was asked to focus on this feeling for 5 min two or three times a day.

Terri was enthusiastic about this practice, and it was obvious that she was accustomed to doing her homework. She returned, saying that she felt good when she practiced but that she still had headaches. She enjoyed watching the computer screen. After two more practice sessions, when it was obvious that her GSR jumped whenever a practice demand was made, regardless of how gentle or indirect, Terri was asked to be her own coach. The therapist sat away from her so that it was obvious that the therapist was not watching the screen. After 15 min she told the therapist that she had "figured out" a way to relax. She described a vacation place with a beach and whirlpool. Her descriptions were kinesthetic: the sand between her toes, the feeling of warm sun, and the splashing of waves. After six practice sessions, it was evident that Terri was in control of her GSR response and that she enjoyed the control she achieved. Her migraine frequency had reduced to once a month. As the therapist began to discuss an approach to pain control, Terri chose the feeling of pushing a button.

Terri was seen monthly over the next 6 months, and she spoke with her therapist by phone every 2 weeks. She was not able to continue on her own as Kevin had, and the therapeutic setting was important to her. Her parents encouraged her and gave her excellent feedback as she demonstrated increased confidence in school, in addition to a reduction in headache episodes. Her learning disabilities and limited visual imagery skills eventuated in a relatively slow therapeutic process. Furthermore, she had developed a conditioned stress response to demands for performance, rendering conventional hypnotherapeutic approaches counterproductive because she associated direct suggestion with performance demands. However, Terri's excellent study habits contributed to her eventual success because she practiced faithfully at home.

Pain

As with adults, children and teenagers in acute pain are the easiest patients to treat with hypnotic techniques. They are highly motivated to feel better, to gain control of their life, and to rid themselves of their discomfort. Whether at the site of an accident or in an emergency room, it is important to speak to the child in acute pain in a way that allows the speaker to be heard, understood, and believed. Because people in acute pain are already in a spontaneous, albeit negative (i.e., acutely focused and believing the worst), hypnotic state (Kohen, 1986b; Olness & Gardner, 1988), it is important that communications are carefully selected and modulated to foster positive feelings and expectations.

For instance, the therapist's empathic statement to the client, "That really hurts," distinguishes the speaker as a good observer, captures the pain patient's attention, and opens the door for additional hypnotic suggestions for comfort and pain relief. For children, these suggestions could be as simple as "and it will probably hurt less soon. I'm glad you came to the doctor" or "It will keep right on hurting until it doesn't need to anymore." This may be followed by an invitation to experience the pain differently, such as "Would it be okay to take your mind somewhere else?" or, more directly, "What will you do when you get home, after this is taken care of?"

Beyond the distraction value of this type of hypnotic suggestion, it offers the expectant reassurance that the child will indeed be going home while also implying that the situation is not as serious as it might have seemed in fantasy. Similarly, a direct "permission" to ignore or dissociate the pain is often easily accepted by the patient in acute pain. Thus, one may say to a child, "Close your eyes . . . find the switch for your leg. . . What color is it in your mind? . . . What shape? Is it a turn or a flip kind of switch? Now, turn it down . . . and then 1–2–3, click off, and notice how different it feels. . . . Good for you!" Adding relaxation, dissociation via leaving to a favorite place, or hypnoanesthesia or analgesia by cleaning the injured part with "special liquid that is cool and comforting" are additional techniques that may be useful when tailored to the child's needs.

For acute discomfort in association with a planned rather than an emergent problem (e.g., for a procedure such as a bone marrow, spinal tap, or venipuncture for blood withdrawal or intravenous hookup), more time is usually available to plan and instigate treatment. This allows for both a creative exploration of the techniques that may be of the greatest benefit to a given child and for practice in preparation for the procedure. Such approaches via RMI may involve making the area numb through transfer of recalled (local) anesthesia (e.g., from a previous dental extraction or suture of a wound), turning off or down of a switch, or taking a trip around the body to reach and put up a temporary protective barrier to prevent the signal from the potential pain site from getting through to the mind. When the procedures required are repetitive, and the anticipated event is emotionally charged by the recalled pain from the prior procedure, the addition of hypnotic amnesia for the prior event may prove effective.

In chronic and recurrent pain, recollections of previous pain affect a child's perceptions of recurrent pain syndromes (e.g., recurrent abdominal pain, migraines, inflammatory bowel disease) as well as perceptions of pain related to chronic illnesses (e.g., back pain, pain from metastatic disease). As with the biobehavioral disorders discussed earlier, the hypnotherapeutic management of chronic or recurrent pain in children is best viewed as one method, technique, or link that is integral to a comprehensive pain-management program individually tailored to the needs of a particular child.

Even during the initial history-taking and rapport-development part of a visit, children with chronic or recurrent pain should be encouraged to describe and characterize their discomfort (we do not use the word *pain* very often, even if the patient does) on a scale from, say, 0–12 or 1–10, identifying the various scale anchors where different effects of the discomfort are perceived. This approach, commonly useful in nonhypnotic or general pain management, can readily be generalized later to the hypnotic environment.

For example, during hypnosis children may be offered several direct or metaphoric options to first see the scale in their imagination (e.g., inner mind, inside thinking) and then to consider adjusting the scale by changing and lowering (or raising) the rating to the level desired. Next, suggestions may be given for children to bring the lower or better number, and associated good feeling achieved, back with them when they "return" from their imagination.

Anxiety

As with other problems, a thorough and sensitive history and assessment of the child, along with careful pacing of the emerging therapeutic relationship, will yield ideas about the proper role of hypnotherapy for a particular child's anxiety. For common performance anxiety such as stage fright, or tachycardia or palpitations before a basketball game, it can be easily demonstrated to the child that his or her response, like a habit disorder, has become a conditioned reaction that is associated with negative expectations and can be controlled and mastered.

Often, this can be readily accomplished by discussing with the child and other family members the common phenomenon of physiological responses to stressful circumstances. An easily understood example is that of flushing or blushing when embarrassed. The therapist can explain to the child that a cycle occurs in which one first experiences something (embarrassing), followed by a feeling reaction (embarrassment), followed by a physical response (blushing) that troubles the child. The therapist can then inquire, "Well, do you stay blushed?" Often children and families remark that they can and do act in some way to relieve the feeling of embarrassment and curtail the blushing episode. This provides the child and parents with an everyday example of how a shift in the way a child feels does in fact provide a shift in the physical response (of blushing) without even thinking about it or modifying the response deliberately.

Such discussion about cognitive mastery then allows the hypnotic approach to reinforce whatever approach one wishes to take to allay anxiety. For example, this may include the "split screen" approach, in which the child imagines himself or herself at home practicing his or her free throws, ballet dance, speech, trumpet solo, and so forth, successfully or flawlessly, and in a side-by-side image sees himself or herself in the auditorium or on the basketball court. Hypnotic suggestions are then offered for the merging of the two screens. Other options include the following: "Just turn down the dial on that nervous feeling from 4 to 3. . . . That's right . . . from 3 to 2 . . . great . . . and either 2 to 0 right away or 2 to 1 and then to 0, whichever you prefer." Inclusion of motivating, ego-strengthening suggestions such as "Run the tape on fast-forward in your mind, see how well you did it, and look at how proud you feel and hear what wonderful things your mom and dad are saying" are often strongly facilitative.

Other anxiety reactions, such as phobias, may require more intensive treatment and incorporate elements of staged desensitization procedures such as "Watch yourself, see how proud you are being with your cousin's new dog . . . and remembering that even though you forgot how you used to be back then [both a suggestion for regression and amnesia] when you were younger and used to be worried [the implication is that the child is older, braver, and it is in the past tense] about dogs."

The use of hypnotherapy as an adjunct to supportive counseling and psychotherapy is often highly effective in managing commonly experienced separation anxieties. These include sadness and symptoms associated with moving away from old friends, starting school, or helping children with the natural but difficult process of grief and bereavement following the death of a significant person or pet. Positive imagery of happy memories, reexperienced by way of age regression, may provide a respite from feelings of sadness and loneliness, as well as a bridge to learning about and accepting death.

Chronic Disease, Multisystem Disease, and Terminal Illness

Much less is known about the influence of hypnosis and self-hypnosis on the progress of malignant disease than about anxiety, for example, but researchers are becoming increasingly aware of the capacity of children with cancer to learn RMI strategies and apply them in a variety of ways to aid in coping with their disease. An informative and optimistic film, *No Fears, No Tears*, prepared by Kuttner (1986), effectively illustrates the range and usefulness of hypnotic techniques for helping children with cancer to manage pain, deal with repeated difficult medical procedures, and cope with the effects of these challenging treatments.

Research (Zeltzer & LeBaron, 1982) also indicates that children are able to use hypnotic skills to reduce nausea and vomiting associated with chemotherapy. Moreover, it has been demonstrated (Olness & Singher, 1989) that children use RMI most effectively when they learn the techniques shortly after their initial diagnosis. With terminally ill children, hypnosis has been a particularly effective adjunctive modality in assisting patients to cope with and traverse the last moments of life (Gardner, 1976).

RESEARCH AND APPRAISAL

Early laboratory research focused on efforts to establish hypnotic susceptibility scales for children. London published the Children's Hypnotic Susceptibility Scale in 1963, and Morgan and Hilgard published the Stanford Hypnotic Clinical Scale for Children in 1979. These scales, modeled on adult hypnotic susceptibility scales, were validated. However, multiple groups have found them to be irrelevant clinically. Efforts to establish various physiological responses (e.g., peripheral temperature, electroencephalographic changes, GSR measures) as surrogate markers for changes in awareness or hypnotic responsivity have proved unproductive.

The inability to document the hypnotic state via a prospective test or concurrent measure has caused considerable difficulty in multidisciplinary studies that demand proof of the hypnotic state. It has been more practical to describe the process of intervention without claims that a different or altered state has been attained in the experimental subject.

A number of clinical research studies (Hilgard & LeBaron, 1984; Olness, 1989; Zeltzer & LeBaron, 1982) in which hypnotherapy in children's pain problems was used have consistently documented the clinical effectiveness of hypnosis. Recently, such studies have attempted to assess predictive factors related to age, sex, previous experience with pain, and differences in subjective experiences of pain.

Most researchers and clinicians (Erickson, 1991) agree that previous experience with pain or painful procedures is an important factor in predicting how quickly children can be expected to learn and respond to training in self-hypnosis. For example, if children with leukemia have the opportunity to learn cyberphysiological pain-management techniques shortly after the diagnosis, they are able to apply their skills more quickly and successfully with less training than are children negatively conditioned to expect pain from procedures (Olness, 1981).

Developmental stages also relate to how children perceive, tolerate, and cope with pain. Preschoolers may view pain as punishment for being bad and may have difficulty in localizing their areas of discomfort (Olness et al., 1989). Studies also reveal that the process of teaching self-regulation skills to children is not limited to structured, stiff, ritualistic inductions (Kuttner, 1988). Storytelling, games, computer games, movement, and spontaneous imagery can all be antecedents to successful programming for desirable therapeutic outcomes in children (Lynn & Rhue, 1991). Of course, children's responsivity to a particular naturalistic approach depends on their preferences, personalities, and past experiences.

A significant difficulty in designing hypnotherapeutic research relates to the fact that some conditions for which hypnotherapy is applied are not well understood in terms of their etiology or pathogenesis (e.g., juvenile migraine, enuresis, Tourette syndrome, warts). Such conditions are lumped into groups, and the interpretation of therapeutic outcome does not take into consideration variability in the etiology of the condition. Thus, response variation may reflect variations in etiology rather than variations in technique or practice or age of the child.

During the late 1980s, there was intense interest in the possibility that humans, via self-regulation methods, could improve immunological functioning. Much of this interest focused on AIDS. Unfortunately, basic laboratory research to document what, if any, individual changes may occur has not been conducted. At present, the only laboratory changes documented with respect to immunoregulation have been in children and adolescents (Hall, Minnes, Tosi, & Olness, 1992; Olness et al., 1989).

Research Needs

The changes documented thus far, which are related to healthy children and adolescents, are primarily of heuristic interest, and it is inappropriate to use these findings as a basis for generalizing to clinical populations and applications. Work with a particular focus on clinical populations remains to be done and will require multiple research groups and extensive funding. To our knowledge, eight institutions are currently implementing the first collaborative research in hypnosis with children. This consortium is examining the effects of hypnotic interventions on warts and physiological changes associated with their disappearance or growth.

Although much remains to be done in terms of prospective, controlled laboratory studies involving cyberphysiological interventions, many clinical applications have been noted anecdotally but have not yet been documented in published prospective studies of hypnotherapeutic applications. Examples include the treatment and evaluation of cystic fibrosis, hypertension, endoscopy procedures, ulcerative colitis, regional enteritis, cardiac arrhythmias, and alopecia areata. For a few clinical conditions, occasional single-case reports exist. If clinicians experienced in applying hypnotherapy with children would document their observations sequentially and include long-term outcomes, this area would advance more rapidly, have a more solid basis for the design of laboratory research, and earn greater credibility among clinical practitioners.

CONCLUSION

When used appropriately with children, hypnotherapy is a useful and efficient strategy. The skilled therapist not only helps the child to apply innate imagination in an enjoyable way but also instills or facilitates a sense of mastery in the child. Hypnotherapy is useful in addressing habit problems, acute and chronic anxiety, acute and chronic pain, biobehavioral disorders, and chronic diseases such as hemophilia or asthma. Techniques must be based on a child's developmental stage and interests.

Unlike the side effects of many therapeutic interventions, the "side effect" or by-product of hypnotherapy is increased versus decreased competence. Although more research is essential in this area, there is now a firm basis of clinical experience from which child health professionals can learn and to which they can also contribute.

REFERENCES

Dikel, W., & Olness, K. (1980). Self-hypnosis, biofeedback, and voluntary peripheral temperature control in children. *Pediatrics, 66,* 335–340.

Erickson, C. J. (1991). Applications of cyberphysiologic techniques in pain management. *Pediatric Annals, 30,* 145–146, 148–150, 152–156.

Gardner, G. G. (1976). Childhood, death, and human dignity: Hypnotherapy for David. *International Journal of Clinical and Experimental Hypnosis, 24,* 122–139.

Gardner, G. G. (1978). Hypnotherapy in the management of childhood habit disorders. *Journal of Pediatrics, 92,* 834.

Haley, J. (1973). *Uncommon therapy: The psychiatric techniques of Milton H. Erickson, M.D.* New York: Norton.

Hall, H., Minnes, L., Tosi, M., & Olness, K. (1992). Voluntary modulation of neutrophil adhesiveness using a cyberphysiologic strategy. *International Journal of Neuroscience, 63,* 287–297.

Hilgard, J., & LeBaron, S. (1984). *Hypnotherapy of pain in children with cancer.* Los Altos, CA: Kaufmann.

Hogan, M., Olness, K., & MacDonald, J. (1985). The effects of hypnosis on brainstem auditory responses in children. *American Journal of Clinical Hypnosis, 27,* 91–94.

Kohen, D. P. (1986a). Application of relaxation/mental imagery (self-hypnosis) to the management of asthma: Report of behavioral outcomes of a two year, prospective controlled study. *American Journal of Clinical Hypnosis, 28,* 196.

Kohen, D. P. (1986b). Applications of relaxation/mental imagery (self-hypnosis) in pediatric emergencies. *International Journal of Clinical and Experimental Hypnosis, 34,* 283–294.

Kohen, D. P. (1986c). The value of relaxation/mental imagery (self-hypnosis) to the management of children with asthma: A cyberphysiologic approach. *Topics in Pediatrics, 4,* 11–18.

Kohen, D. P. (1990). A hypnotherapeutic approach to enuresis. In D. C. Hammond (Ed.), *Handbook of hypnotic suggestion and metaphors* (pp. 489–493). New York: Norton.

Kohen, D. P. (1991). Applications of relaxation/mental imagery (self-hypnosis) for habit problems. *Pediatric Annals, 20,* 136–144.

Kohen, D. P., & Botts, P. (1987). Relaxation/imagery (self-hypnosis) in Tourette syndrome: Experience with four children. *American Journal of Clinical Hypnosis, 29,* 227–237.

Kohen, D. P., Olness, K., Colwell, S., & Heimel, A. (1984). The use of relaxation/mental imagery (self-hypnosis) in the management of 505 pediatric behavioral encounters. *Journal of Developmental and Behavioral Pediatrics, 1,* 21–25.

Kosslyn, S. M., Margolis, J. A., Barrett, A. M., Goldknopf, E. F., & Daly, P. F. (1990). Age differences in imagery abilities. *Child Development, 61,* 995–1010.

Kuttner, L. (1986). *No fears, no tears* (Videotape). Vancouver: Canadian Cancer Society, British Columbia Division.

Kuttner, L. (1988). Favorite stories: A hypnotic pain-reduction technique for children in acute pain. *American Journal of Clinical Hypnosis, 30,* 289–295.

London, P. (1963). *Children's Hypnotic Susceptibility Scale.* Palo Alto, CA: Consulting Psychologists Press.

Lynn, S. J., & Rhue, J. W. (Eds.). (1991). *Theories of hypnosis: Current models and perspectives.* New York: Guilford Press.

Morgan, A. H., & Hilgard, J. R. (1979). The Stanford Hypnotic Clinical Scale for Children. *American Journal of Clinical Hypnosis, 21,* 148–169.

Olness, K. (1975). The use of self-hypnosis in the treatment of childhood nocturnal enuresis. *Clinical Pediatrics, 14,* 273–279.

Olness, K. (1981). Imagery (self-hypnosis) as adjunct therapy in childhood cancer: Clinical experience with 25 patients. *American Journal of Pediatric Hematology/Oncology, 3,* 313–321.

Olness, K. (1989). Hypnotherapy: A cyberphysiologic strategy in pain management. *Pediatric Clinics of North America, 36,* 873–884.

Olness, K., & Conroy, M. (1985). Voluntary control of transcutaneous PO_2 by children. *International Journal of Clinical and Experimental Hypnosis, 33,* 1–5.

Olness, K., Culbert, T., & Uden, D. (1989). Self-regulation of salivary immunoglobulin A by children. *Pediatrics, 83,* 66–71.

Olness, K., & Gardner, G. G. (1988). *Hypnosis and hypnotherapy with children* (2nd ed.). New York: Grune & Stratton.

Olness, K., MacDonald, J., & Uden, D. (1987). Prospective study comparing propanolol, placebo, and hypnosis in the management of juvenile migraine. *Pediatrics, 79,* 593–597.

Olness, K., & Singher, L. (1989). Pain and symptom management training for children with cancer: A five year study. *Topics in Pediatrics, 7,* 2–6.

Thompson, K. F. (1979). The case against relaxation. In G. D. Burrows, D. R. Collison, & L. Dennerstein (Eds.), *Hypnosis: 1979* (pp. 41–45). Amsterdam: Elsevier/North-Holland Biomedical Press.

Zeltzer, L., & LeBaron, S. (1982). Hypnosis and nonhypnotic techniques for fear reduction and anxiety during painful procedures in children and adolescents with cancer. *Journal of Pediatrics, 101,* 1032–1035.

18

HYPNOSIS IN THE TREATMENT OF ANOREXIA NERVOSA

MICHAEL R. NASH and ELGAN L. BAKER

Anorexia and bulimia nervosa are exceedingly complex disorders that frequently involve dramatic dissociative features (Beaumont & Abraham, 1983; Russell, 1979). Dissociation of aspects of interoceptive experience and body image, as well as archaic, enmeshed modes of object relating within the family, figure prominently in most cases of severe anorexia. Because hypnosis itself may involve a dissociative experience (Hilgard, 1977) as well as a regressed mode of relating (Nash, 1988), it is not surprising to find that (a) hypnosis may be particularly helpful in the treatment of eating-disordered patients; and (b) even in the experimental laboratory, certain classes of eating-disordered patients may be more responsive to hypnosis than one would otherwise expect. Following a brief summary of the literature, we present a treatment paradigm that explicitly addresses key aspects of anorexia nervosa from a developmental, ego psychological conceptual framework.

CLINICAL APPLICATIONS

Although references to hypnosis in the treatment of anorexia nervosa are relatively few, they are scattered across a century of distinguished clinical work. Whether the therapy was carried out at the Salpêtrière Clinic in 19th-century France (J. Janet, 1888) or at the Menninger Clinic in America (Brenman & Gill, 1947), strategies of treatment are remarkably similar.

In his 1906 American lectures, Pierre Janet outlined the major symptom picture of "hysterical anorexia" as it was viewed at the Salpêtrière Clinic: self-starvation, binge eating and purging, resistance to treatment, late adolescent onset, family disturbance, dissociation of sensations, and profound underlying psychological conflict (reported in P. Janet, 1924). Earlier, Janet had described his brother's hypnotic treatment of a 25-year-old female anorexic patient (Marcelene) who was hospitalized and tube fed following severe weight loss and self-induced vomiting (J. Janet, 1888; P. Janet, 1925). Marcelene had suffered from this disorder for several years but had become acutely emaciated and weak. Over several hypnotic sessions, J. Janet was able to restore Marcelene to a normal pattern of food intake by suggesting increased attention to her tactile and visceral sensations. This seemingly indirect approach was undoubtedly a clinical application of Pierre Janet's assertion that hysterical pathology was dissociative in nature. The treatment process was stormy, with frequent relapses. At first, Marcelene would eat only while hypnotized; on termination of a session, she reported spontaneous amnesia for the proceedings and returned to her anorexic–bulimic patterns. The therapist was eventually able to extend treatment effects across time by suggesting to Marcelene that she remain hypnotized throughout the year but that she should otherwise behave and feel perfectly normal. The patient quickly regained her strength and normal body weight. However, periodic relapses around menstruation and stressful events necessitated frequent "booster" sessions administered by the therapist.

In his other work with acutely anorexic patients, Pierre Janet emphasized that hypnosis was only a part of a much more comprehensive treatment plan (P. Janet, 1925). The patient should be temporarily isolated from the family; meals should be presented in a simple, routine manner and taken with only a nurse in attendance (the same nurse at all meals); confrontation and pleading should be avoided; and the patient should receive a graduated diet that would "reeducate the appetite and the alimentary functions" (P. Janet, 1925, p. 810). It was only in this supportive inpatient context that hypnosis could be effectively used with the acutely anorexic patient.

Brenman and Gill (1947) reported the case of a 14-year-old anorexic girl who weighed 70 lb at the time of her admission to the Menninger

Clinic. A peculiar hopping compulsion complicated her symptomatology. The patient was particularly resistant to treatment and seemed psychotically inaccessible at times. Accordingly, hypnosis focused on establishing a safe holding environment. During hypnosis, the therapist administered indirect suggestions that eventually led to a complete cessation of the hopping behavior. Following several weeks of comprehensive inpatient care and permissive therapy, the patient's food intake increased markedly. Brenman and Gill speculated that her dramatic response to the suggestions that she stop hopping reinforced her belief that the hypnotist was indeed magically powerful. This in turn led to an experience of increased security and safety in the therapeutic relationship. Although the patient refused subsequent treatment with hypnosis, she became increasingly communicative and responsive to the insight-oriented psychotherapy. Treatment gains proved stable over a long-term follow-up.

Several contemporary clinicians have offered brief reports on their work with anorexic patients. Crasilneck and Hall (1975) treated 70 cases of anorexia nervosa with hypnosis; marked improvement was reported in more than half of the cases. During the acute stages of anorexia, direct suggestions for increased food intake were given (increased hunger, enjoyment of eating). Instructions for self-hypnosis were also included. Following medical stabilization, Crasilneck and Hall involved the patients in an uncovering therapy that focused on the unconscious conflicts that presumably precipitated the condition.

Kroger and Fezler (1976) also briefly described using hypnosis in the treatment of anorexia. Direct suggestions were given for reduced level of anxiety, increased appetite, and pleasant food-related memories. Kroger and Fezler offered several standard images of ingesting appealing food as a means of inducing hunger. For patients who reported an inability to eat because of feeling full, the therapist suggested vivid recall of past hunger: sensations of lightness and emptiness in the stomach.

Thakur (1980) also used direct suggestions for healthier eating habits, increased weight gain, and a more realistic body image. In addition, general feelings of interpersonal competence and assertiveness were suggested. Spiegel and Spiegel (1978) used similar direct suggestions with anorexic patients and emphasized the importance of hypnosis in the early diagnostic process.

Ambrose and Newbold (1980) reported two separate cases of anorexia in young boys who presented with gender confusion and fears of pregnancy. Direct suggestions of increased attention to their own masculinity and reassurance of their male characteristics quickly produced positive results.

Milton Erickson (Erickson & Rossi, 1979) described the successful month-long intensive treatment of an anorexic 14-year-old girl. Using indirect suggestions and paradoxical strategies, Erickson conducted the therapy in four phases:

1. *Distracting frames of reference:* Lectures on oral hygiene and absurdly precise instructions for mouth care were presented.
2. *Depotentiating masochistic defenses:* The patient was instructed to rinse her mouth daily with cod liver oil. Punishment for failure was eating food. The patient, of course, failed.
3. *Therapeutic double bind:* The patient was instructed to oversee her parents' weight gain.
4. *Emotional catharsis:* The therapist provoked the patient by accusing her of being a liar and a coward.

Erickson and Rossi (1979) characterized this type of treatment as essentially involving trance, but it is clear that Erickson's therapy also incorporated the supportive, familial, and dynamic interventions cited as being essential by other clinicians.

The most detailed description of hypnotic treatment of anorexic patients was reported by Gross (1983). Gross treated 50 cases of anorexia on a large adolescent psychiatry unit. Although the hypnotic procedures were tailored to the specific dynamics of the patient, Gross identified six core symptoms that seemed amenable to hypnotic treatment, augmented by self-hypnosis:

1. *Hyperactivity:* Suggestions for relaxation, slowed respiration, and heart rate were administered. Pleasurable feelings were associated with beautiful beach and park settings.
2. *Distorted body image:* Photographs of the patient's own emaciated body were compared with a more healthy body image.
3. *Defect in interoceptive awareness:* Suggestions were given that directed attention to visceral cues, specifically hunger and satiety. Association of hunger with moderate food intake also was suggested.
4. *Family enmeshment:* Suggestions were given for self-assertion and self-esteem. Age progression suggestions were used to facilitate self-sufficiency outside of the family in the future.
5. *Repressed traumatic event:* Age regression suggestions were used to explore underlying dynamics associated with the onset of anorexic symptoms.
6. *Overt and covert resistance to therapy:* Hypnosis was sometimes represented as a means of weight control rather than being explicitly associated with weight gain. Suggestions encouraged an association between better eating habits and improved vocational or athletic performance.

There have been a number of other approaches to the use of hypnosis in treating eating disorders, most notably from cognitive–behavioral (Vanderlinden & Vandereycken, 1988), ego-state (Torem, 1987), and strategic intervention (Yapko, 1986) perspectives. In sum, across a broad range of theoretical orientations and clinical settings, hypnosis has been used with some success. Although scant, the outcome literature illustrates the efficacy and flexibility hypnosis affords the clinician.

Beginning with the work of Pettinati and her colleagues, there has been a mushrooming of interest in the hypnotizability of patients with eating disorders (Pettinati, Horne, & Staats, 1985; Pettinati & Wade, 1986). Only carefully designed clinical research will decide this issue. However, it is interesting to note how this contemporary experimental work dovetails with the historically rooted clinical proposition that hypnosis and pathologies of eating behavior share some underlying shared processes.

CASE MATERIAL

Our treatment approach was used successfully with a group of 36 women (aged 17–31) who presented with a primary diagnosis of anorexia nervosa. Most of the patients were seen initially on an inpatient basis and then followed in outpatient psychotherapy in a treatment program that combined individual and group psychotherapy, along with occasional use of psychotropic medication. We outline the hypnotherapeutic strategies used with the patients.

Typically, hypnosis was introduced as part of a multifaceted intervention based on the proposition that the eating disorder had become a metaphor to symbolize a variety of intrapsychic and interpersonal struggles. Many of the struggles centered around self-pathology, control and power conflicts, and difficulties with the adequate differentiation and integration of a cohesive sense of mature identity. These structural and dynamic difficulties operate with differing valences for different patients. Those who present with anorexia nervosa are a relatively heterogeneous group. Therefore, different aspects of the treatment approach were emphasized more or less with different patients depending on their individual needs and specific treatment responses.

1. *Hypnosis was introduced to patients as a means for gaining enhanced self-control associated with various opportunities for increased security and mastery.* It was not introduced as an opportunity to gain control over eating habits or to restore patients' weight. Most patients were more responsive to this specific conscious introduction of hypnosis as an adjunct to the therapeutic regimen because they were ambivalent about mutually participating in activities designed to alter their eating habits or increase their weight level. Most of the patients readily verbalized feelings of being anx-

ious, apprehensive, and out of control in their lives and were generally willing to participate reciprocally in a program designed to facilitate an increased sense of potency and security. The general idea was also emphasized when hypnosis was introduced that hypnotic ability is something that rests in each individual and can be enhanced through training and practice; therefore, the emphasis was on the development of hypnotic talent as being representative of the growth of the patients' own capacities for self-control.

2. *Structured and permissive induction techniques were used with anorexic patients.* A structured rather than purely permissive induction was indicated to help modulate the regressive experiences that often accompany the trance and that may be frightening or even retraumatizing for many anorexic patients. This permissive approach helps to avoid control struggles and associated resistance around power dynamics and competition. Most patients responded well to an induction that combined relaxation and fantasy, which is also useful for early instruction in self-hypnosis. A recent report (Pettinati, 1982) has suggested that anorexic patients demonstrate a somewhat greater susceptibility to hypnosis than does the normal population. This has been associated with a higher incidence of dissociative experience, as reported during interviews.

3. *Early applications of hypnosis were specifically designed to enhance the patients' sense of personal power, to increase their capacity for autonomous functioning, to support the working alliance, and to provide a generalized sense of ego support leading to increased mastery and positive expectations for behavioral success.* For this reason, instruction in self-hypnosis was introduced early in the treatment, and patients were taught to use self-hypnotic strategies to manage feelings of anxiety or insecurity between sessions. Hypnosis was also used for tension reduction, with specific suggestions being made to help patients to become increasingly aware of their generalized tension level and to learn to manage this through a variety of relaxation strategies. Direct and indirect suggestions were used to provide the patients with a sense of comfort, thereby supporting the ego's emerging capacity for mastery. Directed and structured imagery and fantasies are often useful in indirectly suggesting to patients improved functioning and to support most positive attitudes regarding capacities for self-control and adaptation.

4. *Once patients had learned to use self-hypnosis for relaxation and once hypnotic suggestion and imagery had been established to stabilize and support the working alliance between the therapist and the patient, hypnotherapeutic interventions were directed more specifically at a number of arenas of difficulty that are more directly associated with core pathological features of anorexia nervosa.* Many of the patients had a good deal of difficulty with accurately perceiving sensory stimulation from their bodies. For this reason, many of them were unaware of sensory cues typically associated with physiological functioning. For some patients who presented with more severe forms of preoedipal structural pathology, this defect appeared to have been related

to a more generalized problem with boundary management and maintenance. They defensively avoided awareness of sensory stimulation because this evoked insecurity and anxiety associated at a primitive level with a lack of adequate boundary differentiation and integration. For many of these more borderline-level patients, attention to physical functioning began to arouse concerns about the deterioration of body boundaries and merger with the external environment. For these patients, sensory focusing was preceded by general work on boundary support and management. Both guided imagery and specific sensory exercises were used during hypnosis to support the integrity of boundaries and to communicate through indirect and direct suggestions that body and ego boundaries are constant and dependable.

In addition, many patients had learned to defensively dissociate body and body-related experiences from the conscious perception of self and their intellectualized phenomenological experience of the world. The patients often described, either directly or symbolically, a sense of a split between their "body selves" and their "mind or spiritual selves." When this was the case, the hypnotherapeutic work also needed to address the reintegration of these various phenomenological arenas. Imagery and suggestion were used to reestablish a sense of communication between the mind and body that could not be interrupted by anxiety. When anxiety began to intrude on this work, suggestions for calm and relaxation, as well as fantasy designed to reestablish a soothing and comfortable environment, were interspersed with work directed at reintegration until patients were able to maintain a sense of comfort and continuing security while attempting to reconnect physical and mental representations of self and others.

This approach relies on the therapeutic action of a relaxation-based desensitization paradigm. When this work was successful or for the patients who were less severely disturbed and therefore not in need of attention to boundaries and unmodulated dissociative experiences, the hypnotherapeutic work directly supported patients' improved awareness of their body-based sensory phenomenology. They were taught during hypnosis to more accurately label and attend to muscle tension and related skeletal and visceral sensations. This was related to their experiences of hunger as well as to the careful differentiation of a variety of affective experiences. Patients were encouraged in the trance to recapture the affect associated with being in a variety of different fantasized situations and to learn to deal with this emotional experience adaptively.

Frequently, patients reported that they began to find themselves unable to eat or to experience hunger in family situations that were emotionally charged (i.e., with anger and anxiety). These situations were revivified in the trance, and patients were taught to differentially recognize their affective responses to these situations and to reduce the associated tension. Patients then managed these feelings through more adaptive coping strategies rather than via the restriction of food intake, withdrawal, or dissociation accompanied by distortions in body experience and body image. This pattern of affective differentiation and abreaction was often accompanied by a generalized decrease in tension and improvement in the symptoms associated with distorted eating behaviors and body image.

5. *Body image distortions were also addressed more directly in hypnotherapy.* Patients were asked to represent their conscious and preconscious body images in hypnosis by projecting them onto screens or drawing them on blackboards. Age regression techniques were used to uncover the roots of these distortions in malevolent interactions with family members and the associated development of distorted self- and object representations. We have found that the distortions are often related to split-off aspects of the self-representation that cannot be integrated into a conscious sense of self because they evoke a negative sense of vulnerability and associated negative affect. Once the roots of these distortions have been explicated and explored, interpretative work can be done regarding them in the trance and during nontrance verbal, insight-oriented psychotherapy sessions.

We used directed imagery and fantasy in hypnosis to confront these distortions, to help patients to become increasingly aware of them, and to suggest their amelioration. For instance, distortions in body image drawn on an imaginary blackboard during the trance can be corrected by erasing and redrawing the aspects of the image of the physical self that are particularly distorted. Frequently, patients became anxious and uncomfortable, but relaxation was introduced to restore a sense of comfort and calm. When this had been accomplished, patients could then return to working on correcting distortions in the represented self-image without the intrusion of undue anxiety.

It appears that this work resulted in some generalization of an improved self-image external to the trance. However, more important, patients seemed to be able to learn to think about their physical self and to begin to explore their representations of their body without the same degree of defensiveness and anxiety that characterized attempts at this work prior to the specific use of hypnotic imagery and exploration. Age progression was used to suggest the eventual integration of an adequate and reality-based self-representation and the incorporation of this integrated, accurate, physical representation into the conscious sense of self. This was represented through progressive physical changes or, more symbolically, through natural images of differentiation, integration, and growth, structured through evolving hypnotic fantasy.

6. *This work on distortions in body image and the correction of these was closely associated with a more generalized consideration of the integration of an appropriate and mature sense of personal identity.* Because many anorexic patients experience considerable conflicts around individuation and independence because of their prolonged enmeshment in their families, severe generalized distortions in identity maturation are frequently seen. These

were explored in hypnosis and corrected through the use of direct or indirect suggestions and through the use of specific images and fantasies. It was often useful to suggest specific hypnotically induced dreams during the trance to help clarify, for the therapist and the patient, the conflicts that were associated with defects in identity integration. Once these had been clarified, they were further explored in regular psychotherapy sessions and addressed via hypnotic imagery.

7. *Hypnotic work was also used to explore the relation between negative affect expression and distorted attitudes toward eating, food, and unusual eating behaviors.* The relation between these eating behaviors and their role in controlling or avoiding unacceptable affective experiences were established and connected during the trance through suggestion and imagery. Once this had been done, the unacceptable affect was ventilated and abreacted, resulting in an emerging sense of mastery over those feelings. Dreams and imagery were often useful for this, as were more direct hypnotic abreaction techniques.

8. *As aspects of body imagery and general identity integration were corrected, patients' general capacity for mastery was enhanced.* Work in hypnosis was used to further address concerns related to separation, individuation, integration, and adaptation. Rehearsal in fantasy, age progression, and guided imagery were used to provide patients with a more positive sense of their ability to tolerate the affect associated with maturation and to deal with their increasing stability and individuated integrated identity. Within the context of exploring these issues, we also used an insight-oriented approach in individual therapy and group treatment, with which these patients were usually simultaneously involved.

The use of directed hypnotic experience, imagery, and fantasy, as well as specific suggestions, does not necessarily correct defects in patients' internal representational world, nor does it resolve all aspects of the dynamic conflicts seen in patients who present with anorexia nervosa. However, it does provide an opportunity to address some of the issues that interfere with successful, traditional psychotherapeutic work with these patients, particularly the defensive use of denial and dissociation, which are central to distortions in body image and general self-concept. Until these have been addressed, successful psychotherapeutic work with these patients is significantly compromised.

RESEARCH AND APPRAISAL

Our hypnotherapeutic approach was used successfully with a group of women whose primary diagnosis was anorexia nervosa. Most of the patients were seen initially as inpatients and then were followed in outpatient psychotherapy in a treatment program that combined individual and group psychotherapy and occasional psychotropic medication.

Our work suggests that this sort of hypnotherapeutic approach, when used in conjunction with insight-oriented individual and group therapy and occasional conjoint sessions with families (when the patients are still living at home), is a successful treatment approach. Patients' experiential participation, with an emerging sense of mastery and self-control, avoids many of the struggles that emerge around control issues when patients project parental transferences onto their therapist and attempt to maintain their distorted eating behaviors in an effort to maintain some sense of personal control through manipulating the environment.

Follow-up data at 6 and 12 months indicated that 76% of the patients had a remission of symptoms and stabilized weight gain at an acceptable level. These data were compared with those from a group of 31 women who were treated identically without the use of the hypnotherapeutic paradigm described earlier. Only 53% of the women in this latter group achieved the same level of symptom remission and weight stabilization. The use of medication and days of inpatient and outpatient therapy were essentially the same for both of the groups.

These results, although preliminary, suggest that the introduction of hypnosis into the treatment paradigm improved subjects' treatment responses. Undoubtedly, the therapeutic effects of hypnosis had to do with the specific impact of the techniques used and the more generalized and nonspecific effects of hypnosis in improving the patients' sense of self-mastery and reinforcing the quality of the therapeutic alliance, which is frequently associated with the clinical application of hypnotic techniques. These preliminary data were obtained from a clinical treatment program and did not derive from an actual controlled study. Therefore, the patients in the two groups were not matched or randomly assigned to the treatment conditions. The differences in the therapeutic use of hypnosis were a function of which therapist was primarily involved in the patients' treatment; therefore, other therapist-related effects could also account for the differences in treatment outcome. However, a post hoc analysis suggested that most aspects of the patients' treatment in the two groups were constant and were therefore indicative of some positive effect that might have been specifically attributable to the use of the hypnotic treatment approach. Further controlled investigation is, of course, necessary in order to support this preliminary conclusion.

CONCLUSION

This hypnotherapeutic paradigm provides a more direct avenue for addressing the problems in identity formation that are so frequently encountered with patients with anorexia nervosa. More than simply providing an opportunity for learning adaptive behaviors or for exploring and interpreting the structural and dynamic etiologies of core conflicts, the hypnotherapeutic approach described engages patients experientially in examining, exploring, modulating, and correcting these areas of difficulty. This experientially based use of hypnosis appears to be particularly important in dealing with arenas of structural defect and is also useful in circumventing the extreme defensive denial and control struggles that form the basis for resistance to both behavioral and psychodynamic approaches to psychotherapeutic intervention. For this reason, it appears to augment the patients' ability to use psychotherapy and benefit from treatment in a fashion that is generalized and maintained at a significant level of success.

REFERENCES

Ambrose, G., & Newbold, G. (1980). *A handbook of medical hypnosis.* London: Bailliere Tindall.

Beaumont, P. J. V., & Abraham, S. F. (1983). Episodes of ravenous overeating or bulimia: Their occurrence in patients with anorexia nervosa and with other forms of disordered eating. In P. L. Darby, P. E. Garfinkel, D. M. Garner, & D. V. Coscina (Eds.), *Anorexia nervosa: Recent developments in research* (pp. 149–157). New York: Alan R. Liss.

Brenman, M., & Gill, M. (1947). *Hypnotherapy.* Madison, CT: International Universities Press.

Crasilneck, H., & Hall, J. (1975). *Clinical hypnosis.* New York: Grune & Stratton.

Erickson, M., & Rossi, E., (1979). *Hypnotherapy: An exploratory casebook.* New York: Irvington.

Gross, M. (1983). Hypnosis in the therapy of anorexia hysteria. *American Journal of Clinical Hypnosis, 26,* 175–181.

Hilgard, E. (1977). *Divided consciousness: Multiple controls in human thought and action.* New York: Wiley.

Janet, J. (1888). Un cas d'hystérie grave. *Revue Scientifique, 1,* 616.

Janet, P. (1924). *The major symptoms of hysteria.* New York: Macmillan.

Janet, P. (1925). *Psychological healing* (Vol. 2). New York: Macmillan.

Kroger, W., & Fezler, W. (1976). *Hypnosis and behavior modification: Imagery conditioning.* Philadelphia: Lippincott.

Nash, M. R. (1988, August). Theoretical and research perspectives on developmental aspects of the hypnotic relationship. In E. Baker (Chair), *The hypnotic relationship: A developmental approach.* Symposium conducted at the 96th Annual Convention of the American Psychological Association, Atlanta, GA.

Pettinati, H. (1982, October). *Hypnotic susceptibility in patients with anorexia nervosa and bulimia.* Paper presented at the annual meeting of the Society for Clinical and Experimental Hypnosis, Indianapolis, IN.

Pettinati, H. M., Horne, R. J., & Staats, J. M. (1985). Hypnotizability in patients with anorexia nervosa and bulimia. *Archives of General Psychiatry, 42,* 1014–1016.

Pettinati, H. M., & Wade, J. H. (1986). Hypnosis in the treatment of anorexic and bulimic patients. *Seminars in Adolescent Medicine, 2,* 75–79.

Russell, G. (1979). Bulimia nervosa: An ominous variant of anorexia nervosa. *Psychological Medicine, 9,* 429–448.

Spiegel, H., & Spiegel, D. (1978). *Trance and treatment: Clinical uses of hypnosis.* New York: Basic Books.

Thakur, K. (1980). Treatment of anorexia nervosa with hypnotherapy. In H. Wain (Ed.), *Clinical hypnosis in medicine* (pp. 446–493). Chicago: Yearbook Publishers.

Torem, M. (1987). Ego-state therapy for eating disorders. *American Journal of Clinical Hypnosis, 30,* 94–103.

Vanderlinden, J., & Vandereycken, W. (1988). The use of hypnotherapy in the treatment of eating disorders. *International Journal of Eating Disorders, 7,* 673–679.

Yapko, M. D. (1986). Hypnotic strategic interventions in Texas of anorexia nervosa. *American Journal of Clinical Hypnosis, 28,* 224–232.

Note From the Publisher:

The next page number which will appear after page 394 will be page 425. This is not a printing error. Chapter 19, "Hypnosis in the Treatment of Multiple Personality Disorder," by Richard Horevitz, pages 395–424 from the hardback first edition of this volume, has been deleted based on the strong request of the author, who feels that the research and data since 1993 render certain portions of the chapter invalid. The Publisher has reprinted this paperback edition with the same page numbering as the original edition to preserve consistency in page citations.

20

THE BORDERLINE PATIENT AND THE PSYCHOTIC PATIENT

JOAN MURRAY-JOBSIS

CONCEPTUAL DEVELOPMENTAL MODEL OF THERAPY WITH BORDERLINE AND PSYCHOTIC PATIENTS

The hypnotic work with borderline and psychotic patients discussed in this chapter emphasizes acceptance, support, renurturing, and ego building and is based on a conceptual framework that is rooted in the psychoanalytic and developmental approaches to the treatment of severe disturbance. The symptoms of severe disturbance are considered to be best understood as manifestations of the patient's failure to progress along normal stages of human development (Baker, 1981, 1982; Bowers, 1961, 1964; Brown, 1985; Brown & Fromm, 1986; Kernberg, 1968; Kohut, 1977; Murray-Jobsis, 1984, 1990, 1991b, 1992; Scagnelli, 1975, 1980; Winnicott, 1965).

In the theoretical framework presented here, healthy individuals are viewed as developmentally evolving from an initial period of symbiosis in which the world is experienced from an egocentric viewpoint with initial

---

Joan Murray-Jobsis has previously published under the names Scagnelli and Scagnelli-Jobsis.

expectations and fantasies of omnipotence. The healthy infant is then seen as normally developing the beginnings of awareness of physical separateness between the self and the "significant nurturing other" with the resultant beginnings of symbiotic disillusionment. The infant then develops a greater awareness of separateness with an initial experience of loss, anger, grief, and anxiety. Eventually, the normally developing infant or child evolves to a stage of working through the pain, anger, and anxiety of separation within a warm, supportive, and accepting environment in which the nurturing other is "caring enough." Gradually, the child moves to an acceptance of the "good enough" nurturer or mother, seeing mother as a mixture of good and bad but as basically good and loving and caretaking. Eventually, the child also sees the self as a mixture of good and bad but as basically good and lovable.

At this point in development, the normal child has a healthy acceptance of individuation and separation with the capacity for independent growth. He or she can then evolve to an eventual understanding of the positive aspects of separation as he or she experiences the freedom to go beyond the parent and to explore new environments and relationships.

This process of positive self-awareness and separation–individuation is begun in infancy and is initially worked through at a primary level in the first few years of life in the normal developmental pattern. An extended elaboration of this working-through process of accepting separation and developing the capacity for individuation then typically continues into adolescence and beyond. However, in the case of the severely disturbed patient, significant disruption of the early developmental process of forming a positive sense of self and of separation–individuation is theoretically understood to have occurred. This disruption is evidenced by the following deficits and problems that are frequently characteristic of borderline and psychotic symptomatology: (a) a lack of a separate sense of self, a diffuse negative sense of self, or both; (b) a confused sense of merging between the patients' own and others' feelings; (c) a refusal to acknowledge the loss of the symbiotic fantasy and to work through the pain, anxiety, and anger that accompany that loss; (d) a splitting of the self and the world into "all bad" and "all good" segments (in an attempt to preserve the fantasy of an all good symbiotic nurturer and to contain the anger, anxiety, and despair); (e) a lack of autonomy and independent growth in exploring the environment and human relationships; and (f) intense existential despair, anxiety, or anger related to feeling or being empty or alone.

Within the context of a developmental model, the symptoms of severe disturbance that are listed above can be seen as being related to problems and conflicts around initial awareness of self and issues of separation–individuation. Thus, the symptoms of borderline and psychotic disorders can be understood to be manifestations of a failure to progress along normal stages of human development. The task in therapy with these severely disturbed patients, then, is to correct developmental failures. Within this conceptual framework, the hypnotic therapy described in this chapter is designed to provide, as much as possible, corrective developmental experiences for patients. The permissiveness, the support and acceptance, the renurturing and the ego building, along with the setting of reasonable and stable limits, are all part of providing a "good enough" environment (relationship). This good enough relationship is designed to allow positive bonding and self-awareness; facilitate acceptance of the symbiotic loss and of separateness; promote a working through and acceptance of unresolved feelings of despair, anger, and anxiety; and promote growth into positive autonomy. Thus, the therapy that is described in this chapter attempts to redo the developmental process, rebuild relationships, and re-create some of the nurturing experiences as they "should have been" in order to give patients the missing experiences that will allow them to once again continue to grow. Therapy attempts to fill in the missing corrective life experiences to allow these developmentally sidetracked patients to regain their direction and to reclaim their growth potential.

THEORETICAL MODEL OF HYPNOSIS WITH BORDERLINE AND PSYCHOTIC PATIENTS

In addition to the focus on acceptance and support in order to create a relationship that will foster both therapy and hypnosis and the resultant possibility of renurturing, the clinical work presented in this chapter is also based on a theoretical view of hypnosis as a form of adaptive regression. Such adaptive regression would be purposively initiated and managed regression (as opposed to pathological regression), with the therapist's ego providing some of the adaptive strength that allows patients to use the hypnosis productively rather than chaotically or destructively. In a 1988 theoretical article building on earlier work (Gill & Brenman, 1959; Scagnelli-Jobsis, 1982; Schilder & Kauders, 1926/1956), I proposed that hypnosis is a function of adaptive regression and transference, with the therapist providing an "anchoring ego" that joins forces with the patient's monitoring ego to allow for the creation of a regressed subsystem within the ego (i.e., the hypnotic state). I further proposed that heterohypnosis involves the phenomenon of transference, that it is a relationship-dependent experience, and that an individual's hypnotic capacity may be influenced either positively or negatively by the interaction between the client and the therapist (i.e., the transference). This theory of hypnosis as a function of adaptive regression and transference provides a model of how psychotic and other severely disturbed and ego-impaired patients can use hypnosis successfully and productively. This theory also explains why issues of trust and a positive supportive relationship are given such focus and importance in the clinical work with the psychotic and borderline population (Murray-Jobsis, 1988).

CLINICAL APPLICATIONS

Range of Clinical Applications

Given the conceptual and theoretical models described in the preceding section, it can be seen that clinical hypnosis could be potentially used by any borderline or psychotic patient within the framework of a positive, supportive therapy relationship. However, this statement makes it appear simpler than it is in reality to maintain a therapeutic hypnotic relationship with a severely disturbed patient. Therapists who have worked with psychotic and borderline patients are aware that the development and maintenance of a positive and constructive transference relationship can be extremely difficult and sometimes impossible. Therefore, the development of a therapeutic hypnotic process with these patients (dependent as it is on transference) can be equally difficult and sometimes impossible.

In general, in order to foster a clinical hypnotic relationship with severely disturbed patients, clinical studies indicate that the therapist needs to maintain a supportive and nurturing stance with reliability and consistency, giving acceptance wherever possible. In many cases, both borderline and psychotic patients will have a history of feelings of inadequacy and self-condemnation or self-criticism. These basic negative feelings may be interlaced with defensive feelings of paranoid anger or grandiose superiority, but the underlying and dominant picture will usually involve an excessive lack of self-worth. These patients typically dissimulate and hide their inner feelings with symptomatology because they expect and fear an outside critical, judgmental world. Therefore, an accepting supportive stance is essential for both the therapy and the hypnotic relationship (Murray-Jobsis, 1985; Scagnelli, 1975).

However, in addition to this acceptance and support, it is also essential for the therapist to be able to set limits with consistency and stability. These limits may often be perceived as being unsupportive and nonnurturing by patients and may sometimes result in angry, strained relationships. Nevertheless, the therapist needs to be able to remain supportive while allowing patients to feel their way through their angry, hurt, anxious feelings just as a good parent provides an accepting environment for a child learning to accept limits (i.e., to accept separation and the loss of symbiotic omnipotence). In the long run, the therapist's ability to set limits calmly and consistently can reassure patients of the therapist's ability "to last," to not become overwhelmed by their needs and demands, and to not abandon them. By setting limits, the therapist also demonstrates to patients that he or she will provide closeness but not symbiosis. Thus, it can be seen that the therapist working with clinical hypnosis with psychotic or borderline patients may need to be particularly attentive to the special needs of these patients. However, in spite of the therapist's skill, care, and effort, there will be some patients for whom clinical hypnosis will not be successful. There will be some patients who simply will not or cannot form a positive relationship or place enough trust in themselves or the therapist to allow for the possibility of hypnosis. Therefore, a primary step in determining whether to use hypnosis with borderline or psychotic patients is to assess their willingness to work with hypnosis.

Frequently, patients' willingness to work with hypnosis will be affected by their feelings about the transference relationship in therapy and will center around issues of control and trust. Clinical studies suggest that psychotic and borderline patients are likely to be concerned about the potential loss of control in the hypnotic relationship and to feel conflicted about trusting the therapist's integrity and empathic sensitivity to not abuse his or her position of power and control. Although it is frequently stated in clinical hypnosis that patients are always "in control," the hypnotic relationship nevertheless implies and requires a temporary surrender of leadership, initiative, and some degree of control to the therapist. It is probable that all patients perceive this subtle alteration in the locus of control and struggle with this issue on some level. In the case of psychotic and borderline patients, concerns about loss of control are most likely to be based on fears of incorporation (i.e., loss of integrity of the ego and the sense of self), fears of separation and abandonment, or both. These fears of incorporation and abandonment, and the related confusion over identity and confusion over boundaries between the self and others, are an integral part of the pathology of psychotic and borderline disturbances. These same fears that make the formation of the therapeutic alliance (the positive transference) with severely disturbed patients so difficult in traditional psychotherapy also make formation of an hypnotic interaction difficult (Murray-Jobsis, 1988, 1991a; Scagnelli-Jobsis, 1982).

Some techniques developed in clinical practice that have proved helpful in enabling psychotic and borderline patients to establish a positive transference and to permit the temporary shift of control required for the hypnotic relationship will be described.

First, hypnosis is typically presented to psychotic or borderline patients as autohypnosis, with emphasis being given to the increase in mastery, autonomy, and control that this new skill will provide for patients. Many patients are able to perceive the added control over their environment and themselves that the skill of autohypnosis can potentially afford them. In addition, once patients learn autohypnosis, they realize it is a skill that they can use independent of the therapist and outside of the therapy session. For example, with therapist encouragement, patients frequently begin to use their newly acquired hypnotic skill to reduce their anxiety in between therapy sessions (Scagnelli, 1976, 1980).

In addition, severely disturbed patients are specifically told that they can open or close their eyes whenever they choose. Patients can be encouraged to close their eyes by explaining to them that it is more difficult to maintain hypnosis with the eyes open and more comfortable to allow the eyes to close. With such encouragement, most patients comfortably maintain eye closure. According to clinical and empirical reports, both psychotic and borderline patients typically benefit from the reassurance of control over their own eye closure and respond better to hypnosis when permissiveness regarding eye closure is assured. Psychotic and some borderline patients tend to perceive eye closure as a defenseless and vulnerable posture. Psychotics particularly tend to feel that their inner feelings can be "read" in their eyes and on their faces. Because these patients also tend to view themselves negatively and to expect criticism and condemnation from the outside world, the thought of being "viewed" by others without being able to defend themselves by "reading" the feedback in the other person's face is particularly threatening.

When the therapist specifically allows eye opening, patients will typically close their eyes with less discomfort and fear of intrusion. Sometimes, they will open their eyes initially to "check out the situation" and then comfortably maintain eye closure. When patients open their eyes, the therapist can signal attentiveness without intrusiveness by pointedly looking past the patient and focusing on some point other than the patient's face. The therapist can also signal assurance to the patient by entering hypnosis with the patient and thus modeling the safety of hypnosis and the willingness of the therapist to be momentarily "viewed" by the patient. Thus, the therapist uses his or her own autohypnotic experience to model the safety of hypnosis and of being viewed by another (i.e., of being vulnerable; Murray-Jobsis, 1984, 1991a; Scagnelli, 1976).

Thus, it can be seen that patients' fears concerning the control and trust issues involved in hypnosis should be assumed even when they are not specifically stated by patients and that these issues should be addressed early and receive continuing attention from the therapist. With such attention, patient fears can sometimes be alleviated and acceptance of hypnosis can be promoted.

To summarize, when therapists assess psychotic and borderline patients' potential to use hypnosis, therapists are essentially assessing patients' fears regarding issues of control and trust and their willingness to overcome these fears in order to use hypnosis. The patients' abilities to handle their concerns about control and trust need to be evaluated sensitively and shifted toward greater therapeutic tolerance wherever possible. In the final analysis, patient acceptance of the hypnotic relationship is the primary determinant of the appropriateness of the patient for hypnosis.

An additional factor that may also exclude a severely disturbed patient from clinical hypnosis is high hostility combined with a high probability of destructive acting-out. In the rare cases in which a patient has presented with homicidal or suicidal impulses and with little capacity for control, I have chosen not to use hypnosis in order to avoid introducing a new variable into an already dangerous and unstable situation. However, in my experience, overtly hostile patients also tend to be nonaccepting of hypnosis, and the need to reject such patients is rare.

A final factor of importance that should affect the question of whether to use hypnosis with a psychotic or borderline patient is the therapist's comfort and skill in working with this patient population. Specifically, a therapist should be fully skilled and comfortable in working with psychotic and borderline patients in traditional psychotherapy before considering using hypnosis with them.

General Techniques

In general, supportive techniques of therapeutic and hypnotic interaction are essential in working with psychotic and borderline patients. Such supportive techniques will typically be reflected in a permissive, nonauthoritarian style of hypnotic interaction and are helpful in avoiding patient resistance. Empirical research indicates that psychotic and borderline patients report and evidence increased resistance and noncooperation toward controlling, authoritarian, or intrusive messages or methods (Murray-Jobsis, 1991a). A supportive style is also important because it provides an excellent framework for promoting the nurturance and acceptance that so many severely disturbed patients require as an essential and primary element in developing their capacity for bonding and relationship. A supportive therapeutic relationship also provides the "supportive holding environment" within which the therapist can set the limits that allow patients to tolerate the loss of the symbiotic fantasy and to struggle with the difficult emotional growth of separation–individuation. In maintaining this supportive relationship and environment, it is important for the therapist to be highly consistent and reliable. Because severely disturbed patients typically expect excessive control, intrusiveness, and nonsupport, shifting that pattern of expectations requires much consistency.

In addition to maintaining a supportive therapeutic environment, clinical work also suggests that the therapist working with psychotic and borderline patients needs to develop an empathic capacity and to use this capacity to "empathically mirror" patients' feelings (Murray-Jobsis, 1984, 1991b; Scagnelli, 1980). This process of mirroring allows the therapist to validate patients' experiences and feelings. Frequently, severely disturbed patients have had intense experiences of early childhood pain, anxiety, and rage but have never been allowed by the original environment to define or resolve these experiences. In addition, patients frequently have been alienated from their own original feeling-sense of their early experiences and thereby were alienated from themselves. Therefore, the therapist's skill and capacity to empathize with the feeling elements in patients' experiences become crucial in helping patients to reclaim and validate their identity. The therapist's empathetic identifying with patients' feelings may also help patients to tolerate their feelings and accept them as "not bad."

An example from my practice of empathic mirroring of a patient's feelings may effectively illustrate this technique: In hypnosis, a patient perceived a "searing red mist" locked away in a walled room. With great difficulty, the patient scaled the walls and got close enough to the frightening red mist to see his mother's face within it. He then realized that the searing mist was the pain of "knowing that mother doesn't love me."

Although his mother had been defined on a conscious, adult level as "loving and good," the patient, in hypnosis, had reclaimed his early infant and child awareness of emotional abandonment by his mother. As the therapist, I empathically acknowledged and validated the pain, fear, and despair that was truly part of his past experience. This empathic mirroring allowed him to consciously accept and tolerate his feelings.

It later became clear that his mother's emotional energy had been absorbed by an older sibling and that the patient's relationship with his mother had been limited to a semisymbiotic bond in the service of his mother's emotional needs. With his greater understanding and acceptance of his childhood reality, the patient was eventually able to create a more healthy, adult relationship with his mother that was free of much of the formerly repressed pain and anger and the overcompensating, symbiotic identification with his mother.

The process of empathically mirroring patient feelings allows patients to set their own pace and direction in therapy, thereby making therapy both safer and more likely to achieve progress. Patients will typically move into new material and feelings only when they are ready. However, a therapy situation in which empathic mirroring techniques may not be useful can occur if patients move into hostile, destructive patterns of thought and feelings and appear to have potential for destructive acting-out either against themselves or others. In such instances, therapists can shift away from mirroring techniques and move into reframing, redoing, or methods of helping patients contain affect.

In general, a high degree of empathic capacity can be extremely helpful in working with psychotic and borderline patients. Thus, it can be useful for therapists to enhance their empathic capacity with autohypnosis. Therapists' use of autohypnosis can promote their own creative, nonverbal, symbolic potential and provide greater understanding and communication with patients.

An additional advantage of therapists developing their own autohypnotic capacity is that such autohypnotic work can help therapists to understand themselves and their own limits more clearly. It is important, in working with psychotic and borderline patients, that therapists avoid acting out their own needs on patients. For example, therapists should avoid acting out needs for control or for demanding reassurance of their goodness as therapists. Therapists should resist the role of "savior" and the resultant feelings of anger and rejection of severely disturbed patients when they may "fail to be saved." Therapists who have insight into themselves and their limits can also prevent themselves from becoming overwhelmed by patients' neediness or psychotic feelings and can thereby avoid abandonment of patients out of their own guilt, anger, or desperation.

In addition to a general therapeutic environment of support and empathy, clinical reports indicate that hypnotherapy with psychotic and borderline patients often must focus on creating new relationships and self-experiences. Unlike other more emotionally developed patients, psychotic and borderline patients frequently have such a deficit of positive past experiences of themselves or relationships that therapy focuses on creating new positive experiences. Of course, therapists must still work at recovering past experiences and integrating them into a patient's reinterpreted view of himself or herself. However, in addition, therapists should focus much of the energy and work of therapy on creating new positive experiences as a form of restitution for that which was never given originally to the patient. Therapists create these new experiences of positive relationship and positive self largely through imagery, using hypnosis to role play and re-create nurturing and other developmental experiences in imagery, thereby allowing the patient to build a new internal source of positive experience. Both patient and therapist know that these hypnotic images do not reflect the patient's real past life experiences but are designed as restitution in order to permit a building of a healthier and happier present and future (Erickson & Rossi, 1979; Murray-Jobsis, 1984, 1985, 1986, 1989, 1991b, 1992).

In addition to building positive experiences through hypnosis and imagery, therapists also help patients to build positive experiences through the therapy relationship itself. Because therapists working with borderline and psychotic patients must, in order to be effective, regard those patients with care, respect, acceptance, and affection, patients begin to gradually view themselves with that same sense of care, respect, acceptance, and affection. This slow and painstaking process of building and maintaining a positive therapeutic relationship with severely disturbed patients is probably the most important factor in their eventual success in creating a positive self-concept and sense of relationship and in ultimately developing the potential for a healthy life.

In addition to support, empathy, and a focus on creating new positive experiences, therapeutic work with psychotic and borderline patients also generally requires greater use of indirect hypnotic techniques. Although severely disturbed patients will sometimes respond positively to direct suggestion, they frequently will perceive such direct suggestion as intrusive or controlling. Sometimes, they may simply be unable to follow a direct suggestion and then feel themselves to be a failure. Therefore, it is often beneficial to use indirect and extremely permissive suggestions with severely disturbed patients. For example, metaphoric communication may be used, such as a story about an infant crawling away from mother to explore the toys in another room (as a metaphoric message about the positive aspects of separation–individuation). Also, symbolic language and imagery may be used as a mode of indirect communication. In addition, therapists can offer open-ended suggestions or refer to a fictitious third person when wishing to provide distance and indirection to a communication. Wherever possible, therapists should try to follow the language modality of the patient (i.e., using the mirroring technique) in responding to a patient's communication.

Initial Induction Techniques

Formal induction techniques can be used with most borderline patients and with psychotic patients in remission. Typically, some variation of a progressive relaxation induction can be used and will provide most patients with a comfortable entry into hypnosis as well as a general reduction in anxiety and a sense of general nurturance. An added benefit in using a relaxation induction is that patients learning autohypnosis then also learn techniques for relaxing and reducing anxiety. Other formal induction techniques can be used for the few patients who cannot comfortably work with relaxation (e.g., an induction using an imagery trip or an eye fixation).

Acute, disoriented, psychotic patients, however, may be unresponsive to formal induction techniques. In such cases, indirect hypnotic induction techniques can be used. Such techniques are by their nature not formalized and vary from patient to patient and from therapist to therapist depending on the situation. Examples of such indirect techniques with acutely disoriented psychotics exist in the literature (Berwick & Douglas, 1977; Erickson, 1964, 1965; Murray-Jobsis, 1984; Scagnelli, 1974, 1976, 1980; Vas, 1990; Zeig, 1974; Zindel, 1992). These techniques typically involve various methods of rapidly and dramatically capturing the acute psychotic patient's attention and then moving directly into therapeutic hypnotic messages.

Hypnotic Therapy Techniques

There is a great range of therapy techniques that can be used in hypnosis with psychotic and borderline patients. These hypnotic techniques are generally comparable to similar techniques used in traditional psycho-therapy and range from behavioral modification techniques to uncovering and insight techniques. Individual borderline and psychotic patients will vary in their ability to work with one or several of these techniques.

Relaxation and Anxiety Reduction

In addition to the use of relaxation techniques for induction, these techniques can also be used to help patients reduce their anxiety both in the hypnotic therapy session and in their general life situation. In addition to providing patients with much needed immediate relief from excessive anxiety, such techniques also provide a sense of nurturance from therapists. Clinical experience indicates that these relaxation techniques tend to be reinforcing for hypnosis and tend to produce positive bonding and transference with therapists (Murray-Jobsis, 1984, 1990).

Role Rehearsal for Competence and Mastery

Role rehearsal can be used to help patients to master a situation or task or to help them shift to more constructive patterns of behavior. As an example from my clinical practice, a schizophrenic patient who was depressed and unable to function used role rehearsal to successfully and satisfyingly perform her household tasks (Murray-Jobsis, 1989). Another schizophrenic patient used role rehearsal in hypnosis to practice for an upcoming job interview. A paranoid schizophrenic patient learned to use a variation of desensitization techniques to relocate and eventually ignore his imaginary voices (Zeig, 1974). Another paranoid schizophrenic patient learned to stop shouting back at his imaginary voices with the help of hypnotic desensitization (Murray-Jobsis, 1989). These cases of role rehearsal and desensitization essentially use variations of standard behavior modification techniques. The use of such techniques to create or to shift behavior can be productive and workable with psychotic and borderline patients as long as the patient's agreement and motivation for the behavior change is established.

Dream Production and Projective Techniques

When therapy moves beyond behavior modification and into uncovering techniques, again, many hypnotic techniques are comparable to those used in nonhypnotic psychotherapy. In hypnotic therapy, patients can be requested to produce a dream. The request can be specific to a particular topic or can be nondirective and unstructured. Hypnotic dreams can be as productive and useful as night dreams or directed daydreams in helping patients access new material and insight. In addition to hypnotic dreams produced in the therapy session, patients can also use hypnosis to recall and reexperience dream material from past sleeping or waking experiences.

Dream material, whether produced or recalled in hypnosis, can be interpreted by the patient and the therapist jointly while the patient is still in hypnosis. Later, interpretation in the waking state can be restated and expanded. This process of interpreting newly recovered material both in and out of hypnosis is generally used for all hypnotically accessed material regardless of whether the technique used is dream production, free association, a projective technique, or any other uncovering technique. Because hypnosis tends to produce reductions in anxiety and the critical–judgmental mind, patients may have greater access to conflicted, previously unacceptable or unconscious material and may also be more open to interpretation of this newly accessed material. Therefore, it is essential that therapists working with severely disturbed patients in uncovering and insight work refrain from pushing for interpretations beyond the patients' capacity to handle them. Clinical experience suggests that the empathic capacity of the therapist can be essential at this point in therapy, along with the technique of mirroring, to allow patients to pace the uncovering–insight process (Murray-Jobsis, 1984, 1991b, 1992; Scagnelli, 1976, 1977).

Free Association and Projective Techniques

Free association is commonly used in analytically oriented psychotherapy and is easily and naturally integrated into hypnotic psychotherapy. It is a natural progression when working with a patient in hypnosis to ask the patient to "share with me whatever thoughts, feelings, memories, or images are beginning to flow through your mind." The hypnotic experience tends to produce a suspension of the critical, logical mind and to promote an uncensored flow of associations. Thus, the use of hypnosis tends to produce a spontaneous free flow of thoughts that is naturally amenable to the technique of free association.

In addition, projective techniques can be used to help initiate a free-association process. Because the hypnotic process is one that typically accesses imagery, it lends itself naturally to the use of projective techniques. An example of such a technique would be to request a patient "to image a staircase with 10 steps down and at the bottom of the staircase may be a room of many doors." The patient can use the staircase as a deepening technique and then can begin to image and describe the room and the many doors. The therapist can then suggest that "behind each door there will be some memory, image, or understanding that will be important and useful." The patient can then decide which door to open "this time" and proceed to discover and describe whatever is found there. After helping the patient to begin the process, the therapist can be silent, give occasional reassuring sounds and validation, or give interaction depending on the needs of the patient and the situation (Murray-Jobsis, 1984, 1986, 1991b, 1992).

Age Regression

Age regression in hypnosis can be used to enhance the recall of memories already available to conscious awareness and also to promote the recall of suppressed and repressed material. When conscious memory is assisted by age regression, the result is frequently greater detail and richness of memory and greater access to the feelings associated with the memories. When suppressed memories are assisted by age regression, patients may be able to verbalize and share memories and feeling states that they had never been able to speak about to anyone else. When repressed memories are accessed by hypnotic age regression, previously unaccessed material becomes newly available to patients' conscious awareness for the first time. In each of these cases, new material becomes available to patients, with a resulting possible increase in understanding and insight.

In addition, hypnotic age regression promotes greater access to the emotional impact of remembered events and provides an environment for catharsis and abreaction of emotional material that may never have been dealt with fully in the past. Although some psychotic and borderline patients can handle age regression for uncovering and potential catharsis, others may need to distance themselves from the overwhelming imapct of such an emotional encounter with past memories. Therefore, the importance of mirroring techniques, wherein the therapist follows the patient's pacing and capabilities in working with hypnotherapy, must again be stressed.

Reinterpretation of Negative Material

Hypnotic techniques for promoting reinterpretation of negative material include redoing, reframing, imagery shifting, and creator control. An example from my clinical practice of redoing with a patient who had been sexually molested by her father at age 10 consisted of me being the "mother" in hypnotic imagery and protecting the little girl from daddy, telling him that he must stop or go away, and consoling the little girl. In a similar situation, I used reframing techniques to help another patient. The patient was asked to imagine how she as an adult would respond to a little girl who had been molested by her father. The patient was able to see the lack of power a little girl has with an important adult and was then able to relinquish her guilt about sexual acts with her own father.

An imagery shift is a technique in which hypnotic imagery is used to help patients shift feelings in a positive direction. The therapist suggests that a patient change a negative hypnotic image into a positive image. When a patient can produce such a shift in imagery, a positive shift in feelings will typically occur. In a somewhat similar fashion, the therapist may suggest that patients can shift images that are too frightening or overwhelming. Because patients are the creators of their own imagery, the therapist can suggest that they have "creator control" of those images. In clinical practice, patients have been able to change monsters into foolish little men or to make pursuing witches get stuck in glue. Patients who are able to use this creator control technique to shift frightening imagery generally feel relief and humor in their new images (Murray-Jobsis, 1984, 1986, 1989, 1991b, 1992; Scagnelli, 1974, 1977).

Renurturing

The renurturing techniques developed in hypnotic therapy work are made possible by the unique conditions of the hypnotic experience. Because of the use of imagery, the increased access to feelings, and the temporary suspension of the critical–judgmental mind in the hypnotic state, both the patient and the therapist are able to play out in imagery the parent and child roles that can promote a renurturing healing process. Renurturing in hypnosis is designed to make up for missing essential developmental experiences in the patient's life. In the theoretical developmental model presented earlier in this chapter, the original nurturing experiences were seen as being essential for the original bonding of the infant and his or her future bonding–relational capacity. In addition, the original nurturing experiences provide the foundation for a positive sense of self. Therefore, a technique of renurturing that allows therapists to fill in the missing experiences of nurturing can be seen as being extremely important to the therapy of borderline and psychotic patients, for whom such nurturing deficits are central to their pathology.

In hypnotic renurturing, using the technique of age regression, patients imagine themselves "back there" as the infant or little child. The therapist then creates an imaginary series of nurturing experiences: mother rocking baby in her arms; the baby feeling the self being held warm and secure; mother smiling down at baby; the baby seeing the self in mother's smile; mother loving and holding, warm and secure; the baby feeling the holding arms, warm and secure, loved and loving; the baby hearing the soft rhythmic sounds; feeling the rocking motion; smelling the warmth of mother's breast; tasting the warm sweet milk; always connected and loved even in moments of separation; carrying within the feelings and images of being loved and connected even in the moments of separation; and mother always returning and always there "within us."

The therapist can enrich the renurturing technique with as many sensory perceptions as possible, creating an imaginary nurturing experience for the patient. Both patient and therapist know that the real-life experiences of the patient were most likely different from the imaginary renurturing. They know that they are creating new experiences in imagery that will not change the past but may help make the present and future better. Later, renurturing work can move into imagery of the parent reading stories and tucking the little child into bed. The extent of such renurturing is limited only by the patience and creativity of the patient and therapist.

A variation of this renurturing technique is the technique of "creative self-mothering." In creative self-mothering, patients are encouraged to participate more actively in their renurturing process by visualizing themselves as both parent and child. Patients are asked to see their adult self (sometimes with the therapist as coparent) nurturing their infant or child self. Many patients cannot or will not take such an active role in their own renurturing process. However, when patients are willing to engage in this active reparenting of themselves, it has the added advantage of modeling the beginnings of self-love that can grow into adult self-acceptance (Murray-Jobsis, 1984, 1986, 1989, 1990, 1991b, 1992).

Promoting Separation–Individuation

Following renurturing to promote a sense of connectedness and bonding and a positive sense of self, the next sequential developmental process of separation–individuation can also be promoted in hypnotic therapy work using imagery. The therapist can describe the infant's perceptual world: the infant's view of fingers and hands floating in front of the visual field as if separate and apart; the infant's growing awareness of the difference between self and object as he or she grasps and then lets go; and the infant's beginning exploration of the world of touch and sensation. There can also be a description of the sensations of being stroked and held; the holding arms sometimes leaving but always returning; and a dawning sense of awareness of separateness but always against a background of connectedness and bondedness. Gradually, the infant comes to be aware of those moments of separateness even as he or she sustains within himself or herself the images and the feelings of holding and being held warm and secure, loved and connected even in moments of separation. In this manner, descriptions of the beginning of separation–individuation can be created in hypnotic imagery and sensory experience. This experience of separation can be specifically created in a background of bonding and connectedness.

This early experience of separation can be followed with images of the older infant crawling across the floor, seeing the patterns beneath the fingers, looking back for a reassuring glance at mother, crawling farther around a corner to a newly discovered toy, and beginning to explore the possibilities of adventure in this process of separation. At a later stage, there can be imagery of the child beginning to walk and play with other children. Still later, the child can discover the world beyond the home and mother and eventually begin to discover all of the advantages of separation and autonomy. Again, there can be an endless variety of hypnotic images and experiences that can be tailored to the individual needs of the patient and the creativity of the therapist (Murray-Jobsis, 1990, 1991b, 1992).

CASE MATERIAL

Two cases will be summarized to illustrate the use of some of the hypnotic techniques that were discussed in the preceding section.

Case 1: Jenny

Jenny was an attractive woman in her mid-20s who dressed and looked younger than her years. She had been hospitalized for psychiatric illness three times in the past. She had been diagnosed and treated for manic depression and had eventually been stabilized and discharged on Lithium. Although she was being maintained on Lithium, she nevertheless presented at her initial therapy contact in a general state of emotional crisis, with the potential for imminent disintegration. This crisis had apparently been precipitated by the emergence of repressed memories of past sexual abuse by her uncle.[1]

In one of the early hypnotic sessions, Jenny was able to use hypnosis to permit a regression and to recall an encounter with her uncle. She described him pressing up against her, rubbing against her. She could feel his hardness. Her face and body and voice all indicated anxiety and stress as she related these memories.[2] Through hypnosis, Jenny accessed and described a mixture of feelings: feeling excited and aroused, feeling guilty and bad, feeling frightened, feeling pleased that this important man was

---

[1] It may be important to note that there is little empirical data available regarding the reality (or lack of reality) of repressed memories. In general, the research on child and adult memories confirms reliable memory reports beginning with ages 3 and 4 years (Pillemer & White, 1989). A few studies have reported a capacity for accurate memory in children as young as 2 years (Eisenberg, 1985; Nelson & Ross, 1980). A study by Guenther and Frey (1990) relating specifically to repressed memories suggested that "repressors remember as much about victimization experiences as do non-repressors but are more likely to fill in the missing details . . . with positive reconstructions designed to reduce the overall negative quality associated with victimization" (p. 207). Apart from empirical research, however, clinical case studies generally support the global (if not the specific) validity of repressed memories (Putnam, 1991; Ross, 1989). However, it is important to note, for clinical purposes, that therapists do not emphasize proof of the reality of patients' experiences but work at resolving the underlying conflicting feelings that the remembered experiences evoke.

[2] Recent studies on the validity of hypnotically enhanced recall suggest that there is "no evidence for hypermnesia and that hypnotized subjects can make errors and confabulate" (Watkins, 1989, p. 80). Nash, Drake, Wiley, Khalsa, and Lynn (1986) reported that hypnotically enhanced memories may not be an exact replay of historical events and may produce confabulation that may contaminate later waking memories. Beahrs (1988) further noted that "hypnosis has the potential to irrevocably alter cognition, perception and recall" (p. 18). However, both Watkins and Beahrs emphasized that nonhypnotic (as well as hypnotic) memory can be distorted by suggestion and affect and that hypnotic memory needs to be evaluated on the same basis as nonhypnotic memory for its individual case validity. Again, it is important to note that in the clinical setting, therapists emphasize the resolution of feelings and conflicts that emerge from the memories rather than the validity of the memories themselves.

giving her attention, and later feeling that she did not matter to him at all. With therapist support and reframing, Jenny gradually began to tolerate her feelings and to accept them as understandable for a child in a sexual experience with an adult. This work by Jenny is an example of the increased access to memories and feelings possible in hypnosis and the potential for reframing and reinterpreting information in hypnosis.

In other early hypnotic work, Jenny said that she could not speak to me about events that were beginning to emerge in memory. She said that they were too terrible to talk about. (She was beginning to remember sexual abuse by her father.) As a technique for bypassing her resistance, I suggested that she talk to me about the *feelings* that the memories were arousing rather than about the memories themselves. She said that she felt shock and surprise and then dirty, really dirty inside. She said that she could see a tube running inside her filled with filth. I then suggested that because she was the creator of her imagery, she could also change her imagery and that she could shift the negative images into positive ones and get in touch with the beauty inside herself. She gradually created purple and yellow flowers inside of herself and, in the process of creating the positive imagery, also created a shift toward more positive feelings. This work by Jenny is an example of the hypnotic processes of creator control and imagery shifting.

I then asked Jenny to imagine a TV screen. I suggested that instead of experiencing events happening to herself, she could see them happening to actors on the TV screen, and she could tell me about the story on the screen. Using this distancing technique, Jenny was then able to begin to explore the memories of sexual abuse by her father. She then proceeded to tell a story about an 8-year-old girl with her top off and a man playing with her nipples. In telling the story, Jenny slipped in and out of using the pronoun *I*. She said that she felt frightened and very dirty, very bad inside. She said that she hated that part of her body and felt deformed. I suggested that the little girl really needed to know that her body was not deformed, that it was the man who was abusing her who was deformed, that the little girl (and the adult she is now) were never deformed, and that her body was beautiful. I suggested that such hurtful things should never have happened to the little girl, that the little girl was left with feelings she did not know how to handle, and that we could begin to give understanding and support to the little girl. This work by Jenny is an example of hypnotic reframing, wherein events of the past are redefined and understood in new ways. This work also exemplifies how hypnosis can be used to help patients describe their feelings metaphorically or "in a story" and then receive acceptance and renurturance metaphorically "in their story" so that they can maintain the necessary safety and distance.

Between therapy sessions, I encouraged Jenny to store her anxieties about her emerging memories in an imaginary box that she could put away until our next session. This imaginary box gave Jenny a technique that helped her to contain and manage her anxieties in between our sessions.

After the first few sessions, Jenny's anxiety and agitation, which had been initially high, decreased markedly. She also began to form a positive bond with me. As her sense of bonding and trust increased, her need for defensive distancing decreased.

In general, in response to Jenny's emerging memories, hypnosis and therapy provided an environment of acceptance. In addition, I also gave Jenny messages of specific acceptance of the sexual behavior she was relating to me about "little Jenny." I not only accepted little Jenny's sexual behavior, but I also helped Jenny to reinterpret that behavior as "not bad" (i.e., as the behavior of a child under the influence of an emotionally and physically powerful adult). This acceptance and reinterpretation was initially expressed in the hypnotic relationship when Jenny first presented her memories and later was reinforced in the waking state. It was apparent that hypnosis provided an environment that allowed for the temporary lifting of self-censorship and for the expression of suppressed and repressed feelings, which, in turn, allowed me to give the acceptance and reinterpretation that began the healing process.

In addition to acceptance and reinterpretation, I also used hypnosis to help Jenny image a redoing of some of the memories that she had recalled. Specifically, I suggested that the adult Jenny and I could be with "little Jenny" in imagery as her mother. We would then create together scenes of how we as "mother" would have consoled little Jenny and protected her from any further harm. We would have put a stop to daddy's behavior and reassured Jenny that it was not her fault. This hypnotic work illustrates the process of creative self-mothering and redoing. In this instance, such redoing reinforced for Jenny an acceptance of the innocence of the child and how a child is supposed to be treated. It also helped to create a sense of being loved and cared for in the therapy relationship as the child part of the patient very much needed. The use of hypnosis, with its potential for imagery and its capacity for the temporary suspension of reality, is a tremendous asset in this type of therapy work involving a redoing of past events.

Case 2: Caryl

Caryl was a 26-year-old graduate student studying for a professional degree. Caryl was diagnosed as having a borderline personality disorder and displayed the classic borderline characteristic of splitting, seeing herself and others as alternately all bad or all good. She also described symptoms of feeling great emptiness, neediness, and depression. At times, she exhibited intense anger.

In addition to these borderline characteristics, Caryl also saw herself as having separate personalities and had different names for some of her separate selves. However, because she always seemed to be aware of her separate selves, Caryl did not appear to display the differentiating symptoms of a true multiple personality. One highly coherent personality that emerged was named Chris. Chris was a tough, masculine version of herself who was able to be aggressive. Chris functioned fairly well in the real world and was able to take care of himself. He also never perceived himself to be needy. A second personality was an unnamed, frightened, needy, and depressed child who was not able to function well and was very frightened of the world. A third personality was a woman (perhaps most like the person Caryl presented to the world) who appeared to be reasonably self-assured and well functioning on the surface.

As a result of these separate personalities, Caryl's affect was extremely labile and unpredictable. When acting in the "Chris personality," she would be very angry and aggressive and could be very disruptive of therapy. As the little child she would feel helpless and dependent. At some point she would become guilty and angry over her neediness and shift into her aggressive personality and self-destructive behavior. Her most common self-destructive behavior was to burn herself with a curling iron on the buttocks and thighs. She also expressed suicidal ideation but made no active gestures or attempts.

In the initial stages of therapy, Caryl used hypnosis intermittently for the reduction of anxiety and for general support and acceptance. In addition to alleviating some of her symptoms of neediness and depression, this use of hypnosis also generally increased the bonding and the positive therapeutic alliance between us. However, this use of hypnosis was generally not possible when Caryl was experiencing her angry, aggressive personality. During an aggressive, angry phase, Caryl frequently would refuse hypnosis. On one occasion, when hypnosis was accepted in spite of the anger, Caryl produced a spontaneous levitation of both arms and then stated that she wanted to choke herself. At that point, I moved away from empathic mirroring techniques and instead focused on helping her contain the affect. I gave her suggestions to acknowledge her feelings but to allow her hands to relax. Then, using imagery as a distancing technique, I suggested that she find some place of relaxation where she could distance from the self-destructive feelings. With these suggestions, we were then able to talk about the feelings from a distance without the impulse for action. It became clear, with the aid of hypnosis, that when Caryl was in her angry and aggressive state, she was angry at her dependent needy self and felt destructive impulses toward that self. This insight sparked the beginning of Caryl's gradual ability to control and then to extinguish those impulses.

On one occasion, when Caryl arrived for therapy as the frightened, depressed, needy child, she agreed to explore hypnosis for insight in addition to the familiar nurturing that we had been doing. In hypnosis, using age regression and free association, Caryl relived the feeling experience of being unwanted by her mother and father. She reclaimed no specific imagery memories but was firm in her conviction that her feeling memory of being unwanted was accurate. I then suggested a reframing of those feeling memories. I asked Caryl to image her adult self back there with the infant Caryl. I suggested that the infant was truly lovable, as all infants are, and that it was the parents who were unable to give love, who were flawed. Following these suggestions, Caryl reported a sense of healing and wholeness. Although she had been ambivalent about therapy before, she committed to longer term therapy as a result of this session.

Following this breakthrough in therapy, the main hypnotic technique used in Caryl's case was the technique of renurturing in order to create a positive sense of self. Renurturing work in hypnosis was used to allow Caryl to fill in some of the needs, experiences, and feelings that were missing from her childhood. Although she refused to use creative self-mothering (i.e., she would not or could not see herself mothering her own infant self), she was receptive to renurturing imagery with me as the imaged "mother." I created scenes of my holding the infant Caryl, rocking her, singing to her, and smiling down on her in my arms. In later work, we imaged reading stories together, sitting in a rocking chair and rocking together, and playing games together. I would listen to Caryl's feelings and her talk of school and tell her what a wonderful and special girl she was. In this way, we were able to replace the old feelings of being unwanted by parents and to create new feelings of being wanted and nurtured.

RESEARCH AND APPRAISAL

Although early reports of the use of hypnosis with severely disturbed patients were published more than a century ago, modern use of clinical hypnosis with psychotic and borderline patients began in the mid-1900s with the pioneering work of Lewis Wolberg in 1945 and Margaretta Bowers in 1954. In 1945, Wolberg published an account of the hypnoanalysis of Johan R., a chronic hospitalized patient with a diagnosis of hebephrenic schizophrenia (Wolberg, 1945, 1964). In 1954, Bowers reported on hypnotherapy with 10 psychotic and borderline patients (Bowers, Berkowitz, & Brecher, 1954). In later publications, she summarized hypnotic work with 30 chronic ambulatory schizophrenics and addressed the issues of the use of hypnosis with schizophrenic patients as a general group (Bowers, 1961, 1964). Additional early work describing the use of hypnosis with severely disturbed patients was reported by Erickson (1964, 1965), Reardon (1965), and Biddle (1967).

Building on this early pioneering work of the mid-1900s, several clinicians in the 1970s continued reporting productive clinical work with psychotic and borderline patients (Berwick & Douglas, 1977; Scagnelli, 1974, 1976, 1977; Sexton & Maddox, 1979; Zeig, 1974). By the 1980s, the literature on clinical case reports continued to grow and was augmented by the development of new hypnotic techniques for working with psychotic and borderline patients and by the integration of these techniques into conceptual models that were based on existing psychological theory (Baker, 1981, 1982, 1983; Brown, 1985; Brown & Fromm, 1986; Copeland, 1986; Fromm, 1984; Murray-Jobsis, 1984, 1985, 1986, 1988, 1989, 1991b, 1992; Ratner & Gross, 1991; Rostafinski, 1991; Scagnelli, 1980; Scagnelli-Jobsis, 1982; Vas, 1990; Zindel, 1990).

Concerning the integration of hypnotic techniques with psychotic and borderline patients into established psychological theory, major contributions have been made in the past decade. First, Baker (1981) developed a protocol of seven steps designed for the hypnoanalytic treatment of psychotic patients. He based this protocol on an object relations theoretical model of the deficits in object relatedness and in other ego functions associated with psychotic conditions. The seven-step protocol was designed to enhance the positive aspects of the emerging transference and to support the patient's capacity to maintain real connections with the external environment. Baker's work was later elaborated on and extended by Fromm (1984) and Copeland (1986). Baker (1983) also developed specific techniques for managing the transference on the basis of the ego psychological concepts of separation and attachment conflicts.

Second, Brown and Fromm (1986) developed specific hypnotic techniques for treating psychotic and borderline patients that were based on developmental theory and were intended to promote the formation of boundaries and body image, the development of object and self-representations, and the development of affect (Brown, 1985; Brown & Fromm, 1986).

Third, Murray-Jobsis developed techniques of nurturance for bonding and formation of a positive self-image and techniques to foster separation–individuation that were based on a developmental framework and were aimed at restitution through hypnotic imagery experiences (Murray-Jobsis, 1984, 1986, 1989, 1991b, 1992). Murray-Jobsis also developed a theoretical model of hypnosis as adaptive regression and transference. This model provides a framework for understanding the capacity of borderline and psychotic patients to work with hypnosis (Murray-Jobsis, 1988; Scagnelli-Jobsis, 1982).

In addition to these reports of progress emerging from the clinical use of hypnosis with psychotic and borderline patients, experimental research has also been accumulating concerning the capacity of severely disturbed patients for hypnosis. In the early 1980s, three independent review articles were in agreement regarding the positive hypnotic capacity of psychotic patients (Lavoie & Sabourin, 1980; Pettinati, 1982; Scagnelli-Jobsis, 1982). All three articles reported that the experimental literature supported the conclusion that psychotic patients were capable of hypnosis. They also concluded, however, that there was disagreement in the literature about whether psychotic patients display a hypnotic capacity comparable to that of normal individuals.

Concerning the question of comparability of hypnotic capacity, recent studies have reported different results. In 1982, Spiegel, Detrick, and Frischholz reported research using the Hypnotic Induction Profile (HIP) and concluded that "patients diagnosed as schizophrenic by Research Diagnostic Criteria were clearly less hypnotizable than normal subjects" (p. 435). However, in that same year, Pettinati, Evans, Staats, and Horne reported that scores on the Stanford Hypnotic Susceptibility Scale (SHSS) and the Harvard Group Scale of Hypnotic Susceptibility for a hospitalized psychiatric population (including subgroups of schizophrenic disorders and major depression) were not significantly different from those of the normal students. In that same study, however, significant differences were found between inpatient and normal individuals' scores on the HIP. In 1990, Pettinati et al. published additional results from this earlier study and concluded that "when the same patients were administered different hypnosis scales, the conclusions to be drawn concerning hypnotizability of psychiatric patients were inconsistent across the scales" (p. 72). In addition, an informal exploratory study by Murray-Jobsis (1991a) reported higher than normal scores on both the SHSS and HIP for schizophrenic and borderline patients tested by their clinical therapist. An interaction effect between transference and the patients' hypnotic capacity was suggested as a possible explanation for the elevated scores.

Adding to these inconsistencies in the research reports of the comparative hypnotic capacity of psychotic patients and borderline patients, Spiegel et al. (1982) reported HIP variance for "patients with thought disorder" to be twice as great as the reported HIP variance for normal individuals. However, by contrast, Lavoie and Elie (1985) reported that variance was consistently lower with schizophrenics than with normal groups on Form A of the SHSS.

In conclusion, the majority of the research to date supports the assertion that psychotic and borderline patients have hypnotic capacity. However, there is still an ongoing debate concerning the comparability of psychotic and borderline hypnotic capacity with that of normal individuals. In addition, inconsistencies appear to exist among the hypnotic test scales themselves when measuring the same population. Thus, the experimental research concerning the hypnotic capacity of psychotic and borderline patients is inconclusive, and continued research remains to be done. However, the growing body of clinical reports by therapists already working in the innovative area of hypnotherapy with psychotic and borderline patients may make the experimental question of the hypnotic capacity of these patients academic.

CONCLUSION

The material presented in this chapter explains and describes how traditional psychotherapy techniques and new innovative techniques can be integrated and used with hypnosis in therapy work with borderline and psychotic patients.

This therapy is based on a developmental–psychoanalytic theoretical framework. Developmental deficits in bonding, in the formation of a positive sense of self, and in separation–individuation are presumed to be major elements in the pathology of psychotic and borderline patients. Therefore, hypnotherapy is aimed at creating restitutive and corrective experiences in hypnosis to fill in the missing life experiences. The hypnotic process is uniquely suited to this work of creating new and restitutive experiences because of its access to imagery and symbolic material and its suspension of the logical, critical mind.

Traditional therapy work with this severely disturbed patient population is extremely difficult and requires special skills. Integrating hypnosis into therapy with borderline and psychotic patients also requires the special skills of empathic sensitivity and a capacity to provide nurturance and acceptance with limits and consistency.

REFERENCES

Baker, E. L. (1981). An hypnotherapeutic approach to enhance object relatedness in psychotic patients. *International Journal of Clinical and Experimental Hypnosis, 29*, 136–147.

Baker, E. L. (1982). Therapeutic strategies for the aftercare of the schizophrenic: An object relations perspective. *International Journal of Partial Hospitalization, 1*, 119–129.

Baker, E. L. (1983). The use of hypnotic techniques with psychotics. *American Journal of Clinical Hypnosis, 25*, 283–288.

Beahrs, J. O. (1988). Hypnosis cannot be fully nor reliably excluded from the courtroom. *American Journal of Clinical Hypnosis, 31*, 18–27.

Berwick, P., & Douglas, D. (1977). Hypnosis, exorcism, and healing: A case report. *American Journal of Clinical Hypnosis, 20*, 146–148.

Biddle, W. E. (1967). *Hypnosis in the psychoses.* Springfield, IL: Charles C Thomas.

Bowers, M. K. (1961). Theoretical considerations in the use of hypnosis in the treatment of schizophrenia. *International Journal of Clinical and Experimental Hypnosis, 9*, 39–46.

Bowers, M. K. (1964). The use of hypnosis in the treatment of schizophrenia. *Psychoanalytic Review, 51*(3), 116–124.

Bowers, M. K., Berkowitz, B., & Brecher, S. (1954). Hypnosis in severely dependent states. *International Journal of Clinical and Experimental Hypnosis, 2,* 2–12.

Brown, D. P. (1985). Hypnosis as an adjunct to the psychotherapy of the severely disturbed patient: An affective development approach. *International Journal of Clinical and Experimental Hypnosis, 33,* 281–301.

Brown, D. P., & Fromm, E. (1986). *Hypnotherapy and hypnoanalysis.* Hillsdale, NJ: Erlbaum.

Copeland, D. R. (1986). The application of object relations theory to the hypnotherapy of developmental arrests: The borderline patient. *International Journal of Clinical and Experimental Hypnosis, 34,* 157–168.

Eisenberg, A. R. (1985). Learning to describe past experiences in conversation. *Discourse Processes, 8,* 177–204.

Erickson, M. H. (1964). An hypnotic technique for resistant patients: The patient, the technique and its rationale and field experiments. *American Journal of Clinical Hypnosis, 7,* 8–32.

Erickson, M. H. (1965). The use of symptoms as an integral part of hypnotherapy. *American Journal of Clinical Hypnosis, 8,* 57–65.

Erickson, M. H., & Rossi, E. L. (1979). *Hypnotherapy: An exploratory casebook.* New York: Irvington.

Fromm, E. (1984). Hypnoanalysis with particular emphasis on the borderline patient. *Psychoanalytic Psychology, 1,* 61–76.

Gill, M. M., & Brenman, M. (1959). *Hypnosis and related states: Psychoanalytic studies in regression.* Madison, CT: International Universities Press.

Guenther, R. K., & Frey, C. (1990). Recollecting events associated with victimization. *Psychological Reports, 67,* 207–217.

Kernberg, O. (1968). The treatment of patients with borderline personality organization. *International Journal of Psychoanalysis, 49,* 600–619.

Kohut, H. (1977). *The restoration of the self.* Madison, CT: International Universities Press.

Lavoie, G., & Elie, R. (1985). The clinical relevance of hypnotizability in psychosis: With reference to thinking processes and sample variances. In D. Waxman, P. Misra, M. Gibson, & M. A. Basker (Eds.), *Modern trends in hypnosis* (pp. 41–64). New York: Plenum Press.

Lavoie, G., & Sabourin, M. (1980). Hypnosis and schizophrenia: A review of experimental and clinical studies. In G. D. Burrows & L. Dennerstein (Eds.), *Handbook of hypnosis and psychosomatic medicine* (pp. 377–419). New York: Elsevier/North-Holland Biomedical.

Murray-Jobsis, J. (1984). Hypnosis with severely disturbed patients. In W. C. Wester & A. H. Smith (Eds.), *Clinical hypnosis: A multidisciplinary approach* (pp. 368–404). Philadelphia: Lippincott.

Murray-Jobsis, J. (1985). Exploring the schizophrenic experience with the use of hypnosis. *American Journal of Clinical Hypnosis, 28,* 34–42.

Murray-Jobsis, J. (1986). Hypnosis with the borderline patient. In E. Thomas Dowd & J. M. Healy (Eds.), *Case studies in hypnotherapy* (pp. 254–273). New York: Guilford Press.

Murray-Jobsis, J. (1988). Hypnosis as a function of adaptive regression and of transference: An integrated theoretical model. *American Journal of Clinical Hypnosis, 30,* 241–247.

Murray-Jobsis, J. (1989). Clinical case studies utilizing hypnosis with borderline and psychotic patients. *Hypnos, 16,* 8–12.

Murray-Jobsis, J. (1990). In D. C. Hammond (Ed.), *Handbook of hypnotic suggestions and metaphors* (pp. 326–328). New York: Norton.

Murray-Jobsis, J. (1991a). An exploratory study of hypnotic capacity of schizophrenic and borderline patients utilizing SHSS and HIP in a clinical setting. *American Journal of Clinical Hypnosis, 33,* 150–160.

Murray-Jobsis, J. (1991b, April). *Hypnosis with a borderline and a psychotic patient: Two clinical case studies.* Paper presented at the 33rd Annual Scientific Meeting of the American Society of Clinical Hypnosis, St. Louis, MO.

Murray-Jobsis, J. (1992). Hypnotherapy with severely disturbed patients: Presentation of case studies. In W. Bongartz (Ed.), *Hypnosis: 175 years after Mesmer: Recent developments in theory and application: Proceedings of the 5th European Congress of Hypnosis in Psychotherapy and Psychosomatic Medicine* (pp. 301–307). Konstanz, Germany: Universitätsverlag Konstanz.

Nash, M. R., Drake, S. D., Wiley, S., Khalsa, S., & Lynn, S. J. (1986). Accuracy of recall by hypnotically age-regressed students. *Journal of Abnormal Psychology, 95,* 298–300.

Nelson, K., & Ross, G. (1980). The generalities and specifics of long-term memory in infants and young children. In M. Perlmutter (Ed.), *Children's memory: New directions for child development* (pp. 87–101). San Francisco: Jossey-Bass.

Pettinati, H. M. (1982). Measuring hypnotizability in psychotic patients. *International Journal of Clinical and Experimental Hypnosis, 30,* 404–416.

Pettinati, H. M., Evans, F. J., Staats, J. M., & Horne, R. L. (1982, August). *The capacity for hypnosis in clinical populations.* Paper presented at the Ninth International Congress of Hypnosis and Psychosomatic Medicine, Glasgow, Scotland.

Pettinati, H. M., Kogan, L. G., Evans, F. J., Wade, J. H., Horne, R. L., & Staats, J. M. (1990). Hypnotizability of psychiatric inpatients according to two different scales. *American Journal of Psychiatry, 147,* 69–75.

Pillemer, D. B., & White, S. H. (1989). Childhood events recalled by children and adults. *Advances in Child Development and Behavior, 21,* 297–340.

Putnam, F. W. (1991). Recent research on multiple personality disorder. *Psychiatric Clinics of North America, 14,* 489–502.

Ratner, H., & Gross, L. (1991, April). *Hypnosis in the seriously mentally ill: A series of vignettes.* Paper presented at the 33rd Annual Scientific Meeting of the American Society of Clinical Hypnosis, St. Louis, MO.

Reardon, W. T. (1965). *Modern medical hypnosis* (4th ed.). Wilmington, DE: Group Hypnotherapy Research Center.

Ross, C. A. (1989). *Multiple personality disorder: Diagnosis, clinical features, and treatment.* New York: Wiley.

Rostafinski, T. (1991, April). *Differentiation and integration in the hypnotic treatment of borderline conditions.* Paper presented at the 33rd Annual Scientific Meeting of the American Society of Clinical Hypnosis, St. Louis, MO.

Scagnelli, J. (1974). A case of hypnotherapy with an acute schizophrenic. *American Journal of Clinical Hypnosis, 17,* 60–63.

Scagnelli, J. (1975). Therapy with eight schizophrenic and borderline patients: Summary of a therapy approach that employs a semi-symbiotic bond between patient and therapist. *Journal of Clinical Psychology, 31,* 519–525.

Scagnelli, J. (1976). Hypnotherapy with schizophrenic and borderline patients: Summary of therapy with eight patients. *American Journal of Clinical Hypnosis, 19,* 33–38.

Scagnelli, J. (1977). Hypnotic dream therapy with a borderline schizophrenic. *American Journal of Clinical Hypnosis, 20,* 136–145.

Scagnelli, J. (1980). Hypnotherapy with psychotic and borderline patients: The use of trance by patient and therapist. *American Journal of Clinical Hypnosis, 22,* 164–169.

Scagnelli-Jobsis, J. (1982). Hypnosis with psychotic patients: A review of the literature and presentation of a theoretical framework. *American Journal of Clinical Hypnosis, 25,* 33–45.

Schilder, P., & Kauders, O. (1956). Lehrbuch der hypnose [A textbook of hypnosis]. In P. Schilder (Ed.), *The nature of hypnosis* (G. Corvin, Trans.; pp. 45–184). Madison, CT: International Universities Press. (Original work published 1926)

Sexton, R., & Maddox, R. (1979). Age regression and age progression in psychotic and neurotic depression. *American Journal of Clinical Hypnosis, 22,* 37–41.

Spiegel, D., Detrick, D., & Frischholz, E. (1982). Hypnotizability and psychopathology. *American Journal of Psychiatry, 139,* 431–437.

Vas, J. (1990, August). *Mutually projective identification as a special way of communication between the schizophrenic patient and the therapist during hypnotherapy.* Paper presented at the Fifth European Congress of Hypnosis in Psychotherapy and Psychosomatic Medicine, Konstanz, Germany.

Watkins, J. G. (1989). Hypnotic hypermnesia and forensic hypnosis: A cross-examination. *American Journal of Clinical Hypnosis, 32,* 71–83.

Winnicott, D. W. (1965). *The maturational processes and the facilitating environment.* Madison, CT: International Universities Press.

Wolberg, L. R. (1945). *Hypnoanalysis.* New York: Grune & Stratton.

Wolberg, L. R. (1964). *Hypnoanalysis* (2nd ed.). New York: Grune & Stratton.

Zeig, M. S. (1974). Hypnotherapy techniques with psychotic inpatients. *American Journal of Clinical Hypnosis, 17,* 56–59.

Zindel, P. (1992). Hypnosis in psychotherapy of schizophrenic patients and borderline patients. In W. Bongartz (Ed.), *Hypnosis: 175 years after Mesmer: Recent developments in theory and application: Proceedings of the 5th European Congress of Hypnosis in Psychotherapy and Psychosomatic Medicine* (pp. 309–313). Konstanz, Germany: Universitätsverlag Konstanz.

V

COPING WITH STRESS
AND TRAUMA

21

HYPNOSIS AND STORYTELLING IN THE TREATMENT OF CHILD SEXUAL ABUSE: STRATEGIES AND PROCEDURES

JUDITH W. RHUE and STEVEN JAY LYNN

It is no wonder that the devastating aftereffects of child sexual abuse are emblazoned on the headlines of today's newspapers and popular magazines. Whereas a minority of the public may argue that the problem is sensationalized, there is a growing consensus that child abuse is finally getting the attention it deserves. Indeed, with as many as 1 of every 4 girls (Finkelhor, 1979) and 9%–12% of boys (Herman, 1981; Russell, 1983) being sexually victimized before adulthood, child abuse penetrates deep into the social fabric. The estimate that 150,000–400,000 children are victimized annually (Finkelhor & Hotaling, 1984; Mrazek, 1983) underlines the fact that sexual abuse will touch the lives of many children and their families who contact helping professionals.

This chapter is reprinted in expanded and updated form from the October, 1991 *International Journal of Clinical and Experimental Hypnosis*. Copyrighted by the Society for Clinical and Experimental Hypnosis, October, 1991.

Clinicians who work with abused children are likely to encounter relatively high levels of dissociation, somatization, anxiety, sleep disturbance, tension, sexual problems, anger, and depression (Briere & Runtz, 1987, 1988). Nearly universal repercussions of sexual abuse are diminished self-esteem, guilt feelings, and interpersonal problems (Gold, 1986).

To salve abused children's emotional wounds, many interventions have been used (see Kolko, 1987), including comprehensive multidisciplinary team approaches, family therapy, group psychotherapy, training in specific interpersonal skills, individual play and art therapy, and treatment with psychoactive agents. We have not found any reports in the literature on interventions that specifically incorporated hypnotic and imagination-based methods. This is noteworthy because hypnotic techniques have been used to treat other trauma-related problems and disorders ranging from posttraumatic stress disorders (e.g., MacHovec, 1984; Spiegel, 1988) to global amnesia (e.g., Eisen, 1989) to the aftereffects of adult rape (Dempster & Balson, 1982; Ebert, 1988; Smith, chapter 22 in this book; Valdiserri & Byrne, 1982).

In this chapter, we describe how naturalistic hypnotic techniques that focus on storytelling can be used in the assessment and treatment of the aftereffects of child abuse. Storytelling is actually a well-established method. It was used and written about by Despert and Potter (1936) more than 50 years ago, and it is nicely exemplified by R. Gardner's (1977) psychoanalytic work with children. R. Gardner invited children to make up creative stories with a "beginning, a middle, and an end" that have a "moral"; he treated stories created by children in a manner analogous to adult dream productions. The themes and moral of the story were thought to reveal conflicts, current concerns, and psychodynamics relevant to treatment. Stories generated by children served as stepping stones for stories scripted by the therapist that framed alternative approaches to problems, interpretations of situations, and personal attributions in a positive, constructive manner. Numerous clinicians have found storytelling to be a useful treatment modality and have either patterned their work after R. Gardner's or modified his techniques (Aurela, 1987; Brooks, 1981, 1987; Davis, 1986; Keim, Lentine, Keim, & Madanes, 1987; Lawson, 1987; Levine, 1980).

Storytelling, which accesses imagination and fantasy, has fallen under the rubric of "hypnotic" in the psychological literature. Storytelling is client centered and permissive. Levine (1980), for example, described a hypnotic method in which indirect suggestions embedded in the child's favorite fairy tale were used. Levine noted that formal "trance" was not induced so that issues of depth of hypnotizability of young subjects could be circumvented. Many of the methods we describe can likewise be thought of as naturalistic induction techniques that can be used as the primary treatment modality or in conjunction with other therapeutic interventions. Storytelling provides the therapist with the necessary flexibility to alter the theme, tone, affect, and pacing requisite to promoting maximum involvement in fantasy and suggested experiences. Storytelling can also combine direct and indirect suggestions in creative ways and has much akin with play therapy and with Porter's (1975) guided fantasies that are presented to children as bedtime stories.

Many examples of hypnotic storytelling were presented by G. Gardner and Olness (1981), and Milton Erickson is well known for his creative uses of therapeutic stories and metaphor (see chapter 14 in this book). Hypnotic procedures based on storytelling have been applied to the hypnotic treatment of children in acute pain (Kuttner, 1988) and to children who must endure difficult medical procedures (J. R. Hilgard & LeBaron, 1984).

The therapeutic techniques that we describe appeal strongly to the child's imagination and can evoke a state of intense absorption. In this chapter, we describe how storytelling techniques can be used to treat the sexually abused child. Our approach synthesizes the therapeutic interventions we found to be most effective in our work with 32 children, 4–10 years of age, who were victims of sexual abuse. The methods we describe can also be used with other interventions and can be used to treat physically abused children, posttraumatic stress disorder, dissociative disorders, and short-term reactions to trauma in childhood, all of which require titrating affect, controlling abreaction, and fortifying a sense of personal mastery.

CLINICAL APPLICATIONS

Assessment

Before hypnotherapy or any other treatment is instituted, it is imperative that the clinician conduct a thorough assessment of the abused child. Assessment is an ongoing process that must address the child's willingness and ability to profit from storytelling techniques as well as the details and consequences of the sexual victimization.

We have found that children who enjoy imaginative reading or listening to and telling stories and fairy tales are appropriate candidates for hypnotherapy and storytelling. The following suggest a capacity for imaginative involvements (Lynn, Rhue, & Green, 1988) and augur well for involvement in fantasy and storytelling: intense absorption in make-believe games; the belief that dolls and stuffed animals are alive; imaginary friends, animals, and objects; and pretending, and in some sense believing, to be someone else (i.e., a fairy tale character). To provide guidelines for stories, we ask the children about their favorite fairy tales, story characters, superheroes, and people they admire.

Although there is no substitute for actually experimenting with storytelling, cognitive deficits, poor reality contact, a limited attention span, and an impoverished imaginative life contraindicate storytelling or mitigate its effectiveness. Thus, children with an attention deficit disorder, mentally challenged children, and those with neurological disorders are often better served by other treatment strategies.

The psychological literature provides useful guidelines for assessing potential problems and areas of dysfunction in abused children. According to Browne and Finkelhor (1986), the initial effects of sexual abuse include depression, somatic complaints, anxiety, disturbed interpersonal relations, a decrease in the level of social functioning, and heightened sexual activity and preoccupation. In female victims especially, the most frequent initial reaction is an increase in fearfulness and anxiety. Guilt, self-blame, and problems in trusting others are often preeminent themes if the abuser is the child's parent or has threatened the child with disapproval, blame, or physical harm to themselves or others if the child discloses the abuse. Prolonged or more intensive therapy is likely to be required in cases involving severe abuse.

Nevertheless, it is important to keep in mind that there is no consistent pattern of psychopathology or syndrome associated with sexual abuse. Additionally, problems that need to be resolved may vary as a function of the age of the child. In young sexually abused children, fears and anxieties may be expressed as sleep disturbances, nightmares, compulsive masturbation, precocious sexual play, loss of toilet training, crying with no provocation, staying indoors, and regressed behavior such as finger sucking or clinging (Brant & Tisza, 1977; Gomes-Schwartz, Horowitz, & Sauzier, 1985; Pascoe & Duterte, 1981). In school-age sexually abused children, it may also be necessary to treat depression, school failure, truancy, and running away from home (Justice & Justice, 1979).

Given the diversity of symptoms presented by abused children, it is particularly important that stories told to the child be fashioned to meet the child's unique needs. In each case of abuse, the therapist must conduct a careful analysis of the cognitive, behavioral, and affective consequences of abuse. Rhue and Lynn (1991b) have argued that the following sorts of questions can provide useful information about the aftereffects of abuse: How are the dynamics of the family, trust in others, and the matrix of feelings toward the parents affected? To what extent are feelings of self-blame, anger, shame, badness, or being "damaged" or "broken" present? To what extent is the child's self-esteem and sense of power and control over his or her body affected? Do sexual themes, unusual behaviors, or preoccupations surface?

So that conflicts, attitudes, and behaviors can be targeted for treatment, it is important to have a comprehensive picture of the child's problems. Yet, this information is often easier to secure than are the details of the abuse and the subtle feelings and changes in self-concept associated with it. This is because the very occurrence of abuse, much less the details surrounding it, is often shrouded in secrecy. Particularly if abusers are family members or are close to the child, children are reluctant to discuss sexual abuse and may minimize its frequency, duration, and graphic details. Even if the child is reluctant to disclose the nature or extent of the abuse, the therapist must respect the child's privacy. In fact, nothing must infringe on the child's sense of security and control in the therapeutic relationship. To spare the child the emotional pain of disclosing the abuse before he or she is ready to do so, collateral information sources such as social service agencies should be used. Previous contacts with social service agencies and past treatment of the problem ought to be reviewed. If evidence is secured that abuse is continuing, then it is incumbent on the therapist to prevent continued trauma to the child and to inform responsible family members and the appropriate authorities.

In order to assess the child and initiate treatment, it is not essential that the therapist be absolutely certain that abuse has occurred. Even if it can never be ascertained with certainty that abuse has occurred, the child's account of abuse may nevertheless carry the weight of narrative truth while lacking the stamp of historical truth (Spence, 1989). The therapist must resist the insidious temptation to focus on ferreting out the "reality" of what occurred and thereby impose an agenda that could be disruptive to treatment. Yet, because of the danger of pseudomemory creation (Laurence & Perry, 1983), the therapist must be wary about suggesting or implying that abuse occurred. Until the child is ready to disclose the fact or details of abuse, relationship building and symptom reduction are primary treatment objectives.

Storytelling With Sexually Abused Children

General Considerations

After a thorough assessment, collaborative storytelling can proceed. We do not routinely measure children's hypnotizability; it is only necessary that our clients are absorbed in the story and that they participate in the unfolding narrative and that useful insights and the working through of difficult issues flow from our efforts. Only when children have some knowledge about hypnosis and are not resistant to experiencing it have we defined the procedures as "hypnosis." With children 7 years of age or older, we generally discuss hypnosis with them and make a decision about whether to precede storytelling with suggestions that typically include relaxation and ego-strengthening messages framed in the context of hypnosis. To avoid challenging the client, we rarely use direct ideomotor suggestions for specific responses. We have done so only when there were definite indications of movement in response to suggested images; specific movements were suggested in order to intensify the observed response and to ratify the experience.

Regardless of whether we use an hypnotic induction, we encourage our clients to immerse themselves fully in the imagined events, to have a complete sensory experience of the story, and to identify with characters with whom they feel a sense of kinship. Although we ask clients to close their eyes in order to focus on the story, if children open their eyes, we do not make an issue out of it. Some children, particularly those younger than 8 years of age, spontaneously act out aspects of the story or talk in a particular character's voice. We generally do not discourage these sorts of theatrics. We also use verbal or ideomotor signaling when we are unsure about whether the child is immersed in the story or about which image or character the child finds most congenial and when we wish to establish whether a child is experiencing a particular suggested effect such as relaxation. Stories that initially provoked anxiety but that the child wishes to retell may be preceded by formal or direct relaxation suggestions.

Building a Safe Haven: The Favorite Place

It is essential to build a *safe context* from which feelings about the abuse can be explored. Storytelling techniques permit the child to withdraw from anxiety-provoking material and to proceed at a comfortable, self-controlled pace.

The following vignette illustrates the importance of conveying a sense of control to the child, particularly in the early stages of therapy. Tina, a bright, petite 7-year-old, had been sexually abused for about 6 months by her mother's live-in boyfriend. After having to recount the details of the abuse on several occasions to her mother, the police, and social services staff, Tina began to tearfully withdraw and to refuse to talk whenever anyone tried to discuss the abuse with her. During her initial visit with the therapist, she sat on the far end of the sofa looking frightened and tense. She nodded yes or no responses but refused to say anything other than her name. The therapist assured Tina that she did not need to talk unless she wanted to and that it would be okay just to sit and listen. The therapist recounted a story for Tina and then ended the session.

At the next session, the therapist asked Tina to tell a story. After providing the therapist with numerous rationalizations as to why the story would not be any good (she did not know many good stories, could not tell stories well, always left things out), Tina hesitantly began to recount her story. In her story a beautiful princess lived in a castle with her mother and father. One day an evil witch came and put a spell on the princess and she was very afraid. A wild bear tried to break down the door of the palace to steal the princess. Her parents had a good fairy come and make a thick row of briars and thorns grow around the palace to keep the bear away from the door for 20 years until the evil spell was over and the princess would be safe again. Until then, the princess always had to be very careful because the bear might find a way into the castle. Over time and numerous recountings of this story, Tina made the thorns grow all over to protect the castle and thickened the walls before finally, at the suggestion of the therapist, beginning to make the bear grow smaller and smaller until it was only the size of a bear cub and no longer able to hurt the princess.

To build a safe haven, we encourage children to describe their favorite place. This may be an actual place or a fantasized, idealized place. What is important is that the children feel safe, secure, and comfortable in this place. The therapist may expect a wide range of favorite places, some of them improbable. For example, one child we treated described his favorite place as a large green metal box on wheels that seemed to resemble a habitable dumpster; another child detailed the trappings of an underwater cave protected by friendly dolphins. So as not to provide an excessive degree of structure or to create demands for reporting only positive affect, we avoid suggesting that the child feel "happy" in the favorite place, nor do we stipulate whether the child is alone or with a special companion. We do, however, often suggest that the child fill this place with the trappings and creatures that he or she likes best (e.g., stuffed animals, family pets, imaginary companions, articles of self-defense). When children are highly anxious, we have suggested an imaginary gate or other buffer to control who enters and exits.

One of the challenges confronting the therapist is to monitor and modulate children's affect during the story. To this end, it is sometimes useful to sprinkle direct suggestions for relaxation, comfort, and security into the unfolding narrative. One helpful guide to specific suggestions is children's responses to questions such as "How can you feel even better in this place?" Furthermore, we have found it useful to suggest props or devices, such as magic wands, rings, or magic words with special powers, in order to explore children's wishes (e.g., "What three wishes would you like to be granted") or to create certain effects such as relaxation or amnesia for selected events (e.g., "When the magic wand touches you, you will forget everything about . . . , it will seem as if you dreamed it all, only to recall it perfectly when the magic wand touches you again").

As children become more comfortable and familiar with fantasizing in line with suggested stories, we encourage them to introduce new stories from the safety of their favorite place. We then begin to introduce stories involving children and adults and to have the children suggest various plot endings. Stories begin to take on a more realistic quality, with issues of trust, fear, hurt, guilt, love, caring, and anger introduced. Nevertheless, the children are encouraged to bring imaginary protectors if they feel they are needed.

Brooks (1985) argued forcefully that metaphors contained in children's stories can be construed as dynamic organizers of information and behavior that "provide a window into the child's phenomenal world" (p. 762).

Metaphors can be used productively by the therapist to cement the therapeutic alliance, to educate the children about the agenda of treatment, and to transfer what is learned to events and problems of everyday life. Metaphor serves as a basis of Brooks's (1981) "creative characters" technique in which the therapist selects key issues facing the child and then develops characters in the context of a narrative that reflects core therapy issues. Similarly, Kritzberg (1972) described the development and use of a therapeutic storytelling word game (Tell-A-Story Kit) that uses a stimulus board and serves to stimulate motivation and ideational and verbal productivity and promotes the interpretation and analysis of stories as well as the generalization of what is learned in the story to real-life situations.

We view this forging of a connection between what happens to the story characters and the children's own lives as a crucial step in therapy: At some point we move beyond the metaphor to nitty-gritty, real-life problems and issues. To this end, as rapport with the children builds, we encourage them to relate stories of real-life events that have happened to their friends or to "imaginary friends." The children's stories are not questioned; no effort is made to have them disclose whether described events happened to them or to their friends. Nevertheless, spelling out the metaphor in terms of its connection to real-life events is a treatment objective. To foster this sort of "connection making," we generally sidestep directly interpreting the meaning of the stories. Rather, insight is promoted by nondirective questioning (e.g., "Do you see any connection between what happened to E.T. and yourself?"), with interpretations made following the children's insightful remarks. This process of connection making is a treatment objective that permeates all the techniques we describe in this chapter.

The Favorite Story

When children are pressured to reveal details of the abuse, resistance can be expected. Specifics about abuse may emerge only gradually, with children testing the theapist's reaction to symbolic or "actual" accounts of abusive events. To encourage children to talk about themselves and difficult subject matter, we invite them to share a favorite story with us. Fears can be shared and conquered, anger expressed, revenge extracted, sorrow experienced, and loss mourned, if not on a literal, then on a symbolic level. Children can control the imaginal representation of a feared situation and become desensitized to it by way of repetition. If anxiety mounts to uncomfortable levels, suggestions for imaginal separation from the situation may be initiated by the children or the therapist. As children become emotionally secure and can express feelings associated with the abuse with less distancing, we give direct suggestions to promote a stronger, unified sense of self and wholeness.

The following example illustrates that the details of abuse often emerge gradually after considerable rapport building and mutual storytelling. Teresa, age 8, for 2 months recounted favorite stories that depicted children who were terrified of being lost or hurt. Finally, at the end of one session, she asked the therapist, "Don't these stories disgust you?" The therapist replied that she was not disgusted and that sometimes children were afraid of bad things happening to them. During the next session, Teresa recounted a usual favorite story, but toward the end added a description of how a young girl was told to pull down her pants and "let a monster do things to her privates." Teresa then demanded that the therapist "make up a good story, for goodness sakes" and listened to the therapist's story tight-lipped without a word. At the following session, 1 week later, Teresa said, "That girl in the story last week was my younger sister." Thereafter, she recounted numerous instances of abuse in her stories but clearly and repeatedly announced that all of these happened to her "younger sister." Only after 7 months did she say to the therapist, "A lot of things that happened to my sister happened to me too." Thereafter, Teresa never mentioned her sister but gradually began to enter her own stories as a character. Teresa did not have any siblings.

Protective Images

To alleviate children's anxiety if characters in the story are hurt, molested, or "bothered," or whenever children are particularly anxious, "protective images" or symbols (e.g., E.T., Gandalf, a 10-ft-high velveteen rabbit) can be introduced into their stories. When we are viewed by children as powerful allies and protectors, we ask them if they would welcome our accompanying them, to help them brave whatever threat presents itself. Also, having the means of escape at hand (e.g., flying horses, magic carpets, rocket ships) or a protective buffer (e.g., suit of armor, suit with a "disappearing, vanishing button") between them and a hostile environment can quell anxiety.

The following example illustrates how stories that contain images associated with protection, power, and control can assist the abused child in confronting stressful life situations, including mastering situations related to the legal system. Billie, a 9-year-old boy, was scheduled to testify in criminal proceedings court about the sexual abuse perpetrated by his uncle. Billie had testified in a previous hearing and dreaded the questions asked during cross-examination by his uncle's attorney. He said that he felt as if he were being cut by each question and felt that everyone could see the cuts. The therapist described a superhero who was always protected from hurtful things by an invisible clear plastic shield. Anything that hit the shield simply bounced off and could not hurt the person underneath.

This idea clearly appealed to Billie, and the therapist had him close his eyes, relax, and see the imaginary shield in his mind and describe it. The therapist then had Billie stand up and imagine putting the shield all around him and zipping it up. Next, the therapist had Billie jump around and clap and sing to see all of the things he could do with the shield on. After allowing Billie to look in the mirror to be sure no one could see the shield, the therapist asked Billie to pretend he was watching a TV set of the court room. He could see himself wearing the magic shield that would protect him, but no one else could see it. In watching the courtoom scene, the therapist asked Billie to have the attorney ask him a question that might have been hurtful in the past. Billie said in an accusatory voice, "You made the whole thing up to get even with your uncle for not taking you on vacation, didn't you?" Billie was delighted with the magic shield and the TV to practice scary things. He always insisted on taking the magic shield with him when he left the therapist's office at the end of a session.

Of crucial importance to the restoration of a positive self-image is helping abused children to regain a sense of personal power and control. To do so, we emphasize and reinforce children's freedom to chart the course of the story, to "make it what you want." Children are also invited to select a story from among one or more alternatives for the therapist to tell or to choose a story in which the children and therapist alternate assuming responsibility for the narrative. With practice, working and reworking the feelings and conflicts surrounding the abuse, and with the therapist's attention lavished on the children's imaginal creations, the children typically experience enhanced self-esteem, feelings of mastery, and positive response expectancies about the outcome of therapy that are, not infrequently, mirrored in the stories' content (see Rhue & Lynn, 1991b).

The importance of patience and accepting, valuing, and respecting the children's stories, regardless of the characters' emotions or behaviors, is illustrated in the following example: Susan, age 6, would first tell her story and then have the therapist tell one. She adhered rigidly to this pattern and repeatedly told an angry, violent story in which a helpless child (a young girl) was buried alive by falling furniture as a monster roamed through her home looking for her. Over 13 sessions, Susan's plot remained invariate, although her characters fared differently. At first, Susan had the little girl die under the furniture before the monster could get her, saying that she was "better off dead anyway." As the therapy progressed, and Susan's control and power were suggested in the therapist's stories, the little girl began to find weapons and fight the monster, although both characters suffered in these battles. In the 13th session, the little girl had grown very strong and was able to perceive the approach of the monster from some distance and summon the police so that she would not be harmed. Susan was clearly pleased with herself and had the therapist congratulate her as the monster was taken away. The incongruity of a monster being removed by the police was never discussed, and the next week Susan proposed a new story with less helplessness and violence.

Relieving Guilt Via Metaphor and Reframing

Not infrequently, the legacy of abuse engenders a crippling sense of defeat, guilt, and shame. Many abused children are coerced to keep the abuse secret by physical threats or appeals to protect the abuser from exposure (Geiser, 1979; Justice & Justice, 1979). Although abused children are the victims, not the responsible agents, when the secret is revealed, the children may believe that adults blame them for permitting the abuse to continue.

To alleviate this burden of guilt, in story form, we recast the children's problems as irresolute dilemmas in which they coped as best as they could under difficult, conflictual, and confusing circumstances. The children interact with imaginary characters who are in situations analogous to theirs, give them advice, help them not to blame themselves, and teach them about what adults should and should not do. The story also challenges their perception of badness and uses metaphors to promote insight. Examples include conveying the idea that getting rid of guilt feelings is like getting rid of germs and that children who are recovering from having their tonsils removed require time to recover, just as abused children require time to recover from the effects of abuse. The therapist emphasizes that in each case, the children will eventually feel better (Rhue & Lynn, 1991a). Finally, we have found it useful to tell stories about how other children have coped with physical and psychological problems similar to those of the abused children.

The following example exemplifies how working with metaphors can provide an antidote to feelings of shame associated with abuse and "secret keeping." Corey, age 6, had been molested by a neighbor who babysat for her when her parents were away. Instances of abuse were sporadic over a year and involved masturbation and fondling. The abuser admonished Corey "to keep our secret" and not to tell anyone or she would be taken away and everyone would know what she did. Over the year, Corey began to have nightmares and became enuretic. At school, she was isolated and sad. She frequently experienced headaches and vomiting. Finally, she told her teacher "the secret" and said that she wished to die because she was so ugly. She was sent to the therapist when she began scratching and biting herself.

In therapy, Corey drew pictures of herself and then covered them with black watercolor paints or scribbled over them with her pencil. When asked to describe herself she said, "I'm a stupid little rat." Corey had a fondness for animals, and the therapist felt that it would be helpful to use animals in the therapy. The therapist began to tell Corey stories about Chucky, the wood-chuck who lived in the forest. The therapist had Corey close her eyes and picture Chucky and his forest and listen to the birds that sang in the forest.

The therapist had Corey listen to the story and pretend that she was watching it in a movie theatre. One day, Chucky and another young woodchuck were playing near the pond where Chucky's mother had told him not to play. Chucky slipped and fell and got all muddy. When Chucky saw his reflection in the pond, he made a mistake and believed that he was ruined and that none of the other woodchucks would play with him ever again. He was afraid to tell his mother, and the other woodchuck made him promise not to tell. For days, Chucky walked around feeling sad. Even his mother did not understand what was wrong with Chucky. Then one day it rained in the forest. When the shower was over, everything in the forest looked clean and sparkling. Chucky liked the way everything looked and could not help feeling better, even though he felt like such a mess. Then he went to the pond to get a drink. He could not believe his eyes! He was clean and really quite a good-looking woodchuck! "But I thought I was ruined," he told his mother, "and I was playing too near the pond." His mother was not mad at him. She understood that Chucky had made a mistake when he saw that he was muddy because he did not understand that underneath the mud, he was the same woodchuck that everyone loved. Well, it takes some time for young woodchucks to find out that they are okay after they have been through a bad experience, but sooner or later the truth comes out, and the showers clean them up and they feel much better and know they are good young woodchucks.

The Child as "Teacher"

As children become able to tolerate direct reference to issues of abuse, the therapist's stories begin to tackle emotionally laden issues. An example would be their right to control who touches their body. Children may be asked to suggest stories that would help other abused children know what to do if someone wants to touch them inappropriately or asks them to touch him or her inappropriately.

Promoting Wellness and Good Health

Children who have been sexually abused are at risk for developing physical and psychological problems, including vaginal and urinary tract problems, yeast and ear infections, and psychophysiological illnesses (Adams-Tucker, 1982; Boekelheide, 1978; Sgroi, 1982; Yates, 1982). Trauma, including that produced by sexual abuse, has been theoretically linked to immune system suppression, although the evidence is inconclusive (Walker & Bolkovatz, 1988). The storytelling format can be used to provide suggestions for bodily integrity and good health. Also, we use guided imagery and hyperempiric suggestions (Gibbons, 1979) to teach children how to produce a sense of well-being and relaxation to counteract the effects of stress associated with abuse.

Achieving Appropriate Rewards

Finkelhor and Browne (1985) used the term *traumatic sexualization* to refer to developmentally inappropriate and dysfunctional sexuality that arises from sexual abuse. Sexually abused children are confronted with adult sexual behaviors prematurely. Those who experience physical pain as a result of the sexual abuse may develop an association between fear and sex. In such cases, children may require the therapist's help to separate physical affection and, later, sexuality from pain.

However, in the majority of sexual abuse cases, children experience minimal physical pain; sexual behaviors are instead paired with positive physical sensations, statements of affection and love, and a peculiar specialness: Children learn that sexual activities earn extra attention and material goods. They may, therefore, acquire an inappropriate repertoire of sexual behavior, be confused about their sexual self-concept, and have unusual emotional associations to sexual activities. Storytelling may be used to help children learn appropriate ways of earning material rewards via nonsexual means. Initially, fantasy or cartoon characters may be used in scenarios in which the characters strive to gain rewards such as a new spaceship or a glowing purple turtle. Gradually, the therapist develops more realistic stories of children whose experiences are analogous to those of the abused child. Suggestion and repetition are used to bond positive emotions to age-appropriate methods of coping. Ultimately, sexuality is recast as a gift, not a commodity.

CASE MATERIAL

The Case of Ann

The following is the transcript from portions of the 2nd and the 15th sessions with Ann, age 8. Ann was a bright, verbal child who had been sexually abused by her mother's live-in boyfriend over a period of several months. Evidence of abuse and neglect led to her removal from her mother's home and subsequent placement with foster parents. The boyfriend confessed to fondling Ann, as well as another child, and was sentenced to jail. The foster parents with whom she was placed reported that Ann was enuretic, had frequent and frightening nightmares of being chased and stabbed, and played inappropriately with her dolls (i.e., removing their clothes and sucking their breasts or poking holes between their legs). Despite the boyfriend's confession of abuse, Ann denied being abused, maintaining that he had "tried" but that she had outsmarted him and nothing had happened.

During the sessions, Ann closed her eyes spontaneously. Because Ann was cooperative, motivated to imagine and participate in mutual storytelling, and appeared to be intensely absorbed in the stories, we did not attempt to formally test her hypnotizability or "depth of trance."

Session 2

Therapist: Hello, Ann, I'm glad to see you today.

Ann: What are we going to do? You said we might tell a story together. How are we going to do that?

Therapist: It sounds like you're ready to begin.

Ann: I looked at the books in the library at school and picked out some stories, but you may already know them.

Therapist: You really did get a head start! That was a good idea and I bet that you can use your imagination with those stories you read to make them even better. You said last week that you make up your own stories when you're playing with your dolls.

Ann: Unhuh . . . I don't want to talk about my dolls. Everybody thinks I'm hurting them. I hate them!

Therapist: It sounds like you feel pretty angry at someone.

Ann: No, not really. . . . Can we please talk about something else?

Therapist: OK, we can talk about feeling angry and the dolls when you're ready. Now, let's think of our favorite places. I'll think of my favorite place, a place where I feel very happy and safe, and you think of your favorite place. It doesn't have to be a real place, an imaginary one will do just as well.

Ann: That's easy.

Therapist: Now, let's use our imaginations to put our favorite places in the middle of a wonderful enchanted forest. Then we can take a walk in the enchanted forest and share visits to our favorite places.

Ann: [She closes her eyes and sits back in her seat] You can come to mine and have cookies and Coke with me. Okay?

Therapist: That sounds nice. We'll share a walk in the enchanted forest and then we'll go to your favorite place and have our cookies. Do you want to describe the enchanted forest or do you want me to?

Ann: You do it.

Therapist: Okay. Do you want to walk beside me so we can look at everything together?

Ann: No, I'll stay behind you. That way if anything jumps out and gets you I can run away [giggles]. I'm only joking.

Therapist: Let's open our hands so that we can feel the big shiny key that opens the gate.

Ann: Are you sure it's safe? At night it could be dangerous. You don't know who is in there in the dark. My foster mom had to leave the light on last night because I had a bad dream.

Therapist: It seems that right now you feel better with more light so we can control that. We are the only ones with the magic key and we can make it sunny. You can even have a guard if you want.

Ann: I want a giant dragon with big wings that will eat up anyone who shouldn't be there. Her name will be Silver and she will rip them apart. I saw one on the Saturday morning cartoons.

Therapist: Now we are walking through the enchanted forest. Can you see lots of flowers, red ones and yellow ones and white ones? They look so pretty it makes you feel happy. Can you hear the birds singing?

Ann: Yes, I can see a robin. It's building a nest. Can you see it?

Therapist: Yes. Is that your favorite place I see up there?

Ann: Unhuh, you're the only one I am going to let in and you can't tell anyone about it because X [mother's boyfriend] might find out.

Therapist: You're still a little afraid of him even though you know this is a safe place and he won't bother you any more.

Ann: I'm not afraid of him and I don't want to talk about him. Let's have our cookies.

Therapist: Will you show me around?

Ann: Yes, here's the living room. All of my toys are over here. There are lots and lots of them. Here are my books and my desk so I can do my homework. We can eat our cookies here, but be careful not to spill crumbs or stuff or we might get bugs like we do at home. I know how to fix hot dogs. I cooked for my mom.

Therapist: Do you miss your mom?

Ann: Yeah, she got rid of X [boyfriend] when she found out. She's going to get me back again as soon as she gets our house cleaned up and gets some money.

Ann continued to deny abuse until the 15th session. However, she developed a strong relationship with the therapist, frequently bringing a paper with a good grade or a drawing to the sessions. Her enuretic nights became less frequent, and she stopped exhibiting sexual behaviors in playing with her dolls. Ann's nightmares continued to occur sporadically, particularly around the time of visits at home with her mother.

Session 15

Therapist: Hi, Ann, how are you today?

Ann: I'm okay. I visited with my mom this weekend.

Therapist: How did the visit go?

Ann: Okay. She's getting the house cleaned up and she wants me to come home.

Therapist: How do you feel about going home?

Ann: I don't know. It's hard to talk to her. I don't want to hurt her feelings.

Therapist: Why don't we pretend she's here. Then when you're feeling very safe in your favorite place, you can talk to her and be sure that it won't hurt her feelings.

Ann: [She closes her eyes] I don't know . . . maybe. Let's get the key to the magic gate. Close your eyes.

Therapist: Okay. I'll let you lead the way again this week if you want.

Ann: [Giggling] This gate creaks. I think we need to oil it. Now, I'll close it behind us and we can skip. Careful now so that you don't fall down. Okay, we're here.

Therapist: You certainly know the way these days.

Ann: I learn fast, don't I?

Therapist: Yes, you do. Can you imagine your mom sitting here with us? Maybe she's sitting in the big green chair.

Ann: Yeah, I can see her.

Therapist: What would you like to tell your mom first?

Ann: That I'm not mad at her any more for what X [boyfriend] did.

Therapist: It sounds like you were mad at her for awhile about it.

Ann: Yeah, if she hadn't gone to work and left him there at night with me, it wouldn't have happened. He never came in my room during the day when she was home, just at night.

Therapist: It must have been pretty scary for you, but now you're safe and you can talk about it and not be afraid.

Ann: He said my mom would be real mad at me if she found out.

Therapist: Well, your mom already understands what X did. He admitted to the police that he touched you. Is your mom mad at you now?

Ann: No, she's mad at X. She still loves me.

Therapist: Now, let's talk with your mom.

Ann: Hi, mom.

Therapist: Tell your mom about your feelings.

Ann: Mom, I'm sorry that I've been a little mad at you. I didn't want you to leave and go to work when X was there, but you went anyway. I was so scared. He said you would be mad at me. I'm not mad at you any more and I don't want you to be mad at me.

Therapist: Is there anything else you want to tell your mom?

Ann: Yeah. Mom, please don't let him bother me ever again. That's all.

Ann continued in therapy for an additional 25 sessions. During that time, she was returned to her mother's custody and moved back into her home. Although she experienced several enuretic nights around the time of her move home, these ceased after the 2nd week. Ann continued to use the magic cottage as her safe place and chose it as the setting in which to address anxiety-provoking issues. She gained self-confidence and her grades in school improved dramatically. After the termination of therapy, the therapist occasionally received short letters from Ann, many of which were accompanied by a test paper with a high score.

RESEARCH AND APPRAISAL

Our discussion shows that storytelling capitalizes on children's ability to absorb themselves in make-believe, to move in imagination with a creative narrative that flows jointly from the therapist's suggestions and from the child's storymaking efforts. Because fantasy, imagination, and daydreaming are integral to children's cognitive and affective life, hypnotic techniques are particularly well suited to this population. Klinger (1971) described the twining of fantasy and play involvement in which young children become absorbed in a make-believe world. London, Morgan, and Hilgard (1973) suggested that intensive and extensive childhood imaginative involvements account for the finding that children are more hypnotizable than adults. Similarly, O'Grady and Hoffmann (1984) maintained that children's high level of hypnotizability is a function of their openness to new experience, intensity of feeling, desires for mastery, and their aptitude for altering consciousness. Empirical studies of children have documented a modest association between measures of fantasy and hypnotizability (see LeBaron, Zeltzer, & Fanurik, 1988). This relationship holds for adults; in this population, hypnotizability also has been associated with a propensity for everyday imaginative involvements (see Lynn & Rhue, 1988).

More pertinent to our discussion is the finding that abused children exhibit an aptitude for hypnosis and fantasy involvements. In her intensive interview study of excellent hypnotic subjects, J. R. Hilgard (1970) found that a moderate degree of association ($r = .30$) described the relation between hypnotizability and a history of severe childhood punishment. Wilson and Barber's (1983) later research and J. R. Hilgard's research converged in their identification of fantasizing and involvement in imaginative activities as a means of coping with loneliness and isolation and as an escape from an aversive early life environment. More specifically, Wilson and Barber found that a subset of their fantasy-prone subjects reported being subjected to childhood physical punishment and abuse. Fantasizers' rates of reported abuse exceeded that of non-fantasy-prone subjects. Lynn and Rhue (1988) recently confirmed this observation. Six of the 21 fantasizers we studied reported childhood physical abuse (e.g., broken bones, bruises, burns), whereas none of the non-fantasy-prone subjects reported being abused.

Results of another study (Rhue, Lynn, Henry, Buhk, & Boyd, 1991) suggested that there is a link between fantasy proneness and childhood abuse. We found that students who reported a history of being both physically and sexually abused as children were more fantasy prone than were nonabused respondents who either had experienced the death of a parent before age 10 or were from an intact family. Although subjects in this study who reported abuse were no more hypnotizable than nonabused subjects, several other studies (e.g., Nash & Lynn, 1986; Nash, Lynn, & Givens, 1984) have shown that the majority of subjects who reported being physically abused as children scored as high-hypnotizable subjects as adults. Careful replication of these latter findings, with the effects of presenting the abuse and hypnotizability measures in the same sessions controlled for, is necessary to make firm conclusions about the relation between hypnotizability and child abuse.

Even if the link between hypnotizability and abuse turns out to be weaker than originally believed, fantasy and imaginative abilities, which are so important in lending force and credibility to storytelling, may nevertheless be more reliable by-products of a history of abuse. Indeed, fantasy and imagination serve an adaptive and defensive function for some children as a means of achieving an emotional haven or respite from an abusive environment (E. R. Hilgard, 1986; Lynn & Rhue, 1988). Elsewhere, it has been noted that imagination and fantasy serve an active yet functional role in disavowing negative affect, disowning aspects of the self, and, more generally, regulating internal experiences (Lynn et al., 1988).

Many workers in the field of abuse (see Putnam, 1989) have noted that there is a close connection between the traumatic effects of abuse and dissociation. Recently, a number of investigators have pointed to parallels between dissociation and fantasy in traumatized children. With respect to multiple personality disorder, the most severe and dramatic dissociative disorder, Bowers (1991) noted that "fantasized alternatives to reality . . . can become increasingly complex and differentiated . . . with minimal involvement of executive level initiative and control" (p. 169). Bowers (1991) further commented that "when a seriously disturbed individual is also fantasy-prone, 'multiple personality' may well be the result" (p. 168). Finally, Putnam (1989) noted that childhood fantasy is an important developmental substrate of multiple personality, whereas Young (1988) maintained that "multiple personality reflects the gradual crystallizing of a fantasy that is amalgamated with dissociative defenses" (p. 15).

Lynn et al. (1988) posited that "dissociative cognitive strategies," which abused children report invoking to distance or separate themselves from aversive events outside of their realm of control, can be foremost thought of as a fantasy-based creative activity. An example of such activity would be imagining that the "core self" is separated from the body that is being subjected to abuse. What has been labeled *dissociation* (Spiegel, 1984) can be thought of in this way. Not only may dissociative imaginal and attentional strategies (e.g., amnesia, distraction, motivated forgetting) serve a defensive function, but repeated acts of abuse may spur imaginative activities that mitigate anxiety and guilt and block the pain of punishment.

Fantasy-based dissociations become pathological or dysfunctional when they are automatized by way of repetition, not consciously regulated by the person, and triggered by internal cues or sensations or environmental stimuli that resemble or actuate earlier triggers of psychological coping or escape mechanisms. When avoidance maneuvers that were appropriate in a situation of emotional duress are used in situations in which a threat is not actually imminent, dissociative–imaginative mechanisms become a liability rather than an asset.

There is support for the notion that there is a relation between dissociation and fantasy in adults and children. Green, Kvaal, Lynn, Mare, and Sandberg (1991) administered Wilson and Barber's (1981) measure of fantasy proneness—the Inventory of Creative Memories and Imaginings (ICMI)—to 1,249 college students, along with four measures of dissociation: the Dissociative Experiences Scale (DES; Bernstein & Putnam, 1986), the Perceptual Alteration Scale (PAS; Sanders, 1986), the Dissociative Experiences Questionnaire (DEQ; Riley, 1988), and the Bliss Scale (Wogan, 1991). In line with their predictions, it was found that measures of fantasy proneness and dissociation correlated from .47 (DES and PAS) to .63 (Bliss Scale). The DEQ correlated .59 with the ICMI.

In a second study, Segal and Lynn (in press) found the multiple scores on the DES and the Bliss Scale were moderately associated ($rs = .40-.44$) with two dimensions of daydreaming: positive constructive daydreaming and poor attentional control (Short Imaginal Process Inventory; Huba, Singer, Aneshensel, & Antrobus, 1982). The Bliss Scale was also found to be related to guilty dysphoric fantasy themes. Thus, dissociative experiences are associated with multiple dimensions of imaginative activity.

In a third study (Rhue & Lynn, 1992) with clinical samples of children who were sexually abused, physically abused, and nonabused patients, a measure of dissociation (the Children's Perceptual Scale; Evers-Szostak & Sanders, 1991) correlated .54 with a childhood fantasy inventory and .39 with a children's fantasy-proneness scale (adapted from Wilson & Barber, 1981).

In short, a number of studies indicate that there is considerable overlap among fantasy, imagination, and dissociation in adults and children. Of course, not all abused or fantasy-prone children exhibit dissociation or have well-developed hypnotic abilities. Nevertheless, our review of the research provides some basis for positing that abused children may be particularly well suited to exploit storytelling techniques and benefit from them.

What is needed are controlled outcome studies that compare the effectiveness of distinct strategies and procedures for treating sexual abuse. For example, the effectiveness of storytelling techniques could be compared with supportive therapy and hypnotic or relaxation-based interventions that do not take advantage of storytelling to treat children. At any rate, given the lack of controlled outcome research, it is premature to suggest that storytelling is superior to other therapeutic interventions for treating sexually abused children.

CONCLUSION

Therapy moves in steps from establishing rapport and a sense of safety and security, to mutual storytelling, to the introduction of reality events, to the final step of addressing complex emotional issues of loss, trust, love, and guilt stirred by the abuse. Throughout this process, we emphasize connection making and are cognizant and respectful of children's resistances and needs for support to explore traumatic material. However, the therapist must avoid taxing children's emotional resources by attempting to promote abreactive experiences in cases in which there are clear signs (e.g., nightmares, flashbacks, intrusive thoughts) of posttraumatic stress disorder (see Brown & Fromm, 1986, for a thoughtful discussion). With these children, prolonged and more intensive therapy, aimed at integration rather than abreaction (see Brown & Fromm, 1986), is advisable. Anger toward the therapist, revealed in story content, symbols, or passive–aggressive behaviors, is a notable signal that the therapist is intruding on children's defenses.

With victims of traumatic abuse, we generally do not attempt to hypnotize children until a strong therapeutic alliance is established and posttraumatic and dissociative symptoms are in abeyance. We prefer to use storytelling and metaphors with such children rather than direct, authoritative methods. It is not uncommon for therapy to continue 3 or more years in such cases.

Rather than rigidly compacting therapy into a set time frame or number of sessions, an ongoing evaluation of children's degree of distress, needs, and strengths dictates the investment and time spent in each step of therapy. In making decisions about terminating therapy, the therapist needs to evaluate the children's symptom picture, their level of overall coping, and their social and emotional development. We believe that establishing "insight" into complex emotional issues is unnecessary and unworkable for many children. When the therapist feels that the children are functioning at a developmentally appropriate level and when they no longer exhibit symptoms that hamper their functioning, then it is appropriate to terminate therapy. Nevertheless, follow-up contacts for 1 year or longer are advisable because additional dissociative reactions to trauma may surface that were not apparent during treatment; continuous follow-up serves as a check with regard to later sexual abuse.

The procedures we have outlined can be applied in a flexible manner with children who present with a variety of abuse-related symptoms. Storytelling is best implemented in the context of a theory-driven model of the children's conflicts and the behavioral and dynamic meaning of the abuse-related symptoms. It is our hope that the procedures we have delineated will facilitate access to abused children's experiential world and creative treatment in their behalf. .

REFERENCES

Adams-Tucker, C. (1982). Proximate effects of sexual abuse in childhood: A report on 28 children. *American Journal of Psychiatry, 139,* 1252–1256.

Aurela, A. (1987). A systematic storytelling therapy. *Psychiatria Fennica, 18,* 31–34.

Bernstein, E. M., & Putnam, F. W. (1986). Development, reliability, and validity of a dissociation scale. *Journal of Nervous and Mental Disease, 174,* 727–735.

Boekelheide, P. D. (1978). Incest and the family physician. *Journal of Family Practice, 6,* 87–90.

Bowers, K. S. (1991). Dissociation in hypnosis and multiple personality. *International Journal of Clinical and Experimental Hypnosis, 39,* 155–176.

Brant, R., & Tisza, V. (1977). The sexually misused child. *American Journal of Orthopsychiatry, 47,* 80–87.

Briere, J., & Runtz, M. (1987). Post sexual abuse trauma: Data and implications for clinical practice. *Journal of Interpersonal Violence, 2,* 367–379.

Briere, J., & Runtz, M. (1988). Symptomatology associated with childhood sexual victimization in a nonclinical adult sample. *Child Abuse and Neglect, 12,* 51–59.

Brooks, R. B. (1981). Creative characters: A technique in child therapy. *Psychotherapy: Theory, Research, and Practice, 18,* 131–139.

Brooks, R. B. (1985). The beginning sessions of child therapy: Of messages and metaphors. *Psychotherapy, 22,* 761–769.

Brooks, R. B. (1987). Storytelling and the therapeutic process for children with learning disabilities. *Journal of Learning Disabilities, 20,* 546–550.

Brown, D. P., & Fromm, E. (1986). Hypnotherapy in the treatment of post-traumatic stress disorder. In D. P. Brown & E. Fromm (Eds.), *Hypnotherapy and hypnoanalysis* (pp. 262–327). Hillsdale, NJ: Erlbaum.

Browne, A., & Finkelhor, D. (1986). Impact of child sexual abuse: A review of the research. *Psychological Bulletin, 99,* 66–77.

Davis, J. M. (1986). Storytelling using the child as consultant. *Elementary School Guidance and Counseling, 21,* 89–94.

Dempster, C. R., & Balson, P. M. (1982, August). *Hypnotherapy of the victim experience.* Paper presented at the Ninth International Congress of Hypnosis and Psychosomatic Medicine, Glasgow, Scotland.

Despert, J. L., & Potter, H. W. (1936). Technical approaches used in the study and treatment of emotional problems in children. *Psychiatric Quarterly, 10,* 619–638.

Ebert, B. W. (1988). Hypnosis and rape victims. *American Journal of Clinical Hypnosis, 31,* 50–56.

Eisen, M. (1989). Return of the repressed: Hypnoanalysis of a case of total amnesia. *International Journal of Clinical and Experimental Hypnosis, 37,* 107–119.

Evers-Szostak, M., & Sanders, S. (1991, August). *Hypnotherapy with children and adolescents: Research and practice.* Paper presented at the 99th Annual Convention of the American Psychological Association, San Francisco.

Finkelhor, D. (1979). *Sexually victimized children.* New York: Free Press.

Finkelhor, D., & Browne, A. (1985). The traumatic impact of child sexual abuse: A conceptualization. *American Journal of Orthopsychiatry, 55,* 530–541.

Finkelhor, D., & Hotaling, G. T. (1984). Sexual abuse in the national incidence study of child abuse and neglect: An appraisal. *Child Abuse and Neglect, 8,* 23–33.

Gardner, G., & Olness, K. (1981). *Hypnosis and hypnotherapy with children.* New York: Grune & Stratton.

Gardner, R. (1977). *Therapeutic communication with children: The mutual story-telling technique* (2nd ed.). Northvale, NJ: Jason Aronson.

Geiser, R. L. (1979). *Hidden victims: The sexual abuse of children.* Boston: Beacon Press.

Gibbons, D. E. (1979). *Applied hypnosis and hyperemperia.* New York: Plenum Press.

Gold, E. R. (1986). Long-term effects of sexual victimization in childhood: An attributional approach. *Journal of Consulting and Clinical Psychology, 54,* 471–475.

Gomes-Schwartz, B., Horowitz, J. M., & Sauzier, M. (1985). Severity of emotional distress among sexually abused preschool, school-age, and adolescent children. *Hospital and Community Psychiatry, 36,* 503–508.

Green, J., Kvaal, S., Lynn, S., Mare, C., & Sandberg, D. (1991, August). *Hypnosis, dissociation, fantasy proneness, and absorption: The effects of context.* Paper presented at the 99th Annual Convention of the American Psychological Association, San Francisco.

Herman, J. (1981). *Father–daughter incest.* Cambridge, MA: Harvard University Press.

Hilgard, E. R. (1986). *Divided consciousness: Multiple controls in human thought and action.* New York: Wiley.

Hilgard, J. R. (1970). *Personality and hypnosis: A study of imaginative involvement.* Chicago: University of Chicago Press.

Hilgard, J. R., & LeBaron, S. (1984). *Hypnotherapy of pain in children with cancer.* Los Altos, CA: Kaufmann.

Huba, G. J., Singer, J. L., Aneshensel, C. S., & Antrobus, J. S. (1982). *Short Imaginal Process Inventory.* Port Huron, MI: Research Psychologists Press.

Justice, B., & Justice, R. (1979). *The broken taboo: Sex in the family.* New York: Human Sciences Press.

Keim, I., Lentine, G., Keim, J., & Madanes, C. (1987). Strategies for changing the past. *Journal of Strategic and Systematic Therapies, 6,* 2–17.

Klinger, E. (1971). *Structure and functions of fantasy.* New York: Wiley.

Kolko, D. J. (1987). Treatment of child sexual abuse: Programs, progress, and prospects. *Journal of Family Violence, 2,* 303–318.

Kritzberg, N. I. (1972). TASKIT (Tell-A-Story-Kit): The therapeutic storytelling word game. *Acta Paedopsychiatrica, 38,* 231–244.

Kuttner, L. (1988). Favorite stories: A hypnotic pain-reduction technique for children in acute pain. *American Journal of Clinical Hypnosis, 30,* 289–295.

Laurence, J. R., & Perry, C. W. (1983). Hypnotically created memories among highly hypnotizable subjects. *Science, 222,* 523–524.

Lawson, D. M. (1987). Using therapeutic stories in the counseling process. *Elementary School Guidance and Counseling, 12,* 134–141.

LeBaron, S., Zelter, L. K., & Fanurik, D. (1988). Imaginative involvement and hypnotizability in childhood. *International Journal of Clinical and Experimental Hypnosis, 36,* 284–295.

Levine, E. S. (1980). Indirect suggestions through personalized fairy tales for treatment of childhood insomnia. *American Journal of Clinical Hypnosis, 23,* 57–65.

London, P., Morgan, A. H., & Hilgard, E. R. (1973). Age differences in susceptibility to hypnosis. *International Journal of Clinical and Experimental Hypnosis, 21,* 78–85.

Lynn, S. J., & Rhue, J. W. (1988). Fantasy proneness: Hypnosis, developmental antecedents, and psychopathology. *American Psychologist, 43,* 35–44.

Lynn, S. J., Rhue, J. W., & Green, J. (1988). Multiple personality and fantasy proneness: Is there an association or dissociation? *British Journal of Experimental and Clinical Hypnosis, 5,* 138–142.

MacHovec, F. J. (1984). The use of brief hypnosis for posttraumatic stress disorders. *Emotional First Aid, 1,* 14–22.

Mrazek, P. B. (1983). Sexual abuse of children. In B. B. Lahey & A. E. Kazdin (Eds.), *Advances in clinical child psychology* (Vol. 6, pp. 199–215). New York: Plenum Press.

Nash, M., & Lynn, S. (1986). Child abuse and hypnotic ability. *Imagination, Cognition, and Personality, 5,* 211–218.

Nash, M., Lynn, S. J., & Givens, D. (1984). Adult hypnotic susceptibility, childhood punishment, and child abuse. *International Journal of Clinical and Experimental Hypnosis, 31,* 28–36.

O'Grady, D. J., & Hoffmann, C. (1984). Hypnosis with children and adolescents in the medical setting. In W. Wester & A. Smith (Eds.), *Clinical hypnosis: A multidisciplinary approach* (pp. 181–209). Philadelphia: Lippincott.

Pascoe, D., & Duterte, B. O. (1981). The medical diagnosis of sexual abuse in the pre-menarcheal child. *Pediatric Annals, 11,* 813–817.

Porter, J. (1975). Guided fantasy as a treatment for childhood insomnia. *Australian and New Zealand Journal of Psychiatry, 9,* 169–172.

Putnam, F. W. (1989). *Diagnosis and treatment of multiple personality disorder.* New York: Guilford Press.

Rhue, J. W., & Lynn, S. J. (1991a). Storytelling, hypnosis, and the treatment of sexually abused children. *International Journal of Clinical and Experimental Hypnosis, 39,* 198–214.

Rhue, J. W., & Lynn, S. J. (1991b). The use of hypnotic techniques with sexually abused children. In W. Wester & D. O'Grady (Eds.), *Clinical applications of hypnosis with children* (pp. 69–84). New York: Brunner/Mazel.

Rhue, J. W., & Lynn, S. J. (1992, August). *Fantasy and dissociation of abused and nonabused children.* Paper presented at the 100th Annual Convention of the American Psychological Association, Washington, DC.

Rhue, J. W., Lynn, S. J., Henry, S., Buhk, K., & Boyd, P. (1991). Child abuse, imagination, and hypnotizability. *Imagination, Cognition, and Personality, 10,* 53–62.

Riley, K. C. (1988). Measurement of dissociation. *Journal of Nervous and Mental Disease, 176,* 449–450.

Russell, D. (1983). The incidence and prevalence of intrafamilial and extrafamilial sexual abuse of female children. *Child Abuse and Neglect, 7,* 133–146.

Sanders, S. (1986). The Perceptual Alteration Scale: A scale measuring dissociation. *American Journal of Clinical Hypnosis, 29,* 95–102.

Segal, D., & Lynn, S. J. (in press). Predicting dissociation. *Imagination, Cognition, and Personality.*

Sgroi, S. M. (1982). A conceptual framework for child sexual abuse. In S. M. Sgroi (Ed.), *Handbook of clinical intervention in child sexual abuse* (pp. 62–85). Lexington, MA: Lexington Books.

Spence, D. P. (1989). Narrative appeal versus historical validity. *Contemporary Psychoanalysis, 25,* 517–524.

Spiegel, D. (1984). Multiple personality as a post-traumatic stress disorder. *Psychiatric Clinics of North America, 7,* 101–110.

Spiegel, D. (1988). Dissociation and hypnosis in post-traumatic stress disorders. *Journal of Traumatic Stress, 1,* 17–33.

Valdiserri, E. V., & Byrne, J. P. (1982). Hypnosis as emergency treatment for a teenage rape victim. *Hospital and Community Psychiatry, 33,* 767–769.

Walker, E. A., & Bolkovatz, M. A. (1988). Play therapy with children who have experienced sexual assault. In L. E. A. Walker (Ed.), *Handbook on sexual abuse of children* (pp. 249–269). New York: Springer.

Wilson, S C., & Barber, T. X. (1981). *The Inventory of Childhood Memories and Imaginings.* Unpublished manuscript, Medfield Foundation, Harding, MA.

Wilson, S. C., & Barber, T. X. (1983). The fantasy-prone personality: Implications for understanding imagery, hypnosis, and parapsychological phenomena. In A. A. Sheikh (Ed.), *Imagery: Current theory, research, and application* (pp. 340–390). New York: Wiley.

Wogan, M. (1991). *The Bliss Scale: Development, reliability, and validity.* Unpublished manuscript, Rutgers University, New Brunswick, NJ.

Yates, A. (1982). Children eroticized by incest. *American Journal of Psychiatry, 139,* 482–485.

Young, W. C. (1988). Observations on fantasy in the formation of multiple personality. *Dissociation, 1,* 13–20.

22

HYPNOTHERAPY WITH RAPE VICTIMS

WILLIAM H. SMITH

One of the most significant advances in the field of psychotherapy in recent years is the recognition that generic psychotherapeutic approaches are often ineffective in addressing the treatment needs of particular patient groups and that highly specific treatment approaches can be developed for many psychological disorders. *Rape trauma syndrome* is one such disorder. Many, if not most, women who are raped experience significant psychological trauma in addition to whatever physical injury they may suffer. The resultant symptoms often meet *Diagnostic and Statistical Manual of Mental Disorders* (revised third edition) criteria for posttraumatic stress disorder (PTSD; e.g., anxiety, flashbacks, emotional numbing, sleep disturbance) and may also include eating disorders, substance abuse, and depression (Burge, 1988; Nadelson, 1989). Whether women with a previous history of psychological disturbance or a history of victimization develop more serious symptoms or more persistent ones is somewhat controversial (Frank & Anderson, 1987; Nadelson, 1989), but it is clear that the experience of rape has long-lasting and serious consequences for many of its victims (Santiago, McCall-Perez, Gorcey, & Beigel, 1985). For the thousands of

479

women who are raped each year (Schiff, 1978), effective and efficient means of responding to their treatment needs obviously must be developed and refined.[1]

Because the diagnosis of PTSD is not event specific but describes the symptomatic consequences of any substantial trauma, some clinicians and investigators have preferred the concept and terminology of rape trauma syndrome (Block, 1990; Burgess & Holmstrom, 1974). For purposes of this discussion, I do not attempt to distinguish between these descriptors.

In an acute reaction phase to rape trauma, treatment strategies are typically based on a crisis model: It begins quickly, focuses on immediate issues rather than past difficulties, returns quickly to normal functioning, and includes family and group support. Medication is used sparingly, and placing the victim in a "patient role" is avoided (Nadelson, 1989). Chronic or delayed responses are dealt with through a variety of techniques, including traditional individual and group psychotherapy, family therapy, and psychopharmacology (Evans, 1978). Although there are case reports of using hypnosis during an acute reaction (e.g., Valdiserri & Byrne, 1982), hypnosis is more typically used when the symptomatic reactions have failed to respond to supportive interventions (Ebert, 1988). One interesting case report involved the simultaneous treatment of a rape victim and her spouse that addressed the difficulties so often affecting family members and the victims themselves (Somer, 1990).

CLINICAL APPLICATIONS

The use of hypnosis as it is presented here has evolved from a psychodynamic perspective, but it is somewhat eclectic in approach. Concepts of early developmental conflicts, transference and countertransference, ego mastery, resistance, affect modulation, self-experience, and insight guide the work, but the interventions could no doubt be cast in a different theoretical language. Like psychotherapy, hypnotherapy does not identify a highly specific intervention. It includes a range of possibilities that use phenomena such as heightened bodily awareness and self-control, enhanced responsiveness to suggestion, and lowering of defensive barriers (especially repression and dissociation), leading to the recovery of memories.

Some patients are intrigued when presented with a recommendation for treatment that includes hypnosis, but others are wary. Despite increasing public and professional acceptance and the recent positive portrayal in the popular media, hypnosis is still associated with the supernatural (e.g., contacting the spirit world, vampires, zombies), "brainwashing" and other mind

---

[1]Because more than 90% of rape victims are women (Koss, 1990), I refer to patients in this discussion with feminine pronouns for the sake of simplicity.

control techniques, and stage entertainment involving embarrassing performances by audience volunteers. Even greater apprehension stems from the imagined need to surrender one's will to the control of another, especially after the victim's terrifying experience of helpless vulnerability and exploitation that so devastated her. If the expectation exists and is made explicit that the treatment may involve reexperiencing the traumatic event in a trance, patients may insist on referral to another source of help. Education and reassurance must be provided at this point by whatever clinician or helper is involved. I cannot overemphasize that the goal of hypnosis is to put the patient *more* in control of herself, not *less.* She must understand that if reexperiencing the traumatic event is necessary, it will proceed at a pace and in a fashion tolerable to her. If the therapist is male, the pleasant and comforting experience that hypnosis typically provides may be a crucially important bridge to restoring the patient's capacity to trust men, at least those who are trustworthy.

The initial sessions with the hypnotherapist should be devoted to exploring the patient's knowledge and attitudes about hypnosis, correcting distortions, and providing information. As in any treatment process, some amount of relationship building is necessary to provide an atmosphere of trust and safety. This is not to say that all apprehension can be dispelled but that the patient should feel confident that she is in a professional relationship with a responsible and competent person who will not intentionally harm or exploit her and that she is in no way being coerced.

Is it necessary to conduct a formal assessment of the patient's degree of hypnotizability? Practices vary, but usually the first few inductions will reveal what hypnotic techniques can productively be used, so formal testing is not routinely done. Most people can experience hypnosis to some degree, and most trauma patients prove to be good hypnotic subjects, possibly because of the dissociative experiences that often accompany trauma. In terms of induction techniques, except for the caution that touching the patient may be inadvisable because of the seductive or aggressive meanings it may inadvertently carry, induction procedures are guided by the patient's hypnotic talents and her degree of ego stability. Patients with a tendency to regress require inductions that emphasize the solidarity of boundaries, separateness, and self-control and deemphasize "letting go," "floating," or the experience of involuntariness that may be felt in hand levitation or catalepsies. An unstable patient who may be vulnerable to more instability despite the best efforts of the therapist should be approached carefully. This is also true of a person whose symptoms serve a significant stabilizing role in the personality, a role that will be relinquished only as major reorganization occurs in a long-term treatment process.

The nature and extent of the patient's symptoms will determine how hypnosis is used. Sexual assaults are not all the same: Some are carried out by acquaintances and others by strangers. Some last minutes and others several hours. Varying degrees of physical violence, intimidation, and threat are involved. There may be one attacker or several, and different parts of the body may be abused. Accordingly, there is no one reaction, no universal symptom picture. The world may no longer seem safe, and the person's basic assumptions and values regarding society and her place in it are threatened. Fearfulness, depression, and guilt may be unremitting or episodic. Disillusioned about what she can expect in life, the rape victim may no longer feel in control of her life or even her body; she may hate herself and her sexuality more than she hates her attacker.

The first step in treatment, and one that may be sufficient for those with relatively mild difficulties, is to have relief from anxiety in a trance through experiences involving pleasant memories; being in a safe place alone or with loved ones; and relaxing imagery of beaches, lakes, mountains, or firesides. The patient's discovery that she can exert such control over her bodily experiences and emotional states provides an important step toward regaining the experience of self-mastery. Through guiding her into soothing, peaceful states, the therapist will increasingly be experienced by the patient as benign, well-intentioned, and capable of helpfulness. The therapist is not only doing something *for* her but is teaching her how to do it for herself, putting her increasingly in charge of her own well-being. Training in self-hypnotic techniques that may involve both daily practice sessions and specific cues or signals that can be called on when needed is an integral part of the treatment work (Smith, 1990). There is no evidence that overcoming anxiety caused by trauma can lead to careless exposure to danger.

Most traumatized individuals have an understandable aversion to recalling the details of the event. Many actually *cannot* recall the memories because of a dissociative reaction that accompanies most trauma. By definition, traumatic experiences are those that overwhelm the resources of the ego. Rather than experiencing the event with a normal sense of control, emotional composure, predictability, meaning, and coherence, the patient may experience a sense of detachment, in which some or all emotions are not felt, and subsequent amnesia, either total or partial, for what happened. Some patients have a strong wish to know the truth about what happened, whereas others may want to know (or are being encouraged by others to remember) in order to facilitate legal investigation and prosecution. Because of the vulnerability of memory to distortion in and by hypnosis, its forensic usefulness is controversial and complicated: (a) In many states, hypnotically refreshed or enhanced memories are not admissible as evidence in court. (b) In some states, the memories may be admissible, provided that certain standards or safeguards are met. (c) In still other states, the legal picture is not clear. (For an excellent review of the legal status of hypnosis and guidelines for clinicians dealing with the police and court systems, see Scheflin & Shapiro, 1989.)

The therapeutic value of remembering, along with the role of catharsis or abreaction, has a history dating back to the beginning of dynamic psychiatry. Emotionally laden memories kept out of conscious awareness have been targets for efforts at recall and catharsis since before Freud (Frankel, 1988). In the earlier part of this century, theoretical rationales for incursions into the buried parts of the psyche grew out of psychoanalytic drive theory, which essentially states that traumatic events result in dammed-up energies that, in turn, result in interruptions in the flow of ideas and emotions. Releasing or emptying the blocked and therefore unintegrated and unregulated "affect charge" would result in a normalizing of psychic functions. Later developments in ego psychology, object relations, and self theory have broadened the understanding of the effects of trauma on the individual and her intrapsychic and interpersonal functioning. However, the notion of some still-present emotional energy that must be not only released but mastered and the importance of normalizing the flow of ideas have persisted because of their clinical utility. Therapists now think in terms of *dissociation*, the walling off of some aspects of consciousness from others, of some emotions from others, and of emotions from ideas or elements of identity. During and following trauma, there is a disruption in the continuity and integration of experience. Hypnosis can be a tool for restoring continuity and integration by providing an orderly and coherent flow of ideas and in reestablishing the appropriate links between ideas and the emotions that accompany them. The strength of the once-overpowering emotions can be vitiated by repetition at manageable levels of experience (deconditioning), and the person's sense of mastery and self-esteem can be restored. What are the specific techniques through which these changes are accomplished?

Exploring traumatic material always carries the risk of provoking not only anxiety and depression but suicidal and self-multilative urges, socially destructive acting-out, substance abuse, and even psychotic disorganization. Meager ego resources, including limitations in the capacity for a strong treatment alliance, may dictate slow and lengthy treatment. With every patient, care must be taken to avoid retraumatization. The patient should feel a reliable sense of control over the pace of the recall and should be able to use a signal, such as lifting a finger, to indicate when her discomfort is too great. Age regression techniques, such as turning the pages of a calendar backward, can be used if the rape happened a long time ago. Otherwise, she should simply be instructed to begin relating the memory before the incident began and to proceed slowly. The goal at this stage is a memory with some degree of unpleasant feeling but not significantly distressing.

Some patients have to be encouraged to be fully present in the memory, to describe the event in the first person, and to allow the earlier dissociated emotions to occur, even if in muted form. With other patients, parameters must be introduced to titrate the process, guarding against a tendency to be swept along and engulfed in the stormy tide of painful feelings. Having the episode unfold slowly is almost always an appropriate strategy, giving opportunities for stopping the memory if necessary; to clearly grasp what the sequence of events was; and to "cognize" or "linguistically encode" what before was a terrifying jumble of poorly grasped, incomprehensible perceptions. Watching the event unfold as if it were on a TV screen, even a videotape with the patient holding a remote control, is another helpful approach. Watching it as if it were happening to someone else would be an extreme distancing maneuver, but occasionally it may be necessary. At times, the patient may need to be reminded that what she is recalling is only a memory and not actually happening now, that she is safe in the therapist's office. Eventually, the patient should have the ability to go through the memory with a coherent, first-person account of what happened, with some degree of the normal emotions that were stimulated, and a realistic appraisal of why it happened and what she can do to avoid such an experience in the future.

Prior to beginning the memory recall, an image of a safe place should be developed with the patient, a peaceful sanctuary open to no one but her and her chosen companions. An alternative is one or more especially happy memories. Thus, the distress of recall can be interspersed with these calming, reassuring images. At the end of each hypnotic session, sufficient time should be spent with such images to restore the patient to a state of reasonable if not complete calm. I often suggest ending with the image of her luxuriating in a whirlpool tube or jacuzzi, feeling the comfort of surging water, and enjoying scented soaps or lotions. This tub is described as a healing place where she can feel cleansed inside and out, feeling good about her body and herself.

When coming out of the trance, the patient must *always* be allowed to leave behind any memories that she is not ready to deal with outside of hypnosis. Time should be set aside between the hypnotic work and the end of the session to assess the patient's emotional state. Some reflection on what transpired should take place and decisions should be made, when necessary, about what should happen between sessions. Should the memories be discussed with anyone else? Should self-hypnotic work be carried on? Should the therapist be contacted if unexpected problems arise? Lengthy delays between sessions should be avoided when possible. Hypnosis is rarely used in every treatment session. There must be considerable "processing" of the memories; of the patient's reactions at the time and subsequently; and of what impact the rape had on her self-experience, her expectations of others, and her world view. In and out of the trance, a significant amount of "cognitive restructuring" must take place, regardless of whether abreactive work is part of the treatment (Steele, 1989).

The heightened suggestibility that hypnosis affords may help the patient to accept the explanations and reassurances that the therapist provides.

The verbalization of the event is actually the first step in changing the experience and meaning of what happened. Although it is possible to allow a profoundly embarrassed patient to remember what happened without revealing it to the therapist, this is seldom helpful in the long run. In the telling, there is not only the mastery that words give but a shift from secrecy and isolation to openness and trust. The victim not only expects more harm but also criticism and rejection. She typically feels responsible in some way: "I shouldn't have been there; I shouldn't be pretty; I shouldn't be female; I should have fought harder or screamed louder." There appears to be a phenomenon of "revictimization" in which an earlier, now-unconscious trauma is reenacted through provoking or allowing harm, presumably in an effort to master it. The legitimacy of this concept is supported by the high incidence of rape victims who are also found to be incest victims and by the disconcerting frequency with which some women are attacked more than once (Russell, 1984). This perspective should not be confused with "blaming the victim" but as an attempt to understand complex phenomena that add to the alarming incidence of this tragedy. Most victims are *not* responsible in the usual sense for what befell them, and they very much need to alter this misunderstanding. They also need to realize that they are not being punished for real or imagined misdeeds. Ironically, these attitudes have their adaptive aspect because blaming oneself or feeling punished may be preferable to feeling vulnerable to random, mindless violence in a chaotic world that is indifferent to a person's behavior.

Conscious or unconscious fear of another attck may seriously inhibit the woman's ability to feel appropriate anger at her assailant (Janis, 1958), or such inhibitions may be characterologically or religiously based. Coming to understand that anger, even rage, is not morally wrong but is a normal reaction to a degrading assault can facilitate the experience and expression of anger, which is often obscured by fear. Good judgment can take the place of fear in ensuring safety from further harm, but the reality of vulnerability must be maturely faced. What does it mean that there are predatory people in the world? Why is it that something as vital and precious as sexuality can be so cruelly misused? Because bad things happen in the world does not make the whole world bad. Because sexual parts of the body can be misused does not make all sex bad. And because something bad has happened to the patient does not make her bad. Assimilating the experience into the larger context of her life is a necessary and important task, one that may be aided by the shift from a victim stance to that of a survivor.

When the rape trauma links up with earlier significant conflicts in the patient's life, the treatment work may be somewhat more complicated. If the patient does not make the connection herself spontaneously, exploratory techniques such as the "affect bridge" (Watkins, 1971) may bring to light what previous problems are being stimulated and thereby slowing or halting the treatment progress. The affect bridge is a technique for tracing a contemporary emotion to similar ones in the past. The patient is asked in the trance to recall and reexperience the most recent instance of the troublesome affect in question (e.g., fear, shame, guilt). Once clearly in focus, the feeling is followed back in time like a bridge, taking the person back to the first time the particular emotional reaction was experienced. Thus, the historical roots of what now are irrational or exaggerated reactions may be recalled and understood. This phenomenon, along with the following case example, was elaborated in a previous article (Smith, 1991, pp. 129–131).

CASE MATERIAL

Thinking she was alone in her home, a 30-year-old married woman was investigating a noise when a coat was suddenly dropped over her head by a man hiding in a closet. Wearing only a bathrobe, she was told to stop screaming, was walked over to a nearby bed, pushed down, and subjected to genital intercourse despite her protests and efforts to persuade the assailant to stop. She worried for her life, especially when she learned the telephone wires had been cut. Nothing she said made any difference. Her husband was out of town but her parents were to come over that evening and she also worried for their welfare should the intruder not leave soon. He eventually did leave when he heard her parents approaching. Frightened and upset, she called the police and felt angry for years that a single woman officer was sent to investigate. What could a woman alone do against such a man? The rapist was never found.

The patient's parents and her husband were quite supportive, and her immediate distress subsided. She was a mature and intelligent woman who was very successful in her work and who had been in a beneficial psychotherapy some years ago when she needed help with transient depression and relationship difficulties. The rape had taught her an important lesson: The world was a dangerous place and it made no sense for her ever to be alone again. While this reaction might seem extreme to others, to her it seemed like common sense. Five years went by before she faced up to what an enormous burden she was for her family, who had to accompany her everywhere. Her very cautious attitude might even be a detrimental influence on her child. She could not move around in her own home at night, and would feel a sense of panic at every unfamiliar noise. She also worried that a recommendation for many years of treatment might be made if she sought help, but learned through the popular press that hypnotherapy might be helpful for phobic-type conditions, and that lengthy treatment might not be necessary. The patient was frankly wary of giving up her symptoms and thus being exposed to danger, but accepted my "framing" of the problem as follows: If she had been in an auto accident, giving up driving altogether would be a solution that would greatly inconvenience her, but she could simply become more careful, keeping herself safe by substituting good judgment for fear.

The patient initially was evaluated and found to be emotionally stable and functioning well in most respects. There were no contraindications to an intensive treatment approach and she quickly formed a positive alliance with the therapist. She had read a little about hypnosis and had no significant apprehensions about using it. Several sessions were devoted to reliving the event in trance, never allowing her distress to become overwhelming. We frequently slowed the recall down and had her relax, drawing on the heightened capacity for physical and emotional control the hypnotic state provides. Once able to go through the memory with little distress, she still repeated with emphasis, "Nothing I said made any difference." Using the affect bridge technique and focusing on the feeling of frightened helplessness, she first went back to adolescent years when, to the bewilderment of friends and consternation of parents, she had taken up with a very rebellious young man outside her usual social circle. His wild unpredictability was somehow attractive to her for reasons she could not explain. Going back further in her life shed light on this curious relationship and on a crucial element in her response to the rape: periods of depression of her mother when she was quite young. Her mother's unusual behavior had been a source of considerable anxiety for the patient, especially when, in contrast to the good relationship they usually had, nothing she said made any difference in how her mother behaved. In addition to interpretive work around this issue, the treatment work consisted of (a) the catharsis and abreaction mentioned above, (b) reassuring the patient she had not caused the rape, (c) facilitating her experience of anger at the man who had so devastated her, (d) allowing her to punish him in fantasy if she so chose (which she did not), and (e) praising her for keeping a cool head and not provoking greater harm—even worrying more about her parents' welfare than her own. There was no good reason now for the degree of fear that plagued and controlled her, since her husband, her parents, and her co-workers are actually quite predictable and what she says usually does make a difference. A 5-year follow-up found the patient still delighted with her eight-session treatment, conducted in only three months time. She still is reluctant to enter a dark building at night, but otherwise feels no restrictions on her behavior. She comes and goes without accompaniment, and is comfortable in her own home alone at night. Her family, as you might expect, is pleased as well. Who thinks going into a dark building alone at night is such a good idea anyway?

Clearly, this patient's high level of personality development facilitated the good treatment outcome. Intelligent and psychologically minded, she was able to establish a solid treatment alliance and also had favorable family support. Patients with limited ego resources obviously need more time and additional supportive measures (e.g., medication, relationship therapy) to accomplish significant change. Traumatic experiences, even in adulthood, can exacerbate existing characterological vulnerabilities such as low self-esteem and social isolation. Treatment then becomes more complicated and the focus necessarily broader.

COUNTERTRANSFERENCE ISSUES

A male therapist may feel a strong need not only to be a well-intentioned helper as he is to all of his other nontraumatized patients but to be an antidote to the "poisoning" the patient has received. He will be the proof that all men are not bad and that the patient can be respected, protected, and allowed the dignity that she deserves by a caring man. Supporting such a stance may be a defensive need to "purify" his motives for engaging in this type of treatment. Any voyeuristic interests on his part, much less urges to exploit or dominate, must be vigorously denied. He is only interested in *her* needs, not his own. This paradigm of the patient as innocent sufferer and the therapist as white knight–rescuer has many potential pitfalls. Focusing on the harm she has experienced may blind him to any preexisting personality problems and vulnerabilities she may have and prevent an accurate assessment of her actual treatment needs and resources for making use of therapy. On the other hand, if her strengths are ignored, passivity and dependency may be unwittingly promoted. The therapist may be overindulgent in matters such as requests for extra time, telephone calls, or failure to pay her bill. He may be bewildered when normal resistance phenomena surface, stung by her lack of grateful compliance. The emergence of negative transference, even experiencing the therapist as an abuser, is a predictable part of the process that must be taken in stride.

Peebles-Kleiger (1989) presented a richly detailed account of the advantage of careful attunement to countertransference in using hypnosis with trauma patients. She illustrated how correct management or mismanagement of the inevitable strong emotions that accompany such efforts can spell success or failure for the treatment. However, therapists' reactions to working with victims can reach far beyond countertransference. Their steady exposure to the horrors of their patients' lives can produce what McCann and Pearlman (1990) called *vicarious victimization,* alterations in the therapists' attitudes about themselves and their lives, and even provoke PTSD symptoms in them. Every therapist's caseload should be balanced, whenever possible, with patients who have different degrees of trauma, overall psychological disturbance, and treatment difficulty. There should be a supervisor or peer group with whom the treatment work can be shared. Frequent vacation breaks and a fulfilling personal life are also crucial for therapists who must learn about, empathically acknowledge, absorb, and help their patients to assimilate the outrage that their bodies and minds have suffered.

RESEARCH AND APPRAISAL

To my knowledge, there are no empirical studies comparing the relative effectiveness of treatment incorporating hypnosis with other approaches to helping rape victims. Because such individuals are regularly helped through other means, no claim can be made that hypnosis is an indispensable tool. However, the prominent role of dissociation, both in reaction to trauma and in the perpetuation of symptoms, suggests that the controlled dissociation afforded by hypnosis may provide an especially significant therapeutic ingredient to the treatment work. Perhaps incorporating hypnosis can accelerate treatment progress, or perhaps it will provide greater therapeutic leverage for the more severe or persistent traumatic reactions. At the individual-case-report level, it is clear that hypnosis has seemed useful to clinicians and patients alike, not only with rape victims but with survivors of other trauma and even childhood sexual abuse (Rhue & Lynn, 1991; Spiegel, 1991). As the specific techniques are made manifest in clinical accounts, investigators will be able to devise comparisons, isolating key variables for study.

Apart from comparing techniques of intervention, two other areas seem worthy of research attention. First, what about the sex of the therapist? My experience has been that for rape victims who were willing to accept treatment from a male therapist, a valuable corrective experience was achieved. However, perhaps the potential they had for experiencing safety and trust with a man enabled them to accept the referral in the first place and a female therapist would have gotten similar results. Second, does hypnotizability play a role in how quickly or well the treatment proceeds? Introducing a formal measure of hypnotic capacity at the beginning of treatment would not be likely to be a burden on the relationship and may help predictions of the probable treatment course.

CONCLUSION

Hypnosis has been used extensively with patients suffering from various other forms of posttraumatic disorders, but its application to rape victims is a recent development. To my knowledge, there are no controlled studies comparing hypnotherapy with other forms of treatment for rape trauma, so research is still at the individual-case-study level of exploration of this promising approach. Many characteristics of the hypnotic experience fit the special needs of rape victims and are therefore particularly well suited to treatment efforts with this group. The relaxation of defenses allows recovery of memories when necessary; achieving control over anxiety and greater mastery of self-experience counters the feeling of helplessness; and enhanced positive transference facilitates the development of trust, insight, and correction of distorted cognitions.

REFERENCES

Block, A. P. (1990). Rape trauma syndrome as scientific expert testimony. *Archives of Sexual Behavior, 19,* 309–323.

Burge, S. K. (1988). Post-traumatic stress disorder in victims of rape. *Journal of Traumatic Stress, 1,* 193–210.

Burgess, A. W., & Holmstrom, L. L. (1974). Rape trauma syndrome. *American Journal of Psychiatry, 131,* 981–986.

Ebert, B. W. (1988). Hypnosis and rape victims. *American Journal of Clinical Hypnosis, 31,* 50–56.

Evans, H. I. (1978). Psychotherapy for the rape victim: Some treatment models. *Hospital and Community Psychiatry, 29,* 309–312.

Frank, E., & Anderson, B. P. (1987). Psychiatric disorders in rape victims: Past history and current symptomatology. *Comprehensive Psychiatry, 28,* 77–82.

Frankel, F. H. (1988). The clinical use of hypnosis in aiding recall. In H. M. Pettinati (Ed.), *Hypnosis and memory* (pp. 247–263). New York: Guilford Press.

Janis, J. (1958). *Psychological stress.* New York: Wiley.

Koss, M. P. (1990). Violence against women. *American Psychologist, 45,* 374–380.

McCann, I. L., & Pearlman, L. A. (1990). Vicarious traumatization: A framework for understanding the psychological effects of working with victims. *Journal of Traumatic Stress, 3,* 131–149.

Nadelson, C. C. (1989). Consequences of rape: Clinical and treatment aspects. *Psychotherapy and Psychosomatics, 51,* 187–192.

Peebles-Kleiger, M. J. (1989). Using countertransference in the hypnosis of trauma victims: A model for turning hazard into healing. *American Journal of Psychotherapy, 43,* 518–530.

Rhue, J. W., & Lynn, S. J. (1991). The use of hypnotic techniques with sexually abused children. In W. C. Wester & D. J. O'Grady (Eds.), *Clinical hypnosis with children* (pp. 69–84). New York: Brunner/Mazel.

Russell, D. E. H. (1984). *Sexual exploitation.* Newbury Park, CA: Sage.

Santiago, J. M., McCall-Perez, F., Gorcey, M., & Beigel, A. (1985). Long-term psychological effects of rape in 35 rape victims. *American Journal of Psychiatry, 142,* 1338–1340.

Scheflin, A. W., & Shapiro, J. L. (1989). *Trance on trial.* New York: Guilford Press.

Schiff, A. F. (1978). Rape in the United States. *Journal of Forensic Sciences, 32,* 845–851.

Smith, W. H. (1990). Hypnosis in the treatment of anxiety. *Bulletin of the Menninger Clinic, 54,* 209–216.

Smith, W. H. (1991). Antecedents of posttraumatic stress disorder: Wasn't being raped enough? A brief communication. *International Journal of Clinical and Experimental Hypnosis, 39,* 129–133.

Somer, E. (1990). Brief simultaneous couple hypnotherapy with a rape victim and her spouse. *International Journal of Clinical and Experimental Hypnosis, 38,* 1–5.

Spiegel, D. (1991). Dissociation and trauma. In A. Tasman & S. M. Goldfinger (Eds.), *American Psychiatric Press Review of Psychiatry* (Vol. 10, pp. 261–275). Washington, DC: American Psychiatric Press.

Steele, K. H. (1989). A model for abreaction with MPD and other dissociative disorders. *Dissociation, 2,* 151–159.

Valdiserri, E. V., & Byrne, J. P. (1982). Hypnosis as emergency treatment for a teen-age rape victim. *Hospital and Community Psychiatry, 33,* 767–769.

Watkins, J. (1971). The affect bridge: A hypnoanalytic technique. *International Journal of Clinical and Experimental Hypnosis, 19,* 21–27.

23

HYPNOSIS IN THE TREATMENT OF POSTTRAUMATIC STRESS DISORDERS

DAVID SPIEGEL

Hypnosis has been used in the treatment of those suffering from traumatic experiences for more than 150 years. Early uses involved hypnotic analgesia to help patients through traumatic surgical procedures before the advent of inhalation anesthesia (Esdaile, 1846/1957). Freud began his exploration of the unconscious through the use of hypnosis at a time when he conceptualized and treated hysterical reactions as the aftermath of traumatic experiences in childhood (Breuer & Freud, 1893–1895/1955, 1895/1986). More recently, hypnotic techniques were used during World War II to treat what were then called "traumatic neuroses." Despite the growing acceptance of psychoanalysis as a model for psychotherapy in this era, hypnotic techniques were found to be efficient and effective in helping soldiers with acute combat reactions to work through, control, or put aside the effects of traumatic experiences (Kardiner & Spiegel, 1947). With the substantial growth in the recognition of posttraumatic stress disorder (PTSD) as a diagnosis has come an increased interest in hypnosis as a tool in psychotherapy. In this chapter I outline some of the reasons for this parallel growth and for the utility of hypnosis in the psychotherapy of PTSD.

TRAUMA

Trauma is a sudden discontinuity in physical experience that elicits similar discontinuities in mental experience. Most trauma victims report a sharp contrast between their mental states just prior to the trauma (e.g., "I was driving to the airport so excited about the trip") and during and after it (e.g., "Suddenly this man was in my car with a gun. I couldn't do anything. I can't get him out of my mind. Nothing is the same any more. I can't enjoy anything"). A more classically dissociative example is that of a young man who was struck by a drunken motorcyclist on the highway, suffering severe injuries to both legs, which eventually necessitated an amputation. As he lay on the highway in tremendous pain, friends were urging him to get off the road so he would not be hit again. He found himself thinking about a fishing trip with his father at a mountain lake, walked off the road, and felt no pain until several hours later at the emergency room. Such abrupt shifts in mental state may be adaptive and serve the defensive purpose of separating a person from the full impact of the physical trauma as it is occurring. This adaptive defense may help distance individuals from pain and overwhelming fear. It may also work too well in helping people from consciously working through traumatic memories because they remain largely out of awareness. It is the theme of this chapter that there is much that is spontaneously dissociative in the nature of the acute response to trauma. Furthermore, there are a substantial number of dissociative features in the symptoms of PTSD. This means that hypnosis, a state of artificially induced dissociation (Nemiah, 1985), may be especially relevant and useful in accessing memories of trauma and in helping patients to work them through as part of the treatment of PTSD.

DISSOCIATION DURING TRAUMA

There is evidence that many people dissociate during traumatic experiences. It is not uncommon for rape victims to feel as though they were floating above their body and feeling sorry for the woman being attacked. One young woman who suffered an accidental fall from a third-story balcony described her experience of the event as follows: "It was as if I was standing on another balcony watching a pink cloud float down to the ground. I felt no pain at all and tried to walk back upstairs. It turned out that I had suffered a broken pelvis." It is not uncommon for athletes who have suffered serious injuries during a game to become aware of them only after the game is over. A study of the responses to the Bay Area earthquake provide evidence that two thirds of a sample of normal students experienced some kind of dissociative symptom in the immediate aftermath of the earthquake (Cardeña & Spiegel, 1993). These include experiences of time distortion, unusually intense memories, psychogenic amnesia, depersonalization, and derealization. The relevance of dissociation to trauma was illustrated longitudinally by J. R. Hilgard's (1970) observation that highly hypnotizable students reported a history of more physical punishment in childhood than did their less hypnotizable peers. Several studies have also shown that psychiatric patients with a history of sexual and physical abuse in childhood scored high on measures of dissociation (Chu & Dill, 1990; Herman, Perry, & van der Kolk, 1989). Indeed, dissociative disorders have come to be reconceptualized as chronic PTSDs secondary to physical and sexual abuse in childhood (Frischholz, 1985; Kluft, 1988; D. Spiegel, 1984).

A girl who was a repeated victim of incest by her father used to focus all of her attention on her hand rather than other parts of her body during the sexual assaults. Another patient took herself to an imaginary field full of wildflowers as a way of distancing herself from paternal beatings and sexual abuse. In this sense, dissociation—the disintegration of experience and memory—served as an adaptive defensive function against trauma while it was occurring. This defense, however, can increase the difficulty of integrating and working through these memories subsequent to the trauma. If the traumatic experiences are too easily kept out of consciousness, necessary corrective grief work may be postponed or avoided. For example, it is common for trauma victims to blame themselves inappropriately for events that they could not have foreseen or controlled. This occurs both because people conceptualize true randomness with difficulty and because inappropriately blaming oneself for trauma may be less painful than fully accepting one's complete helplessness at the hands of an attacker or in a natural disaster. Conscious, painful attention to traumatic memories in their aftermath can help to correct these frequent distortions, which may predispose one to the development of PTSD symptoms.

From this viewpoint, trauma can be conceptualized as the experience of being made into an object, devoid of any sense of control. It is indeed helplessness that is the core painful experience defended against by trauma victims. Defenses such as separating oneself from one's body are useful in creating a sense of distance of physical helplessness. Psychological control is maintained when physical control is lost. Ironically, in the individuals who develop PTSD, psychological control is lost when physical control returns. These patients now feel victimized by an intrusive reliving of the traumatic event. When the traumatic memory recurs, it often does so in the present tense. Not only is the memory more intense, but the uncertainty of the outcome, the fear of dying, and the fear of being helpless at the hands of the victimizer or force of nature is relived with all of its original intensity. The memory may be kept out of conscious awareness, and dissociative amnesia may develop. However, the message of this amnesia is that the memory is too horrible to be allowed into consciousness and the emotions associated with it too painful.

Indeed, there is an analogy between the major components of hypnosis and the major symptoms of PTSD. One important component of hypnosis is dissociation, the compartmentalization of components of experience. It is a mechanism consistent with the numbing of responsiveness and loss of pleasure in usually pleasurable activities that typifies PTSD (revised third edition of the *Diagnostic and Statistical Manual of Mental Disorders;* American Psychiatric Association, 1987). PTSD patients dissociate content from affect, often demonstrating demoralization without conscious recollection of the details. Thus, a female rape victim with dissociative amnesia for the rape may find herself unable to tolerate any sexual contact with a loving partner, treating him as though he were the assailant. Another important component of hypnosis is absorption (Tellegen, 1981; Tellegen & Atkinson, 1974). This is a narrowing of the focus of attention at the expense of peripheral awareness (e.g., getting so lost in a good movie or novel that one enters the imagined world and loses awareness of the surroundings in which the story occurs). This absorption in an event is reminiscent of some of the intrusive reliving of traumatic experiences that individuals with PTSD suffer. They may spontaneously relive the trauma as though it were occurring again in the present tense, dissociating awareness that they did indeed survive the trauma, which is analogous to hypnotic age regression (D. Spiegel, 1986). Thus, they experience it with great emotional intensity and without the comforting recognition that they lived through the event. The third important component of hypnosis is suggestibility, which is a heightened responsiveness to social cues in an exaggerated willingness to uncritically accept social input (Cardeña & Spiegel, 1991). This is similar to the stimulus sensitivity typical of individuals with PTSD. A female rape victim may avoid passing near anything that reminds her of the setting in which the rape occurred (e.g., any elevator or park). Thus, there is much about trauma that seems to elicit spontaneous dissociative processes. Therefore, it is logical that hypnosis should be an especially valuable tool in treatment.

CLINICAL APPLICATIONS

The fundamental principles involved in using hypnosis in the treatment of PTSD involve inducing controlled access to traumatic memories and helping patients to control the intense affect and strong physiological responses that may accompany memories of trauma. Hypnotic concentration can then be applied to help patients work through and grieve aspects of the traumatic experience and place the memories into a new perspective, a form of cognitive restructuring.

The psychotherapy of trauma can be understood as an adaptation of the traditional psychoanalytic principle of remembering, repeating, and working through (Freud, 1914/1958). It is necessary to bring into consciousness memories of the traumatic experience, repeat some of the affective and interpersonal quality of the experience, and then work through the material, putting it into a new perspective that makes it less overwhelming and likely to produce symptoms. Another way to conceptualize this is a form of grief work (Lindemann, 1944). Facing the reality of a traumatic experience means grieving certain fantasies of invulnerability and images of the self. Patients suffering with traumatic reminiscences often experience themselves as heavily degraded and humiliated by the traumatic experience and as being a parody of their former self, carrying on a kind of pseudonormal existence in which they pretend that the trauma did not occur. The goal is a redefinition of self that acknowledges the reality of the traumatic experience but puts it into perspective and makes it less damaging to the total view of self. Hypnosis is an effective context within which to perform this psychotherapeutic grief work.

One especially useful way of introducing hypnosis into the therapy is through the use of a clinical hypnotizability scale, such as the Hypnotic Induction Profile (H. Spiegel & Spiegel, 1987) or the Stanford Hypnotic Clinical Scale (E. R. Hilgard & Hilgard, 1975). This form of initial hypnotic induction has several advantages:

1. It provides useful information about the patient's degree of hypnotizability, which is a stable and measurable trait (E. R. Hilgard, 1965; Orne et al., 1979; H. Spiegel & Spiegel, 1987). About 1 in 5 psychiatric outpatients are not hypnotizable, and 1 in 10 are extremely responsive (H. Spiegel & Spiegel, 1987). Patients' performance on a hypnotizability test provides either a tangible demonstration of their hypnotic ability, which is a good starting point for therapy and is often surprising to patients, or it demonstrates that hypnosis is unlikely to be useful. Furthermore, there is evidence, to be discussed in the Research and Appraisal section of this chapter, that patients with PTSD are, as a group, highly hypnotizable. The testing can thus be useful in differential diagnosis as well. Hypnotizability testing provides, with little waste of time, an opportunity to select alternative facilitators of treatment. Thus, the hypnotic induction can be turned into a rational deduction about the patient's resources for change (H. Spiegel & Spiegel, 1980).

2. The atmosphere of testing enhances the treatment alliance and defuses anxieties about loss of control. The therapist's responsibility is to provide a clinically appropriate setting and instructions for the systematic exploration of the patient's hypnotic capacity. This is not a power struggle in which the therapist tries to "get the patient into a trance" and the patient succumbs or resists. The therapist is interested in finding out the results of the test, not in proving how successful he or she is at hypnotizing a patient. Thus, the atmosphere becomes something of a Socratic dialogue, in which both discover what the patient already "knows" (hypnotic capacity) but about which there is little conscious awareness.

The hypnotic state can be used as a means of providing a sense of physical comfort and safety that is dissociated from memories of events in which the physical environment was much different. It is also useful to teach patients from the beginning to enter the state of hypnosis as a state of self-hypnosis so that they feel in control of the transition to this altered mental state. The instructions can be simple:

> All hypnosis is really self-hypnosis. Now that we have demonstrated that you have a good capacity to use hypnosis, let me show you how to use it to work on a problem. While there are many ways to enter a state of self-hypnosis, one simple means is simply to count from one to three. On "one," do one thing: look up. On "two," do two things: slowly close your eyes and take a deep breath. On "three," do three things: let the breath out, let your eyes relax but keep them closed, and let your body float. Then, let one hand or the other float up in the air like a balloon, and that will be your signal to yourself and to me that you are ready to concentrate. (H. Spiegel & Spiegel, 1987, p. 76)

Once in a state of self-hypnosis, patients can be taught to produce a physical sensation of floating, lightness, or buoyancy. Their sense of physical comfort can be reinforced by having them initially imagine that they are somewhere safe and comfortable, such as floating in a bath, a lake, a hot tub, or space. This enhances their sense of control over their body, which is critical when reliving memories of bodily discomfort and damage. Once they have established this physical sense of comfort, they can be told to maintain this state regardless of what other images or thoughts come to them.

There are two basic means of accessing traumatic memories. One involves hypnotic age regression. Subjects are instructed to go back and relive earlier periods of their life as if they were occurring in the present. They are told that when given a signal, such as stroking the side of their eyes, their eyes will open and they will experience the event as though it were occurring in the here and now. Later, when given another signal such as stroking the forehead, their eyes will close and their time orientation will be changed again. The alternative method is to have them picture on an imaginary screen a pleasant scene to establish their ability to visualize in this manner and then a scene taken from the traumatic experience as though they were watching their own videotape of the event.

It is often useful to first go back to some comparatively neutral time prior to the trauma as a means of establishing patients' control over this technique before tapping material with strong affective associations. Then, on the basis of the history obtained, the therapist selects one aspect of the trauma and asks the patient to relive it using hypnotic age regression or to see it as if it were viewed on an imaginary screen (the screen technique). It is useful to have them view the same traumatic event from a different viewpoint (e.g., taking into account what they did to protect themselves during the trauma). It might have been fighting off an assailant, attempting to help a wounded friend, or simply deciding to remain quiet so as not to further provoke an attacker. It is often useful with either age regression or the screen technique to consolidate this restructured perspective by having them visualize a split screen: on the left picturing some aspect of what happened to them during the trauma and on the right side concentrating on their efforts to protect themselves during the traumatic experience. This helps them to face what was done to them and yet see it from a restructured viewpoint, in which they recognize and acknowledge their efforts at self-protection at the same time as they admit that there was a period of time during which they were physically helpless. This often reduces the exaggerated and inappropriate guilt that most trauma survivors feel. The guilt provides them with a fantasy that they could have controlled events over which, in fact, they were helpless. The mental discomfort involved in feeling guilty for not having overcome the trauma is the price that is paid for avoiding the confrontation with the fundamental sense of helplessness that accompanies physical trauma.

Having attended to these two different viewpoints about the traumatic experience, instructions to end the hypnotic exercise can be given. It is often useful during this termination phase to say "you will remember as much of this as you care to remember" as a means of not excessively challenging defenses if the patient wants to keep most or all of the material out of consciousness. It is then useful to debrief patients afterward, discussing their memories of the hypnotic work and what new meaning they have extracted from it. This is also an emotional consolidation phase in the therapy, when patients need time to work through and put into perspective strong emotions that might have been aroused by the hypnotic vivification of the traumatic memories.

Patients who are not overwhelmed by the material, who have good general mental health (i.e., are not suicidally depressed or psychotic), or who have supportive resources available should be taught to continue the therapeutic work as a self-hypnosis exercise at home. The instructions can include a repetition of the self-hypnosis induction, then using the screen technique to visualize contrasting aspects of the trauma: acknowledging and bearing their helplessness while recognizing their efforts to cope with and master the traumatic situation. This can be practiced once or twice a day. Such exercises often have the effect of organizing and containing the traumatic memories, confining them to the self-hypnosis exercises and thereby freeing the patient to deal with other issues the remainder of the time. In this sense, the hypnosis is like a more focused version of psychotherapy in general. Irrational feelings are expected to flourish in the transference while the therapist hopes that the patient's outside life will also improve. In the same way, hypnosis is used as a special state of concentration through which traumatic memories can be accessed and worked through, just as dissociation is often associated with the initial experience of trauma.

This approach to the use of hypnosis in treating PTSD can be summarized as the series of eight "Cs." These principles are presented in approximate temporal order. That is, they are designed to be a series of steps gone through, beginning with the confrontation of trauma and ending with congruence (the integration of traumatic memories). Nonetheless, some will occur together, and some may occur before others. The main point of these principles is to try to provide an organizing framework for therapists in their use of hypnosis in working through traumatic memories.

1. *Confront trauma.* The focus of this work is to help patients to link current symptomatology to a previous traumatic experience and work through that experience. This means that the primary goal of this kind of psychotherapy is not to analyze personality development or long-standing genetic reconstruction of symptoms. Rather, the goal is acute and relatively rapid reversal of posttraumatic stress symptoms. If deeper personality issues then surface, the time to deal with them is after the psychotherapy of PTSD has been completed. To address the personality issues first can have the unfortunate effect of reinforcing inappropriate guilt by implying that if the person had not suffered the preexisting personality problems, the trauma would not have occurred.

2. Find a *Condensation* of the traumatic experience. It is not necessary or even helpful to go through every unpleasant detail of the trauma. It is more helpful to find aspects of the traumatic memory that typify the trauma in the patients' mind and work through them.

3. *Confession.* Patients often have to confess to memories, experiences, and feelings about which they feel deeply ashamed.

They may never have discussed them with anyone else. These memories, experiences, and feelings will be revealed with difficulty. It is also useful to distinguish between genuine guilt over acts performed about which they have reason to feel ashamed (e.g., soldiers who harmed or killed civilians in combat) and events in which the guilt is inappropriate (e.g., a combat soldier who felt that he should have known that a shell would land in one spot rather than another and therefore he might have saved a comrade who was hit).

4. *Consolation.* Therapists should be responsive and empathetic with patients in a professionally appropriate way. Neutrality or silence will be interpreted by patients as rejection. A simple statement of comfort such as "I am terribly sorry this happened to you" can go a long way toward reassuring patients that they are not being rejected by the therapist even though they themselves feel that memories associated with these events make them unacceptable as people.

5. Make *Conscious* previously repressed or dissociated material. Material stored unconsciously is rarely transformed. One can think of consciousness as a kind of processor that allows information to be examined, parsed, and reassembled. The overwhelming sense of having been shown to be a coward, for example, can be matched with memories of having tried to rescue friends or having used considerable ingenuity in protecting oneself during a traumatic experience, thereby transforming traumatic memory. When the material is stored in the unconscious again, it is stored in restructured form.

6. Mobilize and focus *Concentration*. Concentration, because of its intensity and narrowness of focus, provides an opportunity for unearthing memories in considerable detail and then putting them aside again. As a result, many trauma victims fear that they will be flooded with memories and feelings and will never emerge from them again. Hypnosis provides a ceremonial occasion in which the individual can focus intently on the memories with the inference that once they have done so, they can put them aside until the next hypnotic encounter with them.

7. *Control.* Because the key issue in dealing with traumatic memories is helplessness, it is especially important that the process of the psychotherapy give subjects a sense of heightened control over the memories. This means that structuring the occasion as one of inducing self-hypnosis is particularly important because it gives patients a sense of control and mastery. It is important that the old myth that hypnosis is something

done to one person by another be dismissed and that the hypnotic encounter be viewed as an active collaboration in which the therapist helps patients to assess and use their own hypnotic capacity.

8. *Congruence.* The goal is to help patients acknowledge, tolerate, and work through traumatic memories so that they can be integrated into their ongoing view of self without inflicting excessive damage to the self-concept.

There are a variety of other methods that have been used along with hypnosis to treat traumatic experiences. This includes abreaction, referred to by Freud as the "cathartic method" (Breuer & Freud, 1893–1895/1955); the alteration of traumatic memories (Kardiner & Spiegel, 1947); and the use of positive transference to integrate and alter material that leads to self-rejection (Brende & Benedict, 1980). All of these techniques involve using hypnosis to access traumatic memories and associated strong affects related to the traumatic experience and to transform them in some way: in the context of the therapeutic relationship so that they are re-stored in an altered form that makes them more acceptable to conscious awareness.

The traumatic transference is an important consideration. Patients will unconsciously and sometimes consciously identify the therapist with the person who or situation that caused the trauma. Therefore, it is especially important that the therapist be sensitive to patients' identification of them with the trauma and work to maintain the therapeutic alliance despite it. Although the therapeutic alliance can be an important tool in the treatment of trauma (Haley, 1974), unacknowledged or ignored fears regarding the therapist and his or her motivation for addressing the traumatic issues can undermine the psychotherapy.

It is important to note that in some states, a victim or witness who is hypnotized may either not testify as to the hypnotically elicited memories or may in fact be prevented from testifying in court (H. Spiegel & Spiegel, 1987). Therefore, if there is any potential litigation involved regarding the trauma, it is important that patients be informed of potential risks to their testimony and that the patients' attorneys or the district attorney or police be consulted. All encounters in the therapy should be electronically recorded, preferably by videotape. It is also important that the therapist avoid injecting information into the hypnotic recounting of the trauma and to simply set the scene and allow patients to provide all of the associations.

CASE MATERIAL

An Assault Victim

A 32-year-old female nurse was violently assaulted in the early evening as she returned home from shopping. The assailant attempted to drag her up a flight of stairs into her apartment, presumably to rape her. She fought vigorously with him, sustaining, among other injuries, a severe blow on the head. The assailant finally ran away and she called the police. Because she had not been raped, the police made a cursory investigation and left. She then suffered a generalized seizure and was taken to the hospital, where it was discovered that she had incurred a basilar skull fracture. By this time, the assailant was long gone. She had little memory of his features and came to me for evaluation several months later to see whether hypnosis would be helpful in refreshing her memory of his appearance. She also suffered symptoms of PTSD, including numbing of responsiveness, intrusive recollection of the trauma, and discomfort in her apartment.

She proved to be moderately hypnotizable, as assessed by the Hypnotic Induction Profile (HIP), and was encouraged to use the screen technique and to visualize the traumatic event on the screen. She was able to come to grips in hypnosis for the first time with how dangerous the situation had been. Previously, she had blamed herself for fighting back as hard as she did, thereby sustaining serious injury. She looked at her image of him in hypnosis and said, "He's really surprised that I'm fighting that hard, he doesn't expect me to." She then noticed something else: "I don't think he just wants to rape me, I think he wants to kill me. If he gets me upstairs, he's gonna murder me." I had her picture on the right side of the screen her efforts to protect herself and the effect that they had. She emerged from the hypnosis with no clearer visual image of what he had looked like because it was dark at the time of the attack. However, she had a transformed sense of her conduct during the assault. She left with the feeling that she had probably saved her life by fighting as hard as she had. Despite having recognized for the first time the extreme danger she had been in, she emerged with a much clearer sense of her own instinctive skill at self-preservation and, thus, the traumatic memories became more bearable.

A Vietnam Veteran With PTSD

A 45-year-old Vietnam combat veteran had been hospitalized for 5 years following a fugue episode in Vietnam (for a more detailed case description, see D. Spiegel, 1981). Despite a prior excellent service record, he was discharged after this episode and had been chronically depressed and suicidal. He had been diagnosed as psychopathic, depressed, and manic–depressive but had not responded to any psychotropic medications. He related in the interview that he had informally adopted a wounded Vietnamese child who had been killed during the Tet Offensive, and this seemed to have set off the fugue episode, for which he had no conscious memory.

He proved to be extremely hypnotizable on the HIP and relived, with considerable affect, the rocket attack in which the child was killed. He then relived a vivid memory of what had happened during the fugue episode.

After seeing the boy's body, he ran into the jungle and engaged in combat with the Vietcong. I then used hypnotic regression to move him to a time when he buried the boy's body and he tearfully dropped imaginary dirt on the boy's casket. He berated himself for not having taken the child somewhere else before the attack: "If I had just taken you over to the hooch, you wouldn't be there man; it's all my fault." I then asked him to think of a time when he and the child had been really happy together, and he pictured a birthday party he had thrown for the boy several months earlier. He smiled as he relived the boy's delight at the presents he received. The final instruction for the session was picturing on a split screen the boy's grave on the left and that birthday party on the right. I told him that although he had lost the child, no one could take away the happy times they had had together. I told him that he would remember as much as he cared to remember and guided him out of hypnosis. He emerged from 40 min of intense abreactive hypnotic age regression with just an image of a grave and a cake. He practiced this self-hypnosis exercise twice a day and improved substantially over the next several weeks, in conjunction with antidepressant medication. He discontinued the medication after discharge from the hospital and did well for several months until, in a period of 2 weeks, his wife started going out with another man, his police officer brother was killed in the line of duty, and someone shot his dog. He was rehospitalized but recompensated fairly quickly. In the ensuing 14 years, he has done well. Although he has had episodic periods of depression and suicidal ideation that resolve fairly quickly, these periods are related to present circumstances in his life rather than to the traumatic loss, which he feels he has worked through.

Both of these cases illustrate the use of hypnosis in helping trauma victims to work through traumatic memories. First, the hypnosis provided focused and controlled access to the memories through the inference that when the hypnosis was over, the memories would be less prominent in consciousness. This helped to make the painful affect associated with the memories more bearable because it implied that their presence in consciousness would be time limited. Second, the use of the split screen provided an opportunity to acknowledge the reality of the memory while also placing it in a broader perspective. In the case of the assault victim, the terror she experienced in reliving the danger that she had undergone also helped her to reappraise her own role in resisting the assailant. Whereas previously she had felt guilty about having caused her injury, she was able to change the context of the memory of the assailant by recognizing his intention to harm or kill her, and therefore her resistance was something that made her feel that she had possibly saved her life rather than gotten herself hurt even more. This made the original memory more tolerable because she had experienced it in a new context. Similarly, the restructuring with the Vietnam combat veteran helped him to acknowledge and bear the intensity of the loss of this child because he was also able to access memories of happier times with him. This made the loss seem real, but not total. This child was no longer alive, but his memories of happier times were not canceled by the child's death. Thus, hypnosis can help trauma victims to place their memories into a broader perspective, which makes working through them less overwhelming and more tolerable.

RESEARCH AND APPRAISAL

To my knowledge, there have been no randomized outcome trials of hypnosis versus other treatments for PTSD, yet there is accumulating evidence suggesting that hypnosis is highly effective. There are studies showing that hypnotizability is, if anything, elevated among individuals with PTSD. Stutman and Bliss (1985) showed that Vietnam veterans high in PTSD symptomatology had higher scores on the Stanford Hypnotic Susceptibility Scale than did Vietnam veterans who do not suffer from PTSD. D. Spiegel, Hunt, and Dondershine (1988) found that 65 Vietnam combat veterans who were hospitalized with PTSD had extraordinarily high scores on the HIP compared with patients with schizophrenia, affective disorders, and anxiety disorders. They were even significantly more hypnotizable than were a normal comparison population. Thus, the research suggests that patients with PTSD, as a group, are extremely hypnotizable. This is consistent with the theory presented earlier that dissociation is a spontaneous response to trauma and is in turn a component of PTSD. Furthermore, it provides systematic data suggesting that as a group, individuals with PTSD should have extremely high hypnotic capacity and therefore be especially able to effectively incorporate hypnosis into their psychotherapy.

More recent research has indicated that dissociative symptoms are common in the aftermath of trauma (D. Spiegel & Cardeña, 1991). In the wake of physical disasters such as earthquakes (Cardeña & D. Spiegel, 1993), airplane crashes (Sloan, 1988), and tornados (Madakasira & O'Brien, 1987), a substantial proportion of victims reported dissociative reactions including numbing and depersonalization (Feinstein, 1989; Noyes & Kletti, 1977).

Furthermore, the presence of such dissociative symptoms in the immediate aftermath of trauma has been found to predict subsequent PTSD (McFarlane, 1986; Solomon, Mikulincer, & Benbenisty, 1989). Because hypnosis is a form of structured and controlled dissociation, these recent studies provide evidence that many trauma victims enter hypnoticlike states during and immediately after trauma. Therefore, on the basis of state-dependent memory theory (Bower, 1981), it makes sense that psychotherapy using hypnosis would be especially able to facilitate access to congruent mental states and memories and consequently would be helpful in working through the aftermath of trauma.

CONCLUSION

Hypnosis is a state of special relevance to the assessment and treatment of PTSD. The phenomena that constitute hypnosis, dissociation, absorption, and suggestibility are mobilized spontaneously during trauma, during which they may serve as a unique and adaptive defense against overwhelming discomfort. In the aftermath of trauma, however, they may forestall adequate working through of the traumatic experience, thereby predisposing an individual to the development of PTSD. Indeed, many of the symptoms of PTSD are reminiscent of these aspects of hypnotic consciousness. Thus, hypnotic phenomena underlie important aspects of the response to trauma, and recent research shows that patients with PTSD are unusually high in hypnotic capacity. These considerations make hypnosis a natural tool in the diagnosis and treatment of PTSD. It enables individuals to intensely connect with traumatic mental content and to disconnect or dissociate their somatic responses to these memories. Hypnosis therefore provides a means of enhancing control for both patient and therapist of access to traumatic memories and association. This type of psychotherapy requires providing a means for restructuring these traumatic memories and therefore facilitating the grief work necessary to come to a new equilibrium. In this way, the special mental state mobilized during trauma may be used in the service of working through and mastering traumatic memories.

REFERENCES

American Psychiatric Association. (1987). *Diagnostic and statistical manual of mental disorders* (3rd ed., rev.). Washington, DC: Author.

Bower, G. H. (1981). Mood and memory. *American Psychologist, 36,* 129–148.

Brende, J. O., & Benedict, B. D. (1980). The Vietnam combat delayed response syndrome: Hypnotherapy of "dissociative symptoms." *American Journal of Clinical Hypnosis, 23,* 34–40.

Breuer, J., & Freud, S. (1955). Studies on hysteria. In J. Strachey (Ed. and Trans.), *The standard edition of the complete psychological works of Sigmund Freud* (Vol. 12). London: Hogarth Press. (Original work published 1893–1895)

Breuer, J., & Freud, S. (1986). *Studies on hysteria.* New York: Pelican Books. (Original work published 1895)

Cardeña, E., & Spiegel, D. (1991). Suggestibility, absorption, and dissociation: An integrative model of hypnosis. In J. F. Schumaker (Ed.), *Human suggest-*

ibility: Advances in theory, research, and application (pp. 93–107). New York: Routledge & Kegan Paul.

Cardeña, E., & Spiegel, D. (1993). Dissociative reactions to the San Francisco Bay Area earthquake of 1989. *American Journal of Psychiatry, 150,* 474–478.

Chu, J. A., & Dill, D. L. (1990). Dissociative symptoms in relation to childhood physical and sexual abuse. *American Journal of Psychiatry, 147,* 887–892.

Esdaile, J. (1957). *Hypnosis in medicine and surgery.* New York: Julian Press. (Original work published 1846)

Feinstein, A. (1989). Post-traumatic stress disorder: A descriptive study supporting DSM-III-R criteria. *American Journal of Psychiatry, 146,* 665–666.

Freud, S. (1958). Remembering, repeating, and working-through: Further recommendations on the technique of psycho-analysis II. In J. Strachey (Ed. and Trans.), *The standard edition of the complete psychological works of Sigmund Freud* (Vol. 12, pp. 145–156). London: Hogarth Press. (Original work published 1914)

Frischholz, E. J. (1985). The relationships among dissociation, hypnosis, and child abuse in the development of MPD. In R. P. Kluft (Ed.), *Childhood antecedents of multiple personality disorder* (pp. 99–126). Washington, DC: American Psychiatric Press.

Haley, S. A. (1974). When the patient reports atrocities. *Archives of General Psychiatry, 30,* 191–196.

Herman, J. L., Perry, J. C., & van der Kolk, B. A. (1989). Childhood trauma in borderline personality disorder. *American Journal of Psychiatry, 146,* 490–495.

Hilgard, E. R. (1965). *Hypnotic susceptibility.* New York: Harcourt, Brace & World.

Hilgard, E. R., & Hilgard, J. R. (1975). *Hypnosis in the relief of pain.* Los Altos, CA: Kaufmann.

Hilgard, J. R. (1970). *Personality and hypnosis: A study of imaginative involvement.* Chicago: University of Chicago Press.

Kardiner, A., & Spiegel, H. (1947). *War stress and neurotic illness.* New York: Hoeber.

Kluft, R. P. (1988). The dissociative disorders. In J. A. Talbott, R. E. Hales, & S. C. Yudofsky (Eds.), *Textbook of psychiatry* (pp. 557–585). Washington, DC: American Psychiatric Press.

Lindemann, E. (1944). Symptomatology and management of acute grief. *American Journal of Psychiatry, 101,* 141–148.

Madakasira, S., & O'Brien, K. (1987). Acute post-traumatic stress disorder in victims of a natural disaster. *Journal of Nervous and Mental Disease, 175,* 286–290.

McFarlane, A. C. (1986). Post-traumatic morbidity of a disaster. *Journal of Nervous and Mental Disease, 174,* 4–14.

Nemiah, J. C. (1985). Dissociative disorders. In H. I. Kaplan & B. J. Sadock (Eds.), *Comprehensive textbook of psychiatry* (4th ed., Vol. 1, pp. 942–957). Baltimore, MD: Williams & Wilkins.

Noyes, R., & Kletti, R. (1977). Depersonalization in response to life-threatening danger. *Comprehensive Psychiatry, 18*, 375–384.

Orne, M. T., Hilgard, E. R., Spiegel, H., Spiegel, D., Crawford, H. J., Evans, F. J., Orne, E. C., & Frischholz, E. J. (1979). The relation between the Hypnotic Induction Profile and the Stanford Hypnotic Susceptibility Scale, Forms A and C. *International Journal of Clinical and Experimental Hypnosis, 27*, 85–102.

Sloan, P. (1988). Post-traumatic stress in survivors of an airplane crash landing: A clinical and exploratory research intervention. *Journal of Traumatic Stress, 1*, 211–229.

Solomon, Z., Mikulincer, M., & Benbenisty, R. (1989). Combat stress reaction: Clinical manifestations and correlates. *Military Psychology, 1*, 35–47.

Spiegel, D. (1981). Vietnam grief work using hypnosis. *American Journal of Clinical Hypnosis, 24*, 33–40.

Spiegel, D. (1984). Multiple personality as a post-traumatic stress disorder. *Psychiatric Clinics of North America, 7*, 101–110.

Spiegel, D. (1986). Dissociating damage. *American Journal of Clinical Hypnosis, 29*, 123–131.

Spiegel, D., & Cardeña, E. (1991). Disintegrated experience: The dissociative disorders revisited. *Journal of Abnormal Psychology, 100*, 366–378.

Spiegel, D., Hunt, T., & Dondershine, H. (1988). Dissociation and hypnotizability in post-traumatic stress disorder. *American Journal of Psychiatry, 145*, 301–305.

Spiegel, H., & Spiegel, D. (1980). Induction techniques. In G. D. Burrows & L. Dennerstein (Eds.), *Handbook of hypnosis and psychosomatic medicine*. Amsterdam: Elsevier/North-Holland Biomedical Press.

Spiegel, H., & Spiegel, D. (1987). *Trance and treatment: Clinical uses of hypnosis*. Washington, DC: American Psychiatric Press. (Original work published 1978)

Stutman, R. K., & Bliss, E. L. (1985). Post-traumatic stress disorder, hypnotizability, and imagery. *American Journal of Psychiatry, 142*, 741–743.

Tellegen, A. (1981). Practicing the two disciplines for relaxation and enlightenment: Comment on "Role of the Feedback Signal in Electromyograph Biofeedback: The Relevance of Attention" by Qualls and Sheegan. *Journal of Experimental Psychology: General, 110*, 217–226.

Tellegen, A., & Atkinson, G. (1974). Openness to absorbing and self-altering experiences ("absorption"), a trait related to hypnotic susceptibility. *Journal of Abnormal Psychology, 83*, 268–277.

VI

BEHAVIORAL MEDICINE AND SPORTS PSYCHOLOGY

24

HYPNOSIS IN PAIN MANAGEMENT

JOHN F. CHAVES

In this chapter I examine the use of hypnosis in the management of pain. Like previous authors who have dealt with this topic (e.g., D. P. Brown & Fromm, 1987; Crasilneck & Hall, 1975; E. R. Hilgard & Hilgard, 1975; Udolph, 1987), I look at issues pertaining to the management of both chronic and acute pain, review central factors in patient selection and preparation for hypnosis, and examine problems inherent in facilitating the generalization of clinical gains outside of the clinical session as well as related issues. Unlike most previous articles on this topic, however, in this chapter hypnosis is viewed within the cognitive–behavioral perspective rather than traditional hypnotic-state theory (T. X. Barber, Spanos, & Chaves, 1974; Chaves, 1989; Chaves & Barber, 1976; Spanos & Chaves, 1989a, 1989b, 1989c). I briefly examine what that means.

Traditionally, hypnosis has been thought of as an altered state of consciousness or trance state that is created in susceptible individuals by their exposure to a fairly wide range of ceremonies that collectively are known as hypnotic induction procedures. Typically, these ceremonies involve administering suggestions for relaxation, eye closure, and deepening hypnosis to carefully selected individuals, followed by the administration of therapeutically relevant suggestions whose nature varies depending on the patient's needs. Next, the patient may be given suggestions designed to facilitate the maintenance and generalization of therapeutic gains outside of the clinical setting. The ceremony typically concludes with generalized suggestions of well-being, suggestions designed to minimize untoward sequelae and to enhance future responsiveness, eye opening, and the resumption of the normal waking state.

Traditional theories of hypnosis start from the premise that hypnotic induction procedures, like the one outlined earlier, produce beneficial clinical effects because they induce in patients an altered state of awareness, during which they are more responsive than they would otherwise be to the suggestions that are administered. Indeed, it is sometimes asserted that the good hypnotic subject may feel a compulsion to follow the therapist's suggestions and experience the execution of the appropriate response as effortless and involuntary (Lynn, Rhue, & Weekes, 1989; Orne, 1959).

At other times, it is assumed that the kinds of responses achieved with the use of hypnosis could not be achieved without the induction of the hypnotic state (Erickson, 1938a, 1938b). This assumption has dominated thinking about hypnotic pain control for almost 200 years. In fact, early clinical reports of the apparent success of hypnotic or mesmeric procedures in attenuating the pain of major surgery during the preanesthetic era might have played an important role in shaping the view that the hypnotic reduction of pain must involve a powerful and mysterious force (T. X. Barber et al., 1974; Dingwall, 1967; Spanos, 1986).

Historically, the authenticity of the phenomena associated with hypnosis, including pain reduction, has been taken for granted by those working in the field; as a result, clinical interest focused on strategies for enhancing hypnotizability and maximizing hypnotic depth, factors thought to play a significant role in clinical success (J. Barber, 1977, 1980). However, close scrutiny of hypnotic phenomena routinely revealed that the suggested phenomena were rarely the same as their nonsuggested or naturally occurring counterparts, although it frequently took the use of sophisticated experimental designs to demonstrate this (T. X. Barber, 1963; T. X. Barber & Calverley, 1964). Thus, for example, it could be demonstrated that hypnotically "deafened" subjects responded by stuttering and stammering, just like their normally hearing counterparts, when exposed to delayed auditory feedback (T. X. Barber & Calverley, 1964). In a similar fashion, hypnotic blindness can be differentiated from its naturally occurring counterpart (Pattie, 1935). Similarly, E. R. Hilgard's (1986) studies of the "hidden observer" showed that subjects who successfully responded to hypnotic analgesia suggestions retained an awareness of their pain that could be demonstrated when the appropriate suggestions were administered. This is much different from analgesia that is chemically induced.

The hypnotic reduction of pain is more difficult to evaluate than are other forms of suggested sensory alteration. Part of the difficulty can be traced to the enormous variability in the human response to painful stimulation. In both clinical and experimental settings, the nature of the response to painful stimulation varies depending on factors such as the "meaning" of the pain to the patient (e.g., wound-related pain that extricates a soldier honorably from the field of battle vs. the inconvenience of civilian pain that impairs activities of daily living), cultural factors, personality factors, the presence of certain forms of psychopathology (e.g., depression or somatizing personality disorder), and so forth (Melzack & Wall, 1988). Even the widely cited examples of early 18th-century surgery with mesmerized patients can be matched with examples of other nonmesmerized patients who displayed an equally extraordinary lack of reactivity to surgical pain (Lozanov, 1967; Trent, 1946; Tuckey, 1889). These complexities, coupled with the absence of any truly objective measure of pain, have made the evaluation of the role of hypnotic procedures in the reduction of clinical pain extremely complex.

Those who approach the topic of hypnosis from the cognitive–behavioral perspective have emphasized the importance of understanding that pain is a multifaceted and multidimensional experience. Contextual, cultural, interpersonal, and personality variables all have the potential to contribute to the pain reductions that are often observed subsequent to hypnotic interventions. In order to maximize the clinical benefits to patients experiencing pain as well as to aid in theory construction, therapists must try to have a complete understanding of the ways in which all of these variables, and their interactions, contribute to the pain experience and its mitigation. Therefore, I begin with the following premises:

1. Hypnotic procedures are complex, multifaceted clinical interventions that involve many variables that alone or in combination with other contextual, interpersonal, or cognitive variables could be instrumental in the reduction of clinical or experimental pain.
2. It is not necessary to postulate the existence of an altered state of consciousness in order to examine or clinically use hypnotic procedures for reducing pain.
3. Variables that are instrumental in reducing pain may be effective both inside or outside of the hypnotic context.
4. Traditional assumptions regarding the suitability of certain patients for hypnosis are left open to question.

CLINICAL APPLICATIONS

Clinical applications of hypnosis for pain management can be conveniently separated into the following phases: (a) patient selection, (b) preparation, (c) induction procedures, (d) deepening procedures, (e) therapeutic suggestions, (f) posthypnotic suggestions, and (g) termination. Of course, these phases are not in practice as distinct as the listing would imply. In many ways, the phases merge at the margin, in much the same ways as the opening, middle, and end of the game do in chess. Nevertheless, there is some heuristic value in considering the issues involved in each phase separately. I have deliberately chosen widely used terminology, such as "deepening," with the understanding that I do not wish to commit myself to reify these metaphors. I now examine the salient clinical issues involved at each phase, with special emphasis on the implications of the cognitive–behavioral perspective.

Patient Selection

Traditional approaches to the use of hypnosis for pain management have generally emphasized the need to select as candidates patients who are highly hypnotizable and who are not disoriented or psychotic. Reports of clinical successes in working with severely compromised patients (D. P. Brown & Fromm, 1986) have suggested that contraindications for clinical hypnosis may be better framed in terms of the clinician's lack of experience with the specified patient population rather than in psychodiagnostic terms. In general, patients who are appropriate for any psychotherapeutic intervention are potential candidates for hypnotic intervention. The same sorts of issues that may render a pain patient a poor candidate for other forms of psychotherapeutic intervention for pain management, such as pending litigation, would also mitigate against success with hypnotic interventions.

Hypnotizability per se is now seen by those working within the cognitive–behavioral perspective as being less important than it has been traditionally assumed (Bertrand, 1989; D. P. Brown & Fromm, 1986). In part, this is because clinicians no longer view hypnotizability as an immutable trait but as a learnable skill that can be taught to patients who can benefit by the use of the skill. A related consideration is that clinical studies in which patients unselected in terms of hypnotizability were used have shown that even poor subjects could achieve clinically significant gains, as measured by reductions in the use of narcotic analgesics and other indirect measures of quality of life (e.g., Cangello, 1961, 1962).

The importance of hypnotizability probably depends on the nature of the clinical problem. It is doubtful that many poor hypnotic subjects have undergone surgery with hypnosis as the sole anesthetic. On the other hand, suggestions designed to improve exercise tolerance or to improve tolerance for removal of stitches or injections of local anesthetic probably do not require high levels of hypnotizability to achieve clinical success.

Although hypnosis has historically been thought of as a powerful and potentially dangerous intervention that ought to be attempted only under prescribed circumstances, hypnosis is now thought of as one part of a broad spectrum of interventions that, under most circumstances, is benign (Coe & Ryken, 1979). Although it is certainly true that problems involved in the clinical use of hypnosis are much different from those involved in experimental hypnosis, it nevertheless seems appropriate to think of hypnotic procedures as being generally safe when used by trained professionals in a professional context.

Preparation

Virtually all patients can be assumed to have expectations regarding the nature of hypnosis, including impressions about how hypnosis is done, who is responsive to it, what the typical outcomes are, and what dangers are associated with it. Young children learn about hypnosis through the media, whereas adults might have seen stage performances or have friends and neighbors who have had an experience with hypnosis. While conducting a workshop at Great Slave Lake in the Canadian Northwest Territories, I had an opportunity to bring the point home to my fishing companion, an anesthesiologist from California, when I asked our guide, a Cree Indian, what he knew about hypnosis. His eyes lit up as he began to describe the visit of an itinerant hypnotist who had put on a demonstration in Yellowknife several years previously. When asked what it would be like to be hypnotized, the guide articulated the usual range of expectations engendered by stage performances, including the notions that (a) hypnosis is an altered sleeplike state induced by the hypnotist; (b) in this state, subjects are able to do things that they are not capable of doing during the normal waking state; (c) hypnotic subjects are unable to resist the suggestions of the hypnotist; and (d) hypnotic subjects invariably experience posthypnotic amnesia.

Patients who present for clinical hypnosis for pain typically have similar beliefs to those outlined earlier. Sometimes, their expectations regarding matters such as how they will be hypnotized or how they will achieve clinical gains are remarkably specific. One female patient, a 65-year-old nurse who was also trained as a social worker, suffered from breast cancer with widespread bone metastases and consulted me several years ago for pain management. She believed that hypnosis could be useful in helping her to achieve an "out-of-body" experience that, she was convinced, would enable her to deal with her pain. Eliciting this expectation proved to be pivotal in helping her to deal initially with symptoms of depression, including anergia, anhedonia, and dysphoria, as well as other sequelae of her cancer treatment. Success with the management of those issues, in turn, encouraged her positive expectations that she would be able to have the out-of-body experience that she felt was essential for her to achieve relief from her pain. At the time, her pain consisted of a chronic, diffuse, relatively low-level discomfort, on which was superimposed periodic, intense exacerbations that at times required hospitalization. Her hope was that the hypnotically facilitated out-of-body experiences would both diminish the intensity of the chronic component of her pain and reduce the frequency and intensity of the exacerbations. She, from the outset, did not expect that hypnosis could eliminate her pain. For her, pain management was the goal. Working within the framework of this patient's expectations, significant clinical gains were achieved that persisted throughout the course of her terminal illness.

Eliciting patients' expectations regarding hypnosis can be difficult. When asked what they think it would be like to be hypnotized, patients often say they do not know or give a brief, vague answer that can be deceptive, masking an array of undisclosed specific expectations. Patients often want to defer to the clinician's expertise and will prematurely lead them into a lecture about hypnosis that may have no direct relevance to the patients' expectations. This is a trap into which inexperienced clinicians often fall. The consequence is that important preconceptions about hypnosis are frequently not identified and managed effectively. In this context, effective management usually means using one of two strategies: (a) educating patients so that their expectations and their experiences during clinical hypnosis will be congruent or (b) modifying the procedure to achieve the same objective. I present examples of each of these strategies in turn.

Pain patients, as well as others, sometimes approach hypnosis with the belief that it is invariably accompanied by spontaneous amnesia. Clinicians realize that spontaneous amnesia for events during the hypnotic session is a rare phenomenon. The danger is that patients will realize posthypnotically that they are not amnesic and therefore conclude that they were not hypnotized and, accordingly, that they will not benefit clinically from the procedure. This, of course, can be a self-fulfilling prophecy. To minimize this possibility, such patients may benefit from a suggestion to the effect that, to ensure that they derive maximum pain relief, they will remember everything that happens during the hypnotic procedure. Alternatively, they could simply be educated about the rarity of spontaneous amnesia.

Sometimes, patients' expectations can be most easily accommodated by incorporating the expectations into the procedure. Thus, patients who have specific ideas about how hypnosis should be induced, such as with eye closure or with shiny objects, can generally be accommodated without the need for informing them about the possibilities of other induction procedures. Pragmatic considerations generally apply in these situations.

The clinical approaches just suggested are clearly based on the assumption that patients' attitudes, expectations, and beliefs can play an enormous role in determining treatment outcome. Within the cognitive–behavioral approach to hypnosis, these variables have consistently been viewed as being extremely important. Early studies by Barber and his associates (reviewed in T. X. Barber et al., 1974) provided support for this conclusion. More recent studies have provided additional support. Indeed, Kirsch (1985, 1986; Kirsch & Council, 1989) argued that the concept of expectation is pivotal in explaining hypnotic phenomena. Clinicians, then, must be concerned about the identification and proper use of those variables that have the potential to enhance or diminish expectations regarding hypnotic responding and clinical outcomes.

Simply defining a situation as "hypnotic" enhances responses to suggestion; however, when subjects believe that they are being subjected to a test of "gullibility," suggestibility declines precipitously (T. X. Barber & Calverley, 1964). It is not unreasonable to suppose that some pain patients bring these sorts of expectations to the clinical setting. Consider the plight of a typical somatizing type of chronic pain patient whose pain appears to be completely disproportionate to the minimal objective findings seen by his or her physician. Such patients have typically been told that their pain is "all in your head and you are just going to have to live with it." Presenting for treatment with hypnosis places these patients, in their view, in a double bind: If they find relief with hypnosis, it confirms the physician's conclusion that the pain was "all in their heads." Optimal preparation of these patients requires reframing of a successful outcome. One example of this sort of reframing may involve informing the patient that "of course, hypnosis is not very helpful for patients whose pain is emotional because those patients usually have a need to keep their pain. However, it can be helpful for patients with organic pain, like yours."

Beyond efforts to assess pretreatment expectations and beliefs regarding hypnosis, clinicians and researchers are investing new energy in creating positive educational experiences for patients that can augment hypnotic responsivity, particularly for patients who would otherwise not be good hypnotic subjects (Bertrand, 1989). Traditionally, hypnotizability has been viewed as a trait that remains stable throughout most of one's life. Thus, clinicians who approach hypnosis from a state viewpoint typically do not invest much effort in modifying hypnotizability. However, in recent years, data from experimental studies seem to document the finding that hypnotic responsiveness, including both objective and subjective components, can be enhanced with suitable training procedures, such as the Carleton University Skills Training Package, developed by Spanos and his associates (Gorassini & Spanos, 1986; Spanos, Cross, Menary, Brett, & de Groh, 1987; Spanos, de Groh, & de Groot, 1987; Spanos, Robertson, Menary, & Brett, 1986). The application of these kinds of training protocols with clinical populations remains a fertile field for future research.

Induction Procedures

The hypnotic induction procedure itself is often thought to be the centerpiece of the clinical hypnotic intervention. The assumption seems to be that the main clinical issue in the therapeutic use of hypnosis is the successful induction of the hypnotic trance state. Once that is achieved, a successful clinical outcome is often thought to be assured. One clinician who was having difficulties using hypnosis for pain control consulted me to determine what was wrong with his technique. He brought with him an audiotape of his induction procedure, fully expecting that the flaw in his technique must reside there. He was somewhat annoyed when I stopped the tape and insisted that we review the events that had preceded the induction itself in order to evaluate the patient's attitudes, expectations, and beliefs about the impending hypnotic intervention.

As Kroger (1977) noted, the induction of hypnosis is the induction of belief. Typically, the hypnotic induction ritual includes the following elements:

1. The situation is defined as a hypnotic induction procedure.
2. Patients may be asked to close their eyes either as an instruction (i.e., as a voluntary act) or as a suggestion (i.e., in which eye closure is to be experienced as an involuntary act whose occurrence ratifies the onset of the hypnotic state).
3. Suggestions for relaxation are administered and are sometimes accompanied by relaxation-related imagery that, ideally, is personalized to reflect the patient's experiences and values.
4. At times, the induction procedure may entail overt responses from the patient such as arm heaviness or lightness, or responses to challenge suggestions (e.g., "Your hands are stuck together, you cannot pull them apart"). The use of these suggestions is designed to allow the patient to experience what it is like to respond to a hypnotic suggestion and, accordingly, enhance the likelihood of a response to later therapeutically relevant suggestions.

In recent years, arguments have appeared in the literature advocating the use of indirect rather than direct suggestions during the induction phase and at other points during the hypnotic procedure (e.g., Alman & Carney, 1980; J. Barber, 1977; Ficton & Roth, 1985; Stone & Lundy, 1985). Thus, for example, suggestions for eye closure may be given indirectly by the use of phrasing such as "Perhaps you've already noticed how heavy your eyes have become" or "Some people find it easier to visualize while their eyes are closed" rather than more direct wording such as "Your eyes are becoming heavier and heavier." Although most clinicians probably use a mixture of indirect and direct suggestions, the extreme claims for the superiority of indirect suggestions proposed by some in therapeutic hypnosis have not received wide support in the research literature (e.g., Lynn, Neufeld, & Matyi, 1987; Matthews, Bennett, Bean, & Gallagher, 1985).

The essential elements of the hypnotic induction procedure appear to be the creation of a series of experiences for patients that help them to define the situation as hypnotic, facilitate the focusing of attention, and enhance their expectation that it will be possible for them to experience the clinical benefits of participating in the hypnotic procedure. In turn, this requires that the induction procedure have face validity for patients. In other words, the procedure needs to be seen as credible within the framework of patients' expectations regarding hypnosis.

Deepening Procedures

The hypnotic induction procedure tends to lead seamlessly into so-called deepening procedures. The term *hypnotic depth* is a sort of geophysical metaphor that is largely viewed as a social artifact from the cognitive–behavioral perspective (Radke, 1989). The term *hypnotic depth* is frequently used to refer to the degree to which subjects believe that they were hypnotized. Depth, then, varies along a continuum from light to medium to deep. Historically, the concept of depth was not distinguished from the concept of suggestibility. However, in recent years, the term *suggestibility* has come to be used more commonly to refer to the objective behavioral responses to hypnotic procedures, whereas the term *depth* often refers to the phenomenological experience associated with alterations in awareness. Deepening procedures are designed to enhance both of these dimensions of hypnotic depth in order to maximize the likelihood of a positive clinical outcome.

Deepening strategies typically include direct suggestions for enhanced hypnotic depth (i.e., "You are becoming more and more deeply hypnotized"), imagery, and, at times, overt test suggestions designed to strengthen the patient's belief that response to the therapeutic suggestions will be positive. The challenge to the hypnotist is to avoid the experience of failure, which could diminish the patient's response to the therapeutic suggestions. This is typically achieved by strategies such as pseudochallenges (e.g., suggesting that patients cannot pull their hands apart without ever really challenging them to do so). Another strategy is to administer suggestions known to have a high probability of success (e.g., eye closure) while avoiding more difficult suggestions (e.g., negative hallucinations).

In its broadest sense, the selection and sequencing of therapeutic goals can also be viewed as a kind of "megadeepening" procedure, with benefits in responsivity being evidenced from one session to the next. Thus, the pain patient who seeks relief from pain can benefit by the pursuit of less ambitious therapeutic goals initially, such as enhanced exercise, relaxation, appropriate pacing of activities, decreased depression, increased energy, and so forth. Success in the pursuit of these goals can nourish a growing expectation that pain management can ultimately be successful.

Therapeutic Suggestions

The kinds of therapeutic suggestions used for relieving pain are much more critical to the success of the procedure than the kind of hypnotic induction used. In fact, after patient preparation, this is probably the most important phase of the hypnotic intervention. For example, Paul (1969) found that the administration of analgesia suggestions was more important than the administration of a hypnotic induction procedure in reducing experimental pain. Indeed, over the past 20 years, several studies have demonstrated that the administration of suggestions of analgesia, with or without a hypnotic procedure, can reduce experimentally produced pain (e.g., T. X. Barber & Cooper, 1972; Chaves & Barber, 1974b; Chaves & Doney, 1976; Worthington, 1978). Moreover, these and other studies have also revealed that even when external suggestions for pain relief have not been administered, subjects will frequently engage in self-generated cognitive strategies designed to reduce pain (Chaves & Barber, 1974a; Chaves & Brown, 1987). On the other hand, some subjects, referred to as "catastrophizers" (Chaves & Brown, 1978, 1987), spontaneously engage in mental processes that amplify the untoward effects of painful stimulation.

The following examples of spontaneous coping activities were elicited in the Chaves and Brown (1978, 1987) study. All of these patients were describing their mental activities during the administration of a mandibular block injection in preparation for either a restorative dental procedure or an extraction:

> Coper 1: "Just like placid thought, pictures and stuff . . . I let my mind wander . . . think on different things . . . look around and observe things in the room and let them bring my attention to them rather than what's going on in my mouth."
>
> Coper 2: "I just tried in a philosophic way not to identify with the body. You know it is just like a vehicle which is needing some repair and they are doing that mechanical repair. . . . To just negate is not enough . . . you have to have something to engage the mind so . . . I was thinking of a mantra."
>
> Coper 3: "I just try and prepare myself. You know it is going to hurt so I tell myself, 'Just be ready for it—think about something else' . . . and I tense up more or less when he puts it in and then I relax and that's about it."

The catastrophizing ideation elicited in the same study (Chaves & Brown, 1978, 1987) contrasts dramatically with these examples of coping:

> Catastrophizer 1: "How I hate it. I hate having injections. I think, 'Oh, no, here we go again.' I hate it with a passion. . . . Just to see

that great big needle coming down at you, the next thing you know you start going bananas. . . . It's so bad."

Catastrophizer 2: "You wonder what it feels like actually if you did not have any novocaine . . . what would it feel like. . . . You wonder what if it's going to hurt a lot after the injection is in . . . and mostly what I feel when he is giving me the shot is what if it wears off and starts hurting because I'm a chicken. You are concerned alright . . . wondering if something is going to go wrong."

Catastrophizer 3: "Oh, this is terrible because I'd like to kill him. I told him before, I don't like dentists because most of the time they don't care about me . . . and I'm just a blah and they can do anything they want, and I want them to say, 'Oh I know this is going to hurt, but I have to do it' . . . and then a little pat and then I feel better. But I just feel like any minute I'm going to receive a terrific, horrible pain."

Similar narratives have been elicited from chronic pain patients (J. Brown, Chaves, & Leonoff, 1981). The central point is that the hypnotic subject typically does not present the clinician with a tabula rasa on which suggestions can be inscribed without regard for what is already present. Accordingly, it can be extremely valuable to explore the patient's pain phenomenology to help gain an understanding of exactly how the pain is perceived as well as to aid in the identification of preexisting coping strategies or, alternatively, to identify themes related to the patient's manner of catastrophizing. In this way, the development of effective therapeutic suggestions can be a highly personal task that requires careful attention to the patient's pain phenomenology. Indeed, it would not be surprising if the efficacy of these procedures depended, in part, on the careful attention to the patient's experience this strategy requires, although this possibility has not been studied formally to my knowledge.

Once the patient's pain phenomenology has been fully determined, attention can then focus on developing therapeutically relevant suggestions. The central theme here is the development of goal-directed fantasies (Spanos, 1971; Spanos & Barber, 1972). Goal-directed fantasies require patients to imagine situations that, if objectively real, would be consistent with the therapeutic goal of attenuating or abolishing pain. It is irrelevant whether the imagined situation could be objectively real. Thus, for example, imagining that a painful part of the body is disconnected from the rest of the body can be therapeutically beneficial regardless of whether such an "amputation" would be anatomically possible or desirable.

A wide range of strategies can be used for reducing clinical pain. Somewhat different strategies are used for acute and chronic pain. Acute pain, such as that which can occur during painful medical and dental procedures, is frequently accompanied by high levels of anxiety. Accordingly, suggestions for an increased pain threshold and a decreased pain magnitude are often accompanied by suggestions designed to reduce anxiety. This may include direct suggestions for anxiety reduction or less direct procedures such as mental rehearsal of a forthcoming medical or dental procedure with concomitant suggestions for the use of certain cognitive strategies for pain reduction at critical points during the procedure.

In chronic pain, the predominant affect is depression rather than anxiety. Accordingly, pain-related suggestions are frequently embedded in a wider array of suggestions designed to address the presenting symptoms of depression, such as anhedonia, anergia, impaired appetite, and so on.

Another distinction is that in the case of acute pain, it is often possible and desirable to administer hypnotic suggestions prior to pain onset. Although there are relatively few data on this issue, it appears that acute pain may be more effectively managed when suggestions are administered prior to pain onset whenever possible (Chaves & Scott, 1979).

The following strategies can be used for pain reduction with either chronic or acute pain:

1. Numbness: Suggest that a painful part of the body is numb and insensitive—as if it were made of rubber—as if it had been injected with local anesthetic and feels swollen, numb, and insensitive.
2. Distraction: The patient's attention is deflected away from the pain and refocused on another part of the body, his or her breathing, innocuous environmental stimuli, pleasant fantasies, and so on, with additional suggestions for enhanced comfort.
3. Transformation of the pain sensation: Use suggestions designed to reduce the area of pain, to move it to another part of the body where it is more benign, or to alter the quality of the pain sensation.
4. Use direct suggestions for pain attenuation.
5. Perform a cognitive analysis of the pain: Use suggestions designed to analyze the pain sensations into more benign components such as pressure, heat, cold, tingling, throbbing, and so forth.
6. Simple distraction: Facilitating absorption in a pattern of thought leaves less attention available to be focused on the pain.
7. Time distortion: Suggest that episodes of pain will be subjectively brief but that pain-free periods will seem to last forever.
8. Dissociation: Have the patient mentally amputate a body part, have an out-of-body experience, or think about the body in a detached, mechanistic way.

9. Age regression–progression: These suggestions are designed to promote absorption in thoughts, ideas, and feelings that were enjoyable prior to pain onset or that will be enjoyable in the future.

10. Transformation of the painful stimulus into a benign one: Have the patient visualize that an injection is about to be given with a foam rubber needle.

11. Pain acknowledging: Use suggestions designed to acknowledge the pain, reduce catastrophizing, and emphasize the ability to cope with the pain while remaining comfortable.

12. Modification of catastrophizing ideation: Use suggestions that mitigate the specific catastrophizing thoughts or images revealed by the patient.

13. Thermal imagery: This is often used for migraine patients, usually with suggestions for peripheral (hand and foot) warming and central (head) cooling. The rationale for this strategy is that suggestions for warming or cooling produce alterations in the patterns of peripheral and cerebral blood flow that, in turn, are thought to be critical in controlling the neurovascular instability that is believed to be the basis for the underlying pathophysiology of migraine headaches (Diamond & Friedman, 1983). Suggestions for cooling can also be used with patients suffering from causalgic syndromes, sympathetic reflex dystrophy, and some types of central pain, for similar reasons.

These categories do not exhaust the universe of pain-relieving strategies that can be used, although most of the commonly used generic strategies are included. Most commonly, these and related strategies are used in combinations that are relevant to the patient's unique circumstances and coping resources. Clinicians do not know at this time whether these strategies produce their beneficial effects in the same way (e.g., by distracting patients) or whether different strategies work for different reasons. More clinical research, along the lines of that conducted by Wack and Turk (1984), who reported some factor-analytic studies of coping strategies, will be needed to answer that question.

Posthypnotic Suggestions and Termination

Ordinarily, the hypnotic session concludes with suggestions designed to facilitate generalization of therapeutic gains following the termination of the hypnotic session. Commonly, suggestions are administered that certain stimulus cues in patients' homes or work environments will evoke the feelings of well-being and increased comfort experienced during the hypnotic session itself. Sometimes, generalization can be facilitated by teaching patients a self-hypnotic procedure. These have the advantage of enhancing patients' sense of self-control. My own experience, however, indicates that pain patients respond better when they are provided with audiotapes of the hypnotic procedure that they are typically instructed to use on a daily basis. In one previously reported case of phantom limb pain (Chaves, 1986), the use of audiotapes proved decisive in achieving a positive clinical outcome. In each case, the tapes used were recordings of hypnotic procedures used personally with the patient.

The goal of pain management with hypnosis is framed for patients as a skill that will get better with practice. As more is learned about patients' experiences with their pain and their coping mechanisms, as well as their responses to previous hypnotic procedures, new hypnotic procedures will be developed and implemented on an iterative basis. This process continues until diminishing returns cast doubt on the efficacy of continued hypnotic work, although occasional "booster" sessions can be useful. It is not uncommon for patients to report better responses to hypnotic procedures that are conducted "live" rather than taped. I illustrate some of the considerations that have been discussed by providing an illustrative case.

CASE MATERIAL

The patient was a 48-year-old divorced Black woman who presented with phantom limb pain of 4 years' duration. Her right leg had been amputated above midthigh because of an acute circulatory crisis. Several weeks had elapsed prior to the decision to amputate, during which time the patient was in extreme pain that was not well controlled by medication. She became aware of the phantom limb, accompanying stump, and phantom pain immediately following amputation. The stump pain responded to medication and was quickly resolved; however, the phantom pain remained. The patient rated her pain at a constant 65–70 on a 100-point scale and reported that nothing seemed to either exacerbate or diminish it. She had been fitted with three prostheses over the years, none of which was tolerable for her, so she expected she would continue to use a walker for the rest of her life. She was not assertive in her interactions with health care providers, family members, or co-workers.

Her phantom limb was initially described as being somewhat smaller than her actual limb had been. Phenomenologically, she described the following elements of her pain: (a) pain around the medial aspect of her phantom ankle that was characterized as "like biting ants crawling up," (b) pain around her phantom knee and thigh that was described as being "like thousands of tight rubber bands," and (c) the feeling of muscular tension in the phantom limb accompanied by the sensation that the phantom leg was positioned uncomfortably.

Discussions regarding therapeutic goals with this patient focused on pain management rather than elimination. Because of high expectations regarding hypnosis, the patient initially expressed a reluctance to pursue any goal except complete elimination of her pain. I posed questions such as, "Would you feel it worthwhile to work with me if we could reduce your pain by 25%? 50%? 75%?" Presented in this way, the patient agreed that it would be worth it even if the pain reduction achieved was only 25%. We started with the view that we would hope for the best but accept what relief could be achieved.

To help sensitize her to variations in pain levels, I initially asked her to rate her pain levels on an hourly basis. This quickly revealed and helped her to focus attention on subtle variations in her pain levels, of which she had been unaware. It also helped in identifying stressors, many of which involved her difficulties in being assertive. For example, she arrived at one early session about 10 min late, sweating profusely and looking exhausted. She revealed that her son had been unable to find a parking spot in front of the building and therefore had to park at the bottom of a hill some distance from the office. The walk to my office had been extremely arduous for her. When I asked her why she had not asked her son to drop her off, she looked at me with utter astonishment. The thought had never even crossed her mind.

The patient believed that she would be a good hypnotic subject, although she expressed only vague notions about what the hypnotic experience would be like or how hypnosis would be induced. She did believe that hypnosis could "turn off" her pain. I explained that phantom limb pain, although unquestionably real, can sometimes be better thought of as a memory rather than a sensation. Thus, medications that help to relieve other kinds of pain do not seem to help people with phantom pain. However, learning to think about the phantom limb and the pain in new ways could help her to be more comfortable. Hypnosis was presented as a tool that could help her to achieve that goal.

The patient was a willing and capable hypnotic subject who responded readily to an eye-closure induction. However, when attention was focused on her phantom limb, her lower body responded with repeated muscular spasms that seemed to originate in her stump and spread throughout her body. These abated after several trials, which included suggestions for relaxation and diminished awareness of the phantom limb, together with suggestions that the phantom limb was growing smaller.

Initial therapeutic suggestions included greater comfort in being aware of and asking for what she needed and more interest in socializing and other activities that would help her to refocus attention outside of herself. After she reported positive responses to these suggestions, we then moved on to focus on the pain sensations themselves. The ants crawling up her ankle were decapitated and were falling to the floor. With the sharpest scissors in the world she took one rubber band after the other, cutting it and watching it fly across the room. With each of these events, she was encouraged to take a deep breath and feel the relief. Although there were lots of ants and lots of rubber bands, she knew that she could continue her work with them whenever she wished. Diminished awareness of the phantom limb was suggested through images of a dense fog creeping in along the floor and gathering around her phantom foot and moving up and swallowing it. Each hypnotic session was audiotaped, and she was asked to use her tapes a minimum of once each day.

Between hypnotic sessions, other issues were discussed, with emphasis on the problems of being a Black, middle-aged, physically challenged, divorced woman in American society and the implications for employment and social life. Meanwhile, her pain levels were falling to an average of about 30 on the 100-point scale and, for the first time, she reported occasional periods when she was entirely pain free. The phantom limb appeared to be shrinking, a common experience of amputees (Melzack & Wall, 1988; Petrie, 1967). Her pain-free periods made her optimistic that continued work on her hypnotic skills on her own may make her goal of being pain free achievable. However, in the meantime, she was able to enjoy her reduced pain levels. As her general pain levels have diminished, she has become even more sensitive to the role of emotional factors in precipitating exacerbations of her pain. These have also made it clear, to her surprise, that drops in barometric pressure increase her pain.

The combination of her reduced pain and increasing assertiveness led her to another effort, this time successful, to use a prosthesis. She continues to be seen on about a monthly basis while she tackles her next problem: resuming driving her automobile. Fear of painful spasms has been the primary obstacle for her, but she is already driving in parking lots with her son, to prepare for this next step.

Obviously, the therapeutic interaction with this patient has been complex, multifaceted, and consistent with the perspective of D. P. Brown and Fromm (1986), who emphasized the multimodal character of hypnotic interventions for pain management. It is by no means clear which variables were instrumental and which were irrelevant in achieving her clinical goals. Nevertheless, given the intractability of phantom limb pain and the poor clinical results achieved with other treatments for phantom limb pain (Sherman, Gall, & Gormaly, 1979; Sherman, Sherman, & Gall, 1980; Sherman, Sherman, & Parker, 1984), a good case can be made for the use of hypnotic treatment in this case (Chaves, 1986, 1989).

RELATED RESEARCH

The past 30 years of research in clinical and experimental hypnosis probably represents something of a golden era in the field. The field is vigorous, with many active research laboratories producing good fundamental research. Theoretical conflicts are helping researchers to sharpen their views and their arguments and generate new and interesting data. Within this context, research in clinical hypnosis, particularly in pain management, is somewhat disappointing. The clinical literature remains largely anecdotal, and clinical interventions are sometimes not described at all (Chaves, 1989; Wadden & Anderton, 1982). The role of contextual factors in hypnotic pain management is frequently underemphasized even though elaborate preoperative preparation protocols used in some studies clearly included nonhypnotic variables that could have played an important role in reducing pain (Chaves, 1989; J. R. Hilgard & LeBaron, 1984).

Outcome measures are frequently not provided in clinical studies of the use of hypnotic interventions for pain management (Chaves, 1989). Clearly, more systematically gathered data are necessary in which multiple outcome measures are used. Similarly, the assessment of hypnotizability in clinical studies must reflect an awareness of recent evidence that the relationship between hypnotizability and clinical outcome may depend critically on the context in which hypnotizability is assessed (Spanos, 1989).

Preexisting pain-coping strategies have frequently been ignored in designing or assessing pain-management strategies in some of the most systematic studies on hypnotic pain management conducted to date. For example, J. R. Hilgard and LeBaron (1984) found that in baseline pain measures on 63 children undergoing bone-marrow aspiration, the 18 children with the lowest pain levels all reported using spontaneous coping mechanisms to deal with their pain. Yet, in another study designed to evaluate the effects of hypnotic suggestion in reducing pain associated with bone-marrow aspiration, the use of imagery was avoided in the control condition (D. P. Brown & Fromm, 1987; Zeltzer & LeBaron, 1982). The apparent efficacy of hypnotic treatments can be altered by using control conditions that either explicitly include or exclude control subjects who use effective spontaneous coping strategies.

CONCLUSION

In this chapter I have presented a cognitive–behavioral perspective on the clinical use of hypnosis for pain management. The cognitive–behavioral perspective is characterized by a broad-ranging concern for the multifaceted nature of hypnotic interventions (Spanos & Chaves, 1989a,

1989b). The importance of patients' attitudes, expectations, and beliefs are emphasized, as are contextual and cognitive factors that can modulate the pain experience. Particular attention is focused on ways of combining these variables to maximize clinical outcomes. Because the cognitive–behavioral approach does not center on the concept of a hypnotic trance state, researchers search elsewhere in their quest to understand the nature of pain modulation in the hypnotic context.

Although traditional hypnotic-state theorists have sometimes argued that cognitive–behavioral theorists see nothing special about hypnosis (e.g., E. R. Hilgard, 1971), it can be argued that the real disagreement is about where the "specialness" resides. The hypnotic context *is* special in terms of the unique array of attitudes, expectations, and beliefs it engenders, as well as its strategic emphasis on cognitive–behavioral modification. In fact, it has been argued that clinical hypnosis has been an important precursor of contemporary cognitive–behavioral modification (Krasner, 1971).

What is needed now is a greater emphasis on clinical research by those working within the cognitive–behavioral perspective. Although this perspective has had enormous heuristic value for investigators doing basic research in hypnosis, little attention has been given to the clinical implications of this viewpoint. Freedom from a theoretical commitment to the hypnotic trance state may open many new research avenues to those with an interest in clinical hypnosis.

REFERENCES

Alman, G. M., & Carney, R. E. (1980). Consequences of direct and indirect suggestions on success of posthypnotic behavior. *American Journal of Clinical Hypnosis, 23,* 112–118.

Barber, J. (1977). Rapid induction analgesia: A clinical report. *American Journal of Clinical Hypnosis, 19,* 138–149.

Barber, J. (1980). Hypnosis and the unhypnotizable. *American Journal of Clinical Hypnosis, 23,* 4–9.

Barber, T. X. (1963). The effects of "hypnosis" on pain: A critical review of experimental and clinical findings. *Psychosomatic Medicine, 25,* 303–333.

Barber, T. X., & Calverley, D. S. (1964). The definition of the situation as a variable affecting "hypnotic-like" suggestibility. *Journal of Clinical Psychology, 20,* 438–440.

Barber, T. X., & Cooper, B. (1972). Effects on pain of experimentally induced and spontaneous distraction. *Psychological Reports, 31,* 647–651.

Barber, T. X., Spanos, N. P., & Chaves, J. F. (1974). *Hypnotism: Imagination and human potentialities.* Elmsford, NY: Pergamon Press.

Bertrand, L. D. (1989). The assessment and modification of hypnotic susceptibility.

In N. P. Spanos & J. F. Chaves (Eds.), *Hypnosis: The cognitive–behavioral perspective* (pp. 18–31). Buffalo, NY: Prometheus Books.

Brown, D. P., & Fromm, E. (1986). *Hypnotherapy and hypnoanalysis*. Hillsdale, NJ: Erlbaum.

Brown, D. P., & Fromm, E. (1987). *Hypnosis and behavioral medicine*. Hillsdale, NJ: Erlbaum.

Brown, J., Chaves, J. F., & Leonoff, A. (1981, August). *Spontaneous hypnotic strategies in two groups of chronic pain patients*. Paper presented at the 89th Annual Convention of the American Psychological Association, Los Angeles.

Cangello, V. W. (1961). The use of hypnotic suggestion for pain relief in malignant disease. *International Journal of Clinical and Experimental Hypnosis, 9*, 17–22.

Cangello, V. W. (1962). Hypnosis for the patient with cancer. *American Journal of Clinical Hypnosis, 4*, 215–216.

Chaves, J. F. (1986). Hypnosis in the management of phantom limb pain. In T. Dowd & J. Healy (Eds.), *Case studies in hypnotherapy* (pp. 198–209). New York: Guilford Press.

Chaves, J. F. (1989). Hypnotic control of clinical pain. In N. P. Spanos & J. F. Chaves (Eds.), *Hypnosis: The cognitive–behavioral perspective*. Buffalo, NY: Prometheus Books.

Chaves, J. F., & Barber, T. X. (1974a). Acupuncture analgesia: A six factor theory. *Psychoenergetic Systems, 1*, 11–21.

Chaves, J. F., & Barber, T. X. (1974b). Cognitive strategies, experimenter modeling, and expectation in the attenuation of pain. *Journal of Abnormal Psychology, 83*, 356–363.

Chaves, J. F., & Barber, T. X. (1976). Hypnotic procedures and surgery: A critical analysis with applications to "acupuncture analgesia." *American Journal of Clinical Hypnosis, 18*, 217–236.

Chaves, J. F., & Brown, J. F. (1978, August–September). *Self-generated strategies for the control of clinical pain and stress*. Paper presented at the 86th Annual Convention of the American Psychological Association, Toronto.

Chaves, J. F., & Brown, J. M. (1987). Spontaneous coping strategies for pain. *Journal of Behavioral Medicine, 10*, 263–276.

Chaves, J. F., & Doney, T. (1976, April). *Cognitive alteration of pain: The role of strategy relevance, absorption, and expectation*. Paper presented at the annual meeting of the Association for the Advancement of Behavior Therapy, New York.

Chaves, J. F., & Scott, D. (1979, April). *Effects of cognitive strategies and suggested criterion alteration on pain threshold*. Paper presented at the annual meeting of the Eastern Psychological Association, Philadelphia.

Coe, W. C., & Ryken, K. (1979). Hypnosis and risks to human subjects. *American Psychologist, 34*, 673–681.

Crasilneck, H. B., & Hall, J. A. (1975). *Clinical hypnosis: Principles and applications*. New York: Grune & Stratton.

Diamond, S., & Friedman, A. P. (1983). *Headache*. New Hyde Park, NY: Medical Examination Publishing.

Dingwall, E. J. (1967). *Abnormal hypnotic phenomena* (Vol. 1). London: Churchill.

Erickson, M. H. (1938a). A study of clinical and experimental findings on hypnotic deafness: I. Clinical experimentation and findings. *Journal of General Psychology, 19,* 127–150.

Erickson, M. H. (1938b). A study of clinical and experimental findings on hypnotic deafness: II. Experimental findings with a conditioned response technique. *Journal of General Psychology, 19,* 151–167.

Ficton, J. R., & Roth, P. (1985). The effects of direct and indirect hypnotic suggestions for analgesia in high and low susceptible patients. *American Journal of Clinical Hypnosis, 27,* 226–231.

Gorassini, D. R., & Spanos, N. P. (1986). A social-cognitive skills training program for the successful modification of hypnotic susceptibility. *Journal of Personality and Social Psychology, 50,* 1004–1012.

Hilgard, E. R. (1971). Hypnotic phenomena: The struggle for scientific acceptance. *American Scientist, 59,* 567–577.

Hilgard, E. R. (1986). *Divided consciousness: Multiple controls in human thought and action*. New York: Wiley.

Hilgard, E. R., & Hilgard, J. R. (1975). *Hypnosis in the relief of pain*. Los Altos, CA: Kaufmann.

Hilgard, J. R., & LeBaron, S. (1984). *Hypnotherapy of children with pain*. Los Altos, CA: Kaufmann.

Kirsch, I. (1986). Role playing versus response expectancy and explanations of hypnotic behavior. *Behavioral and Brain Sciences, 9,* 475–476.

Kirsch, I., & Council, J. R. (1989). Response expectancy as a determinant of hypnotic behavior. In N. P. Spanos & J. F. Chaves (Eds.), *Hypnosis: The cognitive–behavioral perspective* (pp. 360–379). Buffalo, NY: Prometheus Books.

Krasner, L. (1971). Behavior therapy. *Annual Review of Psychology, 22,* 483–532.

Kroger, W. S. (1977). *Clinical and experimental hypnosis* (2nd ed.). Philadelphia: Lippincott.

Lozanov, G. (1967). Anaesthetization through suggestion in a state of wakefulness. In *Proceedings of the Seventh European Conference on Psychosomatic Research* (pp. 399–402). Rome.

Lynn, S. J., Neufeld, V., & Matyi, C. L. (1987). Hypnotic inductions versus suggestions: The effects of direct and indirect wording. *Journal of Abnormal Psychology, 96,* 76–80.

Lynn, S. J., Rhue, J. W., & Weekes, J. R. (1989). Hypnosis and experienced nonvolition: A social–cognitive integrative model. In N. P. Spanos & J. F. Chaves (Eds.), *Hypnosis: The cognitive–behavioral perspective* (pp. 78–109). Buffalo, NY: Prometheus Books.

Matthews, W. J., Bennett, H., Bean, W., & Gallagher, M. (1985). Indirect versus direct hypnotic suggestions—An initial investigation: A brief communication. *International Journal of Clinical and Experimental Hypnosis, 3*, 219–223.

Melzack, R., & Wall, P. (1988). *The challenge of pain* (2nd ed.). New York: Penguin Books.

Orne, M. T. (1959). The nature of hypnosis: Artifact and essence. *Journal of Abnormal and Social Psychology, 58*, 277–299.

Pattie, F. A. (1935). A report of attempts to produce uniocular blindness by hypnotic suggestion. *British Journal of Medical Psychology, 15*, 230–241.

Paul G. (1969). Physiological effects of relaxation training and hypnotic suggestion. *Journal of Abnormal Psychology, 74*, 425–437.

Petrie, A. (1967). *Individuality in pain and suffering.* Chicago: University of Chicago Press.

Radke, H. L. (1989). Hypnotic depth as social artifact. In N. P. Spanos & J. F. Chaves (Eds.), *Hypnosis: The cognitive–behavioral perspective* (pp. 64–75). Buffalo, NY: Prometheus Books.

Sherman, R. A., Gall, N., & Gormaly, J. (1979). Treatment of phantom limb pain with muscular relaxation training to disrupt the pain-anxiety-tension cycle. *Pain, 6*, 47–56.

Sherman, R. A., Sherman, C. J., & Gall, N. G. (1980). A survey of current phantom limb pain treatments in the United States. *Pain, 8*, 85–100.

Sherman, R. A., Sherman, C. J., & Parker, L. (1984). Chronic phantom and stump pain among American veterans: Results of a survey. *Pain, 18*, 83–96.

Spanos, N. P. (1971). Goal-directed fantasy and the performance of hypnotic test suggestions. *Psychiatry, 34*, 86–96.

Spanos, N. P. (1986). Hypnotic behavior: A social psychological interpretation of amnesia, analgesia and trance logic. *Behavioral and Brain Sciences, 9*, 449–467.

Spanos, N. P. (1989). Experimental research on hypnotic analgesia. In N. P. Spanos & J. F. Chaves (Eds.), *Hypnosis: The cognitive–behavioral perspective* (pp. 206–240). Buffalo, NY: Prometheus Books.

Spanos, N. P., & Barber, T. X. (1972). Cognitive activity during "hypnotic" suggestibility: Goal-directed fantasy and the experience of nonvolition. *Journal of Personality, 40*, 510–524.

Spanos, N. P., & Chaves, J. F. (1989a). The cognitive–behavioral alternative in hypnosis research. In N. P. Spanos & J. F. Chaves (Eds.), *Hypnosis: The cognitive–behavioral perspective* (pp. 9–16). Buffalo, NY: Prometheus Books.

Spanos, N. P., & Chaves, J. F. (1989b). Future prospects for the cognitive–behavioral perspective. In N. P. Spanos & J. F. Chaves (Eds.), *Hypnosis: The cognitive–behavioral perspective* (pp. 437–446). Buffalo, NY: Prometheus Books.

Spanos, N. P., & Chaves, J. F. (1989c). Hypnotic analgesia, surgery and reports of nonvolitional pain reduction. *British Journal of Experimental and Clinical Hypnosis*, 6, 131–139.

Spanos, N. P., Cross, W. P., Menary, E. P., Brett, P. J., & de Groh, M. (1987). Attitudinal and imaginal ability predictors of social cognitive skill-training enhancements in hypnotic susceptibility. *Personality and Social Psychology Bulletin*, 13, 379–398.

Spanos, N. P., de Groh, M., & de Groot, H. P. (1987). Skill training for enhancing hypnotic susceptibility and word list amnesia. *British Journal of Experimental and Clinical Hypnosis*, 4, 15–23.

Spanos, N. P., Robertson, L. A., Menary, E. P., & Brett, P. J. (1986). Component analysis of cognitive skill training for the enhancement of hypnotic susceptibility. *Journal of Abnormal Psychology*, 95, 350–357.

Stone, J. A., & Lundy, R. M. (1985). Behavioral compliance with direct and indirect body movement suggestions. *Journal of Abnormal Psychology*, 94, 256–263.

Trent, J. C. (1946). Surgical anesthesia. *Journal of the History of Medicine*, 1, 505–511.

Tuckey, C. L. (1889). Psychotherapeutics, or treatment by hypnotism. *Woods Medical and Surgical Monographs*, 3, 721–795.

Udolph, R. (1987). *Handbook of hypnosis for professionals* (2nd ed.). New York: Van Nostrand Reinhold.

Wack, J. T., & Turk, D. C. (1984). Latent structure of strategies used to cope with nociceptive stimulation. *Health Psychology*, 3, 27–43.

Wadden, T. A., & Anderton, C. H. (1982). The clinical use of hypnosis. *Psychological Bulletin*, 91, 215–243.

Worthington, E. L., Jr. (1978). The effects of imagery content, choice of imagery content, and self-verbalization on the self-control of pain. *Cognitive Therapy and Research*, 2, 225–240.

Zeltzer, L., & LeBaron, S. (1982). Hypnotic and nonhypnotic techniques for reduction of pain and anxiety during painful procedures in children and adolescents with cancer. *Journal of Pediatrics*, 101, 1032–1035.

25

HYPNOSIS IN THE TREATMENT OF OBESITY

EUGENE E. LEVITT

The causes of obesity or overweight (the terms are sometimes differ-entiated by degree and sometimes used interchangeably) are complex. Many investigations have shown that grossly overweight individuals have more emotional disturbance and more neurotic traits than do people of normal weight, but no study has ever linked obesity to any particular syndrome or specific psychological problem. A circumspect view is that it has multiple causes, including metabolic, neurological, and socioeconomic, as well as psychological, factors (Rodin, 1982; Swanson & Dinello, 1970).

Etiology aside, excessive caloric intake is an endemic problem in the United States. It has been estimated that there are 40 to 80 million obese Americans, depending on the criteria for obesity (Stuart & Davis, 1972). A survey carried out more than 25 years ago indicated that almost 10 million Americans were dieting and that another 42 million were concerned about their weight (Wyden, 1965).

The author gratefully acknowledges the technical and clerical assistance provided by JoAnn Switzer, Jeanne Wilson, and Susan Alloway.

So it is not at all surprising that the recent decades have seen a proliferation of self-administered techniques for losing weight. These range from various types of diets, including some that seem bizarre, to chemical devices and drugs. Fifteen years ago, the Federal Food and Drug Administration estimated that 10 million Americans spend at least a half a billion dollars annually on these regimens (Hafen, 1975).

Overeating, like cigarette smoking, is a pathogenetic behavior that is self-initiated and therefore should be subject to voluntary control. Thus, it is not at all surprising that psychotherapy and behavior modification should be noted among the potential remedial procedures. However, surprisingly little attention has been paid in the medical and psychological literature to the possibilities involved in the use of hypnosis.

Authoritative sources on the treatment of obesity have described remedial procedures that include visceral bypass, jaw wiring, panniculectomy, acupuncture, and drugs, as well as formal psychotherapy and behavior modification (Bray, 1975; Enzi, Crepaldi, Pozza, & Renold, 1981; Garrow, 1978; Kallen & Sussman, 1984; Stunkard, 1976, 1980). Hypnosis was not mentioned in any of these texts. A recent, detailed review of dietary and behavioral treatment approaches did not include any reference to hypnosis (Garner & Wooley, 1991).

Chlouverakis (1975) devoted only a single, short paragraph to hypnosis in his review of treatments of obesity. None of the nearly two dozen articles on obesity treatment in the Hafen (1975) compendium dealt with hypnotherapy. Leon (1976) lumped hypnosis with individual psychotherapy in a brief overview; she concluded that

> the literature on the use of individual psychotherapy and hypnosis in treating obesity suggests that these procedures are effective only in isolated cases. Specific statistics on weight loss and follow-up information is almost uniformly lacking, and the majority of reports are individual case histories. (p. 569)

The present review was undertaken to follow up earlier reviews by Mott and Roberts (1979) and Wadden and Anderton (1982) and to attempt to determine whether there may be a particular weight control program that is potentiated significantly by hypnosis.

TREATMENT PROCEDURES

Specific techniques involved in the reports of the use of hypnosis as a method of treating obesity have varied considerably.

The use of direct suggestions in the trance, as either the primary or the only procedure, was advocated mostly in the earlier reports (e.g., Aja, 1977; Glover, 1961; Kroger, 1970; Spiegel & Spiegel, 1978; Winkelstein,

1959), but almost all hypnotherapy weight control programs include some direct suggestions. Some of the recommended direct suggestions are succinct:

> You will not crave for food that you should not wish to eat (for example sugar and sweets. . .). You will easily remember to avoid these items and you will find your ability to remain on this diet becoming stronger and more automatic each day . . . you will simply not crave these items of food. (Crasilneck & Hall, 1975, p. 160)

At the other end of the spectrum, the suggestions used by Spiegel and Spiegel (1978) require almost five pages of text, over 2,000 words. This approach has been summarized as influencing the patient to "restructure" his attitude toward eating by "relating to his body in a responsible and protective way" and eating "with respect for your body" (Spiegel & DeBetz, 1978).

Most of the direct suggestions are authoritarian and positive. A negative suggestion is sometimes embedded within the positive suggestions in an attempt to create aversion to undesirable foods by associating them with nausea, revulsion, and repugnant tastes and odors (e.g., Barabasz & Spiegel, 1989; Deyoub & Wilkie, 1980; Kroger, 1970; Walker, Collins, & Krass, 1982). The degree of emphasis given to negative suggestion has usually not been noted. M. M. Miller (1974, 1976) is an exception. His technique consisted largely of negative suggestions and was frankly labeled "hypnoaversion." Patients were requested to "relive a past nauseant and highly disagreeable experience of a toxic type," which was then associated with ingestion of high-calorie foods (M. M. Miller, 1974, p. 480).

It is not unusual for a hypnotic approach to be coupled with behavior modification tactics (e.g., Bolocofsky, Spinler, & Coulthard-Morris, 1985; Bornstein & Devine, 1980; Channon, 1980; Collins, Jupp, & Krass, 1981; Wadden & Flaxman, 1981), although the specific behavior-shaping methodology is usually only briefly described. In fact, it is not unreasonable to stipulate that every program that aims to alter eating patterns beyond simply prescribing a diet uses behavior modification tactics, even if they are not formally labeled as such. A theoretical "hypnobehavioral model" for treating obesity was formulated by Kroger and Fezler (1976). Most of the proposed techniques reflect the prototypical work on the shaping of eating behavior (Ferster, Nurnberger, & Levitt, 1962).

Imagery is often used as an adjunct within the weight-control hypnotherapy regimen (e.g., Andersen, 1985; Channon, 1980; Cochrane & Friesen, 1986; Cohen & Alpert, 1978; Goldstein, 1981; Kroger, 1970; Stanton, 1975; Wadden & Flaxman, 1981). The content is variable; an image of the self at the goal weight, and preparing and eating low-calorie foods or generally engaging in healthy eating behavior, is the most common. Imagery in a weight control program was uniquely used by Kline (1982) to "significantly enhance feelings of well-being" by visualizing printed words such as *relax, confidence,* and *patience.*

Ego-enhancing suggestions are given in trance in a number of weight control programs (e.g., Andersen, 1985; Cochrane & Friesen, 1986; Crasilneck & Hall, 1975; Hanley, 1967; Hartman, 1977; Jupp, Collins, McCabe, & Walker, 1986; Stanton, 1975). The actual content of such suggestions is seldom specified, but a logical assumption is that the text is intended to buttress the patient/subject's confidence and belief in his or her capacity to follow the program.

Self-hypnosis is another feature of the weight-control hypnotherapy programs (e.g., Aja, 1977; Andersen, 1985; Brodie, 1964; Deyoub & Wilkie, 1980; Kroger, 1977; Spiegel & Spiegel, 1978). Usually, it has been simply noted that self-hypnosis was taught to the patients/subjects with the direction that the tactic be used when necessary. Kline (1982) specified that self-hypnosis was to be practiced at four points during the day for about 15 min each. Bolocofsky, Coulthard-Morris, and Spinler (1984) prescribed the use of self-hypnosis at least daily for at least 4 days. Bolocofsky et al. (1985) recommended its use before each meal. In some programs, audiotapes were given to the patient/subject (e.g., Cochrane & Friesen, 1986; Davis & Dawson, 1980; Stanton, 1975).

Group procedures have been commonly used (e.g., Andersen, 1985; Barabasz & Spiegel, 1989; Bolocofsky et al., 1984; Channon, 1980; Cohen & Alpert, 1978; Davis & Dawson, 1980; Goldstein, 1981; M. M. Miller, 1974; Stanton, 1975; Wadden & Flaxman, 1981; Winkelstein, 1959). Individual sessions have been less often reported (e.g., Aja, 1977; Bornstein & Devine, 1980; Deyoub, 1979a, 1979b; Deyoub & Wilkie, 1980; Glover, 1961). The preference for group treatment probably reflects an economy of time and effort. Cochrane and Friesen (1986) used a mixed method in which hypnosis was induced in group sessions and deepened in individual sessions. Treatment per se was accomplished in group sessions, but individual hypnotic sessions were "used to facilitate the identification of unconscious weight-related issues" (p. 490).

The Macquarie University Weight Control Program uniquely permitted participants to choose individual or group treatment (Collins et al., 1981). However, there was some confusion on this point in the two outcome reports of the Macquarie program (Jupp et al., 1986; McCabe, Collins, Jupp, Walker, & Sutton, 1983). The later report does not note the structure of the sessions, whereas the earlier report states that subjects were "assigned at random" to either individual or group sessions. However, it would appear that the McCabe et al. subjects were indeed allowed to choose, because there were 34 subjects who underwent individual treatment and only 10 in groups of 5.

In any event, the McCabe et al. (1983) report is the only available comparison of group and individual hypnotherapy for obesity. Group participants had lost a mean of 18.1 pounds at the close of treatment, compared with 15.8 pounds for the individually treated subjects, a difference that is not significant.

The Macquarie program, which appears unfortunately to have ended prematurely, gave an unusually detailed description of treatment procedures. Four "scripts" were formulated with precise verbiage dealing with new eating habits, exercise, coping with tension, and increasing control and self-esteem (Walker et al., 1982). Two other unique features of the Macquarie program were anthropometric measurements of subjects (weight loss was found to be related to arm, leg, torso, and skinfold measurements [Collins, Jupp, & McCabe, 1987] but not to measures of height, the pelvis, body surface area, or fingertip span [McCabe, Jupp, & Collins, 1985]) and the use of a Polaroid television technique that allowed the subject to display his or her perceived current self-image, an ideal self-image, and a treatment goal self-image. Reliability data for this latter innovative tactic have been reported apart from the project (Collins, 1986, 1987). Data from the project itself suggest that this photographic adjunct may have influenced weight loss, but no relationship with outcome has been reported (Collins, McCabe, Jupp, & Sutton, 1983). Summaries of techniques for the hypnotherapy of obesity can be found in Kroger and Fezler (1976) and Pratt, Wood, and Alman (1984).

TREATMENT OUTCOME

Case Reports

The literature includes a number of reports of individual cases of obesity treated by hypnotherapy (e.g., Cochrane, 1987; Crasilneck & Hall, 1975; Erickson, 1960; Hershman, 1955; Kamens, 1966; Kline, 1982; Mott, 1979; Pearce, 1988; Pratt et al., 1984; Winkelstein, 1959; Wollman, 1962). In many of the cases, success was claimed with no more than a few direct suggestions. Other cases were sketchily presented so that not much can be learned from them. Exceptions are the two cases presented by Pratt et al. (1984) and the three cases described by Erickson (1960), which nicely illustrate the application of classical Ericksonian tactics to the hypnotherapy of weight reduction.

Quantified Outcome Reports

Outcome reports of the treatment of obesity using hypnosis are found in a variety of forms. Some, as shown in the previous section, are case reports. Others offer data summaries, but their approach, including the number of sessions, is still tailored to suit the needs of the individual patient/

subject. A few reports are clearly experimental; the treatment procedure is standardized.

Data have been reported in different formats. Beginning weights for a group of patients or subjects are usually given as a mean but sometimes as a percentage overweight. Not all reports give a beginning weight, the number of sessions, the duration of the regimen, and follow-up data. Less than half used control groups, and a majority of the reports failed to indicate whether patient/subject weights were self-reported or measured by the investigator.

Data from 20 reports[1] are presented in Table 1. An attempt will be made to summarize the data from the table but the variations in technique and reporting from report to report render summaries somewhat questionable.

Among the 10 reports giving patient/subject attrition, the mean loss was 22.6%. Losses were due to a variety of causes including premature termination, insufficient responsiveness, and statistical concerns.

The range of pretreatment weights was 154–228 pounds, with a crude median of 182 pounds. The crude median weight loss at the close of treatment for the 16 reports providing this data was 7 pounds. The median follow-up interval for 14 studies was 24 weeks; this is also the modal datum. At follow-up, the median additional weight loss was reported as 10 pounds. All reports showed weight loss at all measurement points, with the exception of the follow-up by Wadden and Flaxman (1981).

Measurement at a follow-up point appears to be time-related. Of the 8 reports published prior to 1980, only half did a follow-up. Among the reports from 1980 to the present, all but one utilized a follow-up. The same time relationship can be found for the use of control groups. Prior to 1980, only a single report employed controls, whereas 7 of the 12 more recent reports used controls. Weight measurement by the investigator, as opposed to self-reports, is found in all but one of the controlled studies, compared with only two of the studies without controls. In summary, the recent studies appear methodologically sounder than the earlier ones.

Among those eight reports giving control group outcomes, four found that the hypnotically treated group lost significantly more weight than did the control patients and subjects. Data from two reports show that the hypnotically treated group lost more weight than did some, but not all, control groups. The group labeled by Goldstein (1981) as "hypnosis-with-proof" lost significantly more weight than did either a conventional hypnosis group or a behavior-modification-without-hypnosis control group. The latter two groups did not differ in weight loss. Goldstein's "proof" was an

---

[1]The reports by Deyoub (1979a) and Deyoub and Wilkie (1980) are treated as separate data collections, but it is possible that there was patient/subject overlap between these reports. Bolocofsky et al. (1984, 1985) presented the same outcome data.

arm levitation suggestion, which was passed by 15 of the 20 subjects in the group. Goldstein's hypothesis was that hypnotherapy is more effective with individuals who are convinced that they are in a trance. Bornstein and Devine (1980) found that a group subjected to hypnosis and modeling through imagery lost more weight than did a control group treated only by behavior management without imagery modeling, but not more than a nonhypnosis group treated by modeling alone. Two other investigations reported completely negative findings.

Hypnotic Susceptibility and Outcome

It is generally believed that weight loss through hypnotherapy is un-related to hypnotic susceptibility (e.g., Fromm, 1987; Wadden & Anderton, 1982). This belief was supported by the conclusions of the influential review by Wadden and Anderton (1982), which was based on the findings of seven reports then available. Six of those seven found no relationship between outcome and susceptibility.[2] However, more recent reports tell another story.

Table 2 summarizes the results of 11 reports of the relationship between outcome and susceptibility. Of the 4 published since the Wadden and Anderton (1982) review, 3 had positive findings. Furthermore, the most recent of these 3 (Barabasz & Spiegel, 1989) is the only one that employed the Stanford Hypnotic Susceptibility Scale: Form C (SHSS:C; Weitzen-hoffer & Hilgard, 1962) as the measure of susceptibility. The SHSS:C is widely regarded as the gold standard of susceptibility scales.

Seven of the reports in Table 2 made use of control groups. In four of them, the outcome–susceptibility correlations were computed separately for experimental and control groups. In two of these reports (Deyoub, 1979a; Wadden & Flaxman, 1981), all coefficients were nonsignificant. In two others (Barabasz & Spiegel, 1989; Deyoub & Wilkie, 1980), the coefficients were nonsignificant only for the hypnotically untreated control groups. Of the remaining three, Bornstein and Devine (1980) and Cochrane and Friesen (1986) reported negative findings, although the latter study referred to a "trend toward greater weight loss with higher susceptibility scores" (p. 492). Neither report indicated that hypnotically treated and untreated data were analyzed separately. J. E. Miller (1975) may have pooled his hyp-notherapy group with a "non-induction" hypnotherapy group, presumably, but not definitely, an unhypnotized control group. If the absence of a

---

[2]Two of the sources in Table 1 of Wadden and Anderton's (1982) review article are unpublished doctoral dissertations (Devine, 1978; J. E. Miller, 1975). The Devine dissertation was published later in abbreviated form; it appears in Table 1 as Bornstein and Devine (1980). The finding that weight loss is unrelated to hypnotic susceptibility, which is questionable, as we shall see, does not necessarily constitute an argument that hypnotic intervention is ineffective as a weight control technique.

TABLE 1
Reports of the Hypnotic Treatment of Obesity Providing Quantified Data

Report	N	Treatment groups	No. of sessions	Follow-up interval (weeks)	Weight loss Close	Weight loss Follow-up	Significant differences
Without control groups							
Winkelstein (1959)	42	H	8	10	23	27	—
Glover (1961)	*	H	*	—	*	—	—
M. M. Miller (1974)	49	H	—	—	4[a]	—	—
Stanton (1975)	10	H + BM	4	96	13	22	—
Aja (1977)	40	H	3	12	13	13	—
Cohen & Alpert (1978)	15	H	8	—	5	—	—
Deyoub (1979b)	20	H	8	—	3	—	—
Davis & Dawson (1980)	6	H + BM	4[b]	68[b]	7	20	—
Channon (1980, 1983)	6	H + BM	—	24	—	21	—
McCabe et al. (1983)	44	H + BM	10	—	16	—	—
Andersen (1985)	30	H + BM	9	9	5	11	—
Jupp et al. (1986)	47	H + BM	13	—	16	—	—
With control groups							
Deyoub (1979a)	17	H	8	16	7	10	H > NT
	35	NT			+2	0	
Deyoub & Wilkie (1980)	17	H	8	8	1	6	NHS > NT[c]
	18	NHS			4	5	
	24	NT			+2	+4	

Study	N	Treatment	Weeks	Follow-up	Loss at close	Loss at follow-up	Results
Bornstein & Devine (1980)	9	CM	8	12	7	15	CM + H > MCM
	9	CM + H			6	18	
	9	MCM			2	4	
	9	MT			2	8	
Goldstein (1981)	20	H	4–16	24	5	25	HP > H[d]
	20	H + P			7	36	HP > BM[d]
	20	BM			5	25	
Wadden & Flaxman (1981)	10	CM	7	6, 16	8	8 6	—
	10	H			7	6 5	
	10	RA			6	6 6	
Bolocofsky et al. (1984, 1985)	52	BM	9	32, 104	7	7 7	BM + H > BM[d]
	57	BM + H			9	18 22	
Cochrane & Friesen (1986)	17	H	8	24	8	17	H > NT
	17	H + AT			7	18	H + AT > NT
	20	NT			+2	1	
Barabasz & Spiegel (1989)	14	BM	1	12	3	3	BM + H + AT > BM
	16	BM + H			—	8	
	15	BM + H + AT			—	14	

Note: Weight losses were computed from pretreatment weight. Treatment code: H = hypnosis; BM = behavior modification; CM = covert modeling; RA = relaxation–attention; MCM = modified covert modeling; NHS = nonhypnotic suggestion; AT = audiotapes; P = "proof"; MT = minimal treatment; NT = no treatment.

*Mean weight loss for 27 subjects at 1 week was 4 pounds; for 25 subjects at 4 weeks, 24 pounds; at 8 weeks, 20 pounds, N not reported; at 10 weeks, 24 pounds for 16 subjects; at 16 weeks, 30 pounds for "fewer than 10" subjects. [b]Mean for the 6 subjects. [c]For means at close; analyses of follow-up data not reported. [d]For follow-up data only. [a]Number of weeks is not reported.

TABLE 2
Relationship of Weight Loss to Hypnotic Susceptibility

Report	Correlation	p	N	Scale
J. E. Miller (1975)	ns	—	30	HGSHS
Cohen & Alpert (1978)	ns	—	15	SHSS:A
Deyoub (1979a)	ns	—	17	BSS
Deyoub (1979b)	.07	ns	20	HGSHS
Deyoub & Wilkie (1980)	.56	.05	17	BSS-O
	.69	.01		BSS-S
Bornstein & Devine (1980)	ns	—	36	HGSHS
Wadden & Flaxman (1981)	ns	—	10	BSS
Andersen (1985)				
(% overweight)	.56	.001	30	SHSS:A
(weight loss)	.80	.001		
(weight loss)[a]	.67	.001		
Cochrane & Friesen (1986)	ns	—	34	BSS
Jupp et al. (1986)	.32	.01	47	HGSHS
Barabasz & Spiegel (1989)	.51[b]	.01	29	SHSS:C

Note: ns = result reported as not significant but coefficient not presented. SHSS:A = Stanford Hypnotic Susceptibility Scale, Form A; BSS = Barber Suggestibility Scale (O = objective part; S = subjective part); HGSHS = Harvard Group Scale of Hypnotic Susceptibility; SHSS:C = Stanford Hypnotic Susceptibility Scale, Form C.
[a]Weight loss with beginning percent overweight held constant. [b]Mean rank order coefficient for two groups.

relationship reported in these three articles is based on pooled hypnotized–unhypnotized groups, it is conceivable that a positive relationship between outcome and susceptibility for the hypnotized group was masked. Simple logic dictates that the outcome–susceptibility relationship should exist only for those patients and subjects exposed to a hypnotic intervention. There is no reason for hypnotic susceptibility to affect the performance of individuals who have not been hypnotized.

All told, it appears that the conclusion that hypnotic susceptibility has no effect on the outcome of hypnotherapy for weight reduction is no longer tenable. The hypothesis proposed by Perry, Gelfand, and Marcovitch (1979) and endorsed by Wadden and Anderton (1982), Bowers (1982), and Spinhoven (1987) that susceptibility does not influence hypnotherapy of self-initiated disorders may well turn out to be specious. At the very least, the issue is again open.

CONCLUSION

Leon's (1976) claim that most of the reports of the hypnotic treatment of obesity are case histories is no longer valid. Most of the publications of the past decade make some attempt at quantification and control, although the methodology still tends to be insufficiently rigorous.

TABLE 3
A Comparison of the Effectiveness of Behavior Modification and Behavior
Modification with Hypnosis

Group	Measures	Time period			
		Treatment		Follow-up	
		Beginning	Close	6 mos.	2 yrs.
Hypnosis and behavior modification	Weight (lbs.)	154	146	136	133
	% overweight	25	18	11	8
	Program usage (per week)	—	14	5	3
Behavior modification	Weight (lbs.)	153	147	146	147
	% overweight	23	18	17	17
	Program usage (per week)	—	14	2–3	<1

Note: Data from Bolocofsky et al. (1985).

Stunkard's (1972) often-quoted assertion that "most obese persons will not remain in treatment. Of those who do remain in treatment, most will not lose much weight, and of those who do lose weight, most will regain it" (p. v) does not appear to be applicable to the patients and subjects who have undergone hypnotherapy for weight loss. If subjects dropped from the studies in Table 1 for statistical reasons are not considered, approximately 80% of the patients and subjects completed the hypnotherapy regimen.

A comparison of the hypnotically treated groups with the control groups in Table 1 strongly indicates that hypnotherapy for weight reduction is effective. Follow-ups suggest that effects are still present as long as 2 years after the close of treatment. Only a few designs permit a comparison with other treatment methods, but these results appear to indicate that hypnotherapy combined with behavior modification techniques is more effective than the latter alone (Barabasz & Spiegel, 1989; Bolocofsky et al., 1984, 1985; Bornstein & Devine, 1980).[3] This potentiation is illustrated by the results of the Bolocofsky et al. (1985) report, shown in Table 3.

The data in Table 3 show that both hypnosis with behavior modification and behavior modification alone brought about a significant weight loss during the 9 weeks of the program, 8 pounds by the hypnosis group and 6 by the behavior modification group. At the 6- and 24-month follow-ups, the behavior modification group manifested no further weight loss. The hypnosis group, however, continued to lose a significant amount over the follow-up time periods.

---

[3]Spinhoven (1987) believes that the effectiveness of the combined hypnosis–behavior modification technique has "not been convincingly demonstrated by controlled outcome studies" (p. 26). The Bolocofsky et al. (1984, 1985) and the Barabasz and Spiegel (1989) reports were not included in Spinhoven's review.

An explanation for the potentiation is contained in the questionnaire information gathered by Bolocofsky et al. (1985) at each of the follow-ups. Subjects were asked how often they followed the rules of the behavior modification program. As Table 3 shows, the hypnosis group had considerably more success. The failure of patients treated by behavior modification alone to continue to practice behavior-changing tactics after the close of treatment was also noted by Channon (1983) at a 6-month follow-up.

One might speculate that hypnosis brings about a fixation of the behavior modification principles, either cognitively or emotionally:

> The hypnobehavioral model is effective, in part, because suggestions given at hypnotic levels are more incisively received and acted upon. Individuals under hypnosis generally respond with a pinpoint precision or literalness to what is being said to them because the greater relaxation, concentration, and exquisite receptivity leads to greater objectivity. (Kroger & Fezler, 1976, p. xii)

Assuming that "suggestions" is the same as "instructions" and allowing some latitude for exaggeration, a hypothesis for the potentiation phenomenon is thus advanced.

Kroger (1970) suggested that group hypnosis treatment is more effective than individual treatment because "group attendance substitutes for eating behavior. . . . There is the emotional contagion inherently present in any group, the desire to please the leader . . . and the competitiveness. . . . The increased socialization . . . is rewarding" (p. 174). On the other hand, individual treatment permits adjustment of technique to suit individual requirements. The only intraprogram comparison found no differential effectiveness (McCabe et al., 1983).

Despite the strong indication of the effectiveness of hypnotic intervention, definitive inferences from the reports discussed in this chapter would be premature. Reviews of the literature seldom substitute adequately for systematic, well-designed research, such as the projects envisioned by Mott and Roberts (1979), Wadden and Anderton (1982), and Spinhoven (1987). Beyond treatment styles, duration, and so forth, there are a number of independent variables that could affect the outcome of hypnotherapy for weight control that have not been carefully examined. For example, a substantial majority of the patients and subjects in the reports in Table 1 were female, an obvious bias. Concern with weight and eating behavior may be correlated with hypnotic susceptibility in women (Groth-Marnat & Schumaker, 1990). It is also possible that overweight women are more hypnotically susceptible (Thorne, Rasmus, & Fisher, 1976; but see also Deyoub, 1978).

National background and socioeconomic status (SES) are known to be related to obesity (Goldblatt, Moore, & Stunkard, 1975; Stuart & Davis, 1972). SES is negatively related to obesity regardless of national descent.

The possible impact of these factors on hypnotherapy for weight loss has been totally unexplored.

Some of the innovative procedures proposed by the Macquarie Weight Control Program (Collins et al., 1981) have yet to be rigorously tested. Goldstein's (1981) "hypnosis-with-proof" hypothesis needs further testing. An interesting little study by Stanton (1976) suggested that paying a fee for the hypnotherapy regimen resulted in significantly more weight loss than did an identical no-fee program. Some of these factors might affect any type of weight loss therapy, but they could also interact significantly with hypnotherapy specifically.

The very definition of the problem remains to be examined with care: What is "obesity" or "overweight"? How does the degree of overweight impact therapy? Should we be dealing with percentage of body fat instead of avoirdupois?

Another conclusion of this chapter was stated over a decade ago:

> Although the clinical reports available suggest that hypnosis may have a place in weight control programs, if and how it may be useful needs to be evaluated by controlled research studies. Because of the complexity of the problem [and] the variety of therapeutic approaches . . . a number of carefully designed studies will be necessary. This research is urgently needed now because of the prevalence of the problem of obesity and the tendency for the desperation of its sufferers to be exploited by extravagant claims of commercialized clinics using hypnosis. (Mott & Roberts, 1979, p. 7)

Despite the ambiguity, the literature permits some tentative inferences that can be guidelines for the practitioner. The relative success of hypnosis plus behavior modification over hypnosis alone is the cornerstone. Research findings and clinical reports suggest that the following tactics, used in conjunction with a hypnotic intervention, have a good probability of bringing about weight reduction: (a) keeping an eating diary; (b) ritualizing eating instances; (c) chewing all food very, very slowly; (d) time-outs from eating during meals; (e) guided or spontaneous imagery—the patient imagines himself or herself as thin, as preparing (or ordering) and eating the proper foods, as rejecting improper foods, as feeling good about losing weight, and as following a diet and exercising; (f) using time distortion to create the false impression of a lengthy meal; (g) transferring glove anesthesia to the stomach to suppress hunger feelings; (h) aversive conditioning to associate improper foods with disagreeable odors or to associate the relief of nausea with not eating those foods (caution: never use aversive conditioning as the only tactic); and (i) self-hypnosis to reinforce all other behaviors.

Behavior-shaping methods that have been used in conjunction with hypnosis have been described in more detail in Kroger and Fezler (1976) and in the scripts of the Macquarie Weight Control Program (Walker et al., 1982). An excellent presentation of behavioral tactics that are suitable for weight control programs and that can be adapted for use with hypnosis is also available (Brownell, 1991).

HYPNOTHERAPY WEIGHT CONTROL PROTOCOL

This protocol describes in general terms the components of a behavior modification program with hypnosis for weight control, the technique that has been the most successful thus far. It can be arranged for either individual or group treatment. Additional behavior-shaping techniques can be found in Ferster et al. (1962), Kroger and Fezler (1976), Foreyt (1977), Walker et al. (1982), and Brownell (1991).

The Diet

A diet is, of course, a necessary component of any weight control program. Caloric consumption must exceed caloric intake if weight is to be lost. For most overweight persons, a weight loss of 1 to 3 pounds per week is the short-term goal. Obviously, low-calorie, high-bulk food is preferable to high-calorie, low-bulk food. Beyond these dicta, an effective diet and the manner in which it is arranged may vary considerably from person to person. A first step in any weight control program is to determine the most effective food intake pattern that will lead to weight loss, a procedure that is discussed in the next section.

Self-Monitoring: The Diet Journal

At the outset of the program, the patient is required to record all food intake, its circumstances, and the time of day for a 2-week period. The patient is cautioned not to attempt to reduce intake. The journal is then reviewed with the patient with an eye for the junctures of overeating and the type of foods involved. For example, many overweight people take in thousands of calories a week between meals rather than overeating at meals. A typical diet of an overweight person may be characterized by excessive intake of simple sugars or of animal fat. The diet journal permits targeting of foods and times of day that place the patient at risk for weight increase.

After the initial diet journal evaluation, the continued monitoring of eating behavior keeps the patient focused on the task at hand and may furnish an explanation if loss of weight does not occur.

Stimulus Control

This term refers to the manipulation of the circumstances under which eating behavior occurs. A number of techniques have been developed under this rubric.

The eating situation.   Overweight people eat more often and under more different circumstances than normal. Restricting eating times and places can reduce food intake. Eating can be limited to prescribed mealtimes, to a certain room, to a certain table, and even to specified eating utensils.

Eating behavior.   Current theory holds that the hunger feeling is hypothalamically controlled. The reduction of hunger will therefore require that nutrients that are a consequence of eating enter the bloodstream and be detected by the hypothalamus. Eating slowly is desirable because it permits digestion during the course of a meal, conceivably affecting hunger before the meal is actually finished. The gobbler will ingest more food than is actually necessary to relieve hunger.

Chaining.   Putting food into the mouth is the final stage in a chain of events that begins with deciding to buy a certain food and that extends over a possible 10 or 12 steps. The time involved in this chain of events can influence the frequency with which the final stage occurs. Lengthening the chain decreases the tendency to initiate it. This desirable end can be brought about by requiring effort to engage in eating, especially of high-calorie foods, such as by not stocking up on a food and by having foods that require preparation before eating.

Aversive Consequences of Obesity

An effort should be made to sharpen the focus of the patient's motivation for weight loss. Of course, all patients have an idea of their reasons for engaging in a weight control program, but it is often stated in vague terms like "to feel better" or "to look more attractive." Probing and discussion can improve the perception of motivation. Health facts, if not known to the patient, such as the involvement of overweight in malignancies, coronary artery disease, hypertension, and diabetes, can be added. The therapist's awareness of the patient's motivation will be useful during the hypnotic phase of the program.

Exercise

A regimen of regular exercise has several possible desirable consequences. The primary benefit is, of course, consuming calories. The transformation of fatty tissue to lean muscle mass, without weight loss, will enhance the effect of dieting because lean muscle mass uses more carbo-hydrate nourishment than does body fat. Men and younger people, espe-cially, appear to have an autonomic metabolism regulator that slows the metabolic rate when nourishment is reduced. Regular exercise seems to be able to prevent this unwanted consequence of the diet.

Hypnotic Tactics

Hypnotic intervention is used in several ways. Tactics are initiated in heterohypnosis and can then be transferred to self-hypnosis. A major hyp-notic effort is made to reinforce the efficacy of other program components, as suggested by the findings of Bolocofsky et al. (1985; see Table 3). In trance, the patient is reminded to follow the prescribed diet, to engage in stimulus control tactics, and to exercise. The aversive consequences of overeating are emphasized, highlighting the patient's own motivation for weight control.

Hypnosis is also used to promote imaging and confidence. "End-result imagery" (Pratt et al., 1984) is most effective when carried out in trance. The patient is asked to imagine that he or she is standing on scales that announce that the long-range goal weight has been reached, or to imagine looking in the mirror and seeing a slim self. Other images can be tailored to suit the individual patient. The specific wording of the end-result imagery suggestion is not important as long as it is clear and delivered in a non-authoritarian manner. The following language is proposed by Irving Kirsch (personal communication, September 2, 1992):

> Imagine that you are looking in a mirror and see the image of yourself that is reflected in it. But this is not an ordinary mirror; it is a mirror of the future . . . the future that you are now making come true. You can see yourself becoming thinner and thinner in the mirror . . . thin-ner and thinner . . . the pounds melting away like snow on a sunny day. . . . Now you have reached your ideal weight and can see yourself in the mirror of the future . . . and you can take pride now in accom-plishing your goal.

Most patients will have made several unsuccessful attempts to lose weight and keep it off. These failures breed a lack of confidence that can undermine the program. The effort to build confidence is best accomplished in trance. The clinician should suggest that the patient ignore earlier failures and focus on the current regimen, and that this approach will increase the patient's expectation of success. The clinician should stress that he or she strongly believes that the patient will successfully complete the program.

The trance is also a valuable adjunct when the patient has a period in which the short-term weight loss goal has not been achieved. This can prove to be so discouraging that the patient may quit the program. Reas-surance can be provided both in and out of the trance.

REFERENCES

Aja, J. H. (1977). Brief group treatment of obesity through ancillary self-hypnosis. *American Journal of Clinical Hypnosis, 19,* 231–234.

Andersen, M. S. (1985). Hypnotizability as a factor in the hypnotic treatment of obesity. *International Journal of Clinical and Experimental Hypnosis, 33,* 150–159.

Barabasz, M., & Spiegel, D. (1989). Hypnotizability and weight loss in obese subjects. *International Journal of Eating Disorders, 8,* 335–341.

Bolocofsky, D. N., Coulthard-Morris, L., & Spinler, D. (1984). Prediction of successful weight management from personality and demographic data. *Psychological Reports, 55,* 795–802.

Bolocofsky, D. N., Spinler, D., & Coulthard-Morris, L. (1985). Effectiveness of hypnosis as an adjunct to behavioral weight management. *Journal of Clinical Psychology, 41,* 35–41.

Bornstein, P. H., & Devine, D. A. (1980). Covert modeling-hypnosis in the treatment of obesity. *Psychotherapy: Theory, Research and Practice, 17,* 272–276.

Bowers, K. S. (1982). The relevance of hypnosis for cognitive–behavioral therapy. *Clinical Psychology Review, 2,* 67–78.

Bray, G. A. (Ed.). (1975). *Obesity in perspective* (DHEW Publication No. 75-708). Washington, DC: U.S. Superintendent of Documents.

Brodie, E. I. (1964). A hypnotherapeutic approach to obesity. *American Journal of Clinical Hypnosis, 6,* 211–215.

Brownell, K. D. (1991). *The LEARN program for weight control.* Dallas, TX: American Health.

Channon, L. D. (1980). Hypnosis in a self-control behaviour modification programme for weight reduction. *Australian Journal of Clinical and Experimental Hypnosis, 1,* 31–36.

Channon, L. D. (1983). Follow up data in weight control patients. *Australian Journal of Clinical and Experimental Hypnosis, 11,* 115–119.

Chlouverakis, C. (1975). Dietary and medical treatments of obesity: An evaluative review. *Addictive Behaviors, 1,* 3–21.

Cochrane, G. J. (1987). Hypnotherapy in weight-loss treatment: Case illustrations. *American Journal of Clinical Hypnosis, 30,* 20–27.

Cochrane, G., & Friesen, J. (1986). Hypnotherapy in weight loss treatment. *Journal of Consulting and Clinical Psychology, 54,* 489–492.

Cohen, N. L., & Alpert, M. (1978). Locus of control as a predictor of outcome in treatment of obesity. *Psychological Reports, 42,* 805–806.

Collins, J. K. (1986). The objective measurement of body image using a video technique: Reliability and validity studies. *British Journal of Psychology, 77,* 199–205.

Collins, J. K. (1987). Methodology for the objective measurement of body image. *International Journal of Eating Disorders, 6*, 393–399.

Collins, J. K., Jupp, J. J., & Krass, J. (1981). Hypnosis and weight control: A preliminary report on the Macquarie University programme. *Australian Journal of Clinical and Experimental Hypnosis, 9*, 93–99.

Collins, J. K., Jupp, J. J., & McCabe, M. P. (1987). Effective anthropometry in the evaluation of weight loss. *International Journal of Eating Disorders, 6*, 75–82.

Collins, J. K., McCabe, M. P., Jupp, J. J., & Sutton, J. E. (1983). Body percept change in obese females after weight reduction therapy. *Journal of Clinical Psychology, 39*, 507–511.

Crasilneck, H., & Hall, J. A. (1975). *Clinical hypnosis: Principles and applications.* New York: Grune & Stratton.

Davis, S., & Dawson, J. G. (1980). Hypnotherapy for weight control. *Psychological Reports, 46*, 311–314.

Devine, D. A. (1978). Hypnosis and covert modeling in the treatment of obesity. *Dissertation Abstracts International, 38*, 3389B.

Deyoub, P. L. (1978). Relation of suggestibility to obesity. *Psychological Reports, 43*, 175–180.

Deyoub, P. L. (1979a). Hypnosis in the treatment of obesity and the relation of suggestibility to outcome. *Journal of the American Society of Psychosomatic Dentistry and Medicine, 26*, 137–149.

Deyoub, P. L. (1979b). Hypnotizability and obesity. *Psychological Reports, 45*, 974.

Deyoub, P. L., & Wilkie, R. (1980). Suggestion with and without hypnotic induction in a weight reduction program. *International Journal of Clinical and Experimental Hypnosis, 28*, 333–340.

Enzi, G., Crepaldi, G., Pozza, G., & Renold, A. E. (Eds.). (1981). *Obesity: Pathogenesis and treatment.* New York: Academic Press.

Erickson, M. H. (1960). The utilization of patient behavior in the hypnotherapy of obesity. *American Journal of Clinical Hypnosis, 3*, 112–116.

Ferster, C. B., Nurnberger, J. I., & Levitt, E. E. (1962). The control of eating. *Journal of Mathetics, 1*, 87–109.

Foreyt, J. P. (1977). *Behavioral treatments of obesity.* New York: Pergamon Press.

Fromm, E. (1987). Significant developments in clinical hypnosis during the past 25 years. *International Journal of Clinical and Experimental Hypnosis, 35*, 215–230.

Garner, D. M., & Wooley, S. C. (1991). Confronting the failure of behavioral and dietary treatments for obesity. *Clinical Psychology Review, 11*, 729–780.

Garrow, J. S. (1978). *Energy balance and obesity in man* (2nd ed.). Amsterdam: Elsevier/North-Holland Biomedical Press.

Glover, F. S. (1961). Use of hypnosis for weight reduction in a group of nurses. *American Journal of Clinical Hypnosis, 3*, 250–251.

Goldblatt, P. B., Moore, M. E., & Stunkard, A. J. (1975). Social factors in obesity. In B. Q. Hafen (Ed.), *Overweight and obesity: Causes, fallacies, treatment* (pp. 131–136). Provo, UT: Brigham Young University Press.

Goldstein, Y. (1981). The effect of demonstrating to a subject that she is in a hypnotic trance as a variable in hypnotic interventions with obese women. *International Journal of Clinical and Experimental Hypnosis, 29,* 13–23.

Groth-Marnat, G., & Schumaker, J. F. (1990). Hypnotizability, attitudes toward eating, and concern with body size in a female college population. *American Journal of Clinical Hypnosis, 32,* 194–200.

Hafen, B. Q. (1975). Preface. In B. Q. Hafen (Ed.), *Overweight and obesity: Causes, fallacies, treatment* (pp. xiii–xiv). Provo, UT: Brigham Young University Press.

Hanley, F. W. (1967). The treatment of obesity by individual and group hypnosis. *Canadian Psychiatric Association Journal, 12,* 549–551.

Hartman, B. J. (1977). A hypnobehavioral approach to the treatment of obesity. *Journal of the National Medical Association, 69,* 821–824.

Hershman, S. (1955). Hypnosis in the treatment of obesity. *Journal of Clinical and Experimental Hypnosis, 3,* 136–139.

Jupp, J. J., Collins, J. K., McCabe, M. P., & Walker, W. L. (1986). Hypnotic susceptibility and depth: Predictors of outcome in a weight control therapy. *Australian Journal of Clinical and Experimental Hypnosis, 14,* 31–40.

Kallen, D. J., & Sussman, M. B. (1984). *Obesity and the family.* New York: Haworth Press.

Kamens, I. M. (1966). Hypnosis as an adjunct in obesity case histories. *Journal of the American Society of Psychosomatic Dentistry and Medicine, 13,* 5–11.

Kline, M. V. (1982). Hypnotherapy in the treatment of obesity. In B. B. Wolman (Ed.), *Psychological aspects of obesity* (pp. 268–290). New York: Van Nostrand Reinhold.

Kroger, W. S. (1970). Comprehensive management of obesity. *American Journal of Clinical Hypnosis, 12,* 165–176.

Kroger, W. S. (1977). *Clinical and experimental hypnosis* (2nd ed.). Philadelphia: Lippincott.

Kroger, W. S., & Fezler, W. D. (1976). *Hypnosis and behavior modification: Imagery conditioning.* Philadelphia: Lippincott.

Leon, G. R. (1976). Current directions in the treatment of obesity. *Psychological Bulletin, 83,* 557–578.

McCabe, M. P., Collins, J. K., Jupp, J. J., Walker, W.-L., & Sutton, J. E. (1983). The role of sex of therapist and group vs. individual therapy in treatment outcome using hypnosis with obese female patients: A research note. *Australian Journal of Clinical and Experimental Hypnosis, 11,* 107–109.

McCabe, M. P., Jupp, J. J., & Collins, J. K. (1985). Influence of age and body proportions on weight loss of obese women after treatment. *Psychological Reports, 56,* 707–710.

Miller, J. E. (1975). Hypnotic susceptibility, achievement motivation, and the treatment of obesity. *Dissertation Abstracts International, 35,* 3026B–3027B.

Miller, M. M. (1974). Hypnoaversion in the treatment of obesity: A preliminary report. *Journal of the National Medical Association, 66,* 480–481.

Miller, M. M. (1976). Hypnoaversion treatment of alcoholism, nicotinism and weight control. *Journal of the National Medical Association, 68,* 129–130.

Mott, T. (1979). The clinical importance of hypnotizability. *American Journal of Clinical Hypnosis, 21,* 263–269.

Mott, T., & Roberts, J. (1979). Obesity and hypnosis: A review of the literature. *American Journal of Clinical Hypnosis, 22,* 3–7.

Pearce, M. (1988). Eclecticism and hypnosis in the treatment of weight control: A case study. *Australian Journal of Clinical Hypnotherapy and Hypnosis, 9,* 9–11.

Perry, C. W., Gelfand, R., & Marcovitch, P. (1979). The relevance of hypnotic susceptibility in the clinical context. *Journal of Abnormal Psychology, 88,* 592–603.

Pratt, G. J., Wood, D. P., & Alman, B. N. (1984). *A clinical hypnosis primer.* La Jolla, CA: Psychology & Consulting Associates Press.

Rodin, J. (1982). Obesity: Why the losing battle? In B. B. Wolman (Ed.), *Psychological aspects of obesity* (pp. 30–87). New York: Van Nostrand Reinhold.

Spiegel, H., & DeBetz, B. (1978). Restructuring eating behavior with self-hypnosis. *International Journal of Obesity, 2,* 287–288.

Spiegel, H., & Spiegel, D. (1978). *Trance and treatment.* New York: Basic Books.

Spinhoven, P. (1987). Hypnosis and behavior therapy: A review. *International Journal of Clinical and Experimental Hypnosis, 35,* 8–32.

Stanton, H. E. (1975). Weight loss through hypnosis. *American Journal of Clinical Hypnosis, 18,* 94–97.

Stanton, H. E. (1976). Fee-paying and weight loss: Evidence for an interesting interaction. *American Journal of Clinical Hypnosis, 19,* 47–49.

Stuart, R. B., & Davis, B. (1972). *Slim chance in a fat world: Behavioral control of obesity.* Champaign, IL: Research Press.

Stunkard, A. J. (1972). Foreword. In R. B. Stuart & B. Davis (Eds.), *Slim chance in a fat world: Behavioral control of obesity.* Champaign, IL: Research Press.

Stunkard, A. J. (1976). *The pain of obesity.* Palo Alto, CA: Bull.

Stunkard, A. J. (Ed.). (1980). *Obesity.* Philadelphia: Saunders.

Swanson, D. W., & Dinello, F. A. (1970). Severe obesity as a habituation syndrome. *Archives of General Psychiatry, 22,* 120–127.

Thorne, D. E., Rasmus, C., & Fisher, A. G. (1976). Are "fat-girls" more hypnotically susceptible? *Psychological Reports, 38,* 267–270.

Wadden, T. A., & Anderton, C. H. (1982). The clinical use of hypnosis. *Psychological Bulletin, 91,* 215–243.

Wadden, T. A., & Flaxman, J. (1981). Hypnosis and weight loss: A preliminary study. *International Journal of Clinical and Experimental Hypnosis, 29*, 162–171.

Walker, W.-L., Collins, J. K., & Krass, J. (1982). Four hypnosis scripts from the Macquarie weight control programme. *Australian Journal of Clinical and Experimental Hypnosis, 10*, 125–133.

Weitzenhoffer, A. M., & Hilgard, E. R. (1962). *Stanford Hypnotic Susceptibility Scale: Form* C. Palo Alto, CA: Consulting Psychologists Press.

Winkelstein, L. B. (1959). Hypnosis, diet, and weight reduction. *New York State Journal of Medicine, 59*, 1751–1756.

Wollman, L. (1962). Hypnosis and weight control. *American Journal of Clinical Hypnosis, 4*, 177–180.

Wyden, P. (1965). *The overweight society: An authoritative, entertaining investigation into the facts and fallacies of girth control.* New York: Morrow.

26

HYPNOSIS AND SMOKING CESSATION: A COGNITIVE–BEHAVIORAL TREATMENT

STEVEN JAY LYNN, VICTOR NEUFELD, JUDITH W. RHUE, and
ABIGAIL MATORIN

The statistics are staggering. In the United States alone, smoking is responsible for 350,000 deaths per year. One out of four regular smokers dies of a smoking-related disease such as cancer, chronic obstructive lung disease, heart disease, and pregnancy complications. Smokers run a risk of death from coronary heart disease 59% greater than nonsmokers, longtime ex-smokers, or cigar or pipe smokers. Even passive smoking is estimated to kill 46,000 nonsmokers in the United States each year, including 3,000 deaths from lung cancer, 11,000 deaths from other cancers, and 32,000 deaths from heart disease (see Price & Lynn, 1986).

The negative sequelae of smoking are not so surprising when we consider that each puff of a cigarette delivers nicotine and perhaps 3,000 toxic chemicals into the bloodstream. Nicotine, the most active agent in tobacco, is a poisonous alkaloid more toxic than heroin and is sometimes used as an insecticide. The carbon monoxide content of cigarette smoke is considerably higher than that of Los Angeles smog at its worst.

Deaths and other smoking-related problems are especially tragic because smoking is a voluntary behavior that has, until recently, been a socially sanctioned habit. Smoking has now been identified as a powerful addiction (American Psychiatric Association, 1987) based on nicotine dependence. This partly explains why 29 million people continue to smoke despite surveys demonstrating that up to 85% of smokers would like to quit (U.S. Department of Health, Education, and Welfare, 1990).

Because cigarette smoking poses dire risks to health and well-being, the development, implementation, and evaluation of effective treatments is a public health priority. The use of hypnotic techniques to control the use of tobacco was first documented in 1847. Today, hypnosis is a widely used smoking cessation method, among a host of treatments that include aversive conditioning, pharmacology, nicotine replacement, education, group support, behavior modification, and role-playing (Hunt & Bespalec, 1974). A steadily growing research literature has suggested that some individuals profit from hypnosuggestive interventions and achieve their goal of abstinence. Although questions exist about whether hypnosis produces improved outcomes better than nonhypnotic approaches (Wadden & Anderton, 1982), empirical studies reported since 1980, reviewed later in this chapter, have secured abstinence rates ranging from 14% to 61%.

In this chapter, we describe a two-session, cognitive–behavioral smoking-cessation hypnosis intervention (Lynn, Neufeld, & Rhue, 1992) that can serve as a model for the use of hypnosis in the multidimensional treatment of smoking. After presenting the program in detail, we will examine the outcome data not only for this particular treatment program, but for hypnotic smoking cessation treatments in general.

CLINICAL APPLICATIONS

The preliminary single-session version of this treatment was developed in conjunction with the American Lung Association of Ohio. The 2-day workshop, described below, represents a substantial departure from the single-session program and is designed to improve the success rates and favorability ratings of the treatment. We believed that the multiple components of the program and strategies taught were too complicated and perhaps overwhelming to the average participant to convey in a single session. The two-session program was designed to be implemented with groups ranging in size from 5 to 50; however, the procedures can be readily modified and tailored for use on an individual basis. The program was created after a review of the literature suggested that the following treatment components should be part of a self-hypnosis smoking cessation program.

1. *Hypnosis as self-hypnosis.* Training in self-hypnosis is an integral part of a number of smoking cessation treatments (e.g., Barabasz, Baer,

Sheehan, & Barabasz, 1986; Basker, 1985; Powell, 1980). Popular views of hypnosis hold that the hypnotist and hypnotic proceedings can exert a special influence or control over a passive, essentially inert hypnotized individual, and thereby eliminate the desire to smoke. In contrast, the workshop informs participants that hypnosis achieves its sometimes impressive and dramatic effects as a result of their active participation and cognitive involvement. Indeed, hypnosis can appropriately be construed as self-hypnosis (Barber, 1985), a set of skills and self-directed responses to suggestions that can help a motivated person achieve self-control over smoking behavior.

2. *Cognitive and behavioral skills.* Self-hypnosis is described as one of a number of important skills that participants can master. Hypnotic suggestions, when practiced regularly, can replace negative self-talk with positive statements that emphasize the benefits of nonsmoking and the ability to become a nonsmoker. Behavioral and cognitive behavioral techniques such as relaxation, stimulus control, cue-controlled relaxation (i.e., anchoring), and positive self-talk are incorporated into the program in order to promote self-control and teach skills requisite to achieving abstinence.

3. *Education.* Education is an important component of many smoking cessation programs (Botvin & Eng, 1982). In our program, smoking is described as a learned behavior pattern that can be modified by the learning of adaptive behaviors to replace smoking in a person's life. The discussion of smoking as a psychosocial habit is empirically based. Research has confirmed that nicotine has positive psychopharmacological effects, including the paradoxical effect of increasing arousal and decreasing anxiety (Pomerleau & Pomerleau, 1984). Because smokers are well aware of the positive aspects of smoking, any attempt to deny the reinforcing effects of smoking is likely to decrease the credibility of the hypnotist, to lead clients to question their own normality, or both. Nevertheless, the deleterious effects of smoking on neurophysiology and the cardiovascular system are presented for consideration while the participants are encouraged to generate health and personal reasons for abstinence.

4. *Enhancing motivation and self-efficacy.* Enhancing motivation and self-efficacy expectations (Bandura, 1982) are important components of successful smoking cessation programs (see Perry, Gelfand, & Marcovitch, 1979; Perry & Mullen, 1975). In fact, there is a direct relation between increased self-efficacy and maintenance of treatment gains (Bandura, 1982). The importance of motivation was also underlined in our research (Neufeld & Lynn, 1988) on a preliminary version of our workshop: Of the participants abstinent at the 6-month follow-up, all indicated that they were either *strongly* motivated to quit or *somewhat strongly* motivated to quit. That is, all scored at least 3 on a 5-point scale that indexed subjects' motivation to quit.

One of our central treatment goals is giving participants what we term "the edge"—that is, a menu of skills with which to experiment in order to break habitual patterns, cope with withdrawal symptoms, and maintain treatment gains. Withdrawal symptoms, which can be a detriment to participants' resolve to abstain from smoking, are eased by gradually fading nicotine by decreasing cigarette consumption, over a week's time, and by the participants' stepping down to lower nicotine cigarettes. Positive suggestions regarding clients' sense of control, mastery, and positive feelings about being healthy and alive are administered to counterbalance withdrawal-related discomfort.

5. *Being a "nonsmoker."* Research has indicated that the degree to which people see themselves as nonsmokers is a strong predictor of long-term abstinence (Marlatt & Gordon, 1985). One of the main goals of the workshop is to help participants forge a new identity as nonsmokers—to be able to say to themselves, "I am a nonsmoker" and to envision the implications of smoking abstinence. Participants are asked to see themselves as nonsmokers, to experience on a deep level the positive personal and interpersonal benefits of abstinence, and to learn to provide substitute rewards for avoiding tobacco.

6. *Relapse prevention and gain maintenance.* Participants are invited to identify high-risk or trigger situations associated with increased probability or risk of smoking. Identification of trigger situations linked to places, situations, and times characterized by especially powerful smoking cues is facilitated by self-monitoring of smoking behaviors during the week between smoking sessions. At the same time, participants generate coping responses that constitute an alternative to smoking for each of the trigger situations identified.

The degree to which smokers perceive themselves as effective copers in high-risk smoking situations is a significant predictor of long-term abstinence (Marlatt & Gordon, 1985). Hence, participants are asked not only to identify high-risk situations, but also to visualize themselves using personally meaningful, desirable, and effective coping strategies that replace smoking behaviors in those situations.

The maintenance of treatment gains is encouraged by instructing participants to avoid high-risk situations when feasible, teaching participants strategies to cope with smoking urges, and identifying and instituting self-rewards for nonsmoking.

7. *Minimizing weight gain.* One of the most consistent findings in the smoking cessation literature is that weight gain follows smoking cessation and may promote relapse (see Perkins, Epstein, & Pastor, 1990). It therefore follows that efforts should be instituted to help participants minimize the weight gain that can result from the increased caloric intake (Perkins et al., 1990) and decreased metabolic rate (Dallosso & James, 1984) associated with abstinence. Our program uses a minimal intervention that instructs

participants to eat a well-balanced diet from the four basic food groups, to increase nonstrenuous physical activity, and to lose weight slowly and gradually (no more than 2 pounds per week).

8. *Contracting and social support.* In the initial session, participants sign a contract that affirms their intention to quit on the "quit date" of the second session, a week later. The signing of this contract is witnessed by another group member, and participants are instructed to give copies of the contract to a spouse, living partner, or best friend, and to their employer. To promote social support, a "buddy system" is instituted wherein participants are invited to pair up with one another in order to call each other if they wish to rely on another person for social support outside of the family.

CASE MATERIAL

In this section, we present our two-session, group-format smoking cessation program. The success of the workshop depends, in part, on the trainer's ability to engage the group, promote discussion of relevant issues, and integrate the didactic content with the unique concerns of the participants. What follows is the nuts and bolts of our trainer manual. It is not meant to be adhered to slavishly; rather, it is designed to serve as a touchstone for the trainer's creative attempts to promote smoking cessation. The workshop is copyrighted, so permission should be obtained before the training materials and format are used in clinical or research projects.

Description of Session 1

The first session can be completed in about 2 hours; the second session typically requires 1 to 1½ hours to complete. In the first session, the trainer introduces him- or herself to the participants, describes the origins and history of the program, and presents an overview of the workshop. To stimulate group cohesion, participants are invited to introduce themselves and to discuss their reasons for attending the workshop.

The trainer then proceeds along the following lines:

> I am confident that this program will be an educational experience for you. Education, of course, involves learning. Let's get a fix on how you "learned" to smoke, because smoking is not a "natural" act. How many of you felt awkward when you first began to smoke? Did you feel sick or nauseated? It often takes weeks or even months of practice and perseverance to condition your body to learn to accept the noxious agents contained in tobacco smoke. Many of you probably smoked to fill a specific need (for example, be "in" with your friends, remain alert and awake). What were your reasons for smoking? [Discussion follows.]

Initially, many of you probably only smoked in very limited situations. However, as time passed, the strength of your habit grew and you probably extended your smoking to many other situations (for example, on the telephone, at work, after you eat). Each time you lifted a cigarette to your lips, you strengthened your habit.

Just think of how many times you have lifted a cigarette to your lips. Why don't we calculate the number of times you have lifted a cigarette to your mouth: If you smoke a pack a day: (a) 20 cigarettes per pack; average number of inhalations per cigarette is 10. (b) $20 \times 10 = 200$. (c) 365 days a year $\times$ number of years smoked. (d) Multiply figure from b by c = total number of times you have lifted a cigarette to your mouth if you are a pack-a-day smoker. Now that's a habit! The goal of this program is to teach you how to break your habit, or to unlearn your habitual behavior.

We have many ways we will teach you to give you the "edge," the advantage you will need to break this habit. You should know that more than 40 million Americans have successfully quit. So it certainly is possible. We will help you turn that possibility into a personal reality.

We will teach you the skills you need to learn to break habitual patterns, deal with any discomfort you might experience, and maintain the gains you achieve here. We want you to have many skills and techniques you can choose from. Your task will be to find ones that work best for you. We will not only point out some of the costs of smoking, but make you more aware of the benefits of quitting: How being a nonsmoker can fill you with a sense of pride as you learn you are protecting and preserving your health, being more competitive in sports, more kissable, and keeping your house free of smoke odors. We will make any discomfort easier to deal with by gradually fading out nicotine from your life by moving to fewer and fewer cigarettes over the week and changing to lower nicotine cigarettes.

And of course, hypnosis will be one part of the program, one way to give you the edge. If you follow through with this program, we are confident you can quit. We cannot do it for you, but we can make it a lot easier for you to become smoke free for life.

We have learned that motivation is one of the most important factors in being a nonsmoker. The best hypnotist in the world will not help if you are not motivated to quit. I would now like to pass out a 3×5 index card. As you will see, it has a 1–5 scale on it of how motivated you are to quit: 1 = *not at all motivated*; 3 = *somewhat*; 5 = *extremely motivated*. I would like you to complete this scale at the end of our first session. If you are not strongly motivated (at least 3), then you should consider not coming back for the second session, and we will give you a full refund. Our research indicates that successful participants score between 3 and 5 on this scale.

But if you do want to quit, if you are ready to complete the program, then I will ask you to sign a contract and have it witnessed by another group member. The contract will also be signed by your spouse, living partner, or best friend, and also by your employer if you are employed. We want you to enlist their support. We want you to announce your intention to quit. We want them to understand the efforts you are making. We want them to know you are doing your best, and we want them to help you any way they can. How can they help you? Why don't we brainstorm as a group to get some ideas you can share with the people in your life. [Discussion follows.]

At this point, I would like to discuss your previous quitting experiences. If you had been able to quit successfully, you would not be here today. You have heard the phrase "know thine enemy." In order to conquer the smoking habit, it is important that you let go of blaming yourself, cut out the sorts of statements you make to yourself like, "I'm weak," "I have no willpower." If you smoke 15 or more cigarettes a day, you may be physically addicted to nicotine, and it is possible that withdrawal symptoms will occur when you do not receive your dose of nicotine. We will teach you ways to deal with these withdrawal symptoms if you should experience them.

But there is one thing to remember: Even some heavy smokers do not experience withdrawal symptoms, and withdrawal symptoms may not be very intense in even heavy smokers. In fact, 20%–45% of quitters report absolutely no withdrawal symptoms. Our goal is to prepare you for whatever you will face when you quit. This program is designed to help even heavy smokers quit. This program will help you to be a nonsmoker for life.

By gradually cutting down on the number and nicotine content of cigarettes you smoke, any withdrawal you might experience will be reduced in intensity. But what is important to remember is that withdrawal reactions are temporary, and you can learn to combat smoking urges. Consider this: After a month, two thirds of quitters do not report strong urges. In fact, several months after quitting, most ex-smokers feel less anxiety and depression than they did while they were smoking.

Let's focus more on withdrawal reactions now. Withdrawal is actually a sign that your body is coping with your decision to be a nonsmoker. It is a short-term reaction that you can deal with. Some of the reactions are a direct result of the body's healing itself. Let's consider some of the uncomfortable feelings some of you have had, and what you can do about each reaction. [Discussion follows.]

If you have a cough, this can be a healthy signal, a sign that your lungs are cleansing you. Not being able to concentrate is a short-term reaction; it represents your body's adjusting to decreases of nicotine in your body. Feelings of depression may arise because of your mistaken belief that you are losing a friend; actually, you are vanquishing a deadly enemy by quitting. Feelings of anxiety may arise because of the association that you have made between smoking and situations in which you feel anxiety. But once again, this too shall pass; in the long run, you will be a calmer, less anxious person, perhaps on a more even keel than before you started smoking. To combat any feelings of lack of energy, eating right and getting exercise will give you the boost you need. And there's the old cure for problems sleeping—drink milk before you go to bed. It contains a natural sleep-promoting substance—tryptophan—that will also help to calm your nerves. We have no sure-fire cure for irritability, but one reason why we ask you to have other people in your life sign the contract is so they can better understand what you are going through. At any rate, feelings of irritability will pass in a week or two.

What is important to keep in mind is that any discomfort you may experience is short-term, but some of the long-term effects of cigarette smoking are not. [At this point, the trainer reviews the short- and long-term health consequences of smoking.] But the good news is that the body begins to repair itself almost as soon as you stop smoking. After a year of being a nonsmoker, your risk factors for cancer and heart disease return to about what they were before you began smoking. So this should constitute powerful motivation for you to quit.

Some people get discouraged and begin smoking again when they gain a few pounds after quitting. We have some recommendations for you that are simple but effective. First, be sure that you eat a well-balanced diet from the four basic food groups; increase physical activity like walking, jogging, swimming, playing sports; and lose weight slowly, but do not lose more than 2 pounds a week.

Think for a moment about what it would mean to you to be a nonsmoker. I will pass out some index cards, and I would like you to list at least five reasons for quitting, in order of importance. Now visualize two roads: a high road where you imagine your future if you quit successfully. Think of the social rewards, the monetary rewards, and the health rewards. Now imagine a low road where you see your future if you are not truly motivated to quit. The choice is yours. Which road will you walk down?

How many think or fear that you may not be able to quit [show of hands]. Keep your hands up . . . now, if I told you that you would receive a million dollars if you could remain abstinent for a year, do you think you could do it [show of hands]? But a question I would like you to ask yourself is whether your health is worth a million dollars. Close your eyes now and tell yourself all the reasons you have to quit, and see yourself walking down the road of health and well-being as a nonsmoker.

What I would like you to do this week is to review your reasons to quit, and to do this on a frequent basis. Carry your quit card on your person. During this week, I would also like you to identify trigger situations. These are places, situations, and times that are loaded with powerful personal smoking cues. An urge can be thought of as an internal smoking cue or a prompt for you to smoke. Smokers tend to have urges linked with specific experiences. When a specific situation is linked with the feeling or urge to smoke, we call it a trigger situation.

What triggers your desire to smoke? [Encourage discussion.] Now let's brainstorm some ways that you can cope with smoking urges. [Encourage discussion. If not mentioned, the trainer lists a number of coping methods that center around (a) doing something else, (b) "waiting it out," and (c) using distraction and somatic focus techniques. Participants are encouraged to devise their own coping responses that might include exercising, taking a shower or bath, playing a sport, stretching, touching their toes, polishing their glasses, doodling, doing deep breathing, using imagery, bicycling, chewing sugarless gum, exercising with hand grippers or squeezing a rubber ball, playing with worry beads, chewing on carrot or celery sticks, waiting it out, drinking water, or using self-talk or self-hypnotic techniques.] Now on the reverse side of your reasons-to-quit card, write your alternative coping responses in the trigger situations you identified.

One technique that many participants in our workshop have found useful is what we call the "urge zapper." First, say to yourself, "I am aware of an urge to smoke." Second, say to yourself, "NO! I do not have to smoke; I am a nonsmoker," or another key phrase that will help you. Three, read your reasons-for-quitting card. And finally, engage in one of the alternate coping responses on the back of your card.

During this first week, and even thereafter, it is important that you avoid high-risk or trigger situations, when possible. Think about those situations that you can avoid and how you can reduce stress in your life this week. There may, however, be some situations you cannot avoid, so I would like you to anticipate a situation this week, imagine it now, and see yourself coping effectively in this situation.

We recommend that after this week you never put a cigarette to your lips again. However, some people do slip. This does not mean that you are a total failure and that you should end your efforts to quit. A slip can be a learning experience; you can realize you have a choice. A slip is a sign of the strength of the smoking habit. But remember this, a lapse does not mean relapse, which is a return to the original pattern of behavior. Again, you are playing with fire if you think you can control your smoking by "smoking a few here or there." It is our belief that you will begin to feel better sooner when your body is truly convinced that you are serious about quitting. Make that resolve firm! Do it now!

To help you to maintain the important gains you have achieved, it is important that you reward yourself. Make a list of things you enjoy and that are easy to obtain. A few can be expensive, but not all rewards have to be material. Make this list of rewards now on the paper provided. One thing you might wish to do is to put money ordinarily spent on cigarettes in a highly visible container and then spend it for a pleasurable activity when it accumulates.

Self-hypnosis is an important part of this program. It is a skill that you can learn. It can help you to be a nonsmoker by promoting relaxation, by strengthening your motivation to quit, by helping to change your self-image from a smoker to a nonsmoker, and by providing you with a vehicle for administering useful self-suggestions that have the power to change your life.

The trainer answers questions about self-hypnosis and fosters positive attitudes about hypnosis by demystifying hypnosis and correcting misconceptions (e.g., that hypnosis involves a "trance," that contact with reality is lost, or that responses occur compulsively). Hypnosis is framed as involving the willingness to experience and imagine what is suggested and being open to useful suggestions. The trainer then administers the self-hypnosis induction, which consists of suggestions for calmness; deepening and relaxation suggestions of walking 20 steps to a place of safety and security; developing a key phrase to catalyze the motivation and desire to quit smoking; developing a physical anchor (touching first and second fingers together) to access inner strength, and anchoring reasons for quitting; and imaginarily rehearsing resisting smoking urges in a trigger situation and using relaxation/anchoring techniques. After the induction, the trainer provides participants with a self-hypnosis tape that recapitulates the suggestions and recommends practice at least twice daily.

Participants are given a number of instructions for everyday homework that include the following assignments: (a) record the number of cigarettes smoked; (b) practice self-hypnosis; (c) buy cigarettes by the pack, not the carton; (d) start a "butt jar" and place cigarette butts in the jar; and (e) use urge-management techniques when starting reduction.

The following day-by-day assignments are also given: Day 1: Begin recording smoking behavior; review reasons for quitting, keep the quitting card with cigarettes, and read the card before smoking. Day 2: Analyze the habit, write down a list of triggers, and elaborate alternative behaviors; switch to a lower tar and nicotine brand starting the next day; and plan a 10% cigarette reduction for the next day. Day 3: Switch to a lower tar and nicotine brand; reduce cigarettes. Plan another 10% reduction for the next day. Day 4: Reduce cigarettes and plan a 20% reduction for the next day; plan rewards. Day 5: Switch brands; reduce 20%; plan a 20% reduction for the next day; and plan rewards. Day 6: Switch brands; reduce 20%; plan a 20% reduction for the next day; and plan rewards. Quit Day! Second workshop session—clients are instructed to bring an empty pack of cigarettes to the session.

Before the session comes to a close, the trainer passes out the motivation scale and the contracts for participants to complete. At the end of the group, participants are invited to pair up with another person to telephone for support, if they wish to rely on another person for social support outside of the family.

Description of Session 2

Welcome to our second session! By coming here you again affirm your wish to become a nonsmoker. We will start our work today with a quitting ceremony. What we will do is start off by walking one by one to the front of the room, crumpling up your last pack of cigarettes, and throwing it in the wastebasket that you see here. If you would like, feel free to make a statement, a positive affirmative statement about your feelings about quitting as you throw out your last pack. If you are willing, say this in front of the group, along with the statement, "I am a nonsmoker," and we will all show our support by clapping as you toss your last cigarette away.

Before we do this, though, let's briefly review our reasons for quitting. Let's share a bit and talk about what we became aware of during the week, about how our lives can change for the better when we quit. I know that throwing your cigarettes away may seem to some of you like you are losing your best friend. But as we talked about last week, cigarettes are not really your friend but a deadly enemy. Reviewing our reasons for quitting will only firm our resolve. Let's take a few minutes to review our reasons. [Quitting ritual takes place.]

I would like us to start with your experiencing hypnosis again. You have had some practice doing this. I will give you suggestions for deepening this experience you are already familiar with. So just close your eyes now and begin to relax, with nothing to worry, nothing to disturb, moving and moving, and moving into the familiar ground, the territory of your private experience . . . your hypnosis . . . you can close your eyes, yes, you can close your eyes . . . so easily . . . so gently . . . eyes closing, closing, closing. I wonder if you can let yourself go even deeper into your experience, your mind and body working together, your conscious and your unconscious mind working together for your best good, in their own way . . . partners . . . partners to protect your health, your well-being, your life . . . your breath. With each breath you can begin to move deeper and deeper, although you may not know exactly how you do it. But I can tell you one thing, you don't even have to try . . . in fact, you don't even have to do anything but listen to my voice . . . let my voice move with you, with your own sense of what is good for you . . . what you need. You can probably already feel yourself flowing with the experience . . . would you like to imagine a favorite scene, your spot where you feel so centered and so secure? . . . I wonder if you could do that . . . I know you can. And you will find that you will not fall asleep . . . you will remain awake yet so deeply relaxed, just on the edge, with me communicating with the deepest levels of your understanding . . . all the while knowing on that level of deep, perhaps even subliminal awareness . . . you will take the strength that you need from inside yourself . . . to be what you can be . . . to do what you need to do . . . to be a nonsmoker as you were for so many years before you first smoked.

Yes . . . get more and more of a deep fulfilling sense that strength is within . . . you move toward this place in your mind . . . in your imagination . . . in your being . . . this place where you are centered and secure . . . where you can return to anytime you wish . . . anytime you want . . . moving and moving and moving . . . flowing and flowing and flowing . . . change your position anytime you want to go even deeper, go even deeper into your desire to preserve your health to be a nonsmoker . . . get into your need to free yourself from this habit . . . yet nothing to bother now . . . nothing to disturb . . . you can do this . . . you can be smoke free . . . you can do this . . . yes . . . learning to do this . . . more and more . . . more and more . . . on so many levels . . . your mind is calm and clear even as I speak . . . different muscle groups relaxing in their own way . . . I wonder which muscles are more relaxed . . . your neck or your eyelids . . . it doesn't matter for now . . . does it . . . it really doesn't matter . . . as you approach this place . . . or are you there now . . . I don't really know . . . and is your breathing becoming slower . . . as you relax . . . as you let go . . . or are you feeling heavy or light, floating or heavy . . . or perhaps a relaxed, heavy floating feeling all in one . . . can you feel comfort and security wrapping around you like a blanket that is so comfortable . . . or is your conscious mind wandering while your unconscious mind tunes into the deepest meanings, your deepest desires to be a nonsmoker . . . or are you ready to relax even more?

Let's go deeper now . . . or are you so relaxed that you would just like to maintain where you are . . . so comfortable and at ease . . . strength is within . . . you are moving toward that place or maybe you are there . . . you are taking the steps you need to take . . . learning . . . taking just the steps you need to take to get where you are going . . . to where you want to go . . . can you notice some words and images coming easily and naturally to you . . . healing words and images . . . cleansing words and images . . . freeing words and images . . . perhaps a key phrase is coming to you . . . something you can say any time you want . . . any time you wish . . . a phrase that touches the deepest core of your being . . . a phrase that helps to cushion you . . . support you . . . or maybe it's an image . . . I don't know . . . but you can say this phrase or visualize your image any time you want . . . say it now . . . use it to anchor your resolve to be a nonsmoker forever.

As you do this . . . think of all the many reasons you have to quit smoking forever. Can you see a writing board . . . is it black or is it green . . . I don't know . . . write . . . and hear your words reading your reasons . . . write why you will quit smoking . . . listen to your voice saying to yourself . . . talking to yourself . . . about why you will quit smoking . . . think of all the benefits . . . so much to gain . . . health . . . money saved . . . so many benefits . . . you will think of even more reasons . . . let them move you deeper and deeper . . . let them swell your confidence . . . let them help you as you move and step toward your goal, how much your life can mean to you . . . how much you have to look forward to.

Are your hands more relaxed than your feet . . . is your breathing so easy . . . perhaps you can feel your head moving ever so slightly . . . moving up and down ever so slightly . . . it is saying yes, yes . . . your unconscious mind is somehow communicating with your conscious mind your desire to be free of smoking . . . yes . . . yes . . . but you don't even have to do anything for this to happen . . . for you to be free of smoking . . . yes . . . yes . . . you don't even have to move, although you could if you wished . . . to create a sense of yourself, perhaps an image of yourself as a nonsmoker . . . can you see yourself with others . . . or are you alone . . . feeling a sense that you can say yes, yes to your health . . . to your body . . . to your feeling at ease without smoking . . . say yes to yourself . . . yes . . . take a few minutes to see yourself as a nonsmoker . . . see this image unfold . . . it somehow begins to become more and more real to you . . . I don't know exactly how this happens, but notice it happen anyway . . . I wonder whether you can feel a sense of the strength that is within . . . can you feel it . . . or is it becoming so much a part of you that you do not notice it?

So comfortable now . . . your need to smoke . . . any urges to smoke once a part of you are fading . . . they are dissolving . . . detaching from you . . . breaking up . . . like clouds in the wind . . . like clouds on a day that the sun begins to shine through . . . the light . . . the diffuse light . . . the breeze . . . the wind . . . the gentle calm . . . it all helps you to think that you can do so much other than smoke . . . you can see yourself doing something else in situations in which you smoked . . . you know you have the power . . . the power to flow with your strength to resist any urges that come up . . . they will fade . . . fade . . . like clouds in the wind . . . you can use your key phrase now . . . you know your strength is within . . . you can see yourself as a nonsmoker . . . it is coming clearer to you . . . the light is illuminating you, your reasons to quit . . . your will . . . your resolve . . . the power is within you . . . you know that smoking is a poison . . . you respect yourself . . . you will protect your body . . . you need your body . . . it needs you . . . your strength . . . your willpower.

You can think about what you can do besides smoking . . . so many things . . . your conscious working with your unconscious mind to help you to decide what to do . . . you know that you are capable of taking care . . . taking good care . . . of others . . . of yourself . . . you can get in touch with your kindness . . . your caring . . . you can direct this toward yourself . . . you can feel so good . . . you can learn the art of controlling an urge . . . you can learn to ignore it . . . by admitting it, but at the same time remembering your commitment to respect your body . . . lock them together . . . if you emphasize one, you have to ignore the other, and you can commit yourself to your body . . . emphasize your commitment to your body, ignore the urge to smoke . . . you can feel so relaxed and in control . . . your body is so important . . . you are your body's keeper . . . so many things you can do besides smoking as you ignore the urge . . . you notice it passes . . . it fades away . . . like clouds in the wind . . . you can think about how choosing not to smoke . . . and you will do this . . . will lock into your strength . . . your pride. Do this now . . . feel . . . experience . . . get to know yourself . . . you are a nonsmoker . . . see yourself this way . . . experience it.

See yourself in social situations . . . see yourself this way . . . notice others supporting you . . . noticing you are not smoking anymore . . . you feel their respect for you . . . you feel serene . . . calm . . . comfortable . . . nothing to bother you . . . nothing to disturb you . . . feel this sense growing . . . you don't have to do anything now . . . but later today . . . and tomorrow . . . and the tomorrows thereafter you will become more and more aware that you are in control . . . you will avoid one or two or more situations in which in the past you were perhaps likely to think about smoking . . . you will do this . . . you will do this . . . for you care about yourself . . . relax . . . deeper . . . deeper . . . quitting smoking is a way to be good to yourself . . . to care for yourself . . . yes . . . say yes to this.

Feel good about yourself . . . reward yourself for not smoking . . . you are saving money . . . you are preserving your health . . . you are resisting urges . . . you are not gaining weight . . . you are exercising . . . or eating in moderation . . . you are taking care of yourself . . . you feel pride . . . you can reward yourself . . . you do deserve it . . . how can you do this? You want to do this, to be good to yourself . . . so you can think of some things you can do . . . what will it be . . . think of what it will be now . . . no need to deny yourself a reward for not smoking . . . feel good about what you have done . . . about coming here . . . how can you show yourself that you can like yourself . . . yes . . . say yes to liking yourself . . . see yourself as the person you want to be . . . do this now . . . moving and moving toward strength . . . to be that person . . . see that person . . . get a sense for that person's essence.

Can you begin to feel your senses awakening? Begin to let your senses come alive . . . your sense of touch . . . of smell . . . you can begin to smell better . . . you begin to taste . . . really taste . . . you smell fresh . . . you are free of the stench of cigarettes . . . you are free of their clinging odor . . . you are fresh . . . you are beginning to regain your senses . . . you are becoming aware . . . like a newborn baby . . . before your senses were dulled . . . your body is healing . . . healing . . . you are opening up . . . you are able to taste your foods . . . you can chew them slowly . . . with enjoyment . . . you are exercising . . . if you wish . . . you are a nonsmoker today . . . from this moment on . . . say this to yourself . . . yes . . . say yes to it . . . yes. . . .

Go deeper into your hypnosis . . . moving and moving and moving . . . learning and firming your resolve . . . comfort . . . your mind clear and calm, now you are moving and moving and flowing with your experience . . . nothing to bother as you go deeper and deeper and deeper, aware of what you are and what you can be . . . how you can use what you have learned in your life of learnings . . . how you can use what you have learned about self-hypnosis . . . how you will help yourself to remain a nonsmoker . . . as you see yourself not smoking in situations in the past in which you were tempted to smoke, you can see yourself substituting healthy behaviors for smoking . . . you see yourself choosing health and well-being . . . you feel different . . . your senses are alive . . . you feel a sense of pride . . . you are in control . . . you do it . . . you give yourself positive suggestions . . . you use your key phrase . . . your anchor . . . you find many ways to reinforce your sense of accomplishment . . . in this situation in which, in the past, you had thoughts of smoking . . . you realize you can control what you do and what you do not do . . . no longer a slave to smoking . . . yes . . . you are in charge of your life . . . you can say this firmly to yourself . . . I am in charge . . . I am in control . . . my strength is within . . . I am a nonsmoker . . . until you feel even better about what you can do . . . yes . . . capable of so much . . . perhaps now you can absorb the fact that every day of your life you are a nonsmoker . . . you do not smoke when you sleep . . . perhaps for eight hours a day you did not smoke . . . perhaps more . . . perhaps less . . . you do not feel deprived yet you are not smoking . . . you are coping . . . your conscious and unconscious working together . . . your body relaxed . . . your body healing . . . now when you do not smoke during the day . . . your body will heal even more . . . you can relax too . . . with what you have learned . . . with what you have learned.

Perhaps you can let go even more . . . feel time slowing down . . . time slowing down to a most comfortable pace . . . a sense of feeling really good . . . a flowing feeling . . . moving more and more toward hope and peace . . . a sense of feeling worthwhile . . . and as you experience these feelings, what I'd like you to do is to bring your thumb and forefinger together . . . or perhaps you'd like to touch a ring that has special significance for you . . . make your anchor . . . just lightly touch . . . make your anchor and feel so good and relax . . . more and more . . . more and more . . . feel more confident . . . even better . . . flowing wave upon wave . . . gentle relaxation . . . gentle waves of relaxation as you feel calm, and at ease, and secure . . . deep . . . deep . . . so good . . . yes . . . can you feel this in your entire body . . . relax even deeper . . . so deep . . . you can create this feeling . . . your strength . . . your security . . . is within . . . let yourself create these feelings . . . make these feelings move and flow together with your need to be a nonsmoker . . . relaxing . . . coping effectively . . . that anchor . . . a symbol of your conscious and unconscious mind working together . . . your mind and body working together . . . to help you control your thoughts and feelings in ways that are productive . . . good for you . . . for your health . . . for your self-respect.

The more you practice . . . the more you develop your skills, the better you will feel . . . practice early in the morning . . . practice during the day . . . as you do the things you do in your life . . . as you live and learn . . . more and more and more . . . more and more . . . you can give yourself suggestions . . . program your mind . . . to be a nonsmoker . . . tune yourself . . . tune your feelings . . . like you tune a precision instrument . . . an instrument you take good care of . . . each morning . . . and at times during the day . . . use your anchor . . . say your key phrase . . . review your reasons for not smoking . . . if you have any urges . . . use your lifetime of learnings to emphasize your health and well-being as you ignore them . . . remember that strength comes from within . . . you can use your anchor . . . perhaps take a deep breath and hold it in for four counts, and then as you slowly exhale, say your key phrase . . . be sure to anchor those feelings . . . you are a nonsmoker.

Go even deeper . . . deeper still . . . time slowing down . . . calm and at ease . . . anchored . . . grounded in your being . . . centered in yourself . . . visualize yourself in a situation in which you might in the past have been tempted to smoke . . . and anchor your resolve to be a nonsmoker . . . this sense of yourself as a nonsmoker . . . you can feel so good knowing that you can lock your resolve to be a nonsmoker with good feelings . . . and the knowledge that any thoughts of smoking will fade away . . . until they are gone and you can feel good and whole and together . . . with your body . . . with your unconscious . . . working together with your conscious . . . all of your senses working together to help you, helping you to do what you need to do . . . of course, the essence, the basis of suggestion. [Finally, participants are given suggestions to practice self-hypnosis and to use what they have learned in real-life situations, and hypnosis is terminated.]

Preliminary research on the 2-session program indicates that it achieves continuous abstinence rates ranging between 24% and 39%, across trainers, at 6-month follow-up. Even though trainers used the same training manual, somewhat different outcome rates were achieved by different trainers. Significantly, at follow-up, more than a third (36%) of the participants who did not achieve continuous abstinence reported reducing the number of cigarettes smoked per day. Finally, 42% of the nonquitters were interested either in participating in follow-up treatment or in acquiring additional information about other smoking cessation treatments. As will be evident in the next section, the treatment gains associated with our program compare favorably with 2-session group hypnosis treatments. In our research, as in the research described below, abstinence rates were computed on the basis of participants who completed treatment. Dropouts were considered treatment failures.

RESEARCH AND APPRAISAL

In this section, we will review research on hypnosis and smoking cessation. (The studies presented here are summarized in the appendix.) One of the first literature reviews relevant to the use of hypnosis in smoking cessation was compiled by Johnston and Donoghue (1971). Most of the reports they reviewed were anecdotal or clinical in nature and reported success rates as high as 94% (Von Dedenroth, 1964, cited in Johnston & Donoghue, 1971). Unfortunately, the reports presented no experimental evidence to substantiate the claims made, and the treatment procedures were not presented in sufficient detail to replicate.

In their literature review, Hunt and Bespalec (1974) compared six methods of modifying smoking behavior: aversive conditioning; drug therapy; education and group support; hypnosis; behavior modification; and "miscellaneous," including self-control, role-playing, and combination treatments. They concluded that hypnosis "perhaps gives us our best results" (p. 435), with reported success rates varying between 15% and 88%. However, because success rates were similar across studies, they suggested that the choice of treatment was secondary to engaging smokers in treatment.

In 1980, Holroyd published a major review of the hypnotic treatment of smoking in which she examined 17 reports and concluded that more sessions are better than fewer sessions, that individualized treatments are superior to standardized suggestions, and that adjunctive treatment such as telephone contact and counseling increase the likelihood of a successful outcome. She also recommended the inclusion of "intense interpersonal interaction" (p. 353) as part of treatment. Holroyd concluded that when these conditions are fulfilled, more than half of those treated remain abstinent at 6 months.

The reports reviewed by Holroyd were, for the most part, clinical reports. Although few of them were experimental studies, they are noteworthy. Barkley, Hastings, and Jackson (1977) compared group hypnosis with rapid smoking and an attention placebo. MacHovec and Man (1978) compared group and individual hypnosis with true-site acupuncture, placebo-site acupuncture, and no treatment. Pederson, Scrimgeour, and Lefcoe (1975) compared three groups: group discussion, group discussion plus hypnosis, and a waiting-list control group. Success rates for hypnosis in these studies ranged from 0% to 50%, outcomes that were in the lower range of the studies reviewed by Holroyd (1980).

The issue of the role of hypnotizability in determining the outcome of hypnotic smoking cessation treatments was addressed by surprisingly few studies. No evidence in the early studies emerged to support a link between hypnotizability and smoking cessation, although Perry et al. (1979) found evidence for an association between hypnotizability and smoking reduction.

None of the studies reviewed by Holroyd used an independent biochemical measure of smoking status; all relied on self-report. Independent verification of smoking status is an important element of contemporary smoking cessation outcome research and raises questions about the reliability of the findings summarized by Holroyd.

In the research published after 1980, two categories of studies can be identified: (a) clinical reports and quasi-experimental studies and (b) experimental investigations. We will first consider clinical reports, including single-session group treatments, and quasi-experimental studies.

Clinical Reports

Powell (1980) treated 23 subjects with individual hypnosis using Speigel's (1970) eye roll-arm levitation induction, client self-induction, and individualized suggestions, together with instructions to practice self-hypnosis. For subjects who relapsed, an additional technique, flooding and desensitization, was used. The number of sessions was variable and was determined by the subjects. A total of 11 subjects were abstinent after 9 months, 4 of whom received the additional flooding and desensitization treatment.

Sheehan and Surman (1982) reported on the treatment of 100 private patients by two hypnotists. Although there was no limit to the number of sessions subjects could receive, 89% of the patients had two or fewer sessions. Sheehan and Surman used a deep muscle relaxation induction, combined with direct suggestions to stop smoking, motivational suggestions, and aversive imagery. The technique was apparently similar to Speigel's (1970) technique. Two therapists conducted the treatment; one used a 20- to 25-minute induction, whereas the other therapist used a shortened version of the same induction (5 to 10 minutes long). The mean treatment–follow-up interval was 15 months, and the posttreatment assessment was conducted by a nonexperimenter.

Sheehan and Surman (1982) found that 21% of the clients were abstinent, a success rate comparable to that of other brief hypnosis treatments. Although hypnotizability or depth of hypnosis was not evaluated, information was provided about the subjective experience of hypnosis. Of those who were abstinent at follow-up, 10% reported a "significant trance," and 35% felt "not at all or only slightly 'hypnotized.' "

Basker (1985) used a "utilization" induction followed by suggestions that combined positive and aversive covert conditioning based on clients' reasons for quitting. Direct suggestions to reduce smoking urges, ego-enhancing suggestions, and self-hypnosis were also part of the treatment regimen that was conducted over multiple sessions. Although Basker tested his patients with the Stanford Hypnotic Clinical Scale (SHCS; Morgan & Hilgard, 1978–1979), he did not report when this occurred during treatment. Basker reported that of the 60 patients treated, 50% were abstinent after 6 months. Sixty-four percent of high hypnotizable, 45% of medium hypnotizable, and 25% of low hypnotizable participants were abstinent at the follow-up assessment.

Stanton (1985) examined the effect of hypnotizability on smoking cessation. Forty patients received a single 50-minute hypnosis session, as described by Stanton (1978), that was modified to include the Stanford

Hypnotic Arm Levitation Induction and Test (Hilgard, Crawford, & Wert, 1979). At 12 months, 62% were abstinent. There was no relationship between hypnotizability and abstinence.

Baer, Carey, and Meminger (1986) examined the role of hypnotizability in smoking cessation and relapse following the use of hypnosis for smoking cessation. In the first session, the clients (N = 172) were administered the SHCS. In the second session, an eye fixation induction, combined with Speigel's (1970) method, was used. Subjects were also instructed in the use of self-hypnosis. Treatment was provided by both experienced and inexperienced hypnotists.

Baer et al. (1986) found that at 6 months, none of the low hypnotizables were abstinent. In contrast, after 1½ years, medium and high hypnotizable subjects achieved abstinence rates in the "20–30%" range. After 3 months, the abstinence rates of patients treated by experienced hypnotists and patients treated by inexperienced hypnotists was comparable.

More recently, Marriot and Brice (1990) reported on 34 clients, randomly selected from files, who had attended a single-session hypnotic treatment for smoking cessation. The individualized treatment was described as "Ericksonian" and included techniques taken from Lazarus (1973), Bandler and Grinder (1975), and Hartland (1973) (all cited in Marriot & Brice), as well as aversive, smoking-related suggestions. Clients were instructed in relaxation and were encouraged to practice this daily to reduce withdrawal reactions. Follow-up at 12 weeks revealed that 29% of the clients were abstinent.

Finally, Crasilneck (1990) reported on his experience in treating 4,355 clients in his private practice over a 35-year period. He reported an 81% abstinence rate after a year on a sample of 100 clients who received three individual hypnosis sessions (consisting of relaxation and hypnotic phenomena, plus direct suggestions for minimal cravings, appetite and weight maintenance, increased exercise, self-hypnosis sensory acuity, and improved sleep) on consecutive days, with a fourth session 21 days after the third session. An average weight gain of 4 pounds was reported. Crasilneck emphasized the importance of exercise, self-hypnosis, Nicorette and sugarless gum, cinnamon sticks, and, if requested, extra sessions.

Unfortunately, Crasilneck (1990) did not detail his clients' characteristics, nor did he describe his method of collecting follow-up data. For example, it was not indicated whether the abstinence rate was based only on those clients contacted for follow-up, or if the entire sample was considered, with nonresponders counted as smokers.

Single-Session Group Hypnosis

Results of single-session group sessions, often conducted as part of the proprietary of for-profit or nonprofit programs, were the subject of several reports (Neufeld & Lynn, 1988; Owens & Samaras, 1981; Vermont Lung Association, 1981; Wagner, Hindi-Alexander, & Horowitz, 1983). Procedures are difficult to compare, given the variability in the extent to which they were reported. Abstinence rates ranged from 14% (Vermont Lung Association, 1981) to 18.5% (Neufeld & Lynn, 1988) after 6 months.

Quasi-Experimental Research

Barabasz et al. (1986) treated 307 patients in the context of a quasi-experimental design. Clients received various combinations of hypnotic and restricted environmental stimulation therapy (REST; Best & Suedfeld, 1982), which were administered individually and in a group format, by both experienced and inexperienced hypnotists and in single and multiple sessions. Hypnosis was conducted in five phases, which included rapport building and discussion about the nature of hypnosis; an "imagination exercise"; the administration of the SHCS; Speigel's (1970) procedure, individualized if necessary; and self-hypnosis training.

Follow-up ranged from 4 to 19 months and used self-reports. Abstinence rates ranged from a low of 4% after 4 months for individual hypnosis conducted by inexperienced interns to 47% after 19 months for patients treated with a combination of individual hypnosis conducted by an experienced hypnotist and REST. After 13 months, a no-treatment control group achieved a 6% abstinence rate. Finally, hypnotizability and smoking cessation were found to be correlated.

Experimental Investigations

Javel (1980) used volunteers recruited from Veterans Administration patients and staff. He compared a group to whom hypnosis was administered on an individual basis with two other groups: one given an identical procedure, except that the "trance" induction was omitted, and a waiting-list control group. Suggestions included ego-enhancing suggestions (Stanton, 1978) and Speigel's (1970) suggestions. The therapist followed up with a phone call every other day for a week.

Each group consisted of 10 subjects. Six of the induction group, 4 of the no-induction group, and none of the waiting-list controls were abstinent after 3 months. Follow-up was conducted by phone. It was concluded that treatment was more effective than no treatment. Although the treatment groups were not found to be statistically different, the small sample size placed constraints on this comparison.

Cornwell, Burrows, and McMurray (1981) compared the effects of hypnosis administered during a single session versus hypnosis administered during multiple sessions. The relationship between hypnotizability and outcome was examined, and a biochemical measure of smoking status was used. Nineteen subjects were assigned to a single-session hypnosis session using an eye-fixation induction and Speigel's (1970) suggestions; to a second group using four identical sessions; or to a waiting-list control group. A $50 deposit was collected and refunded after 2 months, contingent on tobacco abstinence. Hypnotizability was evaluated, following an initial interview, with the use of the SHCS.

Follow-up after 2 months revealed 60% abstinence in the multiple-session group, 40% abstinence in the single-session group, and 0% abstinence in the control group. The treatment groups achieved significantly higher abstinence rates than did the control group, but the treatment groups were indistinguishable. No correlation was found between hypnotizability and outcome.

Schubert (1983) assigned 87 subjects to hypnotherapy, systematic desensitization, or a waiting-list control group. Subjects received individual treatment for 4 weekly sessions. The treatments were identical except that the hypnotic induction was replaced by a relaxation procedure in the desensitization procedure. Treatment suggestions were designed to alter subjects' perceptions of themselves in relation to their smoking habits. Subjects maintained phone contact of an unspecified nature during the treatment period and the 4-month follow-up. At follow-up, subjects were tested with the Harvard Group Scale of Hypnotic Susceptibility.

Schubert found that 41% of the hypnotized subjects and 38% of the systematic desensitization subjects were abstinent after 4 months, compared with a rate of only 7% for the control subjects. Hypnotizability was related to a reduction in cigarettes smoked, but not to cessation.

Rabkin, Boyko, Shane, and Kaufert (1984) randomly assigned 168 subjects to an individual, single 30-minute hypnosis session; a group behavioral treatment; group health education; or a waiting-list control. Hypnosis featured Speigel's (1970) method. The groups were composed of 8 to 10 subjects and met five times over a 3-week period. A serum thiocyanate level was drawn initially and at 3 weeks. Self-report data at 6 months revealed that 21.4% of those hypnotized, 19% of the behavior modification group, and 21.4% of the health education group were abstinent.

T. B. Jeffrey, Jeffrey, Grueling, and Gentry (1985) assigned 35 smokers to a group-hypnosis smoking cessation program and 30 smokers to a waiting-list control group. Over a 2.5-week period, treatment subjects attended four 1-hour sessions, which were conducted by two therapists. Treatment consisted of a general discussion of smoking and cessation, training in cognitive–behavioral strategies, and 15 minutes of hypnosis featuring an eye fixation and relaxation induction coupled with suggestions derived from Crasilneck and Hall (1975), Speigel (1970), and Stanton (1978) (all cited in Jeffrey et al.). The suggestions were designed to promote maintenance of smoking cessation, relaxation, and feelings of mastery. Follow-up data were collected at 3 months using self-report data. No control smokers stopped smoking, whereas 31% of those treated were abstinent at follow-up.

Lambe, Osier, and Franks (1986) randomly assigned volunteers to a hypnosis group or a no-treatment control group. Hypnosis consisted of two 40-minute sessions, 2 weeks apart, during which subjects were taught self-hypnosis. They were called three times over 4 months to encourage abstinence and the use of self-hypnosis. After 3 months, the hypnosis group had a 21% abstinence rate, compared with 0 for the control group.

Frank, Umlauf, Wndelich, and Ashkanazi (1986) randomly assigned 63 subjects to one of four conditions: (a) two 1-hour group hypnotic treatments; (b) four 1-hour group hypnotic treatments; (c) two 1-hour group hypnosis sessions and two 1-hour sessions of behavior treatment; or (d) four 1-hour group hypnosis sessions followed by a booster session. The group hypnosis sessions were based on Sanders's (1977) mutual group hypnosis method and Speigel's (1970) suggestions. Subjects were compensated for participation but were required to provide a deposit that could be recouped by abstinence.

Follow-up data at 3 months was derived from saliva thiocyanate for a subset of subjects. At 6 months, data were secured by phone interview and self-monitoring cards. No between-group differences in cessation outcomes were evident. Regardless of group assignment, 19% of subjects were abstinent at the 6-month follow-up. Cessation was positively correlated with education and satisfaction with treatment, and negatively correlated with imagery ability and the presence of another smoker at home.

Hyman, Stanley, Burrows, and Horne (1986) randomly assigned 60 volunteers to hypnosis, focused smoking, attention placebo, or waiting-list control groups. A refundable deposit, not contingent on cessation, was collected. Data on smoking history and demographics were collected, as was baseline serum thiocyanate.

All treatment subjects were seen individually for four weekly sessions. Hypnosis consisted of an induction derived from Weitzenhoffer and Hilgard (1967), combined with Speigel's (1970) suggestions. Hyman et al. (1986) reported that treatment was superior to no treatment, but that no between-group outcome differences emerged. After 6 months, 33.3% of subjects treated were abstinent, leading the authors to conclude that nonspecific treatment effects were responsible for cessation.

L. K. Jeffrey and Jeffrey (1988) randomly assigned 120 volunteers either to a group hypnosis plus behavioral program, with the requirement that they be abstinent for 48 hours prior to treatment, or to an identical program without the abstinence requirement. Treatment consisted of five sessions over a 2½-week period. Each session included group discussion, presentation of behavioral control strategies, and hypnosis. At a 3-month follow-up, there was no between-group difference in abstinence rate: Across groups, 36.7% were abstinent.

In a recent study, Holroyd (1991) examined the relation between hypnotizability and treatment outcome in a sample of 91 clients seen in her private practice. Her clients received four individual hypnosis sessions using individualized procedures. They were then divided into treatment groups on the basis of two variations in the procedure she adopted. The first and second sessions were spaced 2 to 3 days apart, with the duration between later sessions determined by whether subjects were abstinent. Group assignment was based on whether clients were abstinent for 24 hours prior to treatment, and on variations in payment arrangements. All subjects were tested with the SHCS (Morgan & Hilgard, 1978–1979). Subjects were also asked to maintain telephone contact daily or weekly depending on their need for support. The abstinence rate at 6 months was 16%, and hypnotizability was not correlated with abstinence or with measures of expectancy and motivation.

Summary and Implications

Abstinence rates for the reports reviewed ranged from 4% (Barabasz et al., 1986) to 90% (Crasilneck, 1990). What accounts for the wide variability in outcome rates? "Hypnosis" is a catch-all phrase for a variety of procedures that bear little resemblance to one another beyond the label "hypnosis." What suggestions are used and how hypnosis is presented to clients varies across studies. Systematic comparisons of well-defined and carefully described hypnotic procedures are virtually nonexistent. In fact, it is very difficult to interpret the meaning of discrepant outcome rates because studies, as a rule, differ in terms of the types of procedures involved, the outcome measures used, and the intensity of the treatment administered.

Holroyd (1980) identified several factors that she believed were associated with positive treatment outcomes: length of time in treatment, intense interpersonal interaction, individualized tailoring of procedures, and adjunctive treatment such as telephone follow-up and counseling. Together, these could be thought of as measures of treatment intensity.

Three studies compared single-session with multiple-session treatment and booster sessions. Cornwell et al. (1981) found no statistical difference when comparing a single session with four sessions, although a small sample size limited the power of this study. Frank et al. (1986) found no difference between two sessions, on the one hand, and four sessions plus a booster session, on the other. Barabasz et al. (1986) found no difference between a single session and a single session followed by a booster session.

When abstinence rates are compared across studies, single-session interventions achieved rates between 4% (Barabasz et al., 1986) and 62% (Stanton, 1985). Multiple sessions achieved rates between 17% (Frank et al., 1986) and 60% (Cornwell et al., 1981). Williams and Hall (1988) reported 45% abstinence with 2½ hours of hypnosis, whereas Frank et al. (1986) reported 17% abstinence after 4 hours of hypnosis. However, when only the most carefully designed studies are considered, higher rates are associated with multiple sessions (Cornwell et al., 1981; Hyman et al., 1986). Furthermore, Barabasz et al. (1986) noted that it may be appropriate to offer follow-up sessions to those who are having difficulty with abstinence. Thus, although the data do not clearly indicate an advantage for multiple sessions, there may be clinical indications for using more than a single session on an individual basis.

Barabasz et al. (1986) compared treatment administered in a group format with treatment administered on an individual basis. Clients who received group and individual treatments administered by experienced clinicians had comparable abstinence rates that exceeded the abstinence rate of clients who received individual treatment administered by inexperienced clinicians. Thus, therapist experience rather than treatment modality emerged as an important variable. Baer et al. (1986), however, failed to find an advantage for experienced clinicians.

If we compare outcomes across studies, individually administered treatment outcomes range from 4% (Barabasz et al., 1986) to 60% (Javel, 1980). Other abstinence rates reported for individually administered treatments are 41% (Schubert, 1983), 33% (Hyman et al., 1986), and 21% (Rabkin et al., 1984; Sheehan & Surman, 1982). Group outcomes range between 14% (Vermont Lung Association, 1981) and 60% (Cornwell et al., 1981), with Barabasz et al. (1986) reporting 36% and Frank et al. (1986) reporting 17% abstinence. Thus, there is no clear evidence for an advantage to individual versus group hypnotic smoking-cessation treatment.

The least intense form of treatment, the single-session, large-group hypnotic treatment (Neufeld & Lynn, 1988; Owens & Samaras, 1981; Vermont Lung Association, 1981; Wagner et al., 1983), consistently had the lowest success rates; none were greater than 20%. It appears that there is no simple, direct relation between treatment length and intensity of treatment outcome. However, it seems clear that the most minimal treatments achieve no more than 20% abstinence rates. To maximize therapeutic gains, treatment needs to be intensified in some way (e.g., individual treatment, multiple sessions, or individualized suggestions). Such treatment enhancements do not, however, guarantee better outcomes (e.g., Frank et al., 1986).

One reason why variable outcomes across studies are the rule rather than the exception is that demand characteristics may influence clients' self-reports. For example, certain clients may feel obligated to report cessation despite a failure to achieve abstinence. One way of controlling for the vagaries of self-report is to use a biochemical measure of treatment success. Assuming that the use of a biochemical measure of smoking status provides a basis for placing confidence in outcome rates, it is worthwhile to examine the outcomes of studies (Cornwell et al., 1981; Frank et al., 1986; Hyman et al., 1986; Rabkin et al., 1984) using biochemical measures. The outcome (60%) of Cornwell et al. (1981) may be an overestimate of ultimate treatment success insofar as follow-up was at 2 months, and relapse has been shown to progress in a negatively accelerating curve until approximately 6 months (Hunt & Bespalac, 1974). The three remaining studies, representing the most carefully controlled investigations to date, suggest that abstinence rates in the range of 17% (Frank et al., 1986) and 33% (Hyman et al., 1986) are realistic estimates of treatment success.

An important question is whether hypnotizability moderates treatment gains. If hypnosis makes a unique contribution to treatment, then hypnotizability would be expected to be related to treatment outcome. Unfortunately, an unambiguous picture has failed to emerge; instead, the data are mixed. Whereas Barabasz et al. (1986), Basker (1985), and Baer et al. (1986) found a relationship between hypnotizability and abstinence, Cornwell et al. (1981), Stanton (1985), and Holroyd (1991) found no such relationship. These differences may be due to different measures of hypnotizability and differences in the timing of the measurement of hypnotizability. All of these studies except Stanton (1985) measured hypnotizability with the SHCS early in the treatment process. Contextual variables and expectancies have not been examined as possible factors moderating the relation between hypnotizability and abstinence. However, it is possible that the association between hypnotizability and smoking cessation rates depends on subjects' implicit and explicit perceptions of the connection between the hypnosis components of treatment and outcome.

Sheehan and Surman's (1982) data suggest that hypnosis can be viewed as helpful for smoking cessation even in the absence of an experience labeled as "trance." This suggests that hypnotizability may not be required to achieve abstinence in hypnosis smoking-cessation programs. In fact, measuring hypnotizability may well inhibit participants who become discouraged because they perceive that they were not hypnotized and, therefore, are not amenable to treatment.

Other than hypnotizability, only two individual difference variables—depression and absorption—have been studied in relation to smoking cessation. Barabasz et al. (1986) found that depression was correlated with outcome, and noted that several subjects required treatment for significant depression prior to achieving abstinence. Barabasz et al. also reported a positive relation between absorption and outcome. However, Frank et al. (1986) reported a negative correlation between outcome and imagery ability.

Differences in client characteristics that pertain directly to smoking may affect treatment outcome. For example, Williams and Hall's (1988) clients reported an average smoking history of approximately 8 pack-years, compared with studies treating more "hard-core" smokers (e.g., Frank et al., 1986), whose subjects had an average history of 31 pack-years. Although some studies did not report smoking history data, it is reasonable to assume that smokers with a relatively short smoking history would achieve higher abstinence rates than would more long-term smokers. Indeed, Williams and Hall (1988) reported a success rate of 45%, compared with Frank et al. (1986), who reported a 17% abstinence rate.

The available evidence is consistent with Hunt and Bespalec's (1974) conclusion that hypnosis and nonhypnotic treatments produce equivalent gains. The studies that compared hypnosis with other treatments found no superiority for any of the treatments examined. These findings support an approach to smoking cessation wherein smokers are offered a variety of treatments to choose from on the basis of personal preferences and expectancies of therapeutic gain (Neufeld & Lynn, 1988).

Nevertheless, well-controlled studies in this research area are lacking, so that firm conclusions about the relative effectiveness of diverse treatments and the superiority of hypnotic treatments cannot be made. However, from the relatively few available controlled studies, one conclusion can be drawn: No treatment control groups appear to be superfluous, insofar as in the absence of treatment, clients generally show no change in smoking behavior. Studies that compare well-defined and replicable hypnotic and nonhypnotic treatments should report subject characteristics including smoking history; previous quitting attempts; and clients' social support, motivation, and reasons for quitting. Ideally, biochemical measures of abstinence should be used, and follow-up should extend to at least 6 months and include information about withdrawal symptoms, reasons for relapse, and weight gain. Finally, measures of hypnosis should be administered in order to ascertain the exact role of hypnotizability in treatment success.

CONCLUSION

In this chapter, we presented a cognitive–behavioral smoking-cessation treatment that can be administered on a group or individual basis. We provided a detailed description of our program so that clinicians can use the procedures we developed to their advantage, or modify them according to their individual preference. Our literature review indicates that our treatment program fares about as well or somewhat better than the average single-session smoking cessation treatment and many of the more intensive treatment programs. Nevertheless, the available research indicates that many questions regarding the variables that mediate treatment efficacy remain unanswered and await carefully controlled outcome research.

Because hypnosis-based treatments can be relatively brief and inexpensive, in terms of therapist and client involvement, they may represent an excellent entry-level treatment for smoking. For individuals who do not succeed in brief, low-intensive treatments, a "stepped care" approach to smoking cessation (Glasgow, Schafer, & O'Neil, 1981) may be worthwhile. Such an approach acknowledges the need to provide programs that appeal to different individuals who have the opportunity to participate in more expensive and intensive treatments when brief interventions fail.

REFERENCES

American Psychiatric Association. (1987). *Diagnostic and statistical manual of mental disorders* (3rd ed., rev.). Washington, DC: Author.

Baer, L., Carey, R. J., & Meminger, S. R. (1986). Hypnosis for smoking cessation: A clinical follow-up. *International Journal of Psychosomatics, 33,* 13–16.

Bandura, A. (1982). Self-efficacy mechanism in human agency. *American Psychologist, 37,* 122–147.

Barabasz, A. F., Baer, L., Sheehan, D., & Barabasz, M. (1986). A three-year follow-up of hypnosis and restricted environmental stimulation therapy for smoking. *International Journal of Clinical and Experimental Hypnosis, 24,* 169–181.

Barber, T. X. (1985). Hypnosuggestive procedures as catalysts for all psychotherapies. In S. J. Lynn & J. P. Garske (Eds.), *Contemporary psychotherapy: Models and methods.* Columbus, OH: Merrill.

Barkley, R. A., Hastings, J. E., & Jackson, T. L. (1977). The effects of rapid smoking and hypnosis in the treatment of smoking behavior. *International Journal of Clinical and Experimental Hypnosis, 25,* 7–17.

Basker, M. A. (1985). Hypnosis in the alleviation of the smoking habit. In D. Waxman, P. C. Misra, M. Gibson, & M. A. Basker (Eds.), *Modern trends in hypnosis.* New York: Plenum Press.

Best, J., & Suedfeld, P. (1982). Restricted environmental stimulation therapy and behavioral self-management in smoking cessation. *Journal of Applied Social Psychology, 12,* 408–419.

Botvin, G. J., & Eng, A. (1982). The efficacy of a multicomponent approach to the prevention of cigarette smoking. *Preventive Medicine, 11,* 199–211.

Cornwell, J., Burrows, G. D., & McMurray, N. (1981). Comparison of single and multiple sessions of hypnosis in the treatment of smoking behavior. *Australian Journal of Clinical and Experimental Hypnosis, 9,* 61–76.

Crasilneck, H. B. (1990). Hypnotic techniques for smoking control and psychogenic impotence. *American Journal of Clinical Hypnosis, 32,* 147–153.

Dallosso, H. M., & James, W. P. T. (1984). The role of smoking in the regulation of energy balance. *International Journal of Obesity, 8,* 365–375.

Frank, R. G., Umlauf, R. L., Wndelich, S. A., & Ashkanazi, G. S. (1986). Hypnosis and behavior treatment in a worksite cessation program. *Addiction Behaviors, 11,* 59–62.

Glasgow, R. E., Schafer, L., & O'Neil, H. K. (1981). Self-help books and amount of therapist contact in smoking cessation programs. *Journal of Consulting and Clinical Psychology, 49,* 659–667.

Hilgard, E. R., Crawford, H. J., & Wert, A. (1979). The Stanford Hypnotic Arm Levitation Induction and Test (SHALIT): A six minute induction and measurement scale. *International Journal of Clinical and Experimental Hypnosis, 27,* 111–124.

Holroyd, J. D. (1980). Hypnosis treatment for smoking: An evaluation review. *International Journal of Clinical and Experimental Hypnosis, 4,* 241–357.

Holroyd, J. D. (1991). The uncertain relationship between hypnotizability and smoking treatment outcome. *International Journal of Clinical and Experimental Hypnosis, 34,* 103–106.

Hunt, W., Bespalec, D. (1974). An evaluation of current methods of modifying smoking behaviors. *Journal of Clinical Psychology, 30,* 431–438.

Hyman, G. J., Stanley, R. D., Burrows, G. D., & Horne, D. J. (1986). Treatment effectiveness of hypnosis and behavior therapy in smoking cessation: A methodological refinement. *Addictive Behaviors, 11,* 355–365.

Javel, A. F. (1980). One-session hypnotherapy for smoking: A controlled study. *Psychological Reports, 46,* 895–899.

Jeffrey, L. K., & Jeffrey, T. B. (1988). Exclusion therapy in smoking cessation. *International Journal of Clinical and Experimental Hypnosis, 37,* 70–74.

Jeffrey, T. B., Jeffrey, L. K., Grueling, J. W., & Gentry, W. R. (1985). Evaluation of a brief group treatment package including hypnotic induction for maintenance of smoking cessation: A brief communication. *International Journal of Clinical and Experimental Hypnosis, 33,* 95–98.

Johnston, E., & Donoghue, J. (1971). Hypnosis and smoking: A review of the literature. *American Journal of Clinical Hypnosis, 13,* 265–272.

Lambe, R., Osier, C., & Franks, P. (1986). A randomized controlled trial of hypnotherapy for smoking cessation. *Journal of Family Practice, 2,* 61–65.

Lynn, S. J., Neufeld, V., & Rhue, J. W. (1992). *A cognitive–behavioral hypnosis smoking cessation program: Treatment manual and procedures.* Unpublished manuscript.

MacHovec, F. J., & Man, S. C. (1978). Acupuncture and hypnosis compared: Fifty-eight cases. *American Journal of Clinical Hypnosis, 88,* 129–130.

Marlatt, G. A., & Gordon, J. R. (1985). *Relapse prevention: Maintenance strategies in the treatment of addictive behaviors.* New York: Guilford Press.

Marriot, J. A., & Brice, G. L. (1990). A single session of hypnosis to stop smoking. *Australian Journal of Clinical Hypnotherapy and Hypnosis, 11,* 21–28.

Morgan, A. H., & Hilgard, J. R. (1978–1979). The Stanford Hypnotic Clinical Scale for Adults. *American Journal of Clinical Hypnosis, 21,* 146–169.

Neufeld, V., & Lynn, S. J. (1988). A single-session group self-hypnosis smoking cessation: A brief communication. *International Journal of Clinical and Experimental Hypnosis, 36,* 75–79.

Owens, M. V., & Samaras, J. T. (1981). Analysis of the Damon smoking control program: A study of hypnosis on controlling cigarette smoking. *Journal of the Oklahoma State Medical Association, 74,* 65–70.

Pederson, L. L., Scrimgeour, W. G., & Lefcoe, N. M. (1975). Comparison of hypnosis plus counseling, counseling alone, and hypnosis alone in a community service smoking withdrawal program. *Journal of Consulting and Clinical Psychology, 43,* 920.

Perkins, K. A., Epstein, L., & Pastor, S. (1990). Changes in energy balance following smoking cessation and resumption of smoking in women. *Journal of Consulting and Clinical Psychology, 58,* 121–125.

Perry, C., Gelfand, R., & Marcovitch, P. (1979). The relevance of hypnotic susceptibility in the clinical content. *Journal of Abnormal Psychology, 89,* 598–603.

Perry, C., & Mullen, G. (1975). The effects of hypnotic susceptibility on reducing smoking behavior treated by an hypnotic technique. *Journal of Clinical Psychology, 31,* 498–505.

Pomerleau, O. F., & Pomerleau, C. S. (1984). Neuroregulators and the reinforcement of smoking: Towards a biobehavioral explanation. *Neuroscience and Biobehavior Review, 8,* 503–513.

Powell, D. H. (1980). Helping habitual smokers using flooding and hypnotic desensitization technique: A brief communication. *International Journal of Clinical and Experimental Hypnosis, 28,* 192–196.

Price, R. H., & Lynn, S. J. (1986). *Abnormal psychology* (2nd ed.). Homewood, IL: Dorsey Press.

Rabkin, S. W., Boyko, E., Shane, F., & Kaufert, J. (1984). A randomized trial comparing smoking cessation programs utilizing behavior modification, health education, or hypnosis. *Addictive Behaviors, 9,* 157–173.

Sanders, S. (1977). Mutual group hypnosis and smoking. *American Journal of Clinical Hypnosis, 20,* 131–135.

Schubert, D. K. (1983). Comparison of hypnotherapy with systematic relaxation in the treatment of cigarette habituation. *Journal of Clinical Psychology, 39,* 198–202.

Sheehan, D. V., & Surman, D. S. (1982). Follow-up study of hypnotherapy for smoking. *Journal of the American Society of Psychosomatic Dentistry and Medicine, 29,* 6–16.

Speigel, H. (1970). A single treatment method to stop smoking using ancillary self-hypnosis. *International Journal of Clinical and Experimental Hypnosis, 18,* 235–250.

Stanton, H. E. (1978). A one-session hypnotic approach to modifying smoking behavior. *International Journal of Clinical and Experimental Hypnosis, 26,* 22–29.

Stanton, H. E. (1985). The relationship between hypnotic susceptibility and smoking behavior. *International Journal of Psychosomatics, 32,* 33–35.

U.S. Department of Health, Education, and Welfare. (1990). *Smoking and health: A report of the surgeon general* (DHEW Publication No. PHS79-50066). Washington, DC: U.S. Department of Health, Education, and Welfare, Public Health Service, Office of the Assistant Secretary for Health, Office on Smoking and Health.

Vermont Lung Association. (1981). *Newsletter, 11,* Issue 4.

Wadden, T. A., & Anderton, C. H. (1982). The clinical use of hypnosis. *Psychological Bulletin, 91,* 215–243.

Wagner, T. J., Hindi-Alexander, M., & Horowitz, M. R. (1983). A one-year follow-up study of the Damon group hypnosis smoking cessation program. *Journal of the Oklahoma State Medical Association, 76,* 414–417.

Weitzenhoffer, A. M., & Hilgard, E. R. (1967). *Revised Stanford Profile Scale of Hypnotic Susceptibility, Form I and II.* Palo Alto, CA: Consulting Psychologists Press.

Williams, J. M., & Hall, D. W. (1988). Use of single session hypnosis for smoking cessation. *Addictive Behaviors, 13,* 205–208.

APPENDIX

Summary of Studies of Hypnosis and Smoking Cessation

Author	Population	Mode	Suggestions	Self-hypnosis	Sessions
Baer et al., 1986	172P	I	S	yes	2
Barabasz et al., 1986	307P	I&G	S	yes	1–4
Basker, 1985	60P	I	Ind	yes	multiple
Cornwell et al., 1981	19V	G	Ind	no	1–4
Crasilneck, 1990	100P	I	Ind	yes	4
Frank et al., 1986	63V	G	Ind	yes	2–5
Holroyd, 1991	91P	I	Ind	no	4
Hyman et al., 1986	60V	I	S	no	4
Javel, 1980	30V	I	S	yes	1
L. K. Jeffrey & Jeffrey, 1988	120V	G	S	no	4
T. B. Jeffrey et al., 1985	65P	G	S	no	5
Lambe et al., 1986	—	I	S	yes	2
Lynn et al., 1992	68P	G	S	yes	2
Marriot & Brice, 1990	34P	I	Ind	yes	1
Neufeld & Lynn, 1988	27P	G	S	yes	1
Owens & Samaras, 1981	486P	G	S	no	1
Powell, 1980	23P	I	S	yes	multiple
Rabkin et al., 1984	168V	I	S	yes	1
Schubert, 1983	87V	I	Ind	no	4
Sheehan & Surman, 1982	100P	I	S	no	1–5
Stanton, 1985	40P	I	S	no	1
Vermont Lung Association, 1981	561P	G	S	no	1
Wagner et al., 1983	783P	G	S	no	1
Williams & Hall, 1988	60V	G	S	no	1

Note: P = patient; I = individual; V = volunteer; G = group; S = standardized; Ind = individualized; TX = treatment; nm = not measured; *not described well enough to determine whether abstinence rate was based on total sample.

Time span	Adjunctive TX	Follow-up (months)	Biochemistry	Hypnotizability	Abstinence rate (hypnosis)
—	no	24	no	+ correlation w/ outcome	18%*
—	no	4–19	no	+ correlation w/ outcome	4%–47%*
—	mult. sessions	6	no	+ correlation implied, not tested	50%
1–4 weeks	no	2	yes	no correlation w/ outcome	multiple sessions 60%; single session 30%
3 weeks	—	12	no	nm	81%
5–11 weeks	no	6	yes	nm	17%
2–4 weeks	—	6+	no	no correlation w/ outcome	16%
4 weeks	no	6	no	nm	33%
1 session	phone	3	no	nm	60%
2.5 weeks	—	3	—	nm	31%
2.5 weeks	no	3	no	nm	37%
2 weeks	phone	3	no	nm	21%
1 week	—	6	no	nm	24%–39%
1 session	no	3	no	nm	29%
1 session	no	6	no	nm	19%
1 session	no	6–9	no	nm	28%
up to 4 months	add TX as needed	9	no	nm	43%
1 session	no	6	no	nm	19%–21%
4 weeks	phone	4	no	+ correlation w/ reduction but not abstinence	41%
1–5 weeks	no	15	no	nm	21%
1 session	no	12	no	nm	62%
1 session	no	12	no	nm	16%
1 session	no	12	no	nm	14%
1 session	no	11	no	nm	45%

27

ASSESSMENT AND TREATMENT OF SOMATIZATION DISORDERS: THE HIGH RISK MODEL OF THREAT PERCEPTION

IAN WICKRAMASEKERA

When somatic symptoms are presented to behavioral medicine practitioners in the absence of any identifiably pathophysiology (e.g., brain tumor), it is assumed that they are caused by psychological factors, and the patients presenting the symptoms are diagnosed as somatizers. Somatizers are estimated to constitute at least 50% of all patients who visit primary care physicians (Barsky & Klerman, 1983; Brown, Robertson, Kosa, & Alpert, 1971; Garfield et al., 1976; Jencks, 1985). They seldom show gross overt psychopathology (Jencks, 1985) and often do not meet the DSM–III–R (American Psychiatric Association, 1987) criteria for somatoform disorders (Katon et al., 1991). Thus, a substantial proportion of patients in the medical and psychiatric health care systems do not fit neatly into existing categories of mental or physical disease. A recent article in the *Journal of the American Medical Association* described somatization as "one of medicine's blind spots" (Quill, 1985).

The diagnosis of somatization by the absence of identifiable pathophysiology is diagnosis by exclusion. Diagnosis by exclusion is irrational because it may be based on inappropriate or insensitive biomedical tests or because the appropriate physical investigation may not be done (Hall, 1980). Thus, the actual prevalence of somatization disorders is not known. Its determination requires not only the exclusion of pathophysiology, but also the identification of psychological factors that can independently drive somatic symptoms. Diagnosis by exclusion is practiced by default because there has been little systematic effort devoted to the identification of specific pyschological and psychophysiological factors that can cause physical symptoms independently of pathophysiology. The high risk model of threat perception (Wickramasekera, 1979, 1984, 1986, 1988) described in this chapter provides an approach to diagnosis by inclusion, because it identifies psychosocial factors in threat perception that are hypothesized to consciously or unconsciously drive somatic symptoms.

There is growing empirical evidence for unconscious or implicit cognition and emotion (Greenwald, 1992; Kihlstrom, 1987, 1991). In somatizers, psychosocial conflicts and perceptions of threat become unconsciously transduced through conditioning and learning mechanisms into somatic and behavioral symptoms (Dollard & Miller, 1950; N. E. Miller, 1992; Wickramasekera, 1968, 1976b, 1988). I have hypothesized (Wickramasekera, 1968, 1972, 1988, 1991b) that over 50% of the psychosocial threats and fantasies that drive somatization are implicit or unconscious. I also believe that physiological monitoring enhances access to and modification of these implicit threats (Shevrin, 1990, 1991; Shevrin & Fritzler, 1968; Weinberger, Schwartz, & Kristeller, 1979; Wickramasekera, 1972, 1976a, 1979, 1988, 1990, 1991a, 1991b), and I predict that within 25 years it will be unethical to do psychotherapy with somatizers without concurrent physiological monitoring. The high risk model of threat perception offers a psychophysiological method of assessing somatization that provides specific and quantifiable targets for therapy. It also includes a Trojan horse method of building a therapeutic alliance with this very large group of patients who are "enormously resistant" (Smith, 1990) to psychiatric but not medical investigation.

The identification of high risk psychophysiological factors that can implicitly or explicitly independently drive somatic symptoms has profound implications for diagnostic practice, as well as for therapy and for primary prevention. For example, it might inhibit the clinician's tendency to submit the patient to extensive physical investigations that could increase the probability of identifying and then surgically treating a false positive physical etiology and producing an iatrogenic condition. An example of this would be unnecessary back surgery for functionally generated benign and self-limiting back pain (Flor & Turk, 1984).

Hypnosis is an essential but insufficient part of the high risk model. Hypnotizability is one of three interacting traits that are hypothesized to predispose individuals to develop somatization disorders. It is not hypnotic ability alone but the company it keeps that generates pathology.[1] For that reason, very high or very low levels of hypnotic ability appear to be more frequent among somatizers than in the general population (Wickramasekera, 1979, 1984, 1991a; Wickramasekera, Atkinson, & Turner, 1992a; Wickramasekera, Ware, & Saxon, 1992b). Besides being an essential part of the diagnostic process, hypnosis is used to treat high hypnotizables. It is also used with biofeedback to even temporarily increase (Wickramasekera, 1971a, 1973) the hypnotic ability of the very low hypnotizables (Zillmer & Wickramasekera, 1987) so that they are more responsive to psychophysiological hypnotherapy of their somatic disorders. The full high risk model of threat-related symptoms has been presented in detail elsewhere (Wickramasekera, 1986, 1988, 1989). This chapter expands on the role played by hypnotizability and the feedback of physiological information to the therapist and the patient in the assessment and treatment of somatization disorders.

A FRAMEWORK FOR DIFFERENTIAL DIAGNOSIS

Some physical complaints can be accounted for by positive physical findings (e.g., a brain tumor or a herniated disc), others by positive psychophysiological findings (e.g., high levels of muscle tension or neuroticism), and still others by a combination of both factors. As shown in Figure 1, patients who present physical complaints can be grouped into four cells (Wickramasekera, 1979, 1986, 1988) on the basis of physical and psychophysiological findings.

Amplifiers

Cell 1 consists of patients with both positive physical findings and positive psychophysiological findings. Empirical studies (Flor & Turk, 1984) have shown that psychosocial factors can amplify sensory signals from pathophysiology, which can account for approximately 50% of the variability from postsurgical measures of acute pain (Taenzer, Melzack, & Jeans, 1986). I have hypothesized (Wickramasekera, 1977b, 1980, 1985) that one subset of these psychophysiological complaints are conditioned responses (CRs) developed secondary to primary pathophysiology (unconditioned stimulus;

---

[1] In fact, high hypnotic ability, in the company of true (low Lie scale score) positive affect (extroversion), can be a "risk factor" for psychophysiological immunity to mental and physical disease (Wickramasekera, 1988, p. 70).

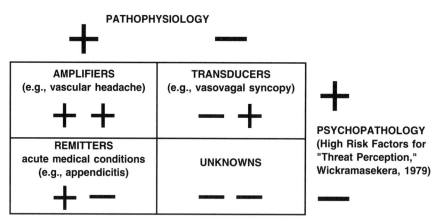

PATHOPHYSIOLOGY

Positive (+) or negative (–) pathophysiological or psychopathological findings.

Figure 1: A model of the relationship between pathophysiology (structural or functional) and psychopathology (Wickramasekera, 1979).

UCS). The onset of an acute episode of tissue damage or infection can function as a UCS for anxiety, depression, or pain. Therefore, the occurrence and severity of these responses are a function not only of pathophysiology (UCS), but also of the neutral stimuli (e.g., medical attention, sick role cues, and health care settings) with which it has been associated. In people who are prone to somatize (Costa & McCrae, 1987), the anxiety, depression, or pain may amplify the pathophysiology and persist as CRs even after the pathophysiology (e.g., brain tumor) has been removed. Pathophysiology (UCS) may be neither an essential nor a sufficient condition for the complaint of chronic low back pain (Wiesel, Feffer, & Tsournas, 1984). I have labeled these patients *amplifiers* because they psychologically amplify pathophysiology.

Transducers

Cell 2 consists of patients with negative physical findings and positive psychophysiological findings. I hypothesize that as children, these patients have learned from adult role models or through operant conditioning to unconsciously transduce psychological conflicts or threats into somatic complaints. I have labeled them *transducers* because they convert psychological information into physiological events. The complaints of these patients frustrate the best diagnostic, surgical, and chemical efforts of physicians. Patients who transduce their psychosocial threats into somatic symptoms present only to primary care physicians or surgeons and are harder to recognize than amplifiers (Drossman, 1978; Smith, 1990). Transducers present few or no psychological symptoms and are also very resistant to psychiatric referral (Smith, 1990). They shop for doctors and insist on extensive, expensive, and unproductive medical tests and procedures to identify a pathophysiologic etiology for their somatic symptoms (Smith, 1990). Psychological, financial, and social incentives for transduction were discussed in Wickramasekera (1988, 1989).

Remitters

Patients in Cell 3 present positive physical findings and negative psychophysiological findings. Effective medical treatment is followed by spontaneous resolution of the acute physical complaint (e.g., appendicitis), without enough time for psychological learning and amplification of the acute physical symptoms. Any secondary psychological symptoms extinguish spontaneously, and no psychotherapy is needed. Current medical education prepares medical doctors to treat effectively only this type of patient.

Unknowns

A patient in Cell 4 presents physical symptoms in the absence of positive physical or psychophysiological findings. These negative findings (Hall, 1980) may be attributed to insensitive or inappropriate physical and/ or psychophysiological tests and examinations. These patients require the most complete and careful medical investigation, particularly if the psychophysiological investigation is negative.

CLINICAL APPLICATIONS

Because of the ineffectiveness, high costs, and iatrogenic injury associated with repeated empirical medical investigations (Drossman, 1978; Relman, 1980; Tancredi & Barondess, 1978) and therapies (e.g., surgery or addictive drugs) of the somatizer, more specific psychophysiological evaluation and therapy for the somatizer is needed. There is also the need for a credible and face-saving rationale for the frustrated and angry physician and the disappointed patient to call a halt to iatrogenic medical investigations. But first, there is a need to convince the patient that some serious undiagnosed pathophysiology (UCS) is very unlikely on the basis of the prior multiple tests and specialist consultations. Furthermore, because the patient's somatic symptoms persist, there is a need to empirically document the fact that an alternative set of specific psychophysiological high risk factors (Wickramasekera, 1979, 1984, 1986, 1988) for psychophysiological amplification or transduction can independently account for this patient's somatic symptoms, in the absence of any pathophysiology. Also, it needs to be shown that the reduction of these specific psychophysiological risk factors is reliably associated with the remission of somatic symptoms. Further specific positive psychophysiological high risk test findings can provide

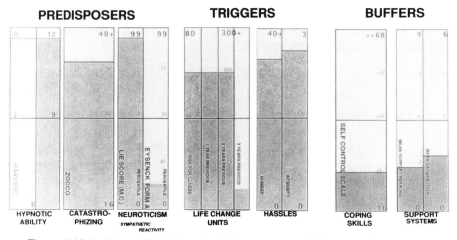

Figure 2: High risk model of threat-related symptoms (Wickramasekera, 1979).

reassurance and independent confirmation of the physician's clinical judgment that no serious pathophysiology was missed and that psychophysiological factors are in fact driving the patient's somatic complaints.

As illustrated in Figure 2, the three components of the high risk model are termed *predisposers, triggers,* and *buffers* of threat perception. Predisposers are personality variables, triggers are situational variables, and buffers are constructs at the interface of personality and situational variables. The three predisposing personality variables are hypnotic ability, catastrophizing, and neuroticism. The two triggering variables are major life change and accumulated minor hassles. The three buffering variables are the availability of support, satisfaction with social support, and coping skills. Buffering variables reduce the probability that the triggering variables will be associated with the onset of somatic or psychological symptoms. Predisposing variables increase the probability that the triggering variables will be associated with these symptoms. The interaction of predisposing, triggering, and buffering variables are thought to account for the bulk of the variance in predicting the onset and stability of clinical symptoms. It has been hypothesized and empirically demonstrated (Wickramasekera, 1990, 1991a) that these risk factors are at least partly independent of each other.

Hypnotic Ability as a Predisposer

Hypnosis can be defined as a mode of information processing in which a suspension of peripheral attention and critical analytic cognition can lead to major changes in perception, memory, and mood in people of high hypnotic ability, which can have major behavioral and biological consequences (Wickramasekera, 1979, 1986, 1988). During hypnosis, these changes appear to occur rapidly, involuntarily, and automatically (Bowers,

1982; Dixon, Brunet, & Laurence, 1990; Sheehan, Donovan, & MacLeod, 1988) and appear to be outside of self-control. Highly hypnotizable persons are prone to perceive "automaticity" or "involuntariness" both outside and inside of hypnosis (Dixon et al., 1990). It is known that the perception of unpredictable and uncontrollable events can amplify pain and fear (Mineka & Kihlstrom, 1978; Thompson, 1981). In turn, pain and fear or the perception of a threat to psychological or physical well-being can trigger the hypothalamic–pituitary–adrenal axis (HPAA) (Harsher-Towe, 1983; Wickramasekera, 1979, 1983, 1986, 1988). Chronic or intermittent triggering of the HPAA may alter the immune system (Dantzer, 1991; Krantz & Manuck, 1984; Mason, 1968; Mathews & MacLeod, 1986). This suggests that in high hypnotizables, implicit (unconscious) or explicit (conscious) threatening situational or interpersonal cues produce aversive changes in perception, memory, and mood. These aversive changes will be amplified if the individual is also high in negative affectivity or neuroticism (Mathews & MacLeod, 1986; Mathews, May, Mogg, & Eysenck, 1990). When these aversive changes are perceived as involuntary, as is likely among persons who are high in hypnotic ability, the changes potentiate fear and pain perception, thereby altering autonomic nervous system (ANS) functions and potentiating the development of stress- (threat-) related disorders. This hypothesized hazardous interaction between high hypnotic ability and high neuroticism or high catastrophizing is depicted in Figure 3. Clinically, this interaction produces the highest level of distress.

Although this sequence of events is more likely to occur among highly hypnotizable individuals when they perceive a threat, it can also occur among those who are low or moderate in hypnotic ability. I have hypoth-

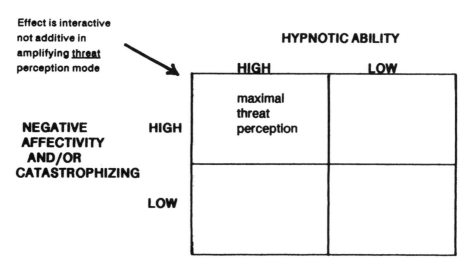

Figure 3: The interaction of hypnotic ability and negative affectivity (or catastrophizing) amplifies threat perception (Wickramasekera, 1979, 1986, 1988).

esized that in all people, the hypnotic mode of information processing is temporarily more likely under certain conditions (Wickramasekera, 1976b, 1977a, 1988). These have been hypothesized to include (a) low levels of psychophysiological arousal (Engstrom, 1976; Wickramasekera, 1971a, 1976b, 1977a); (b) high levels of interpersonal rapport and trust (Wickramasekera, 1969b, 1971b, 1976b); (c) sensory restriction procedures like space flight, automated cockpits of aircraft or nuclear reactors, social and sensory isolation, and so forth (Barabasz & Barabasz, 1989; Wickramasekera, 1969a, 1977a); and (d) high levels of activation of the sympathetic nervous system, such as those that occur during strenuous physical exercise; auto or industrial accidents; warfare; and sexual, physical, or psychological trauma (Banyai & Hilgard, 1976; Gur, 1974; Wickramasekera, 1968, 1972, 1976a). Under these conditions, changes in perception, memory, and mood can also appear to occur involuntarily and suddenly in all people. I hypothesize that all people may be especially vulnerable to implicit maladaptive cognitive learning and conditioning in the four hypersuggestible situations above (Wickramasekera, 1976b, 1979, 1988).

A second mechanism through which high hypnotizables are at risk for stress-related disorders is their hypothesized propensity to surplus pattern recognition, to see "meaning" in a set of data that seem randomly distributed to others (Wickramasekera, 1988). People of high hypnotic ability can also experience hallucinatory or illusory perceptions in one or more sensory modalities (Barber, 1969; Council & Loge, 1988; Hilgard, 1965; Wallace, Garrett, & Anstadt, 1974; Wallace, Knight, & Garrett, 1976; Wilson & Barber, 1982) both in and outside of hypnosis. They are also vulnerable to distortions in memory (Dywan & Bowers, 1983; Laurence & Perry, 1983) and alterations in mood (Crowson, Conroy, & Chester, 1991; Pettinati et al., 1990; Velten, 1968). These false perceptions may be sustained unintentionally (Uleman & Bargh, 1989) by primary or secondary reinforcement mechanisms. High hypnotizables also demonstrate superior response acquisition in operant and responding conditioning situations (Das, 1958; King & McDonald, 1976; Wickramasekera, 1976b). Because of their propensity for surplus pattern recognition, they may be at greater risk of unintentionally perceiving meaning in unrelated events and acquiring maladaptive learned responses (e.g., pain, fear, anxiety, and depressive and phobic behaviors).

Implicit or unconscious cognitive learning of threat is hypothesized to be a third mechanism by which psychophysiological symptoms come to persist without explicit knowledge of reinforcement contingencies (Wickramasekera, 1979, 1986, 1988). However, out of mind (explicit memory) is not out of body (Wickramasekera, 1988). When people confront their mortality in life-threatening situations (auto accidents, sexual abuse or rape, warfare, industrial accidents, etc.), there is massive sympathetic arousal in the microseconds before impact. I have hypothesized that the following series of events occur during this interval (Wickramasekera, 1988), causing posttraumatic stress disorder:

1. The intense perception of terror triggers an altered state of consciousness, like hypnosis, in which negative affect (e.g., terror) expands microseconds of clock time into several minutes of perceived time. The perception of time goes into "slow motion," and cognitive channel capacity and/or cognitive flow rate in short-term memory is temporarily expanded beyond the normal seven (plus or minus two) items (G. Miller, 1956). In recent empirical surveys of over 200 people who had been in auto accidents and had anticipated death at impact, 88% reported a subjective slowing down of time, with many more cognitions than could have occurred in clock time (Wickramasekera, 1990, 1991a). For example, one patient reported that there was enough time to read an entire newspaper while his car was spinning out of control into a line of oncoming traffic at 70 mph on an interstate highway.

2. It is likely that multiple catastrophizing cognitions relating to issues of mortality and life events flood consciousness. I hypothesize that physiology tracks subjective time perception rather than clock time, permitting a greater release of catecholamines and stress hormones than could occur if it tracked clock time.

3. After the accident, when the threat has passed, intense affect and catastrophic cognitions may be repressed into implicit memory, where they may persist for days, weeks, or years. When any remotely related future threat is perceived, these implicit cognitions may amplify it and produce chronic or intermittent activation of the ANS and motor cortex, driving somatic symptoms (e.g., tachycardia, cervical and/or trapezius muscular bracing, etc.). A final common implicit pathway may be established for threat perception. Explicit recall and desensitization of the multiple affective and cognitive components of the repressed terror may be necessary for full extinction of this implicit psychophysiological response.

Empirical studies of posttraumatic stress disorder have documented psychophysiological correlates of explicit traumatic cues (Blanchard, Hickling, & Taylor, 1991). During hypnotic desensitization and flooding procedures, heart rates jumping rapidly from 85 to 180 beats per minute have been observed and recorded, as well as systolic blood pressures jumping from 120 to 210 mmHg. Conditioned implicit cues relating to the perception of time, person, and place during trauma may potentiate state-specific maladaptive autonomic learning (Wickramasekera, 1976b, 1979, 1988) that is resistant to extinction with procedures used in conventional psychotherapy without hypnosis.

Very little is known empirically about people who are very low in hypnotic ability, because they avoid psychological studies and visit mainly the medical sector (Pomerantz & Wickramasekera, 1992; Wickramasekera, 1979, 1986, 1988). However, on the basis of clinical observation and a preliminary empirical study (Pomerantz, 1986), they have been hypothesized to be verbally relatively unaware of threat and to repress or deny the role of psychosocial variables in their own physical symptoms (Wickramasekera, 1979, 1984, 1988) even when they are physiologically activated by the perception of threat (Pomerantz, 1986). Under conditions of high stress, low hypnotizables show reduced explicit (verbal report) but not implicit (e.g., physiological measures) threat perception (Pomerantz & Wickramasekera, 1992), as illustrated in Figure 4. Low hypnotizables explicitly but not implicitly attenuate the perception of threat (see Figure 4). I hypothesize that low hypnotizables "know the words but miss the music." I also hypothesize that they are slow to inhibit critical analytic mental functions or to suspend disbelief. Hence, they tend to be "show me" or "show me again" people (replication). Low hypnotizables may delay in-

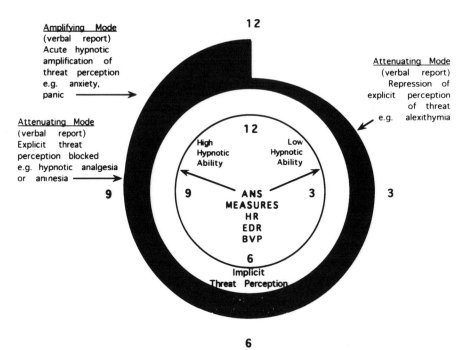

Figure 4: Explicit (conscious) and implicit (unconscious) threat perception in hypnotic ability level (0–12) (Wickramasekera, 1988, 1990). (ANS = autonomic nervous system; HR = heart rate; EDR = electrodermal response; BVP = blood volume pulse.)

vestigating their own physical symptoms, and they typically limit the investigation to medical procedures. Consequently, low hypnotizables seem to present relatively more serious psychophysiological disorders than do high hypnotizables.

Predictions and Findings From High and Low Hypnotic Ability as Risk Factors for Threat Perception

People who are high on hypnotic ability are likely to develop both somatic and psychological symptoms when highly threatened, and to present them in both medical and mental health settings. People who are low in hypnotic ability are predicted to develop primarily or exclusively somatic symptoms and to present them only in medical settings. High levels of threat will be perceived implicitly (with physiological measures) equally well by people of high, moderate, and low hypnotic ability, as shown in Figure 4. Under conditions of high threat, low hypnotizables, compared with high hypnotizables equated on neuroticism, have shown reduced explicit (verbal report measure) but not implicit (e.g., electromyograph; EMG) threat perception (Pomerantz & Wickramasekera, 1992). High and low hypnotizables can both explicitly attenuate (repress) the perception of threat (e.g., hypnotic analgesia or "numbing" in high hypnotizables, and repression of threat in low hypnotizables), but high hypnotizables, in the short run, can repress threat more completely, as shown in Figure 4. High hypnotizables, if they catastrophize, can also amplify threat perception, generating high levels of fear, panic, and pain (see Figures 3 and 4). In moderate hypnotizables, explicit (e.g., verbal report) and implicit (e.g., physiological) measures of threat perception are expected to be less discrepant than in high and low hypnotizables (see Figure 4).

Assessing Risk for Somatization

Risk factors for somatization can be assessed using the following scales and criteria.

Predisposers

Hypnotic ability. Hypnotic ability is measured in my laboratory on the Harvard Group Scale of Hypnotic Susceptibility, Form A (Shor & Orne, 1962) and the Stanford Hypnotic Susceptibility Scale, Form C (Weitzenhoffer & Hilgard, 1962), supplemented by measures of subjective engagement (Kirsch, Council, & Wickless, 1990) and involuntariness (Bates, Dinges, Whitehouse, Orne, & Orne, 1991). Scores of 10 to 12 on either scale indicate a high level of hypnotic ability; scores of 0 to 4 indicate low hypnotizability.

Catastrophizing. Catastrophizing can be defined as an overlearned explicit or relatively conscious tendency to become cognitively absorbed in automatic negative anticipations and negative self-statements ("I can't stand this," "this is horrible," etc.) that keep the limited cognitive resources of attention focused on the negative affective aspects of sensations, their consequences, and their antecedents. Catastrophizing amplifies the threatening properties of even minimally aversive sensory cues (Spanos, Perlini, & Robertson, 1989). This can cause an upward spiral of panic, sympathetic nervous system hyperactivity, muscle contraction, and amplified pain perception (Osterweiss, Kleinman, & Mechanic, 1987). Patients high on catastrophizing are likely to "make mountains out of molehills." Catastrophizing is measured by the Zocco Scale (Zocco, 1984), with scores of 35 and above interpreted as a high level. Catastrophizing about pain can also be measured with the Coping Strategies Questionnaire (Rosenstiel & Keefe, 1983).

Neuroticism/Negative affectivity (Watson & Clark, 1984). Neuroticism has been shown to be related to the number of somatic complaints people present, independent of age and pathophysiology (Costa & McCrae, 1987). Unlike catastrophizing, it appears to be at least partly genetically based (Tellegen et al., 1988). Patients scoring high on neuroticism (N) have enhanced implicit or unconscious memory for threat (Mathews et al., 1990) and a preattentive bias for threatening information (Mathews & MacLeod, 1986). They are more likely to see the glass as half empty rather than as half full and to have excellent unconscious memory for negative events. Hence, it is critical to give them hypnotic suggestions to alter this implicit and explicit "software." I measure neuroticism or negative affectivity on the Eysenck Personality Inventory, Form A (Eysenck & Eysenck, 1968), using a N score of 75% or greater as a criterion.

People who are low on neuroticism but who also score high on the need for social approval (e.g., Marlowe-Crowne, or Lie, scale) are called *repressors.* Repressors are also at risk for somatization because of reduced resistance to infection and inhibition of pain perception (Jamner, Schwartz, & Leigh, 1988). In a prospective study, Jensen (1987) found that this repressive personality style was correlated with more rapid progression of breast cancer. On the Eysenck scale, I use an N score of 25% or less, combined with a Lie (L) score of 75% or greater, as in indication of repressed neuroticism. Repressed neurotics are unaware of psychological distress but show psychological activation (Weinberger et al., 1979). Out of mind is not out of body. Repressors like low hypnotizables show physiological activation during threat perception. It appears that repression (low N, high L) and the hypnotic analgesia or amnesia of high hypnotizables are orthogonal pathways to blocking the explicit perception of fear and threat. I have seen individual patients (see the case study later in this chapter) who have access to both mechanisms, and in these patients the memory of threat (sexual abuse) can be blocked from both mind and peripheral ANS measures. The Psychophysiological Stress Profile (Wickramasekera, 1988) is used to determine the patient's most reactive organ system or window of physiological vulnerability; it is a physiological (implicit) measure of threat perception (see Figure 4) or negative affectivity. The identification of the most reactive sympathetic nervous system response (e.g., skin temperature or skin conductance) enables one to target it for reduction through hypnotherapy or biofeedback, depending on the individual patient's hypnotic ability level (Zillmer & Wickramasekera, 1987).

Triggers

Life changes and hassles. A review of the literature indicates that only about 10% of the variance in predicting symptoms is accounted for by major life change (Rabkin & Struening, 1976). More recently, an accumulation of minor daily hassles was shown to be strongly related to somatic symptoms (Sternbach, 1986), even after the effects of major life changes were statistically removed (DeLongis, Coyne, Dakof, Folkman, & Lazarus, 1982; Zarski, 1984). As a patient recently said to me, "It is not the mountain in front of you but the grains of sand in your shoe that can unravel you." There are still several methodological problems that remain to be resolved in the measurement of both major life change and hassles (Lazarus, DeLongis, Folkman, & Gruen, 1985). I measure major life change with the Schedule of Recent Events (Kanner, Coyne, Schaefer, & Lazarus, 1981), using scores of 280 and above as a criterion, and hassles with the Hassles Scale (Kanner et al., 1981), with 30 or more hassles and a mean intensity of 2 or greater indicating a high level of hassles.

Social support. Numerous studies have shown that social support is associated with less physical and mental illness, and in prospective studies it has been found to be causally related to mortality (House, Landis, & Umberson, 1988). I use an N score of 2 or less and a satisfaction score of 3 or less on the Social Support Questionnaire (Sarason, Levine, Basham, & Sarason, 1983) as an indication of low social support.

Coping skills. There is widespread agreement on the importance of individual differences in coping skills for health outcomes (Lazarus & Folkman, 1984), but there is controversy about the best method of measurement. I use the Rosenbaum Scale (Rosenbaum, 1980) to measure coping competence, with low coping skills indicated by a score of +5 or less.

Positive test findings on these high risk factors can provide the physician with a rational explanation of the patient's persisting somatic complaints. They can also provide a diagnosis of somatization by the inclusion, and not merely the exclusion, of pathophysiology. Hence, the physician can feel both medically and legally justified in referring the somatizer for psychophysiological psychotherapy (Wickramasekera, 1976b, 1988, 1989). Positive findings on one or more of these seven risk factors for threat perception is regarded as evidence of somatization. For example, I have seen somatizers for whom all conventional psychological testing (e.g., the Minnesota Multiphasic Personality Inventory, etc.) and the psychiatric interview are negative for psychopathology but who are high on hypnotic ability or are a repressor (high L but low N).

Conscious (Explicit) and Unconscious (Implicit) Threat Perception in Assessment and Therapy

Cognition (e.g., implicit or explicit threat appraisal) plays a critical role (Lazarus, 1991) in the sequence of events that make up psychological stress. The importance of explicit or implicit cognitive activity is that most psychological stress is initiated and maintained not by tissue damage, but by irrational or infantile cognitive (Lazarus, 1991) or emotional (Zajonc, 1984) appraisals of threats to well-being. We explicitly or implicitly assign rigid negative meanings to psychosocial and environmental events over which we have little or no direct control. These cognitive appraisals (Ellis, 1962) generate catastrophizing verbalizations that transduce into "stressors," the inevitable transient events (failure, delays, loss, uncertainty, rejection, etc.) of life. When appraised in short- or long-term memory as threatening, dreadful, or intolerable, these explicit or implicit catastrophizing verbalizations can lead to chronic anger or fear that puts on "red alert" the HPAA (Ewart, Taylor, Kraemer, & Agras, 1991; Krantz & Manuck, 1984; Matthews, Weiss, & Detre, 1986; Palsson, 1992), damaging, for example, the heart, kidneys, or vasculature.

The empirical data from psychophysiological testing and therapy reliably show that patients with physical symptoms are more or less unaware of the chronic physiological activation (cold hands, paradoxical increases in skin temperature response under cognitive stress, wet hands, high EMG in the back or neck, etc.), which varies across organ systems, and may even be mismatched with their presenting clinical symptom. It appears that nature has to hit them on the head with a club (e.g., a symptom) to get their attention to their body. In the medical literature, for example, it is known that people do not perceive hypertension. Lack of subjective perception of objective physiological activation is the rule and not the exception (Wickramasekera, 1976b, 1988) in patients with somatic presentations. Even temporary, explicit and implicit reductions in threat perception can lead to risking new adaptive behaviors and to discovering old "secrets we keep from ourselves."

Preliminary Hypothesized Concepts and Therapy Prescriptions for Use With the High Risk Profile

The high risk model of threat perception can inform the assessment and therapy of any chronic somatic disorder (headache, diabetes, obesity, primary hypertension, etc.) that has features that are amplified or transduced by the perception of threat. The perception of threat is thought to be determined by the predisposers (high or low hypnotic ability; catastrophizing; and neuroticism and self-deception, or L score). It is important to realize that people of high and low hypnotic ability are more alike in some ways than they may appear (see Figure 4), and it is therefore more heuristic to conceptualize the distribution of hypnotic ability as a circle than as a straight line. For example, both high and low hypnotizables are at greater risk for somatization than are moderates, because they are both able to attenuate the explicit (conscious) perception of threat. But they require different management procedures. For example, both high and low hypnotizables can attenuate from consciousness (explicit threat perception; darkest circle in Figure 4) the fact that they are chronically fearful or angry at their supervisor, and transduce this information into a backache. This attenuating mode is less complete in low than in high hypnotizables. This may be an example of the operation of a cognitive inhibition factor in hypnotic ability. However, out of mind is not necessarily out of body (see Figure 4, white circle, or implicit threat perception). At the level of implicit perception, this attenuated perception of explicit threat may be represented as muscular bracing in the paraspinalis muscles or as an elevated heart rate associated with hypnotic analgesia during surgery. High hypnotizables can amplify explicit threat perception, particularly if they are also high on catastrophizing or neuroticism. For example, high hypnotizables can use the fantasy factor in hypnotic ability to invoke gruesome images of metastasizing, undiagnosed brain tumors during a vascular headache (see the amplifying mode in Figure 4).

The implicit threat perception (HPAA) is thought to be identical in people of all levels of hypnotic ability (see implicit threat perception in Figure 4). For example, a surgical incision will alter heart rate, electrodermal response (EDR), and blood volume pulse equally in all people with intact nervous systems. However, the conscious or explicit perception of threat is significantly cognitively–emotionally attenuated in low hypnotizables and can be to an even greater extent attenuated in high hypnotizables (e.g., hypnotic analgesia, hypnotic amnesia, etc.) (see Figure 4). The attenuating mode can be total in high hypnotizables but incompletely attenuated in low hypnotizables. However, high hypnotizables can also very significantly amplify (see Figure 3) the perception of threat, particularly if there is a statistical interaction between high hypnotic ability and high neuroticism (or high catastrophizing). In high hypnotizables, this amplified interaction appears to occur involuntarily and acutely, generating upward spirals of anxiety, fear, and panic. If the threat cannot be removed (in 4 to 6 months), chronic depression and, finally, entrance into sick role behavior (Sternbach, 1974) can follow. Low hypnotizables have to learn, through physiological self-monitoring of their own body or through biofeedback, to discover what is threatening to them outside of their explicit consciousness. This is truth detection, and it has to be done cautiously. For example, many people have primary labile or stabile hypertension and are unconscious of it. Explicit perception of and repeated testing for hypertension can create an iatrogenic cardiac neurosis in high hypnotizables. Low hypnotizables can learn to recognize the discrepancies among their verbal report, motor behavior, and physiology through biofeedback. The therapist can also learn to recognize these discrepancies in his patients through physiological monitoring with biofeedback instruments. Confronting these discrepancies can be like opening up a sunroof in the patient's head. Low hypnotizables require a formal and systematic Trojan horse role induction to change their beliefs about mind–body interaction. They need to start out with the type of biofeedback that their stress profile reveals to be their window of vulnerability.

It also is possible to use the first three high-risk factors (hypnotic ability, catastrophizing, and neuroticism) together with the L score on the Eysenck Personality Inventory to construct partial profiles, with the following hypothesized prescriptions for clinical management (psychometrically it is important to note that hypnotic ability, neuroticism, and the L score are empirically orthogonal; Wickramasekera, 1990):

1. *High hypnotizability, low catastrophizing, low neuroticism, high L.* I have found this type of patient to score in the normal range or below on conventional psychological tests, but to be at great risk for transducing psychosocial threat into somatic symptoms and to be relatively unaware of both experimental and acute clinical pain and anxiety. This patient has at least two mechanisms to block pain or fear from explicit perception or consciousness: high hypnotic ability (see Figure 4) and high repression (low N and high L). Nevertheless, the stress of cold pressor or surgical pain will be evidenced in implicit perception by a rise in systolic or diastolic blood pressure, heart rate, or EDR (see Figure 4). This patient will profit from hypnotherapy (e.g., psychodynamic or Gestalt) with physiological monitoring by the therapist and delayed biofeedback (Zillmer & Wickramasekera, 1987) for the patient. This type of patient is prone to serious medical disorders (e.g., cancer, vasovagal syncopy, and silent ischemia associated with heart disease), particularly after age 40, when abusive life-style factors start to override "good genes."

2. *Low hypnotizability, low catastrophizing, low neuroticism, and high L.* This patient requires a Trojan horse role induction, as described below, and immediate biofeedback (Zillmer & Wickramasekera, 1987) prior to

any psychotherapy. For treatment to be effective, this patient must be able to shift rapidly and reliably (with immediate biological feedback) into a state of low physiological arousal and to subjectively perceive and label muscular and vascular changes (muscle tension reducing, hand cooling or warming, etc.). The patient needs to verbalize and to feel this shift in perception (e.g., I feel heavy, I feel light, I feel numb, I feel disoriented) before any psychotherapy can start. Conventional psychotherapy without this preparation and experience in enhanced perception of cognitively induced alterations in somatic sensations will trigger immediate "dropping out."

3. *High hypnotizability, high catastrophizing, high neuroticism, and high L.* Because of the high probability of explicit defensiveness (both N and L are high), this profile type requires a gradual approach (e.g., Rogerian) to deeper psychotherapy issues. This patient first needs a cognitive–behavioral approach focused on the presenting somatic symptoms and aimed at reducing conscious catastrophizing cognitions. Specific item analysis of the hassle and catastrophizing scales can provide a general direction to the cognitive–behavioral intervention component. There is a high probability that the patient's chronic psychological and somatic complaints will have eroded and alienated support systems, which will need resuscitation and cultivation. After a trusting and strong therapeutic alliance is built, hypnotherapy can start slowly. Hypnotic suggestions to selectively focus on and retain positive memories and emotions should be used to reprogram this patient's preattentive bias for threatening information. When the patient is less highly defensive and less highly neurotic, it may be time to use hypnoanalysis to access the unconscious resistance to greater levels of social intimacy, social support, and interpersonal vulnerability. Unconscious intrusions from childhood may occur at this point. This patient also needs to assimilate a deeper cognitive schema, such as a rational–emotive philosophy (Ellis, 1962), to immunize against future threats and to prevent relapses into pretherapy baseline high catastrophizing and high neuroticism. These patients have major "boundary" issues and intense positive and negative transference. There is generally little that can be done to prevent or control major life change except to boost psychological immunity through increasing cognitive and behavioral adaptive coping skills and reducing "acting out."

The Referral and the Trojan Horse Procedure

Somatizers, particularly those with low hypnotic ability, are committed to a pathophysiologic explanation and chemical or surgical resolution of presenting somatic symptoms. They need a personal demonstration that their cognitions and emotions can alter their physiology. This process of changing the patient's "software" is called the Trojan horse role induction.

The referral to a psychotherapist is perceived by the patient as a rejection by the primary care physician and a challenge to the reality of the patient's somatic complaint. The somatizer typically perceives the psychological distance between the primary care physician's office and a psychologist's office as several light-years. There is a need to reduce both the psychological and the physical distance between the medical doctor's and the psychotherapist's offices and procedures. The psychological distance is reduced through a set of psychophysiological demonstrations and a role-induction technique called the Trojan horse procedure (Wickramasekera, 1979, 1988, 1989). Using the Stress Profile (Wickramasekera, 1979, 1988), the Trojan horse procedure provides objective and quantitative evidence in a psychophysiology laboratory (a) that cognitive threat responses can alter the patient's biological functions; (b) that the patient's body is chronically or intermittently on "red alert;" and (c) that the patient is psychologically unaware or desensitized to this chronic, abnormal, and activated psychophysiological state (e.g., chronically cold or wet hands, hypertension, muscle bracing, etc.).

The goal of the Trojan horse procedure is to circumvent and disengage the psychological defenses of denial and skepticism with regard to mind–body interaction. For example, if the patient has superior hypnotic ability, one can use hypnotic suggestion to demonstrate an involuntary catalepsy in a region of the patient's body far removed from the area of the presenting symptoms. This provides "ocular proof" of psychological control of physiology. For patients of moderate or low hypnotic ability, biofeedback instruments can be used to demonstrate the dramatic effects of cognitive stress generated by simple mental arithmetic on blood pressure, heart rate, blood volume pulse, muscle tension (EMG), skin conductance, and so forth.

Skeptical somatizing patients, particularly those of low hypnotic ability, believe nothing that they are told and less than half of what they can be shown (they seem to be from Missouri, the "show me" state). Psychophysiological demonstrations provide a startling and face-saving rationale for the somatic symptoms. Once engaged in a therapeutic alliance to reduce ego-alien somatic symptoms, the patient can be led by the psychophysiological therapist out of the somatic closet onto the psychotherapy couch.

The Trojan horse procedure provides a psychophysiological bridge from the biomedical model, in which the patient is a passive recipient of medical services, to the biopsychological model (Engel, 1977), in which the patient is an active coinvestigator of his or her own mind–body interaction. The biopsychological model is an educational one in which the doctor is really a teacher (as the word "doctor" originally implied) and the patient is a student.

Hypnotic Ability and Psychophysiological Psychotherapy

In people with high hypnotic ability, psychological and physiological functions are cognitively closer to each other, at least in an informational exchange and processing sense, both in and out of hypnosis (Wickramasekera, 1976b, 1988, 1991b). In people of low and moderate hypnotic ability, biofeedback instruments, combined with low arousal training or sensory restriction, can bring these functions cognitively closer (Barabasz & Barabasz, 1989; Engstrom, 1976; Wickramasekera, 1969a, 1971a, 1976b, 1977a), although this conclusion has been disputed (Perlini & Spanos, 1991; Radtke, Spanos, Armstrong, Dillman, & Boisvenue, 1983).

Psychophysiological hypno- or psychotherapy (Wickramasekera, 1976b, 1988, 1990, 1991a) is a clinical tool with which to investigate the unconscious (implicit) cognitive and affective mechanisms through which perceptions of threat become transduced or amplified into somatic symptoms. These mechanisms are believed to be amplified, more frequent, and more observable in people of high hypnotic ability. Psychophysiological hypnotherapy is verbal self-exploration in a trusting relationship (Wickramasekera, 1969a, 1969b, 1971b), facilitated by low physiological arousal (indexed by low EMG or low skin conductance, high peripheral skin temperature, high blood volume pulse, etc.) or sensory restriction procedures. I hypothesize that when hypnotic ability is even temporarily increased (Wickramasekera, 1977a) by these means, expanded and more plastic cognitive/affective networks of meaning emerge (Wickramasekera, 1969a, 1969b, 1971b, 1976b, 1988), and these facilitate the conditioned extinction of emotions and motivations or the cognitive reframing of perceptions of threat. As Rescorla (1988) pointed out, the subject in current Pavlovian conditioning is not a passive respondent but an active participant learning relations between events, as in parallel distributed processing (PDP) models in cognitive neuroscience.

The goal of psychophysiological psychotherapy is to inhibit cognitive stereotypy and to increase cognitive creativity. The protocol arranges conditions to increase the probability of cognitive creativity in the patient. The standard protocol for psychophysiological psychotherapy is illustrated in Figure 5. Each session begins when the technician (or therapist) instruments the patient (4 min) and collects approximately 3 minutes of baseline physiological data with the patient's eyes open, followed by 3 minutes with eyes closed. I use the J&J (Model 1330) system, which provides on-line TV monitoring, storage, and data reduction (means, ranges, standard deviations, etc.) on up to 10 channels of physiology or motor behavior. Immediately after baseline data collection, there is 25 minutes of psychotherapy (the risk profile determines whether Rogerian, Gestalt, psychodynamic, or cognitive–behavioral strategies will be most fruitful) in which

A. Initial Interview		1 hour
B. Testing on High Risk Profile and Psychophysiological Stress Profile		5 hours
C. Feedback on test results to patients. Candidacy accepted or rejected for psychophysiological psychotherapy.		1 hour

2. STANDARD PROTOCOL FOR PSYCHOPHYSIOLOGICAL PSYCHOTHERAPY

Technician:	1. Instrumentation	4 minutes
	2. B^1 (eyes open)	3 minutes
	3. B^2 (eyes closed)	3 minutes
Therapist:	4. S^1 Hypno or Psychotherapy	25 minutes
	5. R^1 Hypnosis/Biofeedback (self-soothe)	15 minutes
	6. S^2 Inquiry	10 minutes
		60 minutes

Figure 5: Assessment and protocol for psychophysiological psychotherapy. Goal: to inhibit cognitive stereotypy and promote cognitive creativity in threat perception.

conflicts and threats are explored with physiological monitoring. This is followed immediately by 15 minutes of "self-soothing," or the induction of a state of low physiological arousal. During this phase, the patient is instructed to put everything previously discussed "on the back burner, if not off the stove."

For patients of low or moderate hypnotic ability, low arousal induction is accomplished through biofeedback of the patients' most reactive organ system (muscle tension, skin conductance, skin temperature, etc.), as determined from their diagnostic psychophysiological stress profile. Individualized physiological goals (e.g., reduce heart rate to a mean of 60 beats per minute, or increase hand temperature to 94° F) may be set for each session. For high hypnotizables, low arousal training starts with hypnotic verbal instructions aimed at reducing frontal or trapezius EMG or increasing hand temperature, as determined by the stress profile. High hypnotizables are given delayed feedback to verify their approximation to their physiological goal (Zillmer & Wickramasekera, 1987) (for example, raise hand temperature reliably [on 80% of trials] to 94 °F).

During self-soothing, patients are to "let go" of the prior psychotherapy material. If their "dragons" (i.e., the conflicts and threats explored during psychotherapy) return in new symbolic disguises, they are to regard them with detached curiosity and allow them to cognitively rotate from 180 to

360 degrees, so that they can be viewed from multiple perspectives. I hypothesize that a physiologically relaxed state can disrupt the tendency toward cognitive stereotypy and disinhibit fresh cognitive representations of the old problems and anomalous input from the unconscious mind. Cognitive stereotypy can be defined as thinking in a "rut." Intense emotional conflicts recollected in tranquility can disrupt cognitive stereotypy and promote cognitive creativity. Low arousal induction has also been hypothesized to enhance the extinction and interpretation of maladaptive, recursive loops of cognition, emotion, and behavior termed *core conflictual relationships* (Luborsky, 1976).

For example, when a female (age 36) patient who was referred by a gastroenterologist because she suffered from episodic (1 to 3 times per month), life-threatening constriction and shutdown of her colon (which had not responded to multiple medical investigations by gastrointestinal specialists and subspecialists, to medications, or to surgery) was in the detached neutral hypnotic phase, she had the following experience: A childhood memory of anxiously chasing her younger brother through a grade-school yard to retrieve her gloves intruded into consciousness. This younger brother had died at age 6, and the patient's mother had verbally blamed (for many years) the patient (her oldest child), only 2 years older than her brother, for a trivial neglect associated with his death. Her brother escapes with the gloves, and she next sees herself as an adult "standing by a heavy metal door" through which she cannot pass because her hands had been "chopped off into bloody stumps at the wrists." Many people pass by her and open and close the door, but they seem unaware of her predicament. Her dead 6-year-old brother appears and "opens the door" for her. These apparently unrelated cognitions spontaneously emerged despite the fact that in the prior psychotherapy phase there was no discussion of her dead brother but intensive discussion of her chronic murderous rage at her mother. Incidentally, this "cognitive intrusion" and the psychotherapeutic processing of it were correlated with a clinically significant drop to zero in the base rate of her episodes of bowel constriction. This complete remission lasted 8 months. It appears that implicit strangulation of her gastrointestinal tract had become the final pathway for multiple current psychosocial stressors.

During psychotherapy and the low arousal procedure (self-soothing), changes in physiology are tracked on the computer screen and monitored by the therapist. These changes can signal the conscious or unconscious emergence of cognitive intrusions, about which the patient can be later or immediately questioned. There may also be questions about subtle intrusive images, thoughts, or feelings, perceived by the patient but not signaled to the therapist by physiological changes on the TV monitor. The psychophysiological psychotherapist also watches the TV monitor for basic phenomena like individual response specificity (i.e., the patient's most reactive or threat-vulnerable organ system), for situational response specificity, and for autonomic balance (Andreassi, 1980). The therapist is essentially watching for how, where, and when the explicit and implicit perceptions of threat occur physiologically and where there are desynchonies between organ systems and the verbal report. Patients are also asked periodically during the session to monitor their subjective level of distress on a visual analogue scale, which is tracked along with their physiology on the TV screen. Patients can be monitored verbally, behaviorally, and physiologically, with each channel supplementing and complementing the information given by the others. Empathic "listening" is amplified by technology, and the therapist's pattern recognition skill increases with experience. The therapist can also print or store a screen that seems meaningful.

The 1, 2, 3 self-hypnosis technique (Wickramasekera, 1988) is taught to and audiotaped for all patients. This technique consists of rolling the eyes up into the head, closing the lids, breathing deeply, and exhaling slowly (Spiegel & Spiegel, 1978), plus suggestions of heaviness, lightness, or detachment in various body parts. Patients are instructed to listen to a 10-minute audiotape at least twice daily and to practice an abbreviated version of the tape (2 min duration) 10 times per day. They are told that their compliance with "homework" will be verified at each session by pre-therapy baseline physiological monitoring. The tape contains suggestions tailored to correct their "software programs," as determined from their individual high risk profile. For example, a patient high on negative affectivity may be given hypnotic suggestions for better retention of positive memories in everyday life and for noticing that the "glass is half full" even in respect to small details. A patient high on repression will be given judicious suggestions in the opposite direction (e.g., to notice when he or she is having angry or hurt feelings and to access gradually any relevant repressed traumatic memories).

CASE MATERIAL: PSYCHOPHYSIOLOGICAL DIAGNOSIS AND HYPNOTHERAPY

A 30-year-old married pharmacist, the mother of 2 children (ages 2 and 4 years), presented with episodic vasovagal syncopy, dizziness, bilateral headaches, tinnitus, episodic blurred vision, and episodic problems with sensorimotor coordination, all of which had had a sudden onset 12 months earlier. These symptoms became more frequent and intense at both home and work, with apparently no relationship to any recognizable stressor. Multiple medical tests (magnetic resonance imaging, EEG, spinal taps, etc.) and consultation with specialists and subspecialists (two cardiologists, two neurologists, one endocrinologist, etc.) were negative. The patient was referred by a neurologist who had prescribed Bellergal and secured a 50%

reduction in only the syncopy. Three months prior to referral, the patient had tried to reduce the Bellergal, with a significant amplification of the syncopy that lasted 1½ months. The patient was back on the Bellergal at the time of referral. Because the patient and her neurologist were uncomfortable with an "empirical therapy" that had not significantly improved her other somatic symptoms, she was referred to me for evaluation of "continuing ANS dysfunction, etiology undetermined."

On the high risk model, the patient was positive for only two risk factors: repressed neuroticism (Eysenck N = 3%, L = 98%) and hypnotic ability (Harvard scale = 10; Stanford scale, Form C = 9). Her Bowers (1982) "involuntariness" (classical suggestion effect) score was 46/60, and her Kirsch et al. (1990) score was 48/60. It is likely that these two risk factors (high hypnotic ability and repressed neuroticism), operating either additively or interactionally, powerfully blockade explicit perceptions of threat from consciousness and drive them into implicit perception (chronic ANS dysfunction). Repressed neuroticism can disregulate ANS functions (Jamner et al., 1988; Jensen, 1987; Weinberger et al., 1979). The patient's psychophysiological stress profile showed modest pretherapy autonomic lability only in skin conductance (4.07–9.11 microhms). Pretherapy, she showed stable and low baselines in heart rate (62–89 beats per minute) and frontal EMG (.89–5.92 microvolts) and high normal and stable skin temperature (range = 89–92 °F). All of the above indicates a general parasympathetic dominance (high vagal tone), which was consistent with her denial of any explicit psychological distress during the stress profile or prior to therapy. Her SCL–90 scores were all in the average or low range prior to therapy. Her pretherapy SCL–90–R score provides no basis for any DSM–III–R diagnosis (the general severity index was less than 63, and all primary clinical dimensions were less than 63).

During the initial interview (prior to testing), the patient denied to me, as she had done with the prior medical specialists and her internist, any awareness of psychosocial stress in any areas of her life (marriage, sex, children, job, parents, etc.). In fact, she seemed, clinically, remarkably psychologically healthy, as confirmed by all but two risk factors (the high L score on the Eysenck Personality Inventory, and high hypnotic ability). The patient was trained in the office in self-hypnosis with the 1,2,3 technique (Wickramasekera, 1988), and a cassette tape was made of the 1,2,3 procedure for home practice twice daily. Using this procedure, she learned in three sessions to voluntarily and reliably warm her hands at least 7 °F. This rapid learning of ANS control was consistent with her high hypnotic ability.

During the psychotherapy phase (S[1]; see Figure 5) of the second session of psychophysiological psychotherapy (July 10), the patient reported that her somatic symptoms had started suddenly while registering her oldest son in a nursery school program 12 months before. While elaborating on this topic, she showed a 4 °F drop in skin temperature and a 50-point drop in blood volume pulse. I pointed this out to her without comment and printed and stored the screen.

During the low arousal phase (R^1) of the same session, I instructed her in hypnosis to return as a calm, detached spectator to the nursery school registration memory (12 months before) and to observe the situation. She moved from this low arousal phase into the inquiry phase (S^2) with an intrusive memory image of herself as "a sad child in nursery school" looking out of a window at other children playing in the yard, but confined to the classroom by a "scary male principal." While presenting these explicit memories, her heart rate elevated to 90–95 beats per minute. At the termination of this second session, I suggested in the inquiry (S^2) outside of hypnosis that other memories from this period of her childhood might return during the coming week and that she should record them and bring them to her third session.

The patient returned to the third session very agitated, with a written record of several vivid memories of sexual abuse by the male nursery school principal that had intruded during self-hypnosis. Repeated use of the low arousal procedure (self-hypnosis) was associated with more spontaneously occurring, concrete childhood memories of sexual abuse by the same person, whose voice was familiar but whose face she could not see and whose name she did not know. These memories of sexual abuse and other threatening perceptions started to intrude into consciousness at routine and unexpected times outside of the self-hypnosis episodes (e.g., at work, while cooking, while dressing her children, etc.). For example, she recalled the abuser calling her "my beautiful little girl" and giving her a flower.

Independent support of her recollections came several weeks later from her mother's testimony that 2 years after the patient had entered elementary school, the principal of her prior nursery school was convicted of child molestation. Her mother explicitly denied discussing the news report of the principal's conviction in the presence of any of the children and reported that her husband was still unaware of the event. The mother also reported at least two episodes of abnormal psychological reactions in the patient (severe nightmares at age 6 or 7, and social phobia around age 5) that were investigated medically and had remitted spontaneously.

Within four sessions of starting to unload and process the intrusive perceptions and childhood memories, the patient terminated the Bellergal, with continued progressive decline in all of her somatic symptoms. There was an episode of total syncopy and a fall when a particularly disturbing memory (her bleeding vagina was washed in a bathtub by the abuser) passed from implicit to explicit memory. The patient had previously reported that whenever she first entered a bathtub she would feel temporarily disoriented. As the unconscious intrusive perceptions and memories of childhood and adolescence came "out of her body" (i.e., her somatic symptoms extinguished) and "into her mind," her level of psychological distress increased, as documented by large changes in various psychological test scores. For example, her Beck depression score was 4 pretherapy and 13 posttherapy. In other words, her psychological distress was negatively correlated with her somatic distress.

In the course of psychophysiological psychotherapy, the patient's perspective of her parents, her husband, and her whole life changed significantly. She appeared to have passed from uncritical acceptance, affection, and happiness to sadness about her life and anger at her parents and her husband for their neglect of her emotional needs (e.g., intimacy) and for the subordination of her personal identity to her roles as daughter, wife, and mother. She became more assertive and unaccepting of her husband's and her parents' unwritten code of never discussing anything unpleasant, deep, or painful about personal feelings. She considered divorcing her husband and felt he had "used" her. She plans to quit the pharmacy and apply to medical school.

RESEARCH AND APPRAISAL

In a sample of 83 consecutive patients with typical somatization symptoms (vascular headache, lower back pain, primary hypertension, irritable bowel, etc.) seen in a behavioral medicine clinic prior to therapy, 32% were high and 28% low on hypnotic ability (Wickramasekera, 1984, 1991a). This can be compared with lower rates of high and low hypnotizability in a control group of student volunteers (Kirsch et al., 1990). A chi-square test indicated that the two groups were significantly different in the distribution of their hypnotizability scores ($\chi^2 = 17.90$, $p < .001$).

The mean age of the patient sample was 40 years, and that of the comparison group was 19.6 years. Hypnotic ability is known to decline with age; there should be fewer highs in patients 20 years older than the 19.6-year-old college students. Hence, the overrepresentation of highs in the patient sample, despite a stringent criterion (scores of 12–10 on the Harvard scale, Form A), is doubly surprising. Thus, both high and low hypnotizability can be considered risk factors for somatization.

This finding is consistent with reports of high hypnotic ability in other ANS-mediated somatic symptoms, like chronic pain (Remler, 1990; Stam, McGrath, Brooke, & Cosier, 1986). For example, Remler (1990) found that in a sample ($N = 53$) of older (mean age = 41 years) volunteer pain patients in an anesthesiology pain clinic, 46% were lows and 55% were highs on the Stanford Form C. Wickramasekera, Ware, and Saxon (1992) found that in a sample of carefully EEG-defined insomnia patients (latency to Stage 2) in which pathophysiology (sleep apnea, myoclonus, etc.) was ruled out, 50% were highs, 40% were lows, and 10% were moderates on the Harvard test. The Harvard scores of these insomniacs correlated significantly (.001) at .83 with a subjective involvement measure (Kirsch et al., 1990) of hypnotic ability. Wickramasekera, Atkinson, and Turner (1992) found in a sample of obese patients (mean body mass index [BMI] = 38.0) that the mean Harvard score was 7.4 (SD = 2.7) and that in a matched community control group of nonobese subjects (mean BMI = 26.3) the mean Harvard score was 5.02 (SD = 3.1). The Harvard scores (.001) and the BMI scores (.001) were significantly different in the obese subjects and the controls. The correlations between the Harvard scores and the Kirsch et al. (1990) measures ranged between .83 and .81 (significant at the .001 level) for the obese and control subjects, respectively. The correlations between the Harvard test and a measure of "involuntariness" (Bates et al., 1991) ranged between .76 and .82 (significant at the .001 level) for the obese and control groups, respectively.

Our findings on high hypnotic ability and symptoms are consistent with similar reports (Andersen, 1985; Crowson et al., 1991; Pettinati et al., 1990; Stam et al., 1986; Velten, 1968) on mood alterations, affective disorders, substance abuse, obesity, and chronic pain. The overrepresentation of people with high hypnotic ability among somatizing patients may account in part for the epidemic of empirical relaxation and imagery techniques in contemporary nontheoretically driven "stress management" clinics. Because of the close cognitive connection between their psychological and physiological functions, highly hypnotizable patients respond to any verbal relaxation instructions, regardless of whether they are packaged as "Jacobsonian relaxation instructions," "autogenic training," "meditation," "guided imagery," or "neurolinguistic programming." The skeptical low hypnotizables can learn to connect cognition to physiology, through mechanistic biofeedback and behavioral techniques (Wickramasekera, 1976b; Zillmer & Wickramasekera, 1987).

The high risk model offers an alternative to blind empirical groping. Analysis of the same patient sample (Wickramasekera, 1991a) showed that all seven factors in the high risk model are orthogonal, except for negative affectivity, hassles, and catastrophizing, which correlate substantially (.52 to .57; Wickramasekera, 1990, 1991a). There has been very extensive and independent empirical research on the other nonhypnotic factors in the high risk model. This research documenting their relationship to somatic and psychological symptoms was reviewed earlier in this chapter in the presentation of the high risk model, and elsewhere (Wickramasekera, 1986, 1988).

Empirical research on the Trojan horse procedure is at a clinical observational level (Wickramasekera, 1979, 1988). In the 1979 study, I gave an unsystematic role induction to a consecutive series of 20 patients with typical psychophysiological disorders, resulting in a 60% patient retention rate ("retention" being surviving 1 hour of initial interview, 4 hours of testing, 1 hour of feedback of test results, and at least 10 sessions of psychophysiological psychotherapy). Note that this is a very stringent definition of retention. In a later study (Wickramasekera, 1988) of a comparable series of 20 consecutive patients seen by the same author, but with a more systematic and specific role induction, the retention rate was 83% and the dropout rate 17%. Phillips (1985) reported that 50% of all patients who presented themselves to a community mental health clinic (mainly with psychological symptoms) did not return after the first visit. Thus, it is likely that the dropout rate after the first visit for somatizers at community mental health clinics is much higher, even if they go to the first interview.

CONCLUSION

The high risk model and the Trojan horse procedure significantly enhance the face validity, therapeutic efficacy, and therapeutic alliance of the assessment and therapy of somatizing transducers and amplifiers. Controlled, empirical support for the hypothesized potent statistical interactions among risk factors is still fragmentary.

Patients may enter therapy to learn psychophysiological skills that can replace pills. However, extinguishing symptomatic fires with psychophysiological skills, without identifying and defusing the matches (explicit or implicit perceptions of threat), inevitably leads to new psychological, behavioral, or somatic symptoms. Intrusions of implicit trauma, anomalous phenomena, or developmental issues from implicit memory and the unconscious occur reliably. These intrusions need to be assimilated into explicit memory and digested while new adaptive coping behaviors are constructed. This is why I speculate that mindless, empirically groping stress management with or without "hypnosis" is iatrogenic for many somatizers. Putting out the fire without finding the matches is not enough, because out of mind is not necessarily out of body.

The high risk model appears to carve psychophysiological reality at its natural joints, in terms of the underlying mechanisms that drive somatic and psychological symptoms. For example, an irritable bowel and a vascular headache look very different topographically, but may stem from the interaction of one or more of the same seven underlying high risk factors. Hence, any intervention based on psychodynamic or cognitive behavioral models is unlikely to have durable effects unless it concurrently alters one or more of the seven basic mechanisms that mediate psychophysiological amplification and transduction.

The high risk model permits "psychoarchaeology" to proceed with some specific empirical quantitative markers of somatization. It is theorized that changes in these risk factors directly and specifically targeted by psychophysiological psychotherapy will be related to changes in implicit and explicit threatening perceptions, memories, and moods, and to alterations in the HPAA, the neuroendocrine system (e.g., cortisol, adrenocorticotropic hormone), and perhaps even select immune parameters (Naliboff et al., 1991).

REFERENCES

American Psychiatric Association. (1987). *Diagnostic and statistical manual of mental disorders* (3rd ed., rev.). Washington, DC: Author.

Andersen, M. S. (1985). Hypnotizability as a factor in the hypnotic treatment of obesity. *International Journal of Clinical and Experimental Hypnosis, 33,* 150–159.

Andreassi, J. L. (1980). *Psychophysiology: Human behavior and physiological response.* New York: Oxford University Press.

Banyai, E., & Hilgard, E. R. (1976). A comparison of active-alert hypnotic induction with traditional relaxation induction. *Journal of Abnormal Psychology, 85,* 218–224.

Barabasz, A. F., & Barabasz, M. (1989). Effects of restricted environmental simulation: Enhancement of hypnotizability for experimental and chronic pain control. *International Journal of Clinical and Experimental Hypnosis, 37,* 217–231.

Barber, T. X. (1969). *Hypnosis: A scientific approach.* New York: Van Nostrand Reinhold.

Barsky, A. J., & Klerman, G. L. (1983). Overview: Hypochondriasis, bodily complaints, and somatic styles. *American Journal of Psychiatry, 140,* 273–283.

Bates, B. L., Dinges, D. F., Whitehouse, W. G., Orne, E. C., & Orne, M. (1991, October). *Assessing nonvolitional experience with the Harvard Group Scale of Hypnotic Susceptibility, Form A and the Carleton University Responsiveness to Suggestion Scale.* Paper presented at the 42nd Annual Scientific Meeting of the Society for Clinical and Experimental Hypnosis, New Orleans, LA.

Blanchard, E. B., Hickling, E. J., & Taylor, A. E. (1991). The psychophysiology of motor vehicle accident related post-traumatic stress disorder. *Biofeedback and Self-Regulation, 16,* 449–458.

Bowers, P. (1982). The classic suggestion effect: Relationships with scales of hypnotizability, effortless experiencing and imagery vividness. *International Journal of Clinical and Experimental Hypnosis, 30,* 270–279.

Brown, J. W., Robertson, L. S., Kosa, J., & Alpert, J. J. (1971). A study of general practice in Massachusetts. *Journal of the American Medical Association, 216,* 301–306.

Costa, P. T., & McCrae, R. R. (1987). Neuroticism, somatic complaints, and disease: Is the bark worse than the bite? *Journal of Personality, 55,* 299–316.

Council, J. R., & Loge, D. (1988). Suggestibility and confidence in false perceptions: A pilot study. *British Journal of Experimental and Clinical Hypnosis, 5(2),* 95–98.

Crowson, J. J., Conroy, A. M., & Chester, T. D. (1991). Hypnotizability as related to visually induced affective reactivity. *International Journal of Clinical and Experimental Hypnosis, 39,* 140–144.

Dantzer, R. (1991). Stress and disease: A psychobiological perspective. *Annals of Behavioral Medicine, 13,* 205–210.

Das, J. P. (1958). Conditioning and hypnosis. *Journal of Experimental Psychology, 56,* 110–113.

DeLongis, A., Coyne, J. C., Dakof, G., Folkman, S., & Lazarus, R. S. (1982). Relationship of daily hassles, uplifts, and major life events to health status. *Health Psychology, 1,* 119–136.

Dixon, M., Brunet, A., & Laurence, J. R. (1990). Hypnotizability and automaticity: Toward a parallel distributed processing model of hypnotic responding. *Journal of Abnormal Psychology, 99,* 336–343.

Dollard, J., & Miller, N. E. (1950). *Personality and psychotherapy.* New York: McGraw-Hill.

Drossman, D. A. (1978). The problem patient: Evaluation and care of medical patients with psychosocial disturbances. *Annals of Internal Medicine, 88,* 366–372.

Dywan, J., & Bowers, K. (1983). The use of hypnosis to enhance recall. *Science, 22,* 184–185.

Ellis, A. (1962). *Reason and emotion in psychotherapy.* New York: Stuart.

Engel, G. L. (1977). The need for a new medical model: A challenge for biomedicine. *Science, 196,* 129–136.

Engstrom, D. R. (1976). Hypnotic susceptibility, EEG-alpha and self-regulation. In G. E. Schwartz & D. Shapiro (Eds.), *Consciousness and self-regulation* (pp. 173–222). New York: Plenum Press.

Ewart, C. K., Taylor, C. B., Kraemer, H. C., & Agras, W. S. (1991). High blood pressure and marital discord: Not being nasty matters more than being nice. *Health Psychology, 10,* 155–163.

Eysenck, H. J., & Eysenck, S. B. G. (1968). *Eysenck Personality Inventory, Form A.* San Diego, CA: Educational & Industrial Testing Service.

Flor, H., & Turk, D. C. (1984). Etiological theories and treatments for chronic back pain: 1. Somatic models and interventions. *Pain, 19,* 105–121.

Garfield, S. R., Collen, M. F., Feldman, R., Soghikian, K., Richart, R. H., & Duncan, J. H. (1976). Evaluation of an ambulatory medical care delivery system. *New England Journal of Medicine, 294,* 426–431.

Greenwald, A. G. (1992). New Look 3: Unconscious cognition reclaimed. *American Psychologist, 47,* 766–779.

Gur, R. C. (1974). An attention-controlled operant procedure for enhancing hypnotic susceptibility. *Journal of Abnormal Psychology, 83,* 644–650.

Hall, R. C. W. (Ed.). (1980). *Psychiatric presentation of medical illness: Somatopsychic disorders.* New York: SP Medical & Scientific Books.

Harsher-Towe, D. (1983). *Control of electromyographic activity in subjects demon-strating high and low levels of hypnotizability*. Unpublished doctoral dissertation, Virginia Consortium for Professional Psychology, Norfolk.

Hilgard, E. R. (1965). *Hypnotic susceptibility*. New York: Harcourt, Brace & World.

House, J. F., Landis, K. R., & Umberson, D. (1988). Social relationships and health. *Science, 241,* 540–545.

Jamner, L. D., Schwartz, G. E., & Leigh, H. (1988). The relationship between repressive and defensive coping styles and monocyte, eosinophile, and serum glucose levels: Support for the opiod peptide hypothesis of repression. *Psychosomatic Medicine, 50,* 567–575.

Jencks, S. F. (1985). Recognition of mental distress and diagnosis of mental disorder in primary care. *Journal of the American Medical Association, 253,* 1903–1906.

Jensen, M. R. (1987). Psychobiological factors predicting the course of breast cancer. *Journal of Personality, 55,* 317–342.

Kanner, A. D., Coyne, J. C., Schaefer, C., & Lazarus, R. S. (1981). Comparison of two modes of stress measurement: Daily hassles and uplifts versus major life events. *Journal of Behavioral Medicine, 4,* 1–39.

Katon, W., Lin, E., VonKorff, M., Russo, J., Lipscomb, P., & Bush, T. (1991). Somatization: A spectrum of severity. *American Journal of Psychiatry, 148,* 34–40.

Kihlstrom, J. F. (1987). The cognitive unconscious. *Science, 237,* 1445–1452.

Kihlstrom, J. F. (1991, March). *The emotional unconscious.* Paper presented at the Annual Meeting of the Association for Applied Psychophysiology and Bio-feedback, Dallas, TX.

King, D. R., & McDonald, R. D. (1976). Hypnotic susceptibility and verbal conditioning. *International Journal of Clinical and Experimental Hypnosis, 24,* 29–37.

Kirsch, I., Council, J. R., & Wickless, C. (1990). Subjective scoring for the Harvard Group Scale of Hypnotic Susceptibility, Form A. *International Journal of Clinical and Experimental Hypnosis, 38,* 101–111.

Krantz, D. S., & Manuck, S. B. (1984). Acute psychophysiologic reactivity and risk of cardiovascular disease: A review and methodologic critique. *Psychological Bulletin, 96,* 435–464.

Laurence, J. R., & Perry, C. (1983). Hypnotically created memory among highly hypnotizable subjects. *Science, 222,* 523–524.

Lazarus, R. S. (1991). *Emotion and adaptation*. New York: Oxford University Press.

Lazarus, R. S., DeLongis, A., Folkman, S., & Gruen, R. (1985). Stress and adaptational outcomes: The problem of confounded measures. *American Psychologist, 40,* 770–779.

Lazarus, R. S., & Folkman, S. (1984). *Stress, appraisal and coping*. New York: Springer.

Luborsky (1976). Helping alliance in psychotherapy. In J. L. Claghorn (Ed.), *Successful psychotherapy* (pp. 92–116). New York: Brunner/Mazel.

Mason, J. W. (1968). "Over-all" hormonal balance as a key to endocrine organization. *Psychosomatic Medicine, 30,* 791–808.

Mathews, A., & MacLeod, C. (1986). Discrimination of threat cues without awareness in anxiety states. *Journal of Abnormal Psychology, 95,* 131–138.

Mathews, A., May, J., Mogg, K., & Eysenck, M. (1990). Attentional bias in anxiety: Selective search or defective filtering? *Journal of Abnormal Psychology, 99,* 166–173.

Matthews, K. A., Weiss, S. M., & Detre, T. (Eds.). (1986). *Handbook of stress, reactivity and cardiovascular disease.* New York: Wiley.

Miller, G. (1956). The magical number seven, plus or minus two: Some limits on our capacity for processing information. *Psychological Review, 63,* 81–87.

Miller, N. E. (1992). Some examples of psychophysiology and the unconscious. *Biofeedback and Self-Regulation, 17,* 89–107.

Mineka, S., & Kihlstrom, J. F. (1978). Unpredictable and uncontrollable events: A new perspective on experimental neurosis. *Journal of Abnormal Psychology, 87,* 256–271.

Naliboff, B. D., Benton, D., Solomon, G. F., Morley, J. E., Fahey, J. L., Bloom, E. T., Makinodan, T., & Gilmore, S. L. (1991). Immunological changes in young and old adults during brief laboratory stress. *Psychosomatic Medicine, 53,* 121–132.

Osterweiss, M., Kleinman, A., & Mechanic, D. (Eds.). (1987). *Pain and disability: Clinical, behavioral, and public policy perspectives.* Washington, DC: National Academy Press.

Palsson, O. (1992). *The psychological and psychophysiological effects of stress reduction by means of a group hypnosis intervention.* Unpublished doctoral dissertation, Virginia Consortium for Professional Psychology, Norfolk.

Perlini, A. H., & Spanos, N. P. (1991). EEG alpha methodologies and hypnotizability: A critical review. *Psychophysiology, 28,* 511–530.

Pettinati, H. M., Kogan, L. G., Evans, F. J., Wade, J. H., Horne, R. L., & Staats, J. M. (1990). Hypnotizability of psychiatric inpatients according to two different scales. *American Journal of Psychiatry, 147,* 69–75.

Phillips, E. L. (1985). *A guide for therapists and patients to short term psychotherapy.* Springfield, IL: Charles C Thomas.

Pomerantz, B. S. (1986). *Stress and relaxation effects in high and low hypnotizables: Physiological and subjective measures.* Unpublished doctoral dissertation, Virginia Consortium for Professional Psychology, Norfolk.

Pomerantz, B. S., & Wickramasekera, I. (1992, August). *Hypnotic ability as a risk factor for psychopathology and pathophysiology.* Paper presented at the 100th Annual Convention of the American Psychological Association, Washington, DC.

Quill, T. E. (1985). Somatization disorder: One of medicine's blind spots. *Journal of the American Medical Association, 254,* 3075–3079.

Rabkin, J. F., & Struening, E. L. (1976). Life events, stress, and illness. *Science, 194,* 1013–1020.

Radtke, H. L., Spanos, N. P., Armstrong, L. A., Dillman, N., & Boisvenue, M. E. (1983). Effects of electromyographic feedback and progressive relaxation on hypnotic susceptibility: Disconfirming results. *International Journal of Clinical and Experimental Hypnosis, 31,* 98–106.

Relman, A. S. (1980). The new medical–institutional complex. *New England Journal of Medicine, 303,* 963–970.

Remler, H. (1990). *Hypnotic susceptibility, suggestion and compliance with treatment in patients with chronic pain.* Unpublished doctoral dissertation, Virginia Consortium for Professional Psychology, Norfolk.

Rescorla, R. A. (1988). Pavlovian conditioning. *American Psychologist, 43,* 151–160.

Rosenbaum, M. (1980). A schedule for assessing self-control behaviors: Preliminary findings. *Behavior Therapy, 11,* 109–121.

Rosenstiel, A. K., & Keefe, F. J. (1983). The use of coping strategies in chronic low back pain patients: Relationship to patient characteristics and current adjustment. *Pain, 17,* 33–44.

Sarason, I. G., Levine, H. M., Basham, R. B., & Sarason, B. R. (1983). Assessing social support: The social support questionnaire. *Journal of Personality and Social Psychology, 44,* 127–139.

Sheehan, P. W., Donovan, P., & MacLeod, C. M. (1988). Strategy manipulation and the Stroop effect in hypnosis. *Journal of Abnormal Psychology, 97,* 455–460.

Shevrin, H. (1990, October). *The physical reality of the unconscious.* Paper presented to the Los Angeles Psychoanalytic Society.

Shevrin, H. (1991). Discovering how event-related potentials reveal unconscious processes. *Biofeedback, 19,* 12–15.

Shevrin, H., & Fritzler, D. (1968). Visual evoked response correlates of unconscious mental processes. *Science, 161,* 295–298.

Shor, R. E., & Orne, E. C. (1962). *Manual: Harvard Group Scale of Hypnotic Susceptibility: Form A.* Palo Alto, CA: Consulting Psychologists Press.

Smith, G. R. (1990). *Somatization disorder in the medical setting.* Rockville, MD: U.S. Department of Health and Human Services.

Spanos, N. P., Perlini, A. H., & Robertson, L. A. (1989). Hypnosis, suggestion, and placebo in the reduction of experimental pain. *Journal of Abnormal Psychology, 98,* 285–293.

Spiegel, H., & Spiegel, D. (1978). *Trance and treatment: Clinical uses of hypnosis.* New York: Basic Books.

Stam, H., McGrath, P., Brooke, R., & Cosier, F. (1986). Hypnotizability and the treatment of chronic facial pain. *International Journal of Clinical and Experimental Hypnosis, 34,* 182–191.

Sternbach, R. A. (1974). *Pain patients: Traits and treatment.* New York: Academic Press.

Sternbach, R. A. (1986). Pain and "hassles" in the United States: Findings of the Nuprin Pain Report. *Pain, 27,* 69–80.

Taenzer, P., Melzack, R., & Jeans, M. E. (1986). Influence of psychological factors on postoperative pain, mood and analgesic requirements. *Pain, 24,* 331–342.

Tancredi, L. R., & Barondess, J. A. (1978). The problem of defensive medicine. *Science, 200,* 879–882.

Tellegen, A., Bouchard, T. J., Wilcox, K. J., Segal, N. L., Lykken, D. T., & Rich, S. (1988). Personality similarity in twins reared apart and together. *Journal of Personality and Social Psychology, 54,* 1031–1039.

Thompson, S. C. (1981). Will it hurt if I can control it? A complex answer to a simple question. *Psychological Bulletin, 90,* 89–101.

Uleman, J. S., & Bargh, J. A. (1989). *Unintended thought.* New York: Guilford Press.

Velten, E. (1968). A laboratory task for induction of mood states. *Behavior Research and Therapy, 18,* 79–86.

Wallace, B., Garrett, J. B., & Anstadt, S. P. (1974). Hypnotic susceptibility, suggestion and reports of autokinetic movement. *American Journal of Psychology, 87,* 117–123.

Wallace, B., Knight, T. A., & Garrett, J. B. (1976). Hypnotic susceptibility and frequency reports to illusory stimuli. *Journal of Abnormal Psychology, 85,* 558–563.

Watson, D., & Clark, L. A. (1984). Negative affectivity: The disposition to experience aversive emotional states. *Psychological Bulletin, 96,* 465–490.

Weinberger, D. A., Schwartz, G. E., & Kristeller, J. L. (1979). Low-anxious, high-anxious, and repressive coping styles: Psychometric patterns and behavioral and physiological responses to stress. *Journal of Abnormal Psychology, 88,* 369–380.

Weitzenhoffer, A. M., & Hilgard, E. R. (1962). *Stanford Hypnotic Susceptibility Scale, Form C.* Palo Alto, CA: Consulting Psychologists Press.

Wickramasekera, I. (1968). Sexual exhibitionism: The application of learning theory to the treatment of a case of sexual exhibitionism. *Psychotherapy: Theory, Research and Practice, 5,* 108–112.

Wickramasekera, I. (1969a). The effects of sensory restriction on susceptibility to hypnosis: A hypothesis, some preliminary data, and theoretical speculation. *International Journal of Clinical and Experimental Hypnosis, 17,* 217–224.

Wickramasekera, I. (1969b). Reinforcement and/or transference in psychotherapy and hypnosis. *American Journal of Clinical Hypnosis, 12,* 137–139.

Wickramasekera, I. (1971a). Effects of EMG feedback training on susceptibility to hypnosis: Preliminary observations [Summary]. *Proceedings of the 79th Annual Convention of the American Psychological Association, 6,* 783–784.

Wickramasekera, I. (1971b). The effects of "hypnosis" and task motivational instructions in attempting to influence the voluntary self-deprivation of money. *Journal of Personality and Social Psychology, 19,* 311–314.

Wickramasekera, I. (1972). A brief (2 session) technique for controlling a certain type of sexual exhibitionism. *Psychotherapy, Research and Practice, 9,* 207–210.

Wickramasekera, I. (1973). Effects of EMG feedback on hypnotic susceptibility: More preliminary data. *Journal of Abnormal Psychology, 82,* 74–77.

Wickramasekera, I. (1976a). Aversive behavior rehearsal for sexual exhibitionism. *Behavior Therapy, 7,* 167–176.

Wickramasekera, I. (1976b). *Biofeedback, behavior therapy and hypnosis.* Chicago: Nelson Hall.

Wickramasekera, I. (1977a). On attempts to modify hypnotic susceptibility: Some psychophysiological procedures and promising directions. *Annals of the New York Academy of Sciences, 296,* 143–153.

Wickramasekera, I. (1977b). The placebo effect and biofeedback for headache pain. In *Proceedings of the San Diego Biomedical Symposium* (pp. 193–201). New York: Academic Press.

Wickramasekera, I. (1979, March). *A model of the patient at high risk for chronic stress-related disorders: Do beliefs have biological consequences?* Paper presented at the Annual Convention of the Biofeedback Society of America, San Diego, CA.

Wickramasekera, I. (1980). A conditioned response model of the placebo effect: Predictions from the model. *Biofeedback and Self-Regulation, 5,* 5–18.

Wickramasekera, I. (1983, August–September). *A model of people at high risk.* Paper presented at the International Stress and Tension Control Society, University of Sussex, Brighton, England.

Wickramasekera, I. (1984). A model of people at high risk to develop chronic stress-related symptoms. In F. J. McGuigan, W. Smye, & J. M. Wallace (Eds.), *Stress and tension control, 2.* New York: Plenum Press.

Wickramasekera, I. (1985). A conditioned response model of the placebo effect: Predictions from the model. In L. White, B. Tursky, & G. E. Schwartz (Eds.), *Placebo: Theory, research, and mechanisms.* New York: Guilford Press.

Wickramasekera, I. (1986). A model of people at high risk to develop chronic stress-related somatic symptoms: Some predictions. *Professional Psychology: Research and Practice, 17,* 437–447.

Wickramasekera, I. (1988). *Clinical behavioral medicine: Some concepts and procedures.* New York: Plenum Press.

Wickramasekera, I. (1989). Enabling the somatizing patient to exit the somatic closet: A high-risk model. *Psychotherapy: Theory, Research, Practice, and Training, 26,* 530–544.

Wickramasekera, I. (1990, March). *Psychophysiological monitoring as another royal road to the unconscious.* Paper presented at the annual meeting of the Association for Applied Psychophysiology and Biofeedback, Washington, DC.

Wickramasekera, I. (1991a, March). *Psychophysiological monitoring: Another "royal road" to the unconscious mind.* Paper presented at the annual meeting of the Association for Applied Psychophysiology and Biofeedback, Dallas, TX.

Wickramasekera, I. (1991b). The unconscious, somatization, psychophysiological psychotherapy and threat perception: Footnotes to a cartography of the unconscious mind. *Biofeedback, 19,* 18–23.

Wickramasekera, I., Atkinson, R., & Turner, M. (1992). *Body mass index and hypnotic ability.* Paper presented at a symposium on "Hypnotic Ability as a Risk Factor for Psychopathology and Pathophysiology" at the 100th Annual Convention of the American Psychological Association, Washington, DC.

Wickramasekera, I., Ware, C., & Saxon, J. (1992). *EEG defined insomnia and hypnotic ability with a pathophysiology excluded.* Paper presented at a symposium on "Hypnotic Ability as a Risk Factor for Psychopathology and Pathophysiology" at the 100th Annual Convention of the American Psychological Association, Washington, DC.

Wiesel, S., Feffer, H., & Tsournas, N. (1984). *The incidence of positive CAT scans in an asymptomatic group of patients.* Volo Award paper presented at the Annual Meeting of the International Society for the Study of Lumbar Spine, Montreal, Quebec, Canada.

Wilson, S. C., & Barber, T. X. (1982). The fantasy-prone personality: Implications for understanding imagery, hypnosis and parapsychological phenomena. In A. A. Shiekh (Ed.), *Imagery: Current theory, research and application* (pp. 340–390). New York: Wiley.

Zajonc, R. B. (1984). On the primacy of affect. *American Psychologist, 39,* 117–123.

Zarski, J. J. (1984). Hassles and health: A replication. *Health Psychology, 33,* 243–251.

Zillmer, E. A., & Wickramasekera, I. (1987). Biofeedback and hypnotizability: Initial treatment considerations. *Clinical Biofeedback and Health, 10,* 51–57.

Zocco, L. (1984). *The development of a self-report inventory to assess dysfunctional cognitions in phobics.* Unpublished doctoral dissertation, Virginia Consortium for Professional Psychology, Norfolk.

28

PSYCHOLOGICAL TREATMENT OF WARTS

SUSAN C. DuBREUIL and NICHOLAS P. SPANOS

Numerous case studies and several experiments have indicated that suggestive procedures may be effective in treating a variety of dermatological disorders, including congenital ichthyosiform erythrodermia of Brocq (fish skin disease; Mason, 1955; Wink, 1961), psoriasis (Frankel & Misch, 1973), genital herpes (Longo, Clum, & Yaeger, 1988), and warts (e.g., Couper & Davies, 1952; Obermayer & Greenson, 1949). Some dermatological disorders, such as fish skin disease, are so rare as to preclude multisubject experimental studies regarding the effects of psychological treatment. Other disorders, like psoriasis, are relatively common. Nevertheless, controlled experiments assessing the effects of psychological treatments for this disorder are nonexistent. One experiment (Longo et al., 1988) assessed the effects of psychological treatment on the frequency and severity of genital herpes outbreaks. In this case, however, verbal report was the only criterion for assessing the severity and frequency of outbreaks, and, consequently, the extent to which reporting biases influenced the validity of the results remains impossible to determine.

In contrast with other skin disorders, warts have been studied fairly extensively. Warts are a relatively common disorder (Lynch, 1982), and wart loss can be easily and objectively assessed. For these reasons, warts have been the most popularly studied dermatological disorder with respect to psychological intervention.

Common warts (verruca vulgaris) result from infection of the papova virus. This virus has the ability to replicate in the nucleus of epidermal cells, and it now appears likely that the same virus is responsible for all of the common types of infectious warts (White & Fenner, 1986).

Anecdotal reports of the successful treatment of warts with procedures that, today, are classified as psychological (e.g., charms, prayers, and magical amulets) go back to antiquity (Zwick, 1932). The first modern investigator to make self-conscious use of psychological procedures in treating warts appears to have been the French physician Bonjour (1929). Bonjour believed that the skin was an organ that expressed psychic processes in terms of somatic symptoms, and that many skin disorders had psychological causes. Beginning in 1888, Bonjour developed a procedure that entailed drawing an outline of the patient's infected hand on a piece of paper and marking off the warts. Next, while the patient was blindfolded, Bonjour would touch the patient's warts with some instrument while giving suggestions that the warts would no longer be felt and would disappear. Bonjour claimed a high rate of success for his procedure, and believed that suggestion operated by cutting off the blood supply to warts.

Another early advocate of suggestion in the treatment of warts was Bruno Bloch (1927). Although Bloch used various suggestive procedures, one of his favorites involved having blindfolded patients place their infected hands into an "electric machine." When switched on, the apparatus made a humming noise but did nothing else. In addition to this "electric treatment," Bloch also painted patients' warts with methylene blue or some other innocuous substance. Following removal of the blindfold, patients were instructed not to touch the warts until the blue color had disappeared. Bloch reported a success rate of over 50% after 1 month following treatment. Interestingly, he claimed that success was not diminished by explaining to his more educated patients that they were, in fact, being treated by suggestion.

Bloch (1927) believed that patients varied in suggestibility and that his and other wart treatments were most effective with the most suggestible patients. However, he also believed that the demeanor and attitude of the therapist were particularly important in influencing patients' suggestibility. Thus, Bloch believed that any wart treatment would be made more effective if the therapist exuded confidence in the efficacy of treatment.

Obermayer and Greenson (1949) and McDowell (1949) published the first reports of cases involving hypnotic procedures in suggestion-based treatment for wart loss. Since the 1960s, hypnotic treatment has become the most popular form of psychological intervention for inducing wart loss.

THEORETICAL ACCOUNTS

Attempts to account theoretically for the role of hypnotic and other suggestive influence on wart regression have been limited both by the lack of systematically collected data demonstrating the existence of such an effect and by the lack of credible formulations to explain how psychological influences can produce physiological effects. Nevertheless, at least five more or less distinct psychological hypotheses have been proposed.

The first of these hypotheses holds that hypnotic and suggestive treatments achieve their effects through expectancy. In its strongest version, this hypothesis states that response expectancies constitute both the necessary and sufficient conditions for psychologically produced wart remission (Kirsch, 1985).

The second psychological hypothesis emphasizes patient suggestibility as a relatively stable attribute. In modern variants of this hypothesis, suggestibility is equated with hypnotizability (also called hypnotic susceptibility; Bowers, 1977; Bowers & Kelly, 1979; Wadden & Anderton, 1982). According to this notion, highly hypnotizable individuals, to a greater extent than low hypnotizables, possess the ability to "translate" the verbal messages contained in suggestions into immunological or other physiological processes that contain or kill the wart virus.

A third hypothesis is based on the psychoanalytic notion of conversion. According to this notion, an outbreak of warts serves an unconscious defensive function. By developing warts, the patient's psychological equilibrium is somehow maintained, and anxiety is minimized (e.g., an outbreak of anal warts in a man prevents him from fulfilling an unconscious, anxiety-producing wish for homosexual anal intercourse). Conversely, uncovering the unconscious conflict and concomitantly reducing the level of anxiety through psychotherapy can result in wart remission (Ewin, 1974).

A fourth hypothesis emphasizes the role of imaginal processes in wart remission (Achterberg, 1985; Barber, 1984). According to this hypothesis, suggestive influences elicit therapeutic images that, in turn, elicit the physiological processes that lead to wart regression.

A fifth hypothesis holds that wart remission that appears to be treatment related can be explained in terms of spontaneous remission. Because warts tend to spontaneously remit, the end of treatment and spontaneous remission will occur simultaneously in some proportion of treated patients. According to this hypothesis, the occurrence of such instances leads investigators to conclude erroneously that the treatment caused the remission (Stankler, 1967).

Much of the research used in support of these various hypotheses has involved inadequate methodologies. In many instances, case histories or studies lacking treatment control groups serve as the only bases of support.

METHODOLOGICAL CONSIDERATIONS

The studies of Rulison (1942) and Massing and Epstein (1963) still serve as the most comprehensive data sets available concerning the natural history of untreated warts. In Rulison's study ($N = 921$), wart duration ranged from 1 month to 28 years. On average, however, warts spontaneously disappeared 2 to 3 years following their initial occurrence. Massing and Epstein reported a somewhat shorter duration for warts, on the basis of their sample of 168 untreated cases. Fifty-one percent of their subjects showed complete remission after 1 year, and a further 16% exhibited partial remission. At the 2-year follow-up, 67% of the original sample showed complete remission, and 15% showed partial remission. After 2 years, only 18% of the sample remained status quo. The differences in these reports, together with the wide variability found for wart duration in both reports, constitute one of the major research problems in this area.

Much of the evidence concerning the efficacy of suggestion-based treatment for wart remission is based on case histories, anecdotal reports, and quasi-experimental research. All of these research procedures lack appropriate no-treatment conditions for evaluating the influence of spontaneous remission. Given the variable course of normal wart regression, spontaneous remission cannot be ruled out as an explanation for wart loss in any study that does not include untreated control subjects.

A within-subject approach to control for spontaneous remission has been used in numerous studies (e.g., Sinclair-Gieben & Chalmers, 1959). These studies used subjects with bilateral warts and aimed the therapeutic suggestions at the warts on only one side of the body. Selective regression of the warts on the treated side was then taken as evidence of a treatment effect. However, failure to obtain selective regression was interpreted as treatment failure. Such an interpretation is problematic. For example, some evidence (e.g., Surman, Gottlieb, Hackett, & Silverberg, 1973) has indicated that suggestions aimed at only one side of the body produce significant wart regression on the untreated side of the body as well as on the treated side. Consequently, without a no-treatment control group, the results of within-subject experiments that fail to find a selective treatment effect remain ambiguous.

Subject demographics, including type of warts, duration of presenting warts, and subject age and gender are often not reported. In addition, very few studies have randomly assigned subjects to treatment groups. Consequently, in quasi-experimental studies it is not clear that the groups have been equated on these variables. Another problem area concerns subject attrition. Some studies report a high rate of attrition, without adequate follow-up of subjects who failed to complete treatment (e.g., Stankler, 1967). Thus, it is impossible to determine if subjects who completed treatment differed from those who did not.

Descriptions of the treatment regimens used in most of the studies in this area are inadequate. For example, the nature of hypnotic suggestions for wart loss, the degree of subject involvement in treatment (e.g., whether they were required to practice their treatments on a daily basis), and the number of treatment sessions are often unclear from published reports.

Different criteria for determining the success of various treatments are used across studies. For example, in one study treatment was considered successful only if subjects exhibited complete remission (Stankler, 1967). In other studies, success was equated with an arbitrary percentage of wart loss (e.g., Surman et al., 1973, in which 75% resolution was considered a success). Still others used a continuous index of wart loss (e.g., Spanos, Williams, & Gwynn, 1990).

Most of the work in this area has suffered from one or more of these inadequacies. These deficiencies hinder comparisons among studies and limit conclusions concerning the relative effectiveness of different psychological treatments. Fortunately, more recent research in this area has used stronger methodological designs (e.g., Spanos, Stenstrom, & Johnston, 1988; Spanos et al., 1990).

CLINICAL APPLICATIONS

Traditional medical interventions appear to be relatively ineffective in treating warts. Of 160 patients who sought treatment in Rulison's (1942) study, no more than 55% experienced successful results, and reoccurrences following more radical treatment (e.g., surgery) were not uncommon. Others have reported that warts often reoccur within weeks or months of medical intervention (Bunney, 1982). In addition to being relatively ineffective, medical interventions, such as surgery or liquid nitrogen, are costly and can result in disfigurement.

Psychological interventions, on the other hand, are expedient, may be self-administered, and do not result in scarring. Psychological treatments for warts invariably involve a suggestive component. The two most commonly used psychological treatments in this area are placebos and hypnotherapy. In placebo interventions, the suggestion for wart loss is usually indirect and the subject is not instructed to play an active role in his or her treatment. In this respect, placebos typically mimic traditional medical treatments in which the patient is required to develop little, if any, psychological involvement in or control over the treatment.

Contemporary hypnotherapy, on the other hand, usually involves overt suggestions for wart loss that call for the active participation of subjects in imagery-based suggestions. The hypnotic induction typically consists of repeated instructions for relaxation, drowsiness, and focused attention. At a minimum, the induction procedure is followed by suggestions that the wart is shriveling up, shrinking in size, and disappearing. Suggestions for wart loss are often accompanied by directions to focus on the infected area and to attend to "prickling and tingling" sensations that, it is suggested, accompany wart loss. For example, the suggestions used by Spanos et al. (1988) were as follows:

> Notice that the skin on and around the warts on your hand is beginning to feel warm and a little tingly. The skin around the warts on your hand is beginning to tingle.
>
> Notice the sensations around the warts on your hand; you can feel the tingling, prickling sensation around the warts on your hand, you know that this sensation will cause the warts on your hand to disappear. . . . As you feel these sensations you can see the warts on your hand shrinking in size and dissolving away, shrinking in size and dissolving away. . . .

Still other treatment regimes incorporate a more extensive use of imagery-based suggestion. For example, in addition to imagining cure-related sensations, subjects treated in several recent studies were asked to create an imaginary treatment agent, which they repeatedly imagined attacking and destroying the wart virus. Subjects were also directed to imagine the infected area clear of warts and in a natural, healthy state.

This chapter will review the literature on the psychological treatment of warts, and has been divided into sections that discuss case studies, comparison studies, and experiments that included no treatment control groups. A summary of the studies under review is presented in the appendix.

CASE STUDIES

As discussed earlier, Bloch (1927) treated his patients using a credible display of a simulated medical procedure that included covering the warts with methylene blue. Following the treatment session, patients were told that they were not to touch or wash the wart or surrounding areas until the wart disappeared. Of the 179 patients who were available for a 3-month follow-up, 78.5% were wart-free. Of these subjects, about 30% lost their warts within 2 weeks following the treatment session, an additional 43% showed complete remission within 1 month, and a further 18% lost their warts within 3 months of treatment.

Vollmer (1946) used Bloch's treatment and in some cases used additional mechanical aids to enhance subjects' expectancies of treatment success. He treated over 100 children, most of whom had plana juvenus on the hands or face. Although Vollmer failed to include summaries of his data, he reported that the majority of his clients were cured within 7 weeks following treatment and that many lost their warts much sooner (i.e., within

4 days after treatment). The average follow-up period was about 3 months; however, follow-up status was based on subjects' verbal reports rather than on physical examination. Vollmer reported that the changes in wart histology observed in his patients were similar to those seen during spontaneous remission. In contrast with Bloch (1927), Vollmer concluded that suggestion merely expedited spontaneous remission.

Several authors have offered psychodynamic explanations for the wart loss that accompanied psychotherapeutically oriented interventions. In these cases, treatment consisted of clinical interviews that led the subject to acknowledge that the warts served a psychologically based function. In the majority of reported cases, psychodynamically oriented psychotherapy was used in conjunction with hypnotic suggestions for wart loss. Sheehan (1978) reported the case of a young girl who was initially unresponsive to multiple hypnotic sessions involving suggestions for wart loss. Subsequently, however, the girl was led to acknowledge that she believed that the warts had been a "gift" from her grandfather, who was now ill. Consequently, following a hypnotic induction, suggestions were given that her warts would disappear upon either the death of her grandfather or his return to stable health. Three weeks following the death of her grandfather, the girl was wart-free.

Ewin (1974) reported four cases of genital/anal warts that regressed following treatment with a combination of hypnotic procedures and psychotherapy. In one case, a homosexual male client exhibited a 50% reduction in a rosette of anal warts following a session in which he was led to admit that he did not need the warts as protection against anal intercourse. At a second session, hypnotic suggestions for wart loss were given, and several weeks later the patient showed complete remission.

Several case histories involving suggestion-based hypnotic treatment as the only intervention have also been reported. Obermayer and Greenson (1949) published a case study of a young woman with juvenile planar warts of 2 years duration. Over the course of 3 weeks, she participated in three hypnotic treatment sessions. Obermayer and Greenson reported that 2 weeks following the final treatment session, the woman was completely wart-free. Her wart-free status was also maintained at a 6-month follow-up.

In the same year, McDowell (1949) reported the case of a 32-year-old woman who had warts on her hands, face, and neck of 8 months duration. She participated in three hypnotic treatment sessions involving suggestions for wart loss. McDowell reported that at the third treatment session, the patient's hands were 98% clear and her face was 50% clear. Eighteen days following the first treatment session, the woman reported being completely free of warts.

More recently, Clawson and Swade (1975) reported three cases involving the use of hypnotic suggestions. In each case, a hypnotic induction was followed by repeated suggestions to inhibit the flow of blood to each wart. In one case, an 18-year-old woman with hundreds of common and flat warts showed complete remission following 2 months of weekly hypnotic sessions. The woman was still wart-free 3½ years later. The second case involved a 4-year-old boy with multiple warts on his hands and lower lip. One month following a single treatment session, his hands were improved by 50% and his lip was completely wart-free. The boy was "rehypnotized" at this point, and 1 month following this second treatment session, he was completely wart-free. The third case involved an 11-year-old boy who showed complete remission of multiple warts within 2 months following three treatment sessions.

Tasini and Hackett (1977) reported similar findings concerning the effectiveness of hypnotic treatment. Treatment was administered to one male and two female immunodeficient children. The mean number of treatment sessions was three, and the children showed complete remission within 1 month, 3 months, and 7 months of the first treatment session. Follow-up ranged from 4 to 8 months, and all three patients maintained their wart-free status.

These case studies suggest that psychological treatment may be an effective means of treating warts. However, in addition to the standard criticisms about anecdotal research (e.g., no control), another major criticism of case reports in this area has been the absence or unclarity of information concerning wart duration. In many cases where duration was reported, it was beyond the average time of spontaneous remission. In the cases reviewed above, wart duration ranged from 2 to 51 months. Rulison (1942), however, reported that warts tend to spontaneously remit between 24 and 36 months. Therefore, the spontaneous remission of warts cannot be ruled out as an explanation for wart loss in anecdotal reports.

An added difficulty occurs because clinicians are unlikely to report unsuccessful cases involving psychological treatment. This fosters the impression that psychological treatments for wart loss rarely result in failure, even though controlled experiments indicate that the failure rate is substantial (e.g., Spanos et al., 1990).

RESEARCH AND APPRAISAL

Between-Groups Comparison Studies

Allington (1934) compared the effectiveness of sulpharsphenamine ($n = 80$) and placebo injections (tap water; $n = 84$) for inducing wart regression. The treatment and comparison groups failed to differ significantly on wart loss. Unfortunately, Allington failed to include a no-treatment control group. Consequently, the effectiveness of these treatments relative to subjects who did not receive treatment could not be assessed, and the possibility that remission was spontaneous cannot be ruled out.

Using nonstandardized criteria for assessing hypnotizability, Asher (1956) compared 17 high hypnotizable, 8 light hypnotizable, and 8 unhypnotizable subjects. All subjects were given at least 4 weekly hypnotic treatment sessions. Of the 17 high hypnotizables, 11 showed complete remission, 4 showed partial remission, and 2 showed no change. Fifty percent ($n = 4$) of the light hypnotizables lost all of their warts, and the remainder showed no improvement. None of the unhypnotizable subjects lost warts. Unfortunately, Asher confounded hypnotizability level with length of treatment. The high and light hypnotizable subjects received a greater number of treatment sessions than did the unhypnotizables. Consequently, the reasons for the greater remission in hypnotizables as compared with unhypnotizables remain unclear.

Ullman and Dudek (1960) categorized subjects as either "good" or "poor" hypnotic subjects. However, their criteria for determining the level of hypnotizability were not reported. Subjects were administered one hypnotic treatment session and were recontacted for follow-up 4 weeks later. Of the 15 good hypnotic subjects, 8 showed complete remission, 1 showed partial remission, 4 had warts that had decreased in size, and 2 subjects did not improve. In contrast, only 2 of 47 poor hypnotic subjects showed complete remission, and 42 subjects exhibited no improvement.

Chandrasena (1982) reported an uncontrolled study involving 32 subjects who attained what she labeled "stage 1" of hypnotic responding. She reported that the criteria for assessing hypnotizability were based on a condensed version of the Stanford Hypnotic Susceptibility Scales, Forms A and B (Weitzenhoffer & Hilgard, 1959). However, her criteria included responses to suggestions for anesthesia and motor activity (i.e., walking), which are not included in either of the Stanford scales. Thus, the criteria for assessing hypnotizability in this study remain unclear. Twenty-seven of these subjects had both palmar or plantar warts and common warts, and 5 subjects had only common warts. The subjects attended an average of 8.8 hypnotic treatment sessions, which included suggestions that the wart would "crumble and fall off." Fifty-six percent of the subjects showed at least a 50% reduction in the baseline area covered by warts. Chandrasena also reported a relationship between hypnotizability assessed during the initial treatment session and wart loss: 80% of the subjects who met her hypnotizability criteria for stage 2 or 3 showed a minimum reduction of 50% in the baseline area covered by the warts, whereas less than 17% of the subjects who attained a hypnotizability rating of stage 1 showed a comparable reduction in their warts.

Within-Subject Comparison Studies

Hellier (1951) examined the effectiveness of X-ray treatment using 74 subjects with bilateral warts as their own control. He administered X-rays to the subjects' right hands. Without their knowledge, he then turned off the X-ray machine and repeated the treatment on the left hand. Two subjects showed complete remission on the treatment side only; however, 27 subjects showed complete bilateral wart loss. Because X-ray treatments can produce systemic changes in immune functioning, it cannot be concluded that the loss of warts that occurred on the placebo-treated left hand resulted from psychological factors.

Stankler (1967) used subjects as their own control in two separate studies designed to investigate the effects of implicit suggestion. In one study, 61 subjects self-administered daily applications of a "proven topical treatment" (tap water) to the side of their body with the most warts. Over the course of 3 months, warts on the other side were given no treatment. Of the 45 subjects who completed treatment, 5 exhibited complete bilateral wart loss within 2 months, and an additional 10 subjects showed complete bilateral remission within 3 months.

Using subjects as their own control in a second study, Stankler (1967) treated 30 subjects with a nonfunctional "ray" machine. Again, the treatment side was the side with the most warts. Of the 22 subjects who completed the second study, 7 showed complete remission. In both studies, wart loss was measured dichotomously: Subjects were considered successful only if they lost all of their warts on the treatment side, the control side, or both sides. None of the subjects in either study exhibited unilateral wart loss. This failure to find a side-specific effect for treatment prompted Stankler to conclude that wart loss was due to spontaneous remission. Such a conclusion is, however, not warranted. As described earlier, evidence indicates that suggestion-based treatment effects generalize from the targeted area to other infectious sites. Consequently, studies that aim a treatment at only one side of the body and use the other side as a control may yield misleading findings. Unambiguous findings require the inclusion of a no-treatment control group. Unfortunately, Stankler did not include such a group in either experiment.

Clarke (1965) argued in a similar vein to Stankler that the loss of warts following suggestive treatment coincides with the "natural life's end" of the wart virus. In one experiment, Clarke administered an electric shock to warts on one side and left the remaining side untreated. He monitored the subjects' progress at regular intervals for at least 3 months and reported that 19 subjects improved. However, only 21.0% of these subjects lost warts on the treated side only, 31.6% lost warts only on the untreated side, and 47.4% of the improved subjects lost warts on both the treated and untreated sides. The remaining 43 subjects (69.4%) showed no improvement.

In a second study (Clarke, 1965), 22 subjects were administered a combination of X-ray, placebo X-ray, and no treatment, and served as their own controls. Fifty percent of the subjects showed no change; however, 18% lost all of their warts, 23% lost warts on the treatment side only, and 9% of the subjects failed to lose warts on the treated side but lost warts left untreated or treated by placebo.

Sinclair-Gieben and Chalmers (1959) administered hypnotic treatment to 10 subjects whom they classified, on the basis of nonstandardized criteria, as able to achieve "moderate" to "deep" hypnosis, and 4 subjects who were classified as "lightly" hypnotizable. All subjects had bilateral warts, but hypnotic treatment was targeted unilaterally toward the side with the most warts. Within 3 months, 7 of the 10 hypnotizable subjects showed complete remission, and 2 subjects had lost all but "one big wart" on the treatment side only. None of these subjects lost warts on the control side, and none of the low hypnotizables lost any warts.

Johnson and Barber (1978) randomly assigned 22 subjects to either hypnotic or nonhypnotic treatment conditions. Subjects in the hypnotic group were administered a hypnotic induction before imagery-based suggestions for wart loss. In lieu of the induction procedure, subjects in the comparison group were told that they would receive a treatment called "focused contemplation." The subjects in both treatments who had bilateral warts were given suggestions that the warts would disappear on only one side. Following treatment, all subjects were told to practice the suggestions daily. Johnson and Barber reported that there were no between-groups differences with respect to age, number of presenting warts, or duration of the warts. At a 6-week follow-up, 3 of the 11 hypnotic subjects were wart-free on the treatment side, whereas none of the subjects in the focused contemplation group showed any change. This difference between groups did not, however, attain statistical significance.

Two of the three wart-free subjects showed treatment-specific unilateral loss. The third subject had facial warts and could not be treated unilaterally. The authors hypothesized that the successful subjects had higher motivation and stronger expectancies for treatment success than did the unsuccessful subjects. Consequently, they hypothesized that "believed in efficacy" was the mediating factor in wart loss. Unfortunately, they provided no independent assessments of subjects' motivations and expectancies. In addition, the small sample size, lack of systematic assessment, and absence of a no-treatment control group limit the conclusions that can be drawn from their findings.

Tenzel and Taylor (1969) preselected subjects with bilateral warts who had passed the posthypnotic suggestion on the Stanford Hypnotic Susceptibility Scale, Form A. Treatment was randomly assigned to one side of the body. The subjects were administered a hypnotic induction procedure and told that each wart that was touched would tingle briefly, begin to regress, and be gone within 2 weeks. Subjects were then awakened, and a placebo treatment that included painting the wart with fluoroscene was administered to the warts on the control side. Five weeks following treatment, none of the 20 subjects showed any change in the condition of their warts.

In summary, nine separate within-subject experiments used subjects with bilateral warts and administered a psychological treatment to only one side of the body. Only one of those studies (Sinclair-Gieben & Chalmers, 1959) obtained significantly greater remission of the treated than the untreated side. In that study, the side that received the treatment was not chosen randomly. Instead, treatment was always aimed at the side that initially had the most warts. As we shall see, this confound may have influenced the results obtained by Sinclair-Gieben and Chalmers.

Controlled Studies

Memmesheimer and Eisenlohr's (1931) treatment consisted of a placebo topical application (methylene blue) plus explicit suggestions for wart loss. These investigators conducted the first controlled experiment in this area. One hundred and forty subjects with flat and common warts were evenly distributed between the treatment and control groups. Within 1 month following treatment, 14 of the treatment subjects and only 2 of the control subjects were wart-free. Three months after treatment, an additional 3 subjects in each group showed complete remission. Although the subjects in the treatment condition clearly outperformed the controls at 1- and 3-month intervals, this difference was not maintained at a 6-month follow-up. At the final follow-up, 17 subjects in the treatment condition and 20 control subjects were wart-free. Memmesheimer and Eisenlohr concluded that suggestive treatment was effective only in expediting spontaneous remission.

Surman et al. (1973) compared a treatment group that received side-specific hypnotic treatment ($n = 17$) with a no-treatment control group of 7 subjects. Treatment was administered weekly for 5 weeks, with a 3-month follow-up. One subject in the treatment condition showed complete remission on the treatment side only, 5 subjects showed complete bilateral loss, 3 exhibited partial bilateral loss (75% resolution), and the remaining subjects failed to improve (<75% resolution). None of the control subjects lost warts, and the difference in wart loss between treatment and control subjects was statistically significant. The findings for Surman et al.'s treatment group were similar to the findings of Stankler (1967). However, inclusion of a no-treatment control condition allowed Surman et al. to conclude that suggestive treatment preceded by hypnotic induction is an effective means of curing warts, even though the data did not support a side-specificity effect. In contrast with Asher (1956), Surman et al. also concluded that hypnotizability was not related to wart loss. At the same time, however, Surman et al. cautioned that insufficient variability in the subjects' hypnotic susceptibility scores, as assessed by a 4-point nonstandardized scale, prevented firm conclusions concerning the relationship between hypnotizability and wart loss.

Spanos et al. (1988) used a mixed design to reexamine the side-specificity issue and to test the efficacy of hypnotic ($n = 22$) and placebo (cold laser; $n = 24$) treatments. A no-treatment control group ($n = 17$) was also included. At baseline, the groups failed to differ on age and on the number or duration of their warts. However, at a 6-week follow-up, subjects given the hypnotic suggestion treatment had lost a greater percentage of their warts than had subjects in the placebo and control conditions. On average, the hypnotic subjects lost 33.7% of their warts, the placebo subjects lost 9.1%, and the control subjects averaged only a 2% reduction.

Hypnotic subjects rated suggested sensations of tingling and prickling as more vivid than did placebo subjects. Furthermore, within the hypnotic condition, subjects who lost warts reported more vivid suggested imagery than did subjects who did not lose warts.

To examine the relative importance of hypnotic procedures in the suggestive treatment of warts, Spanos et al. (1988) conducted a second study. Hypnotic induction plus suggestion, relaxation plus suggestion, suggestion alone, and a no-treatment control group were compared ($n = 19$ per condition). The subjects in the three treatment groups showed more wart remission than did the subjects in the no-treatment group, and the subjects who were administered the hynotic induction lost slightly (but not significantly) fewer warts than did those who received the suggestion-alone treatment. Four subjects in the hypnotic treatment, 6 in the suggestion treatment, and 2 in the relaxation treatment lost warts. None of the control subjects lost any warts. Corroborating their previous findings, Spanos et al. found that subjects who lost warts reported significantly more vivid suggested imagery than did those who did not lose warts.

Spanos et al. (1988) also examined the impact of subjects' beliefs concerning treatment efficacy on wart loss. None of the subjects who held low expectations concerning treatment lost warts. However, subjects with high expectations were equally likely to lose or not lose warts. However, among subjects with high expectations, those who lost warts reported higher suggested imagery vividness than did those who did not lose warts.

In the two Spanos et al. (1988) studies combined, 15 subjects presented with bilateral warts on their hands. For these subjects, treatment was randomly targeted at warts on one hand only. The other hand was left untreated. Preliminary analyses indicated that the subjects lost a greater percentage of warts on the treated side, but overall, subjects had more warts on the hand that received treatment. At the beginning of treatment, 5 subjects had the same number of warts on both hands, 8 subjects had more warts on the treated hand (mean difference = 9.5), and only 2 subjects had more warts on the untreated hand (mean difference = 3). Spanos et al. found that subjects lost more warts on the treated than on the untreated side only when they had more warts on the treated side at the beginning of the study. Spanos et al. concluded that single or small numbers of warts may be more resistant to treatment than are large collections of warts. Consequently, when subjects have differing numbers of warts on each limb, they are more likely following treatment to lose warts on the side with the most initial warts. Nevertheless, firm conclusions concerning the issue of site specificity should await the results of studies that assign subjects to the following treatments: (a) an equal and large number of warts on both limbs, only one limb treated; (b) a large number of warts on one limb, few on the other, treatment aimed at the side with the most warts; (c) a large number of warts on one limb, few on the other, treatment aimed at the side with few warts; (d) an equal number of warts on both sides, both sides treated; (e) an equal number of warts on both sides, no treatment control; (f) a large number of warts on one side, a small number on the other, no treatment control.

In a third study involving a no-treatment control group, Spanos et al. (1990) compared the effectiveness of daily imagery-based suggestions, salicylic acid treatment, and a topical placebo treatment ($n = 10$ per condition). There were no differences with respect to age, number of presenting warts, or pretreatment wart duration among these groups. However, at a 6-week follow-up, subjects in the hypnotic treatment had lost significantly more warts than had subjects in any of the other conditions, who themselves failed to differ. Inconsistent with the expectancy hypothesis, subjects in the three treatments had comparable ratings of perceived treatment efficacy. However, subjects' ratings of sensation vividness were significantly different among treatments. Subjects in the hypnotic treatment reported more vivid sensations—corresponding to the suggestion they were given that healing would be accompanied by tingling, prickling sensations—than did subjects in the other three conditions.

In a controlled study, Spanos, Gabora, DuBreuil, Fisher, and Dewhirst (1991) compared the efficacy of imagery-based suggestions with the combined effects of imagery and rhythmic physical manipulation (gently pushing on the warts). Sixty subjects were evently distributed across the three conditions. Subjects who used the imagery procedure in conjunction with physical manipulation lost a significantly greater percentage of warts than did the subjects who used imagery alone or the controls. However, the results also indicated that subjects in both treatment groups outperformed subjects in the control group when wart loss was classified as (a) no change or worse, (b) warts smaller, or (c) some or all warts gone. Subjects in this study had their warts examined on a biweekly basis to ensure that the treatment effects could not be explained in terms of subjects' self-medicating or physically removing the warts. At none of the sessions did any of the subjects' warts show evidence of self-medication or physical trauma.

In a second study (Experiment 2, Spanos et al., 1991) 90 subjects were randomly assigned to one of four conditions: imagery plus physical manipulation, imagery alone, nonimaginal cognition (i.e., counting pushes) plus physical manipulation, or control. Using the categorical classification of success from the first study (Experiment 1, Spanos et al., 1991), the results indicated that the three treatment groups failed to differ. However, a greater proportion of subjects in the treatment groups showed improvement than did subjects in the control group. Spanos et al. also found a fan-shaped relationship between expectancies of treatment success and improvement. Once again, subjects with low expectations of success never lost warts, whereas those with high expectations sometimes lost warts and sometimes did not.

CONCLUSION

The findings of Tenzel and Taylor (1969) stand alone in failing to find a reduction in warts following hypnotic treatment. None of the 20 subjects in their study lost any warts. The findings of four controlled studies (Spanos et al., 1988, 1990; Surman et al., 1973), however, support the hypothesis that hypnotic suggestions produce wart remission that cannot be accounted for in terms of spontaneous remission, and two of these studies (Spanos et al., 1988, Experiment 1; Spanos et al., 1990) suggest that hypnotic treatment may be more effective in this regard than placebo treatment.

Furthermore, Spanos et al. (1988) found that suggestive treatment without a hypnotic induction procedure was as effective as suggestions preceded by an induction. Subjects administered these treatments showed equivalent levels of wart loss. Failure to find significant differences between hypnotic and nonhypnotic treatments in a wide range of suggested responses is common in both the experimental (Barber, 1969; Barber, Spanos, & Chaves, 1974) and the clinical (Spanos, 1991; Spinhoven, 1988; Wadden & Anderton, 1982) literature.

Sinclair-Gieben and Chalmers (1959) are the only investigators who have reported a side-specific effect for psychological treatment. Surman et al. (1973) also unilaterally administered hypnotic treatment to subjects with bilateral warts. Unlike Sinclair-Gieben and Chalmers, however, they found that wart loss was not limited to the targeted treatment side. Some evidence suggests that cases of multiple and single warts may remiss at different rates. Spanos et al. (1988) provided tentative empirical support for this hypothesis. After controlling for the number of presenting warts on each hand, they found no evidence for a side-specific effect. Taken together, the controlled experiments of Surman et al. and Spanos et al. indicate that suggestive treatments are effective in inducing wart remission but that treatments aimed at only one infected site tend to produce effects that generalize to other infected sites.

The findings concerning the effects of placebo treatments on wart loss have been mixed. Stankler (1967) and Clarke (1965) failed to find a side-specific effect when comparing a placebo administered to one side of the body versus no treatment to the other side. These findings prompted both of these investigators to argue in favor of spontaneous remission. In another study, however, Allington (1934) demonstrated that placebo injections were as effective as medical injections. In all of these studies, the extent of spontaneous remission is unclear because no-treatment control groups were not included. Inconsistent results have also been reported in the literature that included controls. Memmesheimer and Eisenlohr (1931) reported that subjects given a topical placebo along with suggestions that their warts would remiss outperformed subjects in a no-treatment control group at 1- and 3-month intervals. Conversely, Spanos et al. (1988, Experiment 1; 1990) found that subjects administered placebo treatments (cold laser or topical) did not lose significantly more warts than did untreated subjects at a 6-week follow-up. However, Spanos et al.'s (1988, Experiment 1) sample was much smaller than the sample in Memmesheimer and Eisenlohr's study, and there was a nonsignificant trend in the Spanos et al. study for the placebo group to outperform the no-treatment control group. With a larger number of subjects, this trend may have reached significance.

As outlined earlier, several hypotheses have been generated to explain the efficacy of suggestion-based wart treatments. One of these, the notion that treatment effects can be accounted for in terms of spontaneous remission, is no longer tenable. The findings from randomized, controlled experiments now leave little doubt that suggestion-based treatments produce wart regression that is beyond any effects of spontaneous remission.

Kirsch (1985) hypothesized that subjects' expectations that they would lose their warts (response expectancy) were the direct psychological cause of wart loss. This response expectancy hypothesis predicts that expectations of treatment success will correlate very highly with wart loss and that psychological factors such as imagery vividness will not contribute to treatment success beyond the effects of expectancy. Contrary to the expectancy hypothesis, Spanos et al. (1988) found a fanlike, rather than a linear, relationship between treatment expectancies and treatment outcome. Subjects with low expectations for treatment never lost warts, whereas subjects with high expectations sometimes lost warts but often did not. In addition, the vividness of subjects' suggested imagery predicted wart loss in subjects with uniformly high expectancies. In a second study, Spanos et al. (1990) found that ratings of treatment efficacy failed to differ among treatments, even though the hypnotic treatment was more effective than the others.

Thus, although high expectancies of treatment success may be necessary, they are clearly insufficient to produce suggestion-induced wart loss.

Another hypothesis holds that highly suggestible subjects will exhibit a greater degree of suggestion-induced wart loss than will subjects who are less suggestible (Bloch, 1927). In most studies in this area, suggestibility has been equated with hypnotizability. Nevertheless, results concerning the relationship between wart loss and hypnotizability have been mixed. Asher (1956), Ullman and Dudek (1960), and Sinclair-Gieben and Chalmers (1959) all found that high hypnotizables lost significantly more warts than did low hypnotizables. In all of these studies, hypnotizability was assessed using nonstandardized criteria.

On the other hand, Surman et al. (1973) and Spanos et al. (1988) found no relationship between wart loss and hypnotizability. In studies where hypnotizability was measured with standardized assessment instruments following treatment, no significant correlation between hypnotizability and wart loss was found (Spanos et al., 1988, 1990). The inferior performance of low hypnotizables in the studies of Asher (1956), Ullman and Dudek (1960), and Sinclair-Gieben and Chalmers (1959) could be because those subjects developed negative expectations of treatment success on the basis of their knowledge that they were unresponsive to hypnotic procedures. A good deal of research (see Spanos, 1991, for a review) has indicated that subjects' expectations about the relationship between their hypnotizability and their performance in a hypnotic situation substantially influence their responsiveness to suggestions. For instance, Spanos, Kennedy, and Gwynn (1984) found that low hypnotizables given suggestions for analgesia in a hypnotic context reported much less pain reduction than did corresponding high hypnotizables. However, when tested in a nonhypnotic context that was unrelated to their earlier hypnotizability testing, low hypnotizables given analgesia suggestions reported as much pain reduction as did high hypnotizables.

Yet another hypothesis holds that warts may persist in some individuals because they serve some underlying psychodynamic purpose (Ewin, 1974). According to this hypothesis, insight into unconscious conflicts enables individuals to recognize that their warts are no longer necessary. Consequently, the warts remit. Support for this hypothesis has been based solely on case reports that often confound psychodynamic psychotherapy with suggestions for wart loss. The available controlled studies indicate that suggestions for wart regression in the absence of psychodynamic therapy are effective in inducing wart regression. Only controlled experimentation can evaluate whether psychodynamic therapy alone is effective in producing greater-than-control levels of wart regression or whether psychodynamic therapy plus suggestion is more effective in this regard than suggestion alone.

A final hypothesis holds that the vividness of suggestion-related imagery is a key variable in psychologically induced wart regression. Suggestions including an imagery component were more effective than a placebo in two studies (Spanos et al., 1988, Experiment 1; Spanos et al., 1990), and in one study (Spanos et al., 1988, Experiment 2) the addition of hypnotic procedures to the imagery suggestion failed to enhance the effects of the suggestion alone. In several studies, the degree to which subjects rated their treatment-specific imagery as vivid correlated significantly with wart loss (Spanos et al., 1988, 1991). On the other hand, attribute measures of imagery vividness failed to predict wart loss in these studies. Furthermore, Spanos et al. (1991) found that a cognitive intervention (counting while pushing on the warts), designed to foster a strong belief in personal control over treatment outcome while precluding vivid wart-related imagery, led to as much wart regression as did an imagery suggestion. Taken together, the findings of these studies may indicate that vivid suggestion-related imagery and belief in personal control over treatment outcome independently influence wart loss. Alternatively, these findings may indicate that situation-specific measures of imagery vividness function as indirect indexes of subjects' treatment motivations and their beliefs that they have developed control over physiological processes. In short, although the available data indicate that the vividness with which warts are imagined as regressing is associated with treatment success, the interpretation of this finding remains unclear. Further studies that manipulate the imaginal content of suggestions, while equating the extent to which suggestions enhance subjects' motivations and their subjective sense of control, might shed more light on the role of imagery in wart regression.

Research is essentially nonexistent on the physiological mediators of wart loss. Experimental studies that examine the role of immune system functioning are a required step in understanding the physiological processes that mediate the relationship between psychological treatment and the eventual loss of warts.

REFERENCES

Achterberg, J. (1985). *Imagery in healing*. Boston: New Science Library.

Allington, H. V. (1934). Sulpharsphenamine in the treatment of warts. *Archives of Dermatology and Syphilology, 29*, 687–690.

Asher, R. (1956). Respectable hypnosis. *British Medical Journal*, 309–313.

Barber, T. X. (1969). *Hypnosis: A scientific approach*. New York: Van Nostrand Reinhold.

Barber, T. X. (1984). Changing "unchangeable" bodily processes by (hypnotic) suggestions: A new look at hypnosis, cognitions, imagining, and the mind–body problem. In A. A. Sheikh (Ed.), *Imagination and healing* (pp. 69–128). New York: Baywood.

Barber, T. X., Spanos, N. P., & Chaves, J. F. (1974). *Hypnosis, imagination, and human potentialities*. Elmsford, NY: Pergamon Press.

Bloch, B. (1927). Uber die helung der warzin durch suggestion. *Klin Worchenscher,* *6,* 2271–2325.

Bonjour, J. (1929). Influence of the mind on the skin. *British Journal of Dermatology,* *41,* 324.

Bowers, K. S. (1977). Hypnosis: An informational approach. *Annals of the New York Academy of Sciences, 296,* 227–237.

Bowers, K. S., & Kelly, P. (1979). Stress, disease, psychotherapy and hypnosis. *Journal of Abnormal Psychology, 88,* 490–505.

Bunney, M. H. (1982). *Viral warts: Their biology and treatment.* New York: Oxford University Press.

Chandrasena, R. (1982). Hypnosis in the treatment of viral warts. *Psychiatric Journal of the University of Ottawa, 7,* 135–137.

Chertok, L. (1983). Psychoanalysis and hypnosis theory: Comments on five case histories. *American Journal of Clinical Hypnosis, 25,* 209–224.

Clarke, G. H. V. (1965). The charming of warts. *Journal of Investigative Dermatology, 45,* 15–21.

Clawson, T. A., & Swade, R. H. (1975). The hypnotic control of blood flow and pain: The cure of warts and the potential for the use of hypnosis in the treatment of cancer. *American Journal of Clinical Hypnosis, 17,* 160–169.

Couper, L., & Davies, T. (1952). A difficult wart treated by suggestion. *British Medical Journal, 2,* 1398.

Dreaper, R. (1978). Recalcitrant warts on the hand cured by hypnosis. *Practitioner, 220,* 305–310.

Dudek, S. Z. (1967). Suggestion and play therapy in the cure of warts in children: A pilot study. *Journal of Nervous and Mental Disease, 145,* 37–42.

Ewin, D. M. (1974). Condyloma acuminatum: Successful treatment of four cases by hypnosis. *American Journal of Clinical Hypnosis, 17,* 73–78.

Frankel, F. H., & Misch, R. C. (1973). Hypnosis in a case of long-standing psoriasis in a person with character problems. *International Journal of Clinical and Experimental Hypnosis, 2,* 121–130.

Hellier, F. F. (1951). The treatment of warts with X-rays: Is their action physical or psychological? *British Journal of Dermatology, 63,* 193–194.

Johnson, R. F. Q., & Barber, T. X. (1978). Hypnosis, suggestions and warts: An experimental investigation implicating the importance of "believed-in-efficacy." *American Journal of Clinical Hypnosis, 20,* 165–174.

Kirsch, I. (1985). Response expectancy as a determinant of experience and behavior. *American Psychologist, 40,* 1189–1202.

Longo, D. J., Clum, G. A., & Yaeger, N. J. (1988). Psychosocial treatment for recurrent genital herpes. *Journal of Consulting and Clinical Psychology, 56,* 61–66.

Lynch, P. J. (1982). Warts and cancer. *American Journal of Dermatopathology, 4,* 55–59.

Mason, A. A. A. (1955). A case of congenital ichthyosiform erythrodermia of Brocq treated by hypnosis. *British Medical Journal, 2,* 422–423.

Massing, A. M., & Epstein, W. L. (1963). Natural history of warts: A two year study. *Archives of Dermatology, 87,* 306–310.

McDowell, M. (1949). Juvenile warts removed with the use of hypnotic suggestion. *Bulletin of the Menninger Clinic, 13,* 124–126.

Memmesheimer, A. M., & Eisenlohr, E. (1931). Untersuchungen uber die suggestive behandlung der warzen. *Dermatol Zeitchr, 62,* 63–68.

Obermayer, M. E., & Greenson, R. R. (1949). Treatment by suggestion of verrucae planae of the face. *Psychosomatic Medicine, 11,* 163–164.

Reid, S. (1989). Recalcitrant warts: Case report. *British Journal of Experimental and Clinical Hypnosis, 6,* 187–189.

Rowe, W. S. G. (1982). Hypnotherapy and plantar warts. *Australian and New Zealand Journal of Psychiatry, 16,* 304.

Rulison, R. H. (1942). Warts, a statistical study of nine-hundred and twenty-one cases. *Archives of Dermatology and Syphilology, 46,* 66–81.

Sheehan, D. V. (1978). Influence of psychosocial factors on wart remission. *American Journal of Clinical Hypnosis, 20,* 160–164.

Sinclair-Gieben, A. H. C., & Chalmers, D. (1959). Evaluation of treatment of warts by hypnosis. *Lancet, 2,* 480–482.

Spanos, N. P. (1991). Hypnosis, hypnotizability and hypnotherapy: A sociocognitive perspective. In C. R. Snyder & D. R. Forsyth (Eds.), *Handbook of social and clinical psychology* (pp. 644–663). Elmsford, NY: Pergamon Press.

Spanos, N. P., Gabora, N. J., DuBreuil, S. C., Fisher, G., & Dewhirst, B. (1991). *The effects of suggested imagery and physical manipulation on wart regression.* Unpublished manuscript, Carleton University, Ottawa, Ontario, Canada.

Spanos, N. P., Kennedy, S. K., & Gwynn, M. I. (1984). The moderating effect of contextual variables on the relationship between hypnotic susceptibility and suggested analgesia. *Journal of Abnormal Psychology, 93,* 285–294.

Spanos, N. P., Stenstrom, R. J., & Johnston, J. C. (1988). Hypnosis, placebo, and suggestion in the treatment of warts. *Psychosomatic Medicine, 50,* 245–260.

Spanos, N. P., Williams, V., & Gwynn, M. I. (1990). Effects of hypnotic, placebo, and salicylic acid treatments on wart regression. *Psychosomatic Medicine, 52,* 109–114.

Spinhoven, P. (1988). Similarities and dissimilarities in hypnotic and nonhypnotic procedures for headache control: A review. *American Journal of Clinical Hypnosis, 30,* 183–194.

Stankler, L. (1967). A critical assessment of the cure of warts by suggestion. *The Practitioner, 198,* 690–694.

Sulzberger, M. B., & Wolf, J. (1934). The treatment of warts by suggestion. *Medical Record,* 552–557.

Surman, O. S., Gottlieb, S. K., & Hackett, T. P. (1972). Hypnotic treatment of a child with warts. *American Journal of Clinical Hypnosis, 15,* 12–14.

Surman, O. S., Gottlieb, S. K., Hackett, T. P., & Silverberg, E. L. (1973). Hypnosis in the treatment of warts. *Archives of General Psychiatry, 28,* 439–441.

Tasini, M. F., & Hackett, T. P. (1977). Hypnosis in the treatment of warts in immunodeficient children. *American Journal of Clinical Hypnosis, 19,* 152–154.

Tenzel, J. H., & Taylor, R. L. (1969). An evaluation of hypnosis and suggestion as treatment for warts. *Psychosomatics, 10,* 252–257.

Ullman, M., & Dudek, S. Z. (1960). On the psyche of warts: II. Hypnotic suggestion and warts. *Psychosomatic Medicine, 22,* 68–76.

Vollmer, H. (1946). Treatment of warts by suggestion. *Psychosomatic Medicine, 8,* 138–142.

Wadden, T. A., & Anderton, C. H. (1982). The clinical uses of hypnosis. *Psychological Bulletin, 91,* 215–243.

Weitzenhoffer, A. M., & Hilgard, E. R. (1959). *The Stanford Hypnotic Susceptibility Scale, Forms A & B.* Palo Alto, CA: Consulting Psychologists Press.

White, D. O., & Fenner, F. (1986). *Medical virology.* New York: Academic Press.

Wink, C. A. S. (1961). Congenital ichthyosiform erythrodermia treated by hypnosis: Report of two cases. *British Medical Journal, 2,* 741–743.

Yalom, I. D. (1964). Plantar warts: A case study. *Journal of Nervous and Mental Disease, 138,* 163–171.

Zwick, K. G. (1932). Hygiogenesis of warts disappearing without topical medication. *Archives of Dermatology and Syphilology, 25,* 508–521.

Controlled and Uncontrolled Studies on the Psychological Treatment of Warts

Study	N	Subjects	Treatment	Sessions	Follow-Up	Results
Yalom (1964)	1	F; age 30	Psychotherapy	Case studies Not specified	None	Wart size fluctuated in response to psycho-social factors.
	1	F; age 13	HS	5	None	Of 50 presenting warts, only 1 or 2 left after 5 sessions.
Bloch (1927)	179	M, F	Placebo, S	Not specified	3 months	78.5% of subjects cured within 2 to 12 weeks of treatment.
Sulzberger & Wolf (1934)	7	M, F; ages 4–33	Placebo, suggestion	1	None	5 of 7 reported cases showed complete remission.
Vollmer (1946)	>100	M, F; children	Placebo, suggestion	Multiple	None	Reported on 6 of a purported 100 patients. Failures were a "rare exception." Warts often remissed within 4 days, the longest interval being 7 weeks. No formal data presented.
Obermayer & Greenson (1949)	1	F; age 21; dur = 24 mo.	HS plus daily imagery	3	6-month "inquiry"	Complete remission 5 weeks after first treatment session. Wart-free at 6-month inquiry.
McDowell (1949)	1	F; age 32; dur = 8 mo.	HS	3	None	At 3rd session, 11 days after first treatment session, hands 98% clear, face 50% clear. Complete remission 18 days after first treatment session (self-report).
Couper & Davies (1952)	1	M; age 39	Suggestion	1	6 weeks, 7 months	Complete remission 1 month following treatment. Wart-free at 6-week follow-up and "no evidence of reoccurrence" at 7 months.
Surman, Gottlieb, & Hackett (1972)	1	F; age 9; dur = 15 mo.	HS	5	3 months	At 5th session, 26 of 31 warts cleared. Only 2 small warts remained at follow-up.
Ewin (1974)	1	M; age 22; dur = 5 mo.	HS	2	6 years	Genital warts cleared in 1 month.
	1	M; age 43; dur = 2 mo.	HS, PE	2	5 years	Genital warts cleared in 6 weeks.

Study	N	Sex; age	Treatment	Sessions	Follow-up	Outcome
	1	M; age 25	HS, PE	1	1 year	Genital warts cleared within 4 months.
	1	M; age 27	HS preceded by PE	2	3 years	Anal warts cleared within 2 months. All subjects were wart-free at follow-up.
Clawson & Swade (1975)	1	F; age 18	HS	8	3.5 years	All cases showed complete remission within 2 months of first treatment session.
	1	M; age 4	HS	2	2 months	
	1	M; age 11	HS	4	2 months	
Tasini & Hackett (1977)	1	F; age 12	HS	2	8 months	Complete remission within 1 month.
	1	F; age 14	HS	3	8 months	Complete remission within 3 months.
	1	M; age 12; dur = 36 mo.	HS	5	4 months	Complete remission within 7 months.
Sheehan (1978)	1	F; age 14	HS, PE	4 plus daily self-hypnosis	None	All 3 subjects were wart-free at follow-up. Complete remission upon death of grandfather, who had "given" her the warts as a "gift."
Dreaper (1978)	1	M; age 25	HS	1	None	Complete remission within 1 week of treatment.
	1	F; age 59; dur = 51 mo.	HS	Multiple	2 years	All treated warts cleared within 10 months; control wart cleared 2 months later with hypnotic suggestion.
Rowe (1982)	1	F; age 14; dur = 16 mo.	HS	3	None	Hypnosis appeared to have no effect, but 2 weeks later, prior to an appointment with the dermatologist, they "dropped off."
Chertok (1983)	1	F; age 23; dur = 11 years	HS	5	1 year	Warts cleared within 2 months of first treatment session; wart-free at follow-up.
Reid (1989)	1	F; age 14; dur = 48 mo.	HS	3 treatment sessions plus daily "autohypnosis"	2 years	"Practically" clear of warts within 10 weeks of treatment; no reoccurrence at follow-up.
Between-groups comparison studies						
Allington (1934)	164	M, F	Sulpharsphenamine injections; placebo injections	1–3	None	No between-subjects differences.
Asher (1956)	25	M, F; M age 9.5	HS	Weekly	1 month	11 highly hypnotizables showed complete remission, 4 highs improved, and 2 showed no improvement. 4 lightly hypnotizables showed complete remission, and 4 showed no improvement.

(appendix continues)

Controlled and Uncontrolled Studies on the Psychological Treatment of Warts

Study	N	Subjects	Treatment	Sessions	Follow-Up	Results
Ullman & Dudek (1960)	62	M, F; M age 26; M dur = 27 mo.	HS	1	1 month	8, 5, and 2 "good" hypnotic subjects showed complete remission, partial remission, and no change, respectively. 2 "poor" hypnotizables showed complete remission, 3 showed partial remission, and 42 showed no change.
Dudek (1967)	20	M, F; M age 8	Topical placebo plus (a) conditional or (b) unconditional play therapy	2 to 11 weeks	None	10 subjects showed complete remission and 4 subjects showed partial remission. 6 subjects showed no change; however, 5 of these 6 were discharged from treatment after 2 weeks.
Johnson & Barber (1978)	22	M, F; M age 24; M dur = 28 mo.	HS; nonhypnotic suggestion, RA	1 treatment session plus daily imagery	2 weeks, 5 weeks, and 3-month mailed questionnaire	At 6 weeks, 3 of 11 hypnotic subjects showed complete remission, and none of the nonhypnotic subjects showed any change.
Chandrasena (1982)	32	M, F; M age 20; M dur = 20 mo.	HS	M = 8.8	1 month	80% of the highly hypnotizable subjects and 16% of the lightly hypnotizable subjects showed at least a 50% reduction in the area covered by warts at baseline.
Within-subject comparison studies						
Hellier (1951)	74	Not specified	X-ray (right side); placebo X-ray (left side)	4 at 3 exposures each at weekly intervals	None	2 subjects showed complete treatment-specific remission, 1 subject exhibited partial treatment-specific remission, 27 subjects showed complete bilateral remission, and 44 subjects showed no change.
Sinclair-Gieben & Chalmers (1959)	14	M, F; dur ≥ 6 mo.	HS; no treatment	Not specified	None	Of 10 deep hypnotizables, 7 showed complete remission, 2 showed partial remission, and 1 exhibited no change (treatment side only). Of 4 light hypnotizables, none showed any change.

Study	N	Subjects	Treatment/control	Sessions	Follow-up	Results
Tenzel & Taylor (1969)	20	M, F; *M* age 22	HS; topical placebo	1	3 and 5 weeks; 5-month phone inquiry	None of the 20 subjects showed any change at 5 weeks. Of 15 subjects contacted at 5-month follow-up, 9 reported no change, 4 reported complete remission, and 2 reported complete remission on the treatment side only.
Clarke (1965)	62	*M* dur = 11 mo.	Electric shock; no treatment	at least 6	None	19 of 62 improved, of which 4 lost warts on the treatment side only, 6 lost warts on the untreated side, and 9 lost warts on both sides.
Clarke (1965)	22	*M* dur = 3 years	X-ray; placebo X-ray; no treatment	1	None	18% of the subjects showed complete remission, 23% showed treatment-specific remission, and 9% lost warts that were administered placebo treatment or no treatment. The remaining 50% showed no change.
Stankler (1967)	61	M, F; *M* age 16; *M* dur = 1.5 years	Topical placebo; no treatment	2 daily applications	3 months	Of 45 subjects who completed treatment, 15 showed complete bilateral loss.
Stankler (1967)	30	M, F	"Ray" machine; no treatment	1	3 months	Of 22 subjects who completed the study, 7 showed complete bilateral remission.

Controlled studies

Study	N	Subjects	Treatment/control	Sessions	Follow-up	Results
Memmesheimer & Eisenlohr (1931)	140	M, F; children	Suggestion and topical placebo; no-treatment control group	1	1, 3 and 6 months	Of 70 treatment subjects, 11, 3, and 3 showed complete remission at 1, 3, and 6 months, respectively. Of 70 controls, 2, 3, and 15 showed complete remission at 1, 3, and 6 months, respectively.
Surman, Gottlieb, Hackett, & Silverberg (1973)	24	M, F; *M* age 21; *M* dur = 37 mo.	HS; no-treatment control group, RA	5 sessions at weekly intervals	3 months	Of 17 treatment subjects, 1 subject showed complete treatment-specific remission, 5 showed complete bilateral loss, 3 showed partial bilateral loss, and 8 subjects failed to improve. None of the 7 control subjects improved.
Spanos, Stenstrom, & Johnston (1988)	63	M, F; *M* age 30; *M* dur = 73 mo.	HS; placebo; no-treatment control group, RA	1 session plus daily self-treatment	6 weeks	Mean percentage loss for the three groups was as follows: 33.68 hypnotic, 9.08 placebo, and 2.00 control.

(appendix continues)

APPENDIX (continued)

Controlled and Uncontrolled Studies on the Psychological Treatment of Warts

Study	N	Subjects	Treatment	Sessions	Follow-Up	Results
Spanos et al. (1988)	76	M, F; M age 23; M dur = 63 mo.	HS; relaxation plus suggestion (RS); suggestion alone (S); control (C), RA	2 sessions at weekly intervals plus daily self-treatment	6 weeks	21% of the HS subjects lost warts; 31.5% of the S subjects lost warts; 10.5% of the RS subjects lost warts; and none of the control subjects lost warts.
Spanos, Williams, & Gwynn (1990)	40	M, F; age 18–35	HS; topical (T); placebo (P); control (C), RA	1 session plus daily self-treatment	6 weeks	T, P, C < HS on total wart loss.
Spanos, Gabora, DuBreuil, Fisher, & Dewhirst (Experiment 1, 1991)	60	M, F; M age 24	Imagery (I); imagery plus physical manipulation (IP); control (C), RA	$M = 8.60$	6 weeks	C, I < IP on percentage wart loss; C < I, IP on the proportion of subjects who showed at least some improvement.
(Experiment 2, 1991)	90	M, F; M age 23	Imagery plus physical manipulation; imagery; physical manipulation; control	3	6 weeks	Significantly more subjects in the three treatment conditions improved than did control subjects.

Note: M = male; F = female; HS = hypnotic suggestion; S = suggestion; dur = duration; mo. = month(s); PE = psychodynamic explanation; RA = random assignment.

29

HYPNOSIS AND SPORT PSYCHOLOGY

WILLIAM P. MORGAN

It is remarkable that hypnosis has not been used more frequently by workers in the field of sports medicine in general, and sport psychology in particular, because the difference between success and failure is often minuscule. Indeed, the difference between a gold medal in Olympic competition and failure to even qualify for the final event is sometimes less than a hundredth of a second. Hence, any ergogenic procedure that might have the ability to enhance performance by even a small margin (e.g., 0.001%), providing it is legal, would have potential value.

At this point in time, the use of hypnosis has not been banned by the United States Olympic Committee (USOC) or the International Olympic Committee (IOC), nor are there any regulations against the use of hypnosis by other sport governing bodies, such as the National Collegiate Athletic Association (NCAA), or professional organizations, such as the

Preparation of this chapter was supported in part by the University of Wisconsin Sea Grant Institute under grants from the National Sea Grant College Program, National Oceanic and Atmospheric Administration, U.S. Department of Commerce, and from the State of Wisconsin. Federal Grant NA90AA-D-56469, Project R/NI-18.

American Psychological Association (APA) or the American College of Sports Medicine (ACSM). There are, however, many instances where the use of hypnosis in the practice of sport psychology or sports medicine would be questionable from both an ethical and a moral standpoint, and although not in direct violation of existing rules and codes, such actions would potentially violate the "spirit of the law." It is inappropriate, for example, to use drugs such as morphine or novocaine to manage an athlete's pain so that she or he might compete; hence, the use of hypnosis for the same purpose would certainly be questionable. Adherence to the APA's (1990) ethical code of conduct should be viewed as necessary but not sufficient in such a case. It is imperative that psychologists who elect to use hypnosis in the treatment of athletes also become familiar with established ethical and legal guidelines adopted by sport governing bodies (e.g., the NCAA, the IOC, and the USOC) and sport science organizations (e.g., the ACSM).

Hypnosis can also play an important role in exercise and sport science research, and this can be done in two ways. First, hypnosis can be used effectively as a means of manipulating independent variables in exercise science experimentation. Massey, Johnson, and Kramer (1961), for example, conducted an innovative experiment in which subjects were tested on a bicycle ergometer sprint task following a warm-up and a control treatment in the hypnotic state. However, the subjects were given posthypnotic suggestions designed to produce amnesia for the warm-up treatment. In other words, the subjects were presumably unaware of whether or not they had warmed up prior to the test, to control or minimize the influence of "attitude toward warm-up." Sprint times did not differ in the two conditions, and related research (Smith & Bozymowski, 1965) has shown that physical performance in such a setting is influenced by the subjects' attitudes concerning the value and necessity of warm-up.

A second way in which hypnosis can be used in exercise science research involves efforts to ascertain the true limits of human performance. It is known, for example, that attempts to measure maximal physical performance are limited by inhibitory mechanisms. Furthermore, it has been shown that maximal or "supramaximal" efforts are governed by the extent to which disinhibition of these inhibitory mechanisms can be achieved. This phenomenon was demonstrated in a classic experiment by Ikai and Steinhaus (1961), who evaluated the influence of hypnotic suggestions, as well as other treatments designed to provoke disinhibition of inhibitory mechanisms (e.g., alcohol, amphetamines, and loud noises), on maximal elbow flexion strength. Subjects were trained to exert a maximal force against a dynamometer, and it was demonstrated that "maximal" values could be enhanced significantly with each of these procedures. In other words, the functional maximum obtained under usual testing procedures was found to be a pseudomaximum, and subjects were able to draw on reserves. Although the effect of hypnosis was superior to the control, hypnotic suggestion did not differ significantly from gains observed with the other interventions.

The rationale for the clinical applications described in this chapter is based on theoretical formulations advanced by Hanin (1978) and Unestáhl (1981), together with the empirical case studies described by Johnson (1961a, 1961b). Although the theoretical views of Hanin and Unestáhl represent independent proposals, these formulations converge in terms of hypnotic application.

Hanin (1978) presented a theory of performance that maintains that each individual athlete possesses a "zone of optimal function" (ZOF), and this zone is based on the individual's optimal state anxiety level in precompetitive settings. Hanin empirically demonstrated that athletes have their best performances when they fall within this ZOF, and he has operationalized this zone as a given point plus or minus 4 raw score units on the state anxiety scale developed by Spielberger (1983). Although Hanin's theory is based on work carried out with elite Soviet athletes and with the Russian translation of the State–Trait Anxiety Inventory (STAI; Spielberger, 1983), his research has been replicated with elite and nonelite American athletes (Raglin, 1992). The theory advanced by Hanin incorporates retrospective recall of precompetitive state anxiety levels obtained in the nonhypnotic state. There is no mention of hypnotic procedures in this theoretical formulation, but the potential for hypnotic intervention is obvious.

The theoretical views of Unestáhl (1981) are related to those of Hanin (1978) in that both believe that athletes experience unique affective states when having peak performances. Unestáhl has chosen to label this the "ideal performing state" (IPS). Although the theoretical views of Unestáhl are in agreement with those of Hanin with respect to the existence of an ideal or optimal affective state, these theories of performance differ in one respect: Whereas Hanin believes that these states can be accurately recalled, Unestáhl has emphasized that athletes often have selective or even total amnesia after perfect performance, which makes it difficult for them to describe or analyze the IPS afterward. Therefore, Unestáhl has used hypnosis in defining the IPS, and this theory has been applied with several thousand Swedish athletes (Railo & Unestáhl, 1979).

The selected cases described in the next section are based on the assumption that important information associated with athletic competition is sometimes repressed and that this information can be retrieved by means of hypnotic age regression. It is also assumed that efforts to retrieve this repressed material should be of a nondirective nature, and the decision to use this approach is based primarily on the clinical reports described by Johnson (1961a, 1961b). Finally, these applications are based on a multidisciplinary approach that includes medical, physiological, and psychological components. Indeed, I propose that hypnotic applications should not be attempted in sport settings unless it can be shown that pathology does not exist and that the requisite physiological capacity is present.

CLINICAL APPLICATIONS

It is imperative that clinical applications in any area be based on scientific evidence, but there is little clinical research on which to base interventions in the field of sport psychology. However, there has been experimental laboratory research conducted on the use of hypnosis in the enhancement of physical performance, and this research will be summarized in a later section. Although application of the experimental literature in the clinical setting has been attempted, the ecological validity of such an approach remains to be demonstrated. Furthermore, most of the available case material has been based on theoretical, as opposed to empirical, evidence. Selected case material will be summarized in the next section to illustrate examples of clinical applications from the sport psychology literature.

There is an absence of systematic research dealing with the application of hypnotic procedures in exercise and sport settings. However, hypnosis has been used in an effort to resolve various problems associated with performance in sports. Selected examples of these efforts will be summarized below in an effort to illustrate potential clinical applications of hypnosis in sport psychology. In reviewing these examples, it should be kept in mind that the applications are based on theoretical formulations rather than research evidence.

One of the most widely cited cases involved a report by Johnson (1961a), who successfully used hypnosis to treat a baseball player. The player had requested that hypnosis be used to resolve his batting slump. The athlete played for a professional baseball team, and his batting average normally exceeded .300. However, he had not had a hit for the last 20 times at bat, and neither he nor any of his coaches could detect any problems with his swing, stance, and so on. The player had become quite frustrated about his inability to return to his prior performance level, and he had requested that hypnosis be used to resolve the problem. Although the player was unaware of the basis for his performance decrement, and although he was initially unable to offer any explanation for his slump under hypnosis, he eventually provided a detailed analysis of his swing that included the identification of specific problems throughout the analysis. Johnson (1961a) reported that he initially asked the batter under hypnosis to explain the nature of his problem, and the athlete replied that he had no idea why he was in a slump. Johnson then informed the batter that he would gradually count from 1 to 10, and with each number he would become more and more aware of why he could no longer hit effectively. He also informed the player that at the count of 10 he would have complete awareness of why he was in the slump. Johnson reported that at the count of 10 a look of incredulity came across the player's face, and he then proceeded to present a detailed analysis of his swing. This self-analysis under hypnosis included elaboration of specific problems that the player was unaware of in the nonhypnotic state. Johnson asked the batter if he wished to have immediate, conscious recall of his analysis, or simply have the information "just come to him gradually" over time. The player replied that he would prefer to have this information come back to him in time rather than all at once. The player's slump ended at once, and he went on to complete the season with an impressive batting average of .400.

This particular case is instructive in several ways, and sport psychologists who elect to use hypnosis in the treatment of such problems should first consider each of the following points. First, it is widely recognized that players in various sports often have spontaneous remission of problems (e.g., "slumps"), and it would be difficult to argue that a hypnotic intervention was responsible for the resolution of a given problem. Second, the information gained in the hypnoanalysis done by Johnson (1961a) was not available in the nonhypnotic state. Third, the batter demonstrated unusual insight, according to Johnson, because he chose to have the wealth of biomechanical information return gradually. Once a complex motor skill has been learned, athletes are encouraged by coaches to "do it" rather than "think about it." In some ways, the situation is analogous to the problem of "paralysis through analysis," which occurred when the mythical frog asked the centipede "pray tell, which foot do you move first?" As the story goes, the centipede was unable to resume normal locomotion once the question was considered. Fourth, at the completion of the season, the player returned and thanked Johnson for the hypnoanalysis that led to his improved performance. The player was unable to accept the fact that he, not the hypnotist, had performed the analysis.

The efficacy of hypnosis in the treatment of pain has been widely documented, and there is at least one comprehensive report dealing with the use of hypnosis in the management of various problems in sports medicine. Ryde (1964) used hypnosis in the treatment of 35 individual cases involving problems such as tennis elbow, shin splints, chronic Achilles tendon sprain, bruised heels, arch sprains, and other common ailments involving minor trauma. As a matter of fact, Ryde reported that hypnosis was so effective in the treatment of minor trauma resulting from injuries in sports that he offers "to treat these disabilities initially by hypnosis and only proceed with conventional methods, should hypnosis fail or be refused" (p. 244). Although Ryde's report appears to support the value of hypnosis in the treatment of sports injuries, there is no evidence presented to suggest that it is any more effective than a placebo. This is an important consideration because it is known that placebo treatments can be just as effective as morphine in the treatment of moderate pain in anxious patients (Morgan, 1972a). Nevertheless, the report by Ryde should be of interest to most workers in the field of sports medicine, and it should prove to be of particular interest to those in orthopedic medicine and physical therapy. However, the use of hypnosis in the treatment of medical problems associated with sport injuries should only be attempted by, or under the supervision of, an appropriately trained physician.

There has not been a great deal written about the use of psychodynamic approaches involving the use of hypnosis in sport psychology. However, in the review by Johnson (1961b), a number of case studies were summarized dealing with performance decrements in sports as a consequence of aggression blockage. In each of these cases, hypnotic age regression was used in an effort to retrieve repressed material, and this was followed by psychoanalytic interpretation and treatment. Also, posthypnotic suggestion was used to resolve the aggression conflicts. In one case, for example, a cycle of aggression–guilt–aggression was identified, and this cycle was directly associated with performance. The athlete, a pitcher in baseball, performed well when characterized by aggressive affect, but his performance fell when he felt guilty and lacked aggression. This transitory affect was found to be governed by feelings of guilt associated with repressed childhood incidents of aggression. When the athlete felt guilty, his performance declined, and his performance improved as the guilt passed and he became aggressive. The therapy in this case focused on resolution of the repressed guilt. Once this was achieved, the aggression–guilt–aggression cycle was broken and the pitcher's performance became more consistent. This general theme is repeated in the related cases described by Johnson (1961b).

It has been shown by Hanin (1978) that some athletes experience their best performances when precompetition anxiety is low, others when anxiety is high, and other athletes when anxiety is intermediate. This theoretical view is supported by empirical research involving athletes from various sports (Morgan & Ellickson, 1989; Morgan, O'Connor, Ellickson, & Bradley, 1988; Morgan, O'Connor, Sparling, & Pate, 1987; Raglin, 1992). Hence, it would be inappropriate to use psychological interventions designed to either reduce or increase anxiety in *groups* of athletes. In other words, an intervention such as autogenic training or progressive relaxation with athletes in a precompetitive setting would not only be ineffective, it would have the effect of placing a large number of athletes outside of their individual zone of optimal anxiety (ZOA).

The concept of a ZOA for athletes has now been well established (Hanin, 1978; Morgan & Ellickson, 1989; Raglin, 1992), and it is imperative that efforts designed to manipulate precompetition anxiety (up or down) be carried out on an individual basis. The difficulty, of course, involves the determination of an athlete's ZOA, because it would be necessary to evaluate an athlete's anxiety level prior to many competitions in order to arrive at his or her ZOA. Alternatively, one might use hypnotic age regression in an effort to ascertain anxiety levels prior to an athlete's best, usual, and worst performances. Once the individual's ZOA was determined, it would then be possible to strive, with autohypnosis or posthypnotic suggestion, for precompetition anxiety that fell within the athlete's optimal range (i.e., ZOA). Although this view is speculative, it is based on a sound theoretical rationale (Hanin, 1978), together with extensive empirical evidence of an indirect nature (Morgan & Ellickson, 1989; Raglin, 1992).

Despite the compelling support for ZOA theory, it is apparent that sport psychologists are more likely to be consulted about problems involving elevations in precompetition anxiety. Indeed, athletes have been reported to be almost incapacitated at times prior to competition, and these anxiety attacks often prevent customary levels of performance. Although an equal number of athletes may experience inadequately *low* levels of anxiety, this problem tends to be less apparent. One of the best discussions of how hypnosis can be used with athletes in the precompetitive setting was presented by Naruse (1965). Intense anxiety in the precompetitive setting was labeled as "stage fright" by Naruse, who summarized the use of (a) direct hypnotic suggestions, (b) posthypnotically produced autohypnosis, and (c) self-hypnosis in conjunction with autogenic training and progressive relaxation in the treatment of anxiety states in athletes.

There are two important points to be made about Naruse's (1965) report. First, the athletes used in this study consisted of elite performers, and the results may not generalize to pre-elite or nonelite athletes. Second, the actual procedure used with a given athlete in Naruse's study was determined on an individual basis. Furthermore, the unique nature of the athlete's "stage fright" was considered together with the individual's personality structure in deciding on the procedure to be used in a given case. The report by Naruse should prove to be particularly useful to hypnotherapists involved in the treatment of precompetition anxiety in athletes competing at the national or Olympic levels.

It has been emphasized by Vanek (1970) that attempts to manipulate anxiety levels prior to competition must be pursued with caution and that the psychologist should have a complete appreciation for the athlete's psychodynamic nature. Furthermore, Vanek described the case of a heavyweight boxer who experienced an anxiety attack prior to an Olympic contest. The boxer's anxiety was controlled effectively with the administration of a nonhypnotic (autogenic method) procedure. The boxer then proceeded to lose his match to an opponent he had previously beaten in earlier competitions. Vanek reported that follow-up study revealed that the boxer typically experienced anxiety attacks prior to important competitions, but he apparently performed well in this state. Anxiety reduction, in retrospect, was judged by Vanek to be contraindicated. This is an interesting case, and it serves to confirm the ZOA theory described earlier. At any rate, it is apparent that indiscriminant use of psychological procedures designed to relax athletes prior to competition is not appropriate.

A novel approach to performance enhancement using hypnotic control of arousal levels has been described by Garver (1977). This method requires that athletes establish a personal arousal scale ranging from 0 (low) to 10 (high) while in the hypnotic state. The number 10 represents the highest possible level of arousal an athlete might experience, whereas the zero anchor represents the lowest. The athlete is moved up and down this arousal scale in an attempt to experience how different arousal intensities feel. Furthermore, the athlete's optimal level of arousal is defined as the sensations associated with the number 5 on the scale. An effort is made to have the athlete develop conditioned responses or affect for each intensity level, with the idea that these arousal levels can be used posthypnotically during competition. Garver described cases of a gymnast and a golfer who experienced performance problems associated with elevated anxiety and anger, respectively. In these cases, posthypnotic cues and cognitive rehearsal were used to produce preferred arousal levels, and this approach led to enhanced performance.

CASE MATERIAL

The cases reviewed in this section involve athletes from the sports of distance running and baseball. The overall approach used in these cases relied on insight training through hypnotic age regression. The hypnotic procedure can be viewed as nondirective, and it is built on the earlier case reports of Johnson (1961a, 1961b). Also, the theoretical formulations of Hanin (1978) and Unestähl (1981) specified that optimal or ideal affective states characterize peak performance, and both theories maintain that information of this nature can be retrieved. Therefore, efforts were made in these cases to retrieve repressed material by means of hypnotic age regression. A multidisciplinary approach was used in each situation, and these case studies demonstrate that performance decrements in sports are sufficiently complex to rule out simplistic, unidimensional solutions.

Hypnosis was used in an effort to help a distance runner and a baseball player gain insights about problems they were experiencing during competition. In both cases, the athletes were patients under the care of a sports medicine physician[1] who participated in the hypnoanalysis. The author assumed responsibility in these cases for the hypnotic inductions.

---

[1]The author wishes to acknowledge the contribution of Dr. Allan J. Ryan, sports medicine physician, who assumed responsibility for the clinical and medical aspects of the two cases described in this section.

Case 1: Distance Runner

This case represents a common problem in which an athlete is no longer able to perform at his or her customary level. This type of situation is considerably different from the case where an athlete is performing at a given level and wishes to enhance his or her performance. In other words, the present case involved a situation in which an athlete previously performed at an elite level but was now unable to do so.

The case involved a 21-year-old distance runner who had previously established a school and conference record but was unable to replicate the performance. Indeed, the runner was not able to even complete many of his races, much less dominate a given competition. Problems of this nature are usually diagnosed as "staleness" in the field of sports medicine, and the only effective treatment appears to be rest (Morgan, Brown, Raglin, O'Connor, & Ellickson, 1987). However, this was not the problem in the present case. The runner's inability to perform at his previous level was judged by the coach simply to reflect inadequate motivation and unwillingness to tolerate the distress and discomfort associated with high-level performance. On the other hand, the athlete reported that he was willing to do anything to perform at his previous level, and he felt that his principal problem stemmed from inadequate coaching. Although the athlete and the coach were both interested in the restoration of the runner's previous performance ability, they were clearly at odds with one another. Indeed, the conflict had reached the point where the two were unable to discuss the matter, and the runner had turned to his team physician for support. However, a thorough physical examination, including blood and urine chemistries routinely used in sports medicine, failed to reveal any medical problems.

The physician proposed that hypnosis be used in an effort to resolve this problem, and the athlete was eager to try such an approach. However, it seemed appropriate to first evaluate the runner's physical capacity in order to insure that he was actually capable of performing at the desired level. It is well documented that aerobic power is an important factor in successful distance running. Therefore, the runner was administered a test of maximal aerobic power on a treadmill. This required that he run at a pace of 12 miles per hour on the treadmill, and the grade was increased by 2% every minute until he could no longer continue. This test revealed that he achieved a peak or maximal VO_2 of 70 ml/kg · min by the 5th minute of exercise, and his ability to uptake oxygen fell during the 6th minute. In other words, a true physiological maximum, as opposed to a volitional or symptomatic maximum, was achieved. The recorded value of 70 ml/kg · min represents the average reported for elite distance runners, and the runner was therefore physiologically capable of achieving the desired performance level. However, our calculations revealed that it would have been necessary for him to average 96% of his maximum throughout the event to replicate his record performance. This could potentially be problematic because exercise metabolites such as lactic acid begin to accumulate and to limit performance during prolonged exercise at 60% to 80% of maximum in most trained individuals. In other words, it would have been possible for this runner to perform at the desired level, but such an effort would be associated with considerable discomfort (pain).

The runner was observed to score within the normal range on anxiety, depression, and neuroticism as measured by the STAI, the Depression Adjective Check List (DACL), and the Eysenck Personality Inventory (EPI), respectively. He scored significantly higher than the population norms on extroversion (the EPI), but this has been a common finding for many athletes (Morgan, 1980b). He was found to be hypnotizable following preliminary induction and deepening sessions, and he was eager to pursue "insight training" through hypnosis and deep relaxation. The runner was viewed as a good candidate for hypnosis for the following reasons: (a) There were no medical contraindications detected, (b) he possessed the necessary physiological capacity to achieve the desired goal, (c) there were no apparent psychological contraindications, and (d) he was able to enter into a deep trance.

The athlete was next age-regressed to the day of his championship performance, and he was instructed to describe the competition as well as any related events that he judged to be relevant. However, rather than telling him that "the race was about to begin" or instructing him in the customary "on your marks" command, he was asked to recall all events leading up to the race on that day. He was instructed, "For example, try to remember how you felt when you awakened that morning; your breakfast or any foods or liquids you consumed; the temperature before and during the race; the nature and condition of the course; interactions with your coach, teammates, and opponents; your general frame of mind; and then proceed to the starting line *when you are ready.*" The athlete's team physician and the author had previously asked the runner if it would be acceptable for either or both of them to ask questions during the session, and the athlete had no objections. The athlete had a somewhat serious or pensive look, but within a few minutes he began to smile and chuckle, saying that he had false-started. When asked why this was so amusing, he replied that it was "ridiculous since there is no advantage to a fast start in a distance race." This event can be viewed as a critical incident because runners and swimmers will intentionally false start at times in an effort to reduce tension. Others will do this in an effort to upset or "unnerve" their opponents. At any rate, his facial expression became serious once again, and his motor behavior (e.g., grimacing and limb movements) suggested the race had begun. The verbatim narrative follows:

> The pace is really fast. I'm at the front of the pack. I don't think I can hold this pace much longer, but I feel pretty good. The pace is picking

up . . . I don't think I can hold it . . . my side is beginning to ache. . . . I have had a pain in the side many times. It will go away if I continue to press. There . . . it feels good now. The pain is gone, but I'm having trouble breathing. I'm beginning to *suck air* . . . the pain is unbearable . . . I'm going to drop out of the race as soon as I find a soft spot. There's a soft, grassy spot up ahead . . . I'm going to stop and lay in the soft grassy spot . . . wait, I can't, three of my teammates are up on top of the next grade . . . they are yelling at me to *kick* . . . I can't let them down. I will keep going. I'm over the hill now . . . on level grade . . . it feels ok . . . I'm alright. There's another hill up ahead. I don't like hills. . . . It is starting to hurt again . . . I can't keep this up . . . I'm going to find a soft spot again and stop. There's a spot ahead . . . I'm going to quit . . . I'm slowing down . . . this is it. Wait, there . . . I see a television set about ten feet off the ground at the top of the hill . . . hey, I'm on the TV, but this race isn't televised . . . but I can see myself clearly on the TV . . . I'm not here anymore . . . I'm on the TV. Now there's another TV, but to the right of the first one. My parents are on that TV, and they are watching me run this race on the other TV. I can't stop now. I can't let them down. Got to keep going. I'm not here . . . I'm on TV. It's starting to feel better. I feel like I'm in a vacuum now. I can't feel anything. My feet aren't hitting the ground anymore . . . I can't feel the wind hitting me. Hey, I'm a Yankee Clipper . . . I'm on the high seas . . . I'm flying . . . the sails are full . . . the wind is pushing me . . . I'm going to *blow out* . . . I'm going to *kick* . . . I don't feel pain anymore. . . . This is going to be a PB, maybe a record, I'm flying now, there is no one in sight, this is my race, there's the tape, I'm almost there, the tape hit my chest, it feels weird . . . weird . . . weird . . . the tape feels weird . . . that's the end . . . the end . . . the end . . . the end.

The runner appeared to be deeply relaxed at this point, and he had previously agreed to answer any questions we might have following his recall of the race. He was asked, "You almost dropped out of the race twice. Why didn't you simply slow your pace? Would that not have been better than quitting?" The runner replied without any hesitation that "Oh, no, you really have to take pride in yourself to quit. You have to be a *real* man . . . it takes guts to quit. Anybody can continue and turn in a lousy performance. I have too much pride to do that. I would rather quit." Although this view can be judged as somewhat unusual, it is noteworthy that he had dropped out of more races than he had completed during the present season.

The runner was asked to clarify the meaning of selected terms or phrases he had used, and then he was asked the following question: "Would you like to have complete recall for all of this information, or would you prefer to forget about it, or perhaps, have it come back to you gradually?" The decision to ask this question was based on the earlier demonstration by Johnson (1961a) that athletes sometimes do not wish to become aware of repressed material in the posthypnotic state. The decision to ask whether he would prefer that this information gradually return was also based on Johnson's case study, and it was intended to prevent the athlete from becoming overwhelmed or further confused as a result of this previously repressed material. At any rate, the runner responded that he would like to have complete recall following the session. Hence, no effort was made to produce posthypnotic amnesia.

The runner was also asked in the hypnotic state whether he wished to continue with this program of insight training, and he replied that he would like to give this some thought. For this reason, posthypnotic suggestions designed to insure adherence to future hypnotic sessions were not administered. In other words, posthypnotic suggestions designed to produce amnesia regarding the previously repressed material, as well as motivating instructions designed to insure continuation, could have, but were not, administered to the runner. This decision was based on our belief in the efficacy of nondirected approaches in such cases, as well as on a priori contingency agreements with the runner. These agreements were of a generic nature, and they were decided on prior to intervention with hypnosis.

This case serves to illustrate several points that practitioners in sport psychology or sports medicine might wish to consider prior to using hypnosis with an athlete. First, efforts designed to enhance physical performance with hypnosis should not be carried out within a unidimensional context. It is important to first obtain relevant information concerning the athlete's physiological, psychological, and medical state. Second, the decision to proceed with hypnosis should be made after obvious contraindications (i.e., pathophysiology and psychopathology) have been ruled out. Third, peak performances involving the transcendence of usual or customary levels can be associated with cognitive–perceptual processes of a remarkable nature. The record-setting performance of this athlete was found to be associated with considerable pain, but the sensation of pain had been repressed; that is, the runner was unaware of this pain experience in the nonhypnotic state. However, the cognitive–perceptual experience was "replayed" during hypnotic age regression, and the runner elected to have awareness of this experience in the posthypnotic state. It is possible that conscious awareness of this previously repressed material may have provided the runner with insights he previously lacked.

The runner subsequently elected to terminate insight training, and this decision was not congruent with his initial statement that he would do anything to return to his previous level of performance. It should be kept in mind that although he did possess the physiological capacity necessary to perform at a high level, to do so would have been associated with considerable pain. Also, despite the fact that his subsequent performance did not improve, our subjective impression was that he had "come to terms" with the situation. In a sense, then, he did not terminate the insight training we were providing, but rather, the insight he gained resolved the problem—at least from his perspective.

Fourth, it is noteworthy that the athlete's record performance was characterized by the cognitive strategy known as *dissociation* (Morgan, 1984). Runners who use this strategy attempt to ignore sensory input (e.g., muscle pain and breathing distress) by thinking about other activities (i.e., distraction). Other runners have reported that they initiate "out-of-body" experiences by entering the body's shadow cast on the ground in front of them. These cognitive strategies have been labeled as dissociation. Although this strategy can clearly facilitate endurance performance (Morgan, Horstman, Cymerman, & Stokes, 1983), it is not the preferred strategy of elite distance runners (Morgan & Pollock, 1977). Indeed, elite runners have been found to use a cognitive strategy known as *association*, which is based on systematic monitoring of physical sensations, rather than ignoring such input (Morgan & Pollock, 1977; Morgan, O'Connor, Sparling, & Pate, 1987; Morgan et al., 1988).

There is a possibility that this athlete could have been taught to use dissociation (Morgan, 1984), in either the hypnotic or the nonhypnotic state, in an effort to help him cope with the perception of pain during competition. It is also possible that such an approach would have led to enhanced performance, because (a) laboratory research has shown that such an approach is ergogenic (Morgan et al., 1983) and (b) the runner had actually experienced a form of dissociation during his record-setting performance. However, ignoring sensory input while performing at a high metabolic level in a sport contest is not without risk, and such an approach can lead to heatstroke, muscle sprains or strains, and stress fractures (Morgan, 1984). Cognitive strategies designed to minimize or eliminate the sensation of pain and discomfort during athletic competition and training should be used judiciously and with caution.

Case 2: Baseball Player

Hypnotic age regression was used in an effort to resolve a periodic problem experienced by a college baseball player who was an outfielder on a Division 1 team. The player was introduced to the author by his team physician in the hope that hypnosis might be used to improve the player's batting performance. He was regarded as a strong hitter, with the exception that he would "bail out" of the batter's box at times when he was not in apparent danger of being hit by a pitched ball. He had been examined and treated by the team physician and found to be in good physical health, including unimpaired vision. The player was highly regarded by a number of professional baseball teams, and he stood a good chance of earning a professional contract following graduation in 2 months' time. He was highly motivated to solve his batting problem because several professional scouts had arranged visits to campus to observe him play. The coach was somewhat frustrated about the situation, and his only approach had been to instruct the player to "hang in with the pitch." This instruction was of no help to the batter, and the exhortation seemed to exacerbate the problem.

The player was deeply concerned about the possibility that he would bail out of the batter's box during the forthcoming visits by pro scouts. Because the batter had a .315 batting average despite bailing out of the batter's box periodically, it was decided that he would be a possible candidate for hypnoanalysis. A battery of psychological questionnaires was administered to the athlete, and he was found to score within the normal range on measures of state and trait anxiety (the STAI); aggression (the Thematic Apperception Test and a Sentence Completion Test); tension, depression, anger, vigor, and confusion (the Profile of Mood States); and neuroticism–stability and extroversion–introversion (the EPI). Also, his Lie score on the EPI was not remarkable. This screening was followed by administration of the Harvard and Stanford C Scales of hypnotizability on separate days. He was quite responsive, scoring 9 on the Harvard Scale and 10 on the Stanford C Scale.

On the basis of the earlier example described by Johnson (1961a), he was initially age-regressed to a recent game in which the problem occurred, and he was asked to describe the situation. He had previously agreed that he did not object to the team physician or author asking him questions as the analysis proceeded. Although the author assumed responsibility for the hypnoinduction, it was agreed by the athlete, physician, and author that the physician would be responsible for the clinical dimensions of the process. The athlete was unable to provide any detail during this age regression that was not available previously in the waking state. The author indicated that he would count from 1 to 10 and that the player would have recall for relevant information that was not previously available when the number 10 was reached. This, too, was based on the earlier approach successfully used by Johnson. At the count of 10, the athlete began to shake his head from side to side, and he apologized for not remembering additional material. He was assured that such a response was not unusual, and he was given posthypnotic suggestions to the effect that he would feel relaxed and refreshed following the session. It was also emphasized that he would look forward to next week's session.

The player returned a week later, at which time a second age regression was used, but on this occasion he was asked to drop back in time and try to recall any events in his baseball career that were of particular importance to him. Within a brief period of time he described an occasion during his first year at the university in which he was hit on the back as he turned in an attempt to avoid a pitched ball. He thought the ball was going to "break," but it did not, and as he turned away from the ball his left scapula was hit and broken. It is remarkable that he had apparently repressed this event, because it was quite significant. At any rate, he had never mentioned this incident to us during the waking state. He then proceeded to describe a situation in high school when, as a pitcher, he had attempted to "dust off" a batter (i.e., throw at the batter rather than the plate) to distract the batter and increase his apprehension about succeeding pitches. Unfortunately, he hit the batter in the head (helmets were not worn at that time). Although the injury was not serious, the batter did not return to the game, and the athlete reported that he felt bad about the event.

It would have been possible to administer various posthypnotic suggestions, but we decided not to do so for several reasons. The case resembled an earlier one described by Johnson (1961b) in which a pitcher regularly cycled through a guilt–rage–guilt cycle, with performance decrements during the guilt phase and enhanced performance during periods of rage. In the present case, there may have been a fear–guilt–repression cycle in which the batter, presumably at an unconscious level, experienced the fear of being hit, or guilt associated with the injury of his opponent, and these states could have created sufficient psychomotor perturbation to provoke the present problem. Additionally, these affective states may have been repressed periodically, during which time performance was increased. These explanations are purely speculative, and we elected not to build on these hypotheses. We also felt that it would be inappropriate to administer suggestions designed to restrain him in the batter's box, because of the potential for injury from a pitched ball. Rather, we elected to ask the batter if he wanted to have conscious recall of this previously repressed material in the posthypnotic state. He indicated that he would like to recall all of the information, and he was then given the same concluding suggestions administered in the previous session.

In the next and final session, the athlete was asked following the induction to once again drop back in time and recall events in his baseball career that possessed particular meaning to him. He responded to this request by saying,

> Okay, but I want to tell you something first. I think I have solved my "bailing out" problem. I have been using a *closed* stance, and I crowd the plate as much as possible in order to "control" the plate and reduce the pitcher's strike zone. All good batters do this, but you always run the chance of being "beaned." Therefore, I'm changing to an *open* stance with my left foot dropped back so I will have a wide open view of all pitches. I'm a good enough hitter that I can do that without hurting my average.

Because the athlete seemed to have gained insight and resolved the problem, we elected not to proceed with further age regression. We talked with him briefly about his decision, and he was encouraged to review this plan with his coach. He was then given posthypnotic suggestion that he would feel relaxed, rested, and confident about his decision following the session. He was also encouraged to contact us if he had any further problems.

This case can be judged as representing a successful resolution of a presenting symptom, because the batter's performance improved. He was no longer plagued with the problem of bailing out, he completed the remainder of the season with a .515 average, and his overall average ranked near the top for all Division 1 players that year.

RESEARCH AND APPRAISAL

Research involving hypnosis and sport psychology has been restricted to laboratory experimentation in which attempts have been made to elucidate the effectiveness of hypnotic suggestion on the transcendence of baseline measures of physical capacity. There have been two principal methodological problems associated with the published literature that warrant mention from the outset. First, investigators have used laboratory tasks (e.g., grip strength and weight-holding endurance) under controlled conditions, and it is unlikely that any of this work possesses ecological validity. In other words, the results of research involving simple motor tasks performed in the laboratory setting with nonathletes cannot be easily generalized to complex sport skills performed by athletes in emotionally charged competitive settings. Second, there has been a tendency to contrast performances in the laboratory following hypnotic suggestion with control or baseline performances in which suggestion has not been used. This traditional research paradigm has been characterized by the confounding of state (hypnosis vs. control) and suggestion. With very few exceptions, it has been difficult to delineate the effects due to hypnosis versus those due to suggestion, because hypnosis with suggestion has typically been contrasted with nonhypnotic interventions without suggestion. Furthermore, the influence of demand characteristics has been largely ignored in this research literature.

The first comprehensive review of this topic was prepared by Hull (1933), who focused on hypnotic suggestibility and transcendence of voluntary capacity. Hull's principal conclusion was that existing evidence bearing on this question was contradictory. Furthermore, Hull explained the equivocal nature of this experimentation as being due to design flaws. Later reviews by Gorton (1959), Johnson (1961b), Weitzenhoffer (1953), Barber (1966), Morgan (1972b, 1980a), and Morgan and Brown (1983) were inconsistent regarding the ability of hypnotic suggestion to enhance physical performance.

Gorton (1959) indicated that reserves of muscular power exist but that these reserves are not usually available. Gorton proposed that hypnotic suggestion is capable of mobilizing these reserves through the disinhibition of inhibitory mechanisms, with the result that muscular performance is enhanced. This proposal has appeal from a teleological standpoint because it is known that maximal contraction of muscle can result in serious injuries such as bone fractures, dislocations, and muscle tears and strains, as well as damage to ligaments and tendons. Evidence in support of this view is largely indirect, and it derives from complications associated with the use of electroconvulsive shock therapy (ECT) (Gorton, 1959). In other words, the inhibitory mechanisms that limit the expression of "maximal" or "supramaximal" efforts can be seen as protective in nature, and Gorton proposed that ECT, in the initial research and clinical applications, sometimes led to disinhibition of these inhibitory mechanisms, resulting in the injuries cited above.

Other investigators have not been as enthusiastic as Gorton (1959) regarding the effectiveness of hypnosis in facilitating physical performance. Weitzenhoffer (1953), for example, presented a review that failed to support the belief that hypnotic suggestion can enhance muscular performance. This review confirmed the position advanced by Hull (1933) three decades earlier, and Weitzenhoffer reported that contradictory findings in this area may have been due to dissimilar designs.

The next review on this topic was written by Johnson (1961b), and it led to a number of qualified conclusions regarding the efficacy of hypnosis. Johnson reported that direct hypnotic suggestions designed to enhance muscular strength and endurance sometimes work but that suggestions of this type are not consistently effective. It was also pointed out in this review that hypnotic suggestions designed to decrease performance are far more likely to be effective. However, such an effect could be easily produced in the nonhypnotic state with cooperative individuals. The review by Johnson suggests that the efficacy of hypnosis in facilitating muscular performance is contingent on (a) individual differences in various psychological and physiological variables, (b) the context in which hypnosis is used, and (c) the interaction effects of the individual and the situation.

Historically, the most critical review of research in this area was presented by Barber (1966), who concluded that hypnosis, without suggestions for enhanced performance, did not influence muscular strength or endurance. Furthermore, Barber reported that motivational suggestions are generally capable of augmenting muscular strength and endurance in both nonhypnotic and hypnotic conditions. Barber presented a compelling argument in that review, and related writings, regarding the necessity of not confounding hypnosis and suggestion. Typical experimental paradigms have involved the comparison of muscular performance following suggestions of enhanced or decreased capacity under hypnosis, on the one hand, with no suggestions under control or nonhypnotic conditions, on the other. There have been exceptions to this generalization, and one of the earliest examples was the finding by Nicholson (1920) that suggestions given during hypnosis were much more effective than the same suggestions given without hypnosis. Another exception to this generalization is the report by Eysenck (1941) that hypnosis per se resulted in facilitation of muscular endurance. On the other hand, there is evidence that suggestion without hypnosis can lead to enhanced muscular performance (Barber, 1966; Morgan, 1981). Therefore, it is imperative that experimental designs not confound suggestion and procedure.

The reviews presented by Barber (1966), Gorton (1959), Hull (1933), Johnson (1961b), and Weitzenhoffer (1953) dealt primarily with the influence of hypnotic suggestion on muscular strength and endurance. More recent research has focused on the extent to which the hypnotic suggestion of an altered work load can influence the perception of effort, as well as the extent to which perturbation of effort sense is associated with corresponding changes in metabolism. It has been reported, for example, that hypnotic suggestion can influence cardiac output, heart rate, blood pressure, forearm blood flow, respiratory rate, ventilatory minute volume, oxygen uptake, and carbon dioxide production, at rest as well as during exercise (Morgan, 1985). It has also been shown that perception of effort can be systematically increased and decreased during exercise with hypnotic suggestion (Morgan, 1970, 1981; Morgan, Hirota, Weitz, & Balke, 1976; Morgan, Raven, Drinkwater, & Horvath, 1973). Also, when exercise intensity is perceived as being more effortful, there is a corresponding elevation in physiological responses even though the actual work load remains unchanged. A summary of recent reviews by Morgan (1980a, 1985) and Morgan and Brown (1983) follows:

1. Although some investigators have reported that hypnosis per se has no influence on muscular strength and endurance, an equal number have found that hypnosis (without suggestion) can lead to both increments and decrements in muscular performance. The evidence in this area is equivocal.
2. Hypnotic suggestions designed to enhance muscular performance have generally not been effective, whereas suggestions designed to impair strength and endurance have been consistently successful.
3. Individuals who are not accustomed to performing at maximal levels usually experience gains in muscular strength and endurance when administered *involving* suggestions in the hypnotic state. However, suggestions of a *noninvolving* nature are not effective when administered to individuals who are accustomed to performing at maximal levels.
4. Efforts to modify performance on various psychomotor tasks (e.g., choice reaction time) have effects similar to those ob-

served in research involving muscular strength and endurance. That is, efforts to slow reaction time are usually effective, whereas attempts to speed reaction time are not.

5. Case studies involving efforts to enhance performance in athletes by means of hypnosis appear to be universally successful. However, this observation should probably be viewed with caution because therapists and journals are not known for emphasizing case material depicting failures.

6. Hypnotic suggestion of exercise in the nonexercise state is associated with increased cardiac frequency, respiratory rate, ventilatory minute volume, oxygen uptake, carbon dioxide production, forearm blood flow, and cardiac output. These metabolic changes often approximate responses noted during actual exercise conditions.

7. Perception of effort during exercise can be systematically increased and decreased with hypnotic suggestion even though the actual physical work load is maintained at a constant level. Furthermore, alterations in effort sense (i.e., perceived exertion) are associated with significant changes in physiological responses (e.g., ventilation).

CONCLUSION

Hypnosis has been used in the field of sport psychology for a number of years as a research tool in efforts designed to elucidate the mechanisms underlying physical performance. Also, there have been numerous clinical applications designed to enhance performance in sport settings, and these interventions have been based largely on theoretical formulations as opposed to empirical research evidence. These clinical applications have generally been successful, but there has been little attention paid to behavioral artifacts such as expectancy effects, placebo effects, and demand characteristics in this work. Furthermore, there is no evidence that effects obtained with these clinical applications exceed those that one might achieve with the same or comparable approaches in the absence of hypnosis.

Efforts to enhance athletic performance by increasing or decreasing precompetitive anxiety have usually not been effective. This can be explained by the observation that most athletes perform best within a narrow ZOA. Hence, efforts to decrease or increase anxiety in athletes should be discouraged unless the athlete's ZOA is known. It is noteworthy that hypnotic age regression offers considerable promise in defining an individual's ZOA. Furthermore, once this anxiety zone has been established, it can be reproduced with various hypnotic procedures (e.g., autohypnosis and posthypnotic suggestion).

An additional area in which hypnosis has proven to be effective in sport psychology involves the interpretation of decreased performance levels (i.e., slumps and failure) in previously successful individuals. Examples of nondirective hypnotic age regression are presented in this chapter, and these cases emphasize the importance of multidisciplinary approaches. In conclusion, direct hypnotic suggestions of enhanced performance are not likely to be successful, but there are a number of ways in which the hypnotic tool can be used effectively in sport psychology.

REFERENCES

American Psychological Association. (1990). Ethical principles of psychologists (amended June 2, 1989). *American Psychologist, 45*, 390–395.

Barber, T. X. (1966). The effects of hypnosis and suggestions on strength and endurance: A critical review of research studies. *British Journal of Social and Clinical Psychology, 5*, 42–50.

Eysenck, H. J. (1941). An experimental study of the improvement of mental and physical functions in the hypnotic state. *British Journal of Medical Psychology, 18*, 304–316.

Garver, R. B. (1977). The enhancement of human performance with hypnosis through neuromotor facilitation and control of arousal level. *American Journal of Clinical Hypnosis, 19*, 177–181.

Gorton, B. E. (1959). Physiologic aspects of hypnosis. In J. M. Schneck (Ed.), *Hypnosis in modern medicine* (pp. 246–280). Springfield, IL: Charles C Thomas.

Hanin, Y. L. (1978). A study of anxiety in sports. In W. F. Straub (Ed.), *Sport psychology: An analysis of athlete behavior* (pp. 236–249). Ithaca, NY: Movement.

Hull, C. L. (1933). *Hypnosis and suggestibility.* New York: Appleton-Century-Crofts.

Ikai, M., & Steinhaus, A. H. (1961). Some factors modifying the expression of human strength. *Journal of Applied Psychology, 16*, 157–163.

Johnson, W. R. (1961a). Body movement awareness in the non-hypnotic and hypnotic states. *Research Quarterly, 32*, 263–264.

Johnson, W. R. (1961b). Hypnosis and muscular performance. *Journal of Sports Medicine and Physical Fitness, 1*, 71–79.

Massey, B. H., Johnson, W. R., & Kramer, G. R. (1961). Effect of warm-up exercise upon muscular performance using hypnosis to control the psychological variable. *Research Quarterly, 32*, 63–71.

Morgan, W. P. (1970). Oxygen uptake following hypnotic suggestion. In G. S. Kenyon (Ed.), *Contemporary psychology of sport* (pp. 283–286). Chicago: Athletic Institute.

Morgan, W. P. (1972a). Basic considerations. In W. P. Morgan (Ed.), *Ergogenic aids and muscular performance* (pp. 3–31), New York: Academic Press.

Morgan, W. P. (1972b). Hypnosis and muscular performance. In W. P. Morgan (Ed.), *Ergogenic aids and muscular performance* (pp. 193–233). New York: Academic Press.

Morgan, W. P. (1980a). Hypnosis and sports medicine. In G. D. Burrows & L. Dennerstein (Eds.), *Handbook of hypnosis and psychosomatic medicine* (pp. 359–375). Amsterdam, The Netherlands: Elsevier/North-Holland Biomedical Press.

Morgan, W. P. (1980b). The trait psychology controversy. *Research Quarterly for Exercise and Sport, 51,* 50–76.

Morgan, W. P. (1981). Psychophysiology of self-awareness during vigorous physical activity. *Research Quarterly for Exercise and Sports, 52,* 385–427.

Morgan, W. P. (1984). Mind over matter. In W. F. Straub & J. M. Williams (Eds.), *Cognitive sport psychology* (pp. 311–316). Lansing, NY: Sport Science Associates.

Morgan, W. P. (1985). Psychogenic factors and exercise metabolism. *Medicine and Science in Sports and Exercise, 17,* 309–316.

Morgan, W. P., & Brown, D. R. (1983). Hypnosis. In M. L. Williams (Ed.), *Ergogenic aids and sports* (pp. 223–252). Champaign, IL: Human Kinetics.

Morgan, W. P., Brown, D. R., Raglin, J. S., O'Connor, P. J., & Ellickson, K. A. (1987). Psychological monitoring of overtraining and staleness. *British Journal of Sports Medicine, 21,* 107–114.

Morgan, W. P., & Ellickson, K. A. (1989). Health, anxiety, and physical exercise. In C. D. Spielberger & D. Hackbart (Eds.), *Anxiety in sports: An international perspective* (pp. 165–182). Washington, DC: Hemisphere.

Morgan, W. P., Hirota, K., Weitz, G. A., & Balke, B. (1976). Hypnotic perturbation of perceived exertion: Ventilatory consequences. *American Journal of Clinical Hypnosis, 18,* 182–190.

Morgan, W. P., Horstman, D. H., Cymerman, A., & Stokes, J. (1983). Facilitation of physical performance by means of a cognitive strategy. *Cognitive Therapy and Research, 7,* 251–264.

Morgan, W. P., O'Connor, P. J., Ellickson, K. A., & Bradley, P. W. (1988). Personality structure, mood states, and performance in elite male distance runners. *International Journal of Sport Psychology, 19,* 247–263.

Morgan, W. P., O'Connor, P. J., Sparling, B. P., & Pate, R. R. (1987). Psychological characterization of the elite female distance runner. *International Journal of Sports Medicine, 8,* 124–131.

Morgan, W. P., & Pollock, M. L. (1977). Psychologic characterization of the elite distance runner. *Annals of the New York Academy of Science, 301,* 382–403.

Morgan, W. P., Raven, P. B., Drinkwater, B. L., & Horvath, S. M. (1973). Perceptual and metabolic responsivity to standard bicycle ergometry following various hypnotic suggestions. *International Journal of Clinical and Experimental Hypnosis, 31,* 86–101.

Naruse, G. (1965). The hypnotic treatment of stage fright in champion athletes. *International Journal of Clinical and Experimental Hypnosis, 13,* 63–70.

VII

ISSUES AND EXTENSIONS

30

TRAINING ISSUES IN HYPNOSIS

PETER B. BLOOM

Adult education is considerably different from pre-adult education. In adult education, there are no "students." There are adult participants who share their personal experiences with each other on an equal basis. The designated leader, for the purposes of the seminar, is a bit more equal than the others. The experiences that are shared are derived from professional work and personal life, and provide the framework for acquiring new knowledge or skills, such as hypnosis. The knowledge or skills that are to be learned must "make sense" and fit into the participant's life experience, or they will be rejected. Those who develop training programs for the teaching of methods of clinical hypnosis must understand these principles of adult education. If they do, their programs will be successful and flourish.

This chapter will address the training issues that play a role in teaching clinical hypnosis to licensed professionals in psychology, psychiatry, medicine, surgery, and dentistry, and to other qualified health care providers. The selection of qualified participants and skillful teachers, as well as the content of the seminars and workshops, will be addressed. How to obtain

---
I am very grateful to Erika Fromm and Campbell Perry for their helpful criticisms of earlier drafts of this manuscript.

sponsoring organizations and accreditation, establish adequate funding, and decide on the appropriate format will be discussed. The interaction between the content and the context in adult educational experiences will be discussed, and common problems arising in the implementation of these training sessions and suggested resolutions will be presented. Finally, two appendixes will list resources available to potential directors of training programs in clinical hypnosis.

Learning and using hypnosis is, in my opinion, a strategy for learning more deeply about psychotherapy and doctor–patient relationships in medical or surgical specialties. This chapter will address the many opportunities inherent in teaching clinical hypnosis to professional adults.

TRAINING ISSUES IN CLINICAL HYPNOSIS

The Concept of Adult Education: Participant Versus Student

In 1971, Thomas Webster pointed out to me the need to understand the difference between *andragogy* (adult learning) and *pedagogy* (Knowles, 1970, 1980). As discussed earlier, this seemingly innocent concept has profound implications for adult educational programs. In preparing flyers for mailing, for example, the word "student" should never be used. During the seminar, constant attention must be placed on eliciting each participant's relevant experience and applying it to the knowledge and skills imparted. Often, adult clinicians return to their practices unchanged in their attitudes and methods of patient care because integration of new knowledge in the context of the individuals' previous experience has not occurred. In past educational settings as students, prior experiences were not crucial to learning—one merely took notes, studied them, and passed the tests. The task was knowledge acquisition. For adults, however, the task is usually not only learning new ideas and skills, but also utilizing this knowledge in the context of ongoing work and experience. In no other educational experience besides adult education, or andragogy, is this the case.

Adult education is sought by professional health care providers most commonly in continuing education courses, seminars, and workshops. In many states, such postgraduate educational experiences are required for renewal of state licensure. All states require some sort of documentation of these courses, and each professional discipline has established standards and guidelines for accrediting sponsoring organizations and certifying member attendance. The American Psychological Association, the American Psychiatric Association, and the American Medical Association, through the Accreditation Council for Continuing Medical Education, have created such standards and guidelines for their members. Other accrediting bodies are also active in instituting similar programs for family medical practitioners, dentists, social workers, and nurses.[1]

Participant Interest in Hypnosis

A variety of hypnotherapy and psychotherapy models appear elsewhere in this book, and a number of diverse applications of hypnotic methods have been presented. Most clinicians seeking training in hypnosis for the first time are interested in adding a new dimension to their therapeutic armamentarium and hope that, in the course of this training, they will learn more about how to do psychotherapy. Inevitably, as interest in hypnosis grows and introductory skills are mastered, clinicians seek further training in specialized areas reflecting their interests: creativity, dissociative disorders, forensic issues, hypnoanalysis, pain management, psychosis, sports medicine, research methodology, and wellness. For some, the study of hypnotic principles also provides a useful vehicle for examining therapeutic relationships and psychotherapeutic interventions (Bloom, 1990).

Participant Eligibility

It is a maxim that no one should treat a patient/client with hypnosis for any condition for which he or she would not treat them without it. Hypnosis is an adjunct to the treatment process and not a treatment in and of itself. It therefore follows that persons who are eligible to be trained to use hypnotic techniques in clinical practice must be licensed professionals in a variety of psychological and medical disciplines. These professionals include psychologists, psychiatrists, dentists, family medical practitioners, social workers, surgeons, and a variety of medical subspecialists. It is assumed, for instance, that a dentist would use hypnosis in treating temporomandibular joint pain or dental analgesia and, in some cases, in attempting to control excess blood loss when performing dental extractions in hemophiliacs (Dubin & Shapiro, 1974; Thompson & Barnes, 1982). However, dentists would not be expected to use hypnosis in treating a generalized anxiety disorder, even though anxiety may, in part, be evoked by visiting the dentist's office. Generalized anxiety disorder is not a condition that the dentist is licensed to treat.

Examples pertinent to other professions are easily found. For instance, should a psychologist who has just completed an introductory course in hypnosis and who has never treated a severe phobic disorder accept such a patient for treatment? The answer, although obvious, needs to be stated:

---

[1]Information on the individual standards for accreditation, needs assessment, course objectives, and evaluation methods can be obtained by writing to the individual organizations listed in Appendix A.

yes, but only if supervision is obtained from a colleague who is experienced in treating phobic disorders with or without hypnosis.

The American Society of Clinical Hypnosis, the Society for Clinical and Experimental Hypnosis, and the International Society of Hypnosis (ISH), including more than 25 component national constituent societies in 20 countries around the world, have established codes of ethics that define and limit the persons who can be taught hypnosis. Although these codes vary to some degree because of national differences (for instance, in the degree of independent duty given dental hygienists in Sweden, who are eligible for membership in the Swedish Society for Clinical and Experimental Hypnosis, compared with the two U.S. societies, where they are not eligible for training or membership), each code of ethics reflects the universal desire to create and maintain high standards in the training and use of hypnosis.[2]

All doctoral-level professionals trained and licensed to practice psychology, medicine, or dentistry are usually eligible and accepted for training, as are licensed master's-level social workers. There are, however, diverse and traditional national and international guidelines. All national constituent society members of the ISH can teach freely in every national society, and most persons eligible for training and membership in one national constituent society of the ISH are eligible to take a training course in any other national constituent society of the ISH.

Why do we need such rigorous ethical standards and guidelines? Two points of fact are noteworthy: First, legislative bodies worldwide have failed to license hypnosis and hypnotherapy as an adjunctive treatment modality of health care providers. Second, as a result, unlicensed and untrained "hypnotists" advertising their services in telephone books in many cities around the world have proliferated, requiring that professional hypnosis societies assume the responsibility for regulating who can and who cannot be trained to use hypnosis. Although most states in Australia (except for New South Wales) and the province of Ontario in Canada have successfully restricted the use of hypnosis to qualified professionals, most countries, including the United States, have failed to do so. For one thing, a suitable definition of *hypnosis* for legislative purposes has eluded consensus. Even more trying, legalizing the uses of hypnosis has been hindered by a lack of consensus about whether, for instance, managing stress, enhancing self-confidence, or achieving better performance in the workplace constitute problems requiring interventions by licensed professionals. Things are not always what they seem to be, however, and the above "innocuous" problems often turn out to rest on more serious underlying issues that in fact require professional training. Therefore, it is understandable that most legislatures

---

[2]Information on membership requirements, member benefits, and national/international meetings can be obtained by writing or calling the individual organizations listed in Appendix B.

have contented themselves, to date, with establishing laws governing the conditions that can be treated by psychology and medicine, with or without hypnosis, and have left the standards and guidelines for using hypnosis in the treatment of these conditions in the hands of professional hypnosis societies.

Despite certain regulatory efforts, unlicensed and untrained laypersons advertise hypnotherapy for a large variety of emotional and psychosomatic complaints. These advertisements are often listed in the yellow pages in many telephone books around the world, and course announcements are mailed to laypersons offering weekend seminars taught by nonlicensed laypersons, with promises that registrants will be able to "hang out a shingle" and begin lucrative practices upon completion of the short course. Because "hypnosis" or "hypnotherapist" is not a title restricted by license, there is no way to police or censure these "quacks."

One final issue remains to be discussed: At times, qualified psychologists or physicians offer training programs in hypnosis that include laypersons who appear to have a need for specialized skills, such as teachers and athletic coaches interested in enhancing school and athletic performances, respectively. At present, these hypnosis teachers are subject to expulsion from the national societies for unethical practice. However, they often establish their own organizations that, at this writing, fall beyond the purview of generally accepted organizations qualified to teach hypnosis.

The maturing of clinical hypnosis and its supporting research may well result in an increase of applications for training programs. As additional practitioners, accountable to their own professional organizations and licensed by their state, begin to seek training in the use of hypnosis within their usual professional activities, ethical eligibility of a broader number of candidates may occur. If the history of hypnosis and its practice is any guide, the process of expanding such eligibility requirements for training and membership should be carefully monitored and controlled. This field is not yet ossified and remains in constant evolution.

Issues of Seminar Design and Content

The definition of clinical and experimental hypnosis has been evolving for centuries, and any offered here is at best a working one useful for training purposes. I conceptualize hypnosis as an altered state of consciousness (ASC) in which one is absorbed in a variety of mental activities resulting in changes in perception, mood, and memory. The nature of the ASC is highly dependent on the context in which it occurs, and can therefore have different meanings and uses. For instance, ASCs such as religious experiences, meditation, possibly deep reflection (e.g., Aldous Huxley's method for writing, as described to Milton Erickson in 1965), and natural childbirth are each dependent on their particular context for their expression, shape, and refinement.

It is easy to design hypnosis training seminars in which these fundamental concepts are presented—that is, in which hypnosis is presented as an ASC in which changes in perception, mood, and memory can occur within the therapeutic relationship. Techniques of trance induction, deepening, and psychological interventions can be thought of as ways of enhancing the usual experiences of psychotherapy. In addition, these techniques are used to intensify certain attributes of successful psychotherapy: mobilizing unconscious motivations for growth and change and eliminating resistances to such motivations, permitting adaptive "regression in the service of the ego" (Kris, 1935/1952), augmenting a wide variety of behavioral interventions, and enhancing personal creativity.

The teaching of specific techniques in hypnosis, as in other disciplines, is often dependent on the personal preferences of each faculty member. Despite these variations, the use of hypnosis has not changed much in over 200 years. Apparent differences are often the result of relabeling old, established techniques and suggesting that they are new or different when, in fact, they are not. Clinicians new to the field of hypnosis may come to believe that real differences exist in the methods being described, resulting in unnecessary difficulties in communicating among professions in the field (Bloom, 1991). The real danger is that research requiring careful definitions may be shunted aside or even abandoned by some as a result of disputes in terminology. However, I believe that although there are more similarities than differences in how hypnosis is taught, it is beneficial that participants in our training programs learn from a wide variety of faculty to insure a full exposure to the field. It is sufficient for the purposes of this chapter to say that we seek to teach a broad-based approach to the nature of hypnosis and how to use it in a variety of settings. In doing so, we should remember that learning and using hypnotic techniques is dependent on the individual characteristics of the practitioner—the shape given to his or her own individual practice—in the context of the unique concerns and abilities the subject brings to the experience.

Training Opportunities in Graduate and Medical School

In 1983, following Parish's earlier study (1975), Rodolfa, Kraft, Reilly, and Blackmore investigated the status of research and training in hypnosis in accredited clinical/counseling psychology internships. Acknowledging that many clinicians learned these techniques in postgraduate workshops, these authors also noted an increasing acceptance and prevalence of such training programs in graduate schools since 1975. Rodolfa and his colleagues reported that as more internship sites offered training in hypnosis, training became more formalized and research projects conducted at these internship sites increased in number.

A caution is in order. Graduate predoctoral students in clinical psychology, medicine, and dentistry evolve their clinical identity during the arduous process of knowledge acquisition and early clinical practice. If clinical hypnosis enhances preexisting clinical skills, clinical hypnosis training may be best suited for postdoctoral students. Using hypnosis in treatment may therefore not be best learned during graduate training, and may account for the hesitancy to incorporate such training in professional schools.

In my own experience, I deferred my exposure to hypnosis until well into my postgraduate residency years. However, in my teaching since then, I have indeed successfully taught psychology interns and medical students hypnotic skills and techniques, to the advantage of their patients or clients. I believe that in the cases in which the students themselves chose to take my seminars during their graduate school days, they benefitted greatly by learning new skills and by enhancing their appreciation of other areas of their education and training. In the final analysis, the timing of the decision to learn clinical hypnosis probably rests on the individual participant's sense of readiness.

Faculty Selection

The selection criteria for faculty in adult educational experiences may differ somewhat from the criteria used to select faculty in pedagogic settings. Certainly, faculty who teach professional adults methods of clinical hypnosis must include well-known clinicians and not only academicians. A useful concept, stated earlier, is that such a workshop is a gathering of equals, with the designated chairperson being a little more equal than the rest. This special quality of equality must truly be felt by the leader if participant-centered learning is to occur. Otherwise, one creates a context in which students sit at the feet of special experts who are inclined to teach from authority rather than by the Socratic method. Faculty experienced in adult education encourage learning by eliciting knowledge and evoking experience from the participant rather than by relying solely on "inputting" the knowledge by lecture.

Desirable and effective teachers, in addition to a sound knowledge base, demonstrate many of the following characteristics:

1. *The ability to become aware of the participant's individual needs, interests, and experiences with sufficient sensitivity for each participant to feel personally attended to.* With as few as 5 or as many as 100 participants, teachers must be aware of the importance of responding individually to each person and be willing to do so.
2. *Willingness to self-disclose by sharing one's own personal and professional experiences appropriately in the process of adult ed-*

ucation. The resultant modeling and sharing by such disclosure provides poignant enhancement of the adult learning experience, especially in teaching clinical skills such as hypnosis.

3. *Caring for the welfare of each participant.* This important attribute of the effective teacher is conveyed by skillfully guiding each participant through the learning experience while remaining cognizant of his or her defenses, specific emotional vulnerabilities, and irrational fears about hypnosis. Cognizance of the perceived risks in experiencing trance phenomena, for the participants and for their patients/clients, is additionally required.

Professional health care providers are often those who have entered the healing professions in an attempt to understand and master their own problems. They are individuals who then transform their own injuries or illnesses (both psychological and physical) into a life career of helping others. Selecting a good faculty member is based on perceiving the ability to be clinically attuned to these deeper motivations and to respond consciously and intuitively to the needs of each participant. This is truly the art of teaching psychologically or medically oriented continuing education courses: to help participants join intellect and affect so that change in their personal behavior and therapeutic endeavors becomes likely in the future.

4. *Charisma and perceived competence.* It is hard to define charisma; nevertheless, it is a quality that participants look for. It is the "juice" that makes the collegial interaction inviting and successful in much of adult education and that usually supports the perception of faculty competence. It is not, however, a characteristic that leads to inappropriate behavior or compromises autonomy. In these times of sexual abuse among teachers and students, not to mention among professional colleagues with differing power advantages, the need to be alert and cautious is important. But caution aside, I believe that charisma is like the dessert that caps a fine meal—not sufficient sustenance in and of itself, but an enjoyable addition to the pleasures of a good meal. A bit of charisma makes good teachers truly outstanding teachers.

5. *The role of humor.* The presence of humor is the essence of good teaching. Playfully exercising logic in absurd situations, laughing with our patients and clients, and interpreting our participants' foibles with humor enhance all learning. A friend was taking a hypnosis course from me and told a 250-

pound woman to go into a trance by feeling heavier and heavier and heavier. . . . As her eyes opened more widely, I whispered to him, "Say lighter and lighter and lighter, you dummy." I smiled, and so did he, and as he relaxed and changed his wording she feel deeply into a trance. "You dummy" simply meant, "Hey, you already know this stuff— all you really have to do is to tap in and use it in this new context." Humor is the very lubricant for assimilating new ideas in adult education.

6. *Motivating professionals to gain knowledge and skills in new fields.* As our colleagues come to us to learn hypnosis, to enter the world of trance phenomena, metaphors, and images, they may at first feel frightened or embarrassed. They may fear that their friends at home would ridicule them for their interest in hypnotherapy. Some are unprepared for this potential threat to their reputations. Each workshop leader must feel that teaching clinical hypnosis is important and must be able to convey, with conviction, the reality of hypnotic phenomena. Most participants are demonstrating by their attendance that they are self-motivated learners. When the desire to learn is matched by the conviction that such learning is worthwhile, new knowledge and skills are readily gained.

7. *Career growth of the effective teacher.* There is probably no finer way for an adult to learn more about his or her specialty than to teach it with other faculty members. This axiom is especially true not only in teaching hypnosis in one's own city among colleagues, but in teaching at the national and international level. The teacher who also slowly rises from teaching introductory courses to advanced ones, and who makes out of this progression his or her own path of knowledge (not unlike the Eastern Tao), finds satisfaction in his or her career of lifetime learning, while savoring the many opportunities to mentor. Those who perceive teaching this way can elegantly realize the attributes of the effective teacher.

CONTEXTUAL ISSUES IN TRAINING ADULTS IN CLINICAL HYPNOSIS

Practical issues of sponsorship and accreditation, funding, and format go hand in hand with the adult educational issues explored above. Also, certain practical problems arise in individual training sessions. As in any human endeavor, the contextual considerations of the event itself determine the success of any learning experience. For example, the participant can be eligible for training and wish to learn, and the teacher can have the requisite knowledge, sensitivity, humor, and charisma, but if there is not enough money, or if no one is willing to sponsor the learning, there will be no adult continuing education in hypnosis or any other subject.

What is not often fully appreciated, however, is that proper attention to the context of adult learning can create a far better learning experience. For instance, in most conferences, consolidation of learning often occurs over coffee during breaks. At these times, participants sort the wheat from the chaff, encourage each other in accepting new material by sharing the relevancy of it in their own professional lives, and receive a few personal comments from the faculty who circulate during these important times. If fruits and juices are offered or substituted for coffee in the afternoons, if the heating and lighting of the room are attended to with care, and if every projector has a backup with spare bulbs, the tone of excellence and attentiveness will pervade the workshop experience. Furthermore, when universities, recognized national hypnosis organizations, and national professional societies (such as the American Psychological Association and the American Psychiatric Association) sponsor these activities, legitimacy is documented and enhanced through peer review. This, in turn, supports the educational process in a constructive manner. All of these considerations require an attention to detail—which may at first seem tedious but, if accomplished, is a major basis for building a successful educational experience.

Let us now examine four areas worthy of serious attention.

Sponsorship and Accreditation

The American Psychological Association sponsors continuing education for psychologists. The American Medical Association, through the Accreditation Council for Continuing Medical Education, is the medical counterpart, whereas the American Psychiatric Association does the same for psychiatrists if they prefer this alternate accreditation path.

In 1900, Sir William Osler (1849–1919), the leading physician–educator of his time in North America and England, presented a major address in London titled "The Importance of Post-Graduate Study." He said, "More clearly than any other, the physician should illustrate the truth of Plato's saying, that education is a lifelong process" (Uhl, 1986). Osler's statement applies to all of us who care for others.

Since Osler's address, public awareness of physician competence, for example, has increasingly depended on the documentation of continuing medical education (CME). As concerns in the 1960s about further government intervention into credentialing physicians through CME reached major proportions (Carmichael, Small, & Regan, 1972; Coggeshall, 1965; Dryer, 1962; Early, 1968), the American Medical Association seized the initiative to create standards for CME by establishing in 1969 the Physicians Recognition Award as a means of documenting participation in approved CME programs.

The successful introduction of CME programs established by physicians and for physicians became a model for many medical subspecialties. Sister professions throughout the health care field have their own developmental histories. Some organizations, like the American Psychological Association, have developed a thorough and comprehensive program for approving and accrediting continuing education programs for psychologists. Nursing associations and family practice associations have different programs, although all strive to provide lifelong continuing education. All health care providers can now document their own continuing education to risk management programs of malpractice carriers, to state licensing boards, and to the public.

Because most individual training programs in hypnosis are available to a wide spectrum of health care givers, it is important for the sponsoring organizations and program directors to be familiar with the different requirements of as many of the national professional organizations as possible for accrediting these programs.

Funding

Continuing education programs are established in many different settings: universities; county, state, and national professional societies; hospitals; private enterprises; and among small groups of individuals. In each setting, the authority to design and implement adult education programs is derived in large part from control of the financial assets. Because, as is often said in business, "He who has the gold makes the rules," control of funding and spending must rest in the hands of those directly involved in program planning and implementation. Otherwise, noneducational priorities of the sponsoring parent institution may take precedence. These priorities may include marketing, enhancing referral patterns to hospitals, indirect advertising for patients, or other institutional activities.

Ideally, offices of continuing education should be self-supporting in all costs, including salaries. In practice, some salary support is often provided by universities and hospitals that sponsor continuing education programs, and some loss of programmatic autonomy is inevitable. There is no free lunch. The setting of fees and the control of costs, as in any business enterprise, are critical factors. To a degree, they insure the attractiveness of the offerings and, ultimately, the longevity of the sponsoring program.

A brief example of autonomously funding a very small program may be illustrative. A fall and spring workshop can be given by one faculty person, who hires a part-time secretary for 10 hours twice yearly. This teacher can design and mail his or her own announcements on personal letterhead. This can often generate enough revenue from 10 to 15 registrants to cover all costs and to earn a modest honorarium. Accredited sponsorship for these local workshops can usually be obtained from nearby larger sponsors if the workshop syllabus, enrollment criteria, and postconference evaluation tests are approved, and if the accrediting organization is involved in the planning process. Examples of funding larger programs are beyond the scope of this chapter, but they rest equally on maintaining financial authority and controlling costs.

One such example of controlling faculty costs in larger programs is illustrative of the complex issues involved. Faculty honoraria are important; however, in my opinion, they are more "honor" than "aria": Educational offerings are not opportunities for teachers to make money, but are rather opportunities for them to make a professional contribution. Nonetheless, some faculty are truly outstanding and, as a result, are in very high demand. Unless reimbursed properly for their potentially extensive time away from home (the place where they make a living), they cannot respond to every invitation they receive. However, if local faculty development is stimulated, good teachers can be developed into great ones, thereby reducing the cost of recruiting outside experts. It is then not always the case that the best teacher is the one who has traveled the farthest.

Format

The actual format of continuing educational courses in hypnosis is dependent on a number of variables: for instance, the time available to registrants at national meetings away from home versus weekends close to home with only a modicum of freedom from the responsibilities of professional duties. Each format has inherent advantages. One that I particularly like is a weekly evening meeting for 8 weeks (or given during the day if most of the registrants work in the evenings). The best reason for spreading out the learning experience is for participants to have the opportunity to integrate what is learned. To experience a trance for the first time and then to induce it in another is an exciting experience, and it takes a good deal of time and practice to master it. To apply trance phenomena to patients and clients in psychotherapy, dentistry, or a surgical practice requires patience with oneself and with one's patients or clients. Adult education and learning takes time, not because we are older, but because it depends on fully integrating new experiences into our lives at many different levels, both emotional and intellectual.

Another format consideration involves balancing workshop practice time for experiencing hypnotic inductions and techniques with lecture time needed to present didactic material. I have never taught in a hypnosis workshop in which the participants did not desire more practice time than was provided. Is it that we faculty like to talk because we bring a mission to our teaching and a sense of urgency to convey our message? Or is it that our students sense that these new skills require a great deal of practice, and are reluctant to practice independently without supervision, thus insisting on as much practice as possible before leaving? Flexibility is often required to meet the needs of individual groups of participants in this regard.

Problems Arising in Implementing the Training Sessions

1. *Workshop attendance levels vary.* At times, large numbers of participants enroll, whereas on other occasions only a small number do. As a rule, experiential workshops have a special problem with large numbers of participants, and additional faculty are needed to preserve an optimal ratio of 1 faculty to 8–20 participants. At times, however, lectures to larger groups, interspersed with discussions of the participants' own cases, can personalize the group experience. Every attempt must be made not to let large groups become a vehicle for imparting information in the pedagogic way. Informal contact times at lunches and coffee breaks can help individualize the teaching experience.

2. *Multidisciplinary conferences are optimal.* In the field of hypnosis, we have come a long way in eliminating professional boundary issues and the reflexive instinct to protect one's turf. After many years of striving, acceptance of master's-level social workers for training in hypnosis is a recent accomplishment. Whether we will accept psychiatric nurses for hypnotherapy training is at this time not clear. The independent role of nurse practitioners in psychotherapy in the future is even less clear.

    Hypnotherapy has become a "neutral turf" by providing a common ground for a rich exchange of ideas and experience from multiple vantage points. It is as if we multidisciplinary professionals can leave our degrees at the door and enter the educational forum to share our knowledge and experiences. When specific information is degree-dependent (that is, when psychologists present certain historical aspects of learning theory, and when psychiatrists present the current understanding of the physiology of affective spectrum disorder), the diverse resources of knowledge become available to everyone in ways they would never be if homogeneity were the rule. Perhaps we health care professionals need to find more common areas in which to collaborate, but in the meantime, our shared interest in clinical hypnosis provides a very real opportunity for collaboration.

3. *In every conference, a few individual participants create excessive demands on individual faculty members to the detriment of the class as a whole.* If one is teaching alone it may be hard to identify these potential intrusions, especially if the individual is asking the kinds of questions that provide an ongoing basis for the group's discussion. One needs to remember, however, that a response to the right question is not the heart of adult education. Rather, it is the sharing of each participant's experiences in order to provide additional ways of feeling and thinking about one's work and thus to gain new skills in working with patients and clients. The problem of the demanding participant is easier to handle if there are several faculty members present: One can be free to act as an objective observer of the educational process. When the teacher is alone, the problem is often solved by the other participants' discerning the process and taking control of the one who monopolizes the teacher's time. It is an interesting problem in group dynamics.

4. *Faculty are often like attractive dishes on a smorgasbord—you need more than one to enjoy a full meal.* Exposure to many faculty members during larger workshops can provide broader access to teachers in one setting. However, when many faculty members teach in the same course, it is advisable that two faculty members "dominate" so as to provide one or two clear role models for the approach to and utilization of hypnosis in all its aspects. The other faculty can fill more specialized roles and provide adjunctive help in the practice sessions and in lectures on special topics.

    Over time, each participant who wishes to learn hypnosis thoroughly and to use it well should take two or three workshops and expose him- or herself to more than one or two teachers, who can become models with regard to knowledge and personal approach to patient care. Finally, after the clinician is fully trained and is well into the process of polishing and integrating these new skills into the very fabric of his or her particular brand of psychotherapy, he or she should return to the class as teacher. This last step caps the training.

5. *Abreaction, strong emotion, and dysphoric affect are evoked at times in practicing hypnosis and can also occur in the classroom.* Caring attention by the faculty to the uncomfortable participant is called for and, if appropriate, can be conducted as part of the participant's training. Many times, a little time at the coffee break, or after class in follow-up, can provide the teacher with enough information and the opportunity to

restore the participant's calmness needed for ongoing learning. Unlike some others, I do not believe that personal psychotherapy or hypnotherapy for the actual medical or psychological problems of a participant in front of the class has any place in training sessions for teaching clinical hypnosis. Although it is tempting to do this, the incongruity of the treatment in an educational context simultaneously limits both the educational and therapeutic value of the experience.

CONCLUSION

Effective training in clinical hypnosis depends on program directors understanding and utilizing the principles of adult education. Adults learn by integrating new knowledge and skills with previous work experiences that have thus far defined their professional identities. Such learning must make sense or fit before it will be used in subsequent patient/client care.

In hypnosis workshops, the content of the presented material combines with the context of the training to form a whole or gestalt. Each element of this gestalt, content and context, affects the other in the service of the total learning experience. Workshop organizers are wise to insure both the quality of the didactic material and the appropriateness of the setting. The process of effective adult education is complex.

For both the participant and the faculty member, hypnosis continuing education programs for adult professionals can also become significant experiences in learning more deeply about psychotherapy. For each, special opportunities abound for enhancing overall clinical competence while learning how to use hypnosis in therapy.

REFERENCES

Bloom, P. B. (1990). The creative process in hypnotherapy. In M. L. Fass & D. Brown (Eds.), *Creative mastery in hypnosis and hypnoanalysis: A festschrift for Erika Fromm* (pp. 159–168). Hillsdale, NJ: Erlbaum.

Bloom, P. B. (1991). Some general considerations about Ericksonian hypnotherapy. *American Journal of Clinical Hypnosis, 33*, 221–224.

Carmichael, H. T., Small, S. M., & Regan, P. F. (1972). *Prospects and proposals: Lifetime learning for psychiatrists.* Washington, DC: American Psychiatric Association.

Coggeshall, L. T. (1965). *Planning for medical progress through education.* Evanston, IL: Association of American Medical Colleges.

Dryer, B. V. (1962). Lifetime learning for physicians. *Journal of Medical Education, 37*(6, Part 2), 1–334.

Dubin, L. L., & Shapiro, S. S. (1974). Use of hypnosis to facilitate dental extraction and hemostasis in a classic hemophiliac with a high antibody titer to factor VIII. *American Journal of Clinical Hypnosis, 17,* 79–83.

Early, L. W. (1968). The need for and problems of continuing education for psychiatrists. *American Journal of Psychiatry, 124,* 1151–1156.

Erickson, M. H. (1965). A special inquiry with Aldous Huxley into the nature and character of various states of consciousness. *American Journal of Clinical Hypnosis, 8,* 14–33.

Knowles, M. S. (1970). *The modern practice of adult education: Andragogy versus pedagogy.* New York: Association Press.

Knowles, M. S. (1980). *The modern practice of adult education: From pedagogy to andragogy* (rev. and updated ed.). Chicago: Association Press, Follett.

Kris, E. (1952). The psychology of caricature. In *Psychoanalytic exploration in art* (pp. 173–188). New York: International Universities Press. (Original work published 1935)

Parish, M. J. (1975). Predoctoral training in clinical hypnosis: A national survey of availability and educator attitudes in schools of medicine, dentistry, and graduate clinical psychology. *International Journal of Clinical and Experimental Hypnosis, 23,* 249–265.

Rodolfa, E. R., Kraft, W. A., Reilly, R. R., & Blackmore, S. H. (1983). The status of research and training in hypnosis at APA accredited clinical/counseling psychology internship sites: A national survey. *International Journal of Clinical and Experimental Hypnosis, 31,* 284–292.

Thompson, K. (Participant), & Barnes, M. (Producer, Writer, & Director). (1982). *Hypnosis and healing: Can your mind control your body?* [Film; segment featuring K. Thompson]. London: British Broadcasting Corporation.

Uhl, H. S. M. (1986). CME: A brief history. In A. B. Rosof & W. C. Felch (Eds.), *Continuing medical education: A primer* (pp. 8–9). New York: Praeger.

APPENDIX A

Sponsor Accreditation Organizations

Academy of General Dentistry
National Sponsor Approval Program
Department of Continuing Education
211 East Chicago Avenue, Suite 1200
Chicago, IL 60611

Accreditation Council for Continuing Medical Education
51-B Sherwood Terrace
Lake Bluff, IL 60044

American Academy of Family Physicians
Commission on Continuing Medical Education
8880 Ward Parkway
Kansas City, MO 64114

American Psychological Association
APA-Approved Continuing Education Sponsors
750 First Street, NE
Washington, DC 20002

American Psychological Association
Continuing Education Program
750 First Street, NE
Washington, DC 20002

The Collaborative of the National Association of Social Workers and Boston College
  and Simmons College Schools of Social Work
C. E. U. Application
14 Beacon Street, Room 409
Boston, MA 02108

APPENDIX B

Hypnosis Societies

The American Society of Clinical Hypnosis
William F. Hoffmann, Jr., Executive Vice-President
2200 East Devon Avenue, Suite 291
Des Plaines, IL 60018
Tel: (708) 297-3317, FAX: (708) 297-7309

The Society for Clinical and Experimental Hypnosis
Marion Kenn, Administrative Director
128-A Kings Park Drive
Liverpool, NY 13090
Tel and FAX: (315) 652-7299

The International Society of Hypnosis
Robb O. Stanley, BSc(H), D. Psych., Administrative Officer
Edward Wilson Building
Austin Hospital
Heidelberg, Victoria 3084
Australia
Tel: 61-3-459-6499, FAX: 61-3-459-6244

31

CROSS-CULTURAL PERSPECTIVES ON HYPNOTIC-LIKE PROCEDURES USED BY NATIVE HEALING PRACTITIONERS

STANLEY KRIPPNER

The term *hypnosis* is often used to refer to a variety of structured, goal-oriented procedures in which it is claimed that the suggestibility or motivation of an individual or a group is enhanced by another person (or persons), by a mechanical device, by a conducive environment, or by oneself. These procedures attempt to blur, focus, or amplify attention or mentation (e.g., imagination or intention), leading to the accomplishment of specified behaviors or experiences.

Considerable research data indicate that these behaviors and experiences reflect expectations and role enactments on the part of the "hypnotized" individuals or groups, who attend (often with little awareness) to their own personal needs and to the interpersonal or situational cues that shape their responses (Barber, 1969; Spanos & Chaves, 1989). Other research data have emphasized the part that attention (whether it is diffuse, concentrated, or expansive) plays in hypnosis, enhancing the salience of the suggested task or experience (Krippner & Bindler, 1974). Both of these bodies of hypnosis literature have emphasized the interaction of several variables in hypnosis and can be used to better understand those healing practices used by native practitioners that involve either overt or covert suggestive or motivational procedures.

The historical roots of hypnosis reach back to tribal rites and the practices of shamans (Brown & Fromm, 1986, p. 3). Agogino (1965) stated that "the history of hypnotism may be as old as the practice of shamanism" (p. 31) and described hypnotic-like procedures used in the court of the pharaoh Khufu in 3766 B.C. Agogino added that priests in the healing temples of Asclepius (beginning in the 4th century B.C.) induced their clients into "temple sleep" by "hypnosis and auto-suggestion" and that the ancient druids chanted over their clients until the desired effect was obtained (p. 32). Vogel (1970/1990) pointed out that herbs were used to enhance verbal suggestion by native healers in pre-Columbian Central and South America (p. 177).

Gergen (1985) observed that the terms in which the world is understood are social artifacts, "products of historically situated interchanges among people" (p. 267). Therefore, I use the description "hypnotic-like procedures" because native (i.e., indigenous or traditional) practitioners and their societies have constructed an assortment of terms to describe activities that resemble what Western practitioners refer to as "hypnosis." The term *hypnosis* has a cultural and historical context dating back to Anton Mesmer in the 18th century. To use this term to describe exorcisms, the laying-on of hands, dream incubation, and the like does an injustice to the varieties of cultural experience and their historic roots. "Hypnosis" and "the hypnotic state" have been too often reified (Spanos & Chaves, 1991, p. 71), distracting the serious investigator from ingenious uses of human imagination and motivation that are worthy of study in their own right.

A survey of the social science literature, as well as my own observations in several traditional societies, indicates that there are frequent elements of native healing procedures that can be termed "hypnotic-like." This is due, in part, to the fact that alterations in consciousness (i.e., observed or experienced changes in people's patterns of perception, affect, or cognition—especially awareness, attention, and memory—at a given point in time) are sanctioned and deliberately fostered by virtually all indigenous groups. For example, Bourguignon and Evascu (1977) sampled 488 societies, finding that 89% displayed socially approved altered states of consciousness.

The ubiquitous nature of hypnotic-like procedures in native healing (e.g., Bowers, 1961) is also the result of the ways in which human capacities—such as the capability to strive toward a goal and the ability to imagine a suggested experience—can be channeled and shaped, albeit differentially, by social interactions (Murphy, 1947, Chapter 8). Concepts of sickness and of healing can be socially constructed and modeled in a number of ways. The models found in traditional cultures frequently identify such etiological factors in sickness as "soul loss," "breach of taboo," or spirit "possession," "intrusion," or "invasion"—all of which are diagnosed (at least in part) by observable changes in the victims' behavior as related to their mentation or mood (Frank & Frank, 1991, Chapter 5). Unlike infectious diseases and disabilities resulting from physical trauma, these conditions—including those with a physiological predisposition—are basically socially constructed, just as the changed states of consciousness identified by Bourguignon and Evascu (1977) are shaped by historical and social forces within a culture.

For example, there is no Western equivalent of *wagamama*, a Japanese emotional disorder characterized by childish behavior, emotional outbursts, apathy, and negativity. Nor is there a counterpart to *kami*, a condition common in some Japanese communities that is thought to be caused by spirit possession. *Susto* is a malaise, commonly referred to in Peru and several other parts of Latin America, that is thought to be caused by a shock or fright, often connected with breaking a spiritual taboo. It can lead to dire consequences such as the "loss of one's soul," but there is no equivalent concept in Western psychotherapy manuals.

Cross-cultural studies of native healing have only started to take seriously the importance of understanding indigenous models of sickness and treatment, perhaps because of the prevalence of behavioral, psychoanalytic, and medical models, none of which have been overly sympathetic to the explanations offered by traditional practitioners (Ward, 1989b, p. 9) or to the proposition that Western knowledge is only one of several viable representations of nature (Gergen, 1985). Kleinman (1980) commented that

> the habitual (and frequently unproductive) way researchers try to make sense of healing, especially indigenous healing, is by speculating about psychological and physiological mechanisms of therapeutic action, which then are applied to case material in truly Procrustean fashion that fits the particular instance to putative universal principles. The latter are primarily derived from the concepts of biomedicine and individual psychology. . . . By reducing healing to the language of biology, the human aspects (i.e., psychosocial and cultural significance) are removed, leaving behind something that can be expressed in biomedical terms, but that can hardly be called healing. Even reducing healing to the language of behavior . . . leaves out the language of experience, which . . . is a major aspect of healing. (pp. 363–364)

An example of Kleinman's caveat is the overly facile equation of the Eskimo *pibloktoq* (in which individuals tear off their clothes and wander aimlessly in inclement environments) with a "hysterical disorder" (Gussow, 1985). In much the same way, *hsieh-ping*, a Taiwanese condition marked by disorientation and auditory hallucinations, has been classified as a "depressive condition" (Hughes, 1985). Ward (1989a) pointed out that in both instances, it is incorrectly assumed that mental disorders are universal, although their manifestations may be shaped by culture. Gergen (1990) warned against using these terms as if they depict actual occurrences; the vocabulary of the mental health professions—traditional or Western—simply serves "to render the alien familiar, and thus less fearsome" (p. 358).

The value of a cross-cultural approach is to extend the range of individual and social variation in the scientific search for an understanding of human capacities (Price-Williams, 1975). Therefore, in this chapter I will concentrate on describing the hypnotic-like aspects of native healing procedures (using the definition of hypnosis already stated), only incidentally making interpretive analyses of the procedures themselves from the standpoint of Western medicine and psychotherapy. Most illnesses in a society are socially constructed, at least in part. Alleged changes in consciousness reflect social construction. Because native models of healing generally assume that practitioners, to be effective, must shift their attention and awareness (e.g., "journeying to the upper world," "traveling to the lower world," "incorporating spirit guides," "conversing with power animals," or "retrieving a lost soul"), the hypnosis literature can be instructive. Western hypnotic models are often assumed to represent universal processes; however, native healing procedures are also worthy of appreciation from the perspective of their own social framework.

CLINICAL APPLICATIONS

Winkelman (1984) conducted an archival study of 47 traditional societies, identifying four groups of spiritual practitioners: shamans and shamanic healers, priests and priestesses, mediums and diviners, and malevolent practitioners. With the exception of priests and priestesses, these practitioners purportedly cultivated the ability to regulate or shift their patterns of perception, affect, and cognition for benevolent (e.g., healing or divining) or malevolent (e.g., casting spells or hexing) purposes. In addition, priests and priestesses presided over rituals and ceremonies that often had as their intent eliciting changes in the behavior and experiences of their supplicants for religious purposes.

Hypnotic-like procedures are often apparent in the healing practices of native shamans. Shamans can be defined as socially sanctioned practitioners who purport to voluntarily regulate their attention and awareness so as to access information not ordinarily available, using it to facilitate appropriate behavior and healthy development—as well as to alleviate stress and sickness—among members of their community or for the community as a whole. Among the shaman's many roles, that of healer is the most common. The functions of shamans may differ in various locations, but all of them have been called on to predict and prevent afflictions or to diagnose and treat them when they occur. Shamanic healing procedures are highly scripted in a manner similar to the way that hypnotic procedures are carefully sequenced and structured. The expectations of the shaman's or hypnotist's clients can enable them to decipher task demands, interpret relevant communications appropriately, and translate the practitioner's suggestions into personalized perceptions and images. Just as expectancy plays a major role in hypnotic responsiveness (Kirsch, 1990), it facilitates the responsiveness of the shamans' clients as well as expediting shamanic "journeying." Shamans themselves display what Kirsch (1990), in discussing the hypnosis literature, called "learned skills"; their introduction to hypnotic-like experiences during their initiation and training generalizes to later sessions, and they can ultimately engage in "journeying" virtually at will.

Goodman (1990) has explored the effects of over two dozen "trance postures" on the attention and awareness of native healing practitioners, having taken these postures from petroglyphs, pictographs, and sculptures. The postures' names range from "Bear Posture" to "Birthing Posture," and their users claim that they function as "gateways" to the spiritual realms, where knowledge can be obtained to diagnose, to heal, or to assist their clients and communities in other ways. The use of these postures may shape and bolster relevant expectancies in ways similar to those used by hypnotists (e.g., "close your eyes, take a deep breath, and relax").

Japanese shamans of the Tohoku region believe that they can contact the Buddhist goddess Kan'non, who assists with their diagnosis, producing visual or auditory imagery that the shaman experiences and reports. This is an example of the "translation" that characterizes both hypnotic sessions and shamanic imagination. These shamanic "translations" have been studied by Achterberg (1985), who considers dreams, visions, and similar processes a venerable source of vital information on human health and sickness. So ubiquitous is their process of gleaning pertinent information from fantasy-based symbols and metaphors that I (Krippner, 1987) have suggested that shamans, as a group, might be considered "fantasy prone" (p. 130). Indeed, they frequently resemble the highly hypnotizable individuals who, on the basis of interviews and personality tests, have been designated "fantasy prone" (Lynn & Rhue, 1988).

Furst (1977) has described procedures by which North American Indians sought alternative states of consciousness: "psychoactive plants, animal secretions, fasting, thirsting, self-mutilation, exposure to the elements, sweat lodges, sleeplessness, incessant dancing, bleeding, plunging into ice-cold pools, and different kinds of rhythmic activity, self-hypnosis, meditation, chanting, and drumming" (p. 70). Furst used non-Indian concepts (e.g., "self-hypnosis," "trance," and "meditation") that may not be directly comparable to the original experiences. Nevertheless, he went on to describe the freedom that was typically given by North American Indian shamans to their clients to use "ecstatic trance" to determine their own relationship with the unseen forces of the universe. The analogous hypnotic practices here would be the various nondirective, permissive procedures in which hypnotized clients use their own fantasy and imagery to work toward the desired goals (e.g., Kroger, 1977, Chapter 14).

The Nanaimo Indians of Vancouver Island expect their shamans to fall unconscious during a ceremony in order to incorporate the tutelary spirits necessary for healing to occur (Jilek, 1982, p. 30). Alaskan Eskimo shamans claim to "journey" to the spirit world during a ceremony conducted in a darkened igloo, while they, stripped naked, sing and beat drums (Rogers, 1982, p. 124). Rogers claimed that the shaman's use of rhythmic drumming and monophonic chanting induces "self-hypnosis" (apparently because of their goal-directed nature) as well as placing the client "in a hypnotic trance in which the suggestions of recovery and cure are given" (p. 143). In discussing the Ammassalik Eskimos of eastern Greenland, Kalweit (1988) observed that their "continuous rubbing of stones against each other may be seen as a simple way of inducing a trance. . . . The monotony, loneliness, and repetitive rhythmic movement join with the desire to encounter a helping spirit. This combination is so powerful that it erases all mundane thoughts and distracting associations" (p. 100). Belo (1960) observed similarities between the behavior of Balinese mediums and that of hypnotized subjects. Although there was no trained observer of hypnosis on Belo's field trips, a hypnotic practitioner observed several of her films and claimed to notice similarities between "hypnotic trance" and "mediumistic trance." In these otherwise useful descriptions, we can observe the proclivity of Western observers to use such terms as "hypnosis" and "trance" in describing shamanic procedures rather than simply making comparisons or using the tribe's own explanations.

Kirsch's (1990) discussion of the role of expectancies in hypnosis and psychotherapy is relevant to each of these cases. Hypnosis, like many culturally based rituals, serves to shape and bolster relevant expectancies that reorganize consciousness and produce behavioral changes relevant to the goals of hypnotic subjects and shamanic clients. For example, the ideomotor behavior that often characterizes hypnosis (e.g., arms becoming heavier or lighter, or fingers moving to denote positive or negative responses) resembles the postures, gestures, collapsing motions, and rhythmic movements that occur during many native rituals. In both instances, the participants claim that the movements occur involuntarily. Kirsch suspects that expectancy plays a major role, but admitted that these responses are experienced as occurring automatically, without volition (p. 198).

Navajo Healing Procedures

Despite attempts at acculturation, most Navajo men and women still believe in their traditional cultural myths and participate in the corresponding rituals (Adair, Deuschle, & Barnett, 1988, p. 4). In the Navajo concept of illness, the universe is an interrelated whole in which powers of both good and evil exist in a balanced and orderly relationship. When this relationship is disturbed, disharmony occurs, producing illness. Its cause, therefore, is basically metaphysical; illness takes place when the individual or group is out of harmony with the natural and supernatural worlds (Topper, 1987). Navajos have constructed three major diagnostic categories of mental illness. "Moth craziness" is characterized by fits of uncontrolled behavior (e.g., jumping into fire like a moth), rage, violence, and convulsions; it is attributed to incestuous activities. "Crazy violence" has some of the same external manifestations as "moth craziness" but is due to alcoholism. "Ghost sickness," ascribed to sorcery, manifests itself in nightmares, loss of appetite, dizziness, confusion, panic, and extreme anxiety. When someone knowingly or accidentally breaches taboos or offends dangerous powers, the natural order of the universe is ruptured and "contamination" or "infection" occurs that must be redressed (Sandner, 1979).

When the family has determined that treatment is necessary, a *hataalii*, or "singing shaman," is called in, frequently accompanied by an herbalist and/or a diagnostician (both of whom are of lower status). The herbalists gather plants and make medicines, some of which are used directly and some of which are used ceremonially by the *hataalii*. The diagnosticians are usually women and "listen" to the spirits for a statement of the problem. This procedure resembles self-hypnosis in that it is a self-administered procedure that regulates one's attention and is goal-oriented in nature. Other diagnostic procedures that resemble self-hypnosis include hand trembling, star gazing, candle gazing, and crystal gazing—all of which involve the inward focusing of the practitioner's attention, with the purpose of facilitating insight as to the nature of the problem.

Navajo *hataalii* use a number of therapeutic procedures, most notably one or more of the ten basic "chantways," complex patterns of activities centered around cultural myths in which heroes or heroines once journeyed to spiritual realms to acquire special knowledge. The symptoms for which a given chant is prescribed are based on connections with the specific chant myth. For example, "Hail Way" is prescribed for muscular tiredness and soreness because the hero, Rain Boy, suffered from these symptoms when he was attacked by his enemies; "Big Star Way" protects the client against the powerful influences of the stars and the dangers of the night.

It takes several years to learn major chants, some of which consist of hundreds of songs. Hosteen Klah, a famous Navajo *hataalii* who died in 1937, knew more chants than any other healer of his era, one of them a chant that took 9 days to complete. The effectiveness of the chant is felt to be the result of its accurate performance because this evokes healing power from the spirits. For example, the "Night Chant" uses 24 sequences containing a total of 324 songs; its hero is Dawn Boy, who enters the presence of the gods at a sacred canyon. His song, which must be sung perfectly by the *hataalii* to be successful, appeals to the deities for assistance. One can observe the resemblance of the storytelling aspect of the chant to the use of narrative "teaching stories" in Ericksonian hypnotic procedures (e.g., Erickson, Rossi, & Rossi, 1976). These stories are highly scripted and reflect the society's perspective on human nature (Lynn & Rhue, 1991, p. 402).

Like Milton Erickson's "teaching stories," no formal "induction" procedures are used in chants. However, there is an emphasis on the correctness of the procedures; as a result, the *hataalii* is in an extremely vigilant frame of mind. The ability to master the elements of a "chantway" has been compared with memorizing a Wagnerian opera (Kluckholn & Leighton, 1962, p. 309). An ability to remember the cultural myths used in the "chantway" is mandatory if a *hataalii* is to serve as an educator who can pass traditions and tribal wisdom on to the younger generation (Dixon, 1908).

The absence of a formal "induction" does not prevent the client from becoming receptive to the suggestion and motivated to follow it, just as most, if not all, hypnotic phenomena can be evoked without hypnotic induction (Kirsch, 1990, p. 129). Contributing to this procedure is the multimodal approach that characterizes chants, as well as their repetitive nature and the mythic content of the words, which are easily deciphered by those clients well-versed in tribal mythology. Sandner (1979) described how the various sensory modalities are combined:

> The visual images of the sand paintings and the body painting, the audible recitation of prayers and songs, the touch of the prayer sticks and the hands of the medicine man, the taste of the ceremonial musk and herbal medicines, and the smell of the chant incense—all combine to convey the power of the chant to the patient. (p. 215) . . . A *hataalii* usually displays a highly developed dramatic sense in carrying out the chant but generally avoids the clever sleight of hand effects used by many other cultural healing practitioners to demonstrate their abilities to the community. (p. 241)

The chant is considered by Sandner (1979) to facilitate suggestibility and shifts in attending through repetitive singing and the use of culture-specific mythic themes (p. 245). These activities prepare participants for a healing session that may involve symbols and metaphors acted out by performers, enacted in purification rites, or executed in "sand paintings" composed of sand, corn meal, charcoal, and flowers—but destroyed once the healing session is over. Some paintings, such as those used in "Blessing Way," are crafted from ingredients that have not touched the ground (e.g., corn meal, flower petals, and charcoal). Once again, the client "translates" the symbols and metaphors, but usually not with full awareness of the ongoing process.

There are five steps in the typical "chantway" ceremony: preparation (in which the client is "purified"); presentation of the client to the healing spirits; evocation of these spirits to the place of the ceremony; identification of the clients with a positive mythic theme; transformation of the clients into a condition where ordinary and mythic time and space merge; and release from the mythic world and return to the everyday world where past transgressions are confessed, where new learnings are assimilated, and where life changes are brought to fruition. These steps resemble Kirsch's (1990, p. 163) three phases of the use of hypnosis in psychotherapy: preparation, induction, and application. The client's purification and presentation are analogous to preparation, the evocation of the spirits resembles induction, and the identification and transformation represent clinical application.

Hypnotic-like procedures affect the mentation of both the *hataalii* and the client during the chant. Sandner (1979) pointed out that the *hataalii*'s performance empowers the client by creating a "mythic reality" through the use of chants, dances, and songs (often accompanied by drums and rattles); masked dancers; purifications (e.g., sweats, emetics, herbal infusions, ritual bathings, and sexual abstinence); and sand paintings. Joseph Campbell (1990) described the colors of the typical sand painting as those "associated with each of the four directions" and a dark center: "the abysmal dark out of which all things come and back to which they go." When appearances emerge in the painting, "they break into pairs of opposites" (p. 30).

In the context of this "mythic reality," especially as made visible in the designs constructed in sand by the *hataalii*, the client is taken into "sacred time" and is able to bring a total attentiveness to the healing ceremony. This resembles the focusing of attention characteristic of many hypnotic procedures, and the presence of culturally significant symbols may maximize clients' imagination and motivation, empowering their self-healing capacities through an identification with symbols held to have therapeutic consequences. This provides the "credible rationale" that Kirsch (1990) has found to enhance treatment effectiveness.

The client follows a specific regimen for the next 4 days to protect members of the community from his or her newly acquired powers. The role of the community is important in another way: The chants are attended by large numbers of people, many of whom might be asked to participate. This type of participation appears to increase the clients' sense of personal power, magnify their imagination as they attend to the chants, and provide social reinforcement and increased motivation.

The mentation of the practitioner, the client, and the community may all be affected by the ceremony. Not only do clients believe that they derive "energy" from the sand painting by sitting on it, but the *hataalii* is dusted with the decorated sand and touched with feathers and other "power objects," and clients claim to feel the power emanating from the sand painting (Sandner, 1979). This resembles the enhancement of imagination common to several hypnotic procedures, and is probably further augmented by the repetitive chanting.

In addition to the "chantway," there are other hypnotic-like healing procedures used by the Navajo *hataalii*, one of which is a prayer session. For example, sacred corn pollen may be sacrificed during a time of prayer in an attempt to foster the influence of the spirits needed to heal the client; this ritual must be performed perfectly and behind locked doors, often at the home of the client. The door to the darkened hogan is fastened to prevent the prayer from "escaping." Sharpened flints are used to expel the evil from both the client and the hogan. Topper (1987) held that these procedures reduce the client's symptoms at the same time that they stabilize the social and emotional condition of the community.

Leighton and Leighton (1941) described the efforts made by the *hataalii* to amplify the anticipation of the client during visits to his or her hogan. They instruct the family to make elaborate preparations for the *hataalii*'s "house call." Upon arriving, the client is told that the prognosis is excellent, thus fostering positive expectations (Torrey, 1986). The most important people in the client's life often join in the prayers, reaffirming the belief that the client will recover.

Topper's (1987) study of Navajo *hataalii* indicated that they also raise their clients' expectations through the example they set of stability and competence. Politically, they are authoritative and powerful; this embellishes their symbolic value as "transference figures" in the psychoanalytic sense, representing "a nearly omniscient and omnipotent nurturative grandparental object" (p. 221). Frank and Frank (1991) put it more directly: "The personal qualities that predispose patients to a favorable therapeutic response are similar to those that heighten susceptibility to methods of healing in nonindustrialized societies, religious revivals, experimental manipulations of attitudes, and administration of a placebo" (p. 184). Suggestion and expectancy are bolstered through reinforcement of the client's belief in the power of the chant and its symbols, a tight structuring of the ceremonial performance, repetition (especially in chants, songs, and prayers), physical exhaustion of the client, the dramatization of a significant event in Navajo mythology, and, on rare occasions, the use of psychotropic herbal substances (e.g., datura) to evoke a physical effect that convinces the client that power is at work.

As important as the impact of the chant and prayers on the *hataalii*'s consciousness may be, Sandner (1979) insisted that the Navajo practitioner "relies on knowledge, not trance phenomena or magical effects. The chant work is a restrained and dignified procedure, and for the most part the medicine man represents for the patient a stable, dependable leader who is a helper and guide until the work is ended" (p. 258). In other words, two crucial factors in the client's treatment appear to be the personal qualities of the *hataalii* and the expectancies of the client; shifts in attending may be more useful in intensifying the abilities of the practitioner and the receptivity of the client than in providing any type of innate therapeutic effectiveness. However, the hypnotic-like procedures strengthen the support by family and community members as well as the client's identification with figures and activities in Navajo cultural myths, both of which are powerful elements in the attempted healing.

Even though hypnotic-like procedures are used by Navajo shamans, they do not consider the "chantway" or the healing prayers to induce an alteration in ordinary consciousness. To deliberately enter an altered state, or to claim that they were in such a condition, would be considered undignified by the Navajo shamans. Nevertheless, the lengthy chants, songs, and prayers are so repetitive and monotonous that an outside observer might justifiably claim that they serve as consciousness-altering procedures. Furthermore, this example demonstrates how each culture constructs the notion of altered states differently; the spectrum of altered states is constricted and narrow among the Navajo, in contrast with the complexities of construction found in many Eastern traditions. Tibetan Buddhism, for example, contains five classes of meditation, each of which includes four levels that may incorporate dozens of specific potential alterations with a variety of outcomes (i.e., ways in which consciousness is reorganized following the meditative procedure) (Brown, 1977).

Afro-Brazilian Healing Procedures

In early West African cultures, an individual was considered to be closely connected with nature, the community, and his or her communal group. Each person was expected to play his or her part in a web of kinship relations and community networks. Strained or broken social relations were held to be the major cause of sickness; a harmonious relationship with one's community, as well as with one's ancestors, was important for health. At the same time, an ordered relationship with the forces of nature, as personified by the *orixas*, or deities, was essential for maintaining the well-being of the individual, the family, and the community. West Africans knew that disease often had natural causes, but they believed that these factors were exacerbated by discordant relationships between people and their social and natural milieu. Long before Western medicine recognized the fact, Africa's traditional healers took the position that ecology and interpersonal relations affected people's health (Raboteau, 1986).

West African healing practitioners felt that they gained access to supernatural power in three ways: by making offerings to the *orixas*, by foretelling the future with the help of an *orixa*, and by incorporating an *orixa* (or even an ancestor), who then diagnosed illnesses, prescribed cures, and provided the community with warnings or blessings. The medium, or person through whom the spirits spoke and moved, performed this task voluntarily, claiming that such procedures as dancing, singing, or drumming were needed to surrender their minds and bodies to the discarnate entities (Krippner, 1989, p. 188). The slaves brought these practices to Brazil with them; despite colonial and ecclesiastical repression, the customs survived over the centuries and eventually formed the basis for a number of robust Afro-Brazilian spiritual movements. Books by a French spiritualist, Alan Kardec, were brought to Brazil, were translated into Portuguese, and became the basis for a related movement (i.e., Kardecism). There were followers of Anton Mesmer in this group, but Kardec proposed that spirits, rather than Mesmer's invisible fluids, were the active agent in altering consciousness, removing symptoms, and restoring equilibrium (Richeport, 1992, p. 170).

Contemporary *iyalorixas*, or *maes dos santos* (mothers of the *orixas*), and *babalawos*, or *pais dos santos* (fathers of the *orixas*), still teach apprentices how to sing, drum, and dance in order to incorporate the various deities, ancestors, and spirit guides. They also teach the *iaos* (children of the *orixas*) about the special herbs, teas, and lotions needed to restore health, and about the charms and rituals needed to prevent illness (McGregor, 1962). The ceremonies of the various Afro-Brazilian groups (e.g., Candomble, Umbanda, Batuque, Caboclo, Quimbanda, and Xango) differ, but all share three beliefs: Humans have a spiritual body (that generally reincarnates after physical death), discarnate spirits are in constant contact with the physical world, and humans can learn how to incorporate spirits for the purpose of healing.

After interviewing 40 spiritistic healing practitioners in Brazil, I (Krippner, 1989) identified five methods of receiving the "call" to become a medium: (a) coming from a family having a history of mediumship, (b) being "called" by spirits in one's visions and dreams, (c) succumbing to a malady or "spiritual crisis" from which one recovers to serve others, (d) having a revelation while reading Afro-Brazilian spiritistic literature or attending spiritistic worship services, or (e) working as a volunteer in a spiritistic healing center and becoming inspired by the daily examples of compassion. If the call is rejected, severe illness or misfortune may result; as one Candomble medium told me, "Once the *orixa* calls, there is no other path to take" (p. 193).

Once the apprentices begin to receive instruction in mediumship, such experiences as spirit incorporation, automatic writing, "out-of-body" travel, and recall of "past lives" lose their bizarre quality and seem to occur quite naturally. Socialization processes provide role models and the support of peers. A number of cues (songs, chants, music, etc.) facilitate spirit incorporation, and a process of social construction teaches control, appropriate role taking, and communal support. Richeport (1992) observed many similarities between these mediumistic behaviors and those of many hypnotized subjects (e.g., dissociation, the positive use of imagination, and frequent amnesia for the experience).

It should be noted that mediums resemble shamans in many ways but lack the control of their attention and awareness that characterizes shamans. For example, shamans are usually aware of everything that occurs while they converse with the spirits, even when a spirit "speaks through" them. Mediums claim to lose awareness once they incorporate a spirit, and purport to remember little about the experience once the spirit leaves. Both shamans and mediums engage in altered states of consciousness, but the shaman's attention, memory, and awareness seem to be enhanced, not restricted. These same facets of mentation appear to be dampened or diffused in mediumship; if there is a shift toward greater focus, it is attributed to the guiding spirit rather than to the medium himself or herself. Finally, it should be mentioned that some practitioners behave like shamans in some situations and like mediums in other contexts.

The traits most admired in mediums resemble those traits that facilitate ordinary social interactions. During a dozen trips to Brazil, I have observed few instances of bizarre behavior during spiritistic ceremonies; indeed, if a spirit seems to be taking control of the medium too quickly, the other mediums may sing a song that will slow down the process of incorporation (Rouget, 1985). Leacock and Leacock (1972) observed that the Brazilian mediums in their study usually behaved in ways that were "basically rational," communicated effectively with other people, and demonstrated few symptoms of hysteria or psychosis. They engaged in intensive training and, as mediums, pursued hard work that often put them at risk with seriously ill individuals (p. 212). These are not likely to be the favorite pastimes of fragile personalities or malingerers.

In 1973, a colleague and I attended an Umbanda ceremony in Sao Paulo, Brazil. Drums were beating, candles were flickering, and the smell of incense was wafting through the room. We took our seats with the other spectators and noticed the gargantuan altar containing dozens of statues of *orixas*, ancestors, and Christian saints—Umbanda being the Afro-American spiritistic movement that has borrowed most heavily from Christianity. A *babalawo* appeared to be in charge of the ceremony, but four other *babalawos* and five *iyalorixas* were playing prominent roles.

As the ceremony continued, a medium began to shake violently, then appeared to demonstrate equanimity as she incorporated the spirit of a *preto velho*, a black slave from Brazil's colonial past. Looked upon as powerful healing spirits, the *preto velhos* are incorporated at least once a month in most Afro-Brazilian spiritistic centers, rotating with such other healing entities as the *caboclos*, or Indians of mixed blood, and the *criancas*, or children who died at young ages.

Other mediums began to engage in automatisms—twitching, writhing, screaming, flailing, and falling to the floor. Once they maintained their composure, they claimed to have incorporated *preto velhos* (or *preta velhas*, the female counterpart), and were able to engage in healing through the laying-on of hands. My colleague and I entered the healing circle, where mediums prayed, sang, and gave us quick massages that were pleasant and pleasurable. (Some spiritistic healers, especially the followers of Alan Kardec, only work with the spiritual body and refrain from touching the client's physical body.) It was not long before many recipients of the healing procedures began to display hypnotic-like behavior including automatisms, conversations with the spirits, and spontaneous chanting and singing.

As the ceremony ended, obeisance was paid to the *exus*, or messengers of the *orixas*; these entities can be mischievous and so must be placated before the session, after the session, or both if the maximum results are to be obtained. Songs, prayers, and offerings of food and drink are sent their way to cajole them and ensure their cooperation. Soon the mediums left the room, doffed their white robes and crucifixes, and joined us for refreshments. They alleged not to have recalled the events of the evening, claiming that as the *pretos velhos* had worked through them, they lost their awareness of the ongoing activities.

In 1991, several colleagues and I attended a Candomble ceremony in Recife, Brazil, again finding ourselves immersed in candlelight, incense, and drumming. Pai (i.e., "Father") Eli, the *babalawo,* had invited us to witness an initiation: A "daughter of the saints" was about to become an *iyalorixa* following a 24-day period of solitude in which her only visitor had been Pai Eli, who had brought food, water, and counsel. As she emerged from her underground room, we noticed that her head had been shaved except for a thin tuft of hair in the middle. This represented a modification of the original ceremony, wherein the skin on top of the head was cut so that the *orixas* could receive a blood offering. We were also told that this temple no longer sacrificed fowl or small animals to the *orixas*, concluding that the previous gift of blood had been merely a metaphor for the vow to live one's life in service and humility, a determination now expressed directly.

For several hours, I (and the others) joined the initiate in a dance around the temple, accompanied by other mediums who were incorporating various entities. Some of them had been initiated years earlier, and continued to venerate the *orixas* who had revealed themselves to them during their revelatory ceremony. For some it had been Oxala, the *orixa* of purity, or Oxum, the *orixa* of the lakes and rivers; for others, it had been Oxossi, the *orixa* of the forest, or Iemanja, the *orixa* of the oceans. Having been silent for 24 days, the initiate's first words would describe the *orixa* who would serve as her benefactor and whose lineage she would join. Finally, the young woman barked the name "Oxumaré," the *orixa* of the rainbow.

The suspense was ended and she was welcomed as the temple's newest *iyalorixa*.

In both of these ceremonies, and in dozens of others that I have witnessed or in which I have participated, a "trance" was supposedly induced by the rhythmic drumming and movement, as well as by the assault on the senses produced by the music, incense, flickering candles, and—in some temples—pungent cigar smoke. But it was apparent to me that powerful demand characteristics were also at work. The very reason for the mediums' presence was the incorporation of spirits; as Kleinman (1980) argued, "providing effective treatment for disease is *not* the chief reason why indigenous practitioners heal. To the extent that they provide culturally legitimated treatment of illness, they *must* heal" (p. 362).

In addition, the community of believers depended on the mothers, fathers, and children of the *orixas* to provide a connection to the spirit world that would ensure the well-being of the temple, prevent illness among those who were well, and bestow healing on those who were indisposed. When one medium incorporated an *orixa*, *preto velho*, *caboclo*, or *crianca*, an entire series of incorporations soon followed, domino-like. Just as many participants in hypnotic sessions seem eager to present themselves as "good subjects" (Spanos, 1989), the mediums in Afro-Brazilian healing sessions may be eager to present themselves as "good mediums" and to enact behaviors consistent with this interpretation. I have also noticed that the presence of visitors appears to increase both the speed and the dramatic qualities of spirit incorporation.

A fairly consistent similarity among mediums is their supposed inability to recall the events of the incorporation after the spirits have departed. However, Spanos (1989) has pointed out that this amnesic quality could just as easily be explained as an "achievement"; each failure to remember "adds legitimacy to a subject's self-presentation as 'truly unable to remember,'" hence as deeply in "trance" (p. 101). In other words, the interpretation of hypnotic phenomena as goal-directed action is helpful in understanding mediumship as an activity that meets role demands, as mediums guide and report their behavior and experience in conformance with these demands. It may be not that they lose control over the behavior as they incorporate a spirit, but rather that they engage in an efficacious enactment of a role that they are eager to maintain.

An alternative point of view would hold that the mediums actually do lose control over their behavior, entering a "trance" or "dissociative state" that allows "hidden parts" of themselves to manifest as secondary personalities or, in the case of the Brazilian mediums, as spirits. But some Brazilian practitioners with whom I have discussed these issues suggested that both the "role-playing" and "dissociative" paradigms describe merely the mechanisms by which a medium actually incorporates the *orixa*, discarnate entity, or spirit. It is the incorporation itself and the subsequent behavior of the spirit that represent the crux of mediumship. Because the possibility of spirit incorporation is hardly open to demonstration at the present time, one can only acknowledge this argument (albeit skeptically) and focus on other aspects of these phenomena.

For example, Afro-Brazilian spiritistic ceremonies enable clients and mediums to arrive at a shared world view in which an ailment can be discussed and treated (Torrey, 1986). In some spiritistic traditions, there are mediums who specialize in diagnosis, mediums who specialize in healing by a laying-on of hands, mediums who specialize in distant healing, and mediums who specialize in intercessory prayer. Treatment may also consist of removing a "low spirit" from a client's "energy field," integrating one's past lives with the present incarnation, the assignment of prayers or service-oriented projects, or referral to a homeopathic physician. All of these procedures contain the possibility of enhancing clients' sense of mastery, increasing their self-healing capacities, and replacing their demoralization with empowerment (Frank & Frank, 1991; Torrey, 1986).

The mediums are not the only ones who appear to manifest hypnotic-like effects. Their clients also demonstrate apparent shifts in consciousness, especially while undergoing crude surgeries without the benefit of anesthetics; however, Greenfield (1992) observed that the Brazilian mediums make no direct effort to alter their clients' awareness. Greenfield, who attributed the benefits of these sessions to the clients' alterations of consciousness, has observed that "no one is consciously aware of hypnotizing . . . patients . . . , and unlike the mediums, patients participate in no ritual during which they may be seen to enter a trance state" (p. 23). However, there are a number of cultural procedures that Greenfield found to be hypnotic-like in nature. One of them is the relationship of client to healer, characterized by trust and resembling "that between hypnotist and client" (p. 23) in that these clients act positively in response to what the medium tells them. Another procedure is a context that allows the client to become totally absorbed in the intervention, a healing ritual that galvanizes the client's attention and distracts him or her from feeling pain. Greenfield added that the spiritistic aspects of Brazilian culture foster "fantasy proneness" because large numbers of people believe that supernatural entities are helping (or hindering) them in their daily lives (p. 24).

Rogers (1982) divided native healing procedures into several categories (p. 112): nullification of sorcery (e.g., charms, dances, and songs), removal of objects (e.g., sucking, brushing, and shamanic "surgery"), exorcism of harmful entities (e.g., fighting the entity, sending a spirit to fight the entity, or making the entity uncomfortable), retrieval of lost souls (e.g., by "soul catchers" or by shamanic journeying), eliciting confession and penance (e.g., to the shaman or to the community), transfer of illness (e.g., to an object or a scapegoat), suggestion and persuasion (e.g., reasoning, use of ritual, and use of herbs), and shock (e.g., a sudden change of temperature or a precipitous physical assault). In all of these procedures, hypnotic-like techniques using symbols, metaphors, stories, and rituals (especially those involving group participation) can play an important role.

CASE MATERIAL

Rolling Thunder

In 1979, I visited Rolling Thunder, an intertribal medicine man living in Carlin, Nevada, where he was directing Meta Tantey ("Go in Peace"), a spiritual community. Much to my surprise, Rolling Thunder asked me to hypnotize one of his clients, William, a young Native American who had sought treatment because of his alcoholism. Rolling Thunder had placed William on a "purifying" diet and had treated him with herbs for approximately 3 months. He had told William that a psychologist was going to hypnotize him at a campfire attended by the entire community.

I assumed that I would meet William before the ceremony so that I could determine his expectations and adapt my intervention accordingly. However, William had a job in the nearby town and was not available until the ceremony began. When I arrived at the campfire, William was already there, seated in a comfortable chair, flanked by some four dozen members of the Meta Tantey community. Drumming, chanting, and singing proceeded for about 90 minutes in preparation not only for my hypnotic procedure but also for a healing session by Rolling Thunder himself.

When the drumming stopped, Rolling Thunder introduced me to the group, and I walked to the center of the circle. I observed that William seemed somewhat apprehensive, probably in anticipation of the event and as a result of the arousing, rhythmic music. I told William that he might feel more comfortable if he closed his eyes, then I suggested that he imagine what it felt like to crave alcohol. He easily recreated this feeling, and I asked him to transform the sensations into an image of some sort. He quickly reported visualizing a horrible monster that was intent on destroying him.

I reminded William that there were some 50 people around the campfire who cared for him and who were concerned for his well-being. I suggested that he imagine that they were giving him a gift that would help him to destroy his enemy. Almost immediately, William reported a mental image of an arrow. Remarking that the gift reflected his Native American heritage, I told William that he could use the arrow to kill the creature. He imagined drawing a bow and shooting the arrow into the monster's heart. The beast collapsed and William reported feeling great relief.

I led William through a brief relaxation exercise prior to the next step of the process. Then I asked him what healthy beverages he enjoyed. He responded with a list of fruit juices and herbal teas, and I had him imagine drinking and enjoying one of these. After he reported carrying out this suggestion, I led him through an exercise that he was to perform in the future. Whenever he desired alcohol, he would convert the craving into the image of his nemesis, shoot it with his bow and arrow, and (either in reality or in his imagination) drink some tea or juice. I told him that the more often he repeated this procedure, the more success he would have combating his yearning for alcohol.

I joined the circle around the campfire and Rolling Thunder stepped forward. Resplendent in a white buckskin suit and a feather headdress, the medicine man asked the group if they had heard the hooting of an owl during the hypnotic session. Various members of the group nodded their heads affirmatively, and Rolling Thunder commented that it was a symbol of death or transformation. Thus, William was engaged in a life-or-death struggle with alcohol, his nemesis. Rolling Thunder added that the owl had hooted seven times; again, several members of the community nodded in assent. The medicine man commented that the number seven is lucky for Native Americans; therefore, William's chances of winning the struggle were quite favorable. Rolling Thunder proceeded to poke William's skin with an eagle feather until his client winced in discomfort. The medicine man then cupped the area with his hands, sucked the skin to "extract" negative material from William's body, and spit a mouthful of dark red fluid into a pail. He explained that this was a "purification" procedure and that the fluid would be taken away and buried.

Frankly, I did not recall an owl hooting—much less hear it hoot seven times. However, I might not have noticed because I was focusing on William and his reactions to my suggestions. Nevertheless, William appeared at the airport when I left Nevada, expressing his thanks intensely with tears in his eyes. He left Meta Tantey the following year and at last report, 2 years later, was still sober. I suspect that my hypnotic intervention played a relatively minor role in William's success story. However, it might have catalyzed the "purification" work he had done with Rolling Thunder before my arrival, and provided him with a vehicle that would help him take an active role in attaining sobriety and remaining sober.

This incident was one of several occasions on which Rolling Thunder called on me to hypnotize one of his clients. He observed my procedures quite carefully; eventually, he carried them out himself. In my conversations with him about hypnosis, I emphasized the importance of evoking expectancy, trust, and rapport—the very factors that Rolling Thunder had been using in his work for decades. I have seen Rolling Thunder establish rapport with his clients, assess their beliefs and expectations, present a rationale for his treatment, and use individually tailored and flexibly administered rituals for producing behavior change, the same strategies that Kirsch (1990) found to characterize both hypnosis and psychotherapy that proved to be effective.

Graywolf

A former resident of Meta Tantey, Graywolf is a shamanic healer whom I visited several times in Oregon. Born as Fred Swinney, Graywolf holds a master's degree in counseling. He integrated shamanic procedures into his practice and his life-style after a number of transformative dreams and visions. Taking the position that dysfunctional behavior is underscored by dysfunctional images of oneself and one's world, Graywolf attempts to assist his clients to identify and transform those models that have permeated cognitive, affective, and physical functioning.

Janis was a client of Graywolf whose behavior reflected an excessive need for approval yet had been punctuated, of late, by unexpected and uncontrollable bursts of rage. One of Graywolf's procedures was hypnotic-like in that it utilized imaginative guided imagery to reach the "upper world," to reach the "lower world," or to "journey" back into a recalled dream. In an "upper world" session, Janis discovered herself as a "deserted child" and gained insight into an important source of her need for approval. In a "lower world" session, Janis began swaying and dipping like a snake. Convinced that she had discovered her "power animal," Janis repeated these movements daily, noticing that her angry outbursts began to diminish. Finding ways to restore self-esteem to her "child," and ways of expressing her "power animal" in her daily behavior, Janis was delighted to observe the termination of her outbursts.

On one occasion, Graywolf guided Janis back into a dream in which she shot her husband because he had not given her an expensive present. By imagining herself moving into the rage, she discovered a dark tunnel at the end of which was a red-faced baby crying desperately. In her fantasy, Janis picked up the baby, held it, and dried its tears. Later, she realized that the baby was herself at a younger age, experiencing a lack of attention that still upset her. The dream was an exaggerated account of her claims on her husband's care and affection; no matter how much he gave her, it was never enough to assuage the needs of the red-faced baby and the deserted child.

Janis understood that her dysfunctional image of being "nice" had begun to break down and that the uncontrolled bursts of rage had signified its demise. By reveling in the image and movements of the snake, rather than in her angry outbursts, she was able to enjoy a part of her that was not necessarily "nice" or "approved" but that was needed for her very survival. Graywolf worked with Janis, exploring the feelings accompanying the snakelike body movements to determine what new self-images they anticipated. An acceptance of her repressed sensuality, self-protection, and authenticity was possible because of her almost instant attraction to her "power animal." Her newly discovered self-acceptance and self-esteem were associated by Janis with a newly discovered enjoyment of life.

In this instance, Graywolf's procedures mirrored the findings of Frank and Frank (1991) that effective treatment procedures involve an emotionally charged, confiding relationship with a helping person in a healing setting; a conceptual scheme or myth that provides a plausible explanation for the client's symptoms and a ritual for resolving them; and a ritual that requires the active participation of both client and helper and that is believed by both to be the means of combating the patient's demoralization. With the help of Graywolf, Janis engaged in rituals that renewed her understanding, confidence, and enjoyment of herself and her life.

RESEARCH AND APPRAISAL

The prestigious *Journal of the American Medical Association* published a report of an apparently successful treatment of systemic lupus erythematosus (SLE) by a native healer (Kirkpatrick, 1981). In early 1977, a 28-year-old Philippine-American woman was diagnosed as having this disease, one which is notably resistant to treatment. After a year of unsuccessful medical attention, the patient returned to the remote Filipino village of her birth, contacting a local healer who then claimed to remove a curse that had supposedly been placed on her by a previous suitor. Within 3 weeks, she returned to face her skeptical physicians. She declined further medication, appeared to be in good health, and 23 months later gave birth to a healthy girl. The physician who authored the report concluded, "It is unlikely that this patient's SLE 'burned out.' . . . But by what mechanism did the machinations of an Asian medicine man cure active lupus nephritis, change myxedema into euthyroidism, and allow precipitous withdrawal from corticosteroid treatment without symptoms of adrenal insufficiency?" (Kirkpatrick, 1981, p. 137).

Kleinman (1980) conducted a follow-up study of 19 clients treated by Taiwanese *tang-kis*, or shamans, at a healing shrine. All clients were visited at their homes 2 months after their initial visit to the *tang-ki*. Interviews could not be held with 7 clients, but of the 12 interviewed, 10 (83%) reported at least partially effective treatment. Six (50%) regarded themselves as completely cured, and 2 (17%) were "treatment failures." The evaluations of family members were also considered, and the mother of one of the "failures" felt that the treatment would have been successful had her daughter continued for a longer period of time. The father of the other failure implied that his daughter's condition had worsened after treatment. Even though the sample was small, Kleinman noted that "there are virtually no other follow-up studies of indigenous practice." Even so, "these findings are in line with our findings from studies of other indigenous healers and our impressions from observation of large numbers of patients treated by

[the] *tang-ki*. . . . Even with these cautions in mind the results are striking" (p. 320).

A follow-up study of individuals treated by a shaman in South Korea was reported by Kim (1973), a psychiatrist. He noted that temporary symptom relief was obtained in the four cases he diagnosed as suffering from psychoneuroses. Of the eight cases he diagnosed as schizophrenic, six deteriorated following the shamanic ceremonies. In commenting on this report, Torrey (1986) claimed that "psychotherapists all over the world . . . are not effective with people who have brain disorders or diseases such as schizophrenia, and in fact some of these individuals may be made worse by psychotherapy" (p. 214).

Spiritualist healers in a rural community in Mexico were investigated by Finkler (1985), who found that their treatments were most effective for nonpathogenic diarrheas, simple gynecological disorders, psychosomatic problems, and mild psychiatric disorders. The former two ailments were treated with teas, enemas, and douches; the latter two by symbolic manipulations and ministrations (pp. 136–137). However, Finkler found that in most cases, by the patients' own accounts, spiritual practitioners failed to heal. Little change was noted in the case of serious physiological symptoms caused by physical or mental illness, probably because

> the living conditions will not have changed. The underlying factors instrumental in producing the disease expressed in physiological or somaticized symptoms continue in effect, including the unceasing flow of untreated sewage waters in the irrigation canals and the unremitting presence of disease vectors in the open garbage pits. Concomitantly, and equally to the point, violent deaths due to alcoholism and violence will continue, given the extant socio-structural conditions. (pp. 136–137)

Finkler also reported that in 50% of the cases, clients of the spiritualist healers claimed that they did not "feel sick," yet still reported symptoms. Of the 108 clients in the study, Finkler judged 30% to have had successful treatments, 35% to have had unsuccessful treatments, and the others to have had inconclusive or unclassifiable results.

Torrey (1986) surveyed indigenous psychotherapists, concluding (on the basis of anecdotal reports) that "many of them are effective psychotherapists and produce therapeutic change in their clients" (p. 205). Torrey observed that when the effectiveness of psychotherapy paraprofessionals has been studied, professionals have not been found to demonstrate superior therapeutic skills. The sources of that effectiveness are the four basic components of psychotherapy: a shared world view, personal qualities of the healer, client expectations, and a process that enhances the client's learning and mastery (p. 207). Strupp (1972) added, "The modern psychotherapist

. . . relies to a large extent on the same psychological mechanisms used by the faith healer, shaman, physician, priest, and others, and the results, as reflected by the evidence of therapeutic outcomes, appear to be substantially similar" (p. 277).

Katz (1982, 1984) conducted a 22-month field study among Fijian healers, recording data on 500 clients in one community who sought help during the course of a year. He noted that in 5% of the interactions, more than one type of healer was consulted. Overall, nearly 79% of the client–healer contacts were with the local nurse and 13% with the traditional healer. However, the latter saw each of his clients more times, so that the actual time spent in the respective healing efforts was about equal. The most frequent complaints were various aches and pains (35%). The nurse saw most of the cuts and wounds, whereas the traditional healer handled all of the requests for help against misfortune. However, Katz noted considerable overlap because of the ways in which clients conceptualized the problems and their etiology.

Additional research projects are needed to follow up the leads provided by these studies, and long-term follow-ups are needed to determine the stability of improvement. Expectation and excitement can produce dramatic short-term effects but may not demonstrate staying power. The hypnotic-like aspects of native healing are possibilities for fruitful investigation. Scales are now available to measure absorption, imagination, suggestibility, and other human capacities that might be related to long-term improvement. Most of these scales are amenable to modification and adaptation to non-Western populations. The instruments developed by Pekala (1991) to observe variations of consciousness are promising candidates for cross-cultural studies, as are the imagery scales developed by Achterberg and Lawlis (1984), which have been used in the prognosis of life-threatening illnesses. These imagery scales are especially suitable for cross-cultural research because they simply ask patients to draw images representing their disease, the treatment they are receiving for the disease, and their body's self-healing capacities. In one study, Achterberg and Lawlis's psychological and imagery measures predicted a disease's progress more accurately than did the patients' blood chemistries (p. 3).

Especially valuable are qualitative analyses of the experiences of both practitioners and their clients. I (Krippner, 1990) used questionnaires to study perceived long-term effects following visits to Filipino and Brazilian folk healers, finding such variables as "willingness to change one's behavior" to significantly correlate with reported beneficial modifications in health. Cooperstein (1992) interviewed 10 prominent alternative healers in the United States, finding that their procedures involved the self-regulation of their "attention, physiology, and cognition, thus inducing altered awareness and reorganizing the healer's construction of cultural and personal realities" (p. 99). Cooperstein concluded that the concept that most closely represented his data was "the shamanic capacity to transcend the personal self, to enter into multiform identifications, to access and synthesize alternative perspectives and realities, and to find solutions and acquire extraordinary abilities used to aid the community" (p. 121). Indeed, the shaman's role and that of the alternative healer are both socially constructed, as are their operating procedures and their patients' predispositions to respond to the treatment. It is important not only to study the effects of the hypnotic-like procedures found in native healing, but to accurately describe them and to understand them within their own framework.

CONCLUSION

After centuries of derision and neglect, the positive contributions of native healers are finally being given serious attention. In 1980, Nigerian legislators passed a law that integrated traditional healers into the state-run national medical health service. In Zimbabwe, the government has encouraged the *ngangas* to set up their own 8,000-member professional association (Seligmann, 1981). In Swaziland, traditional healers have been accorded equal professional standing with Western-oriented medical practitioners. In 1977, the United Malay National Organization, Malaysia's dominant political party, decided to promote the use of *bomohs* in the treatment of drug addicts.

The professionalization of shamanic and other traditional healers demonstrates their similarity to practitioners of Western medicine. Nevertheless, the differences cannot be ignored. Rogers (1982) has contrasted the Western and native models of healing, noting that in Western medicine, "healing procedures are usually private, often secretive. Social reinforcement is rare. . . . The cause and treatment of illness are usually regarded as secular. . . . Treatment may extend over a period of months or years." In native healing, however, "healing procedures are often public: many relatives and friends may attend the rite. Social reinforcement is normally an important element. The shaman speaks for the spirits or the spirits speak through him [or her]. Symbolism and symbolic manipulation are vital elements. Healing is of limited duration, often lasting but a few hours, rarely more than a few days" (p. 169).

Rogers (1982) has also presented three basic principles that underlie the native approach to healing: The essence of power is such that it can be controlled through incantations, formulas, and rituals; the universe is controlled by a mysterious power that can be directed through the meticulous avoidance of certain acts and through the zealous observance of strict obligations toward persons, places, and objects; and the affairs of humankind are influenced by spirits, ghosts, and other entities whose actions, nonetheless, can be influenced to some degree by human effort (p. 43). This worldview—which fosters the efficacy of hypnotic-like procedures—varies from locale to locale but is remarkably consistent across indigenous cultures. The ceremonial activities produce shifts of attending for both the healer and the client. The culture's rules and regulations produce a structure in which the clients' motivations can operate to empower them and stimulate their self-healing aptitudes.

Western practitioners of hypnosis use the same human capacities that have been used by native practitioners in their hypnotic-like procedures. These include the capacity for imaginative suggestibility, the ability to shift attentional style, the potential for intention and motivation, and the capability for self-healing made possible by neurotransmitters, internal repair systems, and other components of mind–body interaction. Hypnosis and hypnotic-like activity are complex and interactive and hence take different forms in different cultures. Yet, as with other forms of therapy, "the mask . . . crafted by the group's culture will also fit a majority of its members" (Kakar, 1982, p. 278).

In Malaysia, a World Federation of Mental Health workshop suggested collaboration between the university's department of psychiatry and the traditional *bomoh* practitioners. The psychiatrists objected, claiming that such a move would only confirm the prejudice against psychiatry as unscientific held by other departments in the medical school (Carstairs, 1973). However, by investigating ways in which different societies have constructed diagnostic categories and remedial procedures, therapists and physicians can explore novel and vital changes in their own procedures—hypnotic and otherwise—that have become obdurate and rigid. Western medicine and psychotherapy have their roots in traditional practices and need to explore avenues of potential cooperation with native practitioners of healing methods that may still contain wise insights and practical applications.

REFERENCES

Achterberg, J. (1985). *Imagery in healing: Shamanism and modern medicine.* Boston: Shambhala.

Achterberg, J., & Lawlis, G. F. (1984). *Imagery and disease.* Champaign, IL: Institute for Personality and Ability Testing.

Adair, J., Deuschle, K. W., & Barnett, C. R. (1988). *The people's health: Anthropology and medicine in a Navajo community* (rev. ed.). Albuquerque: University of New Mexico Press.

Agogino, G. A. (1965). The use of hypnotism as an ethnologic research technique. *Plains Anthropologist, 10,* 31–36.

Barber, T. X. (1969). *Hypnosis: A scientific approach.* New York: Van Nostrand Reinhold.

Belo, J. (1960). *Trance in Bali*. New York: Columbia University Press.

Bourguignon, E., & Evascu, T. (1977). Altered states of consciousness within a general evolutionary perspective: A holocultural analysis. *Behavior Science Research, 12*, 199–216.

Bowers, M. K. (1961). Hypnotic aspects of Haitian voodoo. *International Journal of Clinical and Experimental Hypnosis, 9*, 269–282.

Brown, D. P. (1977). A model for the levels of concentrative meditation. *International Journal of Clinical and Experimental Hypnosis, 25*, 236–273.

Brown, D. P., & Fromm, E. (1986). *Hypnotherapy and hypnoanalysis*, Hillsdale, NJ: Erlbaum.

Campbell, J. (1990). *Transformations of myth through time*. New York: Harper & Row.

Carstairs, G. M. (1973). Psychiatric problems in developing countries. *British Journal of Psychiatry, 123*, 271–277.

Cooperstein, M. A. (1992). The myths of healing: A summary of research into transpersonal healing experiences. *Journal of the American Society for Psychical Research, 86*, 99–133.

Dixon, R. B. (1908). Some aspects of the American shaman. *Journal of American Folklore, 21*(80), 1–12.

Erickson, M. H., Rossi, E. L., & Rossi, S. H. (1976). *Hypnotic realities: The induction of clinical hypnosis and the indirect forms of suggestion*. New York: Irvington.

Finkler, K. (1985). *Spiritualist healers in Mexico: Successes and failures of alternative therapeutics*. New York: Praeger.

Frank, J. D., & Frank, J. B. (1991). *Persuasion and healing* (3rd ed.). Baltimore: Johns Hopkins University Press.

Furst, P. T. (1977). "High states" in culture–historical perspective. In N. E. Zinberg (Ed.), *Alternate states of consciousness* (pp. 53–88). New York: Free Press.

Gergen, K. J. (1985). The social constructionist movement in modern psychology. *American Psychologist, 40*, 266–275.

Gergen, K. J. (1990). Therapeutic professions and the diffusion of deficit. *Journal of Mind and Behavior, 11*, 353–368.

Goodman, F. (1990). *Where the spirits ride the wind*. Bloomington: Indiana University Press.

Greenfield, S. M. (1992). Hypnosis and trance induction in the surgeries of Brazilian spiritist healer–mediums. *Anthropology of Consciousness, 2*(3–4), 20–25.

Gussow, Z. (1985). *Pibloktoq* (hysteria) among the polar Eskimo: An ethnopsychiatric study. In R. C. Simons & C. C. Hughes (Eds.), *The culture bound syndromes* (pp. 271–288). Boston: Reidel.

Hughes, C. (1985). Glossary of "culture bound" or folk psychiatric syndromes. In R. C. Simons & C. C. Hughes (Eds.), *The culture bound syndromes* (pp. 469–505). Boston: Reidel.

Jilek, W. G. (1982). *Indian healing: Shamanic ceremonialism in the Pacific Northwest today.* Blaine, WA: Hancock House.

Kakar, S. (1982). *Shamans, mystics and doctors: A psychological inquiry into India and its healing traditions.* New York: Knopf.

Kalweit, H. (1988). *Dreamtime and inner space: The world of the shaman.* Boston: Shambhala.

Katz, R. (1982). The utilization of traditional healing systems. *American Psychologist, 27,* 715–716.

Katz, R. (1984). Toward a paradigm of healing. *Personnel and Guidance Journal, 61,* 494–497.

Kim, H. (1973). Review of shamanist healing ceremonies in Korea. *Transcultural Psychiatric Research Review, 10,* 124–125.

Kirkpatrick, R. A. (1981). Witchcraft and lupus erythematosus. *Journal of the American Medical Association, 245,* 137.

Kirsch, I. (1990). *Changing expectations: A key to effective psychotherapy.* Pacific Grove, CA: Brooks/Cole.

Kleinman, A. (1980). *Patients and healers in the context of culture.* Berkeley: University of California Press.

Kluckholn, C., & Leighton, D. (1962). *The Navaho.* Garden City, NY: Anchor Books.

Krippner, S. (1987). Dreams and shamanism. In S. Nicholson (Ed.), *Shamanism: An expanded view of reality* (pp. 125–132). Wheaton, IL: Theosophical.

Krippner, S. (1989). A call to heal: Patterns of entry in Brazilian mediumship. In C. Ward (Ed.), *Altered states of consciousness and mental health: A cross-cultural perspective* (pp. 186–206). Newbury Park, CA: Sage.

Krippner, S. (1990). A questionnaire study of experiential reactions to a Brazilian healer. *Journal of the Society for Psychical Research, 56,* 208–215.

Krippner, S., & Bindler, P. (1974). Hypnosis and attention: A review. *American Journal of Clinical Hypnosis, 16,* 166–177.

Kroger, W. S. (1977). *Clinical and experimental hypnosis* (2nd ed.). Philadelphia: Lippincott.

Leacock, S., & Leacock, R. (1972). *Spirits of the deep: Drums, mediums and trance in a Brazilian city.* Garden City, NY: Doubleday.

Leighton, A. H., & Leighton, D. C. (1941). Elements of psychotherapy in Navaho religion. *Psychiatry, 4,* 515–523.

Lynn, S. J., & Rhue, J. (1988). Fantasy proneness: Hypnosis, developmental antecedents, and psychopathology. *American Psychologist, 43,* 35–44.

Lynn, S. J., & Rhue, J. (1991). An integrative model of hypnosis. In S. J. Lynn & J. Rhue (Eds.), *Theories of hypnosis: Current models and perspectives* (pp. 397–438). New York: Guilford Press.

McGregor, P. (1962). *The moon and the two mountains.* London: Souvenir Press.

Murphy, G. (1947). *Personality: A biosocial approach to origins and structure.* New York: Harper & Brothers.

Pekala, R. J. (1991). *Quantifying consciousness: An empirical approach.* New York: Plenum Press.

Price-Williams, D. (1975). *Explorations in cross-cultural psychology.* San Francisco: Chandler & Sharp.

Raboteau, A. J. (1986). The Afro-Brazilian traditions. In R. L. Numbers & D. W. Amundsen (Eds.), *Caring and curing: Health and medicine in Western religious traditions* (pp. 539–562). New York: Macmillan.

Richeport, M. M. (1992). The interface between multiple personality, spirit mediumship, and hypnosis. *American Journal of Clinical Hypnosis, 34,* 168–177.

Rogers, S. L. (1982). *The shaman: His symbols and his healing power.* Springfield, IL: Charles C Thomas.

Rouget, G. (1985). *Music and trance: A theory of the relations between music and possession.* Chicago: University of Chicago Press.

Sandner, D. (1979). *Navaho symbols of healing.* New York: Harcourt Brace Jovanovich.

Seligmann, J. (1981, September 21). The new witch doctors. *Newsweek,* p. 106.

Spanos, N. P. (1989). Hypnosis, demonic possession, and multiple personality: Strategic enactments and disavowals of responsibility for actions. In C. Ward (Ed.), *Altered states of consciousness and mental health: A cross-cultural perspective* (pp. 96–124). Newbury Park, CA: Sage.

Spanos, N. P., & Chaves, J. F. (1989). *Hypnosis: The cognitive–behavioral perspective.* Buffalo, NY: Prometheus Books.

Spanos, N. P., & Chaves, J. F. (1991). History and historiography of hypnosis. In S. J. Lynn & J. W. Rhue (Eds.), *Theories of hypnosis: Current models and perspectives* (pp. 43–78). New York: Guilford Press.

Strupp, H. H. (1972). On the technology of psychotherapy. *Archives of General Psychiatry, 26,* 270–278.

Topper, M. D. (1987). The traditional Navajo medicine man: Therapist, counselor, and community leader. *Journal of Psychoanalytic Anthropology, 10,* 217–249.

Torrey, E. F. (1986). *Witchdoctors and psychiatrists: The common roots of psychotherapy and its future.* New York: Harper & Row.

Vogel, V. J. (1990). *American Indian medicine.* Norman: University of Oklahoma Press. (Original work published 1970)

Ward, C. (1989a). The cross-cultural study of altered states of consciousness and mental health. In C. Ward (Ed.), *Altered states of consciousness and mental health: A cross-cultural perspective* (pp. 15–35). Newbury Park, CA: Sage.

Ward, C. (1989b). Introduction. In C. Ward (Ed.), *Altered states of consciousness and mental health: A cross-cultural perspective* (pp. 8–10). Newbury Park, CA: Sage.

Winkelman, M. (1984). A cross-cultural study of magico-religious practitioners. In R.-I. Heinze (Ed.), *Proceedings of the International Conference on Shamanism* (pp. 27–38). Berkeley, CA: Independent Scholars of Asia.

32

FORENSIC HYPNOSIS: THE APPLICATION OF ETHICAL GUIDELINES

PETER W. SHEEHAN and KEVIN M. McCONKEY

Is it imperative that strict rules concerning professional standards of conduct be formulated and put in place in the forensic setting? The answer must be *yes*, and this answer must be stated even more strongly when hypnosis is involved. It is essential that hypnosis be used "professionally" in the forensic settng. "Professionalism" implies the ability to speak and act authoritatively and responsibly and in a way that is good for the well-being of both individuals and society. Codes of ethics are essential in this endeavor because they guide, regulate, and legitimize the behavior of the professional.

It seems instructive to illustrate at the outset why a code of ethics is warranted in forensic hypnosis.

The preparation of this chapter was supported in part by a grant to both authors by the Criminology Research Council, and in part by grants to each author by the Australian Research Council. We are grateful for that support.

We are also grateful to Amanda Barnier, Scott Ferguson, and Rosemary Robertson for their help in the preparation of this chapter.

HYPNOSIS AND CODES OF ETHICS

Hypnosis is not communication in the usual sense of the word. It often involves an especially close interpersonal relationship (Kleinhauz & Beran, 1981) and, although occurring in a social context, can involve radical changes in ways of thinking (McConkey, 1988). Furthermore, hypnotized people tend not to critically analyze incoming information in detail (Kihlstrom, 1985), and this has important ramifications for the forensic setting. Beliefs of the hypnotist and of clients potentially influence the ways in which hypnotized clients respond. In addition, hypnosis may increase the volume of material recalled from memory, but there is no reliable increase in the accuracy of the material. Experiments demonstrating an increase in the accuracy of recalled material (e.g., Stager & Lundy, 1985) are relatively rare, and the laboratory conditions involved tend to be atypical (McConkey, 1988).

Although caution is recommended (in the form of ethical guidelines) with respect to hypnosis and the courtroom, it seems extreme to take the view that all hypnotically obtained information should be ignored. As Odgers (1988) noted, however, the fact that information is obtained during hypnosis may have a negative effect on the jury, especially in light of common misconceptions about hypnosis. Public conceptions (or misconceptions) regarding hypnosis are well outlined in the literature (e.g., McConkey & Jupp, 1985; McConkey, Roche, & Sheehan, 1989; Wilson, Greene, & Loftus, 1986). For instance, the general public believes that people can remember previously inaccessible material accurately with the aid of hypnosis and that hypnosis can vividly reinstate actual memories of victims or witnesses of crimes.

Risks exist in the forensic use of hypnosis. One example of the questionable use of hypnosis in the forensic setting was presented by Levitt (1990). In that case, hypnosis was used with a sexual assault victim who, up until that time, had been unsure as to the identification of her attacker. However, positive identification of an individual ensued from hypnosis. During the subsequent trial, the victim changed from being certain about this identification back to being uncertain (as she was prior to hypnosis). An appeal on behalf of the defendant was disallowed because it was decided by the court that the witness's uncertainty at trial indicated that the use of hypnosis had had a negligible impact on her memory. This view, however, is questionable, and it can be argued that hypnosis should not have been used in the first place. The need for well-thought-out ethical guidelines is apparent here. Not only did the victim oscillate between being not sure and being absolutely certain, but it is difficult to contend that the hypnotically induced positive identification of the defendant did not ultimately influence the jury, who convicted the defendant entirely on circumstantial evidence.

These same reservations are reflected by an American Medical Association (1985) report that contended that hypnosis can increase confidence in recalling events, with little or no change in the level of accuracy. This report also stated that a large volume of inaccurate material can emanate from hypnosis while confidence levels remain stable. Orne (1979) paralleled these conclusions when he stated that hypnosis can bolster and solidify the memories of a witness (be they tentative or otherwise) by means of the legitimizing impact of the hypnotic procedures. Hypnosis does not necessarily produce new and accurate information, but it can result in witnesses who are less susceptible to cross-examination, because of enhanced beliefs. Despite these problems, the literature warns us against having a closed mind regarding the use of hypnosis in the forensic setting.

Mutter (1990) suggested that "hypnosis can work to uncover repressed memory with proper inquiry techniques" (p. 258), and lucidly demonstrated this view with two case studies. In one case, hypnosis allowed the defendant to relax his mind and examine past events with no specific cuing. This led to the discovery of new physical evidence. In the second case, spontaneous age regression on the part of the hypnotized defendant revealed new information considered important enough by the court to order a stay of execution. The real issue in these cases is what constitutes "proper inquiry techniques." These apparently successful uses of forensic hypnosis must be tempered by the dangers of self-interest when suspects are hypnotized, especially when they may be simulating hypnosis (Orne, 1985). It has been shown very clearly that even experienced hypnotists can be unaware of the true status of the client. Orne (1985) also raised the issue of tactics commonly used by successful interrogators, such as causing psychological needs at the time of the interrogation to surface during the questioning period. The use of such procedures during hypnosis may lead to confessions that are not true.

We will now take a brief look at forensic hypnosis from a legal perspective. Although the central issue from any point of view is the accuracy of hypnotically refreshed memories, the legal profession has been mainly concerned with whether to allow hypnotic evidence and with the best safeguards to preserve the integrity of the information if hypnosis is to be allowed. In our view, there are additional professional issues concerned with the individual's response to hypnosis and his or her welfare after the session. However, as a background to the remainder of the chapter, we will turn briefly to a review of some of the recent history of the use of hypnotically enhanced testimony.

SOME RELEVANT CASES

In 1968, hypnosis was popularly seen as a way of refreshing memory. In particular, two courts of appeal (one in the United States and one in

Canada) allowed hypnotic evidence to influence the decisions made (*Harding v. State of Maryland,* 1968/1969; *R. v. Pitt,* 1968). Many courts subsequently followed the Harding decision in allowing hypnotic testimony; however, there emerged a growing awareness of problems with such testimony. Moreover, research showed that not only does hypnosis increase the likelihood of the production of false, or confabulated, memories, it also tends to increase the confidence of the hypnotized person in those memories (see Pettinati, 1988). Consequently, courts have now become very wary of using testimony derived from hypnotic sessions with witnesses and defendants, with many courts rejecting such testimony (Pinizotto, 1989).

In 1980, the Minnesota Supreme Court (*State v. Mack,* 1980) refused to admit the hypnotic testimony of a witness, and other jurisdictions, such as Pennsylvania, California, New York, and Massachusetts, followed suit. By 1983, the situation was such that the Maryland Court of Appeals reversed the original Harding decision (*State v. Collins,* 1983).

However, as Odgers (1988) concluded, the automatic exclusion of hypnotic evidence is inappropriate because there may be new information uncovered during the hypnosis session that the court may not then take into account, and thus justice might not be served. Furthermore, that information may be crucial evidence, particularly in the case of a traumatic incident, such as rape, resulting in amnesia.

The issue came to a head in 1987 with the case of *Rock v. Arkansas.* That decision mainly concerned the constitutional rights of defendants in criminal cases to defend themselves and to testify on their own behalf. A federal decision deemed it unconstitutional for a state to apply a rule excluding a criminal defendant's hypnotically enhanced testimony, the court noting that no evidence exists to suggest that such testimony is inherently reliable or unreliable. Such a rule was said to be an arbitrary restriction on the right to testify. The decision recommended that inaccuracies be reduced by the use of procedural safeguards concerning the hypnosis session, by the use of corroborating evidence, and also by instruction of the jury by the judge on the nature of hypnotic testimonies and the likely effects. On the basis of the ruling, a trial court was recently required to hold an *in camera,* pretrial hearing to test the reliability and admissibility of evidence after hypnosis (*State v. L.K.,* 1990).[1]

Although specific concerns involved in the matter of hypnosis in the legal setting (e.g., Mutter, 1990) are clearly relevant, the issues—both professional and ethical—are more intricate and complicated than they may appear at first. We now turn to a consideration of hypnosis in the broader context: how the guidelines or ethical principles of professionalism are applicable to the professional practice of forensic hypnosis.

---

[1]Readers interested in further detail on the admissibility of hypnotically enhanced testimony are referred to Shaw's (1991) review of hypnosis in criminal law, Hughes's (1991) article on civil law, and a history and analysis of the issue by Sies and Wester (1985).

PROFESSIONALISM AND ETHICAL CONDUCT

Professional occupations bring with them considerable social advantages and a particular status, and professionals in these occupations are expected to be able to speak and act authoritatively on matters of central importance to their clients (Sheehan, 1978). Professional bodies may endeavor to protect their members from external forces (Anderson & Western, 1972), and members may well have the final word on relevant matters when clients may have no other recourse (Freidson, 1970).

A strong profession must be able to convincingly claim that it has a profound level of knowledge in a given area. Paradoxically, as a sign of the expertise that they do have of this knowledge, professionals must be able to do harm to their clients (Goode, 1969). The literature strongly implies that the practice of forensic hypnosis should be viewed in professional terms; there are, however, certain aspects of the practice of hypnosis that may act effectively to undermine its potential usefulness in the legal field. For example, when hypnosis is performed by someone who lacks "professional psychiatric, medical, psychological, or dental training" (Kleinhauz & Beran, 1981, p. 149), as is often the case with stage hypnotism, grave consequences can follow. Kleinhauz and Beran (1981) gave a very clear example of the kinds of problems that can arise when hypnosis is placed in the hands of an inappropriately qualified individual. In the broader context, another instance in which hypnosis may violate the standards of good professionalism is where it is purportedly used to coerce people into behavior that they would not otherwise engage in, such as antisocial acts or out-of-character sexual behavior (Perry, 1979).

If hypnosis is to be accepted as a professional tool in the legal setting, a fundamental requirement is a comprehensive code of ethics that is designed to protect primarily the client and secondarily the professional members involved. It is important at this point to draw attention to the fact that, in 1979, both the Society for Clinical and Experimental Hypnosis (1979) and the International Society of Hypnosis (1979) detailed their codes of ethics in the form of formal resolutions concerning forensic hypnosis. Both societies stated in their resolutions that they view hypnosis by unqualified people with reservation and concern. Unqualified personnel can have objectives that are incongruent with the needs or health of the client; in the forensic setting, they may also have preconceived ideas regarding guilt and innocence. The societies contended that, when investigative hypnosis is used, it must involve properly trained psychiatrists or psychologists (or, presumably, dentists) who have experience in forensic hypnosis. They also stated that caution must be exercised with respect to what information is conveyed to the client before, during, and after hypnosis and that all interactions with the client at these times must be recorded on videotape.

Orne (1985) noted a number of factors that can pertain to the thrust of the societies' resolutions. For example, apparent aberrations in the very complex area of human behavior are cited, specifically the numerous "confessions" that result from well-publicized crimes, lucidly illustrating variants of behavior that are possible even in the absence of hypnosis. Moreover, Orne goes on to give the example of a person originally classified as a witness by investigative authorities, who then made self-incriminating statements during hypnosis. This effectively changed the status of the person in the investigation, but subsequent investigations cleared the individual as a suspect. Hence, the highly idiosyncratic modes of behavior and thinking of clients during hypnosis (Sheehan & McConkey, 1982) and the apparently inexplicable behavior of some individuals add considerable validity to the concerns expressed in the formal resolutions of the two societies.

Codes of ethics published by professional bodies are typically formulated to define what are "good" or "right" modes of conduct (Steere, 1984); despite this common aim, however, they vary greatly in length. The American Medical Association (1980) managed to outline its objectives in 10 sentences, whereas the American Bar Association (1980) required 48 pages of fine print. The point was made by Keith-Spiegel and Koocher (1985) that codes of ethics are necessarily clumsy instruments because they try to describe everything to everyone. Codes of ethics can also be guilty of being vague or even ambiguous (Keith-Spiegel & Koocher, 1985). Relatedly, Sieber (1982) outlined conditions that can result in ethical problems. These can include unforeseen situations because of inexperience or ignorance and ethical problems that are inadequately anticipated. Furthermore, an ethical problem may be foreseen, but suitable strategies may not be available to avoid it. Additionally, an ethical problem may materialize because of demands by the law or government policy, or because there are insufficient guidelines and laws pertaining to a particular situation.

The resolutions adopted by the Society for Clinical and Experimental Hypnosis (1979) and the International Society of Hypnosis (1979) were initiated primarily because experts in the field foresaw an increase in the number of situations in which hypnosis would be used in an ethically questionable manner. In this sense, the area of forensic hypnosis is fortunate in that it has foreseen a specific problem under specific circumstances, and, thus, the ensuing code of ethics has been able to have a concrete applicability to practice. This is a benefit that Fairbairn and Fairbairn (1987) pointed out may not be the case with all ethics codes. Undoubtedly, it is also important to note that guidelines have emerged in the United States (in particular) and other countries that reflect key legal decisions (Laurence & Perry, 1988; Scheflin & Shapiro, 1989).

A code of ethics that has both specific and broad characteristics and, thus, true applicability to practice is justified in the area of forensic hypnosis for several reasons: There is a very real potential for the misuse (inadvertent or otherwise) of hypnosis; the empirical literature does not necessarily implicate hypnosis as a viable tool to aid memory recall; and the idiosyncratic responsiveness of clients to hypnosis, combined with highly emotive legal cases such as assault, is clearly a potentially dangerous mixture, especially without appropriate guidelines being used for reference.

CLINICAL APPLICATIONS

Forensic hypnosis is subject to all of the major issues that confront practitioners in clinical situations (Sheehan, 1988). The points raised in this section are relevant principles that have been translated from the general clinical situation to the forensic setting. The practice of forensic hypnosis typically relates to a spectrum of clinical applications (Sheehan, 1988) that confront practitioners with a range of issues. The points discussed in this section need to be considered in relation to the forensic setting. Factors that require attention are the choice and the status of the person to be hypnotized, the relationship between emotion and recall in hypnosis, the implication of deception in hypnosis, and the importance of the civil rights of the person who is hypnotized.

To help illustrate the relevance of these factors, we will discuss them in relation to a specific case of suspected child abuse that has been reported by Sheehan, Andreasen, Doherty, and McCann (1986). The case deals with a person suspected of abuse who denied the accusations made against him. The application of hypnosis followed the guidelines for forensic practice set down by the American Medical Association (1985). The hypnosis session was not definitive in relation to the accusations, but it produced useful data for exploring events.

Choice of Person to be Hypnotized

In the forensic setting, individuals generally fall into one of three categories: witness, victim, or suspect. In the case of suspected child sex abuse, for example, the option of hypnotizing a child may not be a viable one because of the child's age. The case recounted by Sheehan et al. (1986) involved a 2½-year-old child, and the difficulties in simply questioning such an infant, let alone during hypnosis, clearly precluded hypnosis as an advisable or even a realistic possibility. There were in this instance no witnesses to the alleged offense(s), so if hypnosis was to be used, the most relevant person was the suspect himself.

A suspect may request hypnosis in the hope that clarification and enhanced recall of events will demonstrate what happened. Significantly, it should be acknowledged that suspects (as well as witnesses and victims) can be strongly motivated by self-interest, with little or no regard for the truth. The possibility of deception also exists. The choice of individual to be hypnotized is thus an important one, and unexpected anomalies, diversions, or biases must be anticipated.

A related point that, although rarely discussed in the forensic literature, needs to be considered is the hypnotizability of the person to be hypnotized. One cannot have an influence on someone who happens to be impermeable to that influence, and then expect relevant data. Thus, the use of forensic hypnosis is limited by the degree of trance that can be experienced by the person involved. It seems reasonable to assert that unless the person to be hypnotized is at least moderately susceptible (on the basis of, say, scores on standard hypnotic test instruments), then the session should not proceed.

Role of Emotion

Questioning a person about a topic that causes him or her to be emotionally aroused may result in subjective, rather than objective answers, that are very difficult to interpret. Despite this, hypnosis can be a viable tool that can be used to help overcome a memory block that is due to strong emotions (Smith, 1983; Udolf, 1983).

When the setting is a forensic (rather than a clinical) one, the occurrence of emotionally charged material may make it difficult for the hypnotist to function objectively or effectively. This may be particularly true for a hypnotist who is not extensively experienced in both the forensic and the clinical settings. Also, it is difficult to deal with information elicited under circumstances that change from being unemotional to suddenly very affect-laden. In this sense, the hypnosis session may give new information a degree of importance that may or may not be warranted. An incident not dissimilar to this occurred with the suspect described in the Sheehan et al. (1986) case. Specifically, two new memories were "brought out" during hypnosis (the suspect unknowingly being observed masturbating by his daughter, and the daughter on another occasion lifting her dress and "inviting" physical contact from the suspect) and communicated upon the termination of hypnosis. Considerable levels of emotion were associated with the relaying of these events. Interestingly, they did not implicate the suspect in illegal activity but went some way toward explaining accusations made against him.

Current guidelines designed for investigative hypnosis do not really take strong emotions into consideration. In particular, specific instruction is needed to indicate that strong affect is not necessarily indicative of an increased likelihood of the validity of statements associated with it. One must be both prepared for the potential heightened impact of strong emotions and alert to the ambiguities of its meaning.

Possibility of Deception

The possibility of deception is a major factor in forensic applications of hypnosis, and it warrants close consideration. The nature of human beings is such that a diverse range of deceptions is often found in their repertoire. The most basic deception related to forensic hypnosis is the feigning of trance. The evidence strongly suggests that it is possible for a highly experienced hypnotist to be unaware of the true hypnotic status of a client (Orne, 1977; Sheehan, 1972). Relatedly, many individuals accused of violent crime (e.g., sexual assault) claim amnesia for crucial events (Parwatikar, Holcomb, & Menninger, 1985), and there is a paucity of literature on the topic of discriminating real from simulated amnesia (Schacter, 1986).

In hypnosis, a client can deceive the hypnotist both intentionally and unintentionally. The client can certainly suffer from authentic memory loss regarding an important event, and while this persists the hypnotist is, in a sense, being deceived, but this may not be intentional on the part of the client. Another way that a client can unintentionally deceive the hypnotist is to recount pseudomemories that are not correct but that the client fully believes to be true (i.e., with subjective conviction).

Clients can also, however, intentionally deceive. For example, they may possess a willful intent to alter the truth, either by having a motivated unwillingness to report information or by reporting information that the client knows is false. The case of intentional deception during hypnosis may be more open to intervention than it at first appears, however. Consider, for example, the case reported by Spiegel and Spiegel (1984) in which it appeared that deception occurred during deep hypnosis. Close inspection of the case revealed that the client may not have been deeply hypnotized; thus, it can be suggested that lying during deep hypnosis is much less likely than faking the actual hypnotic state (Sheehan & McConkey, 1988). If this is the case, then deception in forensic hypnosis may be less likely than it appears. The real problem is that criteria need to be developed and applied that discriminate with a reasonable degree of confidence between deeply hypnotized clients and simulators (see Orne, 1977). It must be remembered that not all hypnotic clients in the forensic setting will be highly hypnotizable, and an important step in reducing the probability of deception in investigative hypnosis is to determine the true hypnotic status of the client. This may also assist in making judgments about the information provided by the person.

Civil Rights

With respect to the civil rights of the person being hypnotized in the forensic setting, it should be noted that current guidelines strongly advocate the absence of investigative personnel other than the hypnotist during the hypnosis session. As the guidelines stand at present, there is no problem with associated individuals being in an observation room. However, when these individuals can be seen in a threatening way by the client (e.g., they are police officers and the client is a suspect), then it could reasonably be argued that the depth of the client's involvement will be reduced. Furthermore, hypnosis involves a focused interpersonal relationship that occurs between two people when there is a hypnotist and one client (see Kleinhauz & Beran, 1981). The implied presence of people who are not involved directly in that relationship may well be contrary to the nature of the interaction between hypnotist and client that occurs during hypnosis.

Moreover, because all sessions should be videotaped anyway, there is ordinarily no justifiable reason for others to be present during the actual forensic session. The material that is captured on videotape should be sufficiently informative to provide an accurate and verifiable record of events. Overall, the inclusion of other individuals in hypnosis sessions is questionable, and in some instances may mean that there is an infringement of civil rights.

CASE MATERIAL

It seems instructive at this point to pursue some of the issues raised by the application of hypnosis in cases of sexual assault. This is an especially problematic area that necessarily demonstrates the adequacy (and inadequacy) of current guidelines.

Some Issues in Cases of Sexual Assault

The literature on rape trauma syndrome (e.g., Knopf, 1978; Nadelson, Notman, Jackson, & Gornick, 1982) clearly indicates that negative self-image results from attempted or actual sexual assault. Thus, it is important clinically to recognize the adaptive significance of changing self-perceptions to increase feelings of self-worth. Used correctly and professionally, hypnosis has the potential to reveal aspects of memory that could tangibly help in sexual assault investigations. There is possible damage, however, to women through the insensitive use of hypnosis when its purpose is investigative rather than clinical. For example, it is often not clear in cases of sexual assault what the real depths of the woman's traumatic reactions are to her highly stressful experience. It must be remembered that investigative hypnosis is not basically geared to provide therapy for the client; rather, it is aimed at isolating reports of events as they might have occurred.

In most cases of sexual assault, hypnosis is used when the corroboration of any information obtained is ordinarily impossible. Where corroboration is difficult, the weight of evidence is thrown on the reports of the victim. If it is assumed that someone who is hypnotized should subsequently not offer testimony, the use of hypnosis may be taking a needed advantage away from the victim.

Questions can also be raised about whether a case of sexual assault should involve a true investigation. There are major concerns that could throw the balance away from an investigative focus onto evidentiary issues. One might also argue that the use of hypnosis in such cases is unacceptably stressful. It is therefore necessary in such cases to provide some means for professional clinical support so as to alleviate experienced stress or any undue pressure created by hypnosis. It is essential, for example, that an experienced clinician be available to provide immediate and continuing care in a way that cannot be provided by the investigative hypnotist because of his or her particular role.

Following consultation about the expectations of the investigator, a decision to proceed has eventually to be made about the use of forensic hypnosis with a sexual assault victim. This is a delicate decision, however, and one needs to carefully consider whether the victim has sought clinical assistance because of the events being investigated and whether she is positively oriented toward the notion that hypnosis could be used to help her understand more fully the events in question and so enable her to regain self-esteem and feelings of competence and control. Although, ethically speaking, explicit guidelines must be followed, this is something of a double-edged sword: Because control is yielded to the "experts," genuine personal problems that may occur for the victim (either immediately or subsequently in court proceedings) can be attributed to the experts and their procedural guidelines.

Consistent with the general literature on rape trauma syndrome and posttraumatic stress disorder, special attention needs to be paid in the preinquiry associated with these cases to the possible symptoms of distress. Such symptoms include disorganization of life-style, indications of depression, recurring images of key past events, somatic complaints, and self-blame (for a comprehensive review, see Frazier & Borgida, 1985). Evidence can be observed of stress associated with traumatic events; of special relevance is the fact that clients may show evidence of memory impairment or of the avoidance of recollections of events. The hypnotist therefore needs to be aware of the network of support available to clients to cope with distress, and pay attention to how supportive and helpful the people are who surround a victim. The degree of stress and the amount of support will influence the exploration of memories of events, and although negative affect is typically the main focus in the crisis counseling of sexual assault, the forensic hypnosis area needs to emphasize more the cognitive aspects of a person's response. All interactions, however, should be supportive and recognize the potential destabilization that may be present.

Overall, one needs to assess whether there is potentially more to gain or to lose in using hypnosis forensically with victims of sexual assault. There are pitfalls for the unwary, but there may be advantages both for the victims themselves, in terms of enhancing their well-being, and for the investigation, in terms of facilitating its progression.

To examine some of these pitfalls, a number of further considerations when using forensic hypnosis with sexual assault victims can be outlined:

1. Who makes the decision to go ahead? This is a critical issue in cases where definite professional/ethical issues are of concern. The same person cannot make both the decision and be the hypnotist, because the amount of information that is needed to make the decision is more than what the hypnotist should have available. Similarly, the decision to go ahead should not be left in the hands of the investigating authority.

2. The choice of hypnotist is a further issue. The facts of some cases could be taken to counterindicate the use of a male hypnotist. Obviously, care should be taken in the choice of the sex of the hypnotist.

3. The issue above is also related to the sex of the accompanying clinician who provides continuing care. The presence of an experienced clinician is frequently implicated, both during the session and during follow-up.

4. It may be important to convey questions and suggestions to the hypnotist during the actual session, and these may originate with the clinician or the investigating authority. Not all questions should be relayed, however, and it may be necessary to use an appropriate "buffer" or "filter" for relevant communications.

5. The technical nature of the situation needs to be perfectly clear, especially when information is revealed that communicates strong feelings of negative self-worth. In this area, special care has to be taken to deal with the client's expressed uncertainty about who is listening and who has access to the recorded material.

6. In a session dealing with sensitive and emotionally charged material, the time required to conduct investigative hypnosis is necessarily long. Breaks are essential, and some monitoring of activity during those breaks is necessary to ensure that unwanted interactions between involved parties do not occur.

7. There are follow-up responsibilities in many cases, and these should be pursued and understood by all parties concerned. One is the provision of clinical care for clients shown to be at risk; another is making sure, as far as possible, that material

collected will not be misused by the investigating authority. Current guidelines say very little about what follows once the actual session has concluded.

RESEARCH AND APPRAISAL

It is evident from the literature cited earlier in this chapter that a significant issue of debate is the extent to which hypnotic memory reports can be considered to relate to the facts as independently established outside of the hypnotic setting. The relevance of this issue pervades the literature. The implications of our understanding of a range of clinical applications and research evidence may be summarized as follows.

Waking memory reports of clients may be inconsistent and not fully believed because of their inconsistency with other, objectively established evidence. In hypnosis, memory reports can be appreciably different from those given either previously or to the hypnotist in the prehypnosis session. In the prehypnosis session, the gist may be the same, but the details of the report need to be explored for accuracy. For example, in the hypnosis session, the report of an attack may be significantly different (e.g., not hit with a bottle but with a fist, or two males present rather than one) from what was said in a prehypnosis session. It is possible that a story reported in hypnosis is a distorted one, but it may also fit substantially with the version of the attack that has been established independently prior to hypnosis. The versions given to the police and in a prehypnosis session may fit well together, and distortion may characterize them both. And although distortion is often associated with hypnotic reports, it may be present out of hypnosis but not within it.

One plausible explanation of this pattern of data is that the story given previously (and perhaps also in the prehypnosis session) has been influenced by factors that distort memory more so than the story that is given during hypnosis. What might be responsible for the closer fit with established facts of the version given in hypnosis is not entirely clear. It could be the removal of external pressure to find a story to describe an assault, the elements of relaxation present in the hypnotic situation, more time being provided (in a relaxed setting) to produce a story, or the fact that questioning itself is less directive (questioning in hypnosis may also be less evaluative than in the standard interrogatory interview).

Major concern is clearly focused in the research literature on the issue of the reliability and accuracy of the information produced during forensic hypnosis. The general view is that hypnosis has a limited use in practice, and accuracy of the reports cannot be guaranteed. There is considerable evidence concerning the limitations of hypnosis, and there is a broad consensus that practitioners of forensic hypnosis should be appropriately qualified.

Some Difficulties With Current Guidelines

The guidelines for forensic hypnosis currently recommended for adoption are clear, but they contain potential difficulties. The whole session is videotaped, only the hypnotist and client are present during the hypnosis session, a memorandum is prepared of "basic facts" of the case for the hypnotist, and the hypnotist is kept unaware of specific (critical) details of the case.

The conduct of a session according to these guidelines raises a number of relevant points, and it seems useful to outline them in light of our experience with clinical applications. These points have wider applications than to cases of sexual assault and are noted here for their general relevance to forensic hypnosis.

1. It is sometimes very difficult to formulate the correct amount of detail for a memorandum to the hypnotist about the case. In certain cases, for example, it might be useful for the hypnotist to know that the client has a record of "inconsistent reporting." However, such information could prejudice the hypnotist about the kind of memory that is being investigated. On the other hand, knowledge of particular memories given in the past could clarify details given in a session in a very useful way. For example, efforts made by the client to recall a car license plate may point to useful strategies for facilitating memory retrieval. In light of the forensic utility of hypnosis as an investigative tool, a case might be made that specific information should be given to the hypnotist between the fact-gathering and the hypnosis components of the session. In this way, future questioning in hypnosis can be more productive.

2. The rights of clients are frequently relevant in individual cases. A false confession can result in a serious injustice as the result of hypnosis. One therefore needs to carefully consider procedures that protect the rights of clients, as well as to ensure that useful information can actually be produced.

3. The guidelines, as they are now formulated, pay relatively little attention to the risks of pursuing particular lines of questioning. It should be noted that when high stress is being experienced, as in cases of sexual assault, a line of inquiry may produce forensically useful material but may also be personally damaging to the client who is experiencing stress.

4. Existing guidelines are not procedurally oriented in ways that address the shifting status of the person who is being hypnotized. At one point in a session, for example, the person

who is hypnotized may assume the status of a neutral witness. At another point in the session, however, that status may alter (e.g., when implied involvement in the events under question becomes evident).

5. It should be further recognized that the time necessary to implement the guidelines in an ethical way is actually quite extensive. Proper guidelines are not easy to implement, and the technical requirements for their application are demanding. This is not an argument for taking less time or using fewer resources, but for the need to educate others (who do apply them).

As with all issues dealing with ethical practice, there are risks associated with guidelines that are not appropriate or are misapplied. We now consider a number of these more closely.

Possible Risks

Although a subject or client may be superficially motivated and cooperative, resistance may be evident to the induction of hypnosis through routine procedures. Consider, for example, clients who state repeatedly during induction that they are not under hypnosis or that their mind is a blank. If this is accepted by the hypnotist, then the session would probably not proceed further. It is essential that the hypnotist be skilled enough to handle resistance of this kind and have available a range of techniques to induce hypnosis and probe resistance if it is judged to be present.

Again, although a client may be consciously motivated and cooperative, he or she may experience substantial difficulty in accessing relevant memories or experiences. There may be attempts to draw the hypnotist away from relevant material, and hypnotists who have not been trained clinically or who have no experience with the forensic setting may not be able to manage this problem. There are techniques, however, that can help (e.g., the use of "hidden observer" procedures and "automatic writing" techniques), and they provide useful ways around resistance that can facilitate access to material that may be psychologically important.

As discussed earlier in this chapter, clients often display emotion in investigative situations, and strong emotion can accompany the memories or experiences that come forward. The balance of forensic and clinical priorities in these circumstances is a difficult one to assess, and judgment about them ought not to be made by a person who has no real knowledge of hypnosis, the clinical aspects of its application, and the possible risks of its application in the forensic setting. The relatively untrained hypnotist may create long-term problems. Even after a session is completed, the nature of the conflict that has been experienced may not be clear. One could be dealing with an unstable personality, or one could be faced with an anxiety reaction to a traumatic episode. Knowledge of these alternatives is important in making decisions about what to do and what not to do in the hypnotic situation, especially where stress is present and being experienced.

Finally, one needs to be alert for the possible sequelae of hypnosis, or for "symptoms" of a client's involvement in hypnosis. A client may wake up with a headache, indicate being sick in the stomach, or express some other clear unease. In such instances, the possibility exists of unsuggested effects. Anticipation of the probability that effects may persist is essential, and appropriate procedures must be used to deal with all outcomes. Again, experience is essential.

CONCLUSION

Broadly speaking, two decisions must be made in relation to the use of hypnosis in the forensic setting. The first is whether to use it. The second is who is best suited to its application under the circumstances.

If the decision has been made to proceed with hypnosis, benefits must be seen in its use. Such benefits may take the form of a refreshed memory that can be checked independently, or a determination of the state of mind of the involved person when the crime was allegedly committed.

A complex set of motivational factors comes into play once the decision to use hypnosis has been taken. There may be (if the person is truly hypnotized) the usual motivational factors associated with hypnosis, such as a desire to please the hypnotist, but there may be other, extrinsic motivational factors at work as well. Victims may in some cases have reasons for wanting innocent people convicted, and this is vividly illustrated in the cases discussed by Orne (1979) and documented by others (e.g., Laurence & Perry, 1988). A suspect may also have a very strong desire to show that he or she is innocent (or even guilty). Finally, it is probably very rare in the forensic setting to find any party who is emotionally neutral.

The question of whether to hypnotize a person who is involved in a criminal case is a difficult one to address. Lying, for instance, is a possibility. Some theorists believe that it is possible to lie while under hypnosis (e.g., Altman & McLeod, 1982; Orne, 1961), whereas others are more hesitant in the matter (e.g., Sheehan, 1989). A further complication is that people in general believe that lying under hypnosis is difficult (McConkey & Jupp, 1985; Wilson et al., 1986), and although most theorists would agree with this, it is the degree of difficulty that is the issue.

Emotional involvement is especially complicated in the case of suspects, who usually have a strong desire to be cleared of a crime. Orne (1985) urged extreme caution in the interpretation of material gleaned from hypnosis used with suspects. Numerous examples of hypnosis being used in this situation have been cited in the literature (e.g., Allison, 1984; Mutter, 1990; Sheehan et al., 1986; Watkins, 1984), with varying degrees of success. Until the 1970s, the main use of hypnosis in criminal cases was with people defending a murder charge, primarily to lift alleged amnesias (Laurence & Perry, 1988). The issue of its use with suspects is not a new one, but with the increase in knowledge about hypnosis and its potential unreliability, much more caution is now advocated.

The guidelines state that the witness or the victim should be evaluated prior to hypnosis. A problem here is that it is implied that suspects are unsuitable for hypnosis. However, victims and witnesses, as well as suspects, may have inappropriate motives. Caution is required with them as well because their motives can bring about unexpected results.

The need for ethical practices is primarily due to the fact that professionalism is lost without guiding principles designed to respect and promote the well-being of all individuals involved. The nature of forensic hypnosis is one of profound complexity, and it clearly needs to be guided by expert, responsible opinion in the form of comprehensive ethical guidelines. Adequate guidelines can act as a brace to support the profession against a wide variety of forces, such as individuals who ask to be hypnotized for unethical reasons or unqualified people who wish to use it on purported witnesses and victims of crime. Although the ethical considerations of the various methods of interrogation that may be used by unqualified people are not directly in the scope of this chapter, they are nevertheless highly relevant.

Existing guidelines are ethically sensitive and go some way toward coping with an area that includes possible deception, abuses of civil rights, and the question of who should be hypnotized and when. However, they ought to be considered only a beginning, because they are not adequate to deal with the full range of situations that can arise.

One specific issue that was discussed in this chapter is emotion and its ethical handling in the forensic setting. With respect to emotion, violence and sex crimes have a special capacity to evoke strong and sudden affect, and this is not fully accounted for in the current guidelines. This must be rectified because affect-laden situations are serious and demand an unerringly ethical response, and because such crimes are among those that are increasing in Western countries and that are likely to reach the courtroom more frequently.

Comprehensive guidelines are clearly needed to increase the likelihood of the successful application of forensic hypnosis and to reduce the possibility of injustices. Failure to do so will directly undermine claims of proper professional conduct. However, guidelines merely focus on the general situation, and the decision to proceed or not to proceed must always be made on an individual basis.

REFERENCES

Allison, R. B. (1984). Difficulties in diagnosing the multiple personality syndrome in a death penalty case. *International Journal of Clinical and Experimental Hypnosis, 32*, 102–117.

Altman, B., & McLeod, G. (1982). Hypnotism: Its utilization in criminal law. *New York Bar Journal, 54*, 377–386.

American Bar Association. (1980). *Model code of professional responsibility and code of judicial conduct.* Washington, DC: Author.

American Medical Association. (1980). *Principles of medical ethics.* Chicago: Author.

American Medical Association, Council on Scientific Affairs. (1985). Scientific status of refreshing recollection by the use of hypnosis. *Journal of the American Medical Association, 253*, 1918–1923.

Anderson, D. S., & Western, J. S. (1972). Professional socialization. In F. J. Hunt (Ed.), *Socialization in Australia* (pp. 288–306). Sydney, Australia: Angus & Robertson.

Fairbairn, S., & Fairbairn, G. (1987). *Psychology, ethics and change.* London: Routledge & Kegan Paul.

Frazier, P., & Borgida, E. (1985). Rape trauma syndrome evidence in court. *American Psychologist, 40*, 984–993.

Freidson, E. (1970). *Professional dominance: The social structure of medical care.* Chicago: Aldine–Atherton.

Goode, W. J. (1969). The theoretical limits of professionalization. In A. Etzioni (Ed.), *The semi-professions and their organizations: Teachers, nurses, social workers* (pp. 266–314). New York: Free Press.

Harding v. State of Maryland (1968), 5 Md. App. 230. cert. denied, 395 U.S. 499 (1969).

Hughes, L. R. (1991). Hypnosis in the civil case: The problem of confabulating plaintiffs and witnesses. *Florida Bar Journal, 65*, 25–30.

International Society of Hypnosis. (1979). Resolution. *International Journal of Clinical and Experimental Hypnosis, 27*, 453.

Keith-Spiegel, P., & Koocher, G. P. (1985). *Ethics in psychology: Professional standards and cases.* New York: Newbery Award Records.

Kihlstrom, J. F. (1985). Hypnosis. *Annual Review of Psychology, 36*, 385–418.

Kleinhauz, M., & Beran, B. (1981). Misuses of hypnosis: A medical emergency and its treatment. *International Journal of Clinical and Experimental Hypnosis, 29*, 148–161.

Knopf, O. (1978). Sexual assault: The victim's psychology and related problems. *Mount Sinai Journal of Medicine, 45*, 1–13.

Laurence, J. R., & Perry, C. (1988). *Hypnosis, will, and memory: A psycho-legal history.* New York: Guilford Press.

Levitt, E. E. (1990). A reversal of hypnotically "refreshed" testimony: A brief communication. *International Journal of Clinical and Experimental Hypnosis, 38,* 6–9.

McConkey, K. M. (1988). A view from the laboratory on the forensic use of hypnosis. *Australian Journal of Clinical and Experimental Hypnosis, 16,* 71–81.

McConkey, K. M., & Jupp, J. J. (1985). Opinions about the forensic use of hypnosis. *Australian Psychologist, 20,* 283–291.

McConkey, K. M., Roche, S. M., & Sheehan, P. W. (1989). Reports of forensic hypnosis: A critical analysis. *Australian Psychologist, 24,* 249–272.

Mutter, C. B. (1990). Hypnosis with defendants: Does it really work? *American Journal of Clinical Hypnosis, 32,* 257–262.

Nadelson, C., Notman, M. T., Jackson, H., & Gornick, J. (1982). A follow-up study of rape victims. *American Journal of Psychiatry, 139,* 1266–1270.

Odgers, S. J. (1988). Evidence law and previously hypnotized witnesses. *Australian Journal of Clinical and Experimental Hypnosis, 16,* 91–102.

Orne, M. T. (1961). The potential uses of hypnosis in interrogation. In A. D. Biderman & H. Zimmer (Eds.), *The manipulation of human behavior* (pp. 169–215). New York: Wiley.

Orne, M. T. (1977). The construct of hypnosis: Implications of the definition for research and practice. *Annals of the New York Academy of Science, 296,* 14–33.

Orne, M. T. (1979). The use and misuse of hypnosis in court. *International Journal of Clinical and Experimental Hypnosis, 27,* 311–341.

Orne, M. T. (1985). The use and misuse of hypnosis in court. *Critical Issues in American Psychiatry and the Law, 2,* 211–245.

Parwatikar, S. D., Holcomb, W. R., & Menninger, K. A. (1985). The detection of malingered amnesia in accused murderers. *Bulletin of the American Academy of Psychiatry and Law, 13,* 97–103.

Perry, C. (1979). Hypnotic coercion and compliance to it: A review of evidence presented in a legal case. *International Journal of Clinical and Experimental Hypnosis, 27,* 187–218.

Pettinati, H. M. (Ed.). (1988). *Hypnosis and memory.* New York: Guilford Press.

Pinizotto, A. S. (1989). Memory and hypnosis: Implications for the use of forensic hypnosis. *Professional Psychology, Research and Practice, 20,* 322–328.

R. v. Pitt, 68 D.L.R. (2D) 51 (1968).

Rock v. Arkansas, 107 S.Ct. 2704 (1987).

Schacter, D. L. (1986). Amnesia and crime: How much do we really know? *American Psychologist, 41,* 286–295.

Scheflin, A. W., & Shapiro, J. R. (1989). *Trance on trial.* New York: Guilford Press.

Shaw, G. M. (1991). The admissibility of hypnotically enhanced testimony in criminal trials. *Marquette Law Review, 75,* 1–77.

Sheehan, P. W. (1972). *The function and nature of imagery*. New York: Academic Press.

Sheehan, P. W. (1978). Psychology as a profession and the Australian Psychological Society. *Australian Psychologist, 13*, 303–324.

Sheehan, P. W. (1988). Issues in the forensic application of hypnosis. *Australian Journal of Clinical and Experimental Hypnosis, 16*, 103–111.

Sheehan, P. W. (1989). Lying in hypnosis. In A. F. Bennett & K. M. McConkey (Eds.), *Cognition in individual and social contexts* (pp. 497–506). Amsterdam, The Netherlands: Elsevier.

Sheehan, P. W., Andreasen, A., Doherty, P., & McCann, T. (1986). A case of the application of guidelines for investigative hypnosis. *Australian Journal of Clinical and Experimental Hypnosis, 14*, 85–97.

Sheehan, P. W., & McConkey, K. M. (1982). *Hypnosis and experience: The exploration of phenomena and process*. Hillsdale, NJ: Erlbaum.

Sheehan, P. W., & McConkey, K. M. (1988). Lying in hypnosis: A conceptual analysis of the possibilities. *Australian Journal of Clinical and Experimental Hypnosis, 16*, 1–9.

Sieber, J. E. (1982). Ethical dilemmas in social research. In J. E. Sieber (Ed.), *The ethics of social research: Surveys and experiments*. New York: Springer-Verlag.

Sies, D. E., & Wester, W. C. (1985). Judicial approaches to the question of admissibility of hypnotically repressed testimony: A history and analysis. *De Paul Law Review, 35*, 77–124.

Smith, M. C. (1983). Hypnotic memory enhancement of witnesses: Does it work? *Psychological Bulletin, 94*, 387–407.

Society for Clinical and Experimental Hypnosis. (1979). Resolution. *International Journal of Clinical and Experimental Hypnosis, 27*, 452.

Spiegel, D., & Spiegel, H. (1984). Uses of hypnosis in evaluating malingering and deception. *Behavioral Sciences and the Law, 2*, 51–64.

Stager, G. L., & Lundy, R. M. (1985). Hypnosis and the learning and recall of visually presented material. *International Journal of Clinical and Experimental Hypnosis, 33*, 27–34.

State v. Collins, 296 Md. 680 (1983).

State v. L.K., 244 N.J. Super 261, 582 A.2d 297 (1990).

State v. Mack, 292 N.W. 2d 764 (1980).

Steere, J. (1984). *Ethics in clinical psychology*. London: Oxford University Press.

Udolf, R. (1983). *Forensic hypnosis: Psychological and legal aspects*. Lexington, MA: Lexington Books.

Watkins, J. G. (1984). The bianchi (L.A. Hillside Strangler) case: Sociopath or multiple personality? *International Journal of Clinical and Experimental Hypnosis, 32*, 67–101.

Wilson, L., Greene, E., & Loftus, E. F. (1986). Beliefs about forensic hypnosis. *International Journal of Clinical and Experimental Hypnosis, 34*, 110–121.

AUTHOR INDEX

Numbers in italics refer to listings in reference sections.

Abraham, S. F., 383, *393*

Achterberg, J., 625, 640, 695, 712, *714*

Adair, J., 697, *714*

Adams-Tucker, C., 466, *474*

Adler, G., 143, *145*

Agogino, G. A., 692, *714*

Agras, S., 313, *331*

Agras, W. S., 156, *168*, 600, *615*

Aja, J. H., 534, 536, 540, *549*

Alberts, G., 56, *69*

Alexander, F., 217, *228*

Allington, H. V., 630, 638, 640, *645*

Allison, R. B., 735, *736*

Alman, B., 206, *211*, 537, 548, *552*

Alman, G. M., 518, *528*

Alpert, J. J., 587, *614*

Alpert, M., 535, 536, 540, 542, *549*

Altman, B., 734, *736*

Ambrose, G., 385, *393*

American Bar Association, 724, *736*

American Medical Association, 19, *20*, 721, 724, 725, *736*

American Psychiatric Association, 282, *289*, 312, 319, *331*, 496, 506, 556, *581*, 587, *614*

American Psychological Association, 4, *20*, 650, *668*

Amigó, S., 158, *168*

Andersen, M. S., 38, *50*, 535, 536, 540, 542, *549*, 612, *614*

Anderson, B. P., 479, *490*

Anderson, D., 723, *736*

Anderson, W. L., 158, *170*

Anderton, C. H., 37, 38, 44, *54*, 158, *171*, 219, *231*, 237, *249*, 527, 532, 534, 539, 542, 544, *552*, 556, 583, 625, 637, *643*

Andreasen, A., 725, 726, 735, *738*

Andreassi, J. L., 608, *614*

Andrews, G., 166, 167, *168*

Aneshensel, C. S., 473, *476*

Angus, L. E., 303, *305*

Anstadt, S. P., 594, *619*

Antrobus, J. S., 473, *476*

Araoz, D., 182, *183*, 190, *211*, 352, *354*

Argyle, M., 288, *289*

Armstrong, L. A., 605, *618*

Arrindell, W. A., 312, 313, *331*

Asher, R., 631, 634, 640, 645

Ashkanazi, G. S., 576, 577, 578, 579, *581*, 584

Atkinson, G., 43, *54*, 259, 270, 324, 327, 336, 496, *508*

Atkinson, R., 589, 612, *621*

Aurela, A., 292, *305*, 456, *474*

Averback, A., 101, *117*

Azikri, D., 95, 102, 104, *119*

Baer, D. M., 67, 68, *70*

Baer, L., 176, *184*, 322, 324, *332*, 556–557, 573, 574, 577, 578, 579, *581*, 584

Baisden, B. S., 182, *186*

Baker, E. L., 49, 50, 62, *69*, 143, *145*, 259, 265, 267, 425, 445, *447*

Baker, S., 158, *168*

Bálint, M., 277, *289*

Balke, B., 666, *669*

Balma, D. L., 325, 326, 327, *334*

Balson, P. M., 456, *475*

Baltruweit, W. J., 19, *22*

Bandler, R., 39, 47, *50*, 79, 90, 205, 206, *211*

Bandura, A., 152, *168*, 237, *247*, 557, *581*

Bank, W. O., 208, *211*

Banyai, E., 11, *20*, 143, *145*, 272, 285, 286, 287, 288, *289*, 290, 594, *614*

Barabasz, A. F., 285, 286, 287, *290*, 313, 314, 315, 316, 317, 320, 321, 322, 323, 324, 325, 326, 328, 329, *331*, *332*, *333*, 335, 556–557, 574, 577, 578, 579, *581*, 584, 594, 605, *614*

Barabasz, M., 285, 286, 287, *290*, 313, 316, *231*, 322, 324, 325, *332*, 335, 535, 536, 539, 541, 542, 543, *549*,

739

556–557, 574, 577, 578, 579, *581,*
584, 594, 605, *614*
Barber, J., 49, *50,* 237, 244, *247,* 265, 267,
512, 518, *528*
Barber, T. X., 41, 43, *50,* 77, 78, *90,* 93,
152, 153, 154, *168,* 169, 240, 249,
471, 473, 478, 511, 512, 516–517,
520, 521, *528, 531,* 557, *581,* 594,
614, 621, 625, 633, 637, 640, *641,*
646, 664, 665, 666, 668, 691, *714*
Bargh, J. A., 594, *619*
Barkley, R. A., 571, *581*
Barlow, D. H., 156, *168*
Barnes, A. R., 75, *92*
Barnes, M., 675, *688*
Barnett, C. R., 697, *714*
Barnett, E., 340, *354*
Barondess, J. A., 591, *619*
Barrett, A. M., 358, *381*
Barrett, D., 98, *117*
Barrios, A., 87, *90*
Barsky, A. J., 587, *614*
Barton, R. D., 157, 163, 164, *170*
Basham, R. B., 599, *618*
Basker, M. A., 557, 572, 579, *581,* 584
Bates, B. L., 166, *168,* 246, *247,* 597, 612,
614
Baucom, D. H., 226, *228*
Beahrs, J. O., 440n, *447*
Bean, W., 207, *213,* 518, *531*
Beaumont, P. J. V., 383, *393*
Beck, A., 152, 157, *168,* 215, 216, 219,
221, 228, 342, 344, *354*
Beck, B. E. F., 298, *305*
Beigel, A., 479, *490*
Bellack, A. S., 154, 165, *168*
Belo, J., 696, *715*
Benbenisty, R., 505, *508*
Benedict, B. D., 502, *506*
Bennett, H., 207, *213,* 518, *531*
Benton, D., 614, *617*
Beran, B., 95, 102, 104, *118, 119,* 720,
723, 728, *736*
Bergan, J. R., 67, *70*
Bergin, A. E., 56, *69*
Berkowitz, M. K., 444, *448*
Bernard, M. E., 174, *183*
Bernheim, H., 32, 42, 46, *51,* 174, *183*
Bernstein, E. M., 473, *475*
Bernstein, G. S., 66, 67, *69*

Bertrand, L., 30, *54,* 80, *90,* 235, *247,* 514,
517, *528*
Berven, N. L., 66, *70*
Berwick, P., 434, 444, *447*
Bespalec, D., 556, 571, 579, 580, *582*
Best, J., 574, *581*
Betts, G. H., 327, *332*
Bibb, B. C., 19, *21*
Biddle, W. E., 444, *447*
Bindler, P., 692, *716*
Biran, M., 226, *228*
Biró, G., 280, *289*
Bischofshausen, S., 302, *305*
Blackmore, S. H., 678, *688*
Blanchard, E. G., 595, *614*
Bliss, E. L., 143, *145,* 253, 267, 325, 326,
327, *332, 336,* 505, *508*
Bloch, B., 624, 628, 629, 639, *641,* 644
Block, A. P., 480, *490*
Bloom, E. T., 614, *617*
Bloom, L. J., 74, *90*
Bloom, P. B., 675, 678, *687*
Boekelheide, P. D., 466, *475*
Boisvenue, M. E., 605, *618*
Bolkovatz, M. A., 466, *478*
Bolles, R. C., 152, *169*
Bolocofsky, D. N., 535, 536, 538n, *541,*
543, 544, 548, *549*
Bonjour, J., 624, *641*
Borgida, E., 729, *736*
Bornstein, P. H., 535, 536, 539, *541,* 542,
543, *549*
Botts, P., 372, *380*
Botvin, G. J., 557, *581*
Bouchard, T. J., 598, *619*
Bourguignon, E., 692, 693, *715*
Boutin, G. E., 182, 183, 227, *229*
Bower, G. H., 505, *506*
Bowers, K., 41, *51,* 79, *90,* 190, *211,* 218,
222, 229, 246, *247,* 472, *475,* 542,
549, 594, *615,* 625, *641*
Bowers, M. K., 425, 444, *447, 448,* 692,
715
Bowers, P., 592, 609, *614*
Boxer, A. M., *252, 263,* 264, 265, *267*
Boyd, P., 292, *308,* 471, *478*
Boyko, E., 575, 578, *583,* 584
Bozymowski, M. F., 650, *670*
Bradley, P. W., 654, 661, *669*
Braid, J., 27, *51*
Brant, R., 458, *475*

Bray, G. A., 534, *549*

Brecher, S., 444, *448*

Brende, J. O., 502, *506*

Brenman, M., 24, 25, 44, 45, *51, 52,* 60, 61, *70,* 98, 102, 114, *118,* 128, 140, 142, *146,* 190, *212,* 384, *393, 427, 448*

Brentar, J., 98, 99, 100, 105, 112, 116, *117,* 117, *119,* 142, *145*

Brett, P. J., 238, 241, 245, 249, 517, *532*

Breuer, J., 493, 502, *506*

Brice, G. L., 573, *582,* 584

Briere, J., 456, *475*

Brodie, E. I., 536, *549*

Brody, N., 87, *92*

Brooke, R., 611, 612, *168*

Brooks, R. B., 292, *305,* 456, 461, 462, *475*

Brooks, S., 75, *92*

Brown, A., 312, 313, 324, 325, 326n, 327, 328, 330, *333*

Brown, D. K., 67, *70*

Brown, D. P., 25, 26, 39, 40, *51,* 58, 59, 61, *70,* 124, 129, 143, *145,* 252, 263, 264, 265, 267, 279, 289, 297, 298, *305,* 315, *333,* 425, 445, 448, 474, *475,* 511, 514, 526, 527, *529* 692, 701, *715*

Brown, D. R., 657, 664, 666, 669

Brown, J., 521, *529*

Brown, J. F., 520, *529*

Brown, J. M., 520, *529*

Brown, J. W., 587, *614*

Brown, M., 34, *54*

Brown, P., 292, 302, 304, *306*

Browne, A., 458, 467, *475*

Brownell, K. D., 546, *549*

Brunet, A., 296, *306,* 593, *615*

Bryant, R. A., 19, *21,* 142, *146*

Buhk, K., 292, 308, 471, *478*

Bunney, M. H., 627, *641*

Burge, S. K., 479, *490*

Burgess, A. W., 480, *490*

Burke, J., 339, *355*

Burnes, D., 342, *354*

Burrows, G., 95, 101, 102, 103, *118,* 325, 326, 329, *334,* 340, *354,* 574, 576, 577, 578, 579, *581,* 582, *584*

Bush, T., 587, *616*

Bushnell, J., 315, 325, 326, *333*

Buza, K., 329, *335*

Byrne, J. P., 456, 478, 480, *491*

Cabianca, W., 67, *71*

Calverley, D. S., 512, 517, *528*

Cameron, O., 312, *337*

Campbell, J., 699, *715*

Çangello, V. W., 514, *529*

Cardeña, E., 324, *336,* 495, 496, 505, *506,* 508

Carey, R. J., 573, 578, 579, *581,* 584

Carkhuff, R. R., 66, 67, *72*

Carlson, B., 98, 99, 100, 105, *117,* 117, *119,* 142, *145*

Carmichael, H. T., 682, *687*

Carney, R., 206, *211,* 518, *528*

Carrington, P., 265, *267*

Carstairs, G. M., 714, *715*

Cautela, J. R., 265, *267*

Chalmers, D., 626, 633, 634, 637, 639, *642,* 646

Chandrasena, R., 646, 631, *641*

Channon, L. D., 535, 536, 540, 544, *549*

Chaves, J. F., 5, 20, *22,* 43, 50, 77, 78, 90, *92,* 152, 165, *170,* 240, *247,* 511, 512, 516–517, 520, 521, 522, 524, 526, 527, 528, *529, 531, 532,* 637, 640, 691, 692, *717*

Chertok, L., *641,* 645

Chester, T. D., 594, 612, *615*

Chevron, E., 342, *355*

Chlouverakis, C., 534, *549*

Chu, J. A., 495, *507*

Cikurel, K., 272, 285, 287, *289*

Claiborn, C. D., 220, *229*

Clark, L. A., 598, *619*

Clarke, G. H. V., 632, 633, 638, *641,* 647

Clarke, J. H., 237, *247*

Clawson, T. A., 629, *641,* 645

Clement, C. A., 302, *306*

Clum, G. A., 227, *230,* 623, *641*

Cochrane, G. J., 535, 536, 537, 539, 541, 542, *549*

Coe, W., 43, *53,* 77, *91, 92,* 95, 96, 99, 100, 105, ·*117,* 117, 152, *170,* 205, *211,* 236, *247,* 515, *529*

Coggeshall, L. T., 682, *687*

Cohen, N. L., 535, 536, 540, 542, *549*

Cohen, S. B., 40, *51*

Cole, J., 302, *305*
Collen, M. F., 587, *615*
Collins, J. K., 535, 536, 537, 540, 542,
    544, 545, 546, *549*, 550, *551*, *553*
Collison, D. R., 37, *51*
Colwell, S., 367, *381*
Comer, S. L., 19, *22*
Conn, J. H., 104, *118*
Conroy, A. M., 594, 612, *615*
Conroy, M., 372, *381*
Cook, E. W., III, 313, 327, *333*
Cooper, B., 520, *528*
Cooper, L. F., 264, *267*
Cooperstein, M. A., 712, *715*
Copeland, D., 256, *267*, 445, *448*
Corley, D., 182, *183*
Cormier, L. S., 67, *71*
Cormier, W. H., 67, *71*
Cornwell, J., 574, 577, 578, 579, *581*, 584
Cosier, F., 611, 612, *618*
Costa, P. T., 590, 598, *614*
Coué, E., 174, *183*
Coulthard-Morris, L., 535, 536, 538n, 541,
    543, 544, 548, *549*
Council, J. R., 11, *21*, 88, 91, 141, 142,
    147, 153, 165, *170*, *171*, 238, *248*,
    517, *530*, 594, 597, 609, 611, *614*,
    616
Couper, L., 623, *641*, 644
Coyne, J. C., 599, *615*, 616
Crasilneck, H., 59, *70*, 218, *229*, 237, *247*,
    251, 258, 264, 265, *267*, 340, *354*,
    385, *511*, *550*, *530*, 535, 536, 537,
    573, 575, 577, *581*, 584
Crawford, H. J., 96, 97–98, 103, *118*, 142,
    146, 302, 306, 312, 313, 323, 324,
    325, 326n, 327, 328, 329, 330,
    331, *333*, *334*, 497, *508*, 573, *581*
Crepaldi, G., 534, *550*
Cross, W. P., 238, *249*, 517, *532*
Crowson, J. J., 594, 612, *615*
Culbert, T., 372, 378, *381*
Curtis, G. C., 312, *337*
Cuthbert, B. N., 313, 327, *333*, *335*
Cymerman, A., 661, *669*

Dakof, G., 599, *615*
Dallosso, H. M., 558, *581*
Daly, P. F., 358, *381*
Dantzer, R., 593, *615*
Dardeck, K., 193, *213*

Das, J. P., 594, *615*
Dash, J., 237, *248*
Davidson, T. M., 246, *247*
Davies, T., 623, *641*, 644
Davis, B., 533, 544, *552*
Davis, J. M., 292, 306, 456, *475*
Davis, S., 536, 540, *550*
Dawson, J. G., 536, 540, *550*
Day, H. D., 205, *212*
de Groh, M., 19, *22*, 517, *532*
de Groot, H. P., 517, *532*
de Jong, R., 227, *229*
DeBetz, B., 535, *552*
Decenteceo, E. T., 219, *230*
Deckert, G. H., 95, 104, *120*
Deikman, A. J., 125, *146*
DeJulio, S. S., 56, *70*
DeLongis, A., 599, *615*, 616
Deltito, J., 176, *184*
Dempster, C. R., 55, 58, 60, 61, 66, *70*,
    71, 456, *475*
Dennerstein, L., 95, 101, 102, 103, *118*
d'Eslon, C., 27, *51*
Despert, J. L., 456, *475*
Detre, T., 600, *617*
Detrick, D., 446, *450*
Deuschle, K. W., 697, *714*
Devine, D. A., 160, *169*, 535, 536, 539,
    541, 542, 543, *549*, 550
Dewhirst, B., 636, 637, 639, 640, *642*, 648
Deyoub, P. L., 535, 536, 538n, 539, 540,
    542, 544, *550*
Diamond, M. J., 42, 43, *51*, 80, *91*, 235,
    236, 245, *247*
Diamond, S., 523, *530*
Dikel, W., 372, *380*
Dill, D. L., 495, *507*
Dillman, N., 605, *618*
Diment, A. D., 141, *146*
Dinello, F. A., 533, *552*
Dinges, D. F., 24, 25, 35, 38, 39, 40, *53*,
    315, *336*, 597, 612, *614*
Dingwall, E. J., 512, *530*
Dixon, M., 296, 306, 593, *615*
Dixon, R. B., 698, *715*
Dlugokinski, L. J., 305, *307*
Doherty, P., 725, 726, 735, *738*
Dollard, J., 588, *615*
Dondershine, H., 325, 330, *336*, 505, *508*
Doney, T., 520, *529*
Donoghue, J., 570, 571, *582*

Donovan, P., 593, *618*
Dorsey, M. F., 67, *70*
Douglas, D., 434, 444, *447*
Dowd, E. T., 4, 175, 182, *185*, 205, *211*, *212*, 217–218, 219, 220, 221, 223, 225, *229*, *230*
Drake, S. D., 440n, *449*
Dreaper, R., *641*, 645
Dreyfuss, D. A., 95, 102, 104, *119*
Drinkwater, B. L., 666, *669*
Drossman, D. A., 590, 591, *615*
Dryden, W., 174, 175, *184*
Dryer, B. V., 682, *687*
Dubin, L. L., 675, *688*
Dubreuil, S. C., 636, 637, 639, 640, *642*, 648
Dudek, S. Z., 631, 639, *641*, *643*, 646
Dunbar, K. D., 49, *54*, 206, *214*
Duncan, J. H., 587, *615*
Duterte, B. O., 458, *477*
Dymond, R. F., 67, *71*
Dywan, J., 594, *615*

Early, L. W., 682, *688*
Ebert, B. W., 456, *475*, 480, *490*
Echterling, L. C., 101, *118*
Edelson, J., 227, *229*
Edelstein, B., 56, *69*
Edelstien, M. G., 57, *70*
Edinger, J. D., 116, *118*
Edmonston, W., 11, *20*
Eisen, M., 60, *70*, 129, 133, 135, 137, *146*, 456, *475*
Eisenberg, A. R., 440n, *448*
Eisenlohr, E., 634, 638, *642*, 647
Eli, I., 95, 103, *119*
Eliade, M., 272, *289*
Elie, R., 446, *448*
Ellickson, K. A., 654, 655, 657, 661, *669*
Ellis, A., 152, *169*, 173, 174, 175, 178, 181, 182, *184*, 215, 216, 219, 221, *229*, 315, 334, 600, 603, *615*
Embry, L. H., 67, 68, *70*
Emery, G., 152, 157, *168*, 342, 344, *354*
Emmelkamp, P. M. G., 312, 313, *331*
Emmerling, D. A., 101, *118*
Eng, A., 557, *581*
Engel, G. L., 604, *615*
Engstrom, D. R., 594, 605, *615*
Enzi, G., 534, *550*
Epstein, L., 558, *582*
Epstein, W. L., 626, *642*

Erickson, C. J., 378, *380*
Erickson, M., 46, 47, 48, *51*, 79, *91*, 188, 189, 190, 191, 192, 193, 206, 209, *212*, 218, 222, 229, 251, 264, *267*, 296, *306*, 341, 345, *354*, 385, 386, *393*, 433, 434, 444, 448, 512, *530*, 537, *550*, 677, 688, 698, *715*
Esdaile, J., 493, *507*
Estabrooks, G. H., 265, *267*
Evans, F. J., 446, *449*, 497, *508*, 594, 612, *617*
Evans, H. I. 480, *490*
Evans, M. B., 302, 303, *306*
Evascu, T., 692, 693, *715*
Evers-Szostak, M., 473, *475*
Ewart, C. K., 600, *615*
Ewin, D. M., 625, 629, 639, *641*, 644
Eysenck, H. J., 151, *169*, 598, *615*, 666, 668
Eysenck, M., 593, 598, *617*
Eysenck, S. B. G., 598, *615*

Fahey, J. L., 614, *617*
Fairbairn, G., 724, *736*
Fairbairn, S., 724, *736*
Falmagne, R. J., 302, *306*
Falzett, W. C., 205, *212*
Fanurik, D., 471, *477*
Faw, V., 99, *118*
Fazio, R. H., 156, *169*
Federn, P., 131, *146*
Feffer, H., 590, *621*
Feinstein, A., 505, *507*
Feldman, R., 587, *615*
Fenichel, O., 125, 128, *146*
Fenner, F., 624, *643*
Ferenczi, S., 124, *146*
Ferguson, J. D., 238, *249*
Ferguson, S. R., 19, *22*
Fernald, P. S., 160, *169*
Ferster, C. B., 535, 546, *550*
Fezler, W., 385, *393*, 535, 537, 544, 545, 546, *551*
Ficton, J. R., 518, *530*
Fiedler, F. E., 67, *70*
Finegold, M., 57, *70*
Finkelhor, D., 455, 458, *475*, *476*
Finkler, K., 711, *715*
Fisch, R., 210, *212*
Fish, J., 76, *91*
Fisher, A. G., 544, *552*
Fisher, G., 636, 637, 639, 640, *642*, 648

Fishers, J. R., 265, 269
Fiske, D. W., 75, 92
Fitzpatrick, J. L., 227, 229
Flaxman, J., 237, 249, 535, 536, 538, 539, 541, 542, 553
Fleming, B., 154, 169
Flor, H., 588, 589, 615
Flynn, D. M., 245, 249
Foenander, G., 325, 326, 329, 334
Folkman, S., 599, 615, 616
Ford, J. D., 56, 70
Fordyce, W. E., 239, 247
Forel, A. H., 46, 51
Foreyt, J. P., 546, 550
Fowler, C. A., 302, 306
Frank, B. M., 227, 229
Frank, E., 479, 490
Frank, J. B., 693, 700, 706, 710, 715
Frank, J. D., 26, 51, 74, 91, 237, 247, 693, 700, 706, 710, 715
Frank, R. G., 576, 577, 578, 579, 581, 584
Frankel, F. H., 39, 40, 51, 127, 146, 324, 325, 326, 327, 328, 334, 483, 490, 623, 641
Franklin, J., 227, 229
Franks, C. M., 110, 119
Franks, P., 576, 582, 584
Frary, R. B., 312, 313, 336
Frauman, D., 106, 142, 148
Frazier, P., 729, 736
Freeman, A., 154, 169
Freidson, E., 723, 736
Fremouw, W. J., 227, 230
Freud, S., 27, 44, 52, 123, 124, 146, 156, 169, 493, 497, 502, 506, 507
Frey, C., 440n, 448
Friedberg, F., 175, 182, 184, 217–218, 219, 220, 221, 230
Friedlander, J. W., 28, 52
Friedman, A. P., 523, 530
Friedman, H., 238, 247
Friesen, J., 535, 536, 539, 541, 542, 549
Frischholtz, M. A., 325, 326, 327, 329, 336
Frischholz, E. J., 325, 326, 334, 446, 450, 495, 497, 507, 508
Fritzler, D., 588, 618
Fromm, E., 25, 26, 39, 40, 43, 49, 51, 52, 58, 59, 60, 61, 70, 102, 103, 104, 106, 107, 109, 110, 112, 113, 118, 124, 125, 126, 127, 129, 133, 135, 140, 141, 145, 146, 252, 256, 257, 263, 264, 265, 266, 267, 268, 279, 288, 289, 290, 297, 298, 305, 315, 333, 425, 445, 448, 474, 475, 511, 514, 526, 527, 529, 539, 550, 692, 715
Fuller, J., 182, 184, 186
Furst, P. T., 695, 715

Gabora, N. J., 636, 637, 639, 640, 640, 648
Gall, N., 526, 531
Gallagher, M., 207, 213, 518, 531
Gardner, G., 33, 52, 257, 268, 357, 367, 374, 377, 380, 381, 457, 476
Gardner, R., 292, 306, 456, 476
Garfield, S. R., 587, 615
Garner, D. M., 534, 550
Garrett, J. B., 594, 619
Garrow, J. S., 534, 550
Garver, R. B., 656, 668
Gearan, P., 166, 169
Geiser, R. L., 465, 476
Gelfand, R., 37, 53, 542, 552, 557, 571, 582
Gendlin, E. I., 67, 71
Gentry, W. R., 575, 582, 584
Gergen, K. J., 692, 693, 694, 715
Gerrig, R. J., 292, 302, 303, 306
Gerschman, J. A., 325, 326, 329, 334
Gerton, M. I., 103, 118
Gfeller, J. D., 242, 245, 246, 248
Gibb, H., 296, 306
Gibbons, D. E., 11, 20, 155, 169, 466, 476
Gibbs, R. W. Jr., 292, 302, 303, 306
Gill, M., 24, 25, 44, 45, 51, 52, 60, 61, 70, 98, 102, 114, 118, 128, 140, 142, 146, 190, 212, 384, 393, 427, 448
Gilmore, J. B., 220, 230
Gilmore, S. L., 614, 617
Givens, D., 471, 477
Glasgow, R. E., 580, 581
Glass, G. V., 3, 19, 22, 116, 120, 153, 166, 167, 170
Glass, L. B., 153, 169
Glover, F. S., 534, 536, 540, 550
Glucksberg, S., 302, 306
Glucksman, M. L., 265, 268
Gold, E. R., 456, 476
Goldberg, G., 95, 102, 104, 119

Goldblatt, P. B., 544, *551*

Golden, W. L., 175, 182, *184*, *185*, 217–218, 219, 220, 221, *230*

Goldfried, M. R., 219, *230*

Goldknopf, E. F., 358, *381*

Goldstein, Y., 15, *20*, 535, 536, 538, 541, 545, *550*

Gomes-Schwartz, B., 458, 476

Goode, W. J., 723, 736

Goodman, F., 695, *715*

Gorassini, D. R., 80, *91*, 166, *169*, 245, 246, 248, 517, *530*

Gorcey, M., 479, 490

Gordon, J. R., 558, 582

Gordon, M. C., 34, *52*

Gormaly, J., 526, *531*

Gornick, J., 728, *737*

Gorton, B. E., 664, 665, 666, 668

Gottlieb, S. K., 626, 634, 637, 639, 642, 643, 644, 647

Gould, R., 260, 268

Granone, F., 237, 248

Gravitz, M. A., 3, 6, 20, 103, *118*

Green, J., 457, 472, 476, 477

Green, J. P., 142, *145*

Green, J. T., 98, 100, 104, *118*, *119*

Greene, E., 720, 734, *738*

Greene, J., 182, *185*

Greenfield, S. M., 706, *715*

Greenson, R. R., 623, 624, 629, *642*, 644

Greenwald, A. G., 588, *615*

Gregory, M. E., 303, 306

Gregson, R. A. M., 324, *332*

Greguss, A. C., 272, 285, 286, 287, 289, 290

Grieger, R., 152, *169*, 174, *184*

Grimm, L. G., 160, *169*

Grinder, J., 39, 47, 50, 79, 90, 205, 206, *211*

Gross, L., 445, 449

Gross, M., 386, 393

Grossack, M., 182, *185*

Groth-Marnat, G., 544, *551*

Grueling, J. W., 575, *582*, 584

Gruen, R., 599, *616*

Gruenberg, E., 339, *355*

Gruenewald, D., 44, *52*, 61, *70*, 264, 265, 268

Grumbles, D., 327, *334*

Gruzelier, J., 272, 285, 287, 289, 329, *333*

Guenther, R. K., 440n, *448*

Guidano, V. F., 216, 217, *230*

Gumm, W. B., 205, *212*

Gur, R. C., 594, *615*

Gussow, Z., 693, *715*

Gwynn, M. I., 19, *22*, 43, *54*, 87, 92, 627, 630, 636, 637, 638, 639, 640, *642*, 648

Gwynne, P. H., 182, *185*, 186

Habeck, B. K., 313, 314, *334*

Haberman, M., 102, *118*

Hackett, T. P., 237, *249*, 626, 630, 634, 637, 639, 642, 643, 644, 647

Hadley, S. W., 116, *118*

Hafen, B. Q., 534, *551*

Hafner, L. P., 88, *91*

Hageman, W. J., 312, *331*

Haley, J., 79, *91*, 188, 191, 206, 210, *212*, 361, 380

Haley, S. A., 502, *507*

Halifax, J., 272, 290

Hall, D. W., 575, 577, 579, *583*, 584

Hall, H., 379, 380

Hall J., 59, *70*, 104, *118*, 218, 229, 251, 258, 264, 265, 267, 340, *354*, 385, 393, 511, *530*, 535, 536, 537, *550*

Hall, R. C. W., 59, *615*

Hamel, J., 98, 109, *119*

Hammer, A. G., 141, *146*

Hammond, C. D., 265, 268

Hammond, D. C., 49, *52*, 192, *212*, 296, 304, 305, 306

Hanin, Y. L., 651, 654, 656, 668

Hanley, F. W., 536, *551*

Harper, R. A., 174, 175, *184*

Harsher-Towe, D., 593, *616*

Hart, H. H., 125, *147*

Hartman, B. J., 182, *185*, 536, *551*

Hartmann, H., 125, *147*

Harvey, R., 166, 167, *168*

Hastings, J. E., 571, *581*

Hazler, R. J., 67, *70*

Healy, J. M., 223, *229*

Heesacker, M., 173, *185*

Heimel, A., 367, *381*

Hellier, F. F., 632, 641, 646

Helstrup, T., 302, *306*

Helzer, J., 339, *355*

Henrich, G., 227, *229*
Henry, D., 205, *212*
Henry, S., 292, 308, 471, *478*
Heppner, P., 173, *185*
Herman, J., 455, 476, 495, *507*
Hersen, M., 154, 165, *168*
Hershman, S., 95, 101, *119*, 537, *551*
Heyman, S., 325, 326n, 327, 328, 330, *333*
Hickling, E. J., 595, *614*
Hilgard, E. R., 4, 7, 11, 20, *20–21*, 28, 30, 31, 32, 33, 34, 35, 39, 40, 41, 52, *53, 54*, 77, 78, 79, 87, *91, 92, 97,* 98, 103, 105, 111, *118*, 120, 127, *147*, 153, 161, *169*, 190, 206, *212, 214*, 236, 238, 248, 264, 265, 268, 272, 282, 285, 286, 287, 289, 290, 321, 324, 326n, 328, 330, *334, 337*, 383, *393*, 471, 472, 476, 477, 497, *507, 508*, 511, 512, 528, 530, 539, *553*, 573, 576, 581, 583, 594, 597, *614, 616, 619*, 631, *643*
Hilgard, J. R., 20, *21*, 34, 35, 36, 37, 39, 43, 49, *52, 53*, 62, 63, *70, 71*, 95, *96, 97–98*, 98, 102, 103, 105, 111, 118, 141, 142, *146, 147*, 207, *213*, 265, 268, 317, 320, 326n, *335*, 377, 378, *380, 381*, 457, 471, 476, 495, 497, *507*, 511, 527, 530, 572, 577, *582*
Hillman, J., 294, *306*
Hindi-Alexander, M., 574, 578, 583, 584
Hingst, A. G., 205, *212*
Hipple, T. E., 67, *70*
Hirota, K., 666, *669*
Hodgins, D. C., 30, *54*
Hoellen, B., 182, *185*
Hoffmann, C., 471, *477*
Hogan, M., 372, *380*
Holcomb, W. R., 727, *737*
Hollander, B., 325, 326, *334*
Holmstrom, L. L., 480, *490*
Holroyd, J., 237, *248*, 256, 265, *268*, 571, 576, 577, 579, *581, 582, 584*
Horne, D. J. de L., 325, 326, *334*, 576, 577, 578, 579, *582, 584*
Horne, R. L., 325, *336*, 387, *394*, 446, *449*, 594, 612, *617*
Horowitz, J. M., 458, *476*
Horowitz, M. J., 294, 298, *307*
Horowitz, M. R., 574, 578, 583, 584
Horowitz, S. L., 329, *334*
Horstman, D. H., 661, *669*

Horvath, S. M., 66, *669*
Hotaling, G. T., 455, *476*
House, J. F., 599, *616*
Howard, L., 182, *185*
Howard, W. L., 227, *230*
Huba, G. J., 473, *476*
Hugdahl, K., 329, *334*
Hughes, C., 693, *715*
Hughes, L. R., 722n, *736*
Hull, C. L., 7, *21*, 153, *169*, 664, 665, 666, 668
Humphreys, A., 313, 329, *334*
Hunt, T., 325, 330, *336*, 505, *508*
Hunt, W., 556, 571, 579, 580, *582*
Hurt, S. W., 252, 263, 264, 265, *267*
Hyman, G. J., 576, 577, 578, 579, *582, 584*

Ikai, M., 650, *668*
International Society of Hypnosis, 723, 724, *736*
Isaacs, C. D., 67, 68, *70*
Iwata, B. A., 67, *70*

Jackson, H., 728, *737*
Jackson, J. A., 237, *247*
Jackson, T. L., 571, *581*
Jacobs, W. J., 216, 217, *230*
Jacobson, E., 154, *169*, 177, 178, *185*
Jacobson, L., 209, *213*
Jacobson, R., 116, *118*
James, W., 4, *21*, 27, *52*, 558, *581*
Jamieson, G. A., 19, *21–22*
Jamner, L. D., 598, 609, *616*
Janet, J., 384, *393*
Janet, P., 102–103, *118*, 384, *393*
Janis, J., 485, *490*
Javel, A. F., 574, 578, *582, 584*
Jeans, M. E., 589, *619*
Jeffrey, L. K., 575, 576, *582, 584*
Jeffrey, T. B., 575, 576, *582, 584*
Jencks, S. F., 587, *616*
Jensen, M. R., 598, 609, *616*
Jeppsen, E. A., 325, 326, 327, *336*
Jilek, W. G., 696, *716*
John, R., 325, 326, *334*
Johnson, L. S., 142, *148*, 238, 248, 264, 266, *268*
Johnson, M., 301, *307*
Johnson, R. F. Q., 633, 641, *646*

Johnson, W. R., 182, *185*, 650, 651, 652, 653, 654, 656, 659, 662, 663, 664, 665, 666, 668
Johnston, E., 570, 571, *582*
Johnston, J. C., 627, 628, 635, 637, 638, 639, 640, *642*, 647, 648
Jones, B., 238, *249*
Judah, S. M., 174, 182, *186*, 227, *230*
Judd, F. K., 95, 101, 102, 103, *118*
Jupp, J. J., 535, 536, 537, 540, 542, 544, 545, 550, 551, 720, 734, *737*
Justice, B., 458, 465, *476*
Justice, R., 458, 465, *476*

Kahn, S., 126, 141, *146*, 256, 263, 266, 267
Kakar, S., 714, *716*
Kallen, D. J., 534, *551*
Kalweit, H., 696, *716*
Kamens, I. M., 537, *551*
Kanfer, F. H., 160, *169*
Kanner, A. D., 599, *616*
Kaplan, G. M., 321, 324, 331, *332*
Kardiner, A., 493, 502, *507*
Katon, W., 587, *616*
Katz, N., 153, 165, *169*, 245, *248*
Katz, R., 712, *716*
Kauders, O., 123, *148*, 427, *450*
Kaufert, J., 575, 578, 583, *584*
Kazdin, A. E., 154, 165, *168*
Keefe, F. J., 598, *618*
Keim, I., 456, *476*
Keim, J., 456, *476*
Keith-Spiegel, P., 724, *736*
Kelly, P., 41, *51*, 625, *641*
Kelly, S. F., 325, 326, 327, *334*
Kemper, S., 296, 302, *307*
Kennedy, S. K., 43, *54*, 639, *642*
Kenny, D. A., 11, *21*, 142, *147*, 153, *170*
Kernberg, O., 425, *448*
Kestenbaum, C., 292, *307*
Keysar, B., 302, *306*
Khalsa, S., 440n, *449*
Kierkegaard, S., 266, *268*
Kiesler, D. J., 67, *71*
Kihlstrom, J. F., 4, *21*, 30, 39, 41, *52*, 153, 169, 218, *230*, 302, *307*, 588, 593, 616, 617, 720, *736*
Kim, H., 711, *716*
King, D. R., 594, *616*
King, N. J., 312, 313, 314, *335*, *336*

King, W., 265, *269*
Kingsbury, S. J., 143, *147*
Kirkpatrick, R. A., 710, *716*
Kirsch, I., 4, 11, 15, 20, *21*, 42, *53*, 88, 89, 91, 92, 141, 142, *147*, 152, 153, 155, 156, 157, 158, 161, 163, 164, 165, 166, 167, *168*, *169*, *170*, *171*, 206, 209, *212*, *213*, 238, 248, 352, 355, 517, 530, 548, 597, 609, 611, 612, *616*, 625, 638, *641*, 695, 696, 698, 699, 708, *716*
Klein, G. A., 302, *307*
Kleinhauz, M., 95, 102, 103, 104, *118*, *119*, 720, 723, 728, *736*
Kleinman, A., 598, *617*, 693, 705, 710, *716*
Klerman, G., 342, *355*, 587, *614*
Kletti, R., 505, *507*
Kline, M. V., 535, 536, 537, *551*
Klinger, E., 471, *476*
Kloosman, A., 14, *22*
Kluckholn, C., 698, *716*
Kluft, R. P., 102, *119*, 143, *147*, 261, *268*, 313, 329, *335*, 495, *507*
Knight, R. P., 45, *51*
Knight, T. A., 594, *619*
Knopf, O., 728, *736*
Knowles, M. S., 674, *688*
Koester, P., 325, 326, 327, *336*
Kogan, L. G., 446, *449*, 594, 612, *617*
Kohen, D. P., 364, 367, 369, 372, 374, 380, *381*
Kohut, H., 425, *448*
Kolko, D. J., 456, *476*
Koocher, G. P., 724, *736*
Kopp, M. S., 329, *335*
Kosa, J., 587, *614*
Koss, M. P., 480n, *490*
Kossak, H. C., 315, *335*
Kosslyn, S. M., 302, *307*, 358, *381*
Kost, P. F., 102, *119*
Kraemer, H. C., 600, *615*
Kraft, W. A., 678, *688*
Kramer, G. R., 650, *668*
Krantz, D. S., 593, 600, *616*
Krasner, L., 528, *530*
Krass, J., 535, 536, 537, 545, 546, 550, *553*
Kratochwill, T. R., 67, *70*
Krippner, S., 692, 695, 702, 712, *716*
Kris, E., 125, *147*, 678, *688*
Kristeller, J. L., 588, 598, 609, *619*
Kritzberg, N. I., 462, *476*

Kroger, W., 78, *91*, 251, 264, 268, 385, 393, 518, *530*, 534, 535, 536, 537, 544, 545, 546, *551*, 696, *716*

Kumar, V. K., 263, 268

Kurzhals, R., 98, 100, 105, *117*, 117, *119*, 142, *145*

Kuttner, L., 359, 377, *381*, 457, 476

Kvaal, S., 113, *119*, 142, *147*, 472, 476

Labelle, L., 19, *21*

Lachnit, H., 296, *307*

Lakoff, G., 301, *307*

Lamb, C. S., 315, *335*

Lambe, R., 576, *582*, 584

Lambert, M. J., 56, *70*

Lambert, M. L., 56, 69

Landes, J., 190, *212*

Landis, K. R., 599, *616*

Lang, P. J., 313, 327, *333*, 335, *337*

Langdell, S., 208, 209, *213*

Langer, S. K., 291, 305, *307*

Lankton, C., 190, 191, 192, 193, 195, 206, 208, *212*, *213*, 292, 299, 305, *307*, 348, *355*

Lankton, S., 190, 191, 192, 193, 195, 197, 206, 208, *212*, *213*, 292, 299, 305, *307*, 348, *355*

Lau, M. M., 67, *70*

Laurence, J., 18, 19, *21*, 296, 306, 459, 476, 593, 594, *615*, *616*, 724, 734, 735, 736

Lavoie, G., 445, 446, 448

Lawlis, G. F., 712, *714*

Lawson, D. M., 292, *307*, 456, 477

Lazar, B. S., 55, 58, 60, 61, 66, *70*, *71*

Lazarus, A. A., 75, 86, 87, 92, 93, 152, 153, 157, 160, 167, *170*, *171*, 241, 248, 314, 328, *335*, *337*

Lazarus, R. S., 599, 600, *615*, *616*

Leacock, R., 703, *716*

Leacock, S., 703, *716*

LeBaron, S., 35, 36, 37, 49, 52, 377, 378, 380, *381*, 457, 471, 476, 477, 527, *530*, 532

Ledwidge, B., 312, *331*

Lefcoe, N. M., 571, *582*

Leigh, H., 598, 609, *616*

Leighton, A. H., 700, *716*

Leighton, D., 698, 700, *716*

Leitenberg, H., 156, *168*

Lentine, G., 456, 476

Leon, G. R., 534, 542, *551*

Leonoff, A., 521, *529*

Lerner, B., 75, *92*

Leuner, H., 265, 268

Levine, E. S., 292, *307*, 456, 477

Levine, H. M., 599, *618*

Levitt, E. E., 19, 95, 101, *119*, 535, 546, 550, 720, *737*

Levitzky, A., 182, *185*

Libet, B., 302, *307*

Lieberman, L. R., 265, *269*

Lin, E., 587, *616*

Lindemann, E., 497, *507*

Lindner, H., 102, *119*

Linehan, M. M., 56, *71*

Liotti, G., 216, 217, *230*

Lipscomb, P., 587, *616*

Loewald, H. W., 125, *147*

Loftus, E. F., 18, *21*, 720, 734, *738*

Loge, D., 594, *614*

London, P., 32, *53*, 377, *381*, 471, 477

Longo, D. J., 623, *641*

Lovaas, O. I., 156, *170*

Lozanov, G., 513, *530*

Luborsky, 607, *616*

Lundy, R. M., 206, *214*, 518, 532, 720, *738*

Lykken, D., 316, 320, *335*, 598, *619*

Lynch, P. J., 623, *641*

Lynn, S. J., 11, *21*, 98, 99, 100, 105, 108, 109, 110, 112, 113, 114, 116, *117*, *119*, *120*, 127, 141, 142, *145*, 153, *161*, *170*, 207, *214*, 235, 242, 245, 246, 248, 263, *269*, 292, 308, 378, *381*, 440n, *449*, 457, 458, 464, 465, 471, 472, 473, 476, 477, 478, 489, 490, 512, 518, *530*, *531*, 555, 556, 557, 574, 578, 580, 582, *583*, 584, 695, 698, *716*

MacDonald, H., 96, 97–98, 103, *118*, 142, *146*, *147*, 148, 238, 248

MacDonald, J., 358, 372, 380, *381*

MacHovec, F. J., 95, 101, 102, 103, 115, *119*, 456, 477, 571, *582*

MacLeod, C., 593, 598, *617*, *618*

Madakasira, S., 505, *507*

Madanes, C., 456, 476

Maddox, R., 444, *450*

Mahoney, M. J., 217, 220, *230*

Makinodan, T., 614, *617*

Makoid, L. A., 302, *305*

Mallet, J. E., 103, *118*

Malott, J. M., 285, 286, *290*
Man, S. C., 571, *582*
Manuck, S. B., 593, 600, *616*
Marcovitch, P., 37, *53*, 542, *552*, 557, 571, *582*
Mare, C., 113, *119*, 142, *147*, 472, 476
Margolis, J. A., 358, *381*
Markell, C. S., 325, 326, 327, *334*
Marks, D. F., 327, *335*
Marks, I. M., 312, 313, 314, *335*
Markus, H., 220, *230*
Marlatt, G. A., 558, *582*
Marriot, J. A., 573, *582*, 584
Maruffi, B., 325, 326, 329, *336*
Marzella, J. N., 182, *186*
Maslow, A., 288, *290*
Mason, A. A. A., 624, *642*
Mason, J. W., 593, *617*
Massey, B. H., 650, *668*
Massing, A. M., 626, *642*
Matarazzo, R. G., 66, 67, *71*
Mathews, A., 593, 598, *617*
Mathews, W. J., 161, *170*
Matthews, K. A., 600, *617*
Matthews, W., 190, 193, 194, 206, 207, 208, 209, *213*, 518, *531*
Mattick, R. P., 227, *230*
Matyi, C. L., 161, *170*, 518, *530*
May, J., 265, 267, 593, 598, *617*
Mays, D. T., 110, *119*
McCabe, A., 303, *307*
McCabe, M. P., 536, 537, 540, 542, 544, *550*, *551*
McCall-Perez, F., 479, *490*
McCann, I. L., 488, *490*
McCann, T., 725, 726, 735, *738*
McConkey, K. M., 4, 19, *21*, 117, *120*, 141, 142, *146*, *148*, 153, *170*, 206, *213*, 257, 266, *269*, 720, 724, 727, 734, *737*, *738*
McCrae, R. R., 590, 598, *614*
McDonald, R. D., 594, *616*
McDowell, M., 624, 629, *642*, 644
McFarlane, A. C., 505, *507*
McGrath, P., 611, 612, *618*
McGregor, P., 702, *716*
McGuinness, T. P., 313, 314, 329, *335*
McLeod, G., 734, *736*
McMullen, L. M., 294, 303, *307*
McMurray, N., 574, 577, 578, 579, *581*, 584

McNeil, D. N., 313, 327, *333*
McNeil, D. W., 327, *335*
McReynolds, W. T., 75, *92*
Means, J. R., 305, *307*
Meares, A., 102, 103, 104, 106, *119*, 126, *147*
Mechanic, D., 598, *617*
Meichenbaum, D., 152, *170*, 215, 216, 219, 220, 230, 315, *335*
Melamed, B. G., 313, 327, *333*, *335*
Melchiori, L., 321, *335*
Melzack, R., 239, 248, 513, 526, *531*, 589, *619*
Meminger, S. R., 573, 578, 579, *581*, 584
Memmesheimer, A. M., 634, 638, *642*, 647
Menary, E. P., 238, 241, 245, 249, 517, *532*
Menninger, K. A., 727, *737*
Mergler, N. L., 303, *306*
Merleau-Ponty, M., 266, *269*
Mészéros, I., 272, 285, 286, 287, 289, *290*
Meyer, D. E., 302, *308*
Meyer, R. G., 49, *54*, 206, *124*
Mihaly, K., 329, *335*
Mikulincer, M., 505, *508*
Milano, M. J., 11, *21*, 112, *119*
Miller, G., 595, *617*
Miller, J., 104, 116, *119*, 539, 542, *550*
Miller, M. F., 285, 286, 287, *290*, 321, *335*
Miller, M. M., 535, 536, 540, *552*
Miller, N. E., 588, 615, *617*
Miller, T. I., 3, 19, *22*, 116, *120*, 166, 167, *170*
Milne, G., 102, *119*
Mineka, S., 593, *617*
Minnes, L., 379, *380*
Minsky, M., 291, *307*
Misch, R. C., 623, *641*
Mitchell, K. M., 67, *72*
Mobayed, C. P., 11, *21*, 142, *147*, 153, *170*
Mogg, K., 593, 598, *617*
Moll, A., 24, 42, 46, *53*
Montgomery, G., 167, *170*
Moon, C., 324, *333*
Moore, M. E., 544, *551*
Moore, R., 190, *212*
Morgan, A. H., 32, 34, *53*, 63, *71*, 207, *213*, 238, *248*, 317, 320, 326n, *335*, 377, *381*, 471, *477*, 572, 577, *582*
Morgan, W. P., 654, 655, 657, 658, 661, 664, 666, *668*, 669
Morley, J. E., 614, *617*

Mosher, D., 161, *170*, 206, 207, *213*
Mott, T., 534, 537, 544, 545, *552*
Mrazek, P. B., 455, *477*
Mullen, G., 557, *583*
Mullin, C., 324, *332*
Munyon, P., 103, *118*
Murdock, M., 87, *92*
Murphy, G., 692, *717*
Murphy, L., 288, *290*
Murphy, M. A., 182, *185*, 227, *230*
Murphy, M. M., 174, 182, *186*
Murray-Jobsis, J., 259, 265, 269, 280, *290*, 425, 428, 429, 430, 431, 433, 434, 435, 436, 437, 438, 439, 440, 445, 446, 448, *449*
Mutter, C. B., 721, 722, 735, *737*

Nadel, L., 216, 217, *230*
Nadelson, C., 479, 480, *490*, 728, *737*
Naliboff, B. D., 614, *617*
Naruse, G., 655, *669*
Nash, M., 18, *21*, 98, 109, *120*, 124, 125, 127, 140, 141, 142, 143, *147*, *148*, 352, *355*, 383, *393*, 440n, *449*, 471, *477*
Neinstein, L. S., 237, *248*
Nelson, K., 440n, *449*
Nemiah, J. C., 494, *507*
Nesse, R., 312, *337*
Neufeld, V., 161, *170*, 518, 530, 556, 557, 574, 578, 580, 582, *584*
Newbold, G., 385, *393*
Newman, M. R., 97, 98, 105, 111, *118*
Nicholson, N. C., 666, *670*
Noble, J. P., 227, *229*
Norcross, J., 66, *71*
Notman, M. T., 728, *737*
Noyes, R., 505, *507*
Nuechterlein, K. H., 265, *268*
Nugent, W., 208, 209, *213*
Nurnberger, J. I., 535, 546, *550*

Oberlander, J. Z., 252, 263, 264, 265, 267, 268
Obermayer, M. E., 623, 624, 629, 642, 644
O'Brien, K., 505, *507*
O'Connell, D. N., 30, 53, 326n, *336*
O'Connor, P. J., 654, 657, 661, *669*
Odgers, S. J., 720, 722, *737*
O'Grady, D. J., 47, *477*
O'Hanlon, W., 190, *213*
Oliveau, D., 313, *331*

Ollendick, T. H., 312, 313, 314, *335*, *336*
Olness, K., 33, *52*, 357, 358, 367, 369, 372, 374, 377, 378, 379, *380*, *381*, 457, *476*
Olson, D. R., 302, *308*
O'Neil, H. K., 580, *581*
O'Neill, M., 321, *332*
Orne, E. C., 78, *92*, 190, *213*, 315, 326n, *336*, 497, 508, 597, 612, 614, *618*
Orne, M. T., 24, 25, 30, 35, 38, 39, 40, 42, *51*, *53*, 77, *92*, 95, 96, 97, 102, 103, 104, 107, 109, 114, 115, *120*, 129, *148*, 190, *213*, 257, 269, 315, 325, 326, 326n, 327, 328, 334, *336*, 497, 508, 512, *531*, 597, 612, 614, 721, 724, 727, 734, *737*
Orne, W. C., 98, *120*
Orvaschel, H., 339, *355*
Osier, C., 576, 582, *584*
Osterweiss, M., 598, *617*
Overholser, J. C., 102, 112, *120*
Owens, M. E., 325, 326, 327, *336*
Owens, M. V., 574, 578, 582, *584*

Palsson, O., 600, *617*
Parish, M. J., 678, *688*
Parisser, R. R., 182, *185*
Parker, L., 526, *531*
Parwatikar, S. D., 727, *737*
Pascoe, D., 458, *477*
Pastor, S., 558, *582*
Pate, R. R., 654, 661, *669*
Patsiokas, A. T., 227, *230*
Pattie, F. A., 512, *531*
Paul, G., 265, 269, 520, *531*
Pearce, M., 537, *552*
Pearlman, L. A., 488, *490*
Pecsok, E. H., 227, *230*
Pederson, L. L., 571, *582*
Peebles, M. J., 143, *148*
Peebles-Kleiger, M. J., 488, *490*
Pekala, R. J., 263, 268, 712, *717*
Perkins, K. A., 558, *582*
Perlini, A. H., 598, 605, *617*, *618*
Perry, C., 4, 18, 19, *21*, 37, 43, *53*, 235, *248*, 325, 326, 334, 459, 476, 542, *552*, 557, 571, 582, *583*, 594, *616*, 723, 724, 734, 735, 736, *737*
Perry, J. C., 495, *507*
Peters, G. A., 67, *71*
Peters, L., 227, *230*
Petrie, A., 526, *531*

Pettinati, H., 325, *336*, 387, 388, *393*, *394*, 445, 446, *449*, 594, 612, *617*, 722, *737*
Petty, J., 205, *211*
Pfeifer, G., 252, 263, 264, 265, 267
Phillips, E. L., 613, *617*
Piccione, C., 34, *53*
Pillemer, D. B., 440n, *449*
Pinizotto, A. S., 722, *737*
Pollock, M. L., 661, 669
Pomerantz, B. S., 596, 597, *617*
Pomerleau, C. S., 557, *583*
Pomerleau, O. F., 557, *583*
Pope, K. S., 264, *269*
Porter, J., 457, *477*
Porush, D., 302, *308*
Potter, H. W., 456, *475*
Powell, D. H., 557, 572, *583*, 584
Pozza, G., 534, *550*
Pratt, G. J., 537, 548, *552*
Pretzer, J., 154, *169*
Pribble, W. E., 242, 245, 246, 248
Price, R. H., 555, *583*
Price-Williams, D., 694, *717*
Prioleau, L., 87, *92*
Putnam, F. W., 440n, *449*, 472, 473, *475*, *477*

Quill, T. E., 587, *617*

Rabkin, J. F., *617*
Rabkin, S. W., 575, 578, *583*, 584
Raboteau, A. J., 701, *717*
Rachman, S., 314, 328, *336*
Radke, H. L., 519, *531*
Radke-Bodorik, H. L., 238, *249*
Radtke, H. L., 30, *54*, 605, *618*
Raglin, J. S., 651, 654, 657, 669, 670
Railo, W. S., 651, 670
Rapaport, D., 125, *148*, 288, *290*
Raskin, N., 56, *71*
Rasmus, C., 544, *552*
Ratkoczi, E., 329, *335*
Ratner, H., 445, *449*
Raven, P. B., 666, 669
Reade, P., 325, 326, 329, *334*
Reardon, J. P., 182, *185*, 186, 227, *230*
Reardon, W. T., 444, *450*
Regan, P. F., 682, *687*
Regier, D., 339, *355*
Rehagen, N. J., 75, *92*
Reid, S., 642, 645

Reilly, R. R., 678, 688
Relman, A. S., 591, *618*
Remler, H., 611, *618*
Rennie, D. L., 303, *305*
Renold, A. E., 534, *550*
Rescorla, R. A., 152, *170*, 605, *618*
Restak, R. M., 128, *148*
Reyher, J., 141, *149*
Rhue, J. W., 11, *21*, 113, *119*, 127, 141, 142, *147*, 148, 153, *170*, 235, 248, 263, 269, 292, 308, 378, *381*, 457, 458, 464, 465, 471, 472, 473, 477, 478, 489, 490, 512, *531*, 556, *582*, 584, 695, 698, *716*
Rich, S., 598, *619*
Richart, R. H., 587, *615*
Richeport, M. M., 702, 703, *717*
Riley, K. C., 473, *478*
Riordan, M. M., 67, *70*
Roberts, J., 534, 544, 545, *552*
Robertson, L. A., 241, 245, *249*, 517, *532*, 598, *618*
Robertson, L. S., 587, *614*
Robins, L., 339, *355*
Robinson, S., 67, *71*
Roche, S. M., 141, *148*, 720, *737*
Rodin, J., 533, *552*
Rodolfa, E. R., 678, *688*
Rogers, C. R., 56, 67, *71*, 75, *92*, 271, *290*
Rogers, M., 173, *185*
Rogers, S. L., 696, 706, 713, *717*
Rosen, H., 102, 104, *120*
Rosenbaum, M., 599, *618*
Rosenstiel, A. K., 598, *618*
Rosenthal, R., 209, *213*
Ross, C. A., 440n, *450*
Ross, G., 440n, *449*
Rossi, E., 79, *91*, 188, 189, 190, 191, 192, 193, 206, 209, *212*, *213*, 218, 222, 229, 264, 269, 296, 298, 300, 306, 308, 341, *354*, 385, 386, 393, 433, *448*, 698, *715*
Rossi, S., 79, *91*, 296, 306, 698, *715*
Rostafinski, T., 445, *450*
Roth, P., 518, *530*
Rothenberg, A., 298, *308*
Rotter, J. B., 288, *290*
Rouget, G., 703, *717*
Rounsaville, B., 342, *355*
Rowe, W. S. G., 642, 645
Rudy, D. R., 182, *185*
Rulison, R. H., 626, 627, 630, 642

Runtz, M., 456, 475
Rush, A. J., 152, 157, 168
Rush, J., 342, 344, 354
Russell, D., 455, 478, 485, 490
Russell, G., 383, 394
Russo, J., 587, 616
Ryan, M., 188, 213
Ryde, D., 653, 670
Ryken, K., 95, 96, 99, 100, 105, 117, 515, 529

Sabourin, M., 445, 448
Sacerdote, P., 257, 265, 269
Sachs, L. B., 158, 170
Salzberg, H. C., 11, 22
Samaras, J. T., 574, 578, 582, 584
Sandberg, D., 473, 476
Sanders, S., 251, 253, 264, 265, 269, 276, 473, 475, 478, 576, 583
Sandner, D., 697, 698, 699, 700, 717
Santiago, J. M., 479, 490
Sapirstein, G., 167, 170
Sarason, B. R., 599, 618
Sarason, I. G., 599, 618
Sarbin, T. R., 28, 43, 52, 53, 77, 91, 92, 152, 153, 170
Sauzier, M., 458, 476
Saxon, J., 589, 611, 621
Sayers, S. L., 226, 228
Scagnelli, J., 259, 269, 425, 428, 430, 431, 434, 436, 438, 444, 445, 450
Scagnelli-Jobsis, J., 427, 429, 445, 450
Schacter, D. L., 727, 737
Schaefer, C., 599, 616
Schafer, L., 580, 581
Scharcoff, J., 205, 211
Scheflin, A. W., 482, 491, 724, 737
Schiefflin, E., 340, 355
Schiff, A. F., 480, 491
Schilder, P., 44, 53, 123, 148, 427, 450
Schoenberger, N. E., 166, 169
Schubert, D. K., 575, 578, 583, 584
Schultz, J., 95, 120
Schumaker, J. F., 544, 551
Schwartz, G. E., 588, 598, 609, 616, 619
Scott, A., 67, 71
Scott, D., 78, 90, 522, 529
Scrignar, C. B., 315, 336
Scrimgeour, W. G., 571, 582
Segal, D., 142, 147, 473, 478
Segal, N. L., 598, 619
Seibel, C. A., 217, 229

Seitz, P. F. D., 104, 120
Seligman, J., 713, 717
Seligman, M., 340, 341, 342, 344, 352, 355
Sellers, D. J., 99, 118
Sexton, R., 444, 450
Sgroi, S. M., 466, 478
Shane, F., 575, 578, 583, 584
Shapiro, D., 265, 268, 269
Shapiro, J. L., 482, 491
Shapiro, J. R., 724, 737
Shapiro, S. S., 675, 688
Sharp, F., 188, 213
Shaw, B., 152, 157, 168, 342, 344, 354
Shaw, G. M., 722n, 737
Sheehan, D., 322, 324, 327, 332, 556–557, 572, 574, 577, 578, 579, 581, 583, 584, 629, 642, 645
Sheehan, P. W., 4, 18, 19, 21–22, 117, 120, 142, 148, 266, 269, 327, 336, 593, 618, 720, 723, 724, 725, 726, 727, 734, 735, 737, 738
Sheikh, A. A., 313, 314, 334
Shengold, L., 253, 269
Sher, T. G., 226, 228
Sherman, C. J., 526, 531
Sherman, R. A., 526, 531
Shevrin, H., 588, 618
Shor, R. E., 43, 53, 60, 71, 78, 92, 98, 120, 125, 127, 133, 143, 146, 148, 190, 213, 259, 266, 269, 326n, 336, 597, 618
Sieber, J. E., 724, 738
Siegelman, E. Y., 294, 303, 308
Sies, D. E., 722n, 738
Silverberg, E. L., 626, 634, 639, 643, 647
Simon, K. M., 154, 169
Simon, M. J., 11, 22
Sinclair-Gieben, A. H. C., 626, 633, 634, 637, 639, 642, 646
Singer, J. L., 264, 269, 473, 476
Singher, L., 377, 381, 381
Sirkin, M. I., 153, 165, 171
Sivec, H., 142, 147
Skrabski, A., 329, 335
Slade, R., 302, 306
Slagle, R. W., 153, 170
Sletten, I., 34, 54
Sloan, P., 505, 508
Small, S. M., 682, 687
Smith, A. H., Jr., 60, 71
Smith, D., 173, 185

Smith, G. R., 588, 590, 591, *618*
Smith, J. L., 650, 670
Smith, M., 3, 19, *22*, 116, *120*, 166, 167, *170*, 298, 300, 308, 726, *738*
Smith, W. H., 456, 482, 486, *491*
Society for Clinical and Experimental Hypnosis, 723, 724, *738*
Soghikian, K., 587, *615*
Solomon, G. F., 614, *617*
Solomon, Z., 505, *508*
Solyom, C., 312, *331*
Solyom, K., 312, *331*
Somer, E., 480, *491*
Soskis, D. A., 237, 238, *248*
Spanos, N. P., 5, 19, *22*, 30, 43, *50*, *53–54*, 77, 78, 80, 87, 90, 91, *92*, 152, 165, 166, *169*, *170*, 236, 238, 240, 241, 245, 246, *248*, *249*, 511, 512, 516–517, 521, 527, 528, *530*, *531*, *532*, 598, 605, *617*, *618*, 627, 628, 630, 635, 636, 637, 638, 639, *640*, 640, *642*, 647, 648, 691, 692, 705, 717
Sparling, B. P., 654, 661, 669
Speigel, H., 572, 573, 574, 575, 576, *583*
Spence, D., 294, *308*, 459, *478*
Spiegel, D., 30, 39, *54*, 126, 143, 148, 219, 230, 258, 269, 324, 325, 326, 327, 329, 330, 334, *336*, 385, 394, 446, 450, 456, 472, *478*, 489, *491*, 495, 496, 497, 498, 502, 503, 505, 506, *508*, 534, 535, 536, 539, 541, 542, 543, 549, *552*, 608, *618*, 727, *738*
Spiegel, H., 30, 39, *54*, 102, *120*, 126, *148*, 219, 230, 258, 269, 325, 326, 327, 329, 334, *336*, 385, 394, 493, 498, 502, *507*, *508*, 534, 535, 536, *552*, 608, *618*, 727, *738*
Spielberger, C. D., 651, 670
Spinhoven, P., 14, *22*, 39, *54*, 87, *92*, 542, 543n, 544, *552*, 637, *642*
Spinler, D., 143, *148*, 535, 536, 538n, 541, 543, 544, 548, *549*
Staats, J. M., 325, *336*, 387, *394*, 446, *449*, 594, 612, *617*
Stager, G. L., 720, *738*
Stam, H., 30, *54*, 611, 612, *618*
Stankler, L., 625, 626, 627, 632, 634, 638, 642, 647
Stanley, R. D., 576, 577, 578, 579, *582*, 584
Stanley, S., 98, 109, *120*, 142, *148*

Stanton, H. E., 174, 182, *186*, 535, 536, 540, 545, *552*, 572, 574, 575, 579, *583*, 584
Statham, D., 19, *21–22*
Steckler, J., 292, *308*
Steele, K. H., 484, *491*
Steere, J., 724, *738*
Stein, D. M., 56, *70*
Steinhaus, A. H., 650, 668
Stenstrom, R. J., 627, 628, 635, 637, 638, 639, 640, *642*, 647, 648
Stern, J. A., 34, *54*
Sternbach, R. A., 602, *618*, *619*
Stevenson, J., 66, *71*
Stokes, J., 661, 669
Stone, J. A., 206, *214*, 518, *532*
Strauss, B. S., 64, *72*
Struening, E. L., *617*
Strupp, H. H., 56, *72*, 116, *118*, 711, *717*
Stuart, R. B., 533, 544, *552*
Stunkard, A. J., 534, 543, 544, *551*, *552*
Stutman, R. K., 325, *336*, 505, *508*
Suedfeld, P., 321, 331, *336*, 574, *581*
Sulzberger, M. B., 642, 644
Surman, D. S., 572, 578, 579, *583*, 584
Surman, O. S., 626, 634, 637, 639, 642, *643*, 644, 647
Sussman, M. B., 534, *551*
Sutton, J. E., 536, 537, 540, 544, *550*, *551*
Swade, R. H., 629, *641*, 645
Swanson, D. W., 533, *552*
Sweetser, E., 305, *308*
Sylvester, D., 313, *331*

Taenzer, P., 589, *619*
Tancredi, L. R., 591, *619*
Tart, C. T., 28, *54*, 324, *336*
Tasinary, L., 302, *306*
Tasini, M. F., 237, *249*, 630, *643*, 645
Tataryn, D. J., 216, 217, *230*
Taub, H. A., 238, *247*
Taylor, A. E., 595, *614*
Taylor, C. B., 154, *171*, 600, *615*
Taylor, R. L., 633, 637, *643*, 647
Tellegen, A., 43, *54*, 259, *270*, 324, 327, *336*, 496, *508*, 598, *619*
Tenzel, J. H., 633, 637, *643*, 647
Thakur, K., 385, *394*
Thomas, R., 265, *269*
Thompson, K., 365, *381*, 675, 688
Thompson, S. C., 593, *619*
Thorne, D. E., 544, *552*

Thyer, B. A., 312, *337*
Tipton, R. D., 142, *148*
Tisza, V., 458, *475*
Tomlin, P., 312, *337*
Topper, M. D., 697, 700, *717*
Torem, M., 387, *394*
Torrey, E. F., 73, 75, 92, 700, 706, 711, *717*
Tosi, D. J., 174, 182, *183, 184, 185, 186,*
    227, *229, 230*
Tosi, M., 379, *380*
Trautt, G. M., 74, *90*
Treiber, R., 227, *229*
Trent, J. C., 513, *532*
Trimble, R. W., 265, *269*
Truax, C. B., 66, 67, 71, *72*
Tsournas, N., 590, *621*
Tuckey, C. L., 513, *532*
Turk, D. C., 523, *532*, 588, 589, *615*
Turner, M., 589, 612, *621*
Túry, F., 279, 285, 286, *290*

U. S. Department of Health, Education,
    and Welfare, 556, *583*
Uden, D., 358, 372, 378, *381*
Udolf, R., 218, 221, *231*, 726, *738*
Udolph, R., 511, *532*
Uhl, H. S. M., 682, *688*
Uleman, J. S., 594, *619*
Ulett, G. A., 34, *54*
Ullman, M., 631, 639, 643, *646*
Umberson, D., 599, *616*
Umlauf, R. L., 576, 577, 578, 579, *581,*
    584
Unestål, L. E., 280, *290*, 651, 656, *670*

Vadász, J., 280, 285, 286, 287, *290*
Valdiserri, E. V., 456, *478, 480, 491*
Van der Does, A. J. W., 14, *22*
van der Ende, J., 312, 313, *331*
van der Kolk, B. A., 495, *507*
Van Dyck, R., 14, *22*
Van Gorp, W. G., 49, *54*, 206, *214*
Vandereycken, W., 387, *394*
Vanderlinden, J., 387, *394*
Vanek, M., 655, *670*
Vas, J., 434, 445, *450*
Velten, E., 174, 175, *184*, 594, 612, *619*
Venables, P., 316, 320, *335*
Vermont Lung Association, 574, 578, *583,*
    584
Vickery, A. R., 153, 165, *171*
Vogel, V. J., *717*

Vollmer, H., 628, *643, 644*
Von Dedenroth, T. E. A., 265, *270*
VonKorff, M., 587, *616*
Vosniadou, S., 303, *308*
Vrana, S. R., 327, *335*

Wack, J. T., 523, *532*
Wadden, T. A., 37, 38, 44, *54*, 158, *171,*
    219, 231, 237, 249, 527, *532, 534,*
    535, 536, 538, 539, 541, 542, 544,
    552, 553, 556, 583, 625, 637, *643*
Wade, J. H., 387, *394*, 449, 594, 612, *617*
Wagner, T. J., 574, 578, *583, 584*
Wales, R., 296, *306*
Walker, E. A., 466, *478*
Walker, M. K., 205, *212*
Walker, W., 141, *146*
Walker, W. L., 535, 536, 537, 540, 542,
    544, 546, *551, 552, 553*
Wall, P., 239, 248, 513, 526, *531*
Wall, V. J., 227–228, *231*
Wallace, B., 594, *619*
Ward, C., 693, *717*
Ward, F., 265, *268*
Ware, C., 589, 611, *621*
Warner, R. E., 173, *186*
Watkins, H., 131–132, 133, *149*
Watkins, J., 56, *72*, 131–132, 133, *149,*
    440n, *450*, 485, *491*, 734, *738*
Watson, D., 598, *619*
Weekes, J. R., 11, *21*, 112, *119*, 127, 141,
    147, 207, *214*, 512, *531*
Weigel, R. G., 74, *90*
Weight, D. G., 264, *268*
Weinberg, L., 219, *230*
Weinberger, D. A., 588, 609, *619*
Weiner, B., 302, *308*
Weiss, E., 131, *149*
Weiss, S. M., 600, *617*
Weissman, M., 339, 342, *355*
Weitz, G. A., 666, *669*
Weitzenhoffer, A., 24, 28, 32, 39, 47, *54,*
    59, *72*, 78, *92*, 97, 103, 104, *120,*
    190, 206, *212, 214*, 282, 287, *290,*
    321, 326n, *337*, 340, *355*, 539,
    553, 576, *583*, 597, *619*, 631, *643,*
    664, 665, 666, *670*
Wert, A., 573, *581*
West, L. J., 95, 104, *120*
Wester, W. C., 722n, *738*
Western, J. S., 723, *736*
White, D. O., 624, *643*

White, R. W., 288, *290*
White, S. H., 440n, *449*
Whitehouse, W. G., 315, *336*, 597, 612, *614*
Wickless, C., 89, *92*, 156, *171*, 597, 609, 611, 612, *616*
Wickramasekera, I., 588, 589, 590, 591, 592, 593, 594, 595, 596, 597, 599, 600, 602, 604, 605, 606, 608, 609, 611, 612, 613, *617*, 619, 620, *621*
Wiesel, S., 590, *621*
Wilcox, K. J., 598, *619*
Wilcox, W. W., 99, *118*
Wiley, S., 440n, *449*
Wilkie, R., 535, 536, 538n, 539, 540, 542, *550*
Williams, G. W., 103, *120*
Williams, J. M., 577, 579, *583*, 584
Williams, V., 87, *92*, 627, 630, 636, 637, 638, 640, *642*, 648
Wilson, G. L., 305, *307*
Wilson, G. T., 226, *228*
Wilson, L., 720, 734, *738*
Wilson, S. C., 78, 90, *93*, 471, 473, *478*, 594, *621*
Wincze, J. P., 156, *168*
Wink, C. A. S., 623, *643*
Winkelman, M., 694, *717*
Winkelstein, L. B., 534, 536, 537, 540, *553*
Winnicott, D., 132, *149*, 252, *270*, 425, *450*
Wiseman, R. J., 141, *149*
Wndelich, S. A., 576, 577, 578, 579, *581*, 584
Wogan, M., 473, *478*
Wolberg, L. R., 24, 43, 54, *56*, 61, *72*, 444, *450*

Wolf, J., *642*, 644
Wolford, G., 302, *306*
Wollman, L., 537, *553*
Wolpe, J., 86, *93*, 151, 152, 153, *171*, 313, 314, *337*
Womack, W., 227–228, *231*
Wong, W. E., 67, *70*
Wood, D. P., 537, 548, *552*
Wooley, S. C., 534, *550*
World Health Organization, 312, *337*
Worthington, E. L. Jr., 520, *532*
Wright, K., 294, *308*
Wright, P., 312, *337*
Wyden, P., 533, *553*

Yalom, I. D., *643*, 644
Yaniv, I., 302, *308*
Yapko, M., 205, *214*, 341, 343, 344, 345, 348, 353, *355*, 387, *394*
Yates, A., 466, *478*
Yeager, N. J., 623, *641*
Young, W. C., 472, *478*

Zaitman, A., 312, *331*
Zajonc, R. B., 600, *621*
Zanna, M. P., 156, *169*
Zarski, J. J., 599, *621*
Zeig, J., 190, *214*, 292, *308*, 344, 348, *355*
Zeig, M. S., 434, 435, 444, *451*
Zeltzer, L., 377, 378, *381*, 471, *477*, 527, *532*
Zillmer, E. A., 589, 599, 602, 606, 612, *621*
Zimbardo, P. G., 34, *53*
Zindel, P., 434, 445, *451*
Zocco, L., 598, *621*
Zseni, A., 280, 285, 286, 287, *290*
Zwick, K. G., 624, *643*

SUBJECT INDEX

Abused children. *See also* Storytelling, with abused children
    assessment of, 457–459
    case material, 460, 462–464, 467–470
    and hypnotizability, 470–472
    research, 470–473
    steps in therapy process with, 473–474
Active–alert hypnosis
    behavioral effects, 277–278, 285–286
    case material, 281–284
    clinical applications, 273, 278–280
    compared to relaxation-based, 272–273
    described, 271–272
    hypnotic suggestion in, 275–276, 286–287
    induction, 273–275
    physiological characteristics of, 287–288
    research, 284–287
    self-hypnosis, 276–277
    transcript, 273–275
Adaptive regression, 44–45, 125
Adaptive synchrony, 128
Addiction, and hypnotizability, 37–38. *See also* Smoking-cessation program
Adult education, principles of 673–675. *See also* Hypnotherapy, training in
Affect bridge (rape trauma syndrome), 485–486, 487
Afro-Brazilian medium (healer), 702–706
Age progression, 345, 390, 523
Age regression, 18–19, 390, 437, 498–499, 523
    possible negative effects of, 104, 113–115
    and sport psychology, 654, 658–659, 661–663, 667
Amplifiers (patients), 589–590
Andragogy (adult learning), principles of, 673–675
Anorexia nervosa, 384–387, 391–393
    case material, 282–283, 387–391

Anxiety. *See also* Phobias
    and acute pain reduction, 521–522
    and child hypnotherapy, 376–377
    precompetition, in sport psychology, 654–656
Arm levitation, transcript, 15
Asthma, and hypnotizability, 37
Attributional style, cognitive model of depression, 342
Autohypnosis, *See* Self-hypnosis

Behavior modification (weight reduction), 535, 543 (table 3), 545
    components of program, 546–548
Behavioral practice, and cognitive–behavioral therapy, 157
Behavior problems (child hypnotherapy), 370–371
Bernheim, Hippolyte, 6
Biobehavioral disorders (child hypnotherapy), 371–374
Biofeedback, 363–364
Borderline patients, 132, 138–139, 389, 425–427. *See also* Borderline/psychotic patients
    case material (self-hypnosis), 260–261
    and RET, 178–182
Borderline/psychotic patients, 427–430
    case material, 440–444
    general treatment techniques, 431–434
    and hypnotherapy, 434–440, 445–446
    research, 444–447
Braid, James, 6, 27
Buffer, of threat perception, 592

Carleton Skill Training Package (CSTP), 80, 165–166
Case material
    abused children, 460, 462–464, 467–470
    active-alert hypnosis, 281–284

Case material (*continued*)
    anorexia nervosa, 282–283, 387–391
    borderline, 260–261
    borderline/psychotic, 440–444
    child hypnotherapy, 372–374
    cognitive restructuring, 223–226
    depression, 348–352
    dysfunctional pain, 242–245
    Ericksonian therapy, 197–205
    healers, native, 707–710
    hypnotherapy, teaching, 63–64
    manic depression, 440–442
    metaphors, 197–205, 295–301
    pain management, 515–516, 524–527
    patient assessment, 63–65
    phobias, 315–324
    psychophysiological psychotherapy, 608–611
    PTSD, 502–505
    rape trauma syndrome, 486–488
    RET, 178–182
    self-hypnosis, 260–263, 322–323
    sport psychology, 652–653, 656–664
    wart regression, 628–630
Catastrophizing, 520–521, 598
Chantway, Navajo, 697–700
Chevreul pendulum (prehypnotic experience), 40
    transcript, 82–83
Child hypnotherapy. *See also* Abused children
    case material, 372–374
    clinical application, 358–361
    categories of, 366
        anxiety, 376–377
        behavior problems, 370–371
        biobehavioral disorders, 371–374
        habit problems, 367–370
        malignant disease, 377
        pain, 374–376
    historical background, 357–358
    induction techniques in, 361–365
    research, 377–379
    transcript, 365
Children, abused. *See* Abused children
Children's Hypnotic Susceptibility Scale, 377–378
Civil rights, and forensic hypnosis, 727–728
Cognitive-behavioral therapy, 511–513. *See also* Pain management
    clinical applications, 154–159

    and cognitive restructuring, 157, 164–165
    comparative effectiveness of, 166–167
    deciding whether to use hypnosis in, 159–161
    historical background, 151–152
    and hypnotic skills training, 161–163, 165–166
    hypnotic versus nonhypnotic, 167–168
    and self-regulation, 158–159
    and smoking-cessation program, 556–559
    and successive approximation, 156–157, 163–164
    view of hypnosis, 152–154, 158, 511–513
Cognitive-developmental therapy, 216–217, 228
    and cognitive restructuring, 219–220
Cognitive events, 220. *See also* Cognitive restructuring
Cognitive models of depression, 342–343
Cognitive restructuring
    case material, 223–226
    and cognitive–behavioral therapy, 157, 164–165
    and cognitive–developmental therapy, 219–220
    and Ericksonian therapy, 220–223
    and rape trauma syndrome, 484–485
    therapeutic effectiveness of, 226–228
    transcript, 164
Cognitive skills model, 236, 240–241
Cognitive therapy, historical background, 215–216
Competence, assessing hypnotherapists', 66–68
Coping strategies, and pain management, 520–521, 527
Core cognitive structures, 220. *See also* Cognitive restructuring
Countertransference, 61, 109, 133, 488–489
Creative Imagination Scale, 78
Cyberphysiology, defined, 358

Deception, and forensic hypnosis, 727
Deepening techniques, transcript, 16, 85–86
Depression, 342–343, 522

case material, 348–352
causal agents of, 339–340
hypnosis in treatment of, 340–342, 352–354
perceptual and behavioral rigidity, 346–348
stable attributional style, 344–346
transcript (for building expectancies), 345–346
Dermatologic diseases, and hypnotizability, 37. *See also* Wart regression
Developed personality, as characteristic of hypnotherapist, 62
Dissociation, 105–106, 472–473, 494–496, 505–506, 522
Domain of hypnosis, 4
Double consciousness, 127
Dream production techniques, 435–36
Dreams, 129–130, 136, 287
Dysfunctional pain, case material, 242–245

Ego activity, 125–126
Ego functions, 125–127, 141–142
Ego passivity, 125–126
Ego receptivity, 125–126, 141–142
Ego states, 131–132, 135–136
Eight "Cs," in PTSD therapy, 500–502
Empathic mirroring (borderline/psychotic patients), 431–433
End-result imagery, and obesity, 548
Entailments, 302
Enuresis, nocturnal, 369–370
Erickson, Milton H., 46–50, 79, 210, 292
biographical sketch, 187–188
Ericksonian therapy
case material, 197–205
clinical applications, 193–196
and cognitive restructuring, 220–223
hallmarks of, 190–193
overview of, 205–211
rationale and philosophy of, 188–190
recursive model of, 194 (figure)
Ericksonian view of hypnotizability, 46–50
Expectancy-management techniques, 42
Expectations, 86, 344, 351–352, 388, 638
client, regarding therapists, 73–75, 77
and hypnotizability, 88–89, 238–240
importance of, 209, 694–696, 700–701
and informed consent, 111–112

in pain management hypnotherapy, 515–517
and self-hypnosis, 81–83, 253–254, 378
techniques for enhancing, 75–77
transcript, 40, 81, 82–83, 345–346
and treatment outcome, 73–74, 87–88
Explicit knowledge, and cognitive-developmental model, 216–217
Exus (messengers of the *orixas*), 704
Eyes-open, focused-attention hypnosis, 322, 324. *See also* Active–alert hypnosis

Fears, intense. *See* Phobias
Forensic hypnosis
clinical applications, 725–728
ethical issues in, 719–721, 732–734
historical background, 721–722
possible risks in, 733–734
and professionalism, 723–725
and rape trauma syndrome, 482, 728–730
and sexual assault, 728–731
Free association techniques (borderline/psychotic patients), 436–437
Freud, Sigmund, 27, 123–124

Grandiosity, as characteristic of hypnotherapist, 61
Grief work, 497
Group therapy, active–alert hypnosis in, 277. *See also* Smoking-cessation program

Habit problems (child hypnotherapy), 367–370
Harvard Group Scale of Hypnotic Susceptibility (HGSHS), 78, 97–99, 218
Hataalii ("singing shaman"), 697–701
Healer, shaman as, 694–696
Healer within, the, 134, 139
Healing procedures, native, 694–695
Afro-Brazilian, 701–707
basic principles of, 713–714
case material, 707–710
Navajo, 696–701
research, 710–713
Heterohypnosis, differentiated from self-hypnosis, 252–253

Hypnoanalysis, 130, 133–134, 137, 145

Hypnobehavioral model, and obesity, 535

Hypnosis. *See also* Active–alert hypnosis; Forensic hypnosis; "Negative effects" of hypnosis

    analogy between, and PTSD, 496, 506

    from cognitive-behavioral perspective, 152–154, 158, 511–513

    compared to hypnotic-like procedures, 691–694

    deepening, 15–16, 85–86, 519–520

    defined, 4, 190, 217–218, 353, 359–361, 592–593. *See also* Hypnotic-like procedures

    historical background, 5–7, 123–124, 692

    increasing responsiveness to, 79–81

    indications and contraindications for use of, 7–10

    misconceptions about, 10–11, 107, 159–160

    with RET, 175–176

    terminating, 17–18, 103

    as tool, 6–7, 143–144, 675

    views of

        cognitive–behavioral therapy, 152–154, 158, 511–513

        Nancy school, 6

Hypnotherapeutic cognitive restructuring, 220–223

Hypnotherapists, 57–62, 66–69, 102. *See also* Hypnotherapy, training in

Hypnotherapy. *See also* Child hypnotherapy

    historical background, 5–7

    reasons therapists avoid, 57

    teaching, 62–63

        case material, 63–64

Hypnotherapy, training in, 59, 67–68, 109–110, 222. *See also* Hypnotic skills training

    contextual issues, 681–682

        format, 684–685

        funding, 683–684

        implementation, 685–687

        sponsorship and accreditation, 682–683

    participant eligibility, 675–677

    role of, in psychotherapy outcome, 56–57

    seminars/workshops, 677–679

Hypnotic Attitudes Questionnaire, 238

Hypnotic Induction Profile (HIP), 30

Hypnotic-like procedures, 691–694. *See also* Healing procedures, native

Hypnotic procedures. *See* Hypnosis

Hypnotic responsiveness. *See* Hypnotizability

Hypnotic skills training. *See also* Hypnotherapy, training in

    and cognitive–behavioral therapy, 161–163, 165–166

    transcript, 161–163

Hypnotic suggestion. *See also* Posthypnotic suggestion

    and active–alert hypnosis, 275–276, 286–287

    and anorexia nervosa, 388–391

    exercising care in making, 107–109

    and obesity, 534–535, 536

    and pain management, 518, 520–523

    transcript, 161

    and wart regression, 629–630, 638

Hypnotic susceptibility. *See* Hypnotizability

Hypnotizability

    correlation between, and negative effects, 97–99

    enhancing, 240–241, 245–246

    importance of assessing, 218, 222

    measures of, 27–34, 30, 377–378, 497–498

        Harvard Group Scale of Hypnotic Susceptibility (HGSHS), 78, 97–99, 218

        Stanford hypnotizability scales, 45, 78, 97–99, 207, 218, 377–378

    therapeutic alliance and, 241–242

    and treatment outcome, 34–38, 50, 80, 237, 328–329

    views of

        Ericksonian, 46–50

        psychoanalytic, 44–46

        social learning, 41–44

        special process, 236

        trait, 27, 39–41

Imagery, 134–135, 141, 365. *See also* Child hypnotherapy; Metaphor

    and anorexia nervosa, 389–391

    and cognitive–behavioral therapy, 155–156

enhancing hypnotizability with, 240–241

and obesity, 535–536, 548

and phobias, 313–315

thermal, and pain reduction, 523

Inductions, 77–79, 83–85, 287. *See also* Transcripts

arm levitation, 15

in child hypnotherapy, 361–365

double hypnotic, 206

eye closure, 14

self-hypnosis, 258–259

standard hypnotic, 11–14

Induction techniques, 46–50, 295–297, 388, 434, 517–519

Informed consent, and expectations, 111–112

Inner child, the, 127, 129, 135–136

Instructions. *See* Transcripts

Interpersonal model of depression, 342–343

Interpretation discrepancy, described, 220

IPS (ideal performing state), described, 651

Irrational Beliefs (IBs), three main categories of, 174–175

Kohnstamm phenomenon, (prehypnotic experience), 40

Liébeault, Auguste, 3, 6

Macquarie University Weight Control Program, 536–537, 545

Malignant disease, and child hypnotherapy, 376–377

Manic depression, case material, 440–442

Mask, as healing metaphor, 134–135

Meaning conjunction, in metaphor sequences, 303

Meaning disjunction, in metaphor sequences, 303

Medium (healer), Afro-Brazilian, 702–706

Mental illness, Navajo diagnostic categories, 697

Mesmer, Franz Anton, 5

Mesmerism, 5–6

Metaphor, 134–136, 293, 301–305, 348. *See also* Child hypnotherapy; Imagery

case material, 197–205, 295–301

and Ericksonian therapy, 206–207, 208

establishing therapeutic context with, 292, 294–295

facilitating induction with, 295–297

and posthypnotic suggestion, 299–301

stimulating problem solving with, 297–299

using, with children, 367–368, 370, 461–462, 464–465

Migraines (child hypnotherapy), 372–374

Nancy school, view of hypnosis, 6

Narcisstic patients, 132, 138–139

Native healers. *See* Healing procedures, native

Navajo healers. *See* Healing procedures, native

Negative affectivity, as risk factor for somatization, 598–599

"Negative effects" of hypnosis

clinical survey data, 101–102

conclusions regarding, 115–117

determinants of, 102–105

in experimental research, 96–101

situations that may promote, 105–110

strategies for limiting, 110–115

Negative transference, clients with history of, 106

Neodissociation theory, 7

Neurolinguistic programming (NLP), 205

Neuroticism, as risk factor for somatization, 598–599

Nurturing adult, the, 135–136

Obesity, 533, 534–539

and behavior modification, 535, 543 (table 3), 545–548

and hypnotic suggestion, 534–535, 536

and hypnotizability, 539–542

Macquarie University Weight Control Program, 536–537, 545

research, 542–546

transcript (end-result imagery), 548

Orixas (deities), Afro-Brazilian, 701–706

Overweight. *See* Obesity

Pacing, as transition to other induction techniques, 79

Pain, 364–365
    and child hypnotherapy, 374–376
    dysfunctional
        case material, 242–245
        and hypnotizability, 238–240
    and expectations, 87–88
    in sport psychology, 653–654
Pain management. *See also* Pain reduction
    case material, 515–516, 524–527
    coping strategies, 520–521, 527
    phases of, 513–514
        deepening, 519–520
        induction, 517–519
        patient selection, 514–515
        posthypnotic suggestions/termination, 523–524
        preparation (expectations), 515–517
        therapeutic suggestions, 520–523
Pain phenomenology, and pain management, 521
Pain reduction, 34–37, 48–49, 238, 521–523. *See also* Pain management
Pathophysiology, and psychopathology, 590
Perceptual and behavioral rigidity, as depression pattern, 346–348
Peripheral pulse volume (PPV). *See* Psychophysiological evaluation
Phantom limb pain, case material, 524–527
Phobias, 313–315
    case material, 315–317
        flight activity, 318–324
        school, 317–318, 323–324
    effectiveness of hypnosis in treating, 329–331
    and hypnotizability, 325–328, 330
    overview of, 312–313
    research, 324–325
Posthypnotic Experience Questionnaire (PEQ), 98, 100
Posthypnotic Experience Scale (PES), 99
Posthypnotic suggestion, 103, 130, 226
    and metaphor, 299–301
    and pain management, 523–524
    transcript, 16–17, 155
Posttraumatic stress disorder. *See* PTSD (posttraumatic stress disorder)
Prayer session, Navajo, 700. *See also* Healing procedures, native

Predisposer, as risk factor of somatization, 592–599
Prehypnotic experiences, 40, 82–83, 294. *See also* Expectations
Primary process thought, 126–127, 141 described, 124–125
Projective techniques (borderline/psychotic patients), 435–437
Psychoanalytic hypotheses, and hypnoanalysis, 140–143
Psychoanalytic view of hypnotizability, 44–46
Psychoarchaeology, 613–614
Psychopathology, 100, 106, 590
Psychophysiological evaluation, 316–318
Psychophysiological psychotherapy, 605–608, 611–613. *See also* Somatization; Threat perception
    case material, 608–611
Psychotherapist, characteristics of, 56–57
Psychotic patients. *See* Borderline/psychotic patients
PTSD (posttraumatic stress disorder), 595. *See also* Rape trauma syndrome; Trauma
    accessing memories, 498–500
    analogy between, and hypnosis, 496, 506
    case material
        assault victim, 502–503
        Vietnam veteran, 503–505
    eight "Cs" in, 500–502
    and hypnotizability scales, 497–498
    and self-hypnosis, 498, 500
Puységur, Marquis de, 5

Questionnaire Upon Mental Imagery (QMI), 327–328

Rape, Victor (peasant), 5
Rape trauma syndrome, 480–482
    and affect bridge, 485–486, 487
    case material, 486–488
    and countertransference, 488–489
    described, 479–480
    and forensic hypnosis, 482, 728–730
    and memory recall, 482–485
Rational–emotive therapy. *See* RET (rational–emotive therapy)
Rational stage-directed hypnotherapy (RSDH), 227
"Regression in the service of the ego," 125

Reinterpretation techniques (borderline/psychotic patients), 437–438
Relaxation, 85, 435
    and cognitive–behavioral therapy, 154–155
    and expectations, 81–83, 86
Relaxation and mental imagery (RMI). *See* Child hypnotherapy
Relaxation-based (traditional) hypnosis, compared with active–alert hypnosis, 272–273
Remitters (patients), 591
Renurturing techniques (borderline/psychotic patients), 438–439
Restricted environmental stimulation (REST), 320–322, 324, 330–31
RET (rational–emotive therapy)
    case material, 178–182
    clinical applications, 176–178
    described, 173–174, 183
    hypnosis with, 175–176
    transcript, 178–181
RMI (relaxation and mental imagery). *See* Child hypnotherapy
Role rehearsal techniques (borderline/psychotic patients), 435
RSDH (rational stage-directed hypnotherapy), 227

Screen technique, and PTSD, 499
Secondary process thought, described, 124–125
Self-control, enhanced, in treating anorexia nervosa, 387–388
Self-hypnosis, 348, 349, 388, 608
    active–alert, 276–277
    with borderline/psychotic patients, 429–430
    case material, 260–263, 322–323
    in child hypnotherapy, 361, 363
    clinical applications, 253–256, 266
    differentiated from heterohypnosis, 252–253
    and expectations, 81–83, 253–254, 378
    induction, 258–259
    interpreting effects of, 265–267
    in Navajo healing procedures, 697
    and PTSD, 498, 500
    research, 263–265

and smoking-cessation program, 556–557
    teaching, 257–259
    by therapist, 430, 432–433
    transcript, 258–259, 498
Self-regulation, and cognitive–behavioral therapy, 158–159
Separation–individuation techniques (borderline/psychotic patients), 439–440
Shamans, 694–696, 703
Skin conductance response (SCR). *See* Psychophysiological evaluation
Smoking-cessation program
    research, 570–572
        clinical reports, 572–573
        comparisons, 577–580
        experimental/quasi-experimental, 574–577
        group hypnosis, 573–574
    transcript
        Session 1, 559–564
        Session 2, 565–570
    treatment components, 556–559
Social learning view of hypnotizability, 41–44
Somatization. *See also* Psychophysiological psychotherapy; Threat perception assessing risk for, 597–600
    risk factors in, 592–597
    and Trojan horse procedure, 603–604
Somatizers, described, 587–589
Special process view of hypnotizability, 236
Spiritual practitioners. *See* Healing procedures, native
Sport psychology
    age regression in, 654, 658–659, 661–663, 667
    case material, 652–653, 656
        baseball player, 661–664
        distance runner, 657–661
    and injuries, 653–654
    research, 664–667
    uses of hypnosis in, 649–652
    and ZOA (zone of optimal anxiety), 654–656, 667
    and ZOF (zone of optimal function), 651
Sports injuries, 653–654
Stable attributional style, as depression pattern, 344–346

Stanford hypnotizability scales, 45, 78, 97–99, 207, 218
    for children, 377–378
Storytelling, with abused children, 466–467
    building a safe context, 460–462
    developing rapport, 462–463
    general considerations, 459–460
    historical background, 456–457
    relieving guilt, 464–465
    suggesting protective images, 463–464
Successive approximation, and cognitive–behavioral therapy, 156–157, 163–164
Suggestion, hypnotic. See Hypnotic suggestion; Posthypnotic suggestion
Suggestive techniques for enhancing expectations, 75–76

Tacit knowledge, and cognitive–developmental model, 216–217
"Teaching stories" (Ericksonian), 698
Therapeutic alliance, and hypnotizability, 241–242
Therapeutic personality qualities, 56–57
Think-with instructions, 78
Threat perception, 592, 599–603. See also Psychophysiological psychotherapy; Somatization
Threat-related symptoms, high risk model of. See Somatization
Thumb sucking (child hypnotherapy), 367–369
Topographic regression, and hypnoanalysis, 141
Training. See Hypnotherapy, training in
Trait view of hypnotizability, 27, 39–41
Trance, 126, 128–129, 193, 364–365
Trance depth, 126–127
Trance logic, the "illogic" of, 129
Transcripts
    active–alert hypnosis, 273–275
    arm levitation, 15
    Chevreul pendulum, 82–83
    child hypnotherapy, 365
    cognitive restructuring, 164
    deepening techniques, 16, 85–86
    end-result imagery (obesity), 548
    expectations, 40, 81, 82–83, 345–346

hypnotic skills training, 161–163
induction, 12–14, 84–85
posthypnotic suggestion, 16–17, 155
RET hypnotherapy, 178–181
self-hypnosis, 258–259, 498
smoking cessation program
    Session 1, 559–564
    Session 2, 565–570
suggestion for unreflective client, 161
terminating hypnosis, 17
wart regression, 628
Transducers (patients), 590–591
Transference, 124, 130–131, 140, 142–143, 502
Trauma. See also PTSD; Rape trauma syndrome
    defined, 482, 494
    dissociation during, 494–496
Traumatic memories, accessing, 498–500
Traumatic sexualization, 466–467
Treatment outcome, 19–20, 24–26
    and expectations, 73–74, 87–88
    and hypnotizability, 34–38, 50, 80, 328–329
    and metaphor, 303–304
Trigger, of threat perception, 592, 599–600

Unknowns (patients), 591

Vicarious victimization, 488–489

Wart regression, 623–624, 625
    case material, 628–630
    clinical applications, 627–628
    and hypnotic suggestion, 629–630, 638
    methodological considerations, 626–627
    research
        between-groups comparison studies, 630–632
        controlled studies, 634–637
        summarized, 637–640
        within-subject comparison studies, 632–634
    transcript, 628
Weight loss, See Obesity

ZOA (zone of optimal anxiety), in sport psychology, 654–656, 667
ZOF (zone of optimal function), in sport psychology, 651

and hypnotic suggestion, 629–630, 638
methodological considerations, 626–627
research
    between-groups comparison studies, 630–632
    controlled studies, 634–637
    summarized, 637–640

within-subject comparison studies, 632–634
transcript, 628
Weight loss. *See* Obesity

ZOA (zone of optimal anxiety), in sport psychology, 654–656, 667
ZOF (zone of optimal function), in sport psychology, 651

ABOUT THE EDITORS

Judith W. Rhue is a professor of family medicine at the Ohio University College of Osteopathic Medicine and has a private practice. She is a member of the American Psychological Association's Division of Psychological Hypnosis, of which she is a fellow. She has received awards for excellence in research from both organizations, as well as an award for the best hypnosis book published during 1991 (*Theories of Hypnosis: Current Models and Perspectives*), bestowed by the Society for Clinical and Experimental Hypnosis. Dr. Rhue serves on the editorial boards of the *International Journal of Clinical and Experimental Hypnosis* and *Contemporary Hypnosis*. She is coeditor of two hypnosis books and a forthcoming book on dissociation (with Steven Jay Lynn), and she has written numerous articles and book chapters on hypnosis, fantasy, and child abuse.

Steven Jay Lynn is a professor of psychology at Ohio University and has a private practice. He is a former president of the American Psychological Association's Division of Psychological Hypnosis; a fellow in the American Psychological Association, American Psychological Society, and Society for Clinical and Experimental Hypnosis; and a diplomate of the American Board of Psychological Hypnosis. He has received two awards from the Society for Clinical and Experimental Hypnosis for research excellence and for the best hypnosis book published during 1991 (*Theories of Hypnosis: Current Models and Perspectives*). An advisory editor of the *Journal of Abnormal Psychology*, the *International Journal of Clinical and Experimental Hypnosis*, and *Psychological Hypnosis*, and a North American editor of *Contemporary Hypnosis*, Dr. Lynn has written or edited textbooks on abnormal psychology, psychotherapy, and dissociation and has published more than 100 articles on hypnosis, child abuse, fantasy, psychotherapy, and behavioral medicine.

Irving Kirsch is a professor of psychology at the University of Connecticut. He is the North American editor of *Contemporary Hypnosis* and a member of the editorial board of the *International Journal of Clinical and Experimental Hypnosis*. Dr. Kirsch is a fellow of the American Psychology Association and the Society for Clinical and Experimental Hypnosis. In 1993, he served as president of the American Psychological Association's Division of Psychological Hypnosis. His book *Changing Expectations: A Key to Effective Psychotherapy* was published in 1990. He has published more than 75 journal articles and book chapters on hypnosis, behavior therapy, anxiety disorders, depression, and expectancy effects, and has presented papers on these topics internationally.